Chapter 24, "Avoiding Design Tragedies," brings you back [obscured] with less lofty ambitions.

Chapter 20: The Huntress	530
Chapter 21: The Diver	540
Chapter 22: The Entrance	554
Chapter 23: The Eagle	566
Chapter 24: Avoiding Design Tragedies	584

Part VI, "The CorelDRAW Freeway," exposes DRAW as the expressway it is, with emphasis on its *exits* and *entrances*— namely, printing, color and prepress theory, importing, and exporting. It ends with our Annual Export Torture Test in *Chapter 30.*

Chapter 25: Print, Darn You!	614
Chapter 26: Working with Color	656
Chapter 27: Turning Gray with Dignity	682
Chapter 28: Preparing for Press	700
Chapter 29: Importing to DRAW	722
Chapter 30: Exporting from DRAW	750

Part VII, "The Supporting Cast," provides a focused and authoritative look at the other modules in the box, including the newly enhanced *PHOTO-PAINT*.

Chapter 31: PHOTO-PAINT	782
Chapter 32: Creating a Presentation	804
Chapter 33: The Utilities	814

Part VIII, "The World of Ventura," offers an overview of the newly acquired and renovated Ventura desktop publishing program, which helps you establish and manage the style and the layout of art and text elements that you have created in DRAW and other programs.

Chapter 34: Publishing Basics	840
Chapter 35: How Ventura Thinks	850

The Appendixes: *Appendix A,* "Advanced Font Management," is a high-level discussion on using PostScript typefaces with DRAW, and *Appendix B* is my traditional "Junk & Miscellany" section, without which no book bearing my name is published. Look to this appendix for, among other things, special installation considerations.

Finally, *Appendix C* highlights "The Companion CD" that may be found on the inside back cover of this book. We really enjoyed writing a book while knowing we would have access to the hundreds of megabytes of space provided by a companion CD. When an idea warranted more illustration than just a print sample and a screen shot, no problem—we just whipped up a DRAW file and placed it on the CD. You'll find dozens of files in the PRACTICE directory alone, with direct relevance to topics and examples presented throughout the book. You'll also find plenty of utilities and fonts to use as you work with the program on your own.

For every kind of computer user, there is a SYBEX book.

All computer users learn in their own way. Some need straightforward and methodical explanations. Others are just too busy for this approach. But no matter what camp you fall into, SYBEX has a book that can help you get the most out of your computer and computer software while learning at your own pace.

Beginners generally want to start at the beginning. The **ABC's** series, with its step-by-step lessons in plain language, helps you build basic skills quickly. For a more personal approach, there's the **Murphy's Laws** and **Guided Tour** series. Or you might try our **Quick & Easy** series, the friendly, full-color guide, with **Quick & Easy References**, the companion pocket references to the **Quick & Easy** series. If you learn best by doing rather than reading, find out about the **Hands-On Live!** series, our new interactive multimedia training software. For hardware novices, there's the **Your First** series.

The **Mastering and Understanding** series will tell you everything you need to know about a subject. They're perfect for intermediate and advanced computer users, yet they don't make the mistake of leaving beginners behind. Add one of our **Instant References** and you'll have more than enough help when you have a question about your computer software. You may even want to check into our **Secrets & Solutions** series.

SYBEX even offers special titles on subjects that don't neatly fit a category—like our **Pushbutton Guides**, our books about the Internet, our books about the latest computer games, and a wide range of books for Macintosh computers and software.

SYBEX books are written by authors who are expert in their subjects. In fact, many make their living as professionals, consultants or teachers in the field of computer software. And their manuscripts are thoroughly reviewed by our technical and editorial staff for accuracy and ease-of-use.

So when you want answers about computers or any popular software package, just help yourself to SYBEX.

For a complete catalog of our publications, please write:

SYBEX Inc.
2021 Challenger Drive
Alameda, CA 94501
Tel: (510) 523-8233/(800) 227-2346 Telex: 336311
Fax: (510) 523-2373

SYBEX is committed to using natural resources wisely to preserve and improve our environment. As a leader in the computer book publishing industry, we are aware that over 40% of America's solid waste is paper. This is why we have been printing the text of books like this one on recycled paper since 1982.

This year our use of recycled paper will result in the saving of more than 15,300 trees. We will lower air pollution effluents by 54,000 pounds, save 6,300,000 gallons of water, and reduce landfill by 2,700 cubic yards.

In choosing a SYBEX book you are not only making a choice for the best in skills and information, you are also choosing to enhance the quality of life for all of us.

TALK TO SYBEX ONLINE.

Don't forget to download the latest info about Ventura, shortly after version 5 has been released.

JOIN THE SYBEX FORUM ON COMPUSERVE®

- Talk to SYBEX authors, editors and fellow forum members.
- Get tips, hints, and advice online.
- Download shareware and the source code from SYBEX books.

If you're already a CompuServe user, just enter GO SYBEX to join the SYBEX Forum. If you're not, try CompuServe free by calling 1-800-848-8199 and ask for Representative 560. You'll get one free month of basic service and a $15 credit for CompuServe extended services—a $23.95 value. Your personal ID number and password will be activated when you sign up.

Join us online today. Enter GO SYBEX on CompuServe. If you're not a CompuServe member, call Representative 560 at 1-800-848-8199

(outside U.S./Canada call 614-457-0802)

SYBEX
Shortcuts to Understanding

MASTERING
CORELDRAW™ 5
SPECIAL EDITION

Rick Altman

SYBEX®

San Francisco ■ Paris ■ Düsseldorf ■ Soest

Acquisitions Editor: Joanne Cuthbertson
Developmental Editor: Steve Lipson
Editor: Carol Henry
Project Editor: Doug Robert
Technical Editor: Dean Denno
Book Designer: Helen Bruno
Production Artist: Lisa Jaffe
Page Layout and Typesetting: Len Gilbert
Proofreader/Production Coordinator: Janet Boone
Indexer: Matthew Spence
Cover Designer: Design Site
Cover and Part Opening Illustrator: David Brickley
Screen reproductions produced with Collage Plus.
Collage Plus is a trademark of Inner Media Inc.

SYBEX is a registered trademark of SYBEX Inc.

TRADEMARKS: SYBEX has attempted throughout this book to distinguish proprietary trademarks from descriptive terms by following the capitalization style used by the manufacturer.

Every effort has been made to supply complete and accurate information. However, SYBEX assumes no responsibility for its use, nor for any infringement of the intellectual property rights of third parties which would result from such use.

Copyright ©1994 SYBEX Inc., 2021 Challenger Drive, Alameda, CA 94501. World rights reserved. No part of this publication may be stored in a retrieval system, transmitted, or reproduced in any way, including but not limited to photocopy, photograph, magnetic or other record, without the prior agreement and written permission of the publisher.

Library of Congress Card Number: 94-67203
ISBN: 0-7821-1508-X

Manufactured in the United States of America
10 9 8 7 6 5 4 3 2

About the Companion CD

Warranty   SYBEX warrants the enclosed CD to be free of physical defects for a period of ninety (90) days after purchase. If you discover a defect in the CD during this warranty period, you can obtain a replacement CD at no charge by sending the defective CD, postage prepaid, with proof of purchase to: SYBEX Inc., Customer Service Department, 2021 Challenger Drive, Alameda, CA 94501. Phone: (800) 227-2346. Fax: (510) 523-2373.

After the 90-day period, you can obtain a replacement CD by sending us the defective CD, proof of purchase, and a check or money order for $10, payable to SYBEX.

Disclaimer   SYBEX makes no warranty or representation, either express or implied, with respect to this software, its quality, performance, merchantability, or fitness for a particular purpose. In no event will SYBEX, its distributors, or dealers be liable for direct, indirect, special, incidental, or consequential damages arising out of the use of or inability to use the software even if advised of the possibility of such damage.

The exclusion of implied warranties is not permitted by some states. Therefore, the above exclusion may not apply to you. This warranty provides you with specific legal rights; there may be other rights that you may have that vary from state to state.

Shareware Distribution   This CD contains, in addition to free art files, various programs that are distributed as shareware. Shareware is a distribution method, not a type of software. The chief advantage is that it gives you, the user, a chance to try a program before you buy it.

Copyright laws apply to both shareware and commercial software, and the copyright holder retains all rights. If you try a shareware program and continue using it, you are expected to register it. Individual programs differ on details—some request registration while others require it. Some request a payment, while others don't, and some specify a maximum trial period. With registration, you get anything from the simple right to continue using the software to program updates.

Copy Protection   None of the programs on the CD are copy-protected. However, in all cases, reselling these programs without authorization is expressly forbidden.

THE CONTENTS OF THE COMPANION CD ARE DISCUSSED IN APPENDIX C.

To the two ladies in my life, Rebecca and Erica. My wife Becky would say that this book took me a lifetime to write—and it did: Our 18-month-old daughter Erica Frances is proof positive.

Acknowledgments

The word he used was *meshuga*—known by those of us who've picked up a little Yiddish to mean "crazy." And my father was looking right at me when he said it.

"How long is that book you're writing?"

"Oh, about a thousand pages."

"A thousand pages on one program?? You must be meshuga!"

What can I say…he was right. You'd have to be a bit crazy to embark upon a project like this. The object of all of this *mishegoss* is one box of software that has taken Windows-based artists and technical illustrators by storm: Version 5.0 of CorelDRAW. The storm is fueled by both enthusiasm and exasperation, and this book addresses the entire spectrum of emotions evoked by the program.

Yes, I'm still crazy after all these years, but at least I'm not crazy enough to think that I could produce this tome all by myself. I had the company of a wonderful team of writers, editors, and artists.

Contributing Writers

A heartfelt thanks to my band of writers. I was fortunate enough to plunk each of them down right in the middle of their respective specialties.

Byron Canfield (Part VI, "The CorelDRAW Freeway"): Byron and I go back to Ventura Publisher days of old, having met at one of the first Ventura Publisher Conferences, held in San Jose. He is the sole proprietor and imaginary ruler (his words) of Canfield Studios in Seattle, Washington, specializing in Ventura Publisher and CorelDRAW production and training. Byron has co-authored three books on Ventura and written numerous magazine articles, and he instructs regularly in computer graphics for the University of Washington. In his spare time, he watches with amazement his two-year-old daughter, Kendra, and also enjoys poking fun at small and defenseless animals (again, his words...).

Wayne Kaplan (Part IV, "Effects and Affects"): I met Wayne Kaplan at a recent CorelDRAW seminar, where he was mesmerizing a crowd with the intricacies of the Extrude function. I hired him on the spot. This self-described burnt-out engineer and ex–tennis instructor found his real calling in freelance computer training and consulting in 1988, working regularly with CorelDRAW, Ventura Publisher, and WordPerfect users from his offices in Huntington Beach, California. He is a member of the national board of directors of the Association of CorelDRAW Artists and Designers, and is a Corel-certified Technical Support Specialist.

Steve Rindsberg (Chapter 25, "Print, Darn You!"): Steve Rindsberg and I have never met. Instead, we have gotten to know each other in true nineties style: by electronic mail. His lucid answers to questions on CompuServe from users with printing problems were all the résumé I needed. He is president of Rindsberg Digital Photography, an imaging service bureau in Cincinnati, Ohio. His schooling is in political science, and he is quick to argue that, in terms of sheer incomprehensibility, neither computers nor electronic output can hold a candle to politics. His driving obsession: "unfettered curiosity about what makes it all tick, and how it can be made to tick better and faster, so I can go home at a reasonable hour once in a while."

Sue Blumenberg (Part VIII, "The World of Ventura"): After working in television for more years than she cares to count, Sue Blumenberg established her own business of technical writing, editing, and publishing. An insatiable curiosity has helped make her one of the true authorities on Ventura Publisher, authoring numerous articles on Ventura, giving presentations at the annual Ventura Publisher Conference, and, now, contributing to this book. You could argue that she had the most difficult assignment of all, trying to cover Ventura during its turbulent on-again, off-again beta cycle.

Gayle Ehrenman (Chapter 31, "PHOTO-PAINT"): Gayle is a writer, editor, and artist, who lives in New York with her cat, Nails. She holds an MFA in Creative Writing from Brooklyn College, CUNY, and has written about image editing and graphics software for *PC Magazine,* where she is currently the Associate Editor for the "After Hours" section of the magazine. Gayle fervently believes that baseball is the mythology of modern life and that one day the New York Mets will be champions again. As you can well imagine, a basis in reality is not a criterion for writing for this book.

Nancy Cedeno (Chapter 32, "Creating a Presentation"): Nancy is a technical writer, still living in her home town of San Francisco. After graduating from college with a degree in Creative Writing, she got hooked on computers when her roommate bought an IBM PC and left her alone with it for the weekend. She describes her discovery of technical writing as something like that old chocolate/peanut butter candy commercial…"Hey, you got technical knowledge all over my writing skills!" She's been using Ventura since version 1.0 and CorelDRAW since 2.0. In her spare time, she goes to baseball games, explores the Internet, and collects hobbies.

Ed Waldorph ("Tracing Your Way" in Chapter 33): Two years in a row, Ed Waldorph was the very first person to sign up for my Northern California CorelDRAW seminars. Both times, he arrived early, sat in the very front row, offered poignant observations and pithy comments, and helped others with their questions. I felt as if *I* should have paid *him* for attending the seminars, instead of vice-versa. After 15 years in law enforcement, Ed decided to determine whether the pen really is mightier than the sword, and converted his computer hobby into a vocation. Ed is founder and partner of Bay West Communications and a principal of RAM Graphics (a digital graphics and desktop publishing company), both located in San Francisco. No stranger to computing, Ed began with the beasts back in the early 1980s, with the 8-bit Ataris and Commodores, packed with a whopping 64K of RAM and connected to a TV set.

Erik Ingenito (Appendix C, "The Companion CD"): Thanks to Erik for diligently putting together the Companion CD at the back of the book and taking care of Appendix C, which explains the contents and use of the CD.

Contributing Artists   My three artists can do what I can't—they can draw straight lines. And curves, blends, and fountains, and beautiful backgrounds, lifelike images, and authentic perspective, etc.

David Brickley: Of all of the work I've seen by CorelDRAW artists, David's is the most "uncomputerlike," and that's a compliment. Until you stand right up next to them, his portraits and renderings look like paintings. Involved in art since his childhood in Washington state, David's career has taken him through advertising, art direction, and graphic design. Now working out of Portland, Oregon, his clients include many of the significant players in the personal computer industry, and his work regularly shows up in Corel's annual Design Contest.

John Brooks: John calls himself a "professional dabbler," and I met him when I needed some quick dabbling done. His 15-minute sketches, logos, and brochure designs convinced me that he was the man to produce the drawing in Chapter 5—the snowboarder that you will get to build yourself. He was once a forensic illustrator, and he was called upon to produce drawings of x-rays and diagrams of accidents. He later took up with CorelDRAW and found somewhat more pleasant avenues for his work. His dabbling also appears in Chapter 11, "Fun with Text," in which I asked him to…have fun with text.

Georgina Curry: Georgina and I met right after she accepted the trophy for Corel's Best of Show, 1993, for her wonderful rendition of actress Clara Bow, the star of Chapter 20. President and co-founder of The Electric Easel in Phoenix, Arizona, Georgina's résumé includes a bachelor's degree in Fine Arts, with an emphasis in drawing, printing, and visual communication design. In addition to her freelance design work, she teaches adult education art courses and has had several gallery showings of her work. Her entrée into self-employment was not without its anxious moments; she recalls, "I knew nothing about computers, and my potential partner knew nothing about graphic arts." Two years later, she is taking home Best of Show. Not bad.

The Editors   Some writers can get by with one editor; I need four. Special thanks to SYBEX developmental editor Steve Lipson for pointing me in the right directions when the road signs were being moved,

Doug Robert for taking the role of project editor to keep this mammoth assignment from bursting at every seam, and to technical editor *Dean Denno* for his exceptionally alert, yet gentle, quality control. *Carol Henry* says that she is just called the "plain old editor," but I prefer Editor Extraordinaire. She is really the one with whom I ran this marathon; her watchful and ultra-accurate eye kept me going when I was on page five million or so and not even a quarter of the way through.

Friends at Corel   I like doing business with Corel, because employee longevity makes it possible for me to make and keep friends there.

I met CEO and founder *Mike Cowpland* on the tennis court. The COMDEX bash he hosted, at which he invited tennis legend Rod Laver to play doubles with us, remains the highlight of both my COMDEX and tennis careers. On the court, Mike gives up about 15 years to me, but little else. The last time we played, the scores were 7-6, 7-6!

You might know *Arlen Bartsch* as Director of Sales & Marketing; I know him as a golfing buddy. He's the guy that kept me company as I wandered into the barranca on the 15th hole at Pebble Beach to look for my ball. He found 10 stray balls, none of them mine; I found a case of poison oak. Becky and I have become fast friends with Arlen, his wonderful wife Dawn, and their great son Aaron.

Fiona Rochester Hennessey started out as a product specialist on the exhausting demo circuit, and is now one of the hardest-working media liaisons in the business. But as far as I'm concerned, her claim to fame will be the outrageous clues she gives when playing guessing games. Quick: What food is brown, bought from a truck, takes vinegar, and is good after skating? Canadians sure love their french fries, but you'd think they'd never seen a McDonald's.

And Finally...   I want to thank three very good friends of mine, Susan Anawalt, David Heckley, and Leslie Vallejo. Our weekly mixed doubles through the spring of 1994 provided my only respite from this writing project. It's a miracle that I only stood them up twice!

CONTENTS AT A GLANCE

Introduction   xxxvii

PART I — Corel's Expanding Horizon

1	The Foundation of CorelDRAW	2
2	A Tour of the Tools	10
3	What's New in CorelDRAW	36
4	Just Click, Baby!	80
5	From Start to Finish: Creating an Illustration	102

PART II — Working with Objects

6	As the Curve Turns	148
7	Understanding Outlines	178
8	Fill 'er Up	192
9	Automate!	234

PART III — Working with Text

10	Taming the Type Monster	268
11	Fun with Text	296
12	Working with Text Styles	332
13	Putting Pedal to Metal	348

PART IV — Effects and Affects

14	Appetizers	364
15	The Envelope, Please	388
16	Metamorphoses	406
17	Energizing with Extrude	440
18	The Power of the Line	474
19	Through the Looking Glass	494

PART V — Doing It!

20	The Huntress	530
21	The Diver	540
22	The Entrance	554
23	Eagle	566
24	Avoiding Design Tragedies	584

PART VI — The CorelDRAW Freeway

25	Print, Darn You!	614
26	Working with Color	656
27	Turning Gray with Dignity	682
28	Preparing for Press	700
29	Importing to DRAW	722
30	Exporting from DRAW	750

PART VII — The Supporting Cast

31	PHOTO-PAINT	782
32	Creating a Presentation	804
33	The Utilities	814

PART VIII — The World of Ventura

34	Publishing Basics	840
35	How Ventura Thinks	850

Appendices

A	Advanced Font Management	880
B	Junk & Miscellany	894
C	The Companion CD	920

Index   961

Table of Contents

Introduction — xxxvii

PART I COREL'S EXPANDING HORIZON

1 THE FOUNDATION OF CORELDRAW — 2
- Drawing versus Painting — 4
  - The Magic of the Curve — 6
- CorelDRAW Is Greater than the Sum of Its Parts — 8
- Typefaces: The Final Frontier — 9

2 A TOUR OF THE TOOLS — 10
- Exploring the Interface — 12
  - The Supporting Characters — 14
  - Understanding Dialog Boxes — 16
  - Working with Roll-Ups — 20
- Exploring the Toolbox — 21
  - The Pick Tool — 21
  - The Shape Tool — 22
  - The Zoom Tool — 22
  - The Pencil Tool — 23
  - The Rectangle and Ellipse Tools — 25
  - The Text Tool — 25
  - The Outline Tool — 26
  - The Fill Tool — 27
- Browsing the Menus — 29
  - The File Menu — 29
  - The Edit Menu — 30
  - The View Menu — 31

The Layout Menu	32
The Arrange Menu	32
The Effects Menu	33
The Text Menu	34
The Special Menu	35

3 WHAT'S NEW IN CORELDRAW — 36

CorelDRAW 4.0	39
The View from the Top in 4.0	39
Text Features New to 4.0	41
New Typefaces	42
Better Defaults	43
More Word Processing Features	44
Friendlier Text Roll-Up	45
Smarter Paragraph Text	46
Text inside Objects	47
Basic Drawing Changes in 4.0	47
Better Node Editing	48
PowerLines	49
Better Fill Options	50
New Effects in 4.0	53
File Menu Functions in 4.0	54
The Object Menu in 4.0	55
Behind the Scenes of 4.0	57
Version 4.0 Miscellany	58
The Bad News	60
CorelDRAW 5.0	63
Ventura Publisher and DRAW 5.0	63
Version 5.0 and Performance	64
5.0's Improved Text Handling	64
5.0's New Tools for Artists and Illustrators	66
Lens	67
PowerClip	68
Better Dimensioning	69
Cosmetic Changes	70
New Grouping Tools in 5.0	70

Changes to the Dashboard in 5.0	71
Redesigned Fill Dialog	72
New Fountain Fill Type: Square	72
Direct Access to MOSAIC	73
Drag and Drop	73
Printing with 5.0	74
Other Good Stuff in 5.0	75
The Bad News in Version 5.0	77

4 JUST CLICK, BABY! 80

Working with Objects	82
Creating, Moving, and Changing Objects	83
Importing Objects	86
Pasting Objects	89
Using the Symbols Library	90
Using Fills and Outlines	90
Selecting Multiple Objects	92
Turning Many Objects Into One	93
Grouping Objects	94
Combining Objects	95
Welding Objects	96
Other Points Of Interest	96
Saving and Opening Files	96
Zooming	97
Arranging Elements	97
Using Undo	99
Copying Attributes	100
Using the Repeat Command	101
Working with Grids and Guidelines	101

5 FROM START TO FINISH: CREATING AN ILLUSTRATION 102

An Overview	105
The Agenda	106
Getting Started	107
Defining the Layers	107
Creating the Layers	108

Creating the Sky	110
Filling the Sky	110
Creating the Cloud	112
Performing the Blend	114
Locking the Layer	117
Creating the Foreground Snow	118
Filling the Slope	120
Extra Credit	122
Bring on the Snowboarder	124
Creating the Tree	126
Importing the Tree	128
Adding Snow to the Tree	128
More Extra Credit	131
The Home Stretch	133
Creating the Text	133
Stretching the Text	137
Adding the Finishing Touches	137
Wrapping Up	143

PART II   WORKING WITH OBJECTS

6   AS THE CURVE TURNS   148

Creating Curves and Lines	151
Drawing in Bezier Mode	155
All about Nodes	156
Types of Nodes	157
Changing Node Types	161
A Blueprint for Painless Drawing	162
Define the Basic Shape	162
Create the Curves	166
Reshape the Curves	166
The Supporting Cast	167
Auto-Reduce	168
Joining and Breaking Paths	170
Other Node Edit Tools	171

Node Miscellany	172
When Curves Aren't Curves (Yet)	173
Converting Objects to Curves	175

7 UNDERSTANDING OUTLINES — 178

Working with Outlines	180
The Outline Pen Dialog	182
Outline Width	183
Arrows	183
Style	185
Color	186
Corners	186
Line Caps	186
Calligraphy	188
The Behind Fill Option	189
Scale with Image Option	189
The Outline Color Dialog	190
Setting the Outline Pen Defaults	191

8 FILL 'ER UP — 192

Understanding Fill Patterns	194
Applying Fills	196
Uniform Fills	197
The Power of CMYK	199
RGB and HSB	201
Using Custom Palettes	202
Creating Your Own Palettes	202
Searching for a Hidden Color	205
Fountain Fills	206
Lines, Rads, Squares, and Cones	208
Choosing Colors	211
Creating the Right Blend	211
Creating Custom Fountains	214
Other Options	217
Pattern Fills	224
Two-Color Patterns	224

Full-Color Patterns	227
PostScript Patterns	229
Texture Fills	230

9 AUTOMATE! — 234

The Foundation of a Style	236
Creating a Graphic Style	238
Design the Object	238
Create and Save the Style	239
Apply the Style to Another Object	241
When and When Not to Use Styles	243
Understanding Templates	245
Modifying the CORELDRW.CDT Defaults	246
Using New Templates	248
Templates in a Teapot	248
Creating Templates as Starting Points	251
Using Your Starting Point	252
Surviving Styles	253
DRAW's New Presets: Have It Your Way	255
Creating a Preset	256
Playing Back a Preset	257
Creating Objects during Recording	258
Creating Text Presets	259
What You Can and Can't Do with Presets	260
Choosing between a Style and a Preset	262
Situations That Call for Styles	262
Situations That Call for Presets	263

PART III WORKING WITH TEXT

10 TAMING THE TYPE MONSTER — 268

Setting Type with DRAW	270
What You Can Do to Text in DRAW	271
Creating Artistic Text	279
Creating Paragraph Text	281

Faster Redraw	282
Much Larger Capacity	282
Better Text Control	282
Irregular Text Wrapping	286
Navigating Your Way	286
Artistic or Paragraph?	291
When to Use Artistic Text	292
When to Use Paragraph Text	292
Switching from One to the Other	294
Remember the Hotkeys	294

11 FUN WITH TEXT 296

Shaping Text around Objects	298
Creating Embossed Text	306
The CorelDRAW Squeeze Play	311
Creating a Text Mask	314
Combining Two Objects	315
Using PowerClips	319
Rules of Thumb for PowerClips	322
Importing Text from Other Programs	323
Fitting Text to a Path	327
Choose Your Curve Wisely	328
Choose Your Type Wisely	328
Keep Your Distance	329
Working with "Untext"	330

12 WORKING WITH TEXT STYLES 332

Creating a Text Style	334
Sharing Text Styles among Objects	336
The Power of the Paragraph	337
Set the Stage	338
Create the Styles	339
Format the Paragraphs	343

13 PUTTING PEDAL TO METAL 348

PostScript vs. TrueType	350

Print Speed	351
Drawing Speed	352
Artistic vs. Paragraph Text	354
Adding Fonts on the Fly	356
What Happens When You Outline Text	356
All in All, DRAW Is Not a Word Processor	359

PART IV EFFECTS AND AFFECTS

14 APPETIZERS — 364

The Effects Menu	366
Basic Transformations	367
Stretch & Mirror	369
Do We Really Need Transform / Stretch & Mirror?	370
Rules of Thumb for Stretch & Mirror	372
Outlines: To Scale or Not to Scale…	372
Absolute Sizing	374
Rotate and Skew	374
Rotations Using the Mouse	375
Skews Using the Mouse	377
Using the Roll-up to Rotate and Skew	377
Rules of Thumb for Rotate and Skew	380
Putting It All into Perspective	380
One-Point Perspective	381
Two-Point Perspective	383
Copying Perspectives	386
Bring on the Steam Shovels	387

15 THE ENVELOPE, PLEASE — 388

Creating an Envelope	390
Enveloping Fundamentals	391
The Keep Lines Check Box	393
All about Mapping Options	395
Another Example of Mapping	397
Rules of Thumb for Mapped Envelopes	399

Unconstrained Envelopes	399
More Ways to Create Envelopes	401
Envelopes and Paragraph Text	403
Text Wrap	405

16 METAMORPHOSES 406

Blending Objects	408
Blending 101	409
Going Deeper with Blends	412
Rules of Thumb for Blending	413
Fringe Players	414
Colors, Colors, Colors	416
Blends That Do Cartwheels: The Rotation and Loop Controls	417
Taking a Different Path	420
Composing Organization Charts	423
The Subtler Side of Blending	425
Compounding, Splitting, and (Con)Fusing Blends	429
More Rules of Thumb for Blending	434
Contours: The Lay of the Land	435

17 ENERGIZING WITH EXTRUDE 440

Extrusions Add Depth and Breadth	442
The Extrude Roll-up	443
Putting Extrusions in Perspective	444
Parallel Extrusions	447
Getting Down to Business	448
Editing the Vanishing Point	452
Color, Shading, and Lights	452
Use Object Fill	452
Solid Fills	454
Adding Realism through Shading	455
Lighting Effects	456
Creating Cutaways and Other Tricks	460
Rules of Thumb for Extruding	461
Vanishing Points Revisited	461
Rules of Thumb for Vanishing Points	463

Rotating Extrusions	464
Rules of Thumb for Rotating	468
Miscellany	468
The Extrude Roll-up Remembers	468
Version 5.0 Has Extrusion Presets	469
Taking Advantage of Common Vanishing Points	469
Warping Objects	471
Extrusions Don't Have to Be Fancy	473

18 THE POWER OF THE LINE — 474

Making Heads or Tails of PowerLines	476
An Exercise with PowerLines	478
Watch Those Nodes	481
Rules of Thumb for PowerLines	482
Speed and Spread	482
What's a Nib, Anyway?	483
The Problem with Pressure	486
Shaping PowerLines with Pressure Edit	486
Saving Your Own PowerLines	490
What Cost, PowerLines?	491
More Rules of Thumb for PowerLines	492
The Kitchen Sink	492

19 THROUGH THE LOOKING GLASS — 494

PowerClips	496
PowerClip Basics	497
Editing PowerClips	500
Avoid Auto-Centering	501
Using the Lock Contents Option	501
Grouping While Editing	501
Extrusions as PowerClips	502
Making PowerClips Jump through Hoops	505
Rules of Thumb for PowerClipping	507
Envelopes and PowerClips	507
Using PowerClips to Incorporate Bitmaps	508
Nesting PowerClips	511

Rules of Thumb for Nesting PowerClips	512
Lenses, Lenses, and More Lenses	513
Combining Lenses	517
Learning to Use the Lenses	519
Using Tinted Grayscale for That Duo-Tone Look	519
Heat Map	520
Color Limit and Color Add	520
Using Brighten to Create Text Backdrops	521
Using Lenses as Windows	521
Putting Lenses to the Test	521
Putting It All Together	524
One Last Thought about Special Effects	524

PART V DOING IT!

20 THE HUNTRESS: BEST OF SHOW, 1993, BY GEORGINA CURRY — 530

Inspired at the Movies	532
The Feathers	534
The Face and Hair	535
The Medallion	536
The Large Beads of the Headdress	537
The Small Beads of the Headdress	538
The Jeweled Headband	538
The Choker	539
The Scarf	539

21 THE DIVER: BEST OF SHOW, 1990, BY DAVID BRICKLEY — 540

A Work in Progress	542
The Genesis of The Diver	544
Doing It!	544
Filling in the Landscape	545
Finding the Leading Character	547
Looking Back	552

22 THE ENTRANCE, BY DAVID BRICKLEY — 554

- In Search of Reference — 556
- From Camera to Computer — 558
  - Setting the Tone — 559
  - Exercising Artist's License — 561
- Peeling the Corner — 561
- Doing It! — 563

23 EAGLE, BY DAVID BRICKLEY — 566

- First Steps: Defining the Project — 568
  - Finding a Good Reference — 570
- Beginning the Sketch — 570
- Getting Down to Business — 571
  - Using XYZ Reference Lines — 571
- Doing It! — 573
  - Refining the Wings — 574
  - Fine-Tuning the Claws: Back to the Drawing Board — 575
- Blending Multiple Colors — 576
- Drawing Three-Dimensional Objects to Make the Jet Engine — 579
- Some Rules of Thumb for Artists and Designers — 582

24 AVOIDING DESIGN TRAGEDIES — 584

- The Look at Me! Syndrome — 587
  - Diagnosing and Treating Look at Me! — 588
  - The Message Is Everything! — 589
  - Bigger Is Not Better — 589
  - Easy on the Attributes — 590
  - Be Brilliant! — 591
- Small Is Beautiful — 592
  - Diagnosing and Treating Pompousitis — 593
  - No Lines Allowed — 593
  - Take the Two-Typeface Challenge — 594
  - Use White Space — 597
  - Relax Your Posture — 597
- "Borrow" Good Design — 598
  - Steal from Yourself, Too — 602

Have a Plan	602
Typography and the Fine Art of Restraint	604
Resist the Temptation to Install All Five Jillion Typefaces	604
Choose the Right Category of Typefaces	606
To Every Face—Kern, Kern, Kern	606

PART VI THE CORELDRAW FREEWAY

25 PRINT, DARN YOU! — 614

Selecting a Printer	617
Setting Up the Page	618
Page Setup, Size Options	619
Page Setup, Layout Options	620
Page Setup, Display Options	620
The Print Dialog	624
Print Range	625
Printer and Printer Quality	626
Printer Color Profile	626
Print to File and for Mac	626
Copies and Collate Copies	627
The Print Preview Area	628
Those Mysterious Buttons under the Print Preview Area	628
Print Options, Layout Page	628
Options, Schmoptions	632
Printing Color Separations	637
Now, about Those Buttons…	642
Troubleshooting Guide for PostScript Printing	646
Hardware Problems	646
Slow Print or No Print At All	647
Complex Curves	648
Bitmaps	649
Fills	653
Embedded .EPS Files	653
If It Still Won't Print	655

26 WORKING WITH COLOR — 656

- The Theory of Color — 658
  - Components of Light — 660
  - Additive Primary Colors — 661
  - Subtractive Primary Colors — 663
- Color Models — 663
  - HSB: Hue/Saturation/Brightness — 664
  - RGB: Red/Green/Blue — 665
  - CMYK: Cyan/Magenta/Yellow/Black — 667
- Other Color Options — 670
  - Spot Color — 671
- Color Trapping — 675
  - How to Apply Trapping — 678
- The Aesthetics of Color — 680
  - Color with Text — 680
  - Color for Realism — 680

27 TURNING GRAY WITH DIGNITY — 682

- Dots All, Folks — 684
- Getting Gray from the Grid — 687
- Setting Line Screens in DRAW — 693
  - Creating Print Files — 695
  - Creating Encapsulated PostScript Files — 696
  - One Print Job, Many Screens — 696
  - Creative Screens — 697
- By the Numbers (Ugh) — 698

28 PREPARING FOR PRESS — 700

- Monitoring Your Monitor — 702
  - Calibrating Your Monitor — 703
- Using the CorelDRAW Color Manager — 704
  - Rolling Your Own… Profile, That Is — 707
- Monitoring Your Scanner — 711
  - Aiming for WYSIWYG — 711
- Printer Calibration — 713
  - The Straight and Narrow — 713

Cancel Hawaii: The Colors Are All Wrong	716
Following Through	717
Basic Imagesetter Operation	718
A Calibration a Day	719
Watching for Poor Output	721

29 IMPORTING TO DRAW — 722

Why Import?	724
What Happens When You Import?	725
Importing Clip Art	726
Adobe Illustrator Files	729
AutoCAD	730
CorelDRAW's CDR Format	730
Computer Graphics Metafile	730
Windows Metafile	733
Importing .EPS Files	733
An EPS Test	735
Importing Bitmap Images	740
Bitmaps and Pieces	741
Importing Linked Data	744
Servers and Clients	745
Creating an OLE Link	745
Editing a Linked Object	746
Linked Files and Embedded Objects	747
Editing a Linked File	748
Editing an Embedded Object	749
Rules of Thumb for Linked vs. Embedded	749
DRAW's Role in OLE	750

30 EXPORTING FROM DRAW — 750

Choose Your Weapon	752
The Third Annual Export Torture Test	753
CGM	756
DXF	758
EPS	758
GEM	761

HPGL	763
PCX and TIFF	763
WMF	767
The Promise of Object Linking and Embedding	769
Summarizing the Torture Test	774

PART VII THE SUPPORTING CAST

31 PHOTO-PAINT — 780

PHOTO-PAINT's Tools	782
Getting Comfortable with PHOTO-PAINT	784
The Tool Settings Roll-up	784
The Zoom Tools	786
The Color Roll-up	787
The Undo Tools	788
Creating an Image	790
When a Whole Image Is Too Much	790
Working with Masks	793
Using the Mask Flyout	793
Creating a Mask	795
Using the Color Mask Roll-Up	796
Working with Objects	798
Enhancing the Image	801
Using the Retouching Tools	801

32 CREATING A PRESENTATION — 804

Step One: The Chart	806
Step Two: The Animation	808
Morphing Around	810
Step Three: The Presentation	812
SHOW's Weaknesses	813

33 THE UTILITIES — 814

Tracing Your Way	816
Why TRACE?	817

A Tour of TRACE	817
The Mechanics of Tracing	819
Presto, Change-o	823
Cleaning Up	825
Moving Uptown	827
Mopping Up with DRAW	828
The Finished Work	829
Cataloging Art with MOSAIC	830
Font Management Made Easy, with Ares FontMinder	833
Adjusting Font Kerning with KERN	836

PART VIII THE WORLD OF VENTURA

34 PUBLISHING BASICS — 840

How to "Publish a Desktop"	842
Choosing Your Weapon	844
Ventura Publisher: Not a Swiss Army Knife	845
Workgroup Publishing	848
Different Strokes for Different Desktops	849

35 How Ventura Thinks — 850

The Roots of Desktop Publishing	852
Enter Ventura	853
Ventura 101	854
Lumped vs. Unlumped Files	854
The Frame Is the Key	857
Modular Components	859
Ventura Productions	859
The Director: The Chapter File	859
The Costume Designer	860
The Cast	862
The Extras	864
Infinite (Almost) Diversity	866
Sharing Style Sheets	866
Presto, Change-o	867

A Rose by Any Other Name…	869
It's HOW Many Pages?	870
Long Document Features	870
Ventura on Auto-Pilot	871
File Management	872
What's New in Ventura 5.0	873
The Game Plan…	873
And the Outcome…	873
A New "Look and Feel"	874
New File Formats	877
New Features	878
Associated Programs	879
And Still on the Wish List…	880

APPENDICES

A ADVANCED FONT MANAGEMENT — 880

Three Things Typographical	883
Sending Text as Curves	884
To Curve or Not to Curve?	886
Downloading Typefaces	887
Converting TrueType Faces	890
Rules of Thumb	891
Making .EPS Files	892
Managing the Backstage Business	892
Managing CORELFNT.INI	893
Managing WIN.INI	894

B JUNK & MISCELLANY — 894

Keeping Two Versions of DRAW	896
Running Two Copies of DRAW 5.0	898
Outies and INIs	899
The COLOR Directory	900
The CONFIG Directory	900
The CUSTOM Directory	902

The PROGRAMS Directory	902
What We Haven't Covered	902
The New Arrange Commands	903
Dimension Lines	907
Print Merge	909
Snapping Objects	909
Layers	911
Extract and Merge Back	912
Object Data	912
Odds and Ends	912
Fast Tool-Switching	913
Movable Rulers	913
Instant Nodes	913
Faking the Quick Copy	913
Removing Guidelines	914
Super-Duper Business Cards	916
Join the CorelDRAW Community	918
That's All, Folks	919

C   THE COMPANION CD   920

What You'll Find on the Companion CD	923
The Utilities	925
Alchemy	926
CDFont	927
Display	927
DragView	927
EPSF	927
FontBook	928
FontName	928
FPower	928
GDS	928
GhostScr	928
J-Pilot	929
Mac-ette	929
MegaEdit	929
NeoBookP	929

NeoPaint	929
NeoShow	930
OKFont	930
Pappren	930
PCS	930
PlugIn	930
PSP	931
Qpeg486	931
RenameTT	931
ROMCAT	932
UC	932
VesaView	933
VuImage	933
Notes	933
Corel Corporation Product Demo	933
Practice Files	934
The Art Gallery	934
Sounds	934
TrueType Fonts	935
List of Files	936
If You Don't Have a CD Player	960
Index	961

Introduction

> When fully installed, CorelDRAW is so big that it should be tested for steroids.
>
> *Rick Altman, March 1991*

The Biggest Gets Bigger

My, how time can change your perspective. The words above were written just a few short years ago to describe Version 2.0 of Corel's rapidly advancing drawing and illustration software. Version 2.0 made news not only for its prowess as an artist's tool, and not only because it came with so many typefaces and so much sample clip art, but also because it was actually more than one program. You see, Corel Corporation placed several other programs in the box along with DRAW 2.0. You got a cute little image-cataloging program called MOSAIC, and a low-end tracing tool called TRACE. This was considered a big deal at the time—extra software at no extra price. My, how time can change your perspective…

With Version 5.0, CorelDRAW has grown in every conceivable dimension: depth and breadth, features, bells and whistles, market share, and, of course, the accompanying consumption of space on your hard drive. CorelDRAW is the clear and obvious leader in Windows-based drawing and illustration software.

With CorelDRAW 5.0, Ventura Publisher will also get a new lease on life, both as a partner in the CorelDRAW box and as a stand-alone product (it's now known as Corel Ventura). PHOTO-PAINT will also try to play in the major leagues now, with a significantly overhauled interface and collection of tools and effects.

What Is CorelDRAW?

What *is* CorelDRAW? Those in the know are already looking forward to this writing team botching the answer to this question. Is CorelDRAW a program that allows you to work with refined curves and objects to produce precise artistic effects? Is CorelDRAW a powerful typographic engine for the creation of logos and other text-based work? Is CorelDRAW actually a collection of seven programs, each covering a particular sect of the graphics industry? Or is CorelDRAW just a tool for driving book authors crazy?

The fact that CorelDRAW is actually all of these things underscores its importance to the computer art community. One way or the other, the programs that constitute the box of software known as CorelDRAW assist in the creation of modern-day graphics. CorelDRAW is the tools with which you can create

- Full-color illustrations
- Complex drawings
- Logos
- Fancy headlines
- Lengthy and complex text-based documents
- Photorealistic images
- Surrealistic images
- Charts, graphs, and pictograms
- Slide shows
- Animation sequences
- Sound bites and film clips
- Libraries of clip art
- High-quality drawings from low-resolution originals

CorelDRAW is actually DRAW, VENTURA, PHOTO-PAINT, CHART, SHOW, MOVE, MOSAIC, and TRACE; and in varying degrees of detail, this book will cover all of these *program modules*.

CorelDRAW Is for Drawing

If there are users out there who have purchased CorelDRAW for the sole purpose of creating slide shows, bar charts, or animations, we haven't met them yet. Though many users do occasionally turn to the expertise of the other CorelDRAW modules, what they really bought CorelDRAW for was one primary function: to draw! Day in and day out, the floating balloon icon is what receives the majority of double-clicks. This lopsided level of attention is not lost on us—in fact, we follow your lead in this regard: The lion's share of this book is devoted to the flagship product, the DRAW module. One of these days, a book proclaiming itself "the definitive reference for Corel's other modules" might reach the shelves, but this isn't it.

Is DRAW easy to use? You're holding a very thick book in your hands and that ought to tell you something, but a majority of users are of the opinion that, yes, DRAW is very easy to pick up and begin using. In fact, Corel owes its phenomenal success in large part to that intangible and mystifying quality we call *intuitiveness* or *user-friendliness*. DRAW is one of those rare programs that makes itself look easy. The menus make sense, the screen icons (what few there are) seem at home, and most of the functions and dialogs invite you to try them before forcing you to retreat to the user's manual.

Don't fool yourself, though. Sooner or later the richness of its color palettes, the intricacies of its global styles, the layers of detail heaped upon its special effects, the mind-boggling power behind its print and export engines—all this can lead to input overload for users, readers and authors alike. But though DRAW's long and winding road seems neverending, embarking on this journey is not the dreadful trip it is with some programs. Your first few steps are easy—Corel has done a fine job at that level. Our job is to smooth out the bumps down the road.

For Whom Does This Book Toll?

From my ongoing series of CorelDRAW seminars, at which I meet a few thousand users every year, I have defined a clear profile of you, the mainstream user: You produce lots of logos, small brochures, and one-page fliers, and you do not have a professional background in the arts. You want to develop a better understanding of CorelDRAW's tools and functions, and learn the hidden treasures that allow for faster and more efficient operation.

This book is written with the following users in mind:

- *Technical illustrators,* who seek to reduce the amount of busy-work involved in producing diagrams, charts, and simple drawings
- *Amateur and budding designers,* who strive to develop an eye for good, clean, simple designs
- *Desktop publishers,* who want a better understanding of DRAW's text-handling capabilities, both inside and outside of Ventura, which is Corel's new industrial-strength document publisher
- *Commercial artists,* who might be auditioning the new version of DRAW for their next double-page spread
- *Fine artists and illustrators,* who don't want a book that tries to teach them their business, but rather one that helps them sharpen their CorelDRAW skills and their understanding of its tools
- *Brand new users,* who want a book that doesn't talk down to them and lead them slowly by the hand, but rather arms them with the information and gives them the practice they need to become self-sufficient
- *And prospective users,* who want to get a sense of what CorelDRAW is all about before they make their purchase.

AUTHOR'S NOTE

NEVER SWITCHED TO VERSION 4? For reasons having to do with price, bugs in Version 4.0, and general satisfaction with the way things were in Version 3.0, many users haven't upgraded since Version 3.0. For you, we've provided additional, extensive coverage in the "What's New" chapter (Chapter 3) of everything you need to know if you're upgrading directly from Version 3.0. Elsewhere in the book, when the differences between what you're reading as a Version 3 upgrader differ substantially from what the Version 4 upgrader needs to know, you'll also find comforting notes of the type you're looking at now.

How to Use This Book

It says something about a book's scope and length when the book comes with instructions to *itself*. ("To use this book, start at the top of the page, read from left to right, and turn pages with your right hand...") But really—since this book addresses users at distinctly different levels of knowledge and skill, you need to know what is what, where, and for whom. We include both tutorial and reference material, and when necessary, we specify right at the top any chapter that is mainly for beginning or mainly for more advanced users.

As you flip through the book, you'll notice *two eight-page sections of full-color illustrations* (starting at page 340 and again at 724). These sections constitute our **Color Gallery,** designed to show things you could only hope to describe otherwise in a two-color book. The illustrations in the gallery are referred to by number in various chapters throughout the book.

In case you've missed it, **The Inside FRONT Cover** gives a run-down of how the book's chapters are arranged. **The Inside BACK Cover** holds the **Companion CD**, without which you'll be missing a lot of freebie software and mega art files, not to mention shareware typefaces and additional product information. The contents of the CD are discussed in Appendix C.

And of course, where would you be without **The Index**—believe it or not, a lot of people forget to use this valuable search tool until someone embarrasses them with a line something like, "Did you look in the index?" Duh. Incidentally, if you discover you can't find something using the index, let the publisher know. SYBEX is always looking to make the information in their books easier to access, and indexes are key to that goal. (Speaking of accessing information, check out the CorelDRAW files and messages in the **SYBEX CompuServe Forum**—and if you don't have a CompuServe account, see the offer at the end of this Intro!)

Upgrading: No Time Like the Present

We know that many CorelDRAW users are a bit gun-shy about new releases of this software, given the pattern of bugs and initial instability established in the 3.0 and 4.0 releases. And we know that many of you rely on books like this one to help you make that buying decision.

For these reasons, we're grateful for our standing policy of writing the introduction *after* writing the main body of the book. We started this project back in January 1994 and finished in July. Much has happened during that period, including another utterly frenetic period of beta testing, in which Corel's engineers turned out new releases almost daily.

Most of all, DRAW 5.0 leaves the starting gate in much better condition than its predecessor, version 4.0, did. If you bought one of the very first packages on the shelf you had to send in your registration card to get the Ventura 5.0 portion of the package, but the short wait proved to be worth the delay. That doesn't mean that there won't be a series of maintenance updates to some of the programs that make up CorelDRAW 5.0—there almost certainly will be at least one to follow the first update of the summer of 1994—but this release has none of the crippling problems that befell 4.0. Bugs, yes—bombs, no.

Does this mean that Corel will stick to its almost maniacal schedule of 12-month overhauls of DRAW? Probably so, despite sentiment from a wide body of users that development be on an 18-month schedule. We authors aren't so crazy about it either—there's no longer time for a vacation.

I hope you enjoy the book. Now if you'll excuse me, I must begin work on the version 6.0 edition…

AUTHOR'S NOTE

With the release of this book, the publisher and I will from time to time be making certain interesting files relating to Corel-DRAW and its updates available on the SYBEX forum on CompuServe. Just type GO SYBEX and browse at will. If you have a modem but you're not already a CompuServe member, you can still try it—for free! Call, toll-free, 800-848-8199 and ask for representative #560. You'll get a personal ID number and password, one FREE month of basic service, a FREE subscription to CompuServe Magazine, and a $15 credit towards your CompuServe connect-time charges.

PART I

COREL'S EXPANDING HORIZON

We used to think that the notion of a computer book being over 600 pages was absurd. Then we met CorelDRAW, the program that seems to stretch into infinity in both its breadth and its depth. As the program extends over all known horizons, so too will this book, with analysis and discussion that should soothe the most savage power user.

But alas, we get ahead of ourselves. Across our close to 1000 pages, there is plenty of time for discussions on advanced usage. This first part of the book is devoted to new users, occasional users, and even prospective users who are still in the throes of a buying decision.

While this is an introduction to the software, our hope is to deliver to you more than just a tutorial on how to click on a button. We intend to provide insight into what CorelDRAW does, why it does what it does, and how it does it. Except when we state otherwise, these first five chapters assume only modest familiarity with CorelDRAW.

CHAPTER 1

The Foundation of CorelDRAW

ONE

When we first started giving our seminars for CorelDRAW users, we were surprised to discover how many users did not understand the essential qualities of the two broad categories of illustration programs. Today, three years later, we still encounter hundreds of users who are unclear on the concept, because many electronic artists simply take for granted what these programs do in the background.

Once the dust settles around all of the jargon, all graphics programs produce art in one of two ways: They produce curves, circles, lines, and rectangles, all based on mathematics; or they produce dots. That's it—curves or dots. The ways in which these programs conduct their business, however, are as different as night and day (though you can sometimes achieve similar results using either method). Let's take a closer look at the two concepts.

Drawing versus Painting

Programs in the first category (graphics based on curves) are called *vector drawing programs* and are said to produce *vector art*. CorelDRAW's main program, DRAW, is a vector drawing program. When you create a circle in a drawing program, the program knows that it is a circle, with x- and y-coordinates, a radius, a circumference, an outline, and an interior color. You can easily change the shape, size, or colors of the circle without compromising its integrity—it still knows that it is supposed to be a circle.

Programs in the second category (graphics based on dots) are called *paint programs* or *image editors* and are said to produce *bitmapped art*. The CorelPHOTO-PAINT module is in this category. When you create a circle in PHOTO-PAINT or some other paint program, you are virtually taking brush to canvas, applying electronic paint to the individual pixels of your electronic canvas. The circle you create here is but a collection of dots, lined up in rows, each dot with a specific color. Taken together, the dots might happen to look like a circle, but there are no essential properties identifying it as a circle. You would not be able to alter it without distorting it.

Vector drawing programs such as DRAW have these characteristics:

- **High Resolution of Printed Output** When you print from DRAW, the objects in your drawing will print at the highest possible resolution. DRAW essentially tells the printer, "Print this object according to the vectors and mathematics I have established, and place the dots as close together as you possibly can."

- **Faster Printing and Screen Drawing** DRAW is not concerned with individual pixels, but rather the shapes themselves. It sends much less information to the printer and the screen than does a paint program.

- **High Level of Editability** Vector art consists of curves, nodes, cusps, and other control points that determine the shape of objects. These control points can be manipulated with ease.

- **Lack of Realism in Drawn Objects** For all its virtues, vector art generally does not look as lifelike as bitmapped art.

In contrast, when you open up PHOTO-PAINT, you are in a different world. When you lay down individual dots on your electronic canvas, you are in fact painting. Paint programs have these characteristics:

- **Finite Resolution** The dots of a bitmapped image are of a fixed size and are a fixed distance from one another. You cannot tell a bitmap to print at 300 dots per inch (dpi) to your laser printer and then 1200 dpi to an imagesetter. The dots are what they are, and no amount of editing or coaxing will make them any smaller or bring them any closer together.

- **Large File Sizes**   Because bitmaps are dots, they consume large quantities of hard drive space, main memory, and display memory. The higher the resolution, the more dots, and the more system resources are required.

- **Pixel Editing**   There are no mathematical control points that describe bitmapped images, but you can control the dots themselves. You can zoom way in on a person's eyebrow and pluck a few hairs that look too long, by just erasing the pixels that represent the hairs.

- **High Degree of Realism**   With control over every dot that makes up an image, you can imitate life at a level beyond vector programs. An image editor and a good scanner together allow you to start the creation process with an actual photograph.

Serious electronic artists will not make an either/or choice about graphics programs; indeed, accomplished CorelDRAW artists will use both DRAW and PHOTO-PAINT, frequently in the same work. It is common today to see electronic art that contains text and complex vector art produced in a drawing program, integrated with a scanned image controlled by a paint program.

The Magic of the Curve

Forgive this oversimplification, but the cornerstone to DRAW can be summed up in one word: *curves*. The essence of DRAW is its ability to create curves, and this is in stark contrast to what a paint program or image editor does—including the one that comes with CorelDRAW.

This bears repeating: Paint programs work with hundreds of thousands or even millions of tiny dots that together form an image that registers with your brain. But the dots don't know that they are supposed to look like something—that happens practically by accident. On the other hand, the basic elements in CorelDRAW are more "intelligent." CorelDRAW knows what a shape is and understands the dynamics responsible for that shape. CorelDRAW's objects have identities and properties;

Drawing versus Painting   **7**

1.1

The left Clinton is made up of curves, the right one of dots.

they are not just a collection of pixels or dots. In Figure 1.1, for example, the curves that form the top-left image of President Clinton are more intelligent and efficient than the dots that make up the lower-right image.

You'll read a lot about curves throughout this text, especially the so-called *Bezier curve* (see Figure 1.2), named after the man who discovered the dynamic relationship that exists between a starting point, an ending point, and the two control points that determine the path taken from start to finish. You don't need to understand the intricacies—just know that Bezier curves get the credit for just about everything that CorelDRAW does right.

8 CH. 1 THE FOUNDATION OF CORELDRAW

1.2
The magic of the Bezier curve

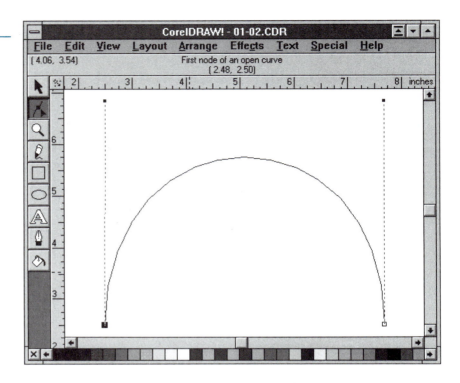

CorelDRAW Is Greater Than the Sum of Its Parts

As with most sophisticated graphics programs, CorelDRAW enters fifth gear when the basic tools of *object creation* are used in conjunction with CorelDRAW's higher-octane features. Creating a simple curve or a rectangle may not be cause for celebration, but applying one of CorelDRAW's *special effects tools* can really turn heads—tools such as Blend, which transforms one object into another, or Extrude, which adds depth and dimension to a shape. There's Radial Fill, which gently changes the fill color from one to another. And Rotate, and Envelope, and Weld, and Combine, and Perspective…the list goes on. As Figure 1.3 shows, the relationship between simple objects and powerful effects tools might be the marriage made in electronic heaven.

1.3

CorelDRAW's special effects steal the headlines every time.

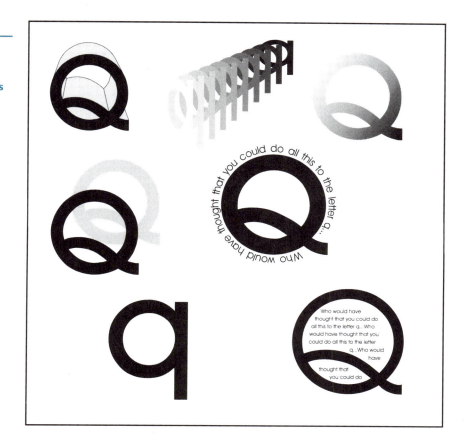

Typefaces: The Final Frontier

Perhaps the most impressive part of CorelDRAW is the way it handles text, or, more appropriately, the way it lets *you* handle text. A mind-boggling number of Type 1 and TrueType faces ship with the product, and its typographic engine allows for the setting of a typeface in point increments as small as .1, and for rotations in equally fine steps. Beyond that, Corel-DRAW allows you to manipulate text as you would other objects, placing on your electronic drafting table all of the special effects for you to use with your text.

This feature is undoubtedly responsible for two things: pure joy on the part of eager users accustomed to far greater constraints on their ability to manipulate type; and some absolutely hideous results from many of those same eager users, who start out blissfully unaware of what's involved in porducing effective art. Indeed, CorelDRAW's contributions to the Desktop Publishing Hall of Shame are substantial, but this is the inevitable price to be paid for software so inviting that practically anyone can use it.

We will close with one last point of irony: CorelDRAW has made a name for itself as an artist's tool despite the fact that a majority of its users are not artists. This demographic distinction is not lost on us, and our intent in this book is to speak to the practical and pragmatic demands and needs of mainstream CorelDRAW users. It is not our hope to convert you into brilliant artists, and frankly, we think we deserve brownie points for not trying. Rather, we hope to broaden your understanding of the software and help you become more efficient and productive.

In our ongoing series of seminars, we have met thousands of skilled CorelDRAW users who turn to the product for technical work, simple logos, sketches, headlines, and other projects that don't require formal training in the arts. These power users enjoy the never-ending search for better and faster ways to pilot the software. We also have encountered accomplished artists (those who really do the program justice) who wouldn't know a keyboard shortcut if it landed on their foreheads. Users in both categories will benefit from a more complete understanding of the inner workings of CorelDRAW, and that is what we intend to deliver.

CHAPTER 2

A Tour of the Tools

TWO

CHAPTER 2

This chapter is for new or occasional CorelDRAW users seeking an overview of the program. In Chapter 3 you'll find the details on features that are new to CorelDRAW 4.0 and 5.0, and Chapter 32 begins an entire part on Ventura Publisher.

As with most Windows programs, all the CorelDRAW modules consist of menus that you pull down, dialog boxes that you invoke, and tools that you click. Almost every function that the modules offer can be accessed from the keyboard as well as with the mouse, and we will likely harp a bit throughout the book on our favorite hotkeys, as we believe them to be invaluable when you're seeking efficiency and economy of motion. (We'll also moan a bit about some strange hotkeys and others that are absent entirely...)

Exploring the Interface

Figure 2.1 shows the essential interface for DRAW, the main module of the CorelDRAW program; for details on many of the basic components of the interface you can consult Chapter 1 of the CorelDRAW 5.0 User's Manual. Your screen might look slightly different from the one we show here, because video cards, color palettes, your Windows Desktop arrangement, and your screen resolution all affect the appearance of Windows applications.

The nine rectangles along the left side of the work area make up DRAW's *toolbox*, and provide access to the most common commands and functions of the program.

DRAW owes much of its success to its relatively clean interface: Even if you have never used a drawing program, we bet you can draw a rectangle in DRAW for the first time without too many wrong turns. And once you know the most basic of maneuvers—click on the tool / move

2.1

DRAW may overwhelm you below the surface, but it won't intimidate anyone at sea level. Since version 1.0, its interface has remained clean and uncluttered.

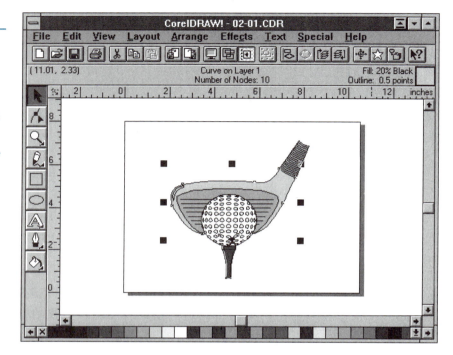

to the page / click and drag—you are all set to create not only rectangles, but ovals, text blocks, lines, and free-form objects. In mastering this maneuver you also automatically know how to zoom in on parts of your drawing. All these operations result from one set of motions:

1. Click on a tool.
2. Move your cursor out to the page.
3. Click and hold the primary mouse button.
4. Drag the mouse across the page.
5. Let go of the mouse button.

We're not exaggerating—once you have learned this simple procedure you have learned about 90 percent of the motions required to drive the program. Of course, this doesn't qualify you as Picasso's protégé just yet, and we acknowledge that this basic skill is more or less equivalent to pressing down on the accelerator and turning the steering wheel to drive your car. Next you'll need to add the vision, the judgment, the experience, and practice, practice, practice.

NEW FOR 5

In addition to all the other features of CorelDRAW's interface, DRAW now offers a Ribbon Bar full of icons allowing quick access to frequently used functions. It's debatable whether the Ribbon Bar actually contributes to DRAW's efficiency and ease-of-use, or just gets in the way and takes space away from the visible work area. As this controversy rages on, we invite you to draw your own conclusions.

The Supporting Characters

Many parts of DRAW's face are leased from Windows 3.1 itself. Like practically every Windows program, DRAW and the other CorelDRAW modules have

- A title bar listing the name of the application and the particular file opened
- A menu bar that provides access to most of the program's functions and commands
- Scroll bars for moving to other parts of a document
- Arrow buttons in the top-right corner, for expanding the DRAW window to cover your entire screen and reducing it down to an icon
- The Control Bar at the top-left, for quickly sizing and closing DRAW

Furthermore, it's difficult to find a Windows program that *doesn't* offer File and Edit as its first two menu bar choices, and which *doesn't* feature some sort of button bar with icons that provide shortcuts to commands and functions. DRAW's menus work just as any Windows user expects: You can pull down a menu by clicking it once, or by pressing the underlined character in combination with the Alt key. (Keep your eye out for those underlined letters—they keep you informed about keystroke alternatives to using the mouse.)

The Status Line DRAW reserves the area immediately below the Ribbon Bar (see Figure 2.1) for communicating with you; this is the *status line*. (On your system, the status line might be at the bottom of the work area, rather than the top.) At the left of this line, DRAW tells you the position of the cursor, and whether Grid Snap—one of the more frequently used functions—is activated.

In the middle, DRAW displays a message; in Figure 2.1, the message is "Curve on Layer 1." At first glance, this message might seem written in a foreign language; actually, DRAW is reminding you of which object is currently selected. You select objects on the page by clicking them, and when you do, they grow small black handles around their perimeters. You can see those handles around the face of the golf club in Figure 2.1. Indeed, that shape is referred to by DRAW as a "curve"; as we established in Chapter 1, without curves, life as CorelDRAW knows it would be impossible.

Toward the right end of the status line, DRAW gives you information about the interior and exterior of the selected object. In this example, DRAW says the face of the golf club has a fill pattern of 20% Black, and has an outline that is colored black and set at .5 point thickness.

The rectangle at the far-right end of the status line changes dynamically to reflect the properties of the currently selected object. If the golf club face were blue, so would be the rectangle. And if the outline were red and 3 points thick (now that's some golf club!), the line around the rectangle would change to reflect those attributes. When objects overlap, sometimes the only way you can tell which object is selected is to watch this little box in the status line. Continuing with our automobile analogy, staying mindful of this box is akin to using your rearview mirror: It's an excellent habit to develop and might save you from some major trouble someday.

The Scroll Bars   DRAW's scroll bars operate just like those in most other Windows programs. The horizontal and vertical scroll bars operate the same way. There are three ways to scroll the screen: You can scroll little by little, by clicking on the small arrow buttons on either end of the scroll bar; you can scroll a lot at a time, by clicking on the gray part of the scroll bar (on your system, the scroll bar may be a different color); or scroll any amount you choose, by clicking and dragging the small rectangle (the *scroll button*) inside the scroll bar.

The Color Palette   At the bottom of the screen resides a different scroll bar: the *color palette,* which provides you with a very easy method of changing the interior fill or the outline color of a selected object. Most color palettes have many more colors than can fit on the screen—hence the presence of the color palette scroll bar. The X button at the left end is for the quick removal of a fill or outline. One palette serves both the outline and the fill, thanks to the fact that PC mice have two buttons: If you click on a color (or the X) with the primary mouse button, you change the interior fill of the selected object; click with the secondary mouse button, and you change the outline.

Have It *Your* Way...   The color palette and the on-screen rulers can be toggled on and off via the View menu, and the status line and Ribbon Bar via the Special / Preferences / View dialog. You can also turn off the page border, and—in DRAW 4.0 and 5.0—the toolbox can be removed, also. By controlling all these screen elements you can make a dramatic change in DRAW's appearance, as you can see if you compare the interfaces in Figure 2.2.

Understanding Dialog Boxes

When you issue commands for actions such as removing the status line or the color palette from the DRAW interface, you are performing the next most common maneuver in the program after the click-and-drag: pulling down a menu and then choosing one of its functions. Clicking on a menu choice will generally produce one of two results: It will either trigger an on/off toggle (as in showing and hiding the on-screen rulers), or it will activate a submenu or *dialog box,* in which a collection

2.2

The DRAW interface. *Top:* with all its essential parts intact. *Bottom:* without the status line, button bar, rulers, color palette, page border, and toolbox

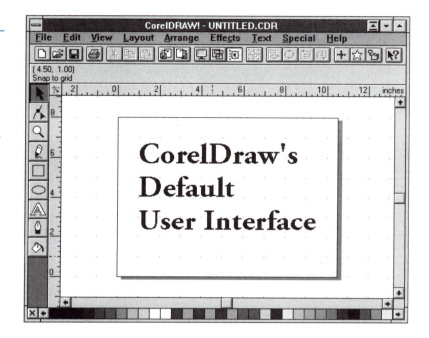

of controls resides. Menu choices that lead to submenus have a right-pointing arrow beside them. Menu choices that evoke dialog boxes—in this book, we say *dialogs* for short—are followed by three dots (an ellipsis). Figure 2.3 shows the result of choosing Special / Preferences. This dialog controls the way many of DRAW's elements behave and appear on screen.

NEW FOR 5

CorelDRAW adopts the new design of "tabbed dialogs," in which electronic file tabs along the top of a dialog box indicate the various places you can go. In Figure 2.3, you are looking at the View settings—you know this because its tab is raised above the others.

2.3

A typical dialog, with fields for entering values, check boxes to click on and off, and buttons for displaying other dialogs

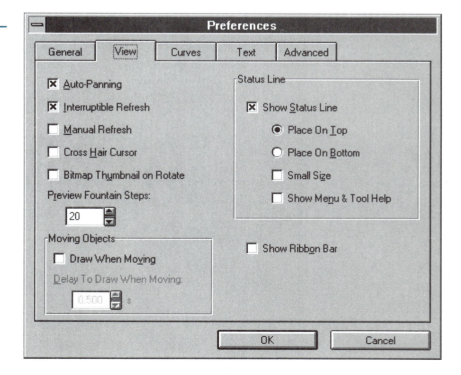

Remember, it makes no difference to DRAW how you open this Preferences dialog. You can use your mouse, clicking once on Special in the menu bar and then on Preferences in the Special menu, or you can press Alt+S for Special and then P for Preferences. Or you can mix and match your keyboard and mouse actions; DRAW doesn't care. (Incidentally, note that the fine art of mnemonics is finally coming to CorelDRAW; in the previous two versions, it was Alt+S and then E to evoke Preferences. This is progress...)

Because the route to this Preferences dialog is heavily traveled by regular DRAW users, the developers assigned a *hotkey* to it: Ctrl+J. DRAW's hotkeys provide you with instant access to a dialog box or command, without having to pull down a menu. Whenever you want to access the Preferences dialog box, typing Ctrl+J will do it, no questions asked. Hotkeys are particularly handy if you just want to check a value for a setting without changing it—Ctrl+J opens the dialog box, and the Escape key closes it.

INSIDE INFO

All of DRAW's keyboard shortcuts (hotkeys) to dialogs are shown on the menus with their functions; for instance, pull down the File menu and you'll see Ctrl+S associated with the Save command. There are probably about 150 different hotkeys across the entire program, including such obscure gems as holding down the Shift key to erase a line drawn with the Pencil tool; or pressing Ctrl+Z to Undo a change and then Alt+Enter to undo the undo.

Understanding what all of DRAW's controls mean can be tricky, but changing them is easy. Here again, DRAW lets you navigate with the mouse or the keyboard within all dialogs. As you can see in Figure 2.3, every field, check box, and button can be accessed with a keystroke (note the underlines). So if you're going to change, say, the Preview Fountain Steps setting from 20 to 24, you have three choices:

- Use the mouse to place the cursor in the box and change it to 24.
- Press Alt+U to highlight the field and press 24 to enter the new value.
- Click on the little up-arrow box to increase the value to 24.

No surprise here—our preference is the second option, using the keyboard. Nothing is faster or easier on your hands and wrists. Try all three and judge for yourself.

WATCH OUT!

When entering values in number fields, make sure the unit of measurement (seconds versus minutes, points versus picas, etc.) is what you want before you change the number. If you do it in the wrong order, DRAW might yell at you.

Working with Roll-Ups

Corel invented these cute little quasi-dialogs for version 3.0, and they quickly became a big hit with users. *Roll-ups* perform many of the same functions as conventional dialogs, but roll-ups are much more interactive. For instance, they don't disappear after carrying out a command, as conventional dialogs do. And because of their diminutive size, you can place roll-ups right next to the object in question, for quick mouse action.

Figure 2.4 shows one of the many roll-ups available to you in DRAW. This one has just presided over the block of text next to it, changing the font to 22-point Berkeley Black. Instead of clicking an OK button to enact a change, you click on one of the Apply buttons. And instead of disappearing promptly, this roll-up sticks around, making a series of tweaks a much friendlier task.

2.4

The Text roll-up is a handy way to edit text, especially if you're making continual and repeated changes. Roll-ups remain on screen until you close them.

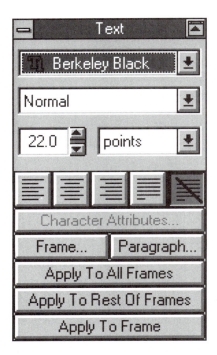

This block of text can be edited very quickly with the Text Roll-up. All of the commands that apply to text can be found in this little dialog.

Exploring the Toolbox

The nine tools that make up the toolbox are the electronic lifeblood of DRAW. You can create hundreds of complete drawings using just these nine tools and none of the commands from the menus (except Save!). Following is a brief rundown 'on each tool.

The Pick Tool

The Pick tool acts as home base for DRAW: It is the tool that you use to select objects before altering them, and it is the active tool every time you start the program. You can select an object by clicking it with the Pick tool, or by dragging across it with a *marquee box* (see Chapter 4). When you drag a marquee around an object or group of objects, you must make sure to completely surround them. Once you have selected an object, you also use the Pick tool to move and/or resize it.

Most advanced DRAW users take the Pick tool for granted—not unlike our relationship with the air we breathe. Many users might not even know this tool's name; they might describe it as "that thing at the top that is always highlighted when you aren't using anything else. You know, the one that pretty much does everything." That about sums up the Pick tool.

Hotkey: the Spacebar (sort of). Unbelievably, Corel developers have never given this most fundamental of tools its own hotkey, but you can toggle between the most recently used tool and the Pick tool by pressing Spacebar.

The Shape Tool

Also referred to as the Node Edit tool, the Shape tool presides over parts of an object, not the whole. Where you would reach for the Pick tool to move or resize an entire curve or a whole string of text, the Shape tool provides access to a part of the curve, or one character in the text string. The parts of a curve are called *nodes*—hence this tool's other moniker—and by adjusting a node, you can change the essential shape of a curve.

In addition to node editing, the Shape tool can edit and kern selected text characters, crop bitmaps, round the corners of rectangles, and turn circles into arcs and pie slices.

Hotkey: F10

The Zoom Tool

The Zoom tool is perhaps the most essential aid to creating and editing illustrations, because it lets you work in the optimum magnification. As shown in the following graphic, this tool is actually a gateway to six separate viewing controls.

- Zoom In, allowing you to define a marquee around the area to magnify

- Zoom Out, which moves out by a factor of two, or returns to the view prior to the last Zoom In
- Actual Size, which lets you display your drawing at the size in which it will print
- Zoom on Selected (new to 5.0), which brings selected objects into the closest possible view
- Fit in Window, which brings all objects in a drawing into the closest possible view
- Show Page, which displays the entire page

Hotkeys: F2 for triggering Zoom In mode, F3 for Zoom Out, Shift+F2 for Zoom on Selected, F4 for Fit in Window, and Shift+F4 for Show Page

The Pencil Tool

If the Pick tool is the essential editing tool, then the Pencil is the essential creation tool. It is the electronic equivalent of the rapidograph or the sketching pencil. DRAW 4.0 added some nice elements to this tool, and 5.0 advanced them a bit, but the Pencil's primary missions are still to support *freehand drawing* and *Bezier drawing*.

Freehand drawing really is like working with a pencil: To draw, you hold the mouse button down and move around the page. If you remember the old Etch-a-Sketch contraptions, you can get a good idea of the type of free-form (and sometimes dreadful) work this tool is capable of.

Bezier drawing creates the smooth curves required by fine art and illustration. When drawing in Bezier mode, you do not hold down the mouse button to create curves. Rather, you click once to define a starting point and then click again to define an ending point. The line that connects the two is treated as a curve whose shape and position can be readily changed. Most of the attractive work you see produced with DRAW makes extensive use of Bezier curves.

Hotkey: F5

NEW FOR 5

The Pencil tool allows you to create lines that automatically calculate distance. These lines, referred to as dimension lines, are quite handy for precision drafting and technical work, as Figure 2.5 shows. Dimension lines were introduced in DRAW 4.0, but their usefulness was hampered by their static nature—that is, the value of the dimension line did not automatically change if you resized the line. In DRAW 5.0, they do.

2.5

Dimension lines make calculating distances as simple as a click and a drag.

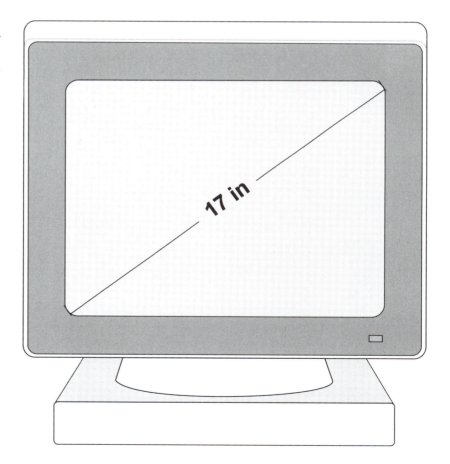

The Rectangle and Ellipse Tools

Probably the first tools every new user reaches for, the simple Rectangle and Ellipse tools produce their respective shapes with simple click-and-drag maneuvers. Once created, these shapes inherit the default outlines and fills that are in effect during the DRAW session.

With both tools, if you hold the Shift key while dragging, the object draws from the center out. If you hold the Ctrl key while dragging, you can create squares and perfect circles.

Hotkeys: F6 for Rectangle, and F7 for Ellipse

The Text Tool

This tool brings the written word to your drawings. By clicking once on the Text icon and then once on the page, you can create *artistic text*, the most versatile of the two text types. This text can be enhanced with all of the special effects DRAW has to offer, such as extrusions, blends, and fitting to a path.

When you click and hold the Text tool, you get a *flyout menu* displaying the other text choice—*paragraph text*. You can create paragraph text by clicking on its tool and then clicking and dragging on the page to create a rectangular frame into which you type text.

Artistic text is designed for headlines and small strings of text; paragraph text can hold thousands of characters and treat them all as one fluid text block.

The Symbols roll-up, shown in Figure 2.6, has taken up new digs in the Special menu.

Hotkeys: F8 for artistic text, and Shift+F8 for paragraph text

NEW FOR 5

Those of you looking for the Symbols roll-up won't find it in the usual place. Formerly the third choice in the Text tool's flyout menu, now it is found under the Special menu. We've always had a soft spot for the Symbols roll-up, but placing it under the Special menu is a bit much. In this context, we suspect that Special means "stuff that doesn't seem to fit anywhere else."

2.6

DRAW's on-line Symbols library has attained "Special" status.

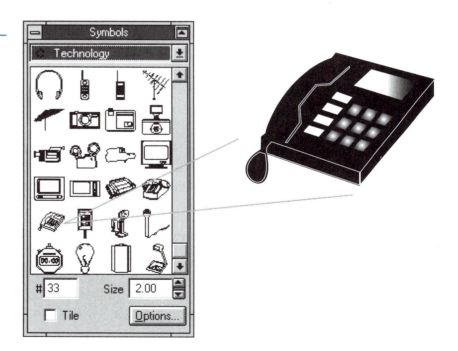

The Outline Tool

The Outline tool (and the Fill tool described just below) are an order of magnitude more involved than the tools examined so far. Simply stated, the Outline tool is the one-stop shop for assigning outline colors and widths to any selected objects, be they curves, rectangles, ellipses, or text characters. You can choose from four preset outline thicknesses, and seven gray-shaded outline colors, as shown in the following graphic. Or you can access the Outline Pen dialog or roll-up and treat yourself to a bevy of controls. Clicking on the X button removes any outline from a selected object (just like the X on the color palette at the bottom).

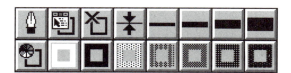

If you use the Outline tool (that is, if you change an Outline setting) without selecting an object, DRAW reminds you that you are about to change the default, which will affect subsequently drawn objects.

Hotkeys: F12 to reach the Outline Pen dialog, and Shift+F12 for the Outline Color dialog.

The Fill Tool

Perhaps the richest of all the tools, the Fill tool is the gateway to some simple chores, such as assigning a pure color to an object, as well as more exotic ones, such as creating a fountain or textured fill. (For simple color fills, you might prefer to use the on-screen color palette.)

As with the Outline tool, assigning a fill affects only the selected object. If no object is selected, the change is made to the default, affecting all subsequent objects. And you can access other dialogs and roll-ups that bring the full power of this tool to your fingertips, just as you can with the Outline tool.

Hotkeys: F11 to reach the Fountain Fill dialog box, and Shift+F11 for the Uniform Fill dialog box.

Figure 2.7 shows one of DRAW's textured fill patterns. Our artistically challenged lead author produced this picture in about 15 minutes.

1. Showing incredible cunning and guile, he calmly retrieved BIG-BEN.CDR from the clip art supplied with the DRAW software.

2.7

Fifteen minutes of fame: DRAW's automated features and clip art library make it easy to produce attractive art.

2. Then he drew a big rectangle and placed it behind Big Ben.
3. Next he clicked on the Fill tool and chose the icon for the Texture Fill dialog (the sixth one on the top row).
4. From Texture Fill he chose the pattern labeled Sky 5 Colors.
5. Then he clicked on the Arrange menu and chose Order, To Back.
6. Last, he saved, printed, and promptly proclaimed it his finest work ever.

You'll find this drawing in the PICTURE directory on the Companion CD of this book, as well as in the Color Gallery as Illustration 1. This is not because your fearless author thinks it is actually worthy of admiration, but because we want to show you how quickly and easily you can bring a couple of elements together into a simple, attractive piece.

Browsing the Menus

As we said earlier, it's possible to produce several simple drawings without knowingly accessing functions from DRAW's pull-down menus—especially if you make a habit of using hotkeys such as Ctrl+S (Save) and Ctrl+P (Print). Nonetheless, it's important for you to understand how the menus are laid out and what kind of logical (and in some cases, illogical) groupings the program employs for its commands.

The File Menu

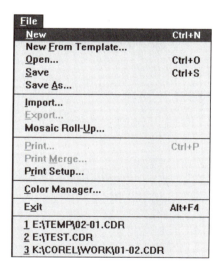

This menu is DRAW's Grand Central Station, where all files enter and exit. As with practically all Windows programs, this is the menu from which you open files, save files, import files, export files, and print files. DRAW 5.0's File menu offers a gateway to CorelMOSAIC, Corel's image cataloging utility, and to a color management utility for calibrating color devices.

Notice the underlines sprinkled throughout this menu, indicating the keyboard alternatives for invoking commands and dialogs, as well as the plethora of hotkeys (Ctrl and Alt key-combinations).

Also, do you notice that the Export command is dimmed? This is DRAW's way of telling you that the command is unavailable. In this instance, you can't use the Export command because there are no objects in this new drawing—nothing created, nothing to export.

The four drawings listed at the bottom of the menu are the four most recently opened files.

Finally, the three dots (…) that follows many of the commands are there to tell you that a dialog or roll-up is lurking underneath. By contrast, commands that perform their entire functions as soon as you activate them—such as Save and Exit—don't have the three dots. (Incidentally, "the three dots" are also known as an *ellipsis*.)

The Edit Menu

Edit	
Undo Move	Ctrl+Z
Redo	Alt+Ret
Repeat Move	Ctrl+R
Cut	Ctrl+X
Copy	Ctrl+C
Paste	Ctrl+V
Paste Special...	
Delete	Del
Duplicate	Ctrl+D
Clone	
Copy Attributes From...	
Select All	
Insert Object...	
Object	▶
Links...	

This menu is in charge of changes, duplications, copying, deleting, cloning, and undoing and redoing all of the above. As with all OLE-compliant programs (that is, programs that support Windows 3.*x* Object Linking and Embedding), the Edit menu is also the headquarters for all Clipboard activity going out to other programs and coming in from the outside world.

The Clone command, introduced in DRAW 4.0, is sure to turn a few heads, as it does Duplicate one better by linking all cloned objects to the original. Change the original, and all the clones change, too.

On this menu, the Paste and Paste Special commands are available, indicating that there is an object on the Clipboard—placed there by DRAW or another program.

The View Menu

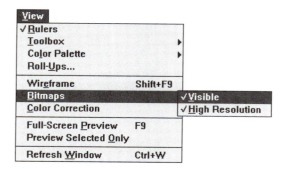

New to 5.0, the View menu is an advanced edition of the old Display menu, and takes charge of on-screen activities. These controls let you control many aspects of the DRAW interface, as well as how much detail to show of the components of your drawing.

One of the new controls, pictured here with its fly-out, lets you control the handling of imported bitmap graphics, giving you the choice of better detail or better performance.

Perhaps the most overlooked and underrated of this support team is the Ctrl+W hotkey, which redraws the screen for you—a frequent requirement when you're working with complex and overlapping elements.

The Layout Menu

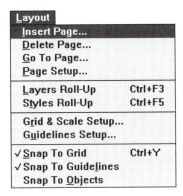

The Layout menu offers controls for elements as fundamental as page size and number of pages, on out to the complex minutiae of laying down the little blue dots that act as guides. Grid, Guideline, and Page setups all reside here, as do the roll-ups for Layers and Styles.

The final three items in the menu toggle the three types of snaps available: grid, guidelines, or objects.

The Arrange Menu

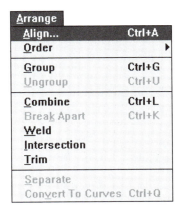

If it needs to be ordered, layered, aligned, collected, taken apart, or put back together again, it is a job for the Arrange menu. Here you can insist that two objects be moved and sized together, with the Group, Combine, or Weld commands, or coupled more exotically with the new Intersection and Trim commands.

Seasoned DRAW users will want to learn the hotkeys for moving objects to the front and back and for moving forward and back one place. These functions are nested a level below the other functions in the Order command.

Also, notice that Ctrl+C and Ctrl+V no longer belong to the Combine and Convert to Curves command, as they did prior to DRAW 4.0. These keystrokes now accommodate the standard Clipboard commands for Copy and Paste. We think you'll like Ctrl+L and Q just as well…NOT!

The Effects Menu

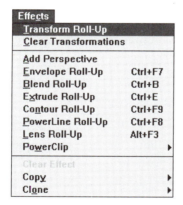

This is DRAW's most happening place, and houses a very lively set of functions. The Effects menu contains the commands that define DRAW's outgoing personality—the blending, extruding, enveloping, skewing, and stretching. Veteran DRAW users will notice not only a few new commands, such as Contour and PowerLine (DRAW 4.0) and Lens and PowerClip (DRAW 5.0), but also an utterly absurd assortment of hotkeys. Ctrl+B and

Ctrl+E, both inherited from 3.0, make nice mnemonic sense, but the others are a complete jumble. If our job as authors is to provide the logic behind decisions like this one, then we resign right now.

The Text Menu

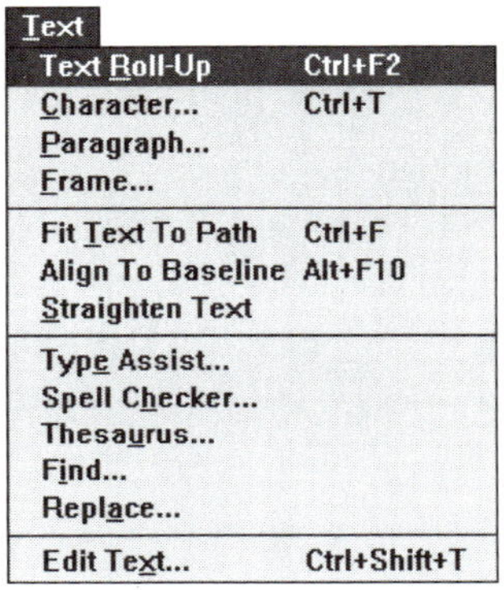

```
Text
Text Roll-Up        Ctrl+F2
Character...        Ctrl+T
Paragraph...
Frame...

Fit Text To Path    Ctrl+F
Align To Baseline   Alt+F10
Straighten Text

Type Assist...
Spell Checker...
Thesaurus...
Find...
Replace...

Edit Text...        Ctrl+Shift+T
```

The Text menu is your supermarket for text formatting and editing. Many of the controls that you need can be found in the Text roll-up, but there are times when the various dialogs for text editing are easier to navigate. The Fit Text to Path command is perhaps the most widely used special effect in all of DRAW history (it's actually a roll-up, but we suspect that the words Fit Text To Path Roll-Up wouldn't fit on the menu).

On the other hand, the Spell Checker and Thesaurus might be the two least-used commands. As DRAW continues to increase its support for text-heavy documents, these word processing features might see more action; as of now, they lie almost dormant, so say our demographic studies. However, the new 5.0 feature, PowerType, promises to vie for Rookie of the Year honors. Figure 2.8 shows its potential value for those seeking the shortest distance between two typewritten points.

2.8

PowerType makes quick work of common expressions and common mistakes.

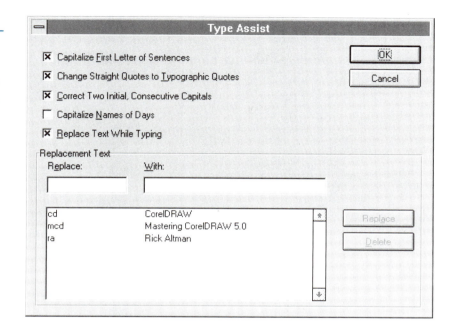

in his book, mcd, author ra says,
"MOst cd users are not professional artists."

In his book, Mastering CorelDRAW 5.0, author Rick Altman says, "Most CorelDRAW users are not professional artists."

You type this

DRAW displays this

The Special Menu

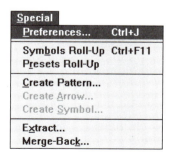

This menu is a cop-out: Herein lie all the things that don't fit anywhere else. The powerful Create Pattern, Arrow, and Symbol commands are mostly for advanced users. Meanwhile, the Extract and Merge-Back functions presume that you use DRAW for fairly high-level word processing tasks. Then there is the good old Preferences dialog, which has a little something for everyone.

In the next chapter, we throw a blanket over all that is new in both DRAW 4.0 and DRAW 5.0.

What's New in CorelDRAW

CHAPTER THREE

CHAPTER 3

This comprehensive chapter is based on two assumptions. First, CorelDRAW users want to know what is in each new version of the program. You might take for granted that all program documentation contains this information, but that point seems to be lost on the documentation developers at Corel Corp. Neither of the Reference Guides for versions 4.0 and 5.0 includes a section detailing new features.

When we called the Corel offices and asked for any available internal documents, we received literature from the marketing department, full of exclamation marks and words such as "impressive," "exciting," and "unique." We then checked the Corel forum on CompuServe—usually a haven for technical notes—but found only a text file called FIFTY GREAT REASONS TO BUY CORELDRAW. Finally, buried deep in the program's on-line help, under the heading Overview, we found a somewhat thin discussion entitled Notes to Upgraders.

Our second assumption is that there are vast numbers of you who are making the jump from CorelDRAW 3.0 directly to 5.0. Therefore, this chapter is divided into two parts: a section that describes changes and additions made to version 4.0, and a section on what's new as of 5.0. Those of you upgrading from version 4.0 might want to pass over the first part of this chapter and go right to the section on new 5.0 features.

Though we expect that all DRAW users will find value in this chapter, it is directed toward experienced users, and we assume a certain level of knowledge of and familiarity with the program. Our only qualification: Don't expect this chapter to be a dry and even-handed recounting of new features. We intend this chapter—indeed, the book in total—to reflect our disposition as users of the software, and we do not hesitate to add our own commentary to the discussion. We won't waste your time by constantly adding "in our opinion," or "if you ask us." We know that you didn't ask us, and you might not give a hoot about our opinions.

But you did buy our book, so now you're stuck with us, bias and all.

AUTHOR'S NOTE

 This chapter focuses on changes to the DRAW module. Part VIII, "The World of Ventura Publisher," includes a complete discussion of Corel's newest family member, Ventura Publisher. We discuss the program's other modules in Part VII, "The Supporting Cast."

CorelDRAW 4.0

It's not enough to say that version 4.0 was CorelDRAW's most dramatic upgrade. DRAW 4.0, released in May of 1993, stands as one of the most ambitious upgrades ever made to any program. In terms of total volume of changes, we place it in the all-time top five upgrades—right up there with dBase IV, DOS 3.3, Ventura Publisher 2.0, and the new Lotus 1-2-3 for Windows.

The View from the Top in 4.0

The two most notable changes made to DRAW 4.0 were its support for *multiple pages* and its incorporation of *templates,* the latter allowing users to globally link common elements across a file, or even a group of files. DRAW 4.0 can create newsletters and other multipage documents, without having to resort to multiple DRAW files or some awkward contortion with the Layers roll-up. And because text elements such as headlines and subheads can be linked to a style, global control is possible over elements that might be pages apart.

These two additions were the harbinger of Corel's move into a fundamentally different arena, owned historically by PageMaker and shared more recently by Xpress for Windows. Though PageMaker will continue to be a close partner to DRAW, it's likely that many DRAW users who have turned to PageMaker for short documents will instead give DRAW a chance to display its multipage prowess.

We, however, use that term *prowess* with fear and trepidation. There are definitely right and wrong times to turn to DRAW for longer projects. Paragraph text flows with acceptable speed from one page to another, but artistic text and independent objects are responsible for interminable delays on many users' systems. One editor, in experiments with 8- and 12-page newsletters, reported load times in excess of 30 minutes for CDR files; other users have enjoyed immensely the ability to produce facing-page ad slicks entirely within DRAW.

Forget about turning a Ventura Publisher-type project over to DRAW, despite the program's boast about support for 999 pages. (Now, of course, you won't have to, with Ventura's inclusion in the CorelDRAW 5.0 box.) DRAW can't touch FrameMaker's document controls, either, or Xpress's typographic precision. In short, documents that span multiple pages and contain artistic text and many other elements will likely prove too taxing—if not for DRAW, then for your patience. Simple layouts containing paragraph text, however, might cater to DRAW's new multipage personality.

The jury is still out on styles, too—but not because of any belief that they are not worthwhile. Quite the contrary: Veteran users have been clamoring for a way to link common elements since version 1.0, and most were happy to see styles in 4.0. Text styles, as shown in Figure 3.1, are exceptionally versatile, offering users the power to

- Incorporate many text elements into a style—typeface, weight, size, spacing, tabs, indents, bullets—and instantly apply them all to selected text.
- Choose which elements to apply to selected text, and which ones not to. For instance, you can ask that only the typeface and size be used from a style, while ignoring tabs and indents.
- Store styles in templates and apply them to multiple files.
- Save any DRAW file as a template to be used globally.
- Assign styles to hotkeys for quick and easy use on selected text.

3.1

Global styles finally came to DRAW with version 4.0.

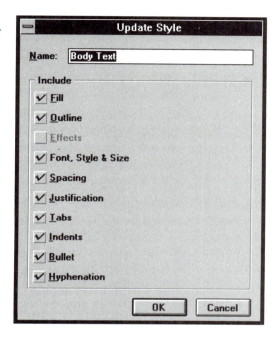

Version 4.0's styles for graphics objects are as convenient as the text styles, though perhaps not quite as dramatic in potential value. Criticism throughout 4.0's reign was centered not on function, but rather implementation. Users have expressed confusion over the extended reach of styles—for instance, how styles become templates, and how templates affect other files. Just about all of us have scratched our heads from time to time over DRAW's messages asking us to save or discard changes made to a template, when we haven't gone near any style elements. We'll get to the bottom of the styles questions in Chapter 9.

These kinks in the styles features remain in DRAW 5.0, but most users are glad to see this powerful capability added to the program.

Text Features New to 4.0

Our surveys show that most people who turn to DRAW do so for projects that in some way involve text. In fact, many DRAW users launch the program just to create headlines or other pieces of text destined for mastheads on newsletters, or for the tops of fliers or corporate reports.

To this wide body of users, the changes made to DRAW 4.0's typographic engine have been of primary interest.

New Typefaces

Let's start with the big stuff: Corel trashed all of its old typefaces and started from scratch, licensing a truckload from Bitstream and ITC. The CD version of CorelDRAW 4.0 shipped with 750 typefaces, and all but 100 of them were from these two reputable typeface vendors. As expected, the approval rating for CorelDRAW's typeface quality was far above that heard when 3.0 was settling in. Though not up to the exceptionally high Adobe Type 1 standard, DRAW 4.0 offered legitimate electronic typography.

DRAW 4.0 and 5.0 still offer support for both TrueType and Type 1 faces, so if you want to continue to use your old 3.0 typefaces, you can. We suspect you won't want to, however, once you browse the improved lineup of typefaces available now. If you can't find the face you're looking for in 4.0 or 5.0, then you'll never be happy.

Wait, we'd better qualify that. If you can't find the face you're looking for, it might be that you *have* looked for it and *really* can't find it. DRAW's current typeface cataloging leaves much to be desired. All of the Bitstream faces have file names such as tt0155m_.ttf, making it next to impossible to hunt down a desired typeface in File Manager and copy it to the hard drive. Figure 3.2 shows what you're in for if you try.

Using Control Panel to solve this problem is not terribly inviting, as it is very slow at compiling all of the names in a given directory, and your only choices are to copy the font into the Windows directory, or run it from the CD—there is no provision to copy it into another directory on your hard drive. Fortunately, the CD offers a separate font installer that makes the task a bit friendlier. All told, however, managing 750 fonts requires a level of support beyond what Corel's architects have designed into 4.0.

For strategies to better manage DRAW's typefaces, see Chapter 13.

3.2

Looking to copy Bauer Bodoni from the CD to your hard drive? Good luck finding it with Bitstream's unfriendly typeface names.

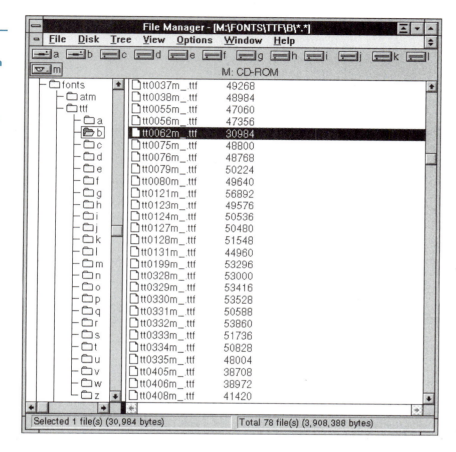

Better Defaults

Thanks to DRAW's styles, you can design starting points that are much better suited for particular projects. For instance, fliers requiring 18-point Erie Black can have their own templates: Open the template, create some text, and it will automatically have the right typeface and size. Other types of work, too, can have templates suited especially for them—each one accessible from the New from Template command on the File menu.

Furthermore, artistic and paragraph text can each have its own set of defaults within the same file. That way, body copy set as paragraph text can default to, say, 12-point Garamond, while artistic text for headlines can default to 24-point Eras Bold.

And remember, text defaults go well beyond merely typeface and size, as discussed at the top of this chapter. DRAW's text styles incorporate tabs, spacing, indents, and even custom bullets.

More Word Processing Features

As DRAW looks more and more like a small document publisher, it is only natural, and essential, that it handle more effectively the rudimentary tasks of word processing. DRAW's Paragraph dialog supports true tabs (not just insertion of spaces), left and right margins, space above and below paragraphs, and—finally!—the option of setting line spacing in points (see Figure 3.3), not just as a percentage of the type size.

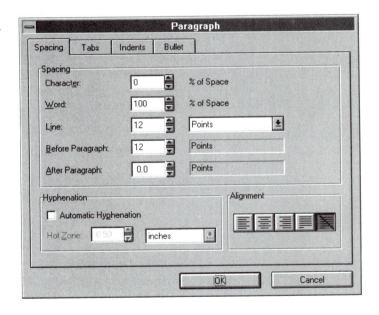

3.3

DRAW users can set a paragraph the normal way, as in "10/12," with 12 points of space before it.

All of this was welcome news for 4.0 users, with one possible exception: Die-hard keyboard users did not like what happened to the Tab key in the Edit Text dialog. Up through version 3.0, you could edit text entirely with the keyboard:

1. Press Ctrl+T to invoke the dialog box.

2. Edit the text in the window.
3. Press Tab to highlight the OK button.
4. Press Enter.

But as of version 4.0, pressing Tab inserts a tab. Sounds logical, we admit, but it hasn't been happy news to those accustomed to the quick Tab/Enter departure from the Edit Text dialog box. The workaround—pressing Alt+F to highlight the font list, and then pressing Enter—is hardly elegant, and requires a healthy dose of unlearning for some. Through Corel's beta forum on CompuServe, many of us pleaded with the engineers to create a Ctrl+Enter keystroke that would trigger OK or Apply in any dialog box or roll-up. We clamored again during the 5.0 beta cycle. To date, Ctrl+Enter sits idle across the CorelDRAW program.

The good news about the venerable Edit Text dialog in 4.0 is that it was relocated to the Text menu where it belongs, instead of in the Edit menu.

Friendlier Text Roll-Up

Version 4.0's Text roll-up provides the same fine preview feature found in the Edit Text dialog. Clicking on the typeface drop-down list triggers a flyout display of the current typeface in the selected weight, as shown in Figure 3.4.

3.4

Flyout typeface preview has come to the Text roll-up.

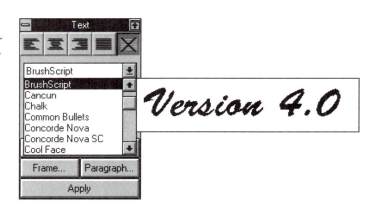

Type styles are grouped into a drop-down style list, and though this makes for a cleaner roll-up, it is not as easy to use as the 3.0 method of clicking on one of the four icons, Normal, Bold, Italic, and Bold-Italic. Sub- and superscripting, manual kerning, and character rotation are all together in a dialog called Character Placement. Curiously, the same was not done for alignment options, whose five icons (Left, Right, Center, Justified, and No Alignment) still reside at the top of the roll-up.

Smarter Paragraph Text

Artistic text remained relatively unchanged in 4.0, but paragraph text received a tremendous shot in the arm. We are fascinated to observe how many DRAW users still don't really know about paragraph text, remaining content for all these years just to click on the icon, click on the page, and begin typing. The particular and often dramatic virtues of paragraph text will be extolled in Part III; following is a brief look at the functionality introduced in 4.0.

Dynamic Text Flow   Paragraph text in 4.0 and 5.0 behaves as do text frames in Ventura Publisher, or text threads in PageMaker: Text can be made to flow from frame to frame, and page to page. When one frame of text is reformatted, reshaped, or edited, the change ripples across all subsequent frames that contain the same text file. Line breaks are automatically recalculated. And because paragraph text resets faster than artistic text, this feature is viable—unlike some of the multipage scenarios discussed earlier in this chapter (such as that 30-minute load time for a newsletter).

Text Enveloping   Though it's not as elegant as PageMaker's Text Wrap command, DRAW 4.0 introduced legitimate text wrap around irregular objects. It's done cleverly—by extending the Envelope function to include paragraphs of text. Simply put, you can node-edit a frame of text as you would any other object. The letter forms themselves don't change, but the frame in which the text resides does. By shaping the frame around an object, you can create a realistic impression that the text is automatically flowing around it.

Figure 3.5 shows both dynamic text flow and enveloping in action: The two text frames are linked, so that the text flows dynamically; and both frames are shaped around the contour of the ellipse.

3.5

Two show-stoppers in 4.0: dynamic text flow between two frames, and envelopes applied to text

Draw brought legitimate text wrap around irregular objects to Version 4.0. It did this in a clever way: by expanding on the Envelope function to include paragraphs of text. Simply put, you can node edit a frame of text as you would most any other object. While the letterforms themselves don't change, the frame in which the text resides does. By shaping the frame around an object, you can create the very realistic impression that the text is automatically flowing around it. This figure shows both dynamic text flow and enveloping in action. While not as elegant as Page-Maker's Text Wrap tool, this two-step process brought to Draw 4.0 legitimate text wrap around irregular objects.

Text Inside Objects

This feature is something less than a true Paste Inside function, in which you can pour text into a frame of any size or shape. Instead, you can apply an existing shape to a paragraph of text. For instance, we could have placed a text frame inside the ellipse of Figure 3.5 and made it follow the inside contour. Once again, DRAW has borrowed the power of the envelope: To make text flow inside of a circle, you create a frame of text, create a circle, and then instruct the frame to look like the circle. Two steps instead of one, but, as with the irregular text wrap, the results are credible.

Basic Drawing Changes in 4.0

As we noted the significant numbers of DRAW users who work primarily with text, so must we acknowledge the artists and illustrators who turn to DRAW for producing sketches, portraits, illustrations, and other works that might not include any text at all. To that camp, the following 4.0 enhancements might be the most salient of all.

Better Node Editing

All node-editing functions have been placed on a roll-up. Before you think this is merely a cosmetic change, remember that roll-ups don't go away when a command is invoked from them. This means you don't have to double-click on a node to change it. Few aspects of DRAW's past have been more responsible for wrist fatigue than those abominable double-clicks on little nodes, only to bring up a dialog that would promptly disappear after each use. We're quick to criticize the use of some of DRAW's roll-ups, but node editing—a mouse-intensive operation that requires constant interaction with a set of controls—is the ideal time to use one.

Although the new Node Edit roll-up captured the headlines for improvements in node editing, there are two other additions worth mentioning:

- **Auto-Reduce.** This nifty, automated tool studies a curve, finding and deleting nodes that are not required. This is great help for users of the TRACE module, who always have to deal with extra nodes added to traced images. Auto-Reduce can be adjusted to sniff out only those obviously useless nodes, or it can be set to be ultrasensitive, indicting and banishing any node that is even suspect.

- **Reshaping Is a Breeze.** You know how you needed to click on a node and then drag the blue control points to change the shape of a curve? No more. As of 4.0, to reshape a curve you can just click and drag right on the curve, at the point you want to change. You no longer need to activate one of the nodes; the curve segment itself can be reshaped.

All told, the drastically reduced need for clicking and double-clicking when creating and editing lines and curves has been a welcome relief to 4.0 users.

PowerLines

One of the new kids on the 4.0 Special Effects block, PowerLines enable you to create lines with variable thicknesses. With PowerLines, it is very easy to create a line that looks like an hourglass—fat at the extremes and thin in the middle. The law governing lines—that they may contain an outline but not a fill—have been overturned. PowerLines act like closed shapes; they can be outlined, filled, edited, and reshaped.

In addition to the numerous presets that DRAW provides in the Power-Lines roll-up, you can create your own PowerLines. Once created, you can apply a PowerLine to an existing conventional line, or draw a new line and have the PowerLine applied automatically.

With PowerLines, it would be quite easy to, for instance, fill a night-time sky with lightning bolts, as shown in Figure 3.6. Here are the steps:

1. Open the PowerLine roll-up from the Effects menu.
2. To create one lightning bolt, choose either the Wedge1 or Wedge2 preset.

3.6

This simple drawing is made even simpler with PowerLines.

3. Click the check box that says "Apply when drawing lines."
4. Create other lightning bolts, just by creating the line segments. The PowerLine engine automatically applies the widths.

You can read a lot more about PowerLines in Chapter 19.

Better Fill Options

DRAW's basic method of creating, editing, and applying fills has remained robust and refreshingly intuitive, and version 4.0 added more power to this operation in the following areas:

Bitmap Fill Patterns   As demonstrated in Chapter 2, DRAW 4.0 came with a host of prefab bitmap textures that can be used to fill any closed object. DRAW's Texture Fill dialog allows you to adjust the colors of each of the components that make up a texture. If you want, DRAW will also roll the dice for you and randomly reassign different colors and densities to each component of a texture.

Conical Fountain Fills   In addition to the now-standard linear and fountain fills, DRAW 4.0 added conical fills, like the one illustrated in Figure 3.7. Implementation is as easy as the other two fills. Too easy, in fact—we fear a wave of unnecessary conical fills will make their way into hundreds of overdesigned drawings.

Multiple Fountains   We are still not exactly sure what to call this 4.0 feature, and DRAW refers to it only as a *custom fountain*. Regardless of its name, though, many of you have been there: You want to create a fountain fill that goes from light blue to dark blue and then back to light blue…or maybe from yellow to red to white to blue…or maybe from 35C14M23Y0B to 72C0M44Y12B to…well, you get the idea. DRAW 3.0 was great at transitioning from one color to the next but had no provision for transitioning more than once. You had to create separate objects—each containing a single transition—and butt them together. DRAW 4.0's improved fountain-fill engine supports multiple transitioning of fill colors. This has been done for the horizon in Figure 3.8, where the sky and ocean meet behind the deserted island. This feature alone was reason enough for many DRAW 3.0 users to move up.

Basic Drawing Changes in 4.0   **51**

3.7

DRAW 4.0 made creating conical fills a one-step process.

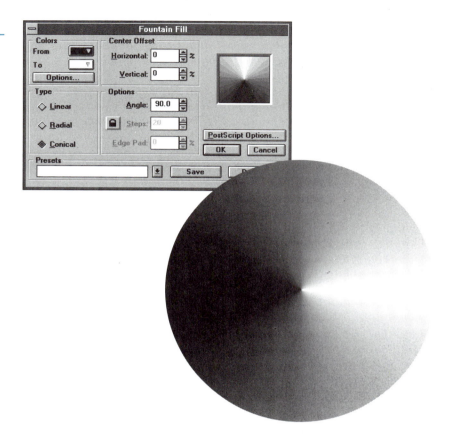

Steps   NBA fans know *steps* as running without dribbling, but to CorelDRAW fans *steps* are the number of increments used to transition from one color to the next. Previously, this capability was available only at the global level for all fountains in a file, or to PostScript printers through a maze of subdialog boxes. The Steps field in 4.0's Fountain Fill dialog lets you set the correct number for each fountain, based on the printer's resolution and/or the design requirements. Figure 3.9 shows Steps in action.

Preset Fountains   Finally, the 4.0 Fountain Fill sports a window of designer fountains (with names such as Ozone Cloud, Pink Neon, and Siren) that you can apply instantly to objects. What's more, a handy Save button lets you store your own fountains for later use.

3.8

No more workarounds—DRAW 4.0 does multiple fountains in the same object.

3.9

Any fountain can have a precise number of steps, be it 250 (top) or 5 (bottom).

New Effects in 4.0

Version 4.0 altered most of the functions under the Effects menu, and the menu was expanded to house all functions even remotely considered a special effect. Here is a brief rundown; for more details, see Part IV.

Envelopes   Version 4.0 gave the Enveloping function the ability to create envelopes from existing shapes, and extended it to handle frames of paragraph text. In addition, there is a collection of preset envelope shapes for quick application to objects.

Blending   Blending received two interesting new tools in 4.0. The new Loop button improves the previous Blend tool's support for rotating intermediate objects between the starting and ending objects, by sending the path itself in a circle. The arc of the circle is determined by the rotation value. The other enhancement to Blend is the set of Split and Fuse commands. Split can effectively turn one blend group into two interconnected ones, where the object that defines the split becomes a movable midpoint, as shown in Figure 3.10. Fuse simply glues the two groups back together as one.

Extrusions   As with many other functions, several presets assist in the creation of quick extrusions. And you can specify a vanishing point in relation to the object's center, in addition to the 0,0 point on the rulers.

3.10

Splitting blends can produce striking effects.

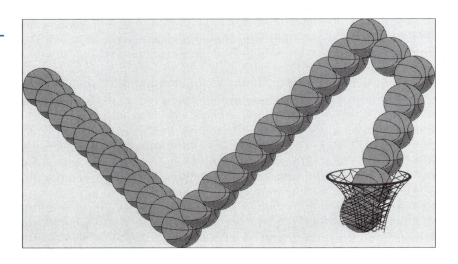

Not big news, perhaps, but this little fix saves the frequent aggravation of having to scroll far off the page to find the vanishing point.

Contours This new 4.0 feature was appreciated immensely by few, and ignored by many—including your lead author, who in the previous version of this book predicted that Contours would prove "to be more of a yawner than a sleeper." True, perhaps...but those who use the feature love it. Essentially a tool for creating a blend with just one object, Contours is often slow and tedious, but results from qualified Contour users are impressive.

Rotate & Skew and Stretch & Mirror These sets of tools were relocated under the Effects menu.

Add Perspective No change.

Copy Effects From This command offers a quick way to copy a perspective or an envelope from one object to another.

Clear Effects The Clear command simply removes whatever special effect has been applied.

File Menu Functions in 4.0

There were three significant changes in 4.0 to DRAW's basic file in/file out capabilities.

- As discussed earlier, a DRAW 4.0 file can be saved as a template, allowing it to serve as a blueprint for other projects. The New from Template command on the File menu is your access to these blueprints.

- There are many new formats under Import. DRAW can import four of the major word-processing formats, including the Big Three under Windows (Ami Pro, Word, and WordPerfect), as well as Rich Text Format. You can also directly import the spreadsheet formats from 1-2-3 and Excel, several new bitmap flavors, Micrografx .DRW files, and—perhaps most important of all—.EPS files. DRAW 4.0 handles this latter format as most other programs do: It places it and prints it, but does not actually read and convert it.

- The Print dialog underwent a complete face-lift. As shown in Figure 3.11, you can preview your file before printing, move the image around the page, and even scale the image up or down.

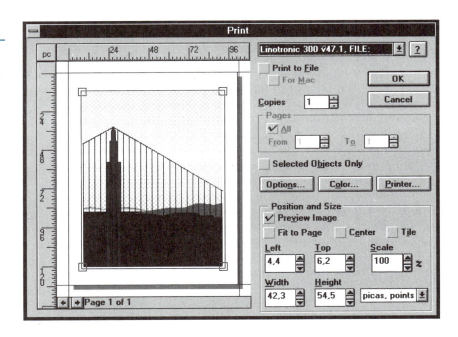

3.11

CorelDRAW's robust print engine is used by all of the 4.0 modules.

The Object Menu in 4.0

DRAW 4.0 assigned a new default role to the secondary mouse button: access to the Object menu. From there, you can get quick access to various tools that are pertinent to the selected object, most notably the Style functions.

We had thought that the big news concerning the Object Menu would be its gateway to the Object Data Manager roll-up, as shown in Figure 3.12.

This roll-up turns DRAW into a graphics database and spreadsheet of sorts, allowing you to assign values to objects and then make calculations against those values. The data assigned to objects can be in the form of numbers, general data, dates, or times. Alas, this feature has gone largely unused by the bulk of DRAW users. Who knows, maybe nobody could come up with a better use for it than our tracking of the Federal Waste Disposal Technology in Figure 3.12.

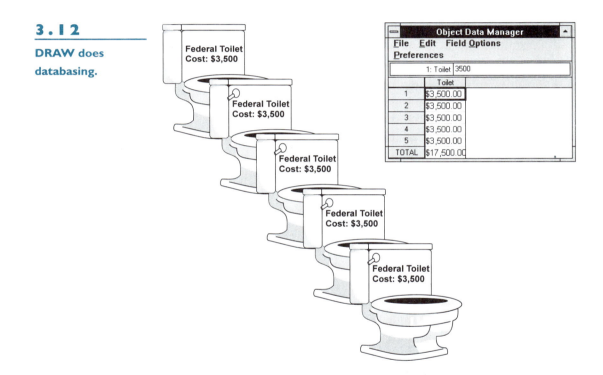

3.12

DRAW does databasing.

The curious aspect of DRAW's Object Data Manager is its access: Like Styles, it is available only through the secondary mouse button (SMB). If you want to return the SMB to your favorite shortcut of old—Full Screen Preview, 2× Zoom, or Node Edit—you can do so without loss of access. But if you do, you must learn to keep separate the two distinct SMB operations: the short click and the long click. More on this in Chapter 9.

Behind the Scenes of 4.0

You could argue that many of DRAW 4.0's most sweeping changes took place backstage, as the architecture for the suite of modules was completely overhauled, mostly for the better. DRAW 4.0 can do so much more than 3.0, and in the same amount of disk space, thanks to much more efficient programming around the common elements of the modules.

For instance, all of the modules in 4.0 use the same File Open, Save, Print, Import, Export, Preferences, and many other dialogs. In Figure 3.13, you may think you see DRAW's familiar Import command dialog, but guess what…it's not. This dialog was invoked from CHART, but it is almost identical to DRAW's.

3.13

Is it DRAW or is it CHART? Only their programmer knows for sure…

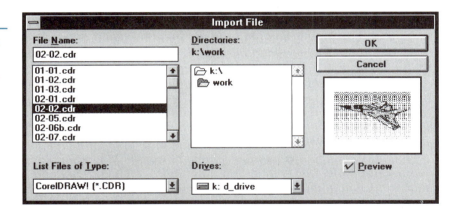

And if you take File Manager for a spin around the 4.0 directories, you will be surprised to find no .EXE files in the DRAW, CHART, SHOW, PAINT, and MOVE directories. More importantly, you'll also find no Dynamic Link Library (DLL) files, the ones responsible for much of a program's operation. Instead, all .EXE files are in the PROGRAMS directory, along with all of the .DLL files that they share. The file responsible for importing .EPS files, IMPEPS.DLL, is used by all of the modules that support that function.

All .INI files are housed in the CONFIG directory, instead of scattered across multiple directories; and shared functions are controlled by just one .INI file, not several. For instance, all font settings are stored in CORELFNT.INI, and universal print settings can be found in CORELPRN.INI.

Version 4.0 Miscellany

Just about every menu and dialog reflected, in some fashion, version 4.0's major overhaul. Following is a collection of other changes and features new to 4.0, listed here in no particular order:

Cloning   You know about copying, you know about duplicating, you know about pasting, and you know about moving an object while leaving an original behind. DRAW 4.0 added one more way you can copy an object: by cloning. Cloning is more than just copying, however; the clone remembers who its master is, and every time the master changes, so does the clone.

Better Undo   In DRAW 4.0 you can change your mind a lot, thanks to multiple levels of Undo. From the default setting of four, you can increase to as many levels of Undo as you can accommodate with available memory.

Selecting Inside a Group   To edit an individual object in a group, you need not ungroup before you can access it. Instead, hold Ctrl while you click on the object, and it will grow circular handles, as shown in Figure 3.14, indicating that it is still a part of the group. You can do pretty much anything to this selected object—move, resize, reshape, fill, rotate, or edit (if text)—except delete it. This little featurette has proven to be one of the true sleepers in 4.0.

Welding   In addition to grouping and combining, you can also weld two objects together. Unlike the Combine command, Weld removes the individual paths of objects that overlap, turning them into one object. As demonstrated in Figure 3.15, Combine maintains the outlines of the individual objects, but Weld melts them together. The resulting curve has just one fill and one outline, taken from the last object selected. Chapter 4 covers Weld and Combine in more detail.

3.14

No more ungrouping just to get at one piece of the puzzle.

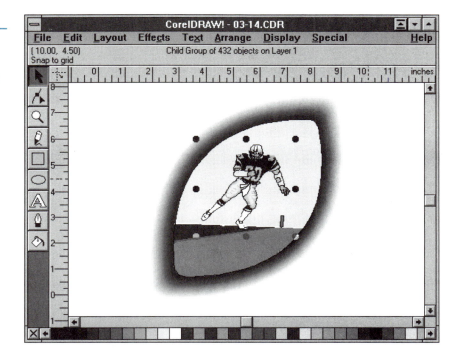

3.15

The difference between combining and welding objects

Floating Toolbox As mentioned in Chapter 2, the toolbox can be peeled from its normal home and moved anywhere on the screen, even outside the DRAW window.

Color Palettes From the Display menu, you can choose among four different color models as your on-screen palette. Version 4.0 also consolidated its Uniform Fill dialog, placing all palettes in a window. Though it's not as easy to change palettes now as it used to be, the dialog is friendlier.

Roll-Up Control As shown in Figure 3.16, you can determine, via the Preferences dialog, how DRAW's roll-ups are to be arranged at startup. By clicking on Current Appearance of Roll-Ups, you can essentially save your desktop in DRAW, just as you do with your Program Manager Desktop. The next time you start DRAW, you'll automatically see the roll-ups you had open when you set Preferences. To return to the desktop as you left it last, choose Appearance of Roll-ups on Exit. And to tuck away the roll-ups in the corners of your screen, choose All Roll-Ups Arranged.

3.16

As far as roll-ups go, you can have it your way in 4.0.

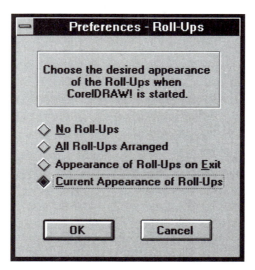

The Bad News

Not all was peaches and cream with version 4.0—indeed, it was a bit of a rocky summer of 1993 for Corel. The company had to sprint to release a maintenance update addressing numerous problems and bugs that were costing many users time and money. Here are the highlights of the lowlights:

V-e-r-r-r-s-i-o–n-n 4 - 0 . . .   DRAW 4.0 won no awards for its speed; in fact, it is slower in almost all measurable areas than all of its predecessors. Slower to load, slower to open a file, slower to copy to the Clipboard, and slower to print.

Inadequate Reference Guide   In an attempt to have one reference guide cover all languages, the 4.0 clip art catalog represents all art categories as icons, not words. There's only one problem: No one has yet figured out just how to use an icon as a subdirectory name. A subdirectory on the 4.0 CD or on your hard drive might be called "PLANT," but you have to search for the corresponding pages represented by a little poppy flower. Once you find your way to the correct part of the catalog, it's still no picnic finding the image you want; each topic is divided into three parts, representing the three vendors supplying clip art.

Bitter Bitmaps   Another so-called improvement that drew a unanimous and collective "uggh" was the support for rotated bitmaps. DRAW 3.0 allowed you to rotate imported bitmaps but wouldn't show them to you, providing you with a gray box instead. DRAW 4.0 makes rotated bitmaps visible—in fact, with great clarity—but at an unbearably high cost to performance. You haven't seen "slow" until you've asked DRAW 4.0 to rotate a high-resolution bitmap.

Figure 3.17 shows a page out of the magazine produced for the International CorelDRAW User Conference. DRAW 3.0 shows each bitmap as a gray box rotated to the correct angle, but the drawing prints correctly and draws in less than 1.1 seconds on screen. DRAW 4.0, on the other hand, requires almost 22 seconds to draw this page. With higher-resolution gray-scale bitmaps, we have waited for minutes, not seconds. In the previous edition of this book we moaned out loud over Corel's failure to make this display option a user-selectable toggle, and what do you know—Corel did just that in 5.0.

3.17

This page draws in about 1 second in DRAW 3.0, as compared to 22 seconds in DRAW 4.0, which insists on rendering all the detail of these rotated bitmaps.

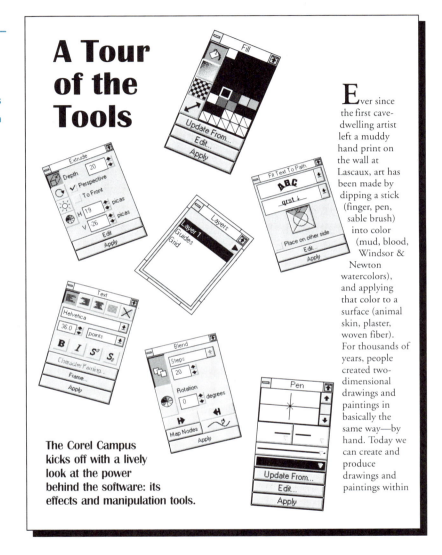

Chump Change, This Ain't Longtime users did not jump for joy over 4.0's $249 upgrade price, particularly when the memory of writing the check for version 3.0 was still fresh in their minds. Corel contends that the value in the 4.0 box is higher than any other software; but users counter that the continuing policy to bundle five major programs does not hold value for the core group, who seek only to work with vector-based drawing tools.

Revisions Needed   For the second consecutive year, Corel hurried a maintenance update out the door within months of shipping the initial product. Before being fixed by this update, some of the problem areas were serious—you know this firsthand if you purchased your copy of DRAW 4.0 between May and August of 1993. Printing and exporting were unreliable, paragraph text spacing would shift upon opening the file, and color separation controls were prone to malfunction. By Revision C, most of the problems were addressed.

CorelDRAW 5.0

Version 4.0 was a true kitchen-sink upgrade, and by comparison, the changes in 5.0 are more modest. Funny…by the standard of just about any other software upgrade, 5.0 would be hailed as a major overhaul. In Corel terms, however, it's only an incremental upgrade, because it adds only a dozen or so features rather than 40 or 50, and only one full-featured application. Here are some of the notable changes, new features, bugs fixed, and, yes, problems created or not yet fixed.

Ventura Publisher and DRAW 5.0

The biggest news about DRAW 5.0 is its incorporation of the venerable and industrial-strength document processing program, Ventura Publisher. Corel acquired Ventura from the Xerox subsidiary that had owned Ventura for almost four years, and in so doing, probably rescued it from death by neglect.

Many of you are already familiar with Ventura; our surveys show a high degree of crossover use between DRAW and Ventura users—undoubtedly one of the factors that persuaded Corel to attempt the acquisition. We have devoted the last part (Part VIII) of this book to Ventura, beginning with Chapter 34.

Version 5.0 and Performance

CorelDRAW users have become sadly accustomed to the reality that with each new version of DRAW will come yet another drain on performance. Indeed, since version 1.1, each new version of DRAW has been slower than its predecessor. The good news here is that the news is not all bad. DRAW 5.0 does require more time to load itself, to open files, and to export certain formats, but other parts of the program are faster than 4.0. Many dialogs are snappier in their response time. More important, text draws and sets more quickly, sometimes much more quickly. Changes to artistic text that took over ten seconds in 4.0 can be performed in DRAW 5.0 in under five. Strings of text that used to get lopped off due to excess length are handled with ease in 5.0 And remember the bitmap example discussed in Figure 3.17? In DRAW 5.0, you can choose to view imported bitmaps in high resolution, low resolution, or no resolution (invisible).

5.0's Improved Text Handling

Both artistic and paragraph text have been treated very kindly by DRAW 5.0. Artistic text draws and sets 50 to 150 percent faster, and artistic strings can now hold up to 8,000 characters before hammering you with the dreaded "text truncated" message.

Paragraph text enjoys several improvements in the area of global handling and flexibility. In Figure 3.18, for instance, the three frames are linked by their text flow (as they were in 4.0), but they can also be linked by their formatting. Any change made from the Text roll-up can be applied to the selected frame, to that frame and all frames hence, or the selected frame and all other frames that share the same text flow, in front of or behind it.

Now the bad news: This helpful feature—applying a particular attribute to every frame linked to a text file—is only available from the Text roll-up, not from any dialog. It's one of several instances in 5.0 where Corel has decided to place a great deal of functionality at your mouse button, but not at your fingertips. The arrangement has not been received well by the advanced users in the CorelDRAW community, many of whom

3.18

From the new Text roll-up, you can change one frame, change many, or change them all.

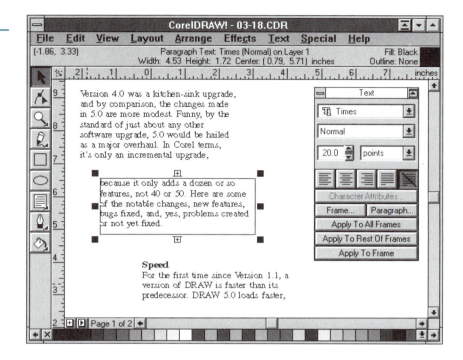

prefer to work the controls from the keyboard. This is not possible with the roll-ups, and so many advanced users choose to use the menus and dialogs instead. But a nice tool like this one can only be reached from the roll-up.

Other improvements to the text engine include the following:

- **Justified Artistic Text.** Previously, only paragraph text could be set with both left and right sides justified.
- **Lines.** Text can now be set with underlines, overscores, or strikeout.
- **On-Screen Tabs.** Tabs were late coming to DRAW at all, and finally, as of 5.0, they reach credible status, thanks to the on-screen ruler that now displays and controls them.

- **Font Substitution.** If you open a drawing that calls for a typeface not installed under Windows, the PANOSE font-matching engine will allow you to substitute a similar one, instead of defaulting to the first face on the list. (We were tired of text from old drawings defaulting to Architecture.)

- **Power Typing.** DRAW 5.0's new TypeAssist command allows you to create abbreviations for common phrases (or automatic corrections for commonly misspelled words). For an example, check out Figure 2.11 in Chapter 2.

- **Better Editing Control.** If you double-click on a word with the Text tool, that word is automatically selected. Furthermore, you can select text with your arrow keys, just as you can in your word processor. Shift+Right and Left, Ctrl+Right and Left, Ctrl+Home, Ctrl+End—they all work according to the Windows standard for text editing. It's now much easier to edit text in DRAW, because you can keep your fingers on the keyboard throughout editing tasks.

AUTHOR'S NOTE

Text handling still has a ways to go. See "The Bad News" at the end of this chapter.

5.0's New Tools for Artists and Illustrators

All throughout the Fall of 1993, Corel's marketing team told us that 5.0 would be a performance upgrade and would not include many new features. Then we got our first beta copy. We could almost hear the Corel marketing folks yelling "PSYCHE!" as we pulled down the Effects menu and saw all the new goodies. Following is a preview of the two significant new special effects that were not supposed to be in 5.0.

Lens

This is one of the best toys to arrive on the CorelDRAW scene in a long time. Now don't misunderstand—by calling Lens a toy, we're not saying that it is useless, or dumb, or not fit for professional artistry. In the right hands, it is a worthy addition to any artist's toolbox. But in just about anyone's hands, it is great fun to use.

What happens when you place a real lens over an object? It acts as a filter or magnifier, depending upon the type of lens. That is exactly how DRAW 5.0's new Lens roll-up works: Any object can act as a lens to an object in back. Figure 3.19 shows one of the eight different Lens effects available: The object in front is acting as a magnifying glass, and the degree of zoom is 2x, as determined in the Amount box.

3.19

With the Lens roll-up, creating filters, transparencies, and enlargements is practically a one-step procedure.

PowerClip

This handy new feature allows you to "hide" one object or group behind another. In its simplest form, the result is much like the effect of using the Combine command to create a mask and then placing an object behind the mask. But the PowerClip tool is easier to use, and its capabilities go well beyond simple masking. PowerClip brings powerful cropping and clipping capabilities to DRAW.

Figure 3.20 shows the result of applying PowerClip to a circle and a string of text, and Figure 3.21 demonstrates PowerClip applied to a bitmap image. We expect this effect to be welcomed by virtually all DRAW artists.

3.20

The PowerClip tool brings clipping paths to DRAW's arsenal.

5.0's New Tools for Artists and Illustrators   **69**

3.21

Any picture can be PowerClipped, including this one of the lead author's 16-month-old daughter.

Better Dimensioning

DRAW's Dimension Line tool allows you to create a line that automatically includes the dimension of that line, in inches, centimeters, feet, miles, or whatever unit of measurement you need. DRAW 5.0's dimension lines are live and dynamic, unlike 4.0's. Now, if you change the length of the line, the dimension automatically changes to reflect the change. Furthermore, you can create dimension lines that are linked to specific objects. That way, when you move the object—the wall of an architectural rendering, for instance—the dimension line moves with it.

This is a significant improvement over the old method of dimensioning. It used to be a tedious and restrictive task: You had to create the object you wanted to size, perfect it, and only then could you draw the dimension line. Now you can draw the dimension line, link it to an object, and never worry about having to make adjustments.

Cosmetic Changes

The only other significant change to DRAW's lineup of effects is a consolidation of the sizing, scaling, rotating, moving, and skewing tools into one Transform roll-up. There is one nice addition: You can now size objects in absolute measurements, instead of just relative measurements. In other words, not only can you ask for a rectangle to be 120 percent bigger, you can also make it exactly 26 picas across and 13 picas deep.

Finally, several of the other effects, such as Extrude and Blend, have seen evolutionary change. Part IV, "Effects and Affects," has all the details.

New Grouping Tools in 5.0

DRAW 4.0 gave us Weld, and now DRAW 5.0 gives us Intersection and Trim. When applied to multiple objects, both Intersection and Trim study the overlapping area. Intersection creates a new object that matches the overlapping area, and Trim cuts out and discards the overlapping area. Figure 3.22 shows how both these tools, and Weld, react differently to text and an overlapping circle.

DRAW users who have been frustrated with the tedium involved in producing transparent effects in objects now have an embarrassment of riches at hand. Thanks to the new Intersection and Lens tools, transparency is easy.

3.22

Intersection and Trim, the two new tools for marrying and divorcing objects.

Changes to the Dashboard in 5.0

DRAW still has the same friendly face as always, but many of its controls have changed—some for the better and some for the worse.

The most obvious modification is the addition of the Ribbon Bar below the menu bar, offering quick access to many common functions and commands. Forgive our bias here, but most of the contributors to this book are underwhelmed by the Ribbon Bar. Setting aside our general disdain for little icons that don't communicate nearly as well as words, DRAW's Ribbon Bar is simply way behind the modern standard for such bars, the best of which allow the user to add and remove icons, and even place custom scripts on the bar. With DRAW's, however, what you see is all you're ever going to get, and so, frankly, we prefer not to see it at all. You'll notice that many of the screen shots in this book show DRAW's main screen without the Ribbon Bar. If you, too, would rather retain this space for the main drawing area, turn the Bar off with Special / Preferences / View / Show Ribbon Bar.

There's plenty of good news, too. DRAW added to its plethora of automation tools an internal scripting tool that allows you to record a series of steps and capture them for later use. DRAW calls them Presets, and they are similar to the presets that 4.0 added to the Fountain Fill dialog. If you use a particular effect in many of your projects—say, a seven-step blend from white to yellow—you can create a preset for it and then recall it quickly any time you want. We would like to access our presets from hotkeys, and have presets available for changes to the interface (Nudge value, color palette, preview fountain steps, snaps, and the like), but we won't look this gift horse in the mouth. DRAW's new Presets (covered in detail in Chapter 9) will prove to be a valuable productivity boost for technical work and other projects involving redundant steps.

Redesigned Fill Dialog

If you never quite understood how the slider bars and boxes worked in the DRAW 4.0 Uniform Fill dialog, join the crowd. As Figure 3.23 shows, this dialog has been revamped with a more intuitive indicator/selector for colors. The old dialog (at the bottom) used four corners of a square and a slider bar in an unsuccessful attempt to illustrate the interplay of the four primary colors: cyan, magenta, yellow, and black. The new dialog uses a three-dimensional axis to represent cyan, magenta, and yellow, and a slider to control the degree of black.

The RGB and HSB color models work in similarly revamped fashion.

New Fountain Fill Type: Square

DRAW 3.0 introduced radial fills, and DRAW 4.0 conical fills. Now DRAW 5.0 ushers in the era of square fountain fills, in which the pattern is produced by a series of gradually changing rectangles. Figure 3.24 shows this new fill effect.

3.23

Out with the old (the 4.0 Uniform Fill dialog, at the bottom) and in with the new (the 5.0 dialog).

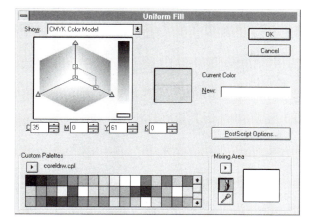

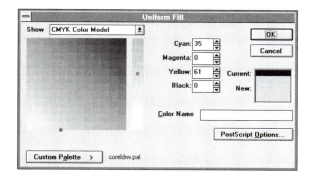

Direct Access to MOSAIC

There's a new roll-up in DRAW 5.0, and it lives in the File menu. The Mosaic roll-up is a little kernel of the MOSAIC module that can be used for finding a file and importing or opening it in DRAW. If you like to use MOSAIC for image management, then you're bound to appreciate the quick access you now have to it.

Drag and Drop

You've read about it in just about every computer magazine, and it's about time that you get to see it in some form. Now .CDR files and importable graphics files can be dragged from File Manager and dumped right onto the DRAW screen. DRAW will automatically incorporate

3.24

DRAW 5.0's new square fountain fill

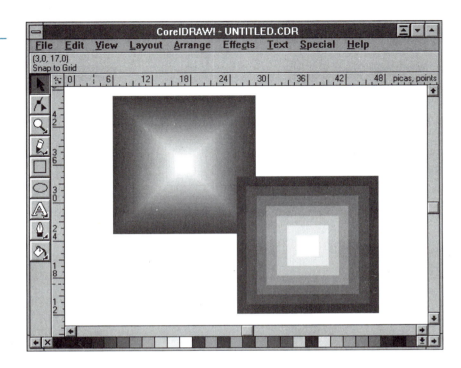

them, as if you have invoked File / Import and gone out and found them. This is ideal for those who keep MOSAIC, File Manager, or a substitute close at hand. We can't show you the dragging and dropping in action, but Figure 3.25 shows the result of it. From File Manager (on the left), BASKET.CDR was imported by the mere act of clicking on the file and dragging it across File Manager's boundaries into DRAW and then releasing the mouse. DRAW's Import command was then immediately invoked, and the image appeared promptly on screen.

Printing with 5.0

The biggest news in the Print department is Corel's move away from its unusual and unpopular method of PostScript typeface management. In versions 3.0 and 4.0, typeface handling was controlled through a private .INI file that had no relevance to how the rest of your Windows applications managed typefaces. DRAW 5.0 now uses the font-handling instructions contained in WIN.INI, just as all your other applications do.

3.25

Drag and drop is now a reality in DRAW. You can find .CDR files in File Manager and dump them onto DRAW in order to import them.

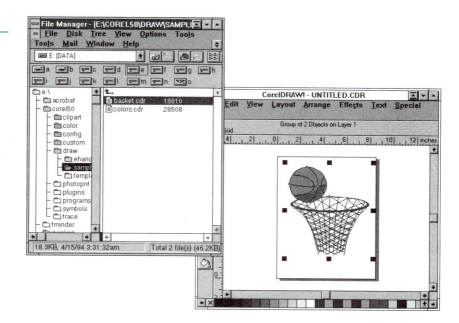

Appendix A explores the old way and the new way of PostScript typeface management (5.0 users can still choose the old method).

Finally, new *imposition controls* greatly facilitate the printing of many standard publications, such as half-sized booklets, saddle-stitched documents, and other projects defined by their "signatures" rather than just their pages. Chapter 25 has all of the details.

Other Good Stuff in 5.0

PostScript Import DRAW 5.0 has more than just the ability to place an EPS image on the page and print it later. Now it can actually interpret the PostScript instructions and provide you with an editable drawing. Don't count on it for one hundred percent reliability, but if you have been supplied with an EPS file and no original source file, DRAW 5.0 just might be able to digest if for you.

Pop-up Tool Help If you let your cursor hang around long enough over one of the tools, the name of the tool will pop up below your cursor. This might appear boring to some of you, but if you are wondering about the function of, say, the fourth tool in the Zoom flyout, putting your cursor on it for a couple of seconds beats looking it up in a book.

Corel's Private File Format   All of the CorelDRAW 5.0 applications are able to share data through a new metafile format known as Corel Presentation Exchange, or CMX, whose initials obviously don't stand for Corel Presentation Exchange, but we're sure stand for something.

Better Clip Art Guide   Hooray, Corel has scrapped the loathsome cataloging system of DRAW 4.0, which saw the clip art reference using useless little icons as its table of contents. Users will now have good old words and phrases to depict categories, and the division by vendor has been eliminated as well.

New Roll-up Controls   Version 5.0 has redesigned roll-up control yet again. With the interactive dialog shown in Figure 3.26, you can determine exactly how you want DRAW to start up each time. Choose your weapons!…er… roll-ups!

3.26

You can tell DRAW 5.0 exactly which roll-ups you want to appear automatically, and whether you want them rolled down and ready for use, or rolled up and tucked away.

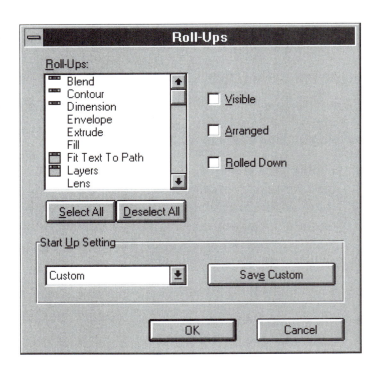

The Bad News in Version 5.0

In almost all respects, version 5.0 leaves the starting gate in better condition than 4.0 did. The feature set appears sturdier, there are fewer bugs, and the new product enjoyed a much more thorough testing cycle. So far, we know of no hidden bombs waiting to explode in the middle of your four-color job, or just as you're extruding four objects to the same vanishing point. To be perfectly honest, though, none of us will be certain of this until DRAW 5.0 has been in the hands of the user community for a few months. What we do know about are features that are absent, shortcomings that haven't been addressed, and users' requests not yet implemented. Here is a brief laundry list.

No Multiple Document Architecture   DRAW 5.0 still does not support the opening of more than one drawing at a time. There is nothing stopping you from retreating to Program Manager and running a second instance of DRAW, but this workaround is almost comical in its inefficiency. Today's word processors, spreadsheets, database programs, presentation software, and page-layout programs all can open multiple documents. Why not DRAW?

No Uninstall   When CorelDRAW installs, it creates its own network of subdirectories, and it also adds quite a few files to your Windows directories and writes directly to WIN.INI. Indeed, as one user described it, "My system is so entangled with CorelDRAW that I can't even breathe for fear of upsetting something."

Yet, version 5.0 offers nothing in the way of an uninstall procedure. The developers have stated that this is "too risky—other applications might use the resource files that we provide." Oh, what a tangled list of files we maul, when we try to uninstall…

No Keystrokes in Roll-Ups   DRAW users who like to keep their fingers on the keyboard or to automate their activities with keyboard macros will continue to be annoyed by the mouse-intensive nature of the roll-ups. Navigation is almost all mouse-driven, and even the Apply button has no keyboard equivalent. The new Transform roll-up has integrated the Move, Size, Skew, and Rotate commands, but by doing so

DRAW 5.0 has robbed users of almost all of their keyboard navigation capabilities. (Incidentally, you also won't like the fact that units of measurement for Move and Size are now fixed, dependent on the Grid Frequency setting, and cannot be changed.)

And as we said earlier, our cries for a Ctrl+Enter key combo to trigger confirmation of the active dialog or roll-up have fallen once again on deaf ears.

Save and Save Again   We think DRAW should allow you to save your drawing only when there is something to be saved. If you have not made changes since your last save, the Save option should be unavailable. This is a minor point to some, but a very large issue for those who work with 2MB and 3MB files, for which the Save command requires several minutes.

No Quick Replacement for Colors   Let's say you have a drawing with 250 objects, and 37 of them are set in PANTONE 455, or a specific combination of the CMYK colors. Now suppose you must change those 37 objects to another color. Good luck. DRAW offers no search-and-replace command for changing color assignments. To change those 37 objects, you have to find them (hidden in groups, embedded in blends and extrusions, on various layers, and so forth), and then manually change their outlines or fills. We'll talk about some of the workarounds for this unpleasantness in Chapter 13, but they are a far cry from a nice little button somewhere that says "Change Color X to Color Y."

No Distribute Command   The Blend tool is very handy for distributing copies of an object evenly across a given area, but what if you want to do this with a square, a circle, a string of text, and then an extruded cone? Your best bet is to set a grid and think good thoughts. We see real value in a Distribute command for evenly spacing objects across a specified area, and we don't see any particular challenge to programming such a tool.

The Bad News in Version 5.0

Text Shortcomings The setting of type continues to be DRAW's weakest suit, and 5.0 continues to lose ground as the other programs in (and out) of the graphics niche become more evolved. To wit:

- **Underlining and strikethrough** are nice additions to 5.0, but there is no provision for adjusting the distance from the underline to the baseline, or the thickness of the line (except for the somewhat vague choices of "thick" and "thin").

- **Justification and letter tracking** are still below the standard of professional typesetting. Figure 3.27 shows a justified paragraph

3.27

DRAW 5.0 still can't quite set paragraph text with the best of them.

PageMaker

CorelDraw 5.0 offers better support for paragraph text, but the proof will be in the pudding, er, printing. This string of 9-point Palatino text has been set justified in DRAW, PageMaker, and Word for Windows. You be the judge.

Word for Windows

CorelDraw 5.0 offers better support for paragraph text, but the proof will be in the pudding, er, printing. This string of 9-point Palatino text has been set justified in DRAW, PageMaker, and Word for Windows. You be the judge…

CorelDRAW

CorelDraw 5.0 offers better support for paragraph text, but the proof will be in the pudding, er, printing. This string of 9-point Palatino text has been set justified in DRAW, PageMaker, and Word for Windows. You be the judge

set in Palatino from three different programs. While PageMaker offers perfect justification and letter spacing without having to add a hyphen, DRAW resorts to a hyphen, and actually places it outside of the right text margin. Discerning eyes might notice other subtle differences in how these three programs craft their letters. We include Word for Windows here to show that DRAW's typesetting is more on a par with its performance than with PageMaker's.

- **Forced justification** is still not supported. The only way to ensure that a short line is stretched all the way to the end is to use a right-aligned tab, and that is decidedly inferior to a standard force-justify command.

- Speaking of **stretching**, there still is no control for condensing or expanding character widths.

- And **forced line breaks** still do not exist. There is no easy way to start a new line without starting a new paragraph.

CorelDRAW will have a wish list for as long as it has customers, so the fact that there are shortcomings is not a surprise. You will have to determine for yourself how significant these failings are, considering how long you have been asking for their improvement and how extensively they will affect your own work. In any case, don't expect these matters to be addressed until May 1995, when Corel is expected to unveil DRAW 6.0. Any interim releases prior to then will most likely consist of bug fixes and performance enhancements, not new features.

Just Click, Baby

CHAPTER FOUR

CHAPTER 4

We mentioned it in Chapter 2, and it bears repeating here: The manual skills required to operate DRAW are not hard to acquire. They consist mostly of clicking, double-clicking, and a bit of dragging. Don't misconstrue this to mean that producing beautiful work in DRAW is easy; manual skills and design expertise are two entirely different things. Only a little can we help you with the latter, but we can get you up and running nicely with the former, and that's what this chapter is all about.

Working with Objects

There are four ways to place an object into a DRAW file: You can create it yourself; you can import a piece of clip art; you can paste it from another program across the Clipboard; or you can get it from DRAW's on-line Symbols library. Regardless of their origin, all these objects behave the same once they arrive—they are all subject to (drumroll, please) *The Laws of DRAW*.

The *Laws of DRAW* proclaim the following:

- Thou shalt be selectable by the mouse.
- Thou shalt be at liberty to move about the page.
- Thou shalt be free to be resized, reshaped, and rotated.
- Thou shalt contain an outline, which can be colored and thickened.
- If thou art a closed object, thou shalt accept an internal color, tint, or pattern.
- Thou shalt be disconnectable.

Only one type of object is exempt from these laws: bitmap images imported or pasted into DRAW (discussed later in the chapter). Bitmap images cannot be filled, outlined, or taken apart, but they can be sized, shaped, and rotated. All the rest follow the CorelDRAW fold.

Creating, Moving, and Changing Objects

If you have used Windows applications at all, you already know how to create an object, and as we said earlier in the book, you could probably get behind DRAW's steering wheel and create an ellipse or a rectangle on your first try. The simple click-and-drag maneuver is all that's required. Creating lines and Bezier curves is a bit more involved than ellipses and rectangles, and that technique will be one of the main players in the next two chapters.

To get started with objects in DRAW, the only other things you need to know are how the click and double-click work: One click selects objects on the page or colors from the on-screen palette; and two quick clicks selects files from various dialogs (Open, Import, Save, Export, and so forth). You'll always know when an object in a drawing is selected, because it grows little black handles around its periphery.

INSIDE INFO

Not quite getting the hang of the double-click? Maybe it's your mouse that needs a bit of taming. Go out to Program Manager, open your Main group, and start Control Panel. Find the Mouse icon, open the Mouse settings, and look for Double Click Speed. By moving the slider in the "Slower" direction, you can make double-clicking easier.

The click-and-drag is the handiest maneuver of all. It is responsible for accomplishing many tasks in DRAW:

- To move a selected object that is filled with a color or shade, click anywhere inside the object and then drag.

- To move an unfilled object, click anywhere on its outline and then drag.
- To change the size of an object, click on one of its handles and drag.
- To rotate or skew an object, select it, click once, and then click and drag on one of the arrows, which operate as shown in Figure 4.1.

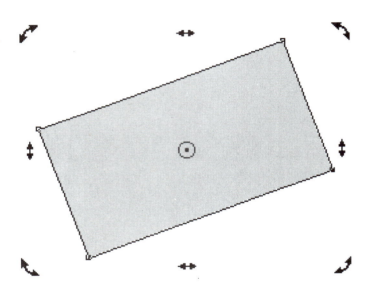

4.1

The click-and-drag technique is responsible for many feats within DRAW, including the rotation of this rectangle.

There are two other handy controls for moving objects. One is the Move control from Effects / Transform, which lets you move an object with an accuracy of .1 point. The other is the use of the Ctrl key while dragging an object. By holding Ctrl as you drag, an object is constrained to move either up and down or side to side, but nothing in between.

You've probably already realized it: DRAW can't do squat to an object on the page until you first select it. That's how you call the object to DRAW's attention. When you have only simple and few objects on a page, selecting the objects is easy; but as your drawing board becomes more crowded, selecting will become more challenging. Selecting is the focus of a discussion in Chapter 20, "Mastering the Tools."

Knowing about Nudge

There is some debate as to how this feature's name is pronounced. Our highly scientific demographic surveys reveal that if you are from the West Coast, you probably pronounce it *nuj,* rhyming with *fudge;* if you are from the East Coast or are familiar with Hebrew or Yiddish, you say *noodge,* sounding like *could* and *would.* However you say it, the definition is the same: to poke or prod—and it is one of DRAW's handiest features, allowing you to move objects with incredible precision.

Nudge, which is always enabled, places the power of motion in the hands of your keyboard's arrow keys: Press the Left Arrow or Right Arrow, and the selected object moves to the left or right (see Figure 4.2). The Up Arrow and Down Arrow work just as easily to move objects up and down. And you can control the *amount* of movement, too, with Special / Preferences / General / Nudge. The beauty of Nudge is how it constrains you to move in only one direction, greatly facilitating the challenging task of placing objects precisely.

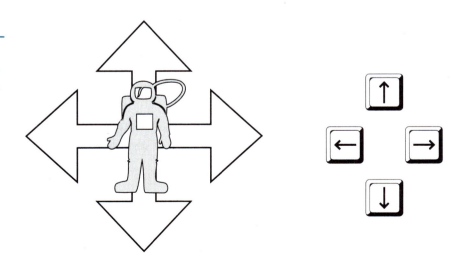

4.2

Using the Nudge feature is the most precise and flexible way to place an object.

Importing Objects

When it comes to incorporating files from other programs, DRAW will digest almost anything that you throw at it. DRAW can accept text files from word processors, tables of numbers from spreadsheets, image files from paint programs, vector art from itself, and even drawings from competing programs. The key requirement is that you first tell DRAW what type of file it is, or at least give DRAW the opportunity to figure it out for itself. But if you try to import a .PCX file while telling DRAW to expect a Word for Windows file, you're asking for trouble.

NEW FOR 5

If you don't feel like changing the file filter every time you go to import a graphic into DRAW, set the filter for All Files. That way DRAW will show you every file that is in a directory, and will determine for itself what each file's format is.

The gateway to all importing is the File / Import dialog shown in Figure 4.3. In this instance, DRAW has its sights set on importing a variety of files from a directory of clip art. Like most programs, DRAW expects certain formats to have particular file name extensions, and it behooves you to follow standard naming conventions when you create your files. We suggest you try importing one of these files now yourself, either from the CorelDRAW CD or from the clip art that is installed from the program disks.

AUTHOR'S NOTE

Whenever an exercise in this book requires a piece of clip art, we have made sure that it is either available in Corel's clip art library, or included on the Companion CD bound with this book.

Here are the steps for importing a .TIF file:

1. In the Import dialog, at the List Files of Type list box, choose TIFF Bitmap.

4.3

DRAW's Import dialog box has the look and feel that veteran Windows users have come to expect.

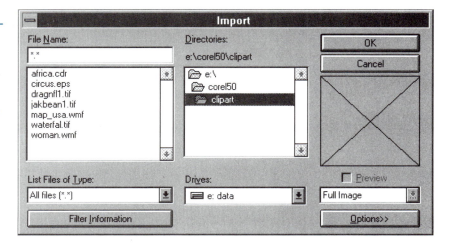

2. Using the Drives and Directories lists, navigate your way to the PRACTICE directory on the Companion CD.
3. Choose one of the files in the Files list box.
4. OK the box.

AUTHOR'S NOTE

There are some instructions in the foregoing procedure that you'll see a lot throughout this book. When we tell you to "use the Drives and Directories lists" (see step 2), remember that the Drive drop-down list behaves as all others in Windows do: You click once to see a list of available drives. The directories for the selected drive appear automatically in the Directories window; you double-click on the desired directory name. When we tell you to "OK the box" (see step 4), remember that when you're choosing files from a list, there are three ways to OK your choice: Highlight the file and then click the OK button, or highlight the file and press Enter, or double-click on the file. All of DRAW's dialogs that involve choosing files work this way. Most experienced users who prefer to keep their fingers on the keyboard as much as possible have already discovered that the dialogs involving file operations can usually be navigated wholly from the keyboard, using the designated hotkeys and the Tab key.

If the file you want does not have a file name extension that DRAW expects, then you'll have to edit DRAW's filter, or ask DRAW to show all files. (DRAW assumes certain extensions for certain formats, such as .TIF for TIFF files, and filters out all the rest.) For instance, say your task is to import a file that you have in the SYSTEM subdirectory under WINDOWS, called SETUP.REG. This is a pure ASCII file, even though it doesn't have a .TXT extension. Here goes:

1. Go to File / Import. (That's shorthand for either "Pull down the File menu and choose Import," or "Press Alt+F and then type I." Your choice).
2. At the List Files of Type box, choose Text.
3. In the File Name text box, change *.txt to read *.reg, and OK the box.
4. Navigate your way to the SYSTEMS directory under WINDOWS.
5. Select the SETUP.REG file and OK the box. DRAW now loads and paginates the file into a paragraph frame.

INSIDE INFO

Advanced users who want DRAW to display more file name extensions with each file format might want to experiment with editing the CORELFLT.INI file. This text file lists many of the default import and export choices, including file name extensions. If you find yourself importing many .DAT ASCII files, for instance, you can edit this line in CORELFLT.INI, TXT=IMPTXT,"Text",*.TXT,6, to read TXT=IMPTXT,"Text", *.TXT;*.DAT,6. Then when you import .DAT files, DRAW will automatically show them to you as ASCII files, along with .TXT files. You won't have to laboriously edit the filter. You can also exclude extensions; for instance, not too many of you name your TIFF files with .CPT extensions, even though PHOTO-PAINT has adopted it as its default extension. If DRAW is running as you edit CORELFLT.INI, you'll need to quit and restart it once for the change to take effect. As always, make a backup copy before editing any of DRAW's .INI files.

Pasting Objects

DRAW's support for the Clipboard has always been robust, and 4.0 continues the tradition. Just about anything that you place on the Clipboard can be brought into DRAW. Try the following, using PHOTO-PAINT or some other paint program that reads .TIF files:

1. Open PHOTO-PAINT or another paint program.
2. From the PRACTICE subdirectory on the Companion CD, select JAKBEAN1.TIF and OK the box.
3. Using the selection tool of your paint program (PHOTO-PAINT calls it the Rectangle Selection tool), select all or part of the image.
4. Choose Edit / Copy.
5. Switch back to the Program Manager and open DRAW.
6. Choose Edit / Paste. On the DRAW screen you will see the image, much like Figure 4.4.

For more Clipboard discussion, and a look at DRAW's support for Object Linking and Embedding (OLE), check out Chapters 27 and 28.

4.4

A clip art image pasted into DRAW

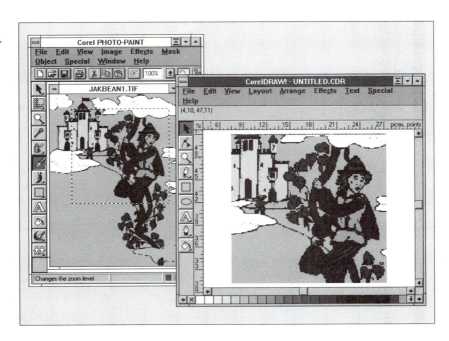

Using The Symbols Library

For an easy starting point to creating a simple drawing, nothing beats DRAW's on-line Symbols library. To access it, choose Special / Symbols Roll-Up, or press Ctrl+F11. From here you can browse through several categories of symbols. When you find one that you like, just drag it out of the roll-up and drop it on the page.

By clicking on the Tile button in the roll-up, you can create a mass of symbols, like the army of snowmen shown in Figure 4.5. When you tile symbols, the one at the top-left is the master, and all others are clones of it. Any change you make to the master changes all the others.

4.5

This horde of snowmen was created in one operation: by choosing and tiling a symbol from the roll-up.

Using Fills and Outlines

One of the first things that new DRAW users do to selected objects is apply fills and outlines, undoubtedly because the controls of the on-screen palette are right there in front of their noses. Although there is considerable depth to the Outline and Fill dialogs and roll-ups, performing the basic moves, as usual, is easy. To create a circle and fill it blue:

1. Use the Ellipse tool to create the circle. To make it a true circle, hold Ctrl while dragging the mouse.
2. Find blue (or a close facsimile) on the color palette at the bottom of the screen, and click it with the primary mouse button, as shown in Figure 4.6. Voilà!
3. To create a blue outline around the circle, click with the secondary mouse button.

4.6

Once an object is selected (note the handles), changing its appearance is easy with the on-screen palette.

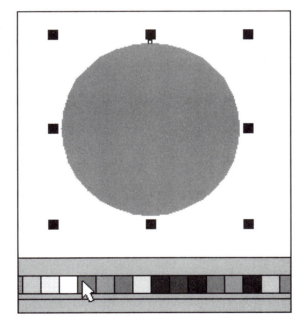

Any object can be outlined, but only objects that are *closed* can be filled. A closed object is one whose outline completely surrounds it, such as a circle or a rectangle. Chapters 7 and 8 offer considerable detail on outlining and filling.

To explore beyond the colors and fills available in the on-screen palette, experiment with the dialogs and roll-ups found under the Outline and Fill tools.

Selecting Multiple Objects

DRAW allows for literally thousands of objects to be selected at one time, for the purposes of grouping, moving, duplicating, deleting, or mass editing of fills and/or outlines.

If the objects are in close proximity and well defined, you can drag a marquee around them to select them. If you need to pick and choose certain objects to select amid others that you don't want to select, the trick is to use the Shift key, like this:

1. Select the first object.
2. Hold down the Shift key.
3. Click on another object. Now both objects are selected.
4. While still holding Shift, click to select as many more objects as you want. As long as you continue to hold Shift, previously selected objects will remain selected. If you click on a selected object while holding Shift, the object becomes deselected.

The one caveat to the above technique is this: If an object does not have a fill, then you will have to click on its outline to select it.

Once you have succeeded in selecting the desired objects, consider grouping them, even temporarily. It's easy to ungroup them later, but not as easy to reselect all of them should they become deselected.

If an object is completely surrounded by a larger object, you might want to take a quick trip into Wireframe view, where only outlines are displayed, no fills. (You toggle Edit Wireframe on and off from the View menu.) Figure 4.7 is a composite of a butterfly image shown in full-color preview (the upper-left butterfly) and a Wireframe view of the butterfly (lower-right). Notice that it is much easier to pick out the individual objects that make up this butterfly when it is displayed in Wireframe. In Wireframe, you need not be concerned with objects that are on top of others—clicking on any part of its outline will select the object.

4.7

Using Wireframe view is often the answer to picking out small pieces of a drawing.

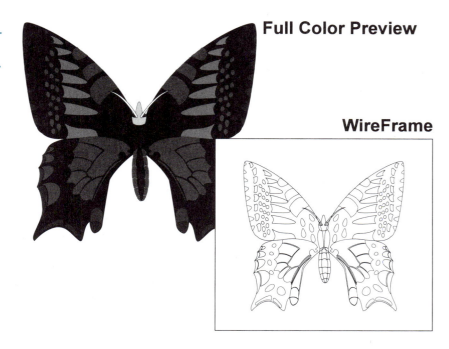

Of course, if you want to select *all* of the objects in your drawing, forget about marquees or Shift+clicks or any of that nonsense, and head straight for the Edit / Select All command.

Turning Many Objects Into One

There are three commands that, in some fashion or another, take multiple objects and lump them together so you can work with them all at once. When used correctly, each of these commands can be enormously helpful in organizing the various elements contained in drawings. The three commands—Group, Combine, and Weld—are found on the Arrange menu.

To select more than one object at a time, click and drag across the desired objects, or select one and hold Shift while selecting others.

Grouping Objects

The most straightforward of the three "lump together" functions, Group, uses an imaginary paper clip or rubber band to collect a set of objects. In other words, the objects are completely independent of one another; they are just being held together so you can move, size, or color them as one object. Grouped objects can always be ungrouped—they maintain almost complete autonomy from the other members of the group. Figure 4.8 includes a set of grouped objects (top left); notice how the members of this group appear the most autonomous of the three sets.

If you apply a fill or an outline to a group, all the objects in the group will receive that fill or outline (unless one of the elements is not closed, in which case it will not be filled).

It's a good idea to get into the habit of grouping objects as soon as their spatial relationship to one another has been established. You can always

4.8

The three commands that join objects can produce startlingly different results.

Grouped Objects

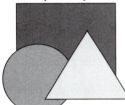

Combined Objects

Welded Objects

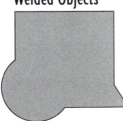

make individual changes later, but to make sure the objects stay put in relation to one another, group them. The two hotkeys for grouping and ungrouping, Ctrl+G and Ctrl+U, will come in handy.

AUTHOR'S NOTE

 **UPGRADING FROM VERSION 3?:** You can select an individual object within a group by holding Ctrl and clicking on the desired object. You'll know when you did it right when you see circular handles (instead of rectangular ones) around the object.

Combining Objects

Combining gives you a less-flexible set of objects than does grouping. First, the objects that are combined lose their individual identities; in other words, rectangles, ellipses, and text characters all become generic "curves" after being combined. The individual components still have their shape and their properties, but they have become fused together.

Since combined objects represent a single curve element, they have only one outline and one fill. Of all the objects in the combined set, the one that was selected last determines the initial outline and fill. Where areas overlap, a "hole" is created, as shown in the middle image in Figure 4.8. To understand this, it helps to think of one object as being the cookie cutter, and the other being the dough: The cutter cuts a hole right through the dough when the two are combined. (We'll return to this cookie-cutter metaphor in Chapter 11, "Fun with Text.")

You can break apart an arrangement of combined objects (and Arrange / Break Apart is in fact the name of the command that does this), but don't expect them to remember how they used to be. Objects you break apart are just curves, and they each inherit the outline and fill of the combined object before it was broken apart. It's not terribly significant that a rectangle becomes a curve (it still looks and acts the same). However, when *text* is combined with other objects and then broken apart, it loses all of its text properties. It may still look like text, because even a text character is actually a collection of curves, but it can never be edited as text again.

Welding Objects

You can take the Weld command almost literally: It takes separate objects and melts them together. As with combining, the last selected object determines the outline and fill for all the objects in the welded set. Unlike the Combine command, however, the Weld command could hardly care less about the points at which welded objects intersect. There are no cookie-cutter holes created, and objects do not get to keep their outlines. As the lower-right image in Figure 4.8 shows, the Weld command is determined to turn all selected objects into one, and in so doing, removes the parts of objects that overlap others.

The Undo command will reverse the Weld effect altogether (assuming you invoke Undo immediately after invoking Weld). Other than that, there is only one way that a Weld can be taken apart, and that is if the welded objects do not touch at all. In that case, the Weld effect is the same as Combine, and the objects can be uncombined. But if they touch at all, welded objects become permanently fused and cannot be taken apart. They truly become one object.

Other Points Of Interest

As you take your first tour of DRAW, there are several other stops you will want to make. As with all the other commands and functions discussed in this chapter, the following are easily learned and performed.

Saving And Opening Files

Saving your work is arguably your most important task in DRAW, without which nothing would be permanent. We won't insult your intelligence by explaining to you how to do it. (The only time we have ever actually done that in a book or magazine article was in 1986, when we attempted to show how to save changes in EDLIN. And no, we don't remember how to do it…)

The key to effective saving is to first establish an organized directory structure. DRAW remembers the directories you last chose for saving and opening files; if you use the same directory for saving, you will have far less navigating to do in DRAW's file windows.

Our only other advice: Remember the hotkey Ctrl+S; it makes saving as automatic as a Joe Montana-to-Jerry Rice touchdown used to be.

Zooming

The easiest way to zoom in on an object is to press F4. This hotkey takes into account all the objects in your drawing and chooses the closest magnification that will allow you to see them all.

If you need to zoom in on just a piece of your drawing, you've got two choices: If you want to zoom in on objects that are selected, click on the Zoom tool and select the fourth icon (the one with the little black squares around the objects), or use the hotkey Shift+F2. If you want to zoom in on a particular collection of objects that may or may not be selected, click on the Zoom tool and then on the plus icon that appears on the flyout. Now any marquee you create on your drawing becomes the zoom area, and DRAW will automatically calculate the magnification.

AUTHOR'S NOTE

And you thought a marquee was just for displaying movie titles! In DRAWspeak, you create a "marquee" around objects when you click and drag diagonally from one corner to the opposite corner, covering the objects entirely. You'll hear that term often when discussing DRAW: "drag a marquee," or "marquee-select an object."

Arranging Elements

When two or more objects are selected, the Arrange / Align command becomes available for duty. With it, you can reposition selected objects so that they line up precisely along their tops, bottoms, or sides.

The Align command can be used even on a single object. When a single object is selected, Align can position the object with respect to the page. Figure 4.9 shows several of the possible ways that objects can be aligned. Notice that in the last image, the basketball is in the center of the backboard both ways—the vertical and horizontal controls are used at the same time.

98 CH. 4 JUST CLICK, BABY!

4.9

All the ways to align a basketball with its backboard

 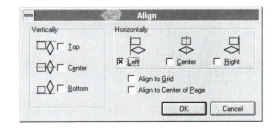

 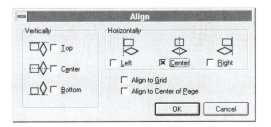

 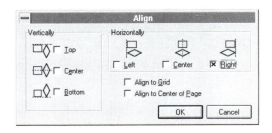

 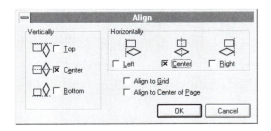

4.9

All the ways to align a basketball with its backboard (continued)

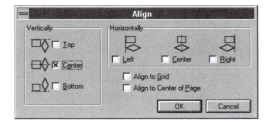

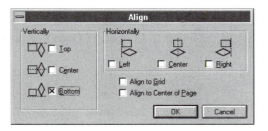

Also, be sure to experiment with the layering commands of To Front, To Back, Forward One, Back One, and Reverse Order, all on the Arrange menu.

Using Undo

DRAW's Undo command has a very good memory, and you can make it even better. In the Special / Preferences / General dialog, you can set the number of *levels* for Undo. Let's say you do the following to a circle: 1) change its color, 2) move it two inches away, 3) make it larger, and 4) delete it. You can undo each of those actions, starting with the most recent and working back in time. Each action is called a level, and the default number of levels for Undo is four. If you have enough computer memory, you can create a safety net that will remember a few dozen of your last actions.

Be aware, however, that you cannot pick and choose the actions that you want to undo; they must be undone in order. For instance, in the example above, you cannot undo the color change without first undoing the move and the resize.

There are four actions that cannot be undone:

- Changes to View settings
- File operations, such as Save, Import, and Export (although DRAW does save backup files, so in the case of Saves, you can retrieve previous versions stored in .BAK files)
- Selection of objects
- Printing (obviously)

Finally, when you save a drawing, DRAW forgets all past actions, regardless of how many Undo levels you have set.

Copying Attributes

With two or more objects in a file, you can take the properties of one object and assign them to another, using the Copy Attributes From command on the Edit menu. To copy attributes:

1. Select the object(s) that you want to have the new attributes.
2. Invoke the Copy Attributes From dialog (select Edit / Copy Attributes From) and choose the particular component(s) you want to apply, be it an outline thickness and/or style, outline color, fill pattern, or text attribute.
3. Click on the object that *already has* the attributes. The selected objects change immediately.

Using the Repeat Command

In conjunction with tedious tasks such as applying special fill patterns or outlines to many objects, or even just careful placement of objects, nothing beats the Edit / Repeat command and its Ctrl+R hotkey. Here is a good use for Repeat:

1. Create a small object.
2. Drag the object a short distance away, and click on the secondary mouse button before releasing the mouse. This creates a duplicate.
3. Press Ctrl+R to repeat the action in step 2 over and over again.

Working with Grids and Guidelines

Setting a good grid, creating guidelines, and activating snap-to points are all important aids in precision work. You can create snap-to points on your page in one of three ways:

- One option is to set a grid, through Layout / Grid Setup, so that objects will snap at intervals that you establish. You can set a large grid, with snap-to points at every inch, or a very small grid, with snaps measured in picas or even points.

- You can quickly create floating guidelines and insist that objects snap to them whenever they are moved close by. To create these guidelines, start on one of the vertical or horizontal ruler lines, and click and drag onto the page. The blue dotted line that follows you is the guideline.

- Or you can ask DRAW to snap objects to the nodes of other objects, thereby allowing you to precisely align objects with other objects.

Grid snap is helpful when all objects of a drawing must conform to the grid. The dotted guidelines are helpful when certain objects must be lined up at various locations. When on, the grid is always there, across the entire drawing; the guidelines, however, can be moved and placed at will.

The Snap To Grid command has a hotkey of Ctrl+Y; we wish Snap To Guidelines and Snap to Objects had them, too.

Now that you've got some exposure to the tools, you're ready to tackle a live project. That is the agenda for Chapter 5.

CHAPTER 5

From Start to Finish: Creating an Illustration

FIVE

CHAPTER 5

If you subscribe to the theory that the only way to learn it is to do it, then this chapter is for you. Here is your opportunity to create an illustration from start to finish. We intend for this to be good exposure for new users, but we are certain that experienced users, also, will benefit from it. In fact, while creating the illustration, our lead author and other advanced users were often found taking notes and inquiring about particular techniques used.

Take a look at our athletic friend in Figure 5.1. If you follow along with this chapter—either by the pictures or the steps—you will witness the creation of the snowy scene in which this snowboarder revels. To use his vernacular (we *think* it's a he…), we invite you to "Go for it!"

If this task intimidates you, we're sure you have lots of company. In fact, to some extent we hope that this project *does* appear daunting when first seen by new users. We want to show how a systematic approach and attention to the individual parts can make any project go more smoothly. And just think how much more satisfying it will be when you complete it.

Having said that, we are just as quick to point out that you're not going to have to create all of the parts from scratch. In fact, the central figure, the snowboarder himself, comes from Corel's clip art library—an ideal place to shop for elements of an illustration. We have broken this project down into well-defined pieces, and we don't expect you to finish the entire thing in one sitting. In fact, it might take a week to complete. Let it.

5.1

Think you could never produce a piece like this? Think again and then try it for yourself.

An Overview

Our snowboarder project will expose you to many of DRAW's tools and functions. To complete this drawing, you will

- Import clip art

- Retrieve a symbol
- Define and manipulate layers
- Scale images
- Create freehand and/or Bezier curves
- Create blends
- Edit curves with the Shape tool
- Create, format, extrude, and apply envelopes to text
- Create a frame around the drawing

As we made our design and implementation decisions, we were mindful of the drawing's purpose as an exercise. For instance, in creating this image you will define several layers, using the Layers roll-up. Were you producing this on your own, you might not need or want as many layers, but the more you have, the more control you have over objects.

Second, although you will be creating the snowboarder in color, we wanted it to also look good in black and white, so our color choices were made with that in mind.

Third, we also wanted you to be able to print your drawing on a standard laser printer, so we have included only a few effects that require a high-resolution output device.

The Agenda

Like most accomplished artists, you will create the background of your image first. After that you will create, in this order:

- The cloud
- The snow in the foreground
- Our flying friend, in position
- The tree
- The GO FOR IT! text

Ready? So go for it!

Getting Started

As with all projects, the approach you take and the work habits you adopt are two of the most important ingredients of a successful illustration. So before you go any further, take all the time you need to get oriented. In so doing, there are several questions you should address:

- **What Size?** Your illustration will be a standard $8\frac{1}{2}$ by 11 inches and have a portrait orientation. Tell that to DRAW right now by choosing Layout / Page Setup, selecting Letter as the page size, and clicking on Portrait.

- **What Name?** This is arbitrary, of course. We have called this file GOFORIT!.CDR, to illustrate that an exclamation mark is legal in file names.

- **Where?** If you haven't already done so, you should establish some sort of directory structure to house your DRAW files—even if it's just a directory called ART or CDR. Once it's created, save your fledgling drawing. The Ctrl+S hotkey will work (if you issue the Save command with an untitled drawing, DRAW treats the Save command as a Save As command). Navigate your way to the directory of your choice, enter a file name, and save the drawing.

Finally, in accomplishing this project you will be frequently moving in and out of the Wireframe view (see the View menu just below), so you'll want to get familiar with the Shift+F9 hotkey that quickly toggles you back and forth between Edit Wireframe and Color Preview.

Defining the Layers

As mentioned, we want you to create separate layers for the various components of this drawing. Some advanced users might argue against the use of extra layers, and we predict that you will, in fact, use them less often as you get more experienced. All well and good—but we find that the Layers feature is an ideal tool for helping new users cope with all the goings-on in a drawing. In particular, we like layers for the following reasons.

Layers Allow Better Definition   As elements overlap in a drawing, it is easy to become confused. If you place overlapping elements on separate layers, you then can lock (so they cannot be selected) or even hide the elements you are not presently working with.

Layers Enable Better Performance   As drawings evolve, they inevitably take longer to draw on screen. By hiding a layer that contains finished elements, you won't have to wait as DRAW renders them each time the screen refreshes.

Layers Are Just Good Form   We believe that the use of layers is simply a good habit to adopt. Many users take for granted and even ignore the handy features of layering. We don't want you to make that mistake.

Is there a downside to using layers? Yes—DRAW does not give very good visual cues to remind you of what layer is active, which makes it too easy to create objects on the wrong layer. Therefore, we will be issuing constant reminders as to which layer is (or should be) the active one.

Creating the Layers

You will create three layers for the various elements of the snowboarder illustration, with the following names:

- The sky and the cloud, named Background
- The snowboarder, named Snowboarder
- The foreground, named Foreground

Here are the steps for creating these layers:

1. Open the Layers roll-up, with Layout / Layers Roll-Up or with Ctrl+F3.

Four layers will be already present: Grid, Guides, Desktop, and Layer 1, which is the default name for the layer on which most elements are placed. The Desktop layer is for multipage projects, similar to PageMaker's Pasteboard. The Grid and Guides layers are for the two on-screen aids you can use for creating precision elements; neither will play major roles here.

2. Click on Layer 1 and then on the right-pointing triangle in the roll-up.

3. From the flyout menu, choose Edit and change the name of the layer to **Background**. OK the Layer Options box.

4. In the roll-up, click again on the triangle and then on New. Replace Layer 1 with the name **Snowboarder**. As soon as you OK the box, this new layer should appear in the roll-up.

5. Repeat step 4 to create the third layer, **Foreground**. Your screen will look like that in Figure 5.2.

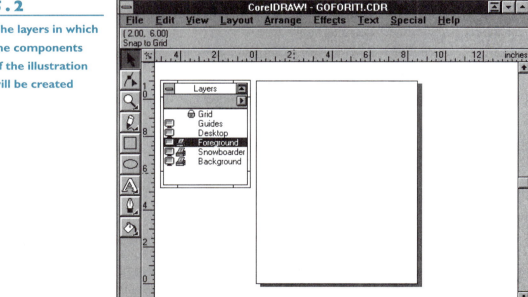

5.2

The layers in which the components of the illustration will be created

Creating the Sky

The sky in the background covers the top two-thirds of the drawing, but you needn't be concerned with fitting it precisely into place and having the elements meet at the horizon. Because the sky is behind the other elements in the drawing, all you have to do is create a full-page rectangle and drop it on the page. Here are the steps:

1. Click on Background in the Layers roll-up (otherwise, your sky will be created on the Foreground, the last layer you created).

2. Using the Rectangle tool from DRAW's toolbox, create the rectangle starting at one corner and moving down to the diagonally opposite one.

Make sure that the rectangle is at least as large as the page on all four sides, but you don't have to worry about aligning it precisely with the page. Before we declare the drawing done, we will apply electronic masking tape to the four sides to give it a nice finished look.

INSIDE INFO

One quick and accurate way to create a full-page rectangle is with DRAW's Add Page Frame command. To do this, go to Layout / Page Setup / Display and then click on Add Page Frame. That instantly creates a rectangle the exact size of the page.

Filling the Sky

Your rectangle probably has an outline and no fill—precisely the opposite of what you want. So...

1. To remove the outline (if there is one), click with the secondary mouse button on the X icon in the on-screen color palette.

2. Open the Uniform Fill dialog, either by pressing the Shift+F11 hotkey, or by clicking on the Fill tool and then the color wheel on the flyout.

3. In the Show drop-down list, set the color model to CMYK.

4. Normally, 100% cyan would produce a fine blue sky, but by adding a bit of magenta in place of some of the cyan, it makes for a better black-and-white printout. So set Cyan to 50%, Magenta to 25%, and the other two colors to 0%.
5. This color won't have an official name, but you can give it one if you want. In the New box, type **Sky**.
6. OK this box. Your screen will look like Figure 5.3.

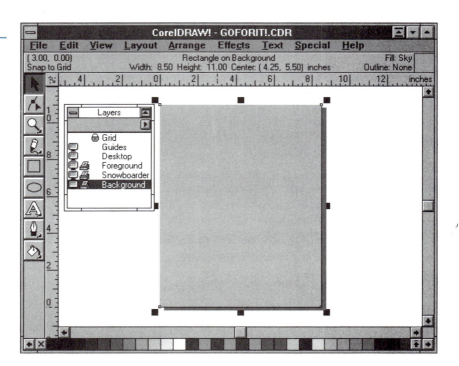

5.3

The sky, courtesy of the Rectangle tool

Notice the status line. It is telling you that the rectangle you created is on the Background layer, that there is no outline, and that the fill is Sky. Had you not designated that name, the status line would simply read "unnamed color."

Creating the Cloud

Study the full drawing in Figure 5.1 and you'll see that the cloud is not a solid object. The inside of the cloud is solid white, but the edges are fuzzy, to give it a wispy look. Creating this type of effect is the domain of the Blend tool, as you shall soon see. Before you can do any blending, though, you must first create the basic shape of the cloud. You have two choices: You can be bold and try your hand with the Freehand Drawing tool, or you can take the easy way out and pull a cloud from the Balloons section of the on-line Symbols library.

We urge you at least to *try* freehand drawing before retreating to the library. We don't suggest that you try to duplicate precisely the cloud we drew; after all, a cloud can have any old shape. Also, don't worry about making it right on your first try, because you can always modify and adjust the shape later. Here goes:

1. Click on the Pencil tool and move out to the point on the page where you want to begin drawing the cloud.
2. Click, hold, and start defining the shape. Keep the mouse button down throughout the process.

As you make the trip around your cloud, don't worry if you accidentally overlap your lines or make a wrong turn—just keep going. Make sure that you finish at the same place where you began.

3. When you have reached the end of the cloud outline, release the mouse. If you were careful to end where you started, then you have created a curve that can be filled, like the one in Figure 5.4.
4. Save with Ctrl+S.

Notice in Figure 5.4 that the cloud extends outside of the rectangle representing the sky. We did this intentionally; in the sample printout, the cloud floats off the picture, giving a sense of motion. Also notice that the Layers roll-up has been, well, rolled up, to get it out of the way. Remember, you can roll it up and down by clicking the small arrow at the top-right, or just by double-clicking on its title bar.

5.4

The outline of the cloud

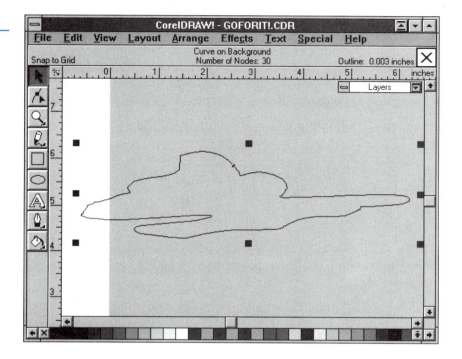

Chances are excellent that your first cloud outline has far more turns and bends than it needs—a result of using relatively crude tools such as the mouse and the Freehand Drawing tool. But not to worry; now comes clean-up time:

5. Switch to the Shape tool, and if your cloud is still selected, all of its curves and bends will be displayed. DRAW refers to these as *nodes*.

6. Click and delete any nodes that you feel are unnecessary or that send the cloud in an undesired direction. If you have many nodes to delete, try marquee-selecting them all and clicking Auto-Reduce from the Node Edit roll-up. You can open the Node Edit roll-up by double-clicking on any node. (You'll learn more about this technique in Chapter 6.)

7. Click and drag any node or any part of the lines in between to change the shape of the cloud.

8. Save.

The curve you have created represents the outer part of the cloud, the fuzzy part. It needs a bluish color that is a bit darker than the background sky, and we hit upon a mixture of cyan and magenta, created as follows:

9. Remove the outline around the curve by clicking the X icon on the color palette (using the secondary mouse button).
10. Open the Uniform Fill dialog (Shift+F11) and set the values as shown in Figure 5.5. OK the dialog.

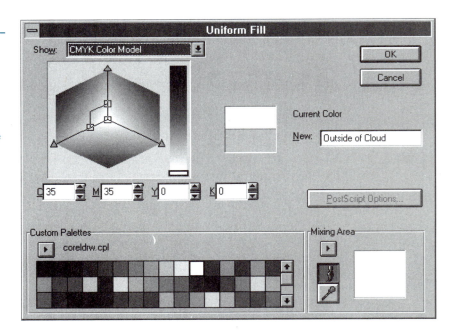

5.5

The Uniform Fill dialog for the outside of the cloud. Notice that your arbitrary Color Name can describe the object instead of the color.

Performing the Blend

DRAW's Blend tool produces smooth transitions from one object to another. Now that you have one cloud created, you need to make another one in order to blend them. But you don't have to re-create the second object from scratch; instead, start with a duplicate of the first one and adjust it from there.

This is a good time to switch to Wireframe view and, if you haven't already done so, to zoom in on the cloud.

1. Press Shift+F9 to switch to Wireframe view.
2. Press F2 and drag a marquee around the cloud to zoom in.
3. Select the cloud. Press + on the numeric keypad to make a quick copy of the cloud directly on top of itself.
4. For this type of blend to work properly, the inner object should be *completely* inside the outer one. To accomplish this, drag the top-left handle just a little bit toward the middle of the cloud. Then repeat this with the bottom-right handle.

By shrinking the cloud down a bit, you have done most of the work, but you'll need to return to the Shape tool and make sure that the inner cloud is entirely within the outer one.

5. With the Shape tool, make sure that every node and every line segment of the duplicated cloud is inside of the original one.

The further inside the original cloud you go to create the duplicate one, the more noticeable the blend will be. You can move and shape the nodes and lines all you want, but don't delete any nodes, because blends work best between objects with the same number of nodes. *Blending is very forgiving*. You needn't concern yourself with how closely the inner curve follows the contours of the outer one.

6. Switch back to the Pick tool, and save the file.
7. Change the fill to solid white by clicking on the white box in the color palette.
8. Return to Color Preview (Shift+F9) and save. Your screen will look like Figure 5.6.
9. Hold Shift and click on the outer cloud. The status line should verify that you have "2 Objects Selected on Background."
10. Open the Blend roll-up (with Effects / Blend or Ctrl+B).
11. Set the number of steps to 30 and click on Apply.
12. Save. Does your screen look like Figure 5.7?

5.6

The two parts of the cloud, ready to be blended together

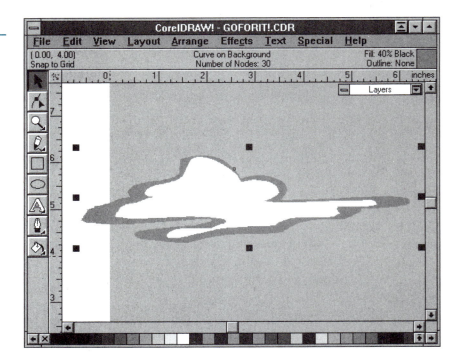

5.7

One outside, one inside, and 28 objects blended in between give this cloud depth and realism.

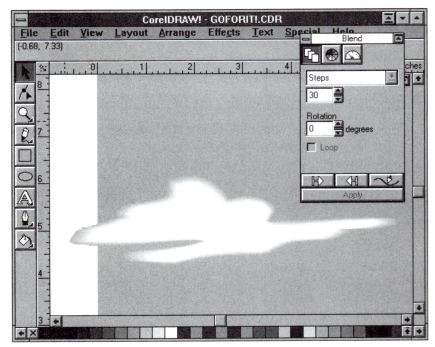

A Word about Blending

Blending two objects together is one of the most popular and heavily used techniques for producing realistic illustrations. This makes sense: In real life, light reflects off every surface, leaving color and hue variants everywhere. DRAW's Blend tool provides a way to simulate that effect, even in a simple implementation like the cloud you just created.

Bear in mind, however, that blending can be taxing on your system. In the case of the cloud, you are working with not just two shapes, but 30, drawing each one in turn, one after the other. And sophisticated blends often call for many more than 30 intermediate steps. Sometimes 50. Sometimes 100.

Our advice is this: When you create a blend, determine the correct number of blending steps necessary—based on print samples and past experience—but don't use that number until your illustration is in its final stages. Instead, substitute a smaller number, say 5 or 10. That way, you won't have to suffer through interminable blending delays, but you'll still be able to get a feel for the image.

Changing the steps of a blend is easy, and you should experiment now with the cloud. If it is not already selected, reselect the blended cloud, open the Blend roll-up again, change Steps to 5, and reapply the blend. Then change to 128 and consider stepping out for coffee...

Locking the Layer

Now that the sky and cloud of your illustration are finished, we recommend that you *lock the layer*. When a layer is locked, DRAW ignores the objects therein; no objects on that layer can be selected or changed, and no new objects can be created on it. Aside from the obvious benefit—insurance against accidentally messing up these objects—locking the layer makes it easier to select other objects in close proximity. Also, because DRAW prohibits creation of objects on locked layers, it's less likely that you might mistakenly create objects on that Background layer.

To lock the Background layer, open the Layers roll-up, double-click on Background, and then check the Locked field. When you return to the page, notice that the cloud is no longer selected. DRAW has automatically deselected it, per the decree that no objects on locked layers are selectable. You'll also see a cute little bicycle lock in the Layers roll-up, next to Background.

Creating the Foreground Snow

Producing the snow in the foreground involves a bit of filling and a bit of blending. The first thing you have to do, of course, is switch to the Foreground layer, or DRAW will bark at you as soon as you try to draw anything. Then it's off to the Pencil tool to create the first curve, the one that represents the horizon of the snow bank. Click and hold on the Pencil tool until the flyout appears, and then choose the second icon, the Bezier tool.

Unlike creating the cloud, where you held the mouse button down for the duration, to create this curve you will leapfrog from point to point, clicking only when you want to add a node. Start on the left side, slightly outside of the page. You should be able to approximate the shape of the slope with four clicks, finishing up slightly off the page on the right side. Use the rulers in Figure 5.8 as a rough guide to positioning the horizon. Then head straight down the right side, staying outside the page boundary, and click once to create that line segment. Click once more below the lower-left page boundary, and finally, click once on your starting point to complete the shape. Eight mouse clicks in all—your screen should look like Figure 5.8.

Each of these segments is a straight line by default, but four of them should be curved to create the contour of the slope. Choose the Shape tool, and press the hotkey, Ctrl+F10, to display the Node Edit roll-up. Drag a marquee across the three nodes in the middle of the slope and the one at the top-right. Then click To Curve in the roll-up.

5.8

Eight clicks of the mouse form the foundation for this snowy slope.

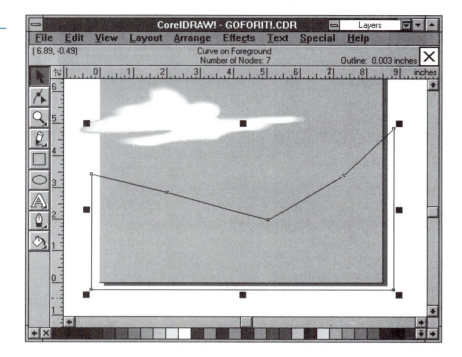

Now that the line consists of curve segments, you can shape it to look like the one in Figure 5.9, by clicking and dragging anywhere on the curve. Shaping Bezier curves takes practice, so give yourself a break if this skill doesn't come to you right away. We know many very talented DRAW users who avoid the Bezier tool because it scares them.

Because your last click was on top of your first node, your shape is automatically closed. You'll know you did it right if you can add a fill pattern to it. Figure 5.9 shows the slope after the curves have been added and the fill changed to solid white.

Notice in Figure 5.9 that the left-hand vertical line is crooked and that the entire object falls off three edges of the page. Because we will be framing the page later, this is of no consequence. Perfectionism brings no added value to this phase of the drawing.

5.9

Now our snow foreground is a closed object and can be filled.

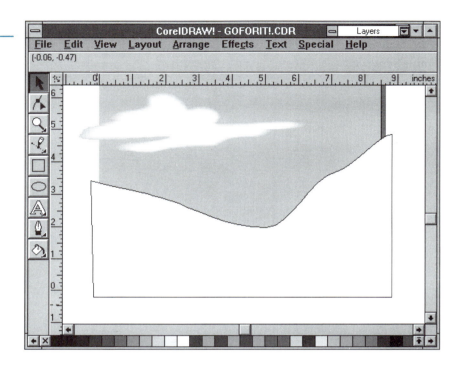

Filling the Slope

Untrained artists would declare this slope done, because the slope is white, and after all, snow is white. But in real life, a snowbank contains many different colors, depending upon reflected light and sun conditions. To make this slope more lifelike, you will start with a fountain fill, and then add a few blends.

The fountain fill is a first cousin to a blend. The fountain fill doesn't need two objects to fill in intermediate steps; it just starts on one side with one color and gradually changes to another color as it moves toward the other side. You determine what those two colors will be, and the direction the color variation will travel. Here goes:

1. Select the slope object with the Pick tool.
2. Remove the outline.

3. Open the Fountain Fill dialog box (click on the third icon of the Fill tool's flyout, or just press the F11 hotkey).
4. Verify that the type of fountain is Linear (in other words, the color changes will follow a straight line from one part of the curve to another).
5. Click on the From button to set the starting color.
6. Click on More to reach the CMYK values. Enter 20% for Cyan, 20% for Magenta, and 0% for both Yellow and Black.
7. OK this subdialog, and verify that the color box next to To is white. If it isn't, change it to white from the pop-up color palette.
8. OK this box, save the file, and see if your screen doesn't look like Figure 5.10. (If your Fountain Fill goes in the wrong direction, return to the dialog and change the angle in 90-degree increments.)

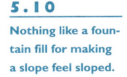

5.10

Nothing like a fountain fill for making a slope feel sloped.

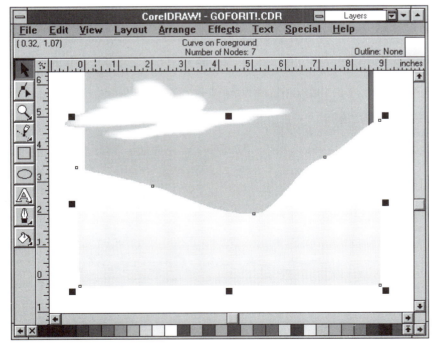

WATCH OUT!

Although most of the effects in this snowboarder drawing will print well on laser printers, fountain fills are the exception. Laser printers cannot show the subtle changes from one color or shade to the next, resulting in blocks of colors instead of smooth transitions. This loathsome condition is called "banding," and is the inevitable result of trying to produce fountain fills at 300 dots per inch. For more on this problem, see Chapter 8.

Extra Credit

The more contour you add to this snow slope, the more lifelike it will appear. And, as in every other worthwhile pursuit in life, this requires more effort. Should you want to proceed further, Figure 5.11 shows two other areas of the snowbank in which blends will add realism.

Using the same click-and-click technique for drawing the main slope, create four curves that approximate the shapes shown in Figure 5.11. When you create the corresponding nodes of objects to be blended, be

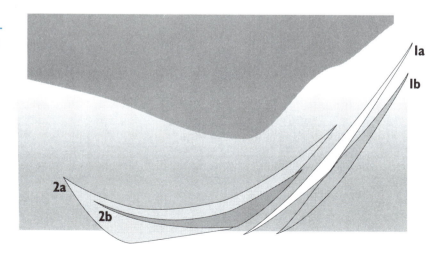

5.11

The four ingredients for cooking up these two blends

sure to create them in the same order. That is, if you start at the top-right of object 1a and proceed clockwise, do the same for object 1b. The four objects are shown here with black outlines for clarity, but you will want to remove all the outlines before blending. Blend objects 1a and 1b together, and then objects 2a and 2b.

The color components for the blends are as follows:

1a	Solid white	
1b	20% cyan, 5% magenta	
2a	15% cyan, 5% magenta	
2b	20% cyan, 5% magenta, 10% black	

Be sure to blend them each with 20 steps. Note that curves 1a and 1b are side-by-side, while curve 2b is contained within 2a. The Blend tool doesn't care.

Figure 5.12 shows a cutaway of the blends in place, and Figure 5.13 offers a print sample of the project thus far.

5.12

The additional blends add realism to the snow.

5.13

This drawing now has its background and its foreground in place.

Bring On the Snowboarder

Now for the main attraction: the man on the snowboard. He is available as SNOWBORD.CDR in the PRACTICE directory of the Companion CD.

As the snowboarder is already in DRAW format, your task is simply to incorporate him into your developing drawing—this is the time to use the Import command.

1. Activate the Layers roll-up (Ctrl+F3) and click on the Snowboarder layer.
2. Go to File / Import and choose CorelDRAW as the file type.
3. Navigate your way to the PRACTICE directory on the CD.
4. Choose SNOWBORD.CDR and OK.
5. Now you might need to position and shrink the snowboarder so he appears in the air and in a plausible size. To shrink him, click and drag his corner handles (not the side handles, as that would distort him). To move him, click anywhere inside him. For more precise positioning, set a Nudge value (Special / Preferences / General / Nudge Factor) of 12 points or so, and use your arrow keys.
6. Save. How close does your screen look to Figure 5.14?

Also on this layer belong the clumps of snow that are flying up all around the snowboarder. Since all of these clumps can come from the same original, creating them is a study in duplicating, sizing, and rotating. To create the first one, use the Freehand Drawing tool to create a closed shape that is somewhere between a rectangle and an oval. Assign it a hairline outline (.2 point) of 50% cyan, and an interior fill of solid white. Then make a quick copy with the + key, and move the copy away. Now make some random changes to the copy, such as resizing, rotation, and reshaping with the Shape tool. Then make a few more copies and change them, too.

Once you have created a few snowflakes, you can begin to duplicate and change them en masse: Switch to Wireframe view, marquee-select a group of them, duplicate the group, move it, resize it, and rotate it as desired. We randomly chose a few flakes and added small percentages of cyan and magenta to their interiors, to show the variety in solar reflection; you're invited to do the same.

5.14

Amazing how a person can bring so much life to an illustration. Note that we have turned the page border off, as it is no longer of use to us.

As your snowflakes get smaller, your Zoom tool becomes more valuable. Remember the Zoom shortcut of F2 and a quick marquee drag over the zoom area. Zoomed in, your screen will look something like Figure 5.15.

Creating the Tree

The challenging part of adding the small tree on the snowbank is not drawing the tree itself. In fact, that part is cake: You just grab it from the on-line Symbols library. The tricky part is the snow that belongs in, on top of, and through the tree. To produce the look of the finished

5.15

Thanks to DRAW's sizing and rotating tools, you can prove that no two snowflakes look alike.

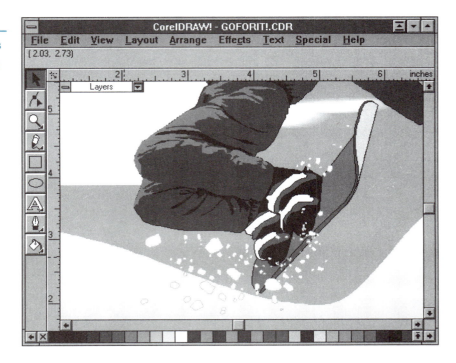

drawing, you will not actually add snow to the tree, technically speaking. Instead, you will take the existing curve shape that defines the horizon, and add to it.

WATCH OUT!

You are now at a point in your drawing where you might find yourself waiting longer than you would like for screen redraws. This is the time to make invisible some of the layers that contain finished elements, for instance, the Background layer and the Snowboarder layer. To do this, double-click on each of these layers' names in the Layers roll-up, and simply uncheck the Visible field. A few of the following screen images in this chapter were taken that way.

Importing the Tree

This is the easy part: Placing the tree on the page is a simple drag-and-drop from the Symbols library. First, make sure you are working on the Foreground layer (just click it once in the roll-up). Open the Symbols roll-up, either from the Special menu or with Ctrl+F11. From the drop-down list of categories, choose Plants. The tree you want is in the second row on the right, Symbol No. 38. Drag it into your drawing and approximate its position. You may need to enlarge it a bit, depending upon the initial size of the symbol when it was dragged out of the library.

As for the color, we found a nice one called Moss Green in DRAW's custom palette, composed of 20% cyan and 60% black. It probably looks like black in this book, and probably prints as black on a black-and-white laser printer. That's okay.

Zoom in on the tree and you'll notice something right away: The tree is not a solid object. If you were to place it below the snow line, you would be able to see the slope through the holes of the tree, and you'll use that to advantage in this next step.

Adding Snow to the Tree

In general, there are two ways to add snow to the tree: The simplistic way is to create a blob of snow and hang it around the tree. The second, more evolved method is to create a curve that represents the snow and merge it with the slope itself. (Do you get the idea that we are steering you toward the second method?) After all, the snow all came from the same place, and it is going to reflect light in the same way—the snow on the tip of the tree should get more sunlight than the snow down the hill.

This is the perfect place to use the Weld command, new as of DRAW 4.0. Here are the steps:

1. Make sure that Foreground is the active layer.
2. Switch to the Pencil tool and try a new method of drawing—the click-and-click technique—to create a series of lines that roughly follow the contour of the tree. Click one to create a

node, then click again in the same spot to create the line segment emanating from the node—two clicks on each node.

3. Continue all the way around the bottom of the tree, making your last click on top of your first click, thereby ensuring that the curve is a closed shape.

4. Switch to the Shape tool, marquee-select the entire curve, and convert nodes to curves so that you can smooth out any parts that need it. Your shape should look similar to the one in Figure 5.16.

5.16

This shape will represent snow hanging on the tree.

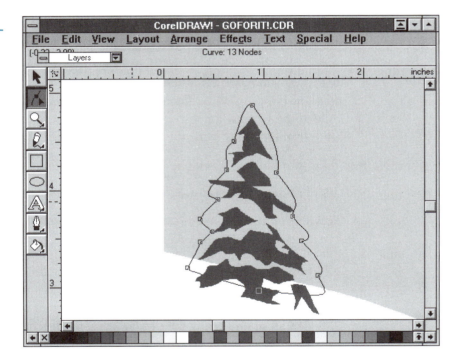

Please notice two things about Figure 5.16. First, it required only 13 nodes to create this shape, each node representing an area where the shape changes direction in some way. Second, we didn't try terribly hard to follow the precise contours of the tree. (After all, gravity and wind conditions determine how snow hangs on a tree, and we humans are not privy to those Laws.) We even allowed one branch on the left to stick through.

AUTHOR'S NOTE

> **We acknowledge that this phase of the project takes new users into unfamiliar and perhaps unfriendly territory, and we expect you to wrinkle your noses a bit over "nodes" and "cusps" and other confusia of curve creation. Have faith—you'll learn a lot more about the different types of nodes in Chapter 6, "As the Curve Turns."**

The one item that will help you shape the snow around the tree is the cusp node. If you have played with DRAW's nodes at all, you have discovered that when you move the little control points that fly out from a node, you affect the curve on both sides of the node. When you shape one side of a node, it can be frustrating to see it move as you begin to work on the next curve segment. That is the time to change the node into a cusp (if it isn't one already). To do that, click once on the node and then on Cusp in the Node Edit roll-up. This one step will allow you to more easily complete the task of shaping the snow around the tree.

Now it is time to weld the new snow with the existing slope:

1. Switch to the Pick tool, and select the snow around the tree.

2. Hold down Shift and select the slope. The order of selection is important—the Weld command uses the last item selected as the determinant of outline and fill. Were you to reverse the order, all of your snow would become invisible.

3. Choose Arrange / Weld and watch the two objects melt into one. Your screen should look like Figure 5.17.

5.17

The snow around the tree and the ski slope have become one, thanks to the Weld command.

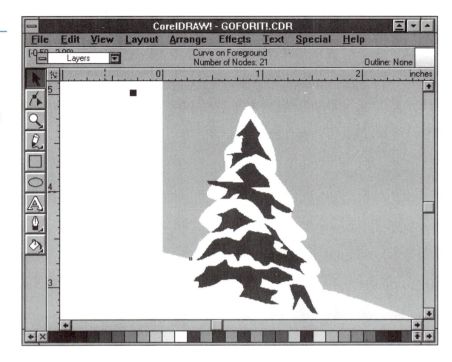

More Extra Credit

Figure 5.18 shows two more blends that you can create to more accurately depict sunlight and shadows. In Image No. 1, you can see the two pairs of curves that will constitute each blend. In Image No. 2, they are colored as intended—the lightest portion being the snowcap that gets the most light at the top-right, and the darkest portion being the area directly under the tree, where the darkest shadows occur. Image No. 3 shows the effect of a 30-step blend on both pairs. The interesting part of this blend is the lower piece of the right pair: It was not given a uniform fill, but rather a fountain fill. In other words, this blend takes place between an object that is white and an object that is itself changing colors. The result is a blended snowcap that gradually blends into the slope.

5.18

Two more blends, each starting from simple curves

1

2

3

The Home Stretch

Up to this point, you have created the background, the foreground, and the snowboarder. Now for the fun part: adding the GO FOR IT! text. We chose the Geometric 231 Heavy typeface, one of the Bitstream display faces that ship with CorelDRAW. Should you want to use it also, it can be found on the CorelDRAW CD or the program disks, and you can install it into Windows using the Fonts option in Control Panel. There, click Add. Then, on the CD navigate to FONTS\TTF\G, or if the typefaces are on your hard drive, move to the directory you designated for typefaces.

INSIDE INFO

If you have ever waited for Control Panel to compile a list of typeface names from one of the CorelDRAW CDs, then you know what torture from boredom is all about. Experienced Windows users may prefer to do an end-run around Control Panel, and manually move the typeface to the hard drive. The crucial piece of information you need to do this is the file name: Geometric 231 Heavy is TT1129M_.TTF (you should have known, right?). Copy that file to the directory in which you house your TrueType faces, and then use Control Panel to install it from there. It is two steps instead of one, but you'll get it done in about one-fifth the time.

Creating the Text

We recommend you continue to hide layers that are not needed. At this point, you need to show the Background layer, but you can hide all the others. Remember to activate and unlock the Background layer before you create the text.

There are two different effects applied to this text: an extrusion and an envelope. Together, they provide depth and dimension. Because you will be applying special effects to the text, you must use artistic rather than paragraph text. Artistic text is the easier one: You just click once on the Text tool, move out to the page, click once, and type the words **GO FOR IT!** (Don't forget the exclamation mark.)

Using the Text roll-up or the Character Attributes dialog (Text / Character command), set the type to Geometric 231 Heavy, at a size of approximately 100 points.

Fill the text with 100% cyan and 50% magenta, and save the file. Before the enveloping process, try vertically stretching the text a bit, by dragging down the lower-middle selection handle. How much stretch to employ is an open question, but too little stretch would be useless and too much stretch could be gross. If this were a recipe, it would read "stretch to taste." Figure 5.19 shows the text after a 140% vertical stretch.

5.19

This text is colored, stretched, and now ready to be enveloped.

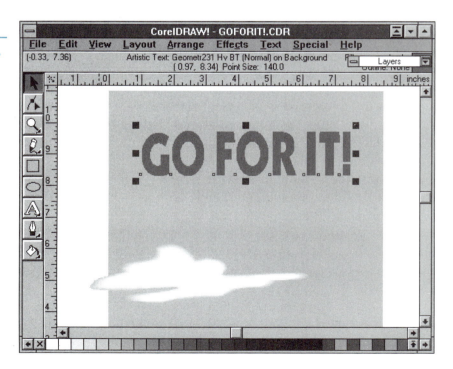

The enveloping involves the following steps:

1. Open the Envelope roll-up (with Effects / Envelope or Ctrl+F7).
2. Switch to Wireframe view for easier envelope editing.
3. In the roll-up, click on the second icon from the left—it has three straight sides and a top side that is gently sloping upward from left to right, representing the kind of change it can make to selected objects.
4. Click on Add New; the selection handles around the text change to nodes.
5. Click the lower-right node and drag it straight down about an inch and a half, according to the on-screen rulers.
6. Click on Apply, and watch the enveloping take place.
7. Drag the top-right node down by about a half-inch, and click on Apply. Your screen should look similar to Figure 5.20.

5.20

The effect of using the Envelope function on a string of text

8. Save the file.

It was not by chance that we had you produce the envelope first, before the extrusion. DRAW does not permit you to envelope extruded text, but doesn't mind if you extrude enveloped text. Got that? Here goes:

1. With the text still selected, open the Extrude roll-up (with Effects / Extrude or Ctrl+E).
2. Of the five icons across the top of the roll-up, choose the second one from the left.
3. Choose Small Back from the drop-down window and set the Depth to 20.
4. Click on Apply, and watch the Extrude tool do its thing.

Without an outline for the text, the extrusion probably looks like a blob (that's a technical term). You can change that by assigning a different color to the extruded portion.

5. In the Extrude roll-up, click the color wheel icon (the one on the far right). Then click the Solid Fill option.
6. Click on the color box below Solid Fill and then on white from the palette.
7. OK the dialog, and click Apply to activate the extrusion changes.
8. Press F12 to reach the Outline Pen settings, click on the color palette at the top-left, and then on More to reach the standard color dialog.
9. Set the color to 100% cyan, 50% magenta, and 0% for yellow and black (the same color of the interior of the text).
10. OK the color dialog, and set the outline width to .5 point.
11. OK this dialog and save the file. Your screen should look like Figure 5.21.

5.21

This text is now enveloped and extruded.

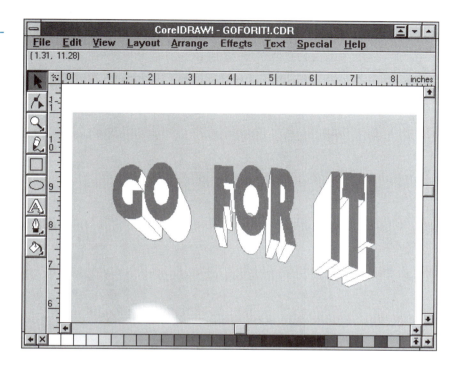

Stretching the Text

Your objective is to make the text as prominent as possible behind the snowboarder. The Pick tool will easily dispose of this chore: First drag the corner handles so that text starts near the top-left and continues until it's near the right edge of the picture. Then drag the middle handle down to stretch the text until the snowboarder covers a portion of it (to do this, you'll need to make the Snowboarder layer visible). Ours ended up looking like Figure 5.22.

Adding the Finishing Touches

All that's left to finish your drawing is placing the frame around the page. Remember at the outset that we told you it was okay for the elements near the edge to actually hang off the page? Now it's time to take

5.22

This text is now enveloped, extruded, and stretched.

care of that by framing (or *masking*) the perimeter of the page. There are three ways to accomplish this:

- You could draw four white rectangles and place them around the edges of the drawing, obscuring all parts of the drawing that hang over the edge. This is the simplest (and most simplistic) method.

- You could draw two rectangles—one exactly $8\frac{1}{2}$ by 11 inches, and one large enough to cover all elements in the drawing—and Combine them together to form a single object containing solid white borders and a hollow interior. This is the standard masking technique that DRAW artists have used to frame their drawings.

Adding the Finishing Touches **139**

- The third way, with DRAW 5.0, is to use the PowerClip tool to "clip" all of the objects in the drawing, so they are contained within the $8\frac{1}{2}$-by-11-inch space.

Figure 5.23 shows the first method of creating rectangles on all four sides of the drawing and turning them solid white. In the top figure, the four rectangles are shown with outlines so you can see where they were drawn. In the lower figure, they are shown with 15% shading so that you can see them; normally, they would be shaded solid white so as to be invisible.

Figure 5.24 shows the first step in creating a mask with the Combine command. The two rectangles are shown with outlines so you can see

5.23

Creating a mask with four solid white rectangles

5.24

Creating a mask with two rectangles that will be combined together

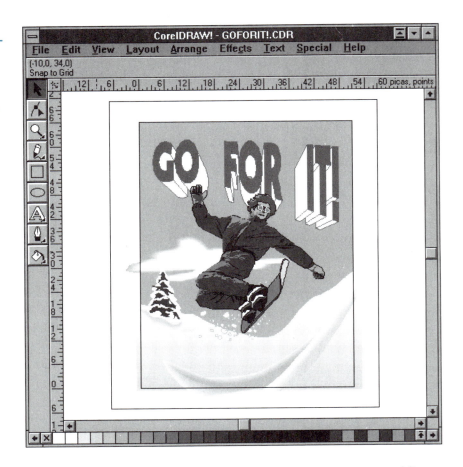

them; when selected and combined, they become one image resembling a picture frame—solid on the outside, hollow on the inside.

Regardless of which of the first two methods you choose, you can make your life easier by setting a grid before you draw the rectangles. Choose Layout / Grid & Scale Setup and set the two Grid Frequency values to 2 per inch. Before you OK the dialog, make sure that the Snap To Grid field is checked. Now the rectangles you draw will snap easily into place. You could also set the grid to 4 per inch or 1 per inch, although the latter might result in a grid too severe for your taste. Make sure to activate the Foreground layer before proceeding.

Advanced or ambitious users might want to try framing this picture with the new PowerClip feature. Here are the basic steps for that method:

1. Use Edit / Select All to select all elements, and then Shift+click on the background to deselect it. Then group all elements together.

2. Choose Effects / PowerClip / Place Inside Container. When prompted with the arrow, click on the background rectangle. You thus define that rectangle as the container inside which all other elements will be placed.

3. Choose Effects / PowerClip / Edit Contents to move the interior contents around in the container. Your screen will look like Figure 5.25.

5.25

With DRAW 5.0's new PowerClip tool, you can define a shape (in this case, the 8½-by-11-inch rectangle) and eliminate all parts of a drawing that fall outside of it.

4. When done, choose Effects / PowerClip / Finish Editing.

The first two masking methods are easier to understand and execute, but not as powerful as the mask created with the PowerClip tool. The rectangles merely cover up the unwanted portions of a drawing; but PowerClip essentially eliminates them. Regardless of the method you have chosen for this drawing, your completed drawing, with all layers made visible, should look like Figure 5.26.

5.26

The completed drawing

Wrapping Up

Here are a few parting thoughts:

Bringing Order to the Order   We suppose it would be nothing short of a miracle if your drawing looked like ours. The most common miscue: layering incorrectly. If your drawing looks more like Figure 5.27 than 5.26, then you either have an object on the wrong layer or a layer in the wrong order (in this case, the cloud is on the Foreground layer instead of the Background layer). To re-layer your image, in the Layers roll-up drag one layer in front of or behind another (the last on the list is the first to be drawn.) To move an object from one layer to another, select it, click on the right-pointing triangle in the roll-up, choose Move To..., and click on the desired layer name.

Changing Backgrounds   You might also enjoy experimenting with a background made from the Texture Fill dialog, like the one shown in Figure 5.28. Texture Fill offers bitmap characteristics and tonal blending that can add realism to drawings.

5.27

This overeager cloud belongs on the Background layer, not the Foreground layer.

Reverse Engineering Is Encouraged Oftentimes, taking a drawing apart is just as educational and enjoyable as putting it together in the first place. If you want to compare yours to ours, you'll find ours named GOFOR-IT!.CDR in the PRACTICE directory of the Companion CD. Also, to see what it looks like in color, check out Illustration 2 in the Color Gallery.

As we conclude this chapter, we are done with what we consider the introduction to DRAW. In the next few chapters, we will examine more closely some of the functions that really make the program tick.

5.28

This background is brought to you by the **Texture Fill** function.

PART II

WORKING WITH OBJECTS

If you worked through the exercise in the last chapter, you survived (we hope) a trial by fire. Hands-on experience is always the best way to learn a subject—whether it's computer software or a game of croquet—and don't let any book author tell you otherwise. The next four chapters will fill in any blanks left by Chapter 5, and serve as a reference for new users who have just finished creating the snowboarder, as well as for experienced users seeking a refresher or a bit of insight to a particular tool or function.

CHAPTER 6

As the Curve Turns

SIX

We proclaimed back in Chapter 1 that the curve is the key to everything in DRAW. Even objects that are called something else—such as rectangles or ellipses—are really curves in disguise. You could argue that even straight lines are treated as curves by DRAW. We admit to using a broad brush to paint this picture, but the point we are trying to make is this: DRAW treats all vector-based objects in essentially the same manner (imported bitmaps are different). Vector-based objects all have exterior outlines that define their shape, as well as interiors that, if closed, can be filled with colors or shades. And—of most relevance to this chapter—all objects created in DRAW contain two components: *paths* and *nodes*.

We hate burdening you with these terms, especially *path*, which has approximately 178 different meanings throughout the computing industry. Here are *our* definitions:

- In DRAWspeak, think of a path as the distance from a start point to an end point. In a rectangle, for instance, any side would be a path; same for a triangle. With an ellipse, the entire shape is one path. A crooked line drawn with the freehand tool might consist of many paths.

- Paths are defined by their start and end points, and those little points are called nodes. A rectangle has four nodes; a circle has just one; your crooked line might have a dozen. Every object you create in DRAW contains these two basic elements, paths and nodes; and in all cases, DRAW provides access to them for editing and reshaping at the most fundamental level.

When you draw with the Pencil tool, you are automatically creating lines or curves…end of discussion. But when you use the other three tools—Ellipse, Rectangle, and Text—you create objects that DRAW treats with a bit more reverence. For instance, ellipses always have one continuous circumference; rectangles always have four sides; and text carries with it a host of special attributes, such as typeface, style, size, and so forth. Until you say otherwise, DRAW identifies these objects as having special properties. When you *do* say otherwise—that is, once you use DRAW's Convert to Curves command—then DRAW lets go of the special properties. These objects are no longer special; they are just curves. You are then free to add a fifth side to a rectangle, turn circles into odd shapes, and commit all sorts of unspeakable crimes on text characters.

Let's start by looking at curves and lines; we'll cover ellipses, rectangles, and text characters later in the chapter.

Creating Curves and Lines

If you worked through Chapter 5, you created and edited curves when you made the snowbank, the cloud, and the snow that hung on the tree. To further explore the dynamics of curves, grab the Pencil tool, choose the freehand drawing mode, and draw a curve on screen. Any curve will do, like the one in Figure 6.1.

Click on the Shape tool, and count for yourself the number of nodes and paths that make up the curve. In Figure 6.1, 15 nodes were required, including the first and last ones, to represent the 14 paths of the curve. We have actually included this inelegant curve on the CD and auxiliary diskette, should you want to use it as you work through this chapter. It is entitled, humbly enough, MSTRPCE1.CDR, and is located in the PRACTICE directory.

Changing the shape of curves got a whole lot easier in DRAW 4.0. In previous versions, the only way to edit a curve was to work with the nodes themselves—and they're pretty small on high-resolution displays. But as of DRAW 4.0, you can click and drag anywhere along the path—welcome news for wrist-weary illustrators.

Because you have used the Pencil tool to draw the curve on your screen, your object is already a curve and is subject to immediate editing. Any node or path can be altered. But before you do that, select each node in turn and

6.1

To enter this drawing in Corel's World Design Contest, send it to…

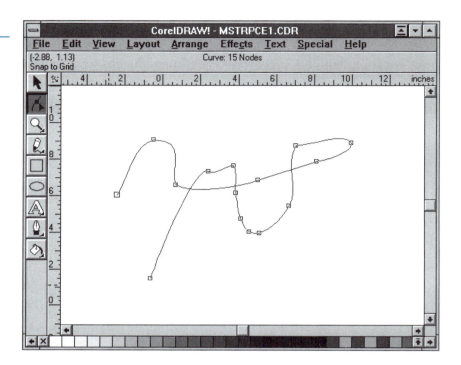

notice the status line. If your curve is anything like ours, the nodes are not all the same, but are listed in the status line as either *smooth* or *cusp* nodes. As you drew your masterpiece, DRAW used discretion (okay, virtual discretion) to determine the type of node to employ at each turn.

DRAW uses smooth nodes where it finds a gradual transition from one path to the other, and cusps to make a sharper turn. Figure 6.2 zeroes in on one of the cusp nodes. Notice how the curve makes almost a 90-degree turn; this is a job for a cusp, and so DRAW automatically uses it.

Our curve also contains a straight line, between the fourth and fifth nodes. We didn't draw it intentionally, but DRAW sensed that the path was close to a straight line and so it forced it to be one. You can choose to draw a series of connected, straight lines in freehand drawing mode, and ultimately, that will be the key to your success as a DRAW user. Instead of holding the mouse button and dragging through the entire curve, you leapfrog from one point to another to draw straight lines. You don't double-click, but you do click twice in a row (there is a difference).

6.2

DRAW sees you turning a sharp corner here, so it automatically uses a cusp node.

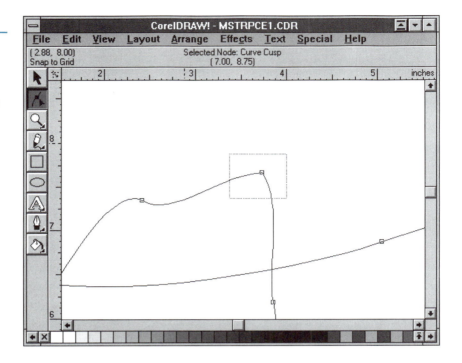

Here is play-by-play commentary of a DRAW user creating a series of straight lines:

> Click to define start point.
>
> Move the mouse.
>
> Click to define end point.
>
> Click at the same place to define new start point.
>
> Move the mouse. Click to define new end point.

Figure 6.3 shows, in rather dramatic fashion, the value of creating straight lines and the folly of not. The top image shows the ease with which you can create a simple outline of an object such as this house, with just a few clicks. On the other hand, as the lower image illustrates quite splendidly, it's not so easy to draw freehand. This is not just another example of our lead author's lack of drawing skills—the most accomplished CorelDRAW artist couldn't do much better with instruments as clumsy as the Freehand Drawing tool and a mouse (drawing tables would yield somewhat better results). That's not what DRAW is all about: When you work in a vector-based application, you are not a painter, and your physical drawing skills are not central to your success. Success in DRAW is determined by how well you can play leapfrog and hop from one point to the next.

INSIDE INFO

DRAW makes decisions about cusps and straight lines based on settings that you control from the Preferences dialog box. From the Curves page, you can set various thresholds that determine DRAW's tendency to use cusp nodes when turning corners and straight lines when going from node to node. With the Corner threshold, the lower the number you enter, the greater DRAW's tendency will be toward creating cusps. With the Straight Line threshold, the lower the number you enter, the greater DRAW's tendency will be toward drawing curves. Other fields in this dialog affect drawing, as well. Press F1 from within the dialog to get descriptions of each field.

6.3

DRAW's tools reward you for taking the most efficient route from one point to the next.

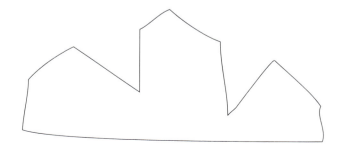

Drawing in Bezier Mode

Creating curves with the Freehand Drawing tool is easy, if inelegant. As we mentioned in an earlier chapter, it's not unlike using an Etch-a-Sketch, with which you move haphazardly from one point to another. Creating curves with the Bezier drawing tool is quite a different experience, both in the way the tool operates and in the results.

We have read all of the books, scoured the CorelDRAW User's Manual, sifted through all of the magazine articles, and taken copious notes at CorelDRAW seminars—and we have reached an inescapable conclusion: It is impossible to teach anyone the Bezier drawing tool. Drawing in Bezier mode is like sculpting with warm jello. Every action has an opposite reaction, and it's doubtful you'll gain any understanding of how the tool works by reading someone else's prose. Therefore, what follows is either another in a string of futile attempts to explain Bezier mode, or the first successful attempt ever (most likely the former).

The Bezier tool doesn't follow every bump and jitter of your mouse through a path. It looks for a beginning point and an end point, and then connects them with one curve. When creating Bezier curves, you do not click and drag across the entire path; rather, you click at the start and end points and drag *once* to shape the curve between the two points.

However—and this is one of several confusing aspects—you can choose *when* to perform the drag. You can either

- Click once to create the start point, and then click and drag on the end point. Or,
- Press and hold the primary mouse button to lay down the start point, drag, and then click once on the end point.

We warned you: This stuff is impossible unless you take hand to mouse. So start DRAW and try the following two maneuvers:

1. From the Pencil tool flyout, choose the Bezier tool (the second one from the left).
2. Click once anywhere on the page.
3. Move the mouse elsewhere.

4. Click and drag. As you drag, you should be creating a smooth curve.

Press the Spacebar twice to disconnect from the curve you just drew. Then try it this way:

1. Click anywhere on the page and drag the mouse away from that point. This time, you are defining the curve as you lay down the start point.
2. Release the mouse and move it elsewhere.
3. Click once. The path between the two points is automatically a curve.

As with the Freehand Drawing tool, you can use Bezier mode to create a series of straight lines, by clicking from one point to the next. But in order to create curves, you must use one of the two methods outlined above. Frankly, we don't expect many users to develop a feel or an appreciation for either of these methods. We'd be happy to help you with the finer points of warm-jello sculpting, but for the majority of DRAW users, the intricacies of the Bezier tool are not worth mastering. This is not to say that you can't use Bezier curves effectively—quite the contrary. In the next section, we recommend a particular strategy for creating simple and effective curves that does not require complete and total mastery of the Bezier tool.

All about Nodes

Curves are formed by the paths that define their shapes, and the paths are connected by nodes. Any time a curve changes its direction (or its *inflection*, to be technical), it does so on a node. This is often obvious, as shown by node 1 in Figure 6.4. In other cases it is quite subtle, as with the soft inflection at node 2. Node 2 marks the point at which the curve changes from moving counterclockwise to moving clockwise.

Nodes and paths are forever editable and changeable, and it is on this last point that we intend to harp. *You don't need to make a curve perfect the first time!* It can always be reshaped later. It is often better to "rough out" a general shape without regard for accuracy, and then go back and

6.4

At nodes 1 and 2 you see different changes in curve inflection. Sometimes it's obvious, and sometimes it's subtle.

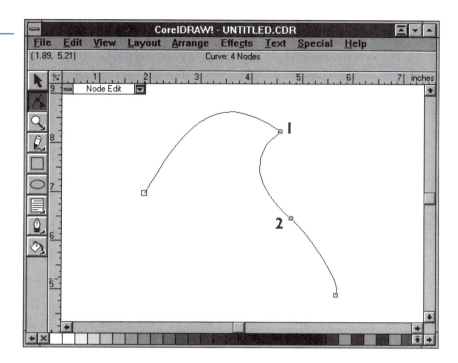

clean it up. Trying to make it perfect the first time will likely take you much longer than making two passes.

Types of Nodes

Before we reveal our recommended strategy for creating and editing curves, we want you to first be aware of the different types of nodes that DRAW employs—symmetrical, smooth, and cusp—even if you don't fully understand them. They are described in the paragraphs that follow.

WATCH OUT!

Remember, editing nodes requires that you use the Shape tool. The Pick tool is for editing the entire curve; the Shape tool provides access to individual nodes.

Symmetrical Nodes   These are perhaps the least friendly of DRAW's three node types. When you reshape a symmetrical node, the paths on each side of the node move equally. To be precise, the two *control points*—the blue dotted lines that emanate from the node—must form a straight line with the node and always remain equidistant from the node, forcing the curvature on both sides to be the same. When you click and drag the control point for a symmetrical node, DRAW will work according to the laws of physics: For every action, there must be an equal and opposite reaction.

To see this at work, draw a curve, switch to the Shape tool, click on a node, and open the Node Edit roll-up. Then change the node to Symmetrical (unless DRAW has made it a symmetrical node already) and reshape one of the paths next to the node. Notice how the other side moves in concert.

Figure 6.5 illustrates this: In the top image, the lower control point for the selected node is about to be dragged downward. Because this is a symmetrical node, the upper control point moves away equally. The result, shown in the lower image, is a curve that maintains symmetry with respect to the node.

Symmetrical nodes are fun to play with, but many users become exasperated at the tendency for symmetrical nodes to change the shape of the adjacent path.

Smooth Nodes   Like symmetrical nodes, smooth nodes assure a gradual transition from one side of the node to the other—but they do not require equal and opposite movement on the opposite side. The control points, though they continue to form a straight line through the node, are not required to be equidistant from the node. Therefore, the curve isn't necessarily mirrored on the other side. Nonetheless, shaping the path on one side of the node *does* affect the other side.

Figure 6.6 shows the dynamics of a smooth node. As the control point is extended downward and at an angle, the opposite control point adjusts only its angle (to maintain the straight line). It does not extend in

6.5

Any change made on one side of a symmetrical node will be mirrored on the other.

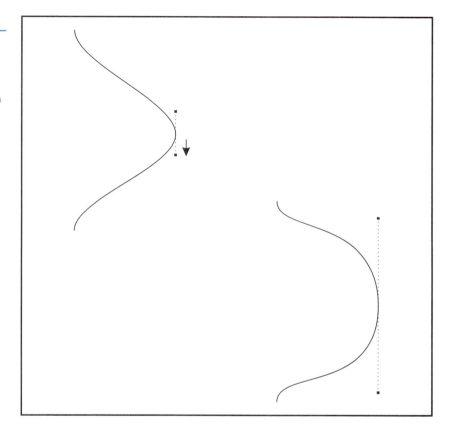

the opposite direction. The curve adjusts to remain smooth (hence the node's name), but there is no mirroring action.

Smooth nodes are handy and efficient when nice, clean curves are sought. For the ultimate in control over nodes, however, read on…

Cusp Nodes This is the don't-mess-with-me type of node. Cusp nodes do not allow movement on one side to affect the other side. The two control points do not have to form a straight line with the node, and can move with complete independence. As Figure 6.7 illustrates, the upper control point doesn't react at all when the lower one is extended out and at a different angle.

6.6

This smooth node does not react equally and oppositely on the other side.

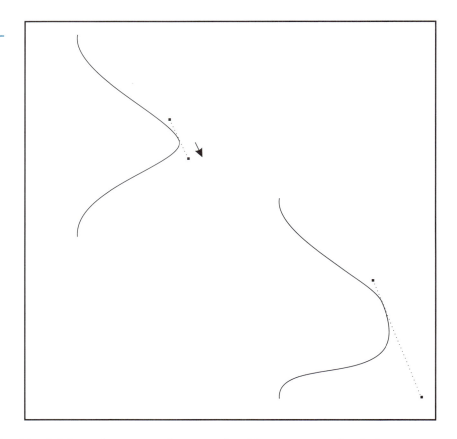

The User's Manual suggests that you should use cusp nodes "when you want a sharp change in direction." We disagree. We think you should consider using cusp nodes *most of the time.* They are the easiest to work with and the friendliest. When you have correctly shaped one side of a node, the last thing you want is for that path to move around when you begin work on the other side of the node. We acknowledge that there are tasks for which smooth nodes are more efficient, but cusp nodes are more predictable and therefore generally easier to work with.

6.7

Cusp nodes feature pairs of control points that don't give a hoot about what the other one is doing.

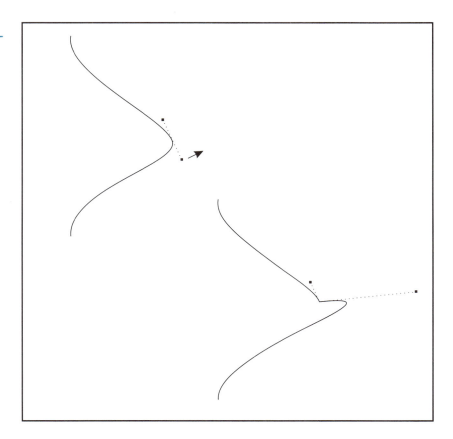

Changing Node Types

You can change node types after you create the curve or as you create it, and we recommend you do it afterward. Why? To force DRAW to create a certain type of node (instead of the type that it would determine on its own), you have to remember an elaborate and precise combination of clicking and dragging. Specifically, after clicking and dragging away from the start point, you must return to the start point and click once to create a smooth node, and twice to create a cusp node, before clicking to lay down the end point of the curve. Otherwise, the next node will be symmetrical.

See what we mean? This is next to impossible to remember—and quite tedious to carry out even if you can remember it. It's easier to let

DRAW create whatever node it wants to; then you can return to the nodes later. If, after creating a series of paths, you know that you want all cusp nodes, you can just marquee-select them, open the Node Edit roll-up, and click on Cusp. Then it's much easier to shape the paths to fit whatever form you seek.

A Blueprint for Painless Drawing

At this point, we want to remind you of the tenor of this book: We are not trying to turn you into master illustrators, but rather want to help you add confidence and skill to whatever sense of design you may already have. As we have watched both new and experienced users fumble with node editing and Bezier curve drawing, we have settled on what we think is the best procedure:

- Lay down the basic shape of the curve as quickly as you can.
- Use cusp nodes to reshape the curve.

Imagine an artist formulating an idea for a painting or a sketch. How fastidious do you think he or she would be at this early stage? Many of our colleagues use the backs of envelopes and the margins of the daily newspaper to sketch out their ideas. When starting out, the artist wants merely to collect thoughts, dump ideas, and allow for inspiration. Making it perfect comes later. And so should it be with you, the DRAW user—even more so, in fact, as modern-day electronic tools make it easier than ever to change your mind and fiddle with elements.

The following sections define our best advice for drawing curves and creating shapes.

Define the Basic Shape

Figure 6.8 shows the intended sketch—a silhouetted image of a little boy at play. Whether you are drawing this from scratch or tracing around a bitmap image already imported into DRAW, your first objective is to define the rough shape with as few nodes as possible. If you would like to follow along, this image is CHILD.CDR in the PRACTICE directory of the Companion CD.

6.8

This silhouetted child makes a good practice court for drawing and shaping curves.

Switch to the Bezier tool and pick a starting point. To produce the shape with the fewest number of nodes, look for the points of inflection—the points on which a curve turns from one direction to another—and click on them. If you do nothing else other than just click, you are well on your way to producing the intended shape. Figure 6.9 shows this process: All paths are created with straight lines. (The final image is in the background in light gray to provide you with a comparison.)

As you can see, this first sketch is grossly inaccurate in some parts. But don't be concerned—your objective is not to create a close sketch, but rather to define the points at which the curve changes shape. You are just laying down nodes. Don't drag the mouse to create any curves at this stage; you want instead to leapfrog from one point to the next, creating nodes and straight lines. These straight lines don't do justice to the

6.9

Using straight lines to define a basic shape

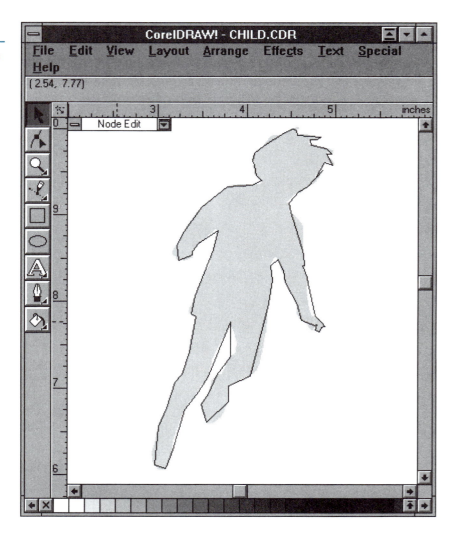

more sweeping curves—for instance, the ones that make up the child's left leg—but that's OK. You're just picking out the places where the curve changes. The more jagged parts, such as the hairline, require more curves. Be careful to complete the overall curve by clicking your final end point right on top of your initial start point.

Figure 6.10 shows exactly the nodes that were used in our version. Estimated time to complete this phase: 10 to 30 minutes.

6.10

Each click of the mouse produced a node—80 in all.

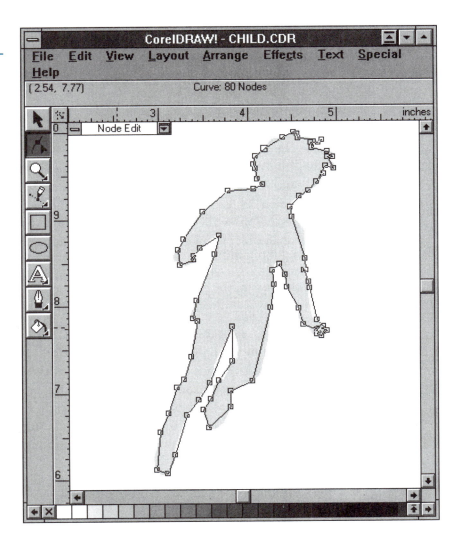

Create the Curves

Because you played leapfrog from one point to the next, every path you created is a straight line. Turning them all into curves is a very simple process. Estimated time to complete this phase: 30 seconds.

1. Select the curve.
2. Choose the Shape tool to make all of the nodes appear.
3. Marquee-select the entire curve.
4. Click on To Curve to change them all from straight lines into curves.
5. Check the Cusp button; if it is available, click on it. (If it isn't available, that means all nodes are already cusps.)

Reshape the Curves

Here is the heart of the project. This is where you turn your collection of lines into the image of a child. If you defined your paths correctly, you should only need to reshape each path to fit that portion of the curve. Inevitably, you will need to reposition nodes and add or remove a few to better follow the curves, but at this point, the project is much more manageable, thanks to your having already defined the basic layout of the curves.

Now zoom in and begin reshaping. Remember, since version 4.0, DRAW lets you click and drag the path itself, not just the nodes.

Keep the Node Edit roll-up near the area you're working on, to reduce excess mouse motion away from the curve. To add a node, click on the approximate desired position on the path, click the + icon on the roll-up, and then promptly turn your new node into a cusp. To remove a node, simply select it and press Delete. You might find it easier to select nodes with marquees than by clicking on them. You'll be your own judge as to how true to the original image your drawing will be. Either way, adjustments are easy with cusp nodes.

Figure 6.11 shows the finished outline side-by-side with the original. Estimated time to complete this phase: 20 minutes to 1 hour.

6.11

Dead ringers: Cusp nodes make it easy to turn lines into curves.

The Supporting Cast

Although learning the different node types and curve editing techniques is top priority in this chapter, several other DRAW features on the Node Edit roll-up are worth attention.

> **What about TRACE?**
>
> You may have been wondering why we haven't advised you to use the TRACE module to automatically create the curve around the child, and we've been begging the question throughout this exercise. If you were to poll the writers on our team for this book, you would not find a consensus on the issue of whether to use the automated TRACE utility or create curves manually. Some believe that TRACE is an excellent starting point; others don't trust it.
>
> TRACE definitely continues to evolve, and version 5.0 is smarter than ever. In conjunction with DRAW's Auto-Reduce tool, TRACE will certainly see more action than in previous versions. Nonetheless, we consider it a necessary fundamental to learn about node editing and curve creation. Nodes and curves are the building blocks of all DRAW's work, and forever sloughing this job off on TRACE is not responsible, in our view.
>
> We think of TRACE as a microwave oven: It is wonderfully convenient and great for simple cooking chores. But to be effective in the kitchen, you must also use the stove, oven, cutting board, and mixing bowls.

Auto-Reduce

A favorite node-editing feature since the release of version 4.0 is DRAW's Auto-Reduce, which studies a curve and sniffs out unnecessary nodes. This new tool is especially helpful with very complex drawings that have pushed printers beyond their limits. By reducing the number of nodes, you automatically reduce the complexity of the drawing.

The simplest way to use Auto-Reduce is to switch to the Shape tool, drag a marquee around the entire figure, and choose Auto-Reduce from the Node Edit roll-up. In Figure 6.12, the fish on top has many more nodes than the one on the bottom.

6.12

Auto-Reduce at work: The original figure (top) contains 55 nodes; the lower figure looks the same with only 26 nodes.

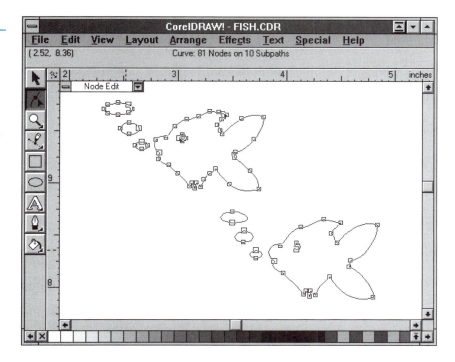

Can you trust Auto-Reduce to maintain the fidelity of your image as it eliminates nodes? Not completely. You can, however, tell DRAW how extensive to be with this crash diet, via a setting under Preferences / Curves / Auto-Reduce. Figure 6.13 shows the consequences of Auto-Reduce with a medium setting and with the maximum setting. When left at the default of .3 point, DRAW reduces the number of nodes by well over half, but the deer barely suffers. You could even argue that the reduced image looks better—with a few nodes knocked out, it's somewhat cleaner.

When Auto-Reduce is increased to 1 point, however, DRAW renders the deer with only 40 nodes instead of the original 170, and here the image is compromised. You can see it in the tail, the ears, and the legs.

6.13

Auto-Reduce is a powerful and helpful tool, but use it with caution.

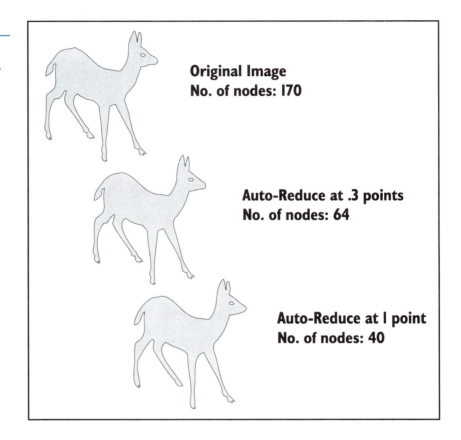

Joining and Breaking Paths

So far, you have worked with paths that have been connected, with each node being one of a continuous train. DRAW's tools enable you to disconnect paths into *subpaths*, and to join two open paths into one.

To break a path, select a node or nodes and click on the top-right icon in the Node Edit roll-up, which represents two objects being separated. The two disconnected subpaths are still part of the same curve, but when a node is broken, the closed shape becomes open and instantly loses its interior fill pattern.

NEW FOR 5

> In previous versions, when you broke a node, DRAW turned it into two nodes, but left them both selected. Thousands of unsuspecting users dragged them together, expecting to see them separate, only to learn that they would first have to deselect them (by clicking away from them) and then reselect just one. Happily, version 5.0 automatically selects just one of the two nodes that are created when one is broken. Sometimes it's the little things that make life with software easier...

Joining nodes is just as easy as separating them: Select any two nodes from separated subpaths, and click on the Join icon next to the Break icon. If you want to join nodes that are from two separate curves, you must first use Combine to integrate them as one curve. Remember, though, that as soon as you do this, the newly combined object gets only one outline and one fill. Once combined, you can select any two end nodes and join them.

Other Node Edit Tools

You'll find the following additional node editing tools available on the Node Edit roll-up.

Rotate   This brings the capabilities of object rotation to selected nodes. Available when two or more nodes are selected, this tool presents you with the familiar arrows that appear around selected objects when you click a second time on the objects. You can rotate or skew the orientation of two nodes just by clicking and dragging.

Stretch   This tool enables you to size selected paths of a curve. This works identically to the interactive stretching you can apply on screen to a selected object, except that this stretching is performed only on two or more selected nodes, instead of on the entire curve.

Align   Selected nodes can be aligned along a straight horizontal line, a vertical line, or right on top of one another.

Elastic Mode   This tool changes the motion of two or more selected nodes when they are moved. Instead of the spacing between the nodes being preserved, the nodes move in direct proportion to the one actually being dragged. Think of it this way: With Elastic Mode on and two or more nodes selected, the node that you choose to drag will move faster than the other selected nodes. If behind the others, it will appear to chase them; if in front of them, it will pull away. It's best to see this one in action:

1. Create a curve with multiple nodes, and switch to the Shape tool.
2. Select two or more nodes.
3. Drag one of the selected nodes, and observe how all selected nodes move equally.
4. Open the Node Edit roll-up and check the Elastic Mode box.
5. Click on one of the selected nodes, and observe this time how the relational motion has changed. The node you are dragging moves faster than the others.

Node Miscellany

Here are some other guidelines to keep in mind as you're working with nodes. Also, Chapter 9 of the CorelDRAW User's Manual shows many good illustrations of node editing in action.

- The first node in a curve is larger than all the others. You can quickly select it by pressing Home. You can select the last node in a curve by pressing End. Ctrl+Home or Ctrl+End selects all nodes.
- Line segments can be recognized by their distinctive nodes, which are hollow and slightly larger when selected.
- You can invoke the Node Edit roll-up with the hotkey Ctrl+F10.

When Curves Aren't Curves (Yet)

Though it's true that all objects created in DRAW have paths and nodes, not all objects behave the same. As we told you at the beginning of the chapter, ellipses, rectangles, and text strings are given special status. They have properties that DRAW considers sacred.

Figure 6.14 shows a rectangle. Hardly front-page news, but we want you to notice a few things. First, in the status line DRAW calls it a rectangle, not just a curve. Practically everything is referred to by DRAW as a curve (or a line, which is really a curve), but this object has special status. Second, although this rectangle clearly contains four nodes, the top-left one of which is selected, the Node Edit roll-up is not interested. All of the options are unavailable. *This rectangle cannot be shaped or node edited;* its shape is sacred.

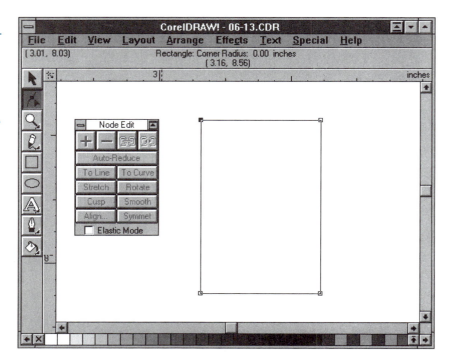

6.14

Subtle signs on DRAW's interface tell you that you are working with a VIO—a Very Important Object.

There is only one thing that can be done with the Shape tool to this rectangle: Its corners can be rounded. By taking any of the four nodes and dragging toward the center, you automatically round all four corners. Ellipses have the same restrictions. The Shape tool cannot be used for node editing, but by clicking on the sole node in an ellipse and dragging it around the circumference, you can create pie slices and wedges. In both the ellipse and rectangle, their essential properties remain intact when you use the Shape tool. Rounded corners or no, DRAW knows to consider this object a rectangle, not just a curve.

Node editing in text strings is somewhat more involved, but the techniques follow this same dynamic. Node editing a character or group of characters is akin to local text formatting: You can adjust letter spacing, control baseline shift, and work with basic formatting such as typeface, style, and size. In Figure 6.15, the first character is crying out to be shifted to the right—a perfect job for the Shape tool. The figure shows that the *K* is already selected, and a simple drag or nudge to the right will close the gap between letters.

6.15

When used with text, node editing can kern and format selected characters.

INSIDE INFO

If ever there's a time to use Nudge or the Ctrl+Drag combination to constrain movement, it's when you're kerning characters. When moving the K in Figure 6.15 closer to the other characters, it is of paramount importance that you keep it aligned on the baseline. You can ensure this by holding Ctrl while you drag the K to the right. If you forget to use the Ctrl key and you suspect that the selected character has wandered off the baseline, then use the Align to Baseline command from the Text menu (hotkey Alt+F10).

In none of these sacred objects can you add a node, shape the path between nodes, or change the basic properties of the object. Rectangles must have four corners, ellipses must have a single path, and text strings a full character set and typeface formatting.

Converting Objects to Curves

But my, how quickly the mighty can fall from grace. It takes but two mouse clicks or one hotkey to knock these privileged classes down a peg. The command responsible for the demotion is called Convert to Curves. Apply this command to a selected rectangle, and you reduce it to a plain old curve. Haunt a circle with it, and you can then add a dozen nodes and disfigure the circle for life. Impose it upon a string of text, and you can never again edit the text.

In each of these events, the object (or string of text characters) becomes a collection of paths and nodes. As Figure 6.16 shows, former text characters get no respect, as their basic shapes and outlines can now be freely altered.

6.16

This text is no longer text—it's a curve.

WATCH OUT!

Before you convert a text string into a collection of curves, make sure the text says what you want it to say. Once converted, there is no turning back (except with Undo).

Figure 6.17 shows a few of the simple shapes that can be created once you give an ellipses and a rectangle a new identity. From the originals (in black), the gray objects were all created just by adding or removing a node or two and doing a bit of reshaping.

6.17

Once you convert to curves, there's no telling what you can do to ellipses and rectangles.

In Chapter 7, you will move back up to the object level and work with whole entities again. But remember what you have read here, because this chapter is analogous to the quantum mechanics of DRAW illustrations. Paths and nodes are the essential building blocks of all objects that can be created with DRAW.

CHAPTER 7

Understanding Outlines

SEVEN

We are covering outlines before fill patterns, but not because we think outlining is more important, or because its tool happens to come first in the toolbox. Compared to DRAW's fill tools, the outlining feature is a second-class citizen, and truth be told, we intend to make quick work of it here before getting to the really good stuff in the next chapter. (We're glad that these tools don't have feelings.) But, to be fair about it, only when they're compared to fill patterns do outlines seem unspectacular.

If you read or browsed Part I of this book, you already have had some exposure to DRAW's Outline Pen, particularly in Chapters 2 and 5. Here in this chapter we assume you have a basic level of familiarity with outlining, put forth in those earlier chapters. Now we'll explore in somewhat more depth the tools and features that lie below the surface.

Working with Outlines

First off, let's define a few terms. Every object created in DRAW has an outer perimeter, but in DRAWspeak, that perimeter is not the outline. Rather, the outline is the visible line that follows the perimeter of the object. According to DRAW, if an object's outline is not "penned in"—that is, the object's outline is not visible—then the object is regarded as simply not having an outline at all. To sum up, when you "add an Outline Pen" to an object, you are giving it an outline. If the Outline Pen has either no width or no color, then the object is said to not have an outline.

Figure 7.1 is a road map to DRAW's outlining tools. Both the flyout menu from the Outline Pen tool and the Pen roll-up provide access to the two main dialogs that control the show. The flyout, in addition to being the gateway to both dialogs and the roll-up, has six preset outline

Working with Outlines **181**

widths, including no outline at all (the X-on-top-of-a-☐). The lower row of the flyout offers five preset shades of gray, as well as solid white and black. Remember, in addition to using the gray outlines, you can always set the color of the Outline Pen by using the on-screen palette and the secondary mouse button.

7.1

A map of the Outline tools

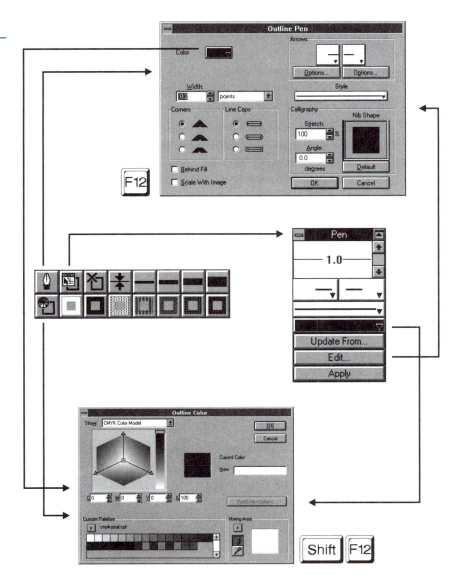

As the road map shows, you can get to the Outline Pen dialog by

- Clicking the first icon in the flyout
- Clicking the Edit button on the roll-up
- Pressing the hotkey F12

The Outline Color dialog can be reached

- From the first (leftmost) icon on the lower row of the flyout
- From the color bar on the roll-up
- With the hotkey Shift+F12
- From the Color button in the Outline Pen dialog

As with the other roll-ups, your rule of thumb for using the Pen roll-up should be based on a question of repetition. If you expect to be tweaking an Outline Pen or color more than a few times, then the roll-up's persistent on-screen presence pays off. If you need to make a one-time change to an outline, the most direct route to the dialogs would be the flyout menu, or better still, the hotkeys.

The Outline Pen Dialog

The Outline Pen dialog is the more heavily traveled, because most users need to adjust an object's outline width more often than its color (most DRAW users don't even work in color). What's more, you can reach the Outline Color dialog from within the Outline Pen dialog. Therefore, you should consider Outline Pen the Grand Central Station for outlining; when in doubt, press F12 and you'll be on the right track.

Through the five presets on the flyout menu, you can set outline widths in the following point sizes: .2 (hairline), 2, 8, 16, and the rather grotesque 24 points. We wish that we could change the value of the presets as we do our car stereo buttons; short of that, widths other than the preset ones must be entered from the roll-up or the dialog. The roll-up is more flexible, but equally arbitrary in its set of choices, offering widths

The Outline Pen Dialog **183**

in fixed increments, depending upon the measuring unit used. We keep coming back to the same conclusion: If you really want control over outlining, reach for the Outline Pen dialog.

Here is a rundown of the settings available to you from Outline Pen, in order of approximate frequency of use.

Outline Width

The Width settings give you total control over an object's outline. You can designate anything from an impossibly thin .1 point to an almost absurd 4 inches. Any of DRAW's four standard measuring units are available. You can dial up the numbers on the little "spin buttons" next to the Width field, or place your cursor in the box and type the value yourself. For the fastest way to change the Outline Width setting, press F12 to invoke the dialog, type in a new Width value, and then OK the dialog. Regardless of whether you choose the fastest or the slowest route, the Width field provides the most flexibility for setting Outline Pen widths.

Arrows

The two Arrows boxes provide access to several dozen arrow styles, ranging from normal-looking arrows to airplanes, a writing hand, and a devil's dagger. The left-hand box is for the arrow at the beginning of your line, and the right-hand box is for the arrow at the end. Bear in mind that if you draw your line from right to left, the boxes operate in reverse—that is, the left box will control the arrow at the right end of the line. If you have painstakingly set up different arrows on both sides, only to discover that you have placed them on the wrong ends, click on one of the Options buttons and choose Swap.

Even if you seek an arrow design that DRAW doesn't offer, you might be able to create it anyway, with the built-in Arrowhead Editor. For example, DRAW doesn't offer an arrow style like the one shown in Figure 7.2—long and thin. But, using the Arrowhead Editor, you can create this arrow from an existing one. Just click on one of the arrow buttons to choose an existing arrow as a starting point, and then click on the corresponding Options button and choose Edit.

7.2

The Arrowhead Editor is responsible for custom arrows like the long, thin arrow shown here.

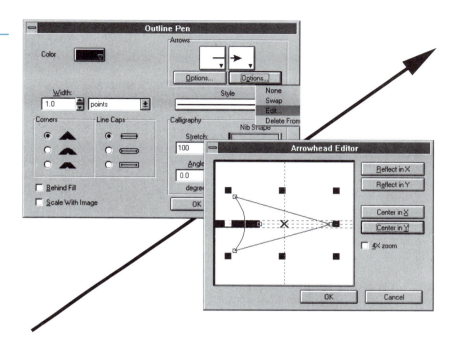

You needn't concern yourself with keeping the arrow precisely in the center of its line—that's what the Center on X and Center on Y controls are for. (Remember your geometry? The x-axis runs along the horizontal, and the y-axis along the vertical.) The Reflect buttons mirror the arrow along each axis. The Reflect in Y button will actually turn the arrow completely around, so it faces the line. (We're still looking for a useful application for this one…)

Finally, if you want a truly exotic arrow, there is nothing stopping you from creating your own. For instance, Figure 7.3 contains a downhill-racer arrow and the steps for designing it.

1. Create the object. (Figure 7.3 shows it being taken from the Symbols Library and flipped, but any single-curved object will do.)
2. Use the Special / Create Arrow command to add the object to DRAW's collection of arrows.

3. Browse the list of arrows and find the new one at the end of the list. You can do this from the Pen roll-up, as shown, or from the Outline Pen dialog.
4. Edit your creation to adjust size and proportion, if necessary.
5. Say Go (or Apply), and voilà.

We leave it to you to come up with custom arrows slightly less absurd than this one.

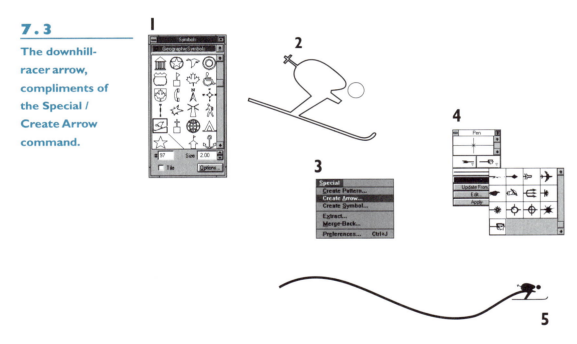

7.3

The downhill-racer arrow, compliments of the Special / Create Arrow command.

Style

This drop-down list displays 15 line choices in addition to a solid line. They are combinations of dots, spaces, and dashes. To use one of them, simply click on it. Your selected object will automatically inherit that line style.

When this feature is used in conjunction with the Line Caps settings, several additional useful styles of dotted and dashed lines can be created.

INSIDE INFO

DRAW's line styles are controlled by an ASCII file, CORELDRW.DOT, through which the size of the dash, the pattern, and the space between dashes can all be controlled. The syntax for customizing lines is not for the neophyte, but the ambitious DRAW user willing to experiment can create custom styles and apply them to any objects with outlines. There are brief instructions embedded in the file. Look for CORELDRW.DOT in the CUSTOM subdirectory under your main CorelDRAW directory. As always, create a backup of your file before you do any editing. You must restart DRAW before any changes to CORELDRW.DOT can take effect.

Color

Your gateway to all of the controls of the Outline Color dialog is the Color drop-down box in the Outline Pen dialog. Begin here, and you can choose among all of the colors in the current palette. If that's not enough, click on More to reach the Outline Color dialog. From there, you can change palettes, choose spot colors, search for names of PAN-TONE colors, or mix your own CMYK, RGB, or HSB values. (For more on the foreign language of color palettes, see Chapter 27.)

Corners

These fields offer three choices for controlling how outlines are drawn on objects with sharp corners. As Figure 7.4 demonstrates, this set of controls operates very intuitively.

Line Caps

These three options determine how the ends of lines are rendered. The first choice (the default) cuts the line off right at the end. The middle option draws round caps that extend beyond the end of the line, and the third control draws square caps that extend beyond the end of the line.

7.4

Changing corners on corners is as easy as a click.

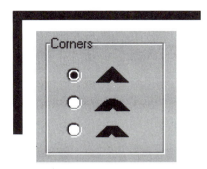

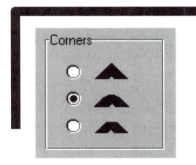

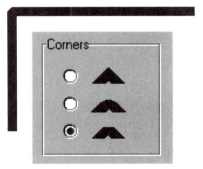

Figure 7.5 shows how your choice of line cap can affect lines that almost join. Notice that the default line cap (the first one) produces poor results; the other two choices produce satisfactory, albeit different, results.

7.5
The influence of Line Caps on lines that almost meet

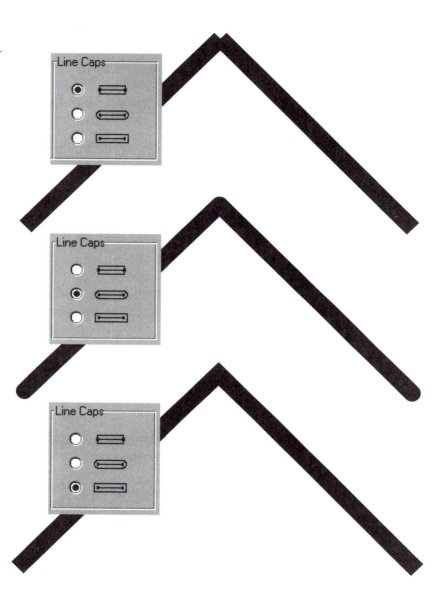

Calligraphy

These settings control the shape and orientation of the Outline Pen, not unlike working with a pressure- and orientation-sensitive ink pen. By adjusting the size and angle of the pen, you can create realistic calligraphic effects. Figure 7.6 shows two such examples with their settings, along with an example of what the default settings produce (top-left).

7.6

Results of various Outline Pen Calligraphy settings

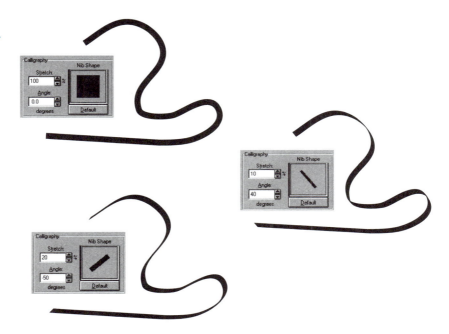

The Behind Fill Option

This field determines the position of the Outline Pen, either in front of a fill pattern or behind it. When an object has no fill pattern, this control is of no consequence. When there is a fill, however, the outline is placed behind the fill (you can witness this as the screen draws), and only half of the outline is visible. Figure 7.7 shows an opportune situation for using this control: with text characters that are kerned so tightly that they appear melted together. Without Behind Fill checked, the outline ruins the effect.

Scale With Image Option

Let's say you create a rectangle and apply an outline width to it. If you then scale the rectangle up by 200 percent, or reduce it by 200 percent, the outline will not change. Therefore, a very small outline might seem

7.7

With the outline *behind* the fill, severely kerned text takes on a whole new look.

Outline in front of fill:

ITS GETTING A BIT CROWDED IN HERE

Outline behind fill:

ITS GETTING A BIT CROWDED IN HERE

out of place once the rectangle is enlarged, or a large outline might look unattractive when the rectangle is reduced. In either case, you can check the Scale With Image option to assure that the Outline Pen remains proportionally correct to the rectangle, regardless of the rectangle's size.

The Outline Color Dialog

The first thing to be said about this dialog is that its name changes: If you invoke it from the flyout, the Outline Pen dialog, or the Shift+F12 hotkey, it is called Outline Color. If you invoke it from the color bar in the Pen roll-up, it is called Select Color.

Except for the advanced use of applying color trapping for offset color printing (discussed in Chapter 27), this dialog doesn't see as much action as Outline Pen. For most users, there is only so much you can do to a line around an object. (This dialog becomes more vital when used to change an object's fill color; in that case, its name is Uniform Fill.) Nonetheless, all of the controls that make this such a robust dialog—choices of palettes, color models, percentages of color values, and custom names—are in fact applicable to outlines, and a full discussion of them is forthcoming in Chapter 8.

Setting the Outline Pen Defaults

With its factory settings, DRAW creates black outlines of .2 point wide for all graphics objects, and no outlines for text. Although it's rare that you'll want outlines around text characters, you might very well want a different default condition for outlines around ellipses, rectangles, and curves.

To change the default outline, proceed as though you are changing an existing object—just don't select it first. When DRAW senses that you have invoked an outline command without selecting an object first, it asks you the question shown below.

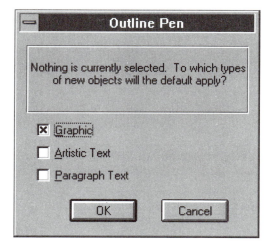

You can permanently change the outline default of three different sets of elements: graphics objects, artistic text, or paragraph text. If you want all three types of elements to have this new default, check all three boxes before continuing.

Be aware that you are not changing the default just for your current DRAW session—your change will affect every subsequent session. If you designate a default of a 2-point blue outline, that's what you'll get for every ellipse, rectangle, and curve that you draw until you again change the defaults.

For more insight into establishing and controlling default settings, check out Chapter 9. And now…on to the superstar fill tools.

CHAPTER 8

Fill 'er Up

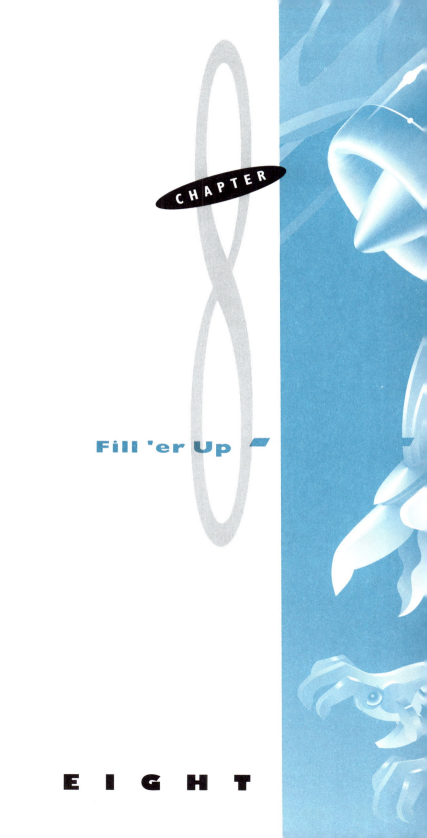

EIGHT

CHAPTER 8

If CorelDRAW were a football team, the nodes and paths we discussed a few chapters ago would be the silent heroes of the team. Though unrecognized and unloved by the fans, these players would be the backbone of the team.

Continuing the analogy, in this chapter we'll look at the headline players, the superstars on the team. They may not be the most valuable performers, but they capture the spotlight with their glamour and charisma. We're talking about DRAW's wildly popular tools for filling objects. Although you could make a strong case that producing the objects in the first place is of paramount importance (using those workhorse paths and nodes), nothing produces oohs and ahhs like a well-executed fountain or radial fill.

As in the previous chapter on outlining, we assume you have a modest familiarity with the fundamentals of filling objects, as introduced in Part I. This chapter picks up from there.

Understanding Fill Patterns

The good news is that there is no large hurdle to learning the concept of applying fill patterns. Any color, shade, or pattern that is inside of an object is considered a fill. The sole requirement is that the selected object must be completely closed before it can accept a fill. There…that's not too hard.

From that simple definition, DRAW's fill tools extend in almost immeasurable depth and breadth. To get an idea, compare Figure 8.1 here with Figure 7.1 in the last chapter; these figures show the road maps for the fill and outline functions, respectively. As you can see, touring the outline tools was a stroll in the park compared to this cross-country trip. There are six separate dialogs that service fill patterns, and up to three levels of subdialogs in some cases.

Understanding Fill Patterns **195**

8.1

The extraordinary depth of DRAW's fill tools is apparent in this road map of the dialogs.

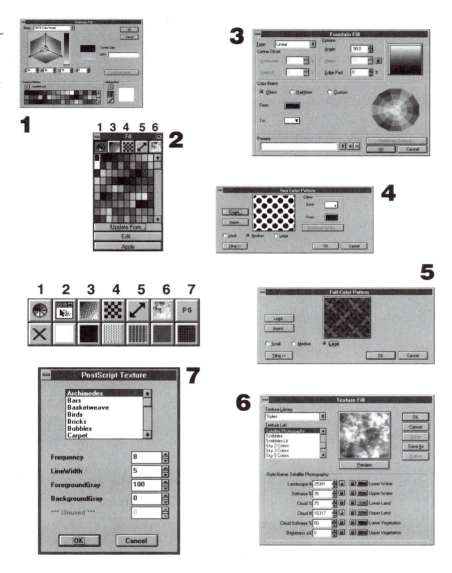

In fact, the network of fill dialogs is so intricate, we need to give you instructions on how to read our map in Figure 8.1. The images labeled 1 through 7 represent the six dialogs and the roll-up, all of which are accessed from the flyout. The smaller numbers above the flyout, also 1 through 7, show you which button invokes which dialog. The Fill roll-up provides access to five of the six dialogs, and the numbers at the top of the roll-up show which ones.

At the risk of oversimplifying, we place DRAW's fill capabilities into four categories:

- **Uniform Fills,** in which a single color or shade covers the entire selected object.
- **Fountain Fills,** in which colors or shades gradually change as they traverse the object. There are four types of fountains: *linear, radial, conical,* and *square.*
- **Patterns,** in which a repeating pattern covers the object. There are three types of patterns: *two-color patterns, full-color patterns,* and *PostScript textures.*
- **Texture Fills,** in which an artistic blend of bitmap images is poured into the object. This feature, introduced in 4.0, was shown off in Chapter 2.

Applying Fills

The bottom row of the Fill flyout is for quick gray-shading of selected objects. The **X** icon lets you remove all fills, and the four icons after the white and black buttons let you fill an object with 10%, 30%, 50%, or 70% black.

The Fill roll-up provides access to uniform fills (dialog 1 in Figure 8.1), fountain fills (dialog 3), two- and full-color patterns (dialogs 4 and 5), and texture fills (dialog 6). Just click one of the roll-up's icons to get access to the basic functions for that fill type. Click the Edit button, and you get the full dialog, with all the bells and whistles.

Just like the Pen roll-up, the Fill roll-up is most handy for quick, frequent changes, where you want the controls right at your mousetips. Otherwise, you may prefer heading straight to the dialogs. We couldn't fit the hotkeys into Figure 8.1: To reach Uniform Fill, press Shift+F11; to reach Fountain Fill, press F11.

Through three versions of the software, the CorelDRAW engineers have made Fountain Fill (F11) more accessible than Uniform Fill (Shift+F11). We wonder why. Do they think users turn to it more often? Are they encouraging the use of fountain fills? Are they aware that botched fountain fills are typical components of electronic drawing disasters? Interesting questions for the ages…

AUTHOR'S NOTE

There is some overlap between the topics in this chapter on fill patterns and the subjects covered in Chapter 26, "Working With Color." Most of the intricate issues of color usage will be covered in Chapter 26. In this chapter we focus more on the operation of the tools than on the theory of using color, but these subjects cannot be completely separated, and we don't try.

Uniform Fills

We submit to you that Uniform Fill is the all-time function leader, based on usage, in the history of CorelDRAW. And if you total up the hours that DRAW users spend filling their objects with solids—be it from this dialog, the roll-up, the flyout, or the on-screen palette—this function wins in a landslide.

The Uniform Fill dialog can change its spots many times (pun intended). Its basic function is helping you choose a specific color, tint, or gray shade to apply to a selected object, and it does this with complete thoroughness. It offers six different industry-standard models for defining colors, as well as an option to use custom palettes with specific color mixtures or names. Of equal (or greater) importance: You can choose shades of gray in increments of 1%, and set precise line screens for projects destined for high-resolution output.

The setup in the Uniform Fill dialog shown at the top-left of Figure 8.1 is considered the standard configuration: showing colors by the CMYK model. Practically any color imaginable can be created by mixing percentages of cyan, magenta, yellow, and black. (CMYK and the other models will be the focus of Chapter 26.) If you are producing four-color work and want direct control over the percentages of those four colors, this is the color model you would use.

If, however, you are under corporate orders to set type in PANTONE 284 (one of over 700 colors defined by the PANTONE Matching System), you can easily switch to another color modeling system. Open the Show drop-down list and choose PANTONE Spot Colors. Check the Show Color Names box, enter **284** in the Search String field, and before you know it, your screen will offer you the list illustrated in Figure 8.2.

8.2

Choosing a PANTONE spot color is as easy as asking for its name.

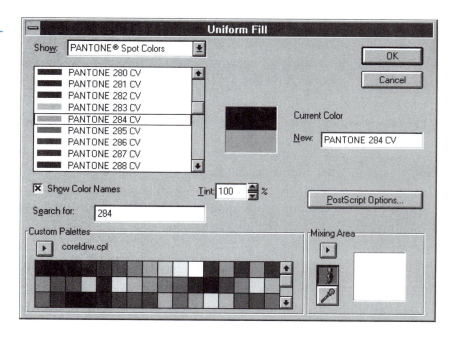

You can also dial up Red/Green/Blue percentages, spin the Hue/Saturation/Brightness wheel, or pick from over 2,000 TruMatch colors. Chapter 26 includes a complete discussion of spot and process colors, and the differences between them.

WATCH OUT!

When you're working with color, if you trust your monitor to show you the color that you'll get on the final printout, you'll be in for a rude and potentially costly surprise. To put it plainly, monitors lie. Certainly they do the best they can, but they emit light and display color very differently from a printing press applying ink to paper. Starting with version 4.0, DRAW has built-in features to compensate for monitor distortion, but during crunch time, when your color projects are on the line, the only things you can really trust are those handy color swatch books from PANTONE and TruMatch, both of which show you exactly what a color will look like when printed. So if you're choosing colors by looking at your monitor and saying, "Gee, that one looks nice—I think I'll use it," you're asking for trouble. More on this in upcoming discussions.

The Power of CMYK

CMYK may not be much in the acronym department (*simic?*), but the CMYK model for choosing colors is perhaps the most popular of all. An exhaustive range of colors can be created by mixing the right percentage of the four primary colors, **C**yan, **M**agenta, **Y**ellow, and Blac**k**. (The **K** represents black in order not to be confused with blue, which is actually not a primary color, but rather a mixture of cyan and magenta.)

The CMYK color model (see Figure 8.3) provides you with the conveniences presented in the following paragraphs.

Precision   If you know the precise percentage of the four colors, you can enter them directly in the boxes provided for each color. But don't bother with the little arrows that increment the percentages; try it this way, instead:

1. Double-click the mouse in the field for Cyan.
2. Type the value desired.

8.3

Setting colors using the CMYK color model

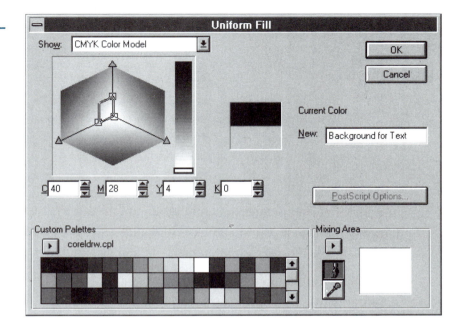

3. Press Tab to instantly jump to the Magenta field.
4. Enter the desired value and press Tab again.
5. Continue through the four color fields, and OK the dialog when done.

Flexibility   When you're looking for a color for an on-screen presentation, you may not much care about its specific composition, but just want it to look good. This is a job for the Uniform Fill dialog's visual selector (at top-left), the color palette (at lower-left), or—new to 5.0—the mixing area (at lower-right). In all three of these, you can browse across the entire spectrum of colors. The preview box in the middle of the dialog shows you the current color for the selected object, and the new one you have chosen or mixed.

The 5.0 visual selector is still a bit daunting but is much more intuitive than previous incarnations. The three-dimensional chart has axes for cyan, magenta, and yellow, and to adjust a particular color you drag a corner of the wireframe rectangle along one of the axes. The slider next to the chart is for independent adjustment of the amount of black to be added.

NEW FOR 5

 Color palette management is much easier in 5.0, as the Uniform Fill dialog includes a visible color palette, from which you can select, add, and reorder the placement of colors.

Notice in Figure 8.3 that DRAW permits you to assign your own names to colors. You can choose a technical name, such as "4Magenta/85Yellow," or one that is more descriptive of the color's use, as shown in the figure. Either way, your new name for the color will appear in the preview box on DRAW's status line whenever you select an object that uses that color.

Gray Shades   You can assign simple shades of gray by entering a percentage of less than 100 for Black and setting the other three colors to 0%.

We chose our words carefully in the foregoing paragraph: *simple shades of gray.* The subject of black-and-white printing can become complex in a hurry. In order to get high-quality resolution output in black and white, you need to know a bit about how PostScript imagesetters render percentages of black, and Chapter 27, "Turning Gray with Dignity," explores this topic. Whether you are sending your work to a 300-dpi laser printer or to a high-resolution imagesetter or film recorder, you need to know how to tell DRAW what to do with all those dots.

RGB and HSB

These two models are based on the belief that a color can be defined in terms of the percentages of red, green, and blue (RGB) that the color contains, as well as by the Hue, Saturation, and Brightness (HSB). The RGB and HSB models are less precise than CMYK; and because DRAW converts colors to CMYK values for color-separation work, anyway, you might as well start with CMYK. For printing to an in-house color printer, or for creating color for on-screen work, these two models work as well as CMYK; just choose the one of the three that seems the most intuitive.

For more information on these color models, see Chapter 26, or consult Chapter 12 of the CorelDRAW User's Manual.

Using Custom Palettes

Although most users rarely change from the default palette, CORELDRW.CPL, the program ships with several other palettes. To use a different palette, click on the little arrow under Custom Palettes, choose Open, and select from the list of either Custom Palettes or Process Palettes. One of our favorites is SMALL.PAL on the Companion CD, which provides shades of gray in increments of 5%, and eight other pure colors that look good on screen. You'll also find a palette on the Companion CD, called GRAY.PAL, which includes white, black, and every shade of gray in between, in 1% increments. To use GRAY.PAL, first copy it into the CUSTOM subdirectory under the main Corel directory on your hard drive. Then open it from there, following the steps set out earlier in this paragraph.

Creating Your Own Palettes

The custom palette is the first of several potentially confusing topics when you're learning to use DRAW's color engine. *As if this CMYK, RGB, PANTONE business weren't enough, you say I can create my own colors, too??* Well, not quite, and herein lies the confusion.

It helps to think of a palette in the literal sense. Imagine you are a painter working on a portrait. You probably have enough paint in your studio to create just about any color you might want, but as you approach a particular project, you choose a few in particular. You dab them on your palette and wield your brush. Your palette is designed to make accessible to you the specific colors you have chosen for this painting. You know you can go get others, but on the palette are the ones you expect to use now.

This analogy holds true in your electronic studio, as well. DRAW enables you to pick out particular colors and add them to a fresh palette. And as with existing palettes, you can assign your own names to these colors.

Let's say you are in charge of a group of newsletters, for three different divisions of a large company. The corporate publishing department has established an official color that you are required to use for the logo and other elements. Beyond that, you have established a few other color standards: yellow tint for frames around text and captions; and a shade of gray for bullets and drop caps. You expect to use these (and only these) colors for the three newsletters.

This is a job for a custom palette. Here is how you would go about creating it:

1. Open the Uniform Fill dialog box. (Select or create an object first, so DRAW won't think you are trying to change the default fill pattern.)

2. At Custom Palettes, click New in the drop-down list. Your screen will look like Figure 8.4. Notice that all of the colors in the palette have vanished.

3. You know the specific CMYK color composition of the predefined logo, as well as for the yellow tint you are using for text boxes. So, from the Show drop-down list, choose CMYK Color Model.

4. Enter **70%** for Cyan and **80%** for Magenta.

5. In the New text box, type **Corporate Logo**.

6. Click the Custom Palettes button and choose Add Color. The new color will promptly appear in the first box on the on-screen palette.

7. Click the Custom Palettes button, choose Save As, and name your palette **NEWSLET**. (DRAW automatically adds the .CPL extension.)

8.4

A fresh palette, just waiting to have some colors added to it.

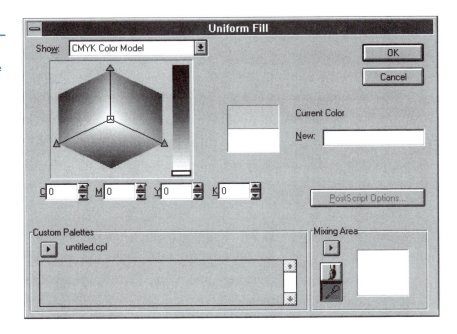

You haven't just "invented" this color—that's not what we mean when we say "creating a custom color"; chances are pretty good that someone, somewhere, has already used 70 Cyan/80 Magenta. But by adding the color and its name to your new palette, you have made it your own and can now easily apply it to elements in your newsletters.

To create the yellow tint for text boxes, follow the steps above, this time setting the color to 0% Cyan, 0% Magenta, 70% Yellow, and 0% Black. The bullets are 50% Black with all other colors at 0%; you will probably want a solid white and solid black in your palette, also. Your Uniform Fill dialog will look like Figure 8.5; to keep this palette for later experimentation, choose Save from the Custom Palettes drop-down list.

At first, you may feel hemmed in by such a small assortment of color choices, especially if you have grown accustomed to seeing an entire row of colors on your palette (even though you probably never use most of them!). But remember, you can always use other colors, even if they are

8.5

Your completed color palette

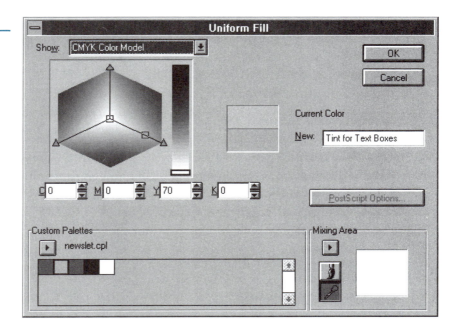

not on your palette: Just return to Uniform Fill and dial in any CMYK or RGB (or other) values you want. When that color isn't named in your custom palette, DRAW refers to it on the status line as "unnamed color." Name or no, DRAW honors the specific mix of colors you have designated for it.

INSIDE INFO

 We have discussed using custom colors in the Uniform Fill dialog—but what about the on-screen palette? It's easy. To place your custom colors on your on-screen palette, choose View / Color Palette / Custom Colors.

Searching for a Hidden Color

If you are using one of the color palettes that represents an established collection of colors—such as PANTONE or TruMatch—you could spend many minutes searching for a color that you know is buried in there somewhere… Remember these two tips for finding colors:

- Click on Show Color Names to get a list of the specific names assigned to the colors.
- Then use the Search For box to locate a color by name. Typing in 586, for instance, would retrieve PANTONE 586 CV, a shade of yellow with a bit of cyan and black mixed in.

Before you begin the next section and wade into the increasingly treacherous waters of fountain fills, it is a good idea to return your palette to its original default: Set Custom Palettes to CORELDRW.CPL, and choose CMYK Color Model from the Show drop-down list.

Fountain Fills

If Uniform Fill is the star of the show, then Fountain Fill is the superstar with the flamboyant personality. It goes to only the most exclusive clubs, stays out late dancing every night, and always seems to be embroiled in some public controversy or another. In the language of the medium, fountain fills are responsible for some of the most fabulous work ever done with DRAW, as well as some of the most fantastic disasters.

Also known as a *gradient fill,* a fountain fill is used to render an object in a constantly changing light. The rendezvous of sky and water at a horizon serves as the classic opportunity to use a fountain fill. When commanded, DRAW starts at one side of the object with one shade or color, and gradually changes it into another color at the other side. You tell DRAW what the colors are, how abruptly or gradually to make the transition, and where to begin making the transition.

Version 4.0 brought many new features to fountains, the most noteworthy being the ability to change from one color to another and then to a third, fourth, fifth, and so on, within the fill. This capability makes Fountain Fill that much more powerful…and that much more dangerous.

Here, we'll discuss not only how to use fountains, but also when and when *not* to use them. We know the hazards all too well to address one topic without the other.

To create a fountain fill, follow these steps:

1. Draw a large rectangle.
2. Open the Fountain Fill dialog. You can do this from the Fill fly-out menu, with the third icon from the left on the top row; or from the Fill roll-up, by clicking the second button in the top row and then the Edit button; or with the hotkey F11.
3. OK the dialog as is, and click Apply in the roll-up (if you used it).

That's it—you have created a fountain, as shown in Figure 8.6. Both the dialog and the roll-up default to a fountain going from white on top to black on the bottom.

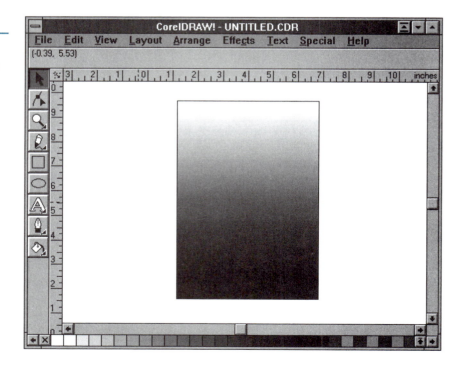

8.6

DRAW's default fountain fill—from white all the way to black

AUTHOR'S NOTE

If you try the fountain in Figure 8.6 on your system, it may look different, because rendering fountain fills is a taxing proposition for video cards. We have produced these screen images using a true-color video driver, capable of displaying over 16 million colors (or in this case, shades of gray). Don't worry if your fountain fills don't look as smooth as the ones shown here; on-screen representation has no impact on printing. You can still get the highest-quality output.

Lines, Rads, Squares, and Cones

Figure 8.7 shows the Fountain Fill dialog, with the Type drop-down list displaying the four types of fountains that you can apply to a closed object. (As stated above, you can reach this dialog box from the Fill flyout, from the Fill roll-up, or with F11.)

8.7

The foot of the fountain

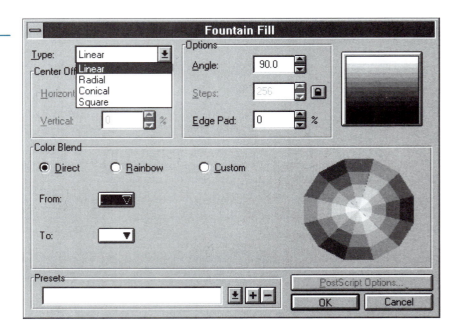

The default fountain is a *linear* fountain fill—one that goes from one side of the object to the other. You can also create fountains that go from the outside to the inside or that spin around the periphery. You'll see all four types—Linear, Radial, Conical, and Square—listed in the dialog, and Figure 8.8 illustrates them.

8.8

DRAW can create four types of fountain fills. Here, from top-left to lower-right, are the linear, radial, conical, and square fountains.

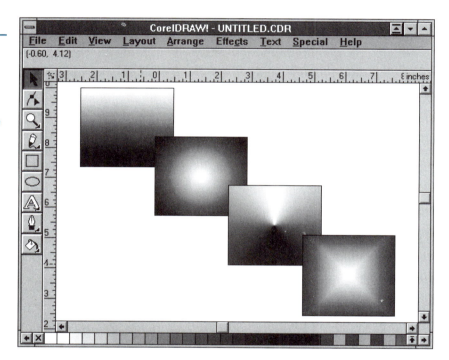

NEW FOR 5

DRAW's square fountain fill is new to 5.0. In this one, the gradations of color are produced by small rectangles that work their way from the outside to the center.

If you haven't noticed already, you soon will: DRAW takes longer to draw fountains to the screen than it does uniform fills. This is especially true of the radial and conical fountains. If the delays are unacceptable, you have three alternatives:

- Switch to Wireframe view, where the fountains won't show.
- Move the filled objects to another layer and hide the layer.
- Reduce the value for Steps, either from the Options box of the Fountain Fill dialog, or from the Preview Fountain Steps box in Special / Preferences / View. This instructs DRAW to transition more bluntly and less often.

Try the last alternative first. If you keep the Steps number at its default of 20, your fountains will draw much faster. As Figure 8.9 shows, they won't look as good, but at least you'll be able to see them; the other strategies require that you hide them altogether. We'll talk more about Steps later in the chapter.

8.9

If fountains become a drag on your system, tell DRAW not to show you so much detail. These 20-step fountains required less than 1 second to draw; the ones in Figure 8.8 needed almost 5 seconds.

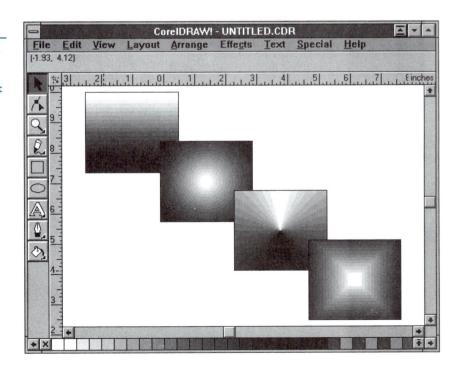

With all four fountain types, the preview box in the dialog gives you a fair approximation of the fill's appearance—at least, of how it would look in a rectangle. Of course, you can apply a fountain fill to any object or collection of curves, so long as they contain closed shapes.

Choosing Colors

Perhaps the most important factor in a fountain fill is your choice of colors or shades, and DRAW doesn't make the choice easy, throwing lots of variables at you. The From and To color buttons display drop-down boxes of all the colors in the currently active palette, so you can determine the start and finish colors for the fountain. If you need more precise control over colors, you can click More from the drop-down list and reach the Uniform Fill dialog. (Its title bar will say Fountain Fill to verify that you are choosing the color for one side of the fountain, but it is identical in every way to the Uniform Fill dialog discussed earlier in the chapter.)

Creating the Right Blend

Once you have chosen the start and finish colors, you can then choose how DRAW will transition from one to the other. The default setting, Direct, takes the shortest possible route from start to finish. Figure 8.10 shows two different fountain fills, both changing from blue to a pale shade of yellow. The top example shows a Direct blend, and the diagonal black line on the color wheel verifies the quick route from one color to another. The lower example is a Rainbow blend, in which DRAW traverses around the perimeter of the color wheel, involving a greater transition of colors. You click the small rotation icons next to the color wheel to determine direction.

To create a rainbow fountain fill, follow these steps:

1. Draw a rectangle or ellipse of any shape, change to the Pick tool, and press F11 to access Fountain Fill.
2. For Color Blend, choose Rainbow.

8.10

The lines on the color wheels determine how many stops these fountain fills will make.

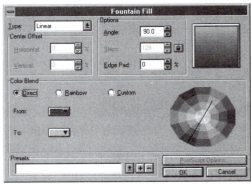

3. Set the From color to blue. You can probably pick it out of the drop-down color palette next to From; if not, click More and enter 100% Cyan and 100% Magenta, leaving the other two colors at 0%.

4. Set the To color to cyan, either from the palette or the Fill dialog.
5. OK your way back out to the page, and notice the fountain fill applied to the object.
6. Make a quick copy of the object by pressing the + key on the numeric keypad, and drag the copy away from the original.
7. Press F11 to reach Fountain Fill, leave the Blend set to Rainbow, but click the other rotation icon.
8. OK back to the page and notice the dramatic difference.

Our black-and-white rendition in Figure 8.11 doesn't do it justice, but you can still get a sense of how many more colors are traversed from start to finish in the lower rectangle. You can open Figure 8.11 from the PICTURES directory of the Companion CD.

8.11

Rainbow fountain fills can be dramatic.

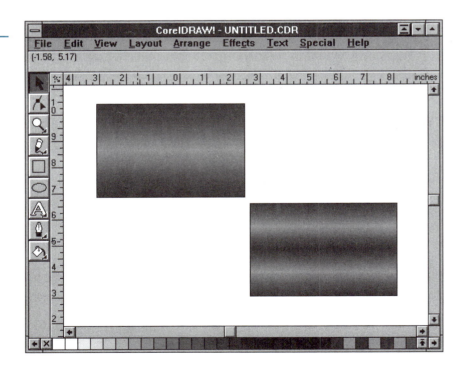

Creating Custom Fountains

Custom fountains were long awaited and oft requested, and they were finally introduced in DRAW 4.0. Users can now create fountains that have start, middle, and finish colors. To make it work, choose Custom under Color Blend, and then designate the intermediate colors—up to 99!

AUTHOR'S NOTE

UPGRADING FROM VERSION 3? If you're used to using DRAW 3.0, you're probably tired of butting together two blends to create a multiple fountain effect. Both DRAW 4.0 and 5.0 do multiple fountains in the same object.

Try creating a fountain that goes from yellow to blue to white:

1. Create an object on the page and invoke Fountain Fill.
2. Click Custom and note that the small square on the left end of the color bar is darkened, indicating that it is the current color.
3. Click on yellow from the palette, or click on the color square next to Current to reach the Fill dialog and set the color to yellow. The left side of the bar will turn yellow.
4. Double-click on the small black square; it changes to a downward-pointing triangle. Drag the triangle into the middle of the color bar. (You can place it *exactly* in the middle by entering 50 in the Position box.)
5. Set the color for the middle to blue, from either the palette or the Fill dialog (under Current).
6. Click on the square on the right end of the color bar and set its color to white. Your screen should look like Figure 8.12.
7. OK your way back out to the page, where your selected object will have a fill like the one in Figure 8.13, which is also included on the Companion CD.

8.12

You can define up to 99 intermediate steps in a fountain.

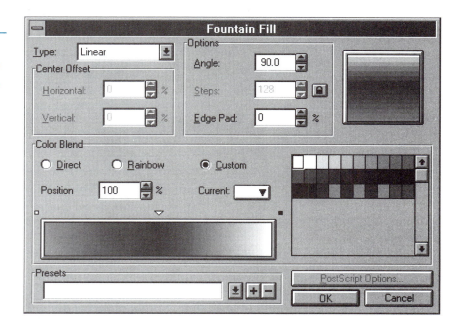

8.13

A three-way fountain, from yellow (top-left) through blue (middle) to white (lower-left). We used a diamond shape to illustrate that you can apply a fountain to any closed object, not just an ellipse or a rectangle.

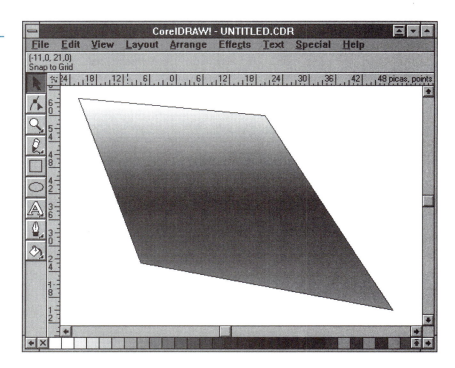

A Word about Choosing Colors

Nothing is more fun and exciting than mixing many colors to produce rainbows and fountains on color displays. Printing them, however, is an entirely different matter, and mistakes can be costly. Before you go wild with fountain fills, you should know both your target output device and your budgetary constraints.

Printing to a Color Desktop Printer: In this case you can go wild. Color laser printers, thermal transfer printers, and ink-based printers can create virtually any color. Limit yourself only by your own imagination and (please!) your own good taste.

Creating Four-Color Separations: If you plan to create four negatives, one for each of the CMYK colors, then you can once again spread your wings. You can be confident that whatever colors DRAW uses as it traverses the rainbow, your four pieces of film negative will be able to represent them.

Creating Spot-Color Separations: Here you must proceed with caution. Covered in detail in Chapter 26, spot-color printing is the method by which you can add just one color to a project, not four. Instead of using the CMYK model, requiring four separate pieces of film, you designate a single color—the spot color—and your print house makes two print runs (black and the spot color), not four.

With spot-color work, you must be careful not to create fountain fills that overstep your bounds. The safest route is to create fountain fills that vary the same spot color. This is easily done:

1. Using the PANTONE Spot Color model, define the From color. Let's say you choose Blue 072.

2. Use the same Blue 072 for the To color, but assign a different tint to it, say 30%. You can set a tint to any spot color, as shown in Figure 8.14.

This gives you a nice fountain, staying entirely within your spot color, Blue 072. The transition will be from 100% to 30%. If you want fancier fountains, you'll have to spring for extra colors, and you know what? They won't necessarily look any better.

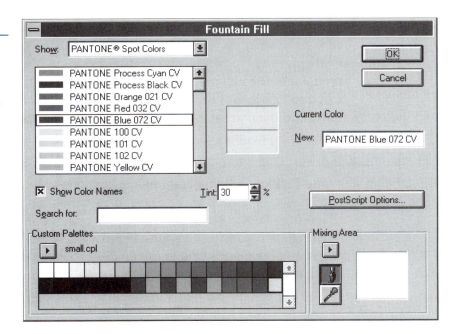

8.14

To create a fountain that is contained within one spot color, use a tint for one side of the color. Here, the To color is being defined as a 30% tint of PANTONE Blue 072.

Other Options

Once you have defined the colors, you still have a treasure chest of fountain toys to play with, all available in the Fountain Fill dialog. The following options all affect how the fountain is displayed and printed:

Angle   When creating any fountains except Radial, you can change the angle of the fountain, by either entering a different value for Angle in the Options box, or directly manipulating the preview box. To do the latter, click and drag in the box, using the secondary mouse button. As you do this, the value in the Angle field automatically adjusts. Conical and square fountains will spin the start point around the center axis as the angle changes. Linear fountains simply change the angle of the fill pattern. Radial fountains do not use the Angle field.

Center Offset   This set of controls affects the center point around which radial, conical, and square fountains are built. Negative values shift the center down and to the left; positive values shift the center up and to the right. As with the Angle option, you can either type values directly into the Horizontal and Vertical fields, or you can move your mouse into the preview box and directly manipulate the center offset. Click and drag with the primary mouse button, and watch the center move and the corresponding Horizontal and Vertical values adjust.

INSIDE INFO

The Ctrl key will constrain mouse movements in the preview box, just as it does on the page. If you hold Ctrl while changing the OFFSET of a radial or conical fountain, the incremental change is constrained to 10%. If you hold Ctrl while interactively changing the angle of a linear or conical fountain, you will notice the ANGLE snapping to even increments. The amount of constraint—15 degrees by default—is controlled by Special / Preferences / General / Constrain Angle.

Steps   The Steps field (under Options) controls the number of *bands* used to display and print a fountain. Fountain fills change from one color or shade to another; the rate at which they change is determined by this value.

This can get confusing, because there are two other places in the program where you can execute this change, and the various controls can interact and affect each other. If you keep the Steps field in its "locked" position (notice the little lock to its right), then the value defaults to that which is set under Special / Preferences / View / Preview Fountain Steps (PFS). That setting is dynamic; change the PFS, and all existing objects with fountain fills will adjust, as long as they were created with the Steps value locked . Furthermore, the Fountain Steps field, under Print/Options/Options, determines the number of steps used during printing. The lock, therefore, is deceiving, because the value is not locked at all, and instead is affected by the PFS setting in Preferences / View and Print/Options/Options.

If you unlock the Steps field in Fountain Fill and enter a value, then you are establishing a permanent and fixed number of fountain steps for displaying and printing that object. So by unlocking the steps value, you are actually locking it; and by unlocking it, you are actually locking it to the settings of PFS and the Print or EPS export dialogs. Sounds like Corel needs to replace its locking analogy…

You're probably a little lost right about now, so here is our recommended strategy for Steps:

- Keep the Steps value in Fountain Fill locked.
- Keep the PFS setting in Preferences / View set to 20.
- Keep Fountain Steps in Print and EPS Export at the optimum setting for printing.

This strategy lets you (1) have fast screen response as the norm with Fountain Steps of only 20, (2) increase all fountain steps in your drawing at once for better screen accuracy, just by increasing PFS; and (3) have complete control over steps during printing or exporting.

Figure 8.15 shows a few of the effects possible by adjusting the Offset, Angle, and Steps values.

8.15

You can change more than just a fountain fill's colors.

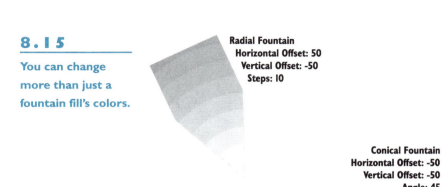

Radial Fountain
Horizontal Offset: 50
Vertical Offset: -50
Steps: 10

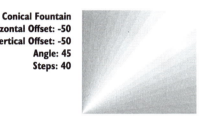

Conical Fountain
Horizontal Offset: -50
Vertical Offset: -50
Angle: 45
Steps: 40

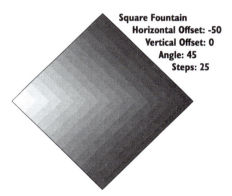

Square Fountain
Horizontal Offset: -50
Vertical Offset: 0
Angle: 45
Steps: 25

Radial Fountain
Horizontal Offset: 17
Vertical Offset: 27
Steps: 128

Edge Pad This setting (under Options) determines the level of the start and finish colors that will be present in the fountain. At its default setting of 0%, the transition from one color to the next is smooth and consistent, and this is fine for most objects. But if you have created a curve that, say, comes to a sharp point at one end, the finish color at that end might not be visible. By adding an Edge Pad value, you tell DRAW to provide more room for the start and finish colors.

Figure 8.16 includes an object in need of an edge pad in order for the entire color span to be displayed. Each of the two images—the Before (top-left) and the After (lower-right)—has a linear fountain fill from dark to light, headed diagonally upward. The Before has no edge padding and, as you can see, the finish color of white is not present. DRAW starts at one edge of the selected object and goes to the other—but what we want to point out is that DRAW starts at the *very* lower-left, where the selection handle is, and goes to the handle on the opposite corner. Because there is no part of the image in that top-right corner, the finish color is not

8.16

Adding an edge pad to the lower-right drawing allows the fountain fill to run its complete course.

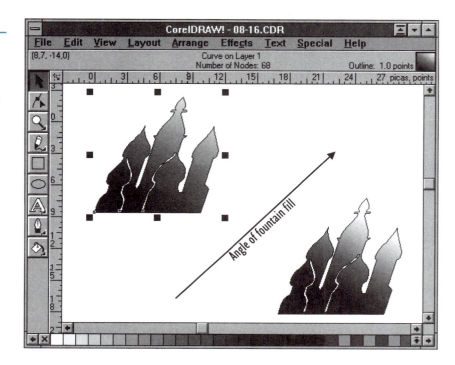

represented. The After image has an edge pad of 20%, effectively bringing the white color further into the fountain fill.

INSIDE INFO

Edge Pad works on both sides—notice there is also extra black on the lower-left side of Figure 8.16's After image. If you only want an edge pad on one side, then you need to take a different approach: Create a custom fountain fill, following the steps presented earlier. Designate an intermediate color for your fountain fill, but keep it the same as the ending color. In effect, you will be creating your own edge pad, but just for one side of the object.

Presets If you need to use a certain fountain fill over and over again, you can capture the settings as *presets* and easily apply them to other objects. This was a very tedious chore prior to 4.0, requiring you to find the object (usually in a different file), copy it to the Clipboard, open the file that has the object you want to fill, paste the object in from the Clipboard, copy its attributes, and then delete the pasted object. Whew!

To create a preset, you simply create the fountain fill, type a name in the Presets field, and click the + (Save) button. Your new settings are available to any closed object within any .CDR file. This holds true until you delete the preset, by selecting it in the Presets drop-down and clicking the – (Delete) button.

AUTHOR'S NOTE

UPGRADING FROM VERSION 3? If you use a particular fountain fill repeatedly, DRAW 4.0 and 5.0 will not only allow you to store all of the settings in a preset, they will let you instantly apply those settings to other objects.

The Last Word on Fountain Fills

Here is our parting thought concerning fountain fills: When in doubt, *don't use them!* We're not kidding. If you are undecided about whether the use of a fountain fill will add any value to your drawing, then it probably won't. In fact, it will probably detract.

We're prepared to be even more direct on this subject: If you output your final work on a 300×300-dpi printer, then you should *never* use fine fountain fills, whose goal is to show a smooth transition from one color to another. Your laser simply can't handle it; even its best effort will portray you as an amateur designer who tried for too much. The only fountain fills you should attempt in this case are ones with low Steps values, designed to have blunt transitions, or ones with very coarse dot patterns. The new crop of 600×600 laser printers can produce credible results, provided you keep the start and finish colors close together, for instance, from 15% to 45%.

Perhaps we have done you a disservice by showing you in this chapter the screen images that fountain fills can produce with a true-color 24-bit video adapter; you'll be hard-pressed to re-create them even on higher-resolution printers. If you expect to use fountain fills regularly for projects destined for film, you should read the discussions about setting PostScript halftone screens in Chapter 27.

When desktop publishing first struck big, we could spot an amateur job from across the building: It had large Helvetica type inside a rounded rectangle with a gray background. Today, the dead giveaway of a bush-league electronic illustration is the misplaced fountain fill. If you want to save the community of electronic designers from this collective reputation, you'll approach fountain fills with caution and restraint.

PostScript Options   This is the place to go for specifying halftone screens and overprint options when a job is destined for high-resolution film and/or color separations. If you work mostly with laser printers—color or black-and-white—this will be unfamiliar terrain for you. If you work regularly with an outside service bureau (or if you *are* a service bureau), then the settings in this relatively advanced dialog are crucial. These options are relevant only if you have installed a PostScript printer driver in Windows.

Chapters 25-27 all contain discussions of the PostScript Options dialog.

Pattern Fills

Would you believe us if we said that you're only two-sixths of the way through DRAW's fill tools? There are four more to go, but rest assured you've covered the two most important ones. The next three tools—the ones that produce patterns—constitute the frills, and in fact these patterns often go largely unused, even by very talented and skilled DRAW users.

Here is a brief run-through of the three tools that produce patterns for your objects.

Two-Color Patterns

Great for simple backgrounds, the Two-Color Pattern dialog comes packed with a few dozen patterns that can be quickly applied to selected objects. You don't need to know anything special to start using these patterns.

1. Create a closed object and make sure it is selected.
2. Invoke the Two-Color Pattern dialog, either from the Fill flyout or from the roll-up and then the Edit button. In both, you click the checkerboard icon. (If you invoke the dialog from the flyout, the bottom half of the dialog is hidden. You can access it by clicking the Tiling button.)
3. Click once on the pattern preview box to see all of the preset choices.
4. Find one you like, and double-click.

5. Click OK (followed by Apply if you used the roll-up), and you have applied a pattern to the selected object.

Figure 8.17 shows a Two-Color Pattern dialog, along with the resulting pattern. All of this dialog's controls invite experimentation. The Colors buttons work just as they do in the Fountain Fill dialog, and the other controls change the pattern's size (the Tile Size settings) and placement (the Offset settings). Notice the PostScript Options button again; we still owe you that discussion on advanced halftone settings, and you'll find it in Chapter 27.

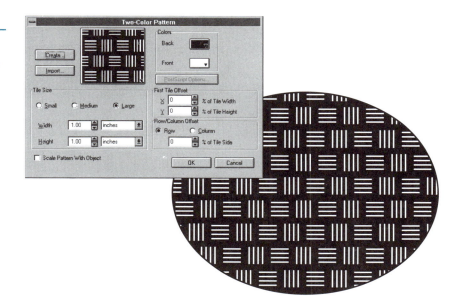

8.17

One of dozens of two-color patterns for you to use

If you can't find the pattern you want, you can always make your own. Any objects you create, paste, or import into DRAW can be turned into a pattern with the Special / Create Pattern command. You are asked to drag a marquee around the area, and DRAW does the rest, creating a pattern from your objects and making them available in the pattern preview box. You can also

■ Import a file—any file, any format—directly into the pattern preview box.

- Create your own pattern from scratch with DRAW's built-in pattern editor, operating at the pixel level. You can get there with the Create button in the dialog.

Clearly, the capabilities of DRAW in this area make it possible to exceed the bounds of good taste. Remember that these patterns render only two colors, and you can't expect that any old image is going to make for a good pattern. At the very least, however, patterns are fun. We certainly enjoyed ourselves when we took our snowboarding friend and put him in the middle of a pelican storm, as shown in Figure 8.18. This was pretty easy; here's what we did:

1. We opened the GOFORIT! drawing and removed the original background and text.

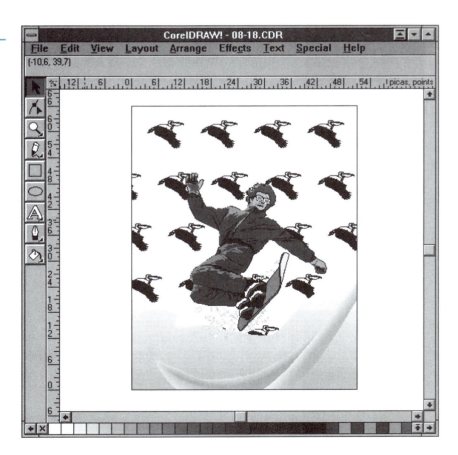

8.18

Alfred Hitchcock plays with CorelDRAW.

2. We created a rectangle behind the remaining images, and then opened the Two-Color Pattern dialog.
3. We imported PELICAN.CDR from the Companion CD.
4. We chose Large for the Tile Size, and offset the rows by 20%.
5. We clicked OK and watched the pelican storm gather.

Adding a background to the pelicans wasn't possible, because that would have constituted a third color. We could have used Black and 50 Cyan/25 Magenta (the color of the sky), but then the white part of the pelicans would have also been the sky color. To provide a background, we would have to turn to…

Full-Color Patterns

Full-color patterns are implemented in essentially the same way as two-color patterns, and from a nearly identical dialog, but there are four differences between the two types of patterns:

- Because full-color images use the entire CMYK spectrum of colors, virtually any color can be represented in a full-color pattern.
- Full-color patterns are saved as DRAW files, but with .PAT extensions instead of .CDR. You can open and edit these files as you would any other DRAW file.
- A full-color pattern cannot have its foreground or background changed, as can two-color patterns. With two colors, that's all there is—a foreground and a background—but with four colors, things aren't so simple. When making your own full-color patterns, you need to define your background and foreground colors—indeed, all of your colors—before you create the pattern.
- Full-color patterns are much more complex and can send a printer to its electronic knees.

To create the pelican storm against a blue sky, we did the following:

1. In an untitled file, we drew a small rectangle. Then we imported the pelican from the Companion CD.

2. We colored the rectangle 50 Cyan/25 Magenta (the same color as the sky), and positioned the pelican in front of the rectangle.
3. We selected Special / Create Pattern, chose Full Color, and drew a marquee around the two objects. Then we saved the pattern as PELICAN.PAT. As Figure 8.19 shows, we were careful to draw the marquee *inside* of the rectangle, so no seams would show in the pattern.

8.19

Defining the area that constitutes the pattern

4. We opened GOFORIT!.CDR, removed the existing background layer, and drew a rectangle behind the other elements. We used the hotkey Shift+PgDn to make sure the rectangle was in the back.
5. We invoked the Full-Color Pattern dialog and continued with the procedure of picking the pattern and adjusting it into place.

Figure 8.20 shows the new pelican storm with a more realistic sky color.

8.20

These lucky pelicans now get to fly in a sky instead of in a white hole.

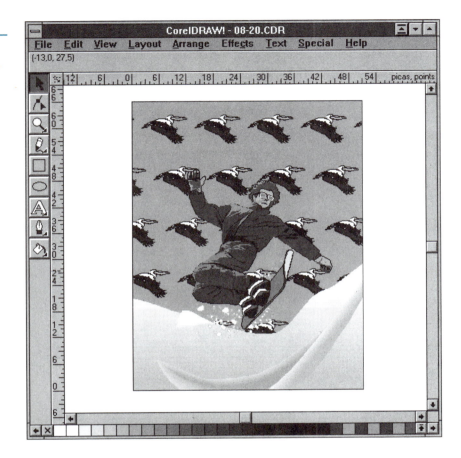

PostScript Patterns

These sophisticated fill patterns are available only to users of PostScript printers. They are essentially little routines written in the PostScript page-description language, and digestible only by PostScript printers. In fact, even your video card can't digest them—PostScript patterns do not appear on screen.

Though you cannot add your own patterns to the ones supplied here, you can alter them significantly, using various controls provided in the PostScript Texture dialog, shown in Figure 8.21.

8.21

Creating sophisticated PostScript fills requires that you fly blind, but the results are worth it for those seeking elaborate fill patterns.

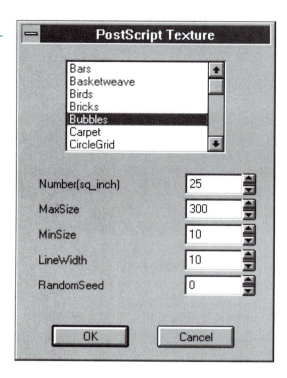

WATCH OUT!

The PostScript Texture dialog is available even without a PostScript printer. It just won't DO anything.

For examples of these intricate patterns, consult Appendix D of the CorelDRAW User's Manual.

Texture Fills

Still the new darling of the Fill family, the texture fill patterns are based on an elaborate library of bitmap images, all produced according to an engine that allows for individual aspects to be adjusted with breathtaking precision.

AUTHOR'S NOTE

UPGRADING FROM VERSION 3? Texture Fills are bitmap images that will display on any screen and print to any laser printer or imagesetter.

Figure 8.22 shows one of the more elaborate textures, called Satellite Photography. Twelve individual properties make up this texture, including such nuances as the Cloud Softness percentage and the color of

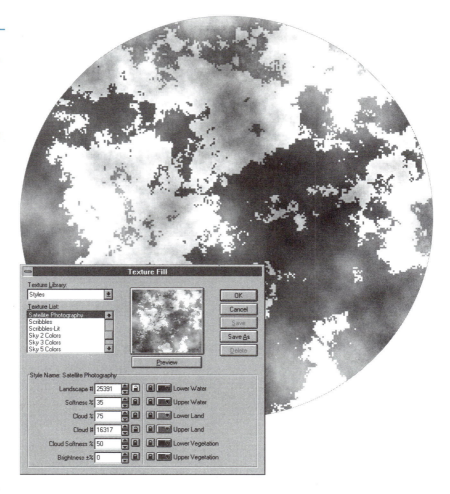

8.22

If you can get past how much fun they are to play with, you might actually create some nice work with DRAW's texture fills.

Upper Vegetation. The 12 components can be adjusted for various aspects, such as color, contrast, and brightness. Also, there are different images for each texture—lots of them. In the case of Satellite Photography, for instance, you can browse among (ready for this?) 32,768 different landscape scenes or cloud formations.

Each of the dialog's controls has a lock icon next to it, but this is a bit misleading. These texture fills have a decidedly video-game nature. The Preview button is intended for you to use as a random generator of different textures. When you click Preview, every element that is not locked will change randomly. The Cloud % value might change from 83 to 17, and the Lower Land color from cyan to orange, and Landscape # from 4,779 to 26,003.

If you have locked all elements, then you can use the Preview button to change one particular aspect: Make the change you want, and click Preview to see your change in the Preview window before placing it into effect. In other words, the lock prevents an element from being randomly changed, but you can always change an element manually, locked or not.

A word of caution: These elaborate textures can devour memory, hard drive space, and printer resources. If you apply them to large objects, or put many of them on a page, be prepared for some backtalk from your hardware. We created a rectangle and filled it two ways, with a simple fill pattern and with a texture; here are the essential statistics of the two operations:

Fill Type	Size of File	Code Sent to Printer	Time to Print
Uniform	13K	23K	4.5 seconds
Texture	201K	147K	17 seconds

We would invite you to browse these textures for yourself, but please don't take us too literally. If you were to view every possible permutation of one of the simpler ones, say Aerial Photography, which has controls for just Texture #, Softness %, Brightness ± %, Background and Foreground…let's see…32,768 textures, 100 percentage points for Softness and Brightness…and 100 percentage points for the four colors…Foreground and Background…well, you would have somewhere around 6,553,600,000,000,000,000,000 variations to look at for the first texture. And then there are 42 more textures in the Texture List, most of which have more permutations than this one. Aren't you glad that you can't add your own…

In the next chapter, we wrap up Part II of this book with a look at DRAW's new controls for linking objects with global styles. All of the outlines and fills that you have explored in the last two chapters can be incorporated into styles and applied across other objects and even across other files.

CHAPTER

Automate!

NINE

We normally resist hyperbole, but DRAW's support for *global styles* and the program's new *presets* just may revolutionize the way its users drive the software. Now when you slave over a hot desktop to produce a perfectly formatted graphic, all of its formatting instructions can be stored away in various containers for later use. DRAW's support for these automated functions extends to both text and graphics elements.

This chapter has two parts: The first part introduces global styles and concentrates on how they are used with graphics objects (in Chapter 11 we'll explore styles and their application to text). The second part studies the new Presets feature, with which users can capture a sequence of commands and play them back quickly.

The Foundation of a Style

Do you use Word for Windows? How about Ami Pro or WordPerfect? PageMaker or Xpress? Ventura Publisher? FrameMaker? If you use any of these or numerous other programs available today, you might already have learned the concept of the style. If DRAW represents your first exposure to styles, you are in for a treat.

The whole idea behind a style is to avoid—forgive the cliché—reinventing the wheel. If you do something right once, you shouldn't have to do it again and again and again, and as of 4.0, DRAW users don't have to any longer. Granted, there have always been tools that allow you to recreate objects, and duplicate formatting from one image or document to another. But styles are in a different class. With a style, you can attach formatting instructions to many objects at once, and ensure that they will all be formatted alike. If you decide to change the style, all objects that use the style will change.

The Foundation of a Style 237

In Chapter 8, we told you that fountain fills can be stored in presets. Styles, too, are storage places, but on a larger scale. The fill, the outline, and any special effects, as well, can all be stored together in these sophisticated presets called styles.

Figure 9.1 shows the steps you take to create and use a style. First, you create the object (step 1) and format it. In this example, you might give the oval a 35% gray shade and a special outline using the Calligraphic Pen. Next (step 2), you hold down the secondary mouse button for a

9.1

The recipe for creating a style

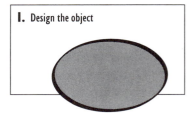

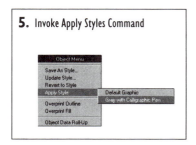
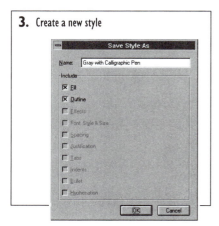

moment to invoke the Object menu, and choose Save As Style. As you create the style, you make up a name for it (step 3) and choose attributes that you want it to include. Any new objects you create (step 4) can instantly be given the attributes of your new style (step 5).

Creating a Graphic Style

Creating a style involves nothing more complicated than creating the prototype object. Once you have that, you can use it as the basis for a new style and begin to apply the style to newly drawn or existing objects. And you don't have to wait until the prototype is perfect before putting it into production, because you can always update the style later as you add or change attributes. You don't need to return to the prototype in order to update the style globally; any object that is connected to a style can be used as the new model for changes to the style. Also, you can format any object independently of the style assigned to that object, and it will keep its "local" formatting until you reapply the style.

PageMaker users will see a similarity in the handling of PageMaker and DRAW styles, because local formatting is easily done in PageMaker, as it is in DRAW. By contrast, Ventura Publisher users have found DRAW's styles to be quite different, because Ventura's tags have historically been more of an all-or-nothing, now-or-never proposition, with only limited local formatting available. (That changes somewhat in DRAW 5.0; see Part VIII of this book.)

Design the Object

There are three elements that can be contained in a graphic style: outlines, fills, and certain special effects. You can use any tool imaginable from the various Fill and Outline dialogs; among the special effects, Perspective, Extrude, and Envelope can be incorporated in a style.

Figure 9.2 shows an object with three separate attributes:

- A full-color pattern
- A thin rule that is set to automatically scale with the image

9.2

This star is just itching to be turned into a style.

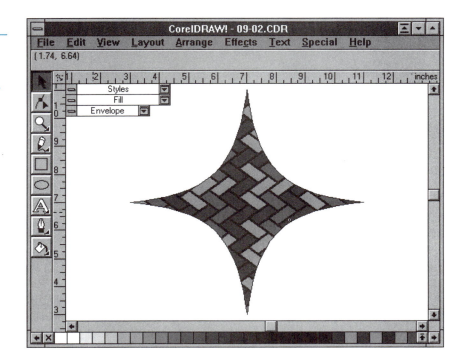

- An envelope that has turned this rectangle into a sharp four-sided star

Because we expect to create many objects that have these attributes, we have found the perfect time to use a style, so that we don't have to spend time reapplying the three individual attributes listed above each time we want the overall star effect. (To follow along with this discussion, create any closed object and apply an outline and a fill, and add either the Perspective, Extrude, or Envelope effect. Don't worry what the object looks like—a filled blob will do nicely.)

Create and Save the Style

To create a style from this star (or your own prototype object), you need to reach the Object menu, which is accessible only one way—from the secondary mouse button.

AUTHOR'S NOTE

 DRAW ships with the secondary mouse button (SMB) set by default to access the Object menu. If you have a favorite SMB shortcut from pre-4.0 days—such as Full-Screen Preview, Node Edit, or 2X Zoom—you can still use it. However, to reach the Object menu you will then have to learn a new maneuver that we refer to as the click-and-hold-for-one-second, for want of any better name. A quick click of the SMB performs the function defined in Special / Preferences / General / Right Mouse Button, and the click-and-hold-for-one-second invokes the Object menu. Make sure you click ON THE OBJECT with the SMB—otherwise, you could use the click-and-hold-for-one-YEAR maneuver, and nothing would happen.

In the Object menu, click Save Style As, and from that dialog, notice that the Effects box is available as one of the three components that can be part of the style. Had you not added a special effect to your prototype, only the first two would be active. We called our style Stars; you can name yours anything (yes, even "Anything").

You can choose how many of the three components are incorporated into your style. If you want just a fill and outline but no special effect, or fill and effect but no outline, that's okay with DRAW. What's more, you can always change your mind later. Updating a style is as easy as creating it in the first place: From the Object menu, choose Update Style instead of Save Style As, whereupon you are presented with the same dialog for choosing the components to include in the style. You can also use Update Style to rename your style.

The Styles Roll-Up   Next, open the Styles roll-up (with Layout / Styles, or Ctrl+F5). As Figure 9.3 shows, the new style name, Stars, is present in the list of styles. Also notice the three buttons above the style names. There is a button for each of the three types of styles that DRAW offers: *artistic text styles, paragraph text styles,* and *graphic styles.* If

9.3

The Styles roll-up provides continual access to the current group of styles.

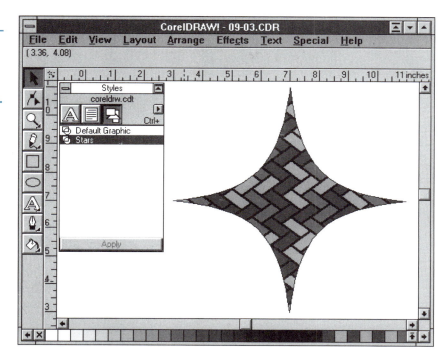

the star (or your own object) is still selected, all you'll see are the graphic styles, but if you deselect the object, DRAW will then show you all styles. The roll-up is really only good for applying styles—it can't create them as the Object menu can—but it allows you to assign hotkeys to styles (more on this soon), and it has the "always present" convenience of a roll-up.

The Styles roll-up also shows the name of the current template, CORELDRW.CDT. You'll be reading more about templates later in this chapter.

Apply the Style to Another Object

Applying a style is easy. Create another closed object, make sure it is selected, click on Stars in the Styles roll-up, and then Apply. Instantly, the new shape takes on the three components stored in the style. This does not mean that the new object will look identical to the original; if its essential shape is different from the first object, it will remain different, even with the style applied. This is not a bug, it's a feature: An object's shape and position are not attributes of a style, nor should they be. The idea here is not to create duplicates (the Clone command does that), but rather to give you the power to take specific attributes and apply them to other objects.

Having said that, though, we must point out the following curious behavior: When a style does not include one of the allowed special effects, then the size, angle of rotation, and horizontal or vertical skew effects are not part of the style. That is, you could resize, rotate, or distort one of the objects governed by the style, then update the style, and yet no other objects that use the style would change. However—and this is a big however—if you *have* incorporated Envelope, Extrude, or Perspective in the style, then suddenly any rotating, sizing, or skewing that you may have done to the master object *is* reflected in the style.

We have forged a theory on why styles work this way: Sizing and shaping of objects are options on the Effects menu. Although you can accomplish them interactively with the mouse, they are actually controlled by the functions in the Transform roll-up. But DRAW doesn't start paying attention to any effects that you add to a style until you use one of the major-league effects (Envelope, Extrude, or Perspective). Once you do, then DRAW picks up on the transformations, as well. Confusing, we agree, but tolerable once you understand the dynamic.

Figures 9.4 and 9.5 show the application of the Stars style in action. Our star continues to drive the style while numerous other objects are created in Figure 9.4, including a text string, a blob, and an alarm clock taken from the on-line Symbols library. Figure 9.5 shows how they all look after the style has been applied. Each one is affected differently by the enveloping, with the wildest effect sported by the text.

Incidentally, notice that even though Stars is a graphic style, we were able to apply it to the text string. Every object in DRAW has a graphics component, including text. Although only artistic text styles were visible in the roll-up when we selected the text, clicking the button for

9.4

Before: One object with a style, and five without it

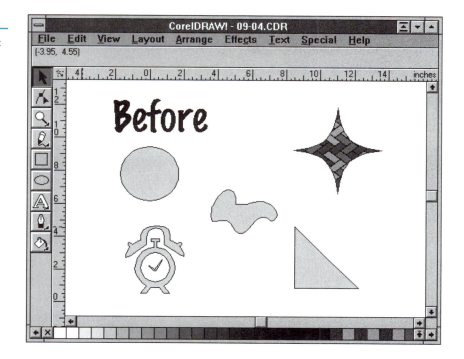

graphic styles provided access to the desired style. Also, note that the text remains fully editable, evidenced by our changing the word *Before* to *After*.

When and When Not to Use Styles

The use of DRAW's styles is certainly a matter of preference, even taste, and if you go with the simple rule of thumb—use styles when they will save you time—you will be ahead of the game. In some instances, however, other strategies might prove more helpful than styles.

Use a style when

- You want to link many objects together. A style's greatest value is the collective control it gives you over multiple objects. You never have to worry about one of them being wrong—they're either all correct or they're all wrong.

9.5

After: Six objects using the same style

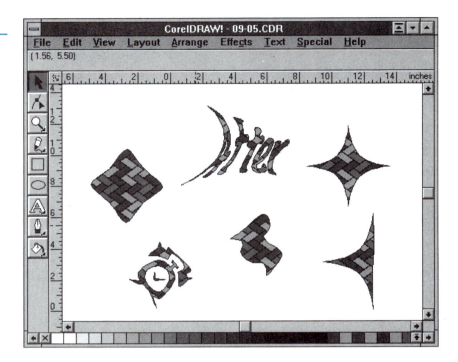

- You have several attributes you want to apply at once. As shown in the earlier examples, nothing saves formatting time like a style.

- You anticipate that you might be changing all instances of one color to another in a complex drawing. Without styles, it would be hell to track down all occurrences of one color and apply another; with styles, this process can be completely automated into one or two steps.

- You want to control elements across multiple pages or even multiple files. Styles are saved in templates, so they can be used across long distances (more about that shortly).

There are times when other tools might work better than styles. Here are the situations where you may want to choose another strategy:

- You already have a custom palette created, and you want to quickly assign colors to objects. Though you could create a style containing a selection of color fills, this job is better suited for a palette.

- You want one or more objects to look *exactly* like an original; this is a job for the Clone command. Clones don't need to be applied or updated; they automatically and instantly take on the entire appearance of the master object.

- You want to borrow just one attribute of a formatted object, and you are not interested in keeping them linked. Though you could apply the style and then strip off the attributes you don't want, that would be wasted effort. The answer here is to use either Edit / Copy Attributes From, or Effects / Copy. Both commands let you choose the particular attribute you want to copy from an existing object. This is better than using a style, if all you want is a piece of the style.

And bear in mind that there are also times when it is better to use a preset than a style; discussion coming up later in this chapter.

Understanding Templates

Styles take the formatting of graphics to a higher level, by offering a link between objects. In turn, styles themselves can be taken to a higher level, thanks to DRAW's use of *templates*. Styles hold collections of formatting information; templates hold collections of styles. Actually, templates can contain the styles *as well as* the objects themselves, and are thus excellent starting points for projects.

Templates can also be aggravating, as DRAW has a tendency to ask you often whether or not you want to save changes you made to a template—when you didn't even know you had a template, let alone made any changes to it. And because templates are separate files, they do require a bit of extra maintenance on your part.

Template files have .CDT extensions instead of the standard .CDR. Even if you never create a template, DRAW still employs one—the default template, CORELDRW.CDT—to preside over your global operations. DRAW opens CORELDRW.CDT every time you start the program, and unless you say otherwise, all style changes are stored there. Our guess is that most users will usually store their changes directly in CORELDRW.CDT, rather than create separate templates, so our discussion will begin there.

Modifying the CORELDRW.CDT Defaults

There are three ways in which you can modify the default set of styles stored in CORELDRW.CDT: by adding a new style, by updating any of the default styles, or by invoking the Fill or Outline commands without having selected an object.

The first method of altering CORELDRW.CDT is to add a new style, following the steps discussed earlier. Anytime you add a new style, you must indicate whether you want to record it in CORELDRW.CDT permanently. Don't worry about forgetting; DRAW will always remind you with the following dialog. In fact, you may have already noticed that DRAW likes to remind you—over and over again (more on that shortly).

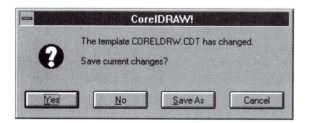

The second way to alter CORELDRW.CDT is to change the Default Graphic style itself, instead of adding a new style. To do this, you can draw a new object (it automatically takes on the Default Graphic style), reformat the object with the desired attributes, and then choose Update Style from the Object menu. From this point on, every graphic you create will start out with these new default attributes. For instance, if you add a fill, outline, or even an extrusion or envelope to the graphic

Understanding Templates 247

and then update the Default Graphic style, then every object you create henceforth automatically inherits that effect.

The third way of altering CORELDRW.CDT, as discussed in Chapters 7 and 8, involves accessing the Fill or Outline dialogs or flyout menus without first selecting an object. DRAW first asks you if you really mean to change the default, and then records your changes as the new Default Graphic style. As with the second method of changing the default, DRAW does not ask you whether or not you want to make these changes permanent; *it just does it.*

WATCH OUT!

When you update the default style—either by using the Object menu or by changing the fill or outline without first selecting an object—DRAW does not ask you whether you want to make these changes permanent; it just does it. Nor do you receive confirmation afterward; DRAW assumes on faith that you know what you are doing (!) and automatically records the change in CORELDRW.CDT.

We know all this information about templates can be confusing—and, unfortunately, it gets worse. So before we continue, here's a summary of the three ways to make changes to DRAW's default set of styles:

- Add a new style, and answer Yes upon closing the file when DRAW asks you if you want to save the changes.

- Draw a new object, format it, and use the Object menu to update the style. DRAW automatically records the change to the default style in CORELDRW.CDT, *without asking you for confirmation.*

- Without selecting an object first, operate the Fill or Outline dialog/roll-up/flyout. DRAW asks you to choose the type of object that will receive this new default, and then automatically records the change in CORELDRW.CDT, *without asking you for confirmation.*

AUTHOR'S NOTE

CORELDRW.CDT is a plain old file, residing on your hard drive like all other files. Therefore, before you start any wild experiments with your default settings, you might want to back up the file first. You'll find CORELDRW.CDT in the DRAW\TEMPLATE subdirectory of your main CorelDRAW directory.

Using New Templates

If you are embarking on a project that requires the addition of many new styles, you might want to store the styles in their own template(s). You must use the Styles roll-up (Ctrl+F5) to do this, because the Object menu does not provide access to template creation (only style creation). After creating a group of styles, click on the right-pointing triangle in the Styles roll-up and choose Save Template from the flyout. To load an existing template into memory, choose Load Styles from the same flyout.

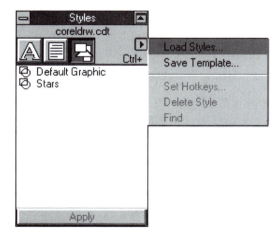

Templates in a Teapot

The actual steps to creating a new template are easily accomplished, but administering your new template is another matter, as DRAW is not at all helpful with keeping you on track. In the last edition of this book, we wrote that this is "nothing we haven't seen before with version 1.0 features." Well, now styles are at their second iteration, but they are no further advanced. Therefore, we cannot retreat from our position that implementation of templates remains awkward and underdeveloped.

For instance, you are likely to be frustrated if you try to create separate template files and attach them to drawings. Suppose you create a small project called HELLO.CDR. You create a few styles and save them as HELLO.CDT. Then you leave the file and return to it later, only to discover that your default style for creating new objects has changed. You had a very specific default style in HELLO.CDT, but now the default looks suspiciously like the one in the most recent template. You think back, but can remember no time when you saved a template under a different name, or anything like that. This is a common snafu with templates.

Here's another one: You open a file that has some styles (other than the default) and you begin work. You make no style changes whatsoever, but when you close the file, DRAW asks you whether you want to save the changes you made to CORELDRW.CDT. Huh?? You answer no, open up another file, print it, close it after making exactly zero changes, and DRAW again asks you what to do with the changes you made to CORELDRW.CDT. Lucky for you, "Format hard drive" isn't a choice, because you just might be frustrated enough to choose it.

Do you find that DRAW is forever asking you to save the template? If so, it is likely the result of what we call the Black Hole of Styles. When you create a style, you do not have to save it in a new template—DRAW stores it directly in the .CDR file. If you *do* create a new template, then DRAW will automatically load that template whenever you open the .CDR file, and other style changes could be stored in the template. But the styles are also stored directly in the .CDR file. You don't need to have a template attached in order to preserve styles in a drawing.

But here's what happens if you *don't* create a template: You open a file with a bunch of styles in it, and DRAW dumps them into the list of styles for the current template, most likely CORELDRW.CDT. "Where did all these styles come from," DRAW asks itself. "The user must have just created them—I'd better ask if I should store them in the template." DRAW doesn't realize that the styles were contained in the drawing itself; it sees a collection of new styles and assumes you just created them and might want to store them in the current template.

Compound this with DRAW's tendency to forget the attributes of the Default style from one template to the next, and we have one potentially dismal situation. If you haven't followed all of this, that's okay—it's not worth reading a second time. Just follow these rules of thumb:

- Try to collect a set of attributes for the Default Graphic style that you can use consistently across all of the templates you create. For instance, you might decide that your Default Graphic style will be solid white with a 1-point black outline, or maybe hollow or a 20% black tint with a .5-point outline. If you keep default attributes the same across all your templates, you won't have to worry about DRAW inadvertently altering them if you switch from one template to another. Therefore, the assumption here is that you…

- Store specialty formats in new styles. If you want to create a style to help you apply a complex extrusion, make it a new style, not part of the Default Graphic style.

- Remember that all styles created in a drawing are stored in the .CDR file. You needn't create a template (.CDT) file in order to have your styles intact. But…

- If you *don't* attach a specific template file to a drawing that has styles in it, DRAW will nag you about changes made to the current template.

- When you save a template, you are essentially creating a duplicate set of styles that can then be used as a starting point by other new drawings.

We're not saying that this is necessarily how Corel's engineers intended for styles to be used. (We may never really know that, as there is little relevant discussion in either the User's Manual or the on-line Help, and numerous calls placed to the development team provided little insight.) Our suggestion is that you keep your expectations low, as the behavior of DRAW styles is…well, pardon the vernacular, but "flaky" comes immediately to mind.

Our recommendations to you will continue to unfold over the course of this chapter, but for now we want to reiterate:

> All styles that you create are stored in the .CDR file itself. By saving a new template, you make it easier for new projects to use the same styles, and you keep DRAW from annoying you about changes made to CORELDRW.CDT (or whatever template is current).

Creating Templates as Starting Points

Our judgment of templates has been somewhat harsh up to this point, but they do have one feature that makes them worth the trouble: DRAW's templates can contain more than just styles; they can contain any element that would normally go into a drawing.

When you issue the Save Template command from the Styles roll-up, notice the With Contents check box below the OK and Cancel buttons. If you check that box, your template is saved with all of the elements in place. Now we're talking! You can use the template to give yourself a major-league running start toward the completion of a repetitive project.

Figure 9.6 shows the completed version of a blank form to be filled out for some extremely important purpose. In completing this, we created styles for the lines and for the text (to be discussed in Chapter 12, "Working with Text Styles"). In this example, though, the format of the lines is not as important as the lines themselves, and, happily, they can be captured in the template.

There are two ways you can create this template. You can use the roll-up and issue the Save Template command, making sure to click on With Contents. Or you can issue a regular File / Save As command and change the file type to CorelDRAW Template, instead of the standard CorelDRAW File. In either case, make sure to save the template in the DRAW\TEMPLATE subdirectory (you'll see why in the next section).

9.6

A completed template, providing a good launch point for the completion of this form

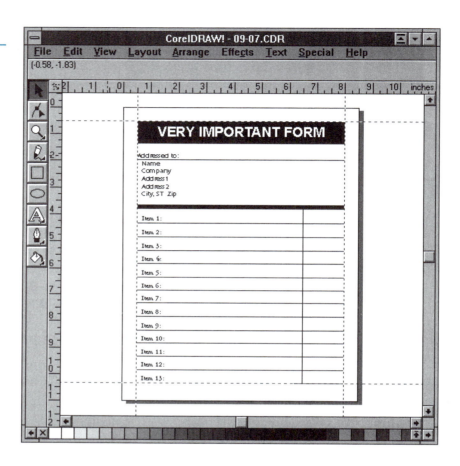

Using Your Starting Point

Now it's time for you to fill out one of your forms—but you don't have to start it from scratch. You don't even have to open the existing file and hope that you remember to save it under a different name with its new contents. Instead, you issue the File / New From Template command and find the template name in the file window. Because you saved it in the default subdirectory, you won't have to navigate to other directories. When you find the file and OK the dialog, DRAW places the entire template—text, lines, and all—on your page. As you can see in Figure 9.6, DRAW does not name the file; it remains untitled. You don't have to worry about changing the template or any existing file; this is its own file, once you give it a name. We see this as an essential value of templates.

WATCH OUT!

> Make sure you use the New From Template command and NOT the File / Open command. DRAW permits you to open templates just like regular files (you first have to change DRAW's file filter to show .CDT files), and then any changes you make are permanently recorded in the template. It's okay to do that consciously—that is, when you really want to change your starting point. Otherwise, however, make sure to use the New From Template command when you want to create a new file from a template.

DRAW ships with several templates that can help inspire you to create your own. Use the New From Template command and browse the .CDT files in the TEMPLATES subdirectory.

Surviving Styles

Until DRAW's implementation of styles evolves, managing your styles and templates will continue to be an inexact science—and that's an understatement. Unless you know which of DRAW's messages to ignore and which to heed, you probably won't enjoy working with these rough gems. Here are some tips to help:

Install the Avant Garde BT and Common Bullets Typefaces

Many of DRAW's templates and sample files expect to find these two typefaces, Avant Garde BT and Common Bullets. If you don't have them installed on your system, DRAW might act as if you do anyway and try to use them for text whose font assignment is unknown. Many, if not most, of DRAW's templates and sample files assume the presence of those two typefaces. As of DRAW 5.0, you can use the PANOSE font substitution to make your own substitution, but we have found that even ardently anti-TrueType users have capitulated and installed these two faces in their environment, just so they don't have to be bothered.

Just Say No! Does DRAW incessantly ask you if you want to save CORELDRW.CDT, even though you made no changes to its styles? Us, too. Tell DRAW no. Tell DRAW you're *not interested.* As we explained earlier, this message occurs when you open a file with styles of its own and they get dumped into memory along with the ones in CORELDRW.CDT. So, DRAW assumes you just created them and might want to save them. Most of the time, that is incorrect.

There is only one time when this message is legitimate: when you have added a style and truly want it included in CORELDRW.CDT. At no other time should DRAW ask you (remember, if you change the Default Graphic style, DRAW saves the template automatically without asking you). Any other time that DRAW asks you, just say no. You won't lose any of your formatting; all styles are recorded in the .CDR file. The only time you would want to save CORELDRW.CDT is when you have added a style.

Interview Yourself DRAW's styles can be enormously powerful when used to help you reach your productivity potential, so ask yourself some questions about your work: Do you regularly need to assign 2-point outlines with round caps? Create a style for them. How about a custom Calligraphic Pen? Create a style. Is there a particular extrusion that you often apply to a logo? Style.

You can add all of these styles to CORELDRW.CDT and have them immediately accessible every time you start the program. Just park them right in CORELDRW.CDT. If you do, it'll be one of those few times when you can answer Yes when DRAW asks you what to do with changes to CORELDRW.CDT.

We will revisit styles in Part III of this book, when we examine DRAW's text engine and how it integrates styles and templates.

DRAW's New Presets: Have It Your Way

How many times have you done this: You're building a complicated extrusion, or perhaps formatting type according to a precise specification. "Shoot," you say to anybody who's listening, "I'm tired of doing this over and over again. Why can't I teach DRAW to do it for me?"

Ask no more. DRAW 5.0's new macro language, called Presets, offers you that very capability. Presets are similar to styles and similar to keyboard macros, but just different enough to have a special mark of distinction. Using presets is like plugging a very efficient tape recorder into your computer—a tape recorder that doesn't pay attention to the individual steps you took to perform a task, but records just the result.

NEW FOR 5

With DRAW's new Presets roll-up, you can record a sequence of commands and then play them back at high speed.

Presets are related to styles, in that both tools allow you to quickly apply formatting to a selected object. At the end of this chapter, we'll outline the essential differences and offer suggestions on usage.

Creating a Preset

Let's say you have a particular effect that you often want to apply to objects on your page, perhaps a ten-step extrusion. You could create a style from it, but then its availability would depend upon which template is in memory. You conclude, therefore, that this is a job for DRAW's new presets, and you are right. Here are the steps you would take to record your extrusion:

1. Open the Presets roll-up (Special / Presets, or Alt+F5).
2. Create the object, or select it if it already exists.
3. In the roll-up, click on the Start Recording button.
4. Fill it with solid blue, or some other dark color.
5. Pull down the Extrude roll-up (Effects / Extrude or Ctrl+E) and begin building your extrusion. For this exercise, produce the following extrusion:
   - Small Back with a depth of 10 (from the second icon of the five across the top)
   - Solid Fill of cyan, or some other light color (from the far-right icon)
6. Click Apply to confirm the extrusion, and then click on Stop Recording from the Presets roll-up.
7. In the Edit Preset dialog, supply a name and an optional description, as shown in Figure 9.7.

Notice that your preset takes its place in the alphabetical list of presets, and the preview window shows a thumbnail of the effect. In the preview, the thumbnail uses the type of object to which you applied the

9.7

Identifying your preset for future use

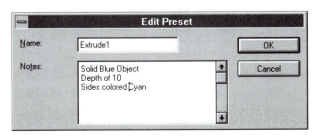

effect, but this doesn't mean you can't apply the preset to another type of object. Also, if you gave your preset a description, it will show up in a flyout window as you browse your list of presets.

Playing Back a Preset

Now it's time to apply your favorite extrusion to another object, and instead of going through all of the motions again, you can ask DRAW to play back your preset:

1. Create a second object, and make it a type different from the original one (rectangle, ellipse, blob, or even just a line).

2. With the new object selected, find the name of your preset in the drop-down list and click Apply. Figure 9.8 shows the preset being applied to a heart taken from the Symbols library.

9.8

With a preset, you can apply effects to new objects at a moment's notice.

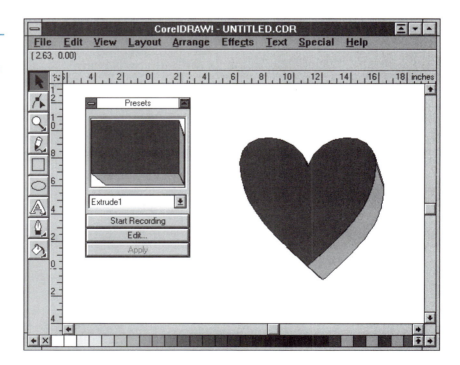

INSIDE INFO

 **Presets are stored in binary form in a file named CORELDRW.PST that resides in the DRAW subdirectory below your main Corel directory. This file cannot be edited, but it wouldn't be a bad idea for you to have a current backup, in case a recording session goes awry.**

Creating Objects during Recording

In the foregoing example, you created a preset that let you apply an extrusion to any selected object. Let's suppose that your requirement is more specific: You have a precise starting point—which includes not only the effect, but the object itself in a known size and shape—that you use for a particular role. The preset created earlier would only address half of the issue; you would still need to create the object.

DRAW might be able to accommodate you, as it allows for the creation of rectangles and ellipses during the recording of the preset. After clicking on Start Recording, you create a rectangle or an ellipse, use the Transform roll-up to set the object's exact size, position, and rotation/skew angle, and then apply whatever effect you want to it. Click on Stop Recording and assign a name to the preset. This preset will automatically create the object and format it.

What's in a Name? You can name your presets anything you want, provided you keep within 32 characters, but it pays off handsomely to plot a bit of strategy. DRAW stores all presets alphabetically, and once you click in the window of names, you can navigate the list by typing characters on your keyboard. Typing *E*, for instance, would whisk you, perhaps, to Extrude1, and *F* would take you to that cool fractal that you recorded last week.

> So when you are asked to supply a name for a preset, don't call it *Set Extrude of 10 Steps,* because you may not remember that a week later. Instead, name it *Extrude: 10 Steps.* Then, when you next create an extrude preset, name it *Extrude: Big Back with Blue Shade.* Maybe there are three specific fractal fills that you use frequently; record these as presets, naming them *Fractal1, Fractal2,* and *Fractal3.* That way, you can browse your fractal fill presets by typing *F* repeatedly until you find the one you want, at which point you can simply press Enter to execute it.
>
> Also, remember that the preview window in the Presets roll-up gives you a visual image of the preset, based on the object that you used initially. So before you record a preset, give some thought to the type of object—rectangle, oval, string of text, or curve—that would best illustrate and represent the effect.

Creating Text Presets

You can create presets that take care of text formatting, but the rules of the road are a bit more strict. Try the following exercise:

1. Create a line of artistic text.
2. Select it and click Start Recording.
3. Using the Text roll-up or the Character dialog, change the face, the style, and the size. It doesn't matter what you change them to, as long as you make some kind of change to all three.
4. Click OK or Apply, stop the recording and assign a name to your preset.

That preset you just made will change any string of artistic text to the specifications that you set. Now try this one:

1. Create a line of artistic text.

2. Select it and click Start Recording.
3. Using the Text roll-up or the Character dialog, change the size to 10 points higher than its current value. Don't make any other changes.
4. Click OK or Apply, stop the recording, and assign a name to your preset.

This preset will change the size of any string of artistic text, but will not change anything else. In other words, the preset recording function does not take note of the current dialog settings; it only pays attention to what you *specifically change.* If you want to create a preset that changes text to 14-point Century Italic, left-aligned, you'll have to make sure that none of those specs are current. You literally have to change the settings in order for the recorder to take note.

Two other points concerning text and presets: First, you cannot apply a preset to paragraph text, only artistic text. You can use either type of text when recording the preset, but DRAW won't let you play back a preset to paragraph text. Second, you can only apply a preset to an entire string of text, not a few characters selected with the Text tool. If you try, DRAW will automatically change to the Pick tool and apply the change to the entire string.

What You Can and Can't Do with Presets

Taking full advantage of presets requires that you know their limitations. DRAW has packed a wallop of power into them, but they are not allowed to tread in certain areas.

You *Can* Use Presets for These Tasks:

- To create rectangles and ellipses
- To change fills and outlines (except custom arrows)
- To apply anything from the Transform roll-up
- For duplicating and cloning
- To convert to curves

- To format text
- To realign or reorder objects
- For blending two objects together

Let's take a closer look at the last two situations. DRAW does not record functions that involve your selecting more than one object, unless you perform some other operation in the middle. For instance, DRAW would bark at you if you recorded a preset that included your creating a second object, selecting it and an existing object, and blending them together. On the other hand, if you were to merely nudge the first object by 1 point, then create the second object, select both, and then blend, DRAW would permit that preset.

So, to record a preset that aligns two objects together, you must take the following steps:

1. Select one object and begin recording.
2. Nudge that object in one direction and then back again.
3. Create the new object.
4. Select both objects and align them.

Watch out—if you try this without step 2, it will fail.

You *Can't* Use Presets for These Tasks:

- To compose or edit text
- When more than one object is selected initially
- To apply two- or full-color patterns
- To apply envelopes or PowerClips

We *Wish* We Could Use Presets for These Tasks:

- To control the interface (We'd like to set grids, change page size, control nudge and fountain stripes, and swap color palettes.)
- To perform file imports and exports
- To record and play back actual keystrokes

Our Other Druthers for Presets We'd also like to be able to manage presets better, by saving them in specific files (like color palettes). Then we could mix, match, and merge them among files. This point came up as we were browsing the many presets that ship with DRAW, ready for use. At first glance, they were impressive and seemed potentially useful...but they were also intrusive. As we started making our own, the list became quite crowded. You can delete presets easily enough, by clicking Edit and using a simple dialog, but then they are gone for good. We'd prefer to treat them like styles and store them in their own templates for specific uses. Maybe in DRAW 6.0...

And finally, we *really* wish we could assign hotkeys to presets, as we can to styles.

Choosing between a Style and a Preset

No doubt there will be plenty of times when you can accomplish the same thing using either a style or a preset. For instance, to quickly create a 3-point outline with a rounded corner, you can either define a style or record a preset. Here are rules of thumb to help you choose the best course of action.

Situations That Call for Styles

- *You have already created and formatted an object* and now you want to capture its formatting for future use with other objects. Creating a preset means you have to go through all of the formatting steps; a style is best in this case because you can use existing objects.

- *You want to format several objects together.* To apply formatting to ten different objects, you can choose either styles or presets, but if you anticipate the format will change in the future, you're much better off using a style. By changing one object and updating the style, the others change automatically; there is no such global link, however, with presets.

- *You want to add an envelope.* You can capture an envelope in a style, but you can't record it in a preset.

Situations That Call for Presets

- *You want to transform an object.* You can record in a preset all of the functions in the Transform roll-up, but a style will ignore these transformations unless you also include an envelope, extrusion, or perspective. Because of the macrolike quality of a preset, you can record an action such as a 20% skew; but a style can only take note of the end result.

- *You want to convert an object to curves.* Again, this is taking an action on the object, rather than applying a format to it. Styles can't do that.

- *You want to create objects automatically.* A preset can actually create a rectangle or an ellipse as part of its playback. We used extensively in this book a preset that merely created a rectangle and then sized it to 26 by 42 picas (the maximum dimension of our figures). Prior to 5.0, we had to create a .CDR file with the rectangle in it and importe it into a drawing-in-progress. Creating a preset is worlds easier.

- *You want to record a blend between two objects.* You have to remember the curious requirement of nudging the original object first when recording the preset; after that, you can use the preset to create a quick blend between an object you select and the one you've recorded in the preset.

- *You might not remember…* The Object menu doesn't give you much opportunity to describe a style—about 30 characters on one line. But the Presets roll-up allows you to store the name of the preset, a nine-line description, and a visual thumbnail of the result. If you find yourself forgetting what a style does and why you defined it in the first place, you might have better luck recording a preset.

Chapter 14 in the CorelDRAW User's Manual offers further detail on the dynamics of presets. Stay tuned as we switch gears now and explore the never-a-dull-moment world of DRAW's text handling.

PART III

WORKING WITH TEXT

Let's start with what Part III is not. It is not a dissertation on typography, and we will not spend pages upon pages discussing x-heights, ascenders, splines, and a host of other topics that make up the specialized field of typography. To take absolutely nothing away from the art of typography, we simply don't believe that it is our place, in a single book purporting to cover how best to use CorelDRAW, to claim that we can teach you all you need to know about fine typography.

Instead we focus here on down-to-earth text issues—matters of technique, strategy, and performance. Many thousands of Corel-DRAW users buy the package just to set type. Nodes, curves, and fountain fills? They could hardly care less—just give them those 825 typefaces, the Text and Effects menu, and they're set for life. In these four chapters, we offer insight into why DRAW's text handling is so popular, and—what's fair is fair—we'll also look closely at the areas that have earned the most criticism.

Love it or hate it, DRAW's text handling is an awesome force to reckon with, responsible for the livelihood of a great many artists, illustrators, T-shirt makers, sign and banner manufacturers, and a host of other DRAW users who take very seriously the business of putting letters down on printed pages.

Taming the Type Monster

CHAPTER 10

TEN

CorelDRAW has two distinct reputations in the electronic publishing and graphics community. On the one hand, it is known as the Typesetting Giant, thanks to the always huge library of typefaces that ships with the program. On the other hand, it is known as something less than a precise, finely honed machine, thanks to a history of offering typefaces that are poorly crafted. DRAW 4.0 and 5.0 have substantiated the first reputation, offering 750 and 827 typefaces, respectively, at no additional charge. Happily, these last two versions of the program have also somewhat allayed the second reputation, by providing typefaces straight from the drafting boards of Bitstream and ITC, two well-respected type foundries.

Setting Type with DRAW

DRAW offers two avenues for creating and manipulating text: *artistic text* and *paragraph text*. Artistic text is created by selecting the Text tool and clicking once. Paragraph text is created by clicking and holding on the Text tool, choosing the Paragraph icon (the right-hand one) from the flyout, and either creating a marquee on the page, or clicking once on the page.

DRAW refers to a unit of artistic text as a *string* of text, and a unit of paragraph text as a *frame* of text. We will too. Both this chapter and Chapter 13 explore the differences between text strings and text frames. First, however, we'll look at the elements that are common to both.

What You Can Do to Text in DRAW

Regardless of how you create text in DRAW, you can do the following things to it.

Change Its Size You can set type as small as .7 point (for the really fine fine print of a contract) or up to 2,160 points (for the Goodyear Blimp). You can resize text characters from the Text roll-up (Figure 10.1), from the Character Attributes dialog (Figure 10.2), or, in the case of artistic text, by dragging its corner selection handles. As of DRAW 5.0, the venerable Edit Text dialog might not see much action anymore; as Figure 10.3 shows, it is now just a big window for text editing, with a gateway to the Character Attributes dialog.

10.1

DRAW's handy Text roll-up places all of the text controls on screen.

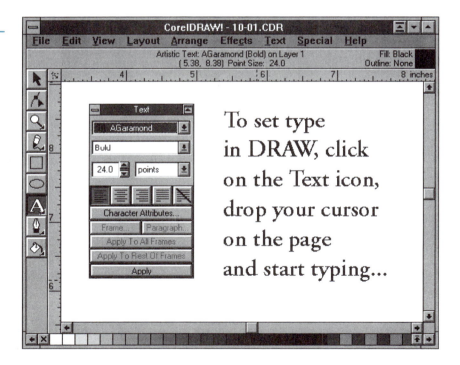

10.2

For the fastest access to DRAW's text formatting tools, use the Character Attributes dialog.

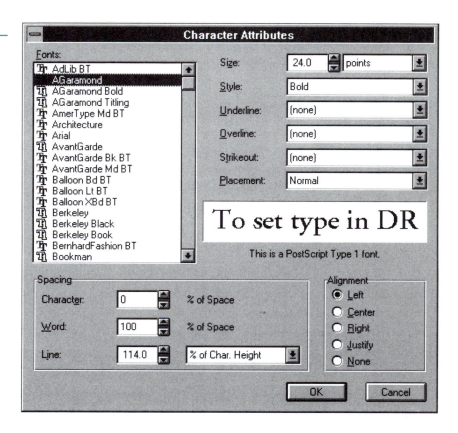

NEW FOR 5

The Character Attributes dialog gets a promotion in 5.0, now providing all typeface, size, weight, positioning, and spacing controls. What used to be a confusing maze of dialogs is now much more streamlined: You can format text from the roll-up or from Character Attributes.

10.3

Will the Edit Text dialog be relegated to second class citizen? You tell us.

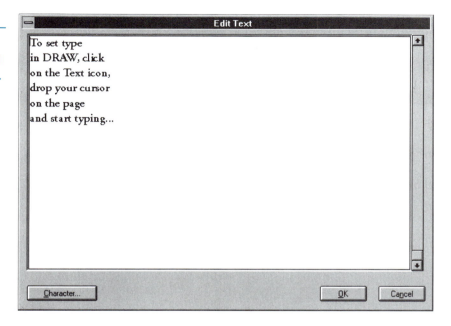

AUTHOR'S NOTE

Rarely are phrases mangled and misused more than the ones that describe type. We have been on our high horses many times concerning the distinction between a **TYPE FAMILY** (a collection of typefaces with a unifying design, such as Helvetica), a **TYPEFACE** (one in a collection, such as Helvetica Medium or Helvetica Bold), and a **FONT** (a typeface set in a specific size, such as 9-point Helvetica Italic). Corel doesn't make it easy for us to be typographically correct in our prose, because the User's Guide contains the common errors of referring to type families as **TYPEFACES**, and to typefaces as **FONTS**. We will do our best, however, and beg for leniency from the Goddess of Prose.

Change Its Style and Alignment Both the Text roll-up and Character Attributes dialog provide full control of typeface selection, style (bold, italic, and so on), size, and alignment (left, center, right, and justified). With the roll-up, you can change font and alignment with the on-screen controls, or click Character Attributes to reach the full dialog of controls.

Adjust Spacing With DRAW's spacing tools, you can adjust the space between characters, between words, and between lines of type. You can do this from the Paragraph dialog (reached via Text / Paragraph or the Paragraph button on the Text roll-up), or from the Character Attributes dialog. The dialog titled Paragraph works for both artistic and paragraph text.

Line spacing (known in the industry as *leading*) can be set in exact measurements of points, or by percentages of the text. The former method—new as of 4.0—provides more precision; the latter offers more flexibility when sizing type.

Figure 10.4 shows text set with various amounts of leading. You would think that 9-point text set with 10 points of lead would correspond to a percentage of *over* 100%, not *under* (97%). But in determining the percentage, DRAW uses the distance from the top of the *tallest character* to the bottom of the *longest descender,* rather than the nominal point size.

10.4

DRAW 4.0 can set text spacing in fixed points, or as a percentage of the type size.

This is 9-point text with 10-point spacing

This is 9-point text with 97% spacing

This is 9-point text with 11-point spacing

This is 9-point text with 106.8% spacing

This is 9-point text with 12-point spacing

This is 9-point text with 116% spacing

This is 9-point text with 13-point spacing

This is 9-point text with 126.3% spacing

Kern Individual Characters You can take any character in a string and move it left, right, up, or down. To do this, choose the Shape tool, not the Pick tool. The Shape tool treats each character in a text

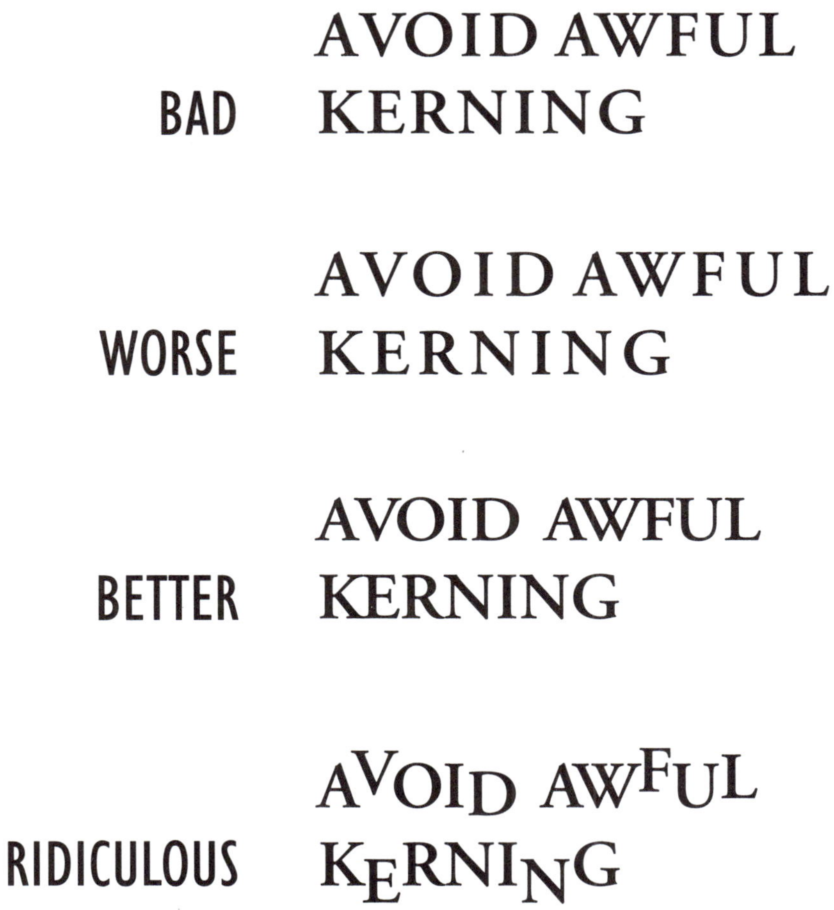

10.5

Character kerning is especially helpful with text set in all caps.

BAD   AVOID AWFUL
           KERNING

WORSE   AVOID AWFUL
           KERNING

BETTER   AVOID AWFUL
           KERNING

RIDICULOUS A^VO_{ID} AW^FUL
            K_ERNI_NG

string as a node, and even provides a node in front of each character. Select the node, and you can drag a character in any direction; or better yet, set a Nudge value and use your keyboard arrow keys. As Figure 10.5 illustrates, this can be put to good use or to positively hilarious use.

Lateral adjustment of characters is called *kerning*; the term is also used as a verb—*to kern* characters means to remove space between the characters. Capital letters, like the ones in Figure 10.5, often need manual kerning to look good. The third example down shows proper kerning for capital letters.

From 3 to 5: Learning TextSpeak

If you have migrated directly from DRAW 3.0 to 5.0, you have been spared the dreadful message that 4.0 users encountered when they opened 3.0 files:

> You are opening a file which uses CorelDRAW! 3.0 text spacing. Do you want to convert it to CorelDRAW! 4.0 spacing?

The choices were Yes, No, or Cancel, but many 4.0 users wished for a choice called Get Lost! or Leave Me Alone. Thankfully, text spacing is handled quite differently in DRAW 5.0. Here is the lowdown on the upgrade and how it affects text spacing:

Text Spacing in 3.0   Version 3.0 supported only one kind of line spacing: as a percentage of the point size. You could set text at 18 points with 100% line spacing, and know it to be roughly equivalent to 18/18. If you wanted 18/20, you would have to get out your calculator to figure out that you had to set the spacing at 111%. Most typographically-aware DRAW users complained that they missed the tried-and-true method of setting line spacing (or leading) in fixed points, but they gradually got used to it.

Then Came 4.0   Version 4.0 brought good news and bad news. You were able to set leading in points (that's good), but you had to wrestle with an entirely new system for calculating leading based on percentage (that's bad). Or you could throw in the towel and tell DRAW 4.0 to keep things the way they were in 3.0. But then, every time you tried to open a DRAW 3.0 file, you would be asked that question: Do you want to convert text spacing?

This scared users. "Convert my text? I should say not!" Yet, regardless of how you answered that question, the text looked the same. By "convert," DRAW 4.0 did not mean that it was going to change the actual line spacing, but rather the way the spacing was calculated. Nonetheless, this made DRAW 4.0 users uneasy.

No More Asking DRAW 5.0 doesn't ask you about it anymore. It supports all three of the line spacing measurements that have arisen since 1992:

- Fixed Points: The traditional and largely preferred way to measure space between lines of type is in the fixed units of measurement that you know as points. If you have set a string of text in 18 points, you can establish that the line spacing be precisely 22 points.
- Percentage of Point Size: This is the DRAW 3.0 way of doing things, in which 18/18 type was considered 100% spacing (and considered by most to be too tight).
- Percentage of Character Height: This system, ushered in by DRAW 4.0, measures the spacing as a percentage of the *character height*—from the highest point to the lowest point. Text set in 18 points and 110% spacing in DRAW 3.0 would look the same as text set in 4.0 or 5.0 with 96% spacing. *Only the measuring system has changed.* If you change the measurement to points, DRAW will calculate a spacing value of about 19.8 points, which is just about dead on.

Serious typographic artists may prefer the precision of points, but many users like keeping spacing as a percentage of the type size. That way, if the size of the type is increased, the spacing will change with it; in fixed-point measurements, you have to change that, too. It's your call—more precision and more effort vs. less precision and more automation.

INSIDE INFO

In addition to the Character Attribute and Paragraph dialogs, DRAW offers on-screen support for character and line spacing. Select the text, artistic or paragraph; then choose the Shape tool and look for the strange-looking arrows at the bottom of the text, one pointing down and one pointing to the right. These allow you to interactively change the line spacing (arrow pointing down) and the character spacing (arrow pointing right). If you do not have a specific number in mind for line and character spacing and are working on the basis of look and feel, you will save a lot of time and mouse activity by using these handy arrow controls.

Like most good typefaces, DRAW's ship with built-in intelligence about which character combinations need more or less space between them—these are referred to as *kerning pairs*. Invariably, however, text set at large sizes or in all caps needs to be scrutinized for proper kerning.

Format Individual Characters In addition to character kerning, DRAW supports character reformatting. To do this, you can reach for the Shape tool again and select the node in front of the character, or choose the Text tool and select characters by dragging across them. Either way, the Text roll-up and the Character Attributes dialog are the gateways for reformatting characters. The Text tool is more intuitive, providing a standard text cursor for selecting text, but the Shape tool has the advantage of allowing you to select noncontiguous characters. Select one character, hold Shift, and then select others anywhere in the string.

Figure 10.6 shows how we recently used character formatting to boost sales of our book.

10.6

Extortion notices, thanks to DRAW's character formatting

B*u*y 500 bo*o*ks f*r*om us or *we* wi**ll** form✽t yo*u*r *h*ard dri∨ε.

WATCH OUT!

Individual character formatting is overridden by changes made to a text string's size or style. In other words, if you format characters using the Shape tool and then format the entire string in the conventional manner, your custom formatting will be lost. Changing the typeface, style, or size after individual formatting spells trouble. Rule of thumb: Format the entire string first, and then reformat the individual characters.

Check for Spelling and Synonyms   DRAW's on-line Spell Checker and Thesaurus will improve all your DRAW documents. To check spelling, select a string or frame of text and choose Text / Spell Checker. You can spell-check an entire string or frame, or any portion of text that you have selected (using the Text cursor). To use the Thesaurus, select a word within a string or frame, and choose Text / Thesaurus. Most users have ignored these two functions, but they might be called into action more often now that DRAW can accommodate large blocks of text. And our prediction is that DRAW users will be pleasantly surprised by the breadth of the program's dictionaries. DRAW's spelling and synonym dictionaries rival those of major word processors.

Creating Artistic Text

Most DRAW users create text in the standard form, artistic text. This is the most intuitive method. You click once on the Text tool (or press F8), move out to the page, and type away. Press Enter when you want a new line. When you're done typing, you decide on the typeface, style, size, and alignment. Select a string of artistic text, and you can size, stretch, skew, and rotate it by tugging on its selection handles.

Artistic text is eligible for all of the cool special effects found in the DRAW's Effects menu, like the extrusion shown in Figure 10.7. For a close look at the Effects menu, see Chapters 14 through 19.

10.7

All of DRAW's effects, including Extrude, can be applied to artistic text.

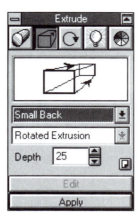

Artistic text also has its limitations. Compared to paragraph text, artistic text is slower to adjust when changed and does not support tabs or indents. Also, artistic text has less capacity for characters in a single string—though DRAW 5.0 does have a much larger appetite for artistic text than any of its predecessors. If you are a veteran DRAW user, you have surely encountered the loathsome error message found in Figure 10.8, and will be relieved to know that it won't rear its ugly head nearly as often anymore.

10.8

Artistic text strings can be longer in 5.0. We won't miss seeing this error message so often; will you?

The party of the first part, not to be mistaken with the party of the second part, shall hold harmless the party of the third party, in so much as the party of the first part participated in, or actively benefitted from the actions prompting..

Creating Paragraph Text

Often neglected by DRAW users, paragraph text and its benefits became increasingly difficult to ignore in version 4.0.

You create paragraph text inside a text frame, instead of directly on the page as with artistic text. A subtle distinction, perhaps, but paragraph text takes on a vastly different personality. Paragraph text supports word wrapping, just like your word processor, to create text that flows freely from one line to the next. The frame determines the shape of the text flow, and you determine the shape of the frame—either when you first create it or when you reshape it later. Figure 10.9 shows three renditions of the same paragraph of text, each one shaped differently.

The chief limitation of paragraph text is its indifference to most of DRAW's special effects. You cannot distort, skew, extrude, or do any of the other gee-whiz stuff to paragraph text. Nevertheless, you'll find a treasure of features hidden within paragraph text, as described in the paragraphs that follow.

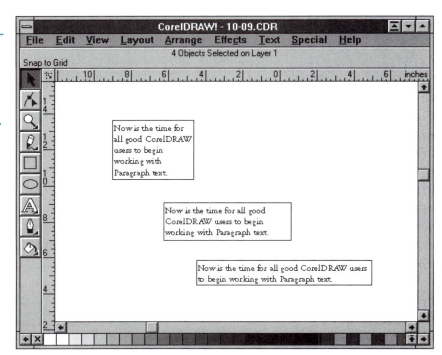

10.9

Dragging the selection handles of paragraph text affects the flow, not the size, of the text.

Faster Redraw

Paragraph text is much faster on the redraw than artistic text. When you change typeface, style, or size, paragraph text adjusts almost instantaneously, while artistic text has to think about it for several seconds. For more detail on the relative performance of paragraph and artistic text, see Chapter 13, "Putting Pedal to Metal."

Much Larger Capacity

Paragraph text is not limited by its nodes, but by its characters. Actually, paragraph text is not much "limited" at all; each paragraph can hold upwards of 4,000 characters, and a frame of text can hold 850 paragraphs.

Better Text Control

Paragraph text offers the kinds of controls you would expect to find in a program that supports large quantities of text. You can set tabs and indents; create left and right margins; set space above and below a paragraph and between the lines of a paragraph; and attach bullet characters to the beginnings of paragraphs. All of this is done through the network of dialogs under the Paragraph option in the Text roll-up, all shown in Figure 10.10. These are not related subdialogs; rather, the dialog has a different page for each of the tabs that appear at the top. All four dialogs emanate from the Paragraph button. (Be sure to appreciate our little emanation lines in the figure, which we spent hours perfecting.)

The Spacing Page This page provides controls for space between characters, words, lines within a paragraph (leading), and space above and below paragraphs (remember, you can have many paragraphs within one frame of text). Alignment controls and hyphenation are here, also.

The Tabs Page These controls work like every other tab function known to computingkind. New to 5.0 are the on-screen rulers and tabs that allow you to adjust tabs and margins interactively.

10.10

The new tabbed dialogs for controlling paragraph text

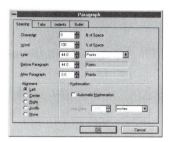

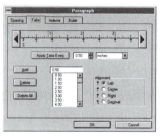

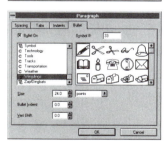

The Indents Page Here you'll find some functions that are a bit curious, requiring five minutes of fiddling. Right Margin is simple, obediently shifting the text in from the right edge of the frame by a specified amount. But First Line, Rest of Lines, and Left Margin are closely interrelated.

If all you want is a simple indent, then just set a value for First Line and be done with it (or just use the on-screen controls, which are explained later in this chapter). However, if you want all of the text moved in from the left margin, or if you want a so-called hanging indent (also known as an outdent), in which subsequent lines are indented from the first line, then you'll need to understand how these three controls interrelate.

When you set a value for Left Margin, it has top priority—the other two controls cannot be set for anything less than the Left Margin's value. In fact, when you enter the Left Margin value, DRAW automatically adds it to First Line and Rest of Lines. If you want the first line indented in addition to whatever margin you have set, then you increase the First Line value. If you want to set a hanging indent, increase the Rest of Lines value.

Figure 10.11 offers a few simple examples of some Indents settings and their results. The shaded rectangles behind the text indicate the boundary of the text frame, so you can see the operation of the Left Margin controls.

The Bullet Page   This set of controls enables you to precede any paragraph with a bullet. Many characters are available to use as the bullets, including such absurdities as those shown in Figure 10.10. In a more sensible vein, you can set standard bullets, as in Figure 10.12.

NEW FOR 5

Corel has listened to those of you who grumbled out loud about not being able to use Zapf Dingbat characters to set bullets. If you have the Zapf Dingbats typeface installed in your system, it shows up in the list of available bullet faces. Even if you didn't have Zapf Dingbat before, you'll inherit a TrueType version of the character set when you install 5.0.

10.11

Controlling margins and indents is not immediately intuitive, but eminently learnable.

> Lorum ipsum dolor sit amet, con; minimum venami quis nostrud laboris nisi ut aliquip ex ea com color in reprehenderit in voluptate

> Lorum ipsum dolor sit amet, con; minimum venami quis nostrud laboris nisi ut aliquip ex ea com color in reprehenderit in

> Lorum ipsum dolor sit amet, con; minimum venami quis nostrud laboris nisi ut aliquip ex ea com color in reprehenderit in

> Lorum ipsum dolor sit amet, con; minimum venami quis nostrud laboris nisi ut aliquip ex ea com color in reprehenderit in

Curiously, one command was left out of the network of Paragraph dialogs and banished to its own lonely dialog: To set the number of columns in a frame and the space in between, choose Text / Frame or click on the Frame button on the roll-up, to get the Frame dialog.

10.12

There's more than one way to create bulleted paragraphs.

- This paragraph is set with its bullet at the left margin, and all other text indented in.

- This paragraph is set without any additional indent, so the bullet seems to just be the beginning of the paragraph.

  - This paragraph is set with an extreme indent, so as to emphatically call attention to the text.

Irregular Text Wrapping

At long last, DRAW 4.0 brought us text wrapping in and around objects. Though not as automatic as some users might like—it's a two-step process—it nonetheless works quickly and easily. The essential gateway for wrapping text both around and inside of objects is the evolution of Envelope to support frames of paragraph text, not just the text itself. Figure 10.13 shows both effects in action: At the top, the text is wrapped around the circle, and below, the text is fitted inside the circle.

Navigating Your Way

We remember a time when the only thing you could do in DRAW while your cursor was in a line of text was type. With version 5.0, you might almost be fooled into thinking you're in your word processor, what with all of the editing, formatting, and navigating commands now at hand. Here is a short laundry list.

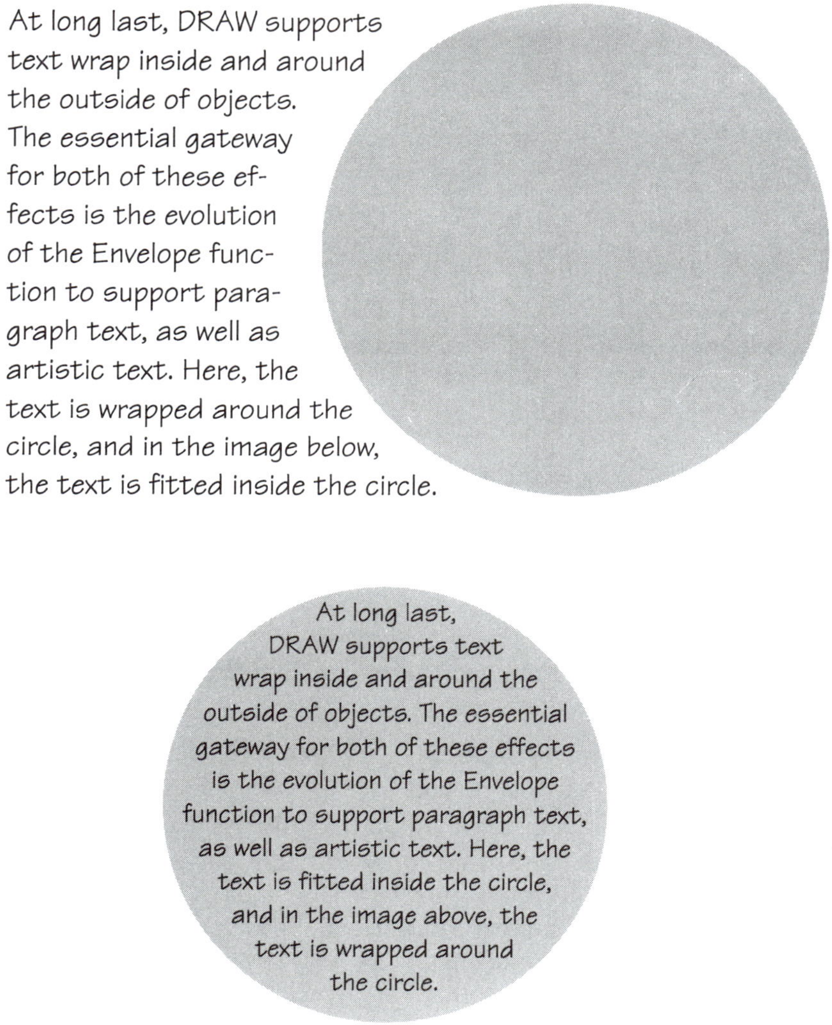

10.13

As of DRAW 4.0, you can wrap text around and inside an object.

At long last, DRAW supports text wrap inside and around the outside of objects. The essential gateway for both of these effects is the evolution of the Envelope function to support paragraph text, as well as artistic text. Here, the text is wrapped around the circle, and in the image below, the text is fitted inside the circle.

At long last, DRAW supports text wrap inside and around the outside of objects. The essential gateway for both of these effects is the evolution of the Envelope function to support paragraph text, as well as artistic text. Here, the text is fitted inside the circle, and in the image above, the text is wrapped around the circle.

On-Screen Controls   It wasn't too long ago that DRAW didn't even have tabs; now there is an almost-full-featured tab settings dialog, and fast and friendly on-screen controls in the ruler. As Figure 10.14 shows, when your cursor is in a frame of paragraph text, you can change tabs (the arrows in the ruler), indents (the small triangles), and margins (the square brackets), just by dragging them to a different position. Tabs, margins, and indents are only relevant for paragraph text.

10.14

On-screen controls make paragraph formatting much easier. (Note: We've misspelled a couple of words here intentionally to set up the topic of the next section.)

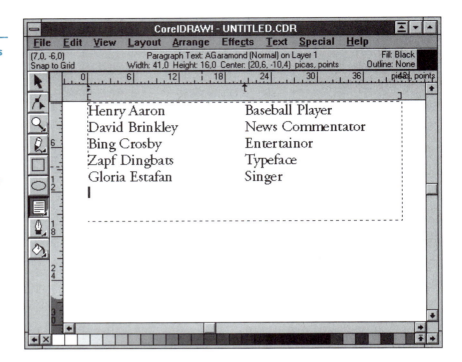

Spell Checking   We used to laugh at DRAW's Spell Check; now we actually use it. Figure 10.15 shows its friendly interface in the process of catching a typo in the celebrity list from Figure 10.14. Too bad it can't detect errors in proper names, too—even famous ones like Gloria's...

Justification of Artistic Text   Artistic text does not automatically break to the next line when it reaches the right margin. That's because

10.15

The more you use DRAW for text, the more you will take advantage of Spell Check.

there *is* no right margin. Since a string of artistic text may continue well past the point where it would fall off the edge of the page, conventional justification has never been supported in artistic text. DRAW 5.0, however, provides a different kind of justification, known as *forced justification*. Here is how it works: Though it is true that there is no right margin to artistic text, if a string contains more than one line, then the line that is longest determines the de facto left and right margin. All other lines of text will be spread out so that they span the entire distance from the beginning to the end of that longest line.

This is easier to demonstrate than to explain. At the top half of Figure 10.16 are six lines of artistic text, set with standard left-alignment. The second line is clearly the longest. When the same string is set justified, as shown at the bottom of the figure, all five of the other lines stretch and claw to reach the end of the second line.

10.16

The top string of text is left-aligned; the bottom is forced-justified. The longest line defines the right margin, to which all other lines must stretch.

It was a dark and stormy night.
Then a shot rang out from the deepest depths of the night.
Suddenly, a scream pierced the midnight sky,
and it became all too clear to our story's two heroes:
That this was the world's worst introduction to a novel.
The end.

It   was   a   dark   and   stormy   night.
Then a shot rang out from the deepest depths of the night.
Suddenly,   a   scream   pierced   the   midnight   sky,
and   it   became   all   too   clear   to   our   story's   two   heroes:
That   this   was   the   world's   worst   introduction   to   a   novel.
The   end.

Where might you use such a feature? Yeah, good question—we know that *use* and *misuse* are potential first cousins. The key is to use lines of text that are close to the same length to begin with; otherwise, you risk lapsing into the type of hilarity displayed in Figure 10.16. In Figure 10.17 you see a way in which we might use forced justification for a banner or placard at next year's International CorelDRAW Conference.

10.17

Forced justification works best when the lines of text are close to the same length.

Editing Controls   There was no real value to having good editing controls in DRAW 3.0 and 4.0 because, most of the time, you could not create text quickly enough to take advantage of them. Text editing in DRAW 5.0 is much faster, and it will pay off for you to practice some of the in-line editing commands that DRAW offers. Odds are, though, you already know them from the time you have put in with your word processor. Here is a summary:

What You Do	What Draw Does
Double-click	Selects the current word
Ctrl+click	Selects the current line (or paragraph, in paragraph text)
Ctrl+Right	Jumps one word to the right
Ctrl+Left	Jumps one word to the left
Home	Jumps to the beginning of the line
End	Jumps to the end of the line
Ctrl+Home	Jumps to the beginning of text string or frame

What You Do	What Draw Does
Ctrl+End	Jumps to the end of text string or frame
Shift+Right	Selects character by character to the right
Shift+Left	Selects character by character to the left
Shift+Home	Selects all text from cursor to beginning of line
Shift+End	Selects all text from cursor to end of line
Ctrl+Shift+Right	Selects word by word to the right
Ctrl+Shift+Left	Selects word by word to the left
Ctrl+Shift+Home	Selects all text from cursor to beginning of text
Ctrl+Shift+End	Selects all text from cursor to end of text

Instant Editing   Through the Special / Preferences / General / Right Mouse Button control, you can set your secondary mouse button (SMB) to take you directly to the Edit Text dialog or to the Character Attributes dialog. Adding to the efficiency of this shortcut is the fact that you don't have to have your cursor touching the text. It can be way on the other side of the screen—as long as the text is selected, one click of the SMB takes you directly into the dialog of your choice.

Artistic or Paragraph?

In some cases, it doesn't matter whether you choose artistic or paragraph text to set type. A standard headline of three or four words at the top of a newsletter is going to look fine regardless of which mode you use to create it. Other times, however, your decision will be crucial to your work flow. Here are our rules of thumb.

When to Use Artistic Text

- When you resize, stretch, and skew: Artistic text can easily be scaled and stretched—you just tug at the selection handles. (Paragraph text can only be resized from the roll-up or dialog, and cannot be stretched or skewed at all.)

- When you mirror, extrude, envelope, or change perspective: These are effects that can be applied to artistic text only. Look again at Figure 10.13 to see how paragraph text can be redirected with the Envelope function; when used with artistic text, Envelope actually bends the characters.

- For editing character shapes: If you want to change the very shape of text characters by converting them to curves and then editing the nodes, you must use artistic text. If you try to choose Arrange / Convert to Curves when working with paragraph text, DRAW just ignores you. In Chapter 11, we will take apart some characters and edit their shapes.

When to Use Paragraph Text

- To set large blocks of copy: As appropriate as artistic text is for the headline to an article, so is paragraph text perfect for the article itself. Paragraph text has a capacity of thousands of characters and hundreds of individual paragraphs, and you can create pages and pages of text.

- To control text flow: Paragraph text can flow from frame to frame and from page to page. Also, you can easily change the length of each line, thanks to the word wrapping used by paragraph text. (The only way to end a line of artistic text is to use a carriage return.)

- To control the baselines of text: We haven't mentioned this yet, but a handy use for paragraph text arises when you want to set text along an angle. Figure 10.18 shows how each type of text responds to a 30% skew, horizontal (above) and vertical (below). With artistic text, the characters themselves skew; with paragraph text, the baseline skews.

10.18

Skewing text produces profoundly different results with artistic and paragraph text.

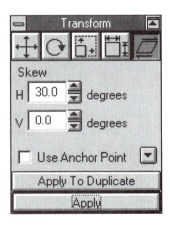

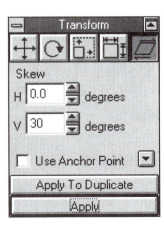

Switching from One to the Other

What happens when you create text in one form and discover that you really need it to be in the other? Would that there were a command to instantly convert artistic text to paragraph, and vice versa. The best we can do is show you how to make the switch without having to reenter the text.

To convert text from artistic to paragraph:

1. Use the Text tool to highlight all of the text.
2. Choose Edit / Cut (or Ctrl+X) to cut the text to the Clipboard.
3. Create a frame with the Paragraph tool, and with the cursor blinking at the top, choose Edit / Paste (or Ctrl+V).

Converting in the other direction, from paragraph to artistic, is handled in the same way—by going through the Clipboard.

Remember the Hotkeys

These shortcuts can make text creation much easier: Press F8 and click once to create artistic text; press Shift+F8 and click once to create paragraph text. You don't have to drag a marquee to create paragraph text—if you have a shape in mind for your paragraph, then go ahead and create the marquee. If not, just click once and let DRAW create a default rectangular shape. You can always change it later.

INSIDE INFO

If you have text currently selected, you can press the appropriate hotkey—F8 for artistic, Shift+F8 for paragraph—and immediately get a text cursor at the end of the line. This is undoubtedly the easiest way to edit text. With one hand on the mouse and the other on the keyboard, select the text, press the hotkey, and you're ready to type.

Follow the simplest of strategies—to use artistic text for display type, and paragraph text for body copy—and you will probably be correct 80 percent of the time. In the next chapter, we'll let artistic and paragraph text run wild. Please wear your seat belts.

CHAPTER 11

Fun with Text

ELEVEN

CHAPTER 11

If you are hoping for one unifying theme to bring together all of the topics in this chapter, we should warn you that the chapter's title is as close as you'll get. As we pulled out that overstuffed file from our desk, entitled "Miscellaneous Text Stuff," we knew this chapter would wander from one idea to the next. One of the tips, about producing embossed text, has been on our "to be written" schedule since Version 2.0 of DRAW.

This chapter doesn't need (deserve?) any more introduction than this. From the first topic to the last, our collective stream of consciousness was our guide. It was our most enjoyable chapter. Dollars to donuts it'll be yours, too…

Shaping Text Around Objects

For years, ever since they saw it showing up in competing software, DRAW users have been clamoring for the ability to shape a paragraph of text around an object—and it arrived with version 4.0. Other programs handle it more automatically than DRAW; nonetheless, DRAW's support for placing text both around and inside of an object is more than adequate.

AUTHOR'S NOTE

UPGRADING FROM VERSION 3? Text can now flow around or inside of an object of any shape. When the text is paragraph text, DRAW allows you to node-edit the frame and completely reshape it. The text doesn't change; the shape of the frame does.

Figure 11.1 is a simple drawing that incorporates the two standard methods of enveloping paragraph text. The paragraph on top is shaped around the horn, and the paragraph below is shaped inside of the piano. Here is a recounting of how we produced this page. You can follow along by opening ENVTEXT1.CDR from the Companion CD, or you can open ENVTEXT2.CDR to study the finished piece.

11.1

This drawing contains text fit around an object, and text fit inside an object.

AUTHOR'S NOTE

ENVTEXT2.CDR is saved with a PowerClip; to get at the component parts, select it and go to Effects / PowerClips / Extract Contents. In either file, ENVTEXT1 or ENVTEXT2, the paragraphs are set in Times Roman; you can have DRAW substitute Times New Roman, if necessary.

1. First, we browsed the on-line Symbols library in search of good curves. From the Music section, we found No. 37 (the horn), No. 75 (the piano), and from MusicalSymbols, No. 38 (the treble clef).

2. Next, we positioned the objects on screen, placed the headline at the top, and fitted a fountain-filled rectangle in the back. We imported both text items and placed them on the sidelines. We set both frames of text for automatic hyphenation with a .25 hot zone (which means any text coming within .25 inch of the margin is eligible for hyphenation). *Hint:* The more hyphenation, the better the fit of the text around the curve. Figure 11.2 shows our screen at the point when we were ready to begin enveloping.

3. For the text on the top, we carefully positioned the top and the left side of the frame, since those sides would stay fixed through the envelope operation. We adjusted the right side so that it would represent the farthest point across the frame to which the text could flow. We did the same thing for the text along the bottom side, and our screen looked like Figure 11.3.

4. In studying the curvature of the horn, we found that there is only one change in direction in the entire shape. It is a very subtle shift in the angle of inflection, highlighted in Figure 11.4. That is the only point along the curve where we needed to place a node.

5. Then we invoked the Envelope roll-up, clicked on the Add New button and the Node Edit icon (the rightmost one). Of the four in the middle of the roll-up, the Node Edit icon provides the most flexibility,

Shaping Text Around Objects **301**

11.2

All of the design elements are in place; let the enveloping begin.

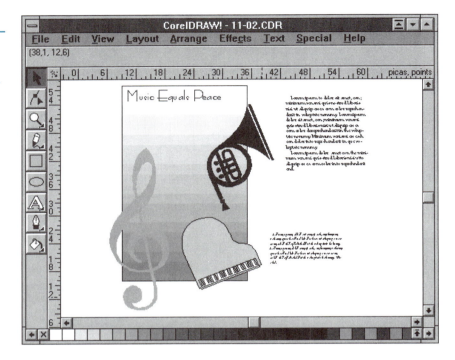

11.3

The top, left, and bottom sides of the frame won't change. All of the enveloping will occur on the right, around the horn.

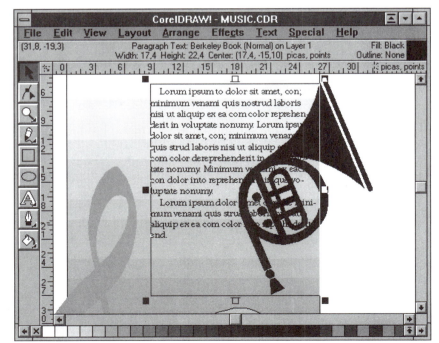

11.4

The highlight shows the one spot where the curve changes direction. That's where the node goes.

allowing editing of the frame just like any other curve. You can adjust nodes in any fashion, add new ones, and change them to and from lines and curves.

6. We dragged the right-side node to the point of inflection, and invoked the Node Edit roll-up in order to convert the node to a cusp node. Then we began shaping the curve of the frame around the horn. We tugged and pulled on the various control points, nudged here and there, and gradually succeeded in fitting the frame around the horn. We knew that we didn't have to get it precisely right, because the text wasn't going to go to the very edge anyway. We clicked Apply, and our screen looked like Figure 11.5.

7. We saved, and scrolled down to study the next one—the text in the piano. In this case, we intended to create an envelope from an existing shape, using the Create From button. The first thing we noticed was that the piano is a compound object, consisting of two combined curves. No good—interior enveloping requires a single curve. So we had to break

11.5

Halfway done

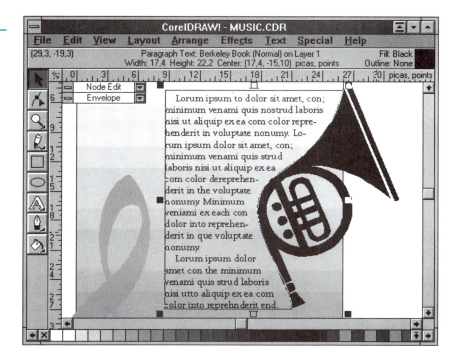

apart the piano to separate out the two objects (and then were careful not to move one without the other). Our next challenge was that we wanted the piano to hang off the drawing, so we needed to shape the text frame so that the text wouldn't flow off the drawing with the piano.

8. We clicked on Create From and then Apply, and the frame instantly took on the shape of the piano, as shown in Figure 11.6.

9. Then we reached for the Pick tool, and with the text already selected, we Shift+selected the piano. Then we went to Arrange / Align and placed the text directly on top of the piano. (Because we selected the text first and the piano second, the text moved and the piano stayed still.)

10. As expected, the text filled the entire piano, including the part that hangs off the edge of the drawing. At this point, we had to get aggressive with the Node Edit tools. We deleted several of the nodes along the right side of the frame, and converted others to line segments. Then we found the lower-left node and dragged it up over the piano's keyboard.

11.6

Two clicks, and the text looks like a grand piano.

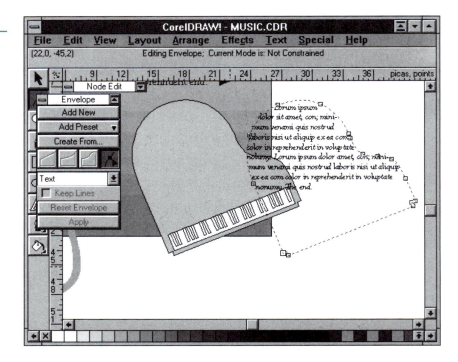

We clicked Apply from the Envelope roll-up, and our screen looked like Figure 11.7. (Notice that both roll-ups are on screen; this procedure requires regular use of both.)

11. Just one more thing to do: At this point, the text flowed all the way out to the edge of the piano—that's bad form. We needed to move the text in a bit. At first we thought we would have to reshape the frame all over again, tugging and pulling at each node to move it in from the piano. Then we realized we were still working with a frame of paragraph text, which is subject to all of the controls in the Paragraph dialog, including margins.

12. For the top margin, we simply added an extra carriage return and formatted it with about 8 points of extra space. For the sides, we went to the Indents page of the Paragraph dialog, and set left and right margins of 1 pica each. That was too much, so we backed off to 6 points each. But that didn't push the first line far enough away from the top of the piano, where it begins to curve inward. So we cheated—we dropped

11.7

This modified shape keeps the text from flowing outside of the drawing or into the piano keys.

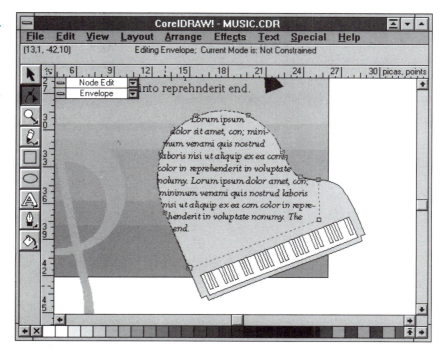

our text cursor in front of the first character and spaced it over. In the case of text enveloping, the end definitely justifies the means, as you can see in Figure 11.8.

WATCH OUT!

Don't make the same mistake we did: If you want to go back and fine-tune the shape of an enveloped frame, DO NOT click on Add New (which is the conventional way of accessing the nodes before creating an envelope). That action will return the frame to its original shape (DRAW thinks you want to start over). Instead, activate the Shape tool, just as if you were editing an existing curve. As far as DRAW is concerned, that's exactly what you are doing—once a frame is enveloped, DRAW thinks of it as just another curve. Only when you are done with node editing should you reach for the Envelope roll-up, and then only to click Apply.

11.8

The finished product of making text flow inside an object and adjusting the margins to fit.

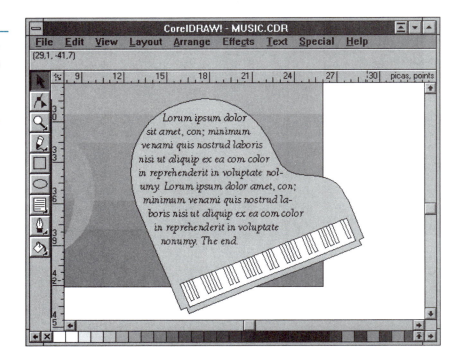

Our final move was to mask all of the objects so that they appeared cut off at the edge of the drawing, just as you did with the snowboarder drawing in Chapter 5. Only this time, we used DRAW 5.0's new Power-Clips command: We selected all of the objects in the drawing except for the background, went to Effects / PowerClips / Paste Inside Container, and then clicked once on the background. You'll be reading a lot more about PowerClips later in this chapter and in Chapter 19.

Creating Embossed Text

Practically every CorelDRAW book on the market includes a tutorial on producing embossed text—the effect shown in Figure 11.9, in which the text appears to be raised off the page. (The black and white highlights are what provide the depth.) We don't pretend to have invented this technique, and we suspect that you have seen it elsewhere and perhaps even produced it. We include the discussion of it here because it is great practice for using hotkeys. In fact, we would argue that producing this embossed text is easy if you know your way around the keyboard, but close to impossible if you don't.

11.9

Creating embossed text involves knowing your hotkeys.

To follow along with this next exercise, open EMBOSS.CDR from the PRACTICE directory on the Companion CD. Figure 11.10 shows your starting point. The typeface is Helvetica Black, and the characters have been

11.10

The four main ingredients for creating embossed text

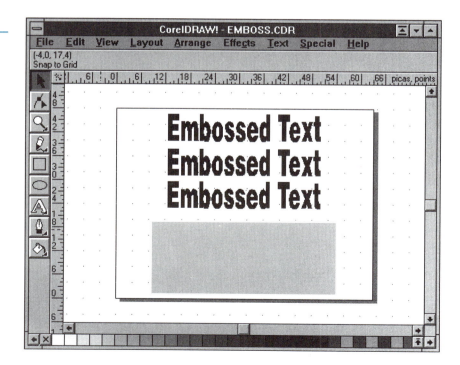

stretched vertically. Though not essential to the task, we converted the text to curves so that your screen will look similar to ours, and you won't have to bother with installing a typeface you might not have.

Two actions are crucial to this procedure: Nudge and the Tab key. As objects overlap (which they soon will), the only way you will be able to pick out individual ones will be with the Tab key, and the only way to reliably move them is with Nudge.

AUTHOR'S NOTE

We suggest that before you start this activity, you go to Special / Preferences / General / Undo and set an Undo level of about 8. That way, it will be easy for you to retrace and repeat your steps with Ctrl+Z. In order to analyze a particular action, you can do it, undo it with Ctrl+Z, redo it with Alt+Enter, and keep rocking back and forth until you understand the dynamics of each move.

Here are the essential steps for creating the embossed text sample:

1. Open EMBOSS.CDR, and make sure that your status line is visible (Special / Preferences / View / Show Status Line).

2. Select the top "Embossed Text" text string and change its color to 20% black, the same color as the background rectangle. If you are using the default CORELDRW.CPL palette, you should be able to pick out 20% black from the on-screen palette. Otherwise, you can go to Uniform Fill, or even use the Copy Attributes From command to clone the shade of the rectangle.

3. Leave the middle text string black, and change the bottom one to white, using either the palette or the Fill flyout.

4. Drag a marquee across all three text strings. (Even though the third one is invisible against the white page, you can still select it. Your selection handles and the status line will confirm that you have selected all three.)

5. Choose Arrange / Align and center the text strings both horizontally and vertically. Press F4 to zoom, and your screen will look like Figure 11.11.

6. With the three text strings still selected, hold Shift and select the rectangle, too.

7. With all four objects selected, repeat the center and middle alignment (if you haven't issued any other commands since the one in Step 5, you can just press Ctrl+R to repeat it).

At this point, your text will be completely invisible—the 20% black rectangle covers the 20% black text, which in turn covers the other text strings. If it weren't for the Tab key, it would be virtually impossible to individually select the text strings; but with Tab, it's easy. Try it now: Press Tab several times, and watch how your screen reacts. Your visual cue is the right side of the status line, which flashes the color of the selected object; that will be your guide as you complete this job.

Three strings of text rolled into one

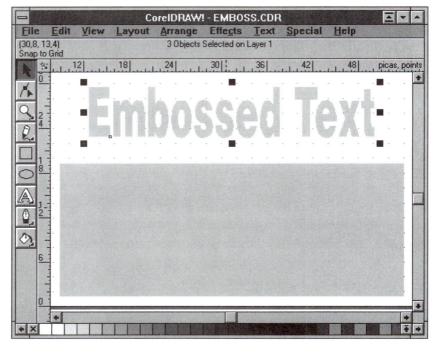

8. Go to Special / Preferences / General / Nudge and set the Nudge value to 1 point.
9. Press Tab until the status line indicates that you have selected the black string of text. This is the text that should be moved down and to the right.
10. Press the Down Arrow twice and Right Arrow twice. Thanks to Nudge, you have insured against any extraneous motion—just 2 points down and 2 to the right. Press F4 to zoom in closer, and what you'll see will look like Figure 11.12.

The shadow of the text takes shape...

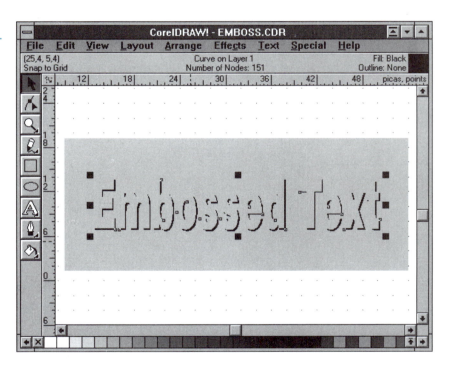

11. Press Tab until you have selected the white string of text.
12. Nudge that text twice to the left and then twice upward.
13. Press Esc to clear the selection, Ctrl+W to redraw the screen (if necessary) and you're done—does your screen look like Figure 11.13?

11.13

Now the text appears raised.

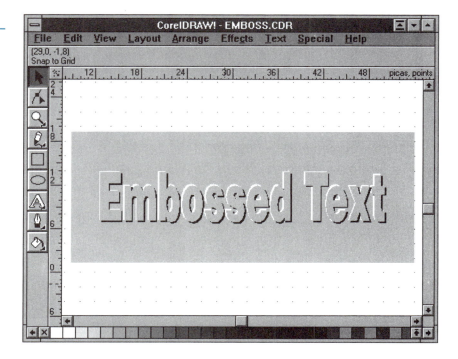

As with any other recipe, use Nudge according to taste. If you want more shadows visible, you might nudge the white and black strings by 3 points instead of 2. For just a sliver of a shadow, try 1 point.

We do not consider creating embossed text to be an advanced or complicated procedure for DRAW users, but we want to reemphasize how difficult this would be without the keystrokes. Imagine selecting individual strings of the overlapping text with the mouse; and once you do manage to select one of them, think about having to move it in tiny but precise increments. Without the keyboard, these tasks would probably earn you a case of arthritis...not to mention teach you a few choice words.

The CorelDRAW Squeeze Play

Here is another technique guaranteed to make your time in front of the computer marginally more amusing. Who knows—you might even find a legitimate use for this one... Figure 11.14 shows the effect of the

Squeeze Play: All the characters appear to melt together. As with embossed text, this is not difficult to re-create, as long as you know to use one important but infrequently used function of DRAW.

11.14

This effect requires one little command. Do you know which one?

First, set up a line of artistic text, and choose a nice fat typeface. (We chose the Type 1 face Helvetica Black; DRAW includes several similar faces in its library.) Enlarge it to about 100 points, choose a light color or shade of gray for the interior, and then add a very thick Outline Pen, say 12 points. We chose to shade the outline 50% black; you can choose any dark color, including solid black. The Uniform Fill (Shift+F11) and Outline Pen (F12) dialogs are the places to go for these tasks. At this point, your text will look quite hideous, as shown in Figure 11.15.

11.15

Ugh!

Now you're going to make this text look even worse, by smashing all of the letters together. To do this, change to the Shape tool and move the funny-looking arrow at the end of the text to the left. Keep going until every character overlaps its neighbor, as shown in Figure 11.16. You could also do this by entering a value in Text / Character / Character. With our 100-point type, we arrived at a Character value of −28.

11.16

Even worse!

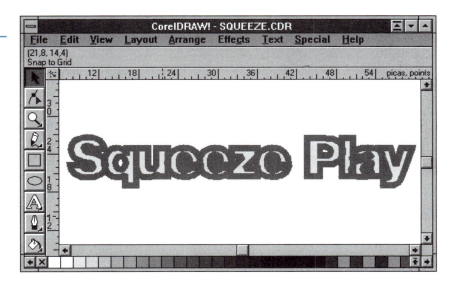

However atrocious your screen might look, DRAW is behaving normally, placing outlines in front of fill patterns by default. However, as long as the large outline sits on top of the text, the result is never going to look good. Your task is to place the outline *behind* the fill, and that is precisely the name of the command that you will use. Return to the Pick tool and reselect the text. Then press F12 to open the Outline Pen dialog, and check the box that says Behind Fill. What a difference! Now the outline draws first and the fill draws afterward, producing the look that you're after.

All that's left for you to do is make sure that each letter touches the one to its right. Use the Shape tool and kern the characters until they all touch; when you're done, your screen should look like Figure 11.17.

11.17

With the outline behind the fill and certain characters kerned, this text just melts together.

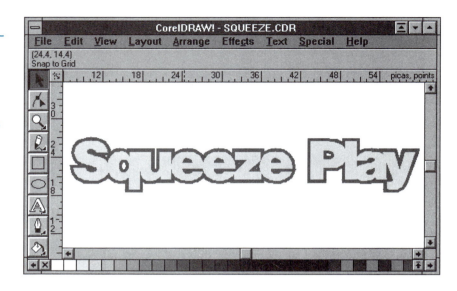

Creating a Text Mask

DRAW 5.0 has an automatic masking feature, called PowerClips. In addition, you can create masks by combining two objects together (what we think of as the old-fashioned way). In the following exercises, you will use both methods of creating a mask, because we think it is important to understand the fundamentals of masking.

One more comment to preface this discussion of masks: It's only here in "Fun with Text" because we are using a string of text as our example; you can use masking—both techniques—with nontext objects, as well. (In fact, truth be told, the string of text you'll be working with here has already been converted to curves, so there…)

Now let's talk about this word, *mask*. We suspect that accomplished artists use the term when they want to intimidate us amateurs. "Oh, we'll just mask off that image, cut an overlay, and place it in the background." Yeah, right—and then we'll call NASA and discuss liquid fuel burn ratios. To understand masking, think of it literally, like a Halloween mask—an object with holes, through which elements behind the mask are visible.

Open ALBERT.CDR from the Companion CD, and you'll see a block of text and a picture of Albert Einstein. Your objective in this exercise is not just to place the text in front of Einstein, but actually to hide Einstein behind it, so that he is peeking through. We remind you of the comparison we drew in Chapter 4: It helps to think of DRAW's Combine and PowerClips commands as giant cookie cutters. The object in front is the cookie cutter, and the one in back is the dough. The cookie cutter slices into and creates a hole in the dough. And so it is with combining and clipping. You will see this phenomenon in action shortly.

Combining Two Objects

The traditional method of creating a mask has been by combining two objects together. Even with DRAW 5.0's new PowerClips command available, you should know how the Arrange / Combine command operates.

1. Draw a rectangle around the letters E=MC^2 (see Figure 11.18). Size the rectangle so that its top is above Einstein's head and its bottom is below the bottom of the picture, as shown in the figure. (On our screen, we turned off the page border by going to Layout / Page Setup / Display and unchecking Show Page Border. You might want to do the same.)

2. Select both the rectangle and the text by dragging a marquee around them both, or by clicking on the rectangle and then Shift+clicking on the text. Your status line will confirm that you have two objects selected.

3. Go to Arrange / Combine and turn these two objects into one (Figure 11.19).

There are three things we want to point out at this stage:

- The status line in Figure 11.19 now says "Curve on Layer 1," instead of "2 Objects Selected." The two objects are now one object.

- Figure 11.19 shows a black rectangle with white lettering; yours might be all white with only a black outline. That's okay—it just means that you selected the text first and the rectangle next,

11.18

The text and the rectangle are the two raw ingredients of the mask.

11.19

When these two objects are combined, a hole is created where the objects overlap.

before combining. When you combine objects into one, they are given a single outline and a single fill, which they inherit from the object that was selected last. To turn the combined curve black, simply change its fill to black.

■ The white lettering in the rectangle is not a white fill, but rather a *hole in the rectangle*—and this is an important distinction. When we demonstrate this technique live at CorelDRAW seminars, we create a small circle, move it to the back, and nudge it across the screen. The circle peeks through the text as it travels across, emphasizing that objects behind the mask do become visible. Figure 11.20 shows how a circle traveling behind the mask peeks through the holes cut out by the text.

11.20

Pass an object underneath a mask and you'll see that the white space is not solid white, but hollow.

Now we have two collective objects: the mask on the right, and the picture of Einstein, which is composed of 165 objects in one group. If you were to place Einstein behind the mask, he would peek through just as the circles did. Here goes:

4. Select the mask and move it to the front (Shift+PgUp). Then Shift+select Einstein (status line: "2 Objects Selected").

5. Go to Arrange / Align and click on both Center buttons. OK the dialog, and press F4 to zoom in. (You'll want to zoom in or out with F4 as needed throughout these steps.) Your screen should look like Figure 11.21.

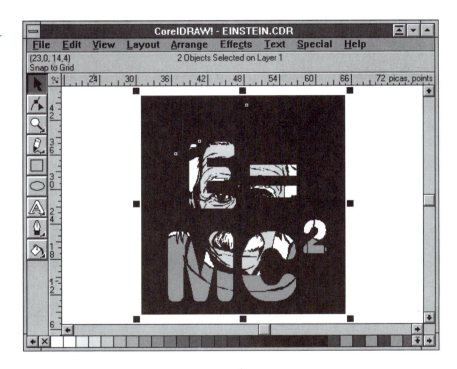

11.21

Einstein peeks through his famous formula.

To complete the effect, select the mask and turn its fill pattern from solid black to solid white, using the on-screen palette or the Fill flyout. Remember the difference between *white* and *hollow:* The area that is filled (the cookie dough) is opaque, regardless of its color. The hole that the cookie cutter produced is open, so the picture underneath shows through, as shown in Figure 11.22.

Creating a Text Mask **319**

11.22

The completed effect of combining two objects (text and a rectangle) and placing a third object (Einstein) in the back

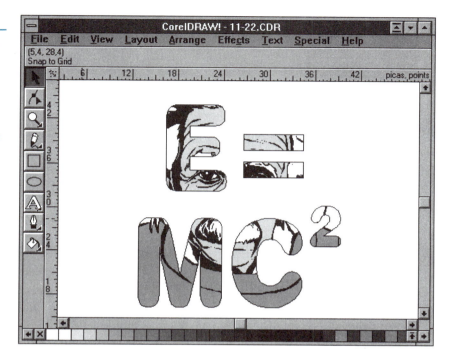

AUTHOR'S NOTE

If you want to save your revised picture of Einstein, remember to use the Save As command and designate a directory on your hard drive. CDs are read-only, so you won't be able to issue the simple Save command.

Using PowerClips

This exciting new feature of 5.0 greatly streamlines the process of masking one object with another, by eliminating the need for the third object. You won't always want to use PowerClips (see "Rules of Thumb for PowerClips" later in this section), but our Einstein illustration is an ideal case.

1. First, one important housekeeping chore: Go to Special / Preferences / General and find the Auto-Center Place Inside field. Make sure that it is unchecked. We'll explain this one shortly.
2. Reopen ALBERT.CDR from the Companion CD.
3. Select both objects and align them on top of each other (Arrange / Align / Center Vertically & Center Horizontally), and then zoom in.

Your initial task here is one of refinement: to make sure that both of Einstein's eyes are visible in the finished picture. You'll need to think in reverse for this—that is, the only parts of Einstein that will eventually show are those that are currently obscured by the text. Try this:

4. Press Esc to clear the selection, and then reselect the text.
5. Move the text down until Einstein's right eye is covered by the bottom part of the *E*. To insure against unwanted lateral movement, use nudge to move the text down, or hold Ctrl while moving (Ctrl+drag permits motion only in up-and-down or side-to-side directions).

In order to cover Einstein's left eye with the equal sign, you have two options: (1) using the Shape tool, select the nodes of the equal sign and move them down; or (2) using the Pick tool, skew the entire string of text down. We have chosen the second option for you, because we believe the skewing of the text does not detract from the illustration, and in fact, adds an interesting element.

6. Select the text, if necessary, and then click again on it to get the rotation handles.
7. Move to the middle handle on the right side (next to the ^{2}), and drag it down. Keep dragging until the equal sign covers Einstein's left eye. Your screen should look like Figure 11.23.
8. Select Einstein, and go to Effects / PowerClips / Place Inside Container. The arrow that appears is your prompt to choose the container.
9. Move the arrow to the text and click once.

11.23

Now that the mask has been positioned, we're ready to PowerClip it.

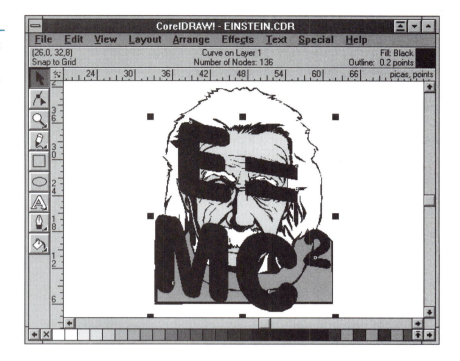

Now the PowerClips function takes over, studying the shape of the container and clipping the picture so that only the parts that overlap the container remain visible. The rest of the picture seems to vanish. Figure 11.24 shows what the final printout would look like. You can read much more about PowerClips in Chapter 19.

Beware of Auto-Place Center Inside Earlier we asked you to go to Preferences and uncheck the curiously named Auto-Place Center Inside check box. When that option is turned on, DRAW automatically centers the image in the container. If you hadn't turned it off, it would have dashed all of your careful efforts to line up Einstein's eyes with the text.

Early feedback is telling us that most DRAW users prefer to keep that option turned off, for precisely the same reasons that you needed to here.

11.24

The finished picture: Einstein has been PowerClipped into his own famous equation for mass and energy.

INSIDE INFO

You probably experienced significant delays waiting for PowerClips to calculate and render your illustration. We have observed that containers made of combined objects slow down the clipping process, as compared to containers that are made of grouped objects. You can see this for yourself by doing the following: Undo the PowerClip (Effects / PowerClip / Extract Contents); select the text and break apart the pieces (Arrange / Break Apart); immediately group them (Arrange / Group); and then select Einstein and repeat the PowerClipping procedure. It should go more quickly this time.

Rules of Thumb for PowerClips

PowerClipping is faster than Combine in creating a mask, but it slows down the works from that point on. Consider it a finishing tool: When you are all done with the image and ready to frame it or contain it, use PowerClips. In fact, we suggested this back in Chapter 5—framing the snowboarder is an ideal time to use PowerClips.

On the other hand, editing the contents within a PowerClipped object is not easy at all, requiring you to enter a special PowerClips editing mode. If it is important that you mask off an object during the middle of a project, you might prefer to use the traditional masking method (with Arrange / Combine), because it provides complete access to the objects that are underneath. That, coupled with the performance hit exacted by PowerClipping, suggests that this tool is best used in the later stages of a project.

Importing Text from Other Programs

Most of the time when DRAW users reach for the Import command, it is for the purpose of incorporating other art into their work. But you can also import text—lots of it, in fact—into a drawing. DRAW can accept large text files in one gulp, it can accept text across the Clipboard, and it can accept text directly into the Edit Text dialog. You can also embed a text object from an OLE-compliant word processor (we'll translate that into English in a moment).

Most of this import/export business is covered in Part VI, "The CorelDRAW Freeway." Our interest here is in determining how intelligent DRAW is in receiving formatted text from other sources. Figure 11.25 shows a simple word-processed letter from a bureaucratic department you should hope never to encounter. The letter contains a variety of small formatting requirements, including

- The company name set in Helvetica Black
- A Dingbat character between the phone and fax numbers
- The body of the letter set in Times Roman
- The dollar amount in the first paragraph, set in bold
- The department's threat of torture set in secret code, using the Symbol typeface
- Wilma's signature in a handwriting face called Briquet

11.25

How accurately can DRAW digest these formatting requirements?

Office of Lost Wages

555 Poverty Lane, Homeless BK 00000
(211) 555-0000 ♦ (211) 555-0001 - fax

Dear Friend:

We are aware of your recent downturn in luck at the gaming tables in Reno and Lake Tahoe. And we agree that if that dealer had only turned up a 7 instead of an 8 on that last hand, you would be cruising the Mexican Riviera right about now. We will look into your allegations of dealing from the bottom of the deck, but in the meantime, you must make arrangements to repay the **$27,500** debt that you have accrued.

If you are unable to do so, then we will have no alternative but to στριγ ψου υπ βψ ψουρ τηυμβσ οϖερ α χλιϕϕ ανδ σειζε ψουρ ηομε ανδ αλλ οϕ ιτσ χοντεντσ.

Yours Truly,

Wilma Banquerupt

Wilma Banquerupt,
Collections Specialist

We sent this letter out of two different word processors, and also copied it to the Clipboard. In DRAW, we imported the word processing versions and then pasted the text from the Clipboard. Figure 11.26 shows our success, or relative lack thereof. The imports from Word for Windows and WordPerfect for Windows yielded results that were close to identical, so we don't make the distinction here.

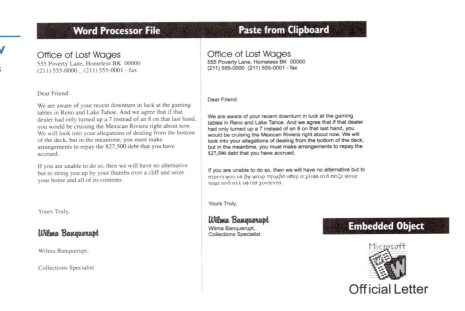

11.26

Results in DRAW are mixed in this Second Annual Import Test.

Let's analyze what happened. First, from neither the word processing file nor the Clipboard paste did DRAW pick up the Helvetica Black company name or the little Dingbat character between the phone and fax numbers (although in the word processor file it got replaced with an underline character). The word processor file has the body typeface correct, and the Clipboard paste picked up the boldface dollar amount. But DRAW didn't pick up the line spacing and neglected to honor the Symbol typeface used to conceal the punishment. The signature, set in Briquet, came out fine in both imports. The bottom line: Both text blocks came into DRAW with imperfect but acceptable results, and either one would provide a better starting point for a text-based project than typing all of the text over again.

Okay, our next topic is...what? Oh, the little Microsoft icon? Oh, that's just an *embedded OLE object* with a *hotlink* back to its *server application*. Oh yeah—we promised you English, didn't we? Okay—that icon is the result of, first, choosing Edit / Insert Object in DRAW, and then opening the file in Word (or your chosen word processor). This so-called embedded object contains the entire letter, plus intelligence about which program produced it. If you double-click on the icon, Windows automatically starts Word and opens the letter. All formatting is impeccably maintained.

This, of course, serves a purpose other than having the actual text dropped on the page. If you want to include notes about a drawing or an image, you can create an embedded text object like this one. Those who want more information can double-click; those who don't, won't. Figure 11.27 shows the action, as Word pops up in its own little window right on the screen.

11.27

An embedded object can contain a link to a text file, worksheet, macro, sound file, video clip, e-mail, or about a hundred other elements from applications that play by the OLE rules.

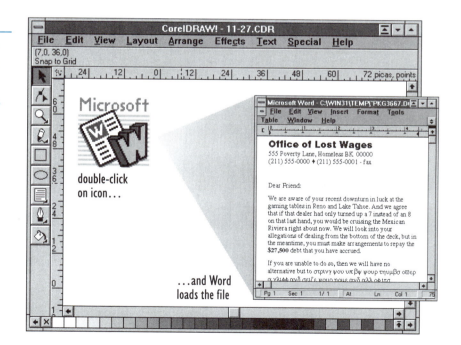

A Note about Performance   In the last edition of this book, we wrote the following about DRAW 4.0 and its efforts with multiple pages of text:

> …we imported into DRAW 4.0 the text for this chapter. DRAW automatically created enough pages to accommodate the text—11 pages in all—and all of the frames were linked together. Initial loading time was about 40 seconds total. But then we adjusted, by about 1 pica, the top margin of the frame on page 1. The text adjustment needed four minutes to ripple through all 11 pages of linked text. We shudder to think how long it would have taken had we done any real editing.

We are delighted to report that we must eat our words. This time around, we found text-flow performance to be significantly improved. We loaded an even larger file into DRAW 5.0: 38 pages of text. Load time was still about 40 seconds, but when we attempted the same 1-pica margin adjustment, the hourglass turned over only three times before presenting us with our page. We changed typefaces, sizes, leading, and left and right margins. We even searched for every occurrence of the word DRAW and replaced it with HOWDY-DOODY. The results in all cases were at nearly word-processor speed.

Fitting Text to a Path

We have reached a firm conclusion concerning the Text / Fit Text to Path command: Practically nobody knows by heart how to use it. There are competent and skilled DRAW users who produce some brilliant work with this command, but if you were to listen closely as they fine-tune an image, you'd probably hear something like this: "Okay, to move the text under the curve instead of over… Let's see, I think it's this one… No, how about this one… Well, maybe it's this one while at the same time you click here… No, how about that one… There, got it!" And just when you think you understand the interplay between the controls in the Fit Text to Path roll-up, DRAW turns your text inside-out or upside-down.

We're not going to waste a bunch of paper describing every turn taken by the Fit Text to Path command (that would not be fun, and is therefore prohibited in this chapter). But we would like to suggest a few rules of thumb and show you both good and bad examples of well-executed text fit to a path.

Choose Your Curve Wisely

Above all, text must be readable. If you lose the message in the medium, you've lost everything. A sure way to do that with the Fit Text to Path command is to choose the wrong path. If your path has sharp corners, the only way the Fit Text effect will work is if the text turns the corner between two words. Even then, you run the risk of the effect overshadowing the message.

And if you, the publisher of *Climber's Quarterly*, get the bright idea of integrating your magazine's theme with your subscription promos, we hope you already have a lot of readers. Figure 11.28 shows the disastrous results of trying to fit text to a path that is too unforgiving. Moral: When in doubt, use rounded corners, not sharp ones.

11.28

Turning sharp corners is too much to ask of fitted text.

Choose Your Type Wisely

The example in Figure 11.28 also makes the mistake of using a typeface whose characters are way too loud. If you are asking text to follow the contour of a crooked path, you need to choose a typeface with better shock absorbers than the ostentatious Expo. Figure 11.29 is marginally better because it uses a more appropriate typeface, Palatino Italic, and employs rounded hills instead of sharp peaks. We have also allowed for more space between words (Text / Paragraph / Word is set to 165%).

11.29

These rounded corners are better, but still too steep.

There is still a bad transition between *best* and *lift,* and the word *off* appears to be hanging by a thread.

Keep Your Distance

What else is wrong with these two whipping posts of examples? The text is sitting right on top of the curve—very distracting. Either the text needs to be lifted off the curve, or the curve needs to be removed altogether. In these examples, the text *is* the curve; it doesn't need any other visual help in showing the path.

Figure 11.30 shows the text being fit to the same path, only here the path is invisible. This makes for a much cleaner look and an almost acceptable product. We made some other modifications, too: We dropped the point size, changed from italic to normal, reduced the word spacing even more, and fiddled with the horizontal offset control in the Fit Text roll-up, in an attempt to rescue the word *lift*—a very difficult task, due to the word's extremely thin characters.

11.30

This text no longer needs its path—it *becomes* the path.

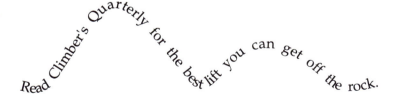

We have intentionally shown you all of the outtakes, so you can witness the typical hit-and-miss process that illustrators frequently adopt. When our lead author takes this route, he likes to call it "floundering," but we'll be more charitable with the efforts of others.

Finally, Figure 11.31 shows a nice variation, using the text orientation control on the roll-up. The vertical skew and the slight upward rotation give the impression that the letters are actually climbing up and down the slopes. By the way, even with the roll-up included in the figure, it's practically impossible for us to show or describe this text orientation control, as there are no words and no good visual clues. Here goes: "You know the first drop-down box with the fat *ABC* letters? Click it and choose the second set of fat letters." There, that's as good as it gets.

11.31

Now we're talking: This text appears to be climbing the mountain.

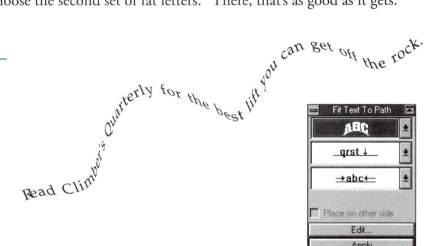

We carefully chose the foregoing example of text fitting that started out with big problems, to show you the pitfalls. Figure 11.32 shows an example that has no problems. Corel's Technical typeface is perfect for text fitting, as its letterforms are agile and appear to be walking an uneven path, anyway. Also, the tree branch in this figure is an ideal path, with smooth and friendly curves. Finally, the text is comfortably moved off the path, making for good integration between the two elements.

Working with "Untext"

What do we mean by *untext*? It's text that is no longer text, stripped of its special status by the Arrange / Convert to Curves command. When you convert text to curves, you gain access to all of its nodes and paths, just like any other type of curve. This opens the door to many fascinating

11.32
This fitted text is an unqualified success.

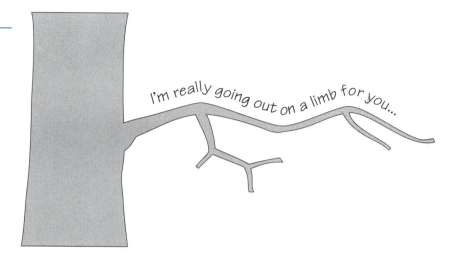

effects, with which you can personalize your text to a level beyond just what the typeface offers. The only problem is that whenever this feature is shown off in public by well-intentioned company representatives or eager users, the result always seems to look something like Figure 11.33. A guest at one of our recent seminars stood up and asked if we could show her how to use the "Text Uglifier tool," so closely identified is this tool with its potentially hideous results.

In many ways, working with converted text requires even more care than working with abstract objects, because readers know how a text character is supposed to look. If you distort a character too much, you can offend your readers' sensibilities, and if you don't change it enough, they might not notice the effect at all and decide instead that you are just using poorly crafted typefaces.

Figure 11.34 shows a couple of simple yet effective examples of text effects. What began as a string of Futura Black became four characters

11.33
The usual result of editing text that has been converted to curves

11.34

When you convert text to curves, don't think you have to do something dramatic. Usually, simpler really is better.

Futura Black Before:

After:

Erie Black Before:

After:

that stayed out in the sun too long. And Erie Black was the source for this creative logo that connects two letters together.

Finished files for all of the effects shown in the foregoing examples can be found in the PRACTICE directory on the Companion CD. Also, you'll find more discussions on text in Chapter 24, "Avoiding Design Tragedies."

Now if you'll excuse us, the fun is over and we have to get back to working—namely, with text styles (Chapter 12).

Working with Text Styles

TWELVE

CHAPTER 12

The essential operation of styles was covered in Chapter 9, "Automate!" where you learned the mechanics of creating styles, updating styles, and saving templates. You also read about the curious and often confusing behavior of templates when applied to or saved with existing files. Little that you will read here in Chapter 12 will mitigate the previous charges we have leveled against templates or, for that matter, the praise given to styles. DRAW's handling of text styles merely adds yet another wrinkle to the story.

Text styles can play an invaluable role in the production of text-intensive work, in which the rigors of text formatting and the importance of a consistent look present substantial challenges. In this chapter, we assume you have read Chapter 9 and understand DRAW's basic approach to styles. As a result, we will keep this discussion short and sweet, concentrating on the potential value of text styles.

Creating a Text Style

In Chapter 9, you were able to create a graphic style just by formatting a graphic and giving its style a name. The steps for building text styles are essentially the same: Create a string or frame of text, format it, invoke the Object menu with the secondary mouse button (SMB), choose Save As Style, and make up a name. As Figure 12.1 shows, there are several attributes that you can include in or exclude from a text style.

As with graphic styles, you can change the default text style—affecting every block of text you subsequently create—or you can create new styles. DRAW pays close attention to the type of text you create, maintaining separate styles for artistic and paragraph text. We think users will appreciate this, because artistic text is generally used for display and headline text, and paragraph text is usually reserved for blocks of body

12.1

Asking for the menu at this restaurant is easy; choosing among the entrees is not so easy. Most patrons just order one of everything.

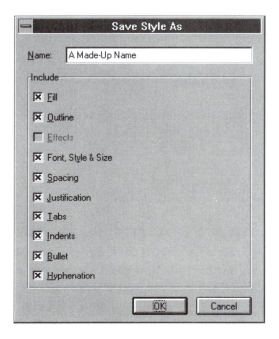

text. In each case, you will probably want different defaults, perhaps 36-point Switzerland Black for artistic text, and 11-point Times or Times New Roman for paragraph text.

AUTHOR'S NOTE

UPGRADING FROM VERSION 3? It used to be a cumbersome, behind-the-scenes maneuver to change the default typeface and size. Now it's easy: Create and format a piece of text, invoke the Object menu, and choose Update Style. Furthermore, you can set the default for ALL text attributes, not just face, style, and size.

The Save Style As dialog shown in Figure 12.1 offers a host of formatting specifications that can potentially be included in a style. Tabs, bullets, indents, and hyphenation are available only to paragraph frames, so they will be dimmed in this dialog when you work with artistic text.

Sharing Text Styles Among Objects

The Update Style and Save Style As dialogs both have options for Fill and Outline, meaning that you can incorporate these attributes into a text style. Fill and Outline are the two attributes available to all three types of styles—graphic, artistic text, and paragraph text—and it is interesting to note that they can be shared among any objects.

You may recall from Chapter 9 how you were able to apply a graphic style to a piece of text to change its fill pattern—remember the crazy four-point star created and applied to several objects, including text? If you have assigned a particular color to a text style, you can apply it to a graphic object as well; the only wrinkle is that you will need to go through the Styles roll-up (Ctrl+F5) to accomplish this, because the Object menu only provides access to styles for the particular object you have selected. In other words, if you have created and selected a rectangle, the Object menu shows you only graphic styles.

To apply to a graphic object a color already assigned to a string of text, select the graphic object and go to the Styles roll-up. DRAW thinks it is doing you a favor by showing you only the graphic styles, but you can override that by clicking on either the artistic text icon or the paragraph text icon. Then you will see all styles in the template, allowing you to pick the one whose color you want to use. Select it and apply it, and your graphic will promptly take on the color of the text.

This is very handy when creating layouts in which your color choices affect many different objects. If you establish a spot color to use throughout a drawing, you can incorporate it into one style and then apply it across the board to all objects (text or graphic). This is easier than using the Copy Attributes From dialog, and much easier than returning to Uniform Fill each time you want to assign the color. The key is to keep the Styles roll-up on screen, so you can reach the styles quickly.

Along with this tip about manipulating the Styles roll-up, however, we must issue the following caveat: Reformatting and updating a text style won't change a graphic object that uses that style. We had hoped to be able to make an unqualified endorsement for this technique, but DRAW's styles just aren't smart enough. If you decide on PANTONE Blue 072 for your spot color, you can incorporate it into a style, let's say a text style, and apply it to all objects, using the roll-up. If you should change your mind about the color, wanting PANTONE 267 instead, you can easily update the text style, and all text strings using the style will change. But any graphic objects using the style will not change; you will need to select each graphic and reapply the style. DRAW does not maintain an automatic link between unlike objects that share a style.

We wish Corel would have made it easier to link up text and graphic objects designed to use the same color. Nonetheless, the basic strategy is sound, with the following qualification: After applying your text format to a graphics object, use that object to create a new graphic style, and apply that style to other graphics objects that you want to have the same fill and outline. Then, if you decide to change the color of the text, you can apply the new text style to just one of the graphics objects and use that object to update the graphic style. All other graphics formatted with the style will then be automatically updated, too.

The Power of the Paragraph

As it ships from the factory, DRAW's "collection" of artistic text styles is meager—there is but one, the Default Artistic Style. For paragraph text, DRAW provides a small running start with three bullet styles, and though they are nothing to fax home about, they do provide good launch points for the creation of your own styles.

DRAW makes it easy to apply paragraph styles, thanks to a set of hotkeys that you can employ and change to suit your needs. Do you use a lot of bullets or boldface headings? How would you like to press Ctrl+1 and instantly add a bullet to your paragraph, or format a line as a heading? This level of control is available only via paragraph styles.

Using a set of styles and hotkeys, it wasn't terribly difficult to create our own rendition of a couple of pages out of this book. Figure 12.2 shows draft copy from two earlier pages, with all elements being controlled by styles. If you want to follow along on screen with this discussion, the file BOOK.TXT is in the PRACTICE directory on the Companion CD.

12.2

DRAW's paragraph styles make these pages much easier to create.

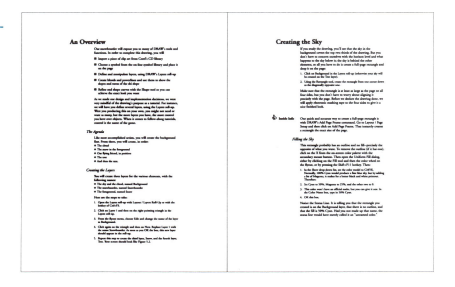

Set the Stage

Begin with the following steps:

1. From a new, empty page, use Layout / Page Setup / Size to set up a standard letter-sized page, with portrait orientation. While you're in Page Setup, go to the Display page and make sure the following three items are checked: Show Page Border, Facing Pages, and the Left First option under Facing Pages.

2. Use File / Save As to save this file as BOOK.CDR.

3. Invoke the Styles roll-up (Ctrl+F5), click on the right-pointing triangle, and choose Save Template.

4. Create a new template named BOOK, and save it in the DRAW\TEMPLATE directory (where all the other .CDT files are).

To make sure that you are on the same page of the playbook as we are, we're going to have you delete all existing styles except for the defaults. We can't assume that your initial template started out the same as ours, so the safest course of action is to start literally from the beginning.

5. Select a style name, click the triangle to get the flyout, and choose Delete Style.

6. Continue deleting styles until the only ones left are the three Default styles (DRAW won't let you delete them).

Create the Styles

The two-page spread in our example requires two headline styles, two bullet styles, a style for numbered steps, and a style for margin notes. We used Corel's Garamond typeface, and if you want your efforts to look similar to ours, you can install that typeface from the CD. Otherwise, choose another standard serif face.

AUTHOR'S NOTE

UPGRADING FROM VERSION 3? When you add a new typeface to your system, you no longer need to close DRAW and reopen it in order to use the typeface. DRAW recognizes it and lets you set type with it immediately.

Before you create any other styles or import any text, you should correctly format the Default style, because all other styles will be spawned from it. The Default style will be used for all standard paragraph text in this document. It will pay off for you to do this *before* you import any text; we'll explain shortly.

1. While your page is still empty, invoke the Text roll-up (Ctrl+F2).

2. Set the font to 10-point Garamond Normal.

3. From the Paragraph dialog, set the spacing value for Line to 12 points, and Before Paragraph to 18 points.

4. From Indent, set Left Margin to 12 picas and Right Margin to 6 picas.

5. Apply these changes; as you do, DRAW will ask you what kind of default you are changing, as shown in Figure 12.3 (because you did not select any text). Click on Paragraph Text.

12.3

Establishing the style for text is best done before you even have any text in your drawing.

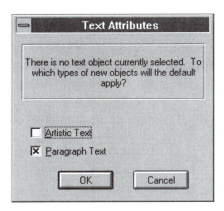

6. Go to File / Import, choose Text as the file type, and select BOOK.TXT from the PRACTICE directory. DRAW will automatically create as many pages as the text needs and, on each page, a frame holding the text.

7. Size each frame so that it is 1 inch from the edge of the page on all sides (there's a good chance that the text will import that way by default).

8. Save.

Notice that all of the text imported as 10-point Garamond (or whatever face you chose for your default), with the various margins that you designated. This is because you set the default before importing. Your screen should look similar to Figure 12.4 (we have outlined the two text frames for clarity).

INSIDE INFO

You might want to change DRAW's Greek Text value in order to see the small type, or you might choose to leave it greeked for faster screen performance. Text greeking is a process whereby DRAW does not try to render text at small sizes (which you couldn't read, anyway), and instead uses little lines and squiggles. To adjust this setting, go to Special / Preferences / Text, and change the Greek Text Below value. The smaller the number, the less text DRAW will greek. We wonder when this phrase might become politically incorrect…

12.4

Because you defined your default style first, the text for this two-page spread comes into DRAW with the main formatting already in place.

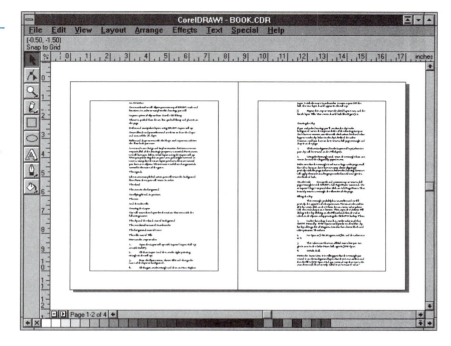

9. Select one of the text frames and invoke the Object menu (by holding down the SMB for a long second).
10. Choose Save As Style, and enter **Head1** as the new style name.
11. Repeat steps 9 and 10 five more times, each time supplying one of the following style names:

    Head2

    Bullet1

    Bullet2

    Steps

    Notes

12. When you're done creating the styles, return the currently selected paragraph to the Default style, either from the Styles roll-up or the Apply Style command on the Object menu.

INSIDE INFO

When you're formatting paragraph text, the selection process is different. You can select the entire frame of text with the Pick tool (just as you would select a circle or a string of artistic text), but to select a specific paragraph within a frame, you use the Text tool. From there, remember this rule: When changing the font, you must select the characters by clicking and dragging across them. When changing any of the paragraph settings, your cursor need only rest anywhere in the paragraph.

13. From the Styles roll-up, choose Set Hotkeys (on the flyout), and specify the keys to be used with Ctrl as shown in Figure 12.5. This step is optional, but highly recommended.

14. Save.

We chose a numbering scheme that seemed logical to us, even though they are mixed up in Figure 12.5: Heading levels first (1 and 2), bullet styles next (3 and 4), then note styles (5) and step formats (6), and then default paragraph text (0). You can certainly come up with your own arrangement. Once you set these up, they appear on the Styles roll-up.

12.5

With these hotkey assignments, your seven styles can be applied instantly to selected paragraphs. Just press Ctrl and the corresponding number.

Format the Paragraphs

Assuming you are already modestly familiar with formatting paragraphs, the rest of this job is really pretty easy. For instance, to assign the Head1 style to the first paragraph, zoom in on it, place your cursor anywhere in the line, and press Ctrl+1. To format it, highlight the entire line and set as follows in the Character and Paragraph dialogs:

Typeface and Size: 20-point Garamond Bold

Spacing: Line: 24 points; Before Paragraph: 24 points

Indents: All values at 6 picas

Once you OK or Apply these changes, record them in the Head1 style, with Object / Update Style. (Remember, the Object menu is invoked with the SMB, unlike the other menus.) Figure 12.6 shows the new format for Head 1. When you encounter the next headline that is to be formatted like this one (it'll be "Creating the Sky"), you can apply the Head1 style by simply placing your text cursor anywhere inside the heading text and pressing Ctrl+1.

12.6

The new Head 1 style

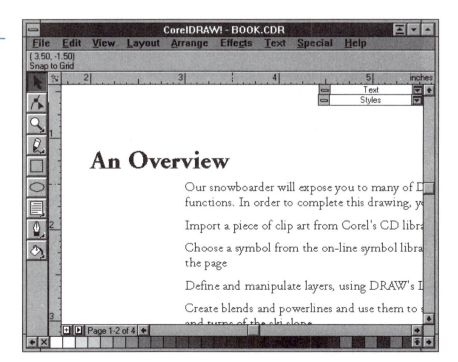

WATCH OUT!

DRAW's Undo command is not very smart with paragraphs of text selected with the Text tool. For instance, if you select an entire frame of text (with the Pick tool) and make three changes to it, you can then undo each one of those changes in sequence. But if you make the same three changes to selected paragraphs within a frame, DRAW will see them all as one operation and undo them all at once. DRAW sees any continuous use of the Text tool as one action, all of which would be undone at the first level of Undo. To separate out parts of a formatting session so you can undo specific actions, either save between steps, or quickly switch to the Pick tool and then immediately back to the Text tool. Remember: When you're using the Text tool, Undo will throw out all parts of a continuous formatting session.

Head2 paragraphs ("The Agenda," "Creating the Layers," and "Filling the Sky") move slightly out to the left and are set in bold italic. The particulars are

>**Typeface and Size:** 12-point Garamond Bold Italic
>
>**Spacing:** Line: 14 points; Before Paragraph: 28 points
>
>**Indents:** First Line, Rest of Lines, and Left Margin all at 10 picas (set Left Margin first; others will automatically adjust)

The Bullet1 paragraphs (the square bullets at the top) need to have their bullet characters assigned. Also, the space around them needs to be set, with a tab (already placed in the file) and a hanging indent. You know the drill by now: Format one of the Bullet1 paragraphs this way and then update the style to change them all. Here are the settings:

>**Typeface and Size:** 10-point Garamond Normal
>
>**Spacing:** Line: 11 points; Before Paragraph: 18 points
>
>**Bullets:** Typeface: Common Bullets; Symbol No. 43; Size: 12 points

Tabs: One tab stop, set at 13 picas (*Hint:* As you set tabs, you may find that the simplest thing to do is first click on Delete All, then enter the desired value, and click Add.)

Indents: First Line and Bullet Indent at 12 picas; Rest of Lines at 13 picas

Figure 12.7 shows the result of the three formats you have established so far.

The Bullet2 paragraphs (with round bullets, in the middle of the first page) have the same requirements as Bullet1, but with a different bullet and slightly different spacing values:

Typeface and Size: 10-point Garamond Normal

Spacing: Line: 12 points; Before Paragraph: 12 points

Bullets: Typeface: Wingdings; Symbol No. 108; Size: 8 points

Tabs: One tab stop, set at 12,9 picas

Indents: First Line and Bullet Indent at 12 picas; Rest of Lines at 12,9 picas

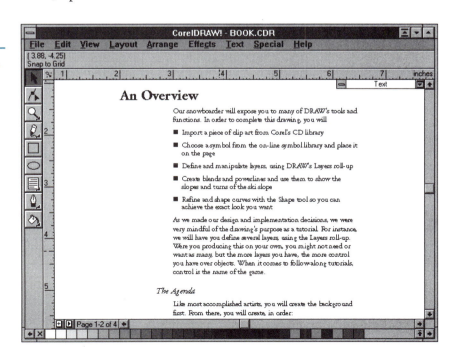

12.7

The Head1, Head2, and Bullet1 formats. The bulleted lists are derived from a combination of bullets, tabs, and hanging indents.

The Steps paragraphs use the same technique of pushing one line out from the rest, as follows:

Typeface and Size: 9-point Garamond Normal

Spacing: Line: 10 points; Before Paragraph: 15 points

Tabs: One tab stop, set at 13 picas

Indents: First and Left at 12 picas; Rest of Lines at 13 picas

Figure 12.8 shows the result of the last two pieces of formatting. Don't forget to save…

The Notes paragraph (which begins with "Inside Info") is a concoction of formatting, designed to appear as if two paragraphs are side by side. Here are the specs:

Typeface and Size: 10-point Garamond Normal

Spacing: Line: 12 points; Before Paragraph: 36 points

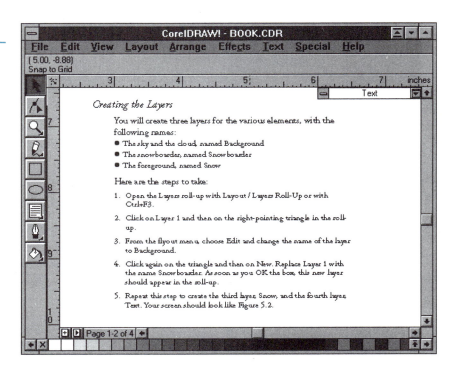

12.8

The second bulleted list and the numbered steps

Bullets: Typeface: Wingdings; Symbol No. 67; Size: 24 points; Vertical Shift: 3 points down (–3)

Tabs: One tab stop, set at 12 picas

Indents: First Line at 6,9 picas; Rest of Lines at 12 picas; Bullet Indent at 5 picas

Figure 12.9 shows the final result.

As mentioned earlier, you can try all these steps yourself using the BOOK.TXT file supplied on the Companion CD. If you would like to work backwards and reverse-engineer any part of this example, you'll also find BOOK.CDR and BOOK.CDT on the CD. As with all other sample data for the book, they are in the PRACTICE directory.

In the next chapter, we explore strategies for advanced users, as we look at several critical issues of typeface performance.

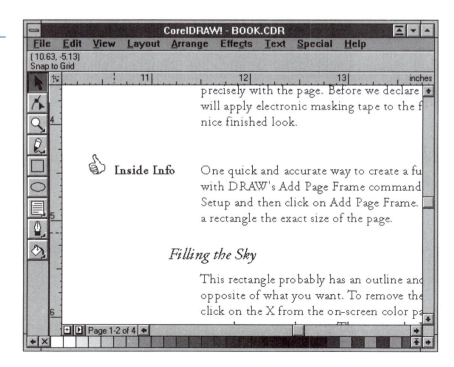

12.9

This Inside Info note is made up of a bullet, a tab, and an outdent.

CHAPTER 13

Putting Pedal to Metal

THIRTEEN

CHAPTER 13

This chapter may hold the record for the most times referenced, alluded to, or teased throughout one book. Here we explore issues, not of typeface aesthetics or operation, but of typeface *performance*. You're either going to produce beautifully typeset work with DRAW or you're not—quite honestly, this variable is largely out of our hands. What we *can* show you is how to produce your typeset work faster, with less effort, and with more confidence.

There are no step-by-step instructions in this chapter, and we assume you already know the basics of typography and typesetting. And while our approach for this chapter reflects our assumption that you know your way around, we do not consider this an "advanced" discussion. We expect that all DRAW users will benefit from better performance, and that the topics brought forth here will be relevant across the board. (We can see the faxes and e-mail now…"Dear Rick, Chapter 13 was over my head and you said it wouldn't be!")

PostScript vs. TrueType

Back in the old days of CorelDRAW (version 3.0 and earlier), the ATM vs. TrueType conflict made for a much livelier debate, with a conclusion that usually went something like this: "Use TrueType fonts for speed, PostScript fonts for precision, and, oh, by the way, *avoid using Corel's typefaces at all costs.*" We're happy to report that these guidelines no longer hold up to close scrutiny—especially the one about Corel's typefaces. Today it's often difficult to tell the difference between Corel's versions of standard typefaces and the real thing.

AUTHOR'S NOTE

 PostScript Type 1 is the FORMAT, and Adobe Type Manager (ATM) is the ENGINE for displaying and printing PostScript typefaces. For you to be able to use PostScript Type 1 faces, DRAW requires ATM to be running on your system. Because of this close link, it has become common to refer to PostScript typefaces as "ATM typefaces" and "ATM fonts," and even though it is not technically precise, we will do so throughout this discussion.

Print Speed

As recently as 1992, TrueType enjoyed significant advantages over ATM in printing speed. TrueType was quicker off the mark than ATM when printing to non-PostScript printers, as well as faster at printing to PostScript devices when nonresident typefaces were used. ATM prevailed only when it could call for a typeface already resident in a PostScript printer, rather than having to download it. Even then, however, the edge was slim.

This situation has changed as of mid-1993 and the advent of ATM 2.5, which is substantially more intelligent in the way it prints to non-PostScript printers. Today the only instance in which TrueType has a clear speed advantage is when printing to a PostScript printer using a nonresident face. The TrueType engine sends only the characters that are required to render the string of text; ATM, by contrast, sends the entire character set, regardless of how many characters are needed.

We were prepared to show you a bunch of charts and graphs offering data on printing from various applications, to various printers, using various typefaces. But we looked at the data and decided to toss it all away, because the conclusions were insignificant. ATM 2.5 and 2.6 were right up there with TrueType in all the tests we conducted, except in the nonresident PostScript typeface department. The moral of this story is clear: If you use ATM and haven't yet upgraded to at least version 2.5, do so right away.

TrueType typefaces have one continuing advantage outside of DRAW: You never have to worry about font downloading. You never have to remember which faces are resident in the printer and which ones must be included with the print job. The TrueType engine sends font information with every print job, completely removing you from the font-handling loop. DRAW 5.0 does a better job than previous versions of streamlining typeface management, and Appendix A covers in detail the issue of using resident PostScript typefaces.

Drawing Speed

Since print speed is less of an issue than it used to be, let's turn our attention to an area of performance that is very much an issue, and arguably more important than print speed: the speed of rendering type on your screen. On this topic, the jury returns an immediate verdict, and if you are running ATM and have PostScript as well as TrueType typefaces installed, you can see this for yourself. Start DRAW, and set the following line of text as artistic text (press F8 and click once on the page):

This is a test of DRAW's text rendering skills.

Get out your stopwatch or your "hippos" (you know, from touch football… "One hippo, two hippo, three hippo, RUN!"). Open the Text roll-up and set the text in 18-point Times Normal (or some other standard ATM font). Count how long it takes. On our system, the hourglass flipped around for 3.6 seconds—which is down, incidentally, from DRAW 4.0's time of 4.6 seconds.

Now Undo (Ctrl+Z) and try it again, this time using Times New Roman or some other TrueType font. (If you're not sure of the format of your typefaces, the Text / Character dialog will identify the format of every typeface.) Was it faster? We'll bet so. On our system it was 1.0, over three times as fast (and down from 2.1 seconds in DRAW 4.0).

These results are not due to some gimmick with Times and Times New Roman. Our tests indicate that TrueType faces, across the board, are faster to draw than ATM faces. To understand the point we're making, it's important that you distinguish between a screen refresh and a font change. If you press Ctrl+W to refresh the screen, it doesn't matter what type of text you have. *But if you change the font in any way,* then its format plays a significant role in screen performance. How significant, you ask? We're glad you did...

We tested the redraw speed for a lengthy string of artistic text, using 15 different typefaces, and the results were unequivocal: All the TrueType faces drew faster than the ATM faces, without exception. Figure 13.1 shows the results, including an almost ridiculous 11:1 performance discrepancy between the fastest typeface (Arial) and the slowest (Garamond). We haven't bothered to include a legend showing you the formats of the various typefaces, because it's obvious: The fast times are all TrueType, and the slow ones are all ATM. The slowest TrueType face outperforms the fastest ATM face by better than 4:1.

How much weight should you assign to this dramatic statistic? There are two mitigating factors: the value you place on typeface fidelity, and the extent to which you use artistic text.

13.1

No question about this one: TrueType faces perform much better on screen than ATM faces.

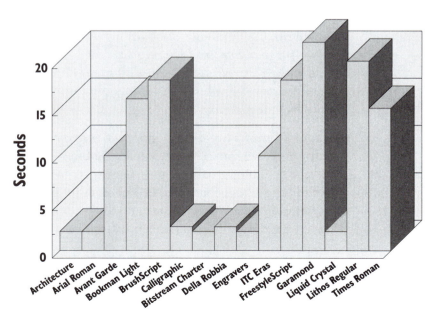

A large body of professional users would trust their work to nothing less than the Adobe library of Type 1 faces. To these users, screen redraw is far less important than the exceptionally crisp output of Adobe Type 1 PostScript typefaces. They remain the standard of excellence throughout the electronic typesetting industry, and they are the de facto language of the service bureau industry.

The second factor, your use of artistic text, needs some elaboration, so keep reading…

Artistic vs. Paragraph Text

This is one of the topics that we have alluded to many times in earlier chapters: the difference between artistic text and paragraph text. There is the obvious difference, that artistic text allows you to do cool stuff to it, and paragraph text allows you to set gobs and gobs of copy. Then there is the less obvious difference: DRAW formats paragraph text on screen much, much faster than it does artistic text.

Want proof? Start DRAW, and open PARATEXT.CDR from the PRACTICE directory. Select the top block of text and reformat it in an ATM typeface. We did this with Palatino, and the text required 14.1 seconds to reformat. Now select the lower block of text and do the same. On our system, the difference was nothing short of unbelievable: .7 seconds—*less than one second* to reformat the lower text. Only one thing could make this text draw almost 20 times faster: paragraph text. In the case of Garamond, which is the worst performer with artistic text, the improvement is almost 30 to 1.

Figure 13.2 shows two distinct groups of performance times. The ones on the left, repeated from Figure 13.1, are the times required to reformat artistic text. The ones on the right are the redraw times for the exact same quantity of text in the exact same typefaces, but set as paragraph text. As you can see, all typefaces perform much faster, and the performance difference between TrueType and Type 1 fonts virtually disappears.

You'll have to decide for yourself how often to use paragraph text. Two drawbacks must be factored into your decision: You lose special effects

13.2

The message is crystal clear: When you have lots of copy to set, use paragraph text.

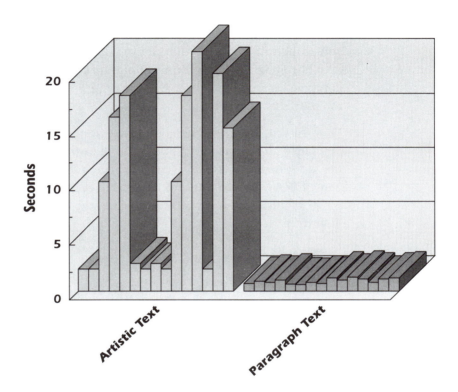

capabilities (except fitting text in and around objects), and won't be able to quickly size and skew text on screen (all text formatting must be done from the roll-up or dialogs). When we lecture before CorelDRAW users, we often find ourselves describing paragraph text at a very basic level to advanced users who have never had the occasion to think about it. They are content to click on the Text tool and start typing, oblivious to the alternative. So our mission here is clear: We want to make you more aware of paragraph text, so you can make an informed decision for yourself as to when and when not to use it.

Adding Fonts on the Fly

Good news for both ATM and TrueType users: You can add fonts to your system without closing and reopening Windows, even without having to close and reopen DRAW. Version 3.0 notifies you when a new typeface is observed in the environment, but requires you to close and reopen the program in order to use it. DRAW 4.0 and 5.0 just add it to the typeface list without complaining. This on-the-fly support is native to TrueType faces; ATM users need to be at least at version 2.5 to enjoy this capability.

Figure 13.3 is an actual snapshot (unretouched!!) of a TrueType face being added to Windows. On the right, Control Panel has just completed the task of adding Corel's Impress to the system. As soon as that happens, DRAW is able to use it. We didn't even have to close and reopen the Text roll-up—the typeface appeared there almost as soon as Windows recorded it.

13.3

New typefaces become available to DRAW as soon as you add them to your system.

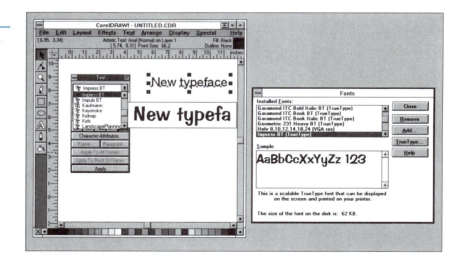

What Happens When You Outline Text

The advice here is simple: Don't do it. Avoid placing an Outline Pen around text unless you are consciously pursuing a special effect in which you want the outline of the text to have a color or shading different from the interior of the text. Don't do it to simulate boldface. When you add outlines to text, you lose out on screen performance, printer performance, and aesthetic appeal.

Let's begin with this last point. We don't mean to be condescending, but we think that there are many users who haven't given this much thought: A bold weight of a given type family is not just a heavier variation of roman, it is a different typeface altogether, with distinctly crafted characters. When you add an outline to a roman face, you are merely drawing a rule evenly around the perimeter of the character. Most typefaces, however, do not have even strokes and weights; their variations are what make them distinctive.

As Figure 13.4 shows, the true bold face on top looks quite different and, in our view, better than the roman face with a thick rule around it. The text string is set in the Palatino family; the single character is set in Times New Roman. With the true bold *e,* you can see how the horizontal stroke and the top of the curve are much thinner than the rest—this is how the typographer designed it. With the outlined *e,* the entire character is bluntly made thicker.

Creating Figure 13.4 was quite frustrating, because we had to sit through interminable delays waiting for the text to draw. Why? Because text with outlines is especially slow to draw and even slower to print. Text that normally draws in a half-second or less bogs down to several seconds when given an outline. Text strings that print in 10–13 seconds require 17–20 with outlines. You'll get no relief from paragraph text in this case; it draws just as slowly. And, unlike the earlier discussion of

13.4

There's true bold (above) and then there's just big and fat.

 Is this type really bold or is it just outlined? bold

 Is this type really bold or is it just outlined? outlined

typeface performance when you're reformatting, this time we are talking solely about redraw speed.

You can press Ctrl+W to redraw the screen and measure the difference. Figure 13.5 shows our findings: Without outlines, the 26 letters of the alphabet draw almost instantly, irrespective of typeface format (ATM or TTF). Print times are also quick and even, at 7 seconds. But add outlines to the text, and there is hell to pay, especially with ATM typefaces.

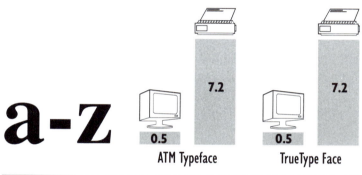

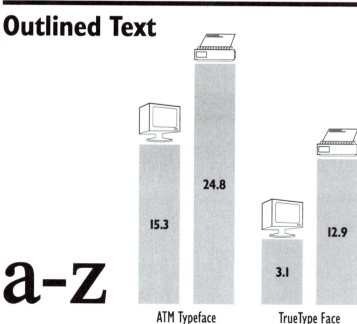

13.5

Adding an outline to text will definitely slow you down, and quite possibly offend your readers' sensibilities. All times shown are in seconds.

To sum up, there appears to be only one legitimate use of outlined text: for creating a typographic effect in which the interior and exterior of the letters are different colors. Don't use outlining to fabricate a bold style for a typeface family that doesn't offer one.

All in All, DRAW Is Not a Word Processor

The final word on performance considerations is this: If you really want to get speedy screen and printer performance with text-intensive projects, do the following:

1. From DRAW, choose File / Exit.
2. From Program Manager, search for a PageMaker, XPress or Ventura Publisher icon.
3. Double-click the icon, and create your text there.

Pardon our sarcasm, but you must face the fact that, regardless of the marketing hype about 999-page support, DRAW does not excel at handling large quantities of text, and probably never will. (And now that Ventura is in the box, DRAW doesn't have to try to be the text monster that it wasn't designed to be.) One DRAW user, Charles Blaum, performed the following tests and shared his findings in the Corel forum on CompuServe:

Task	DRAW	PageMaker
Import a 4K file	37 seconds	5 seconds
Cut 15 lines of text	18 seconds	2 seconds
Scroll one screen of text	9 seconds	Too fast to time
Adjust text block frame	23 seconds	Too fast to time
Change point size	26 seconds	2 seconds
Change face of one line	16 seconds	1 second
Change leading of a block	27 seconds	1.5 seconds
Change to 2 columns	31 seconds	5 seconds
Change to Pick tool	19 seconds	Too fast to time

Enough already with text. In Part IV, we will change gears in a big way and explore DRAW's powerful, exciting, and sometimes dangerous collection of special effects tools.

PART IV

EFFECTS AND AFFECTS

This part begins with a warning. DRAW's special effects can be addicting, once you understand how they work. This is both wonderful and dangerous—you must beware the intoxicating power special effects give you. Enjoy learning them and please have fun with them, but don't overdose. More than a few layouts have been ruined by the abuse or overuse of special effects. You want proof? Browse through just about any computer magazine or the computer ads in your newspaper. You will see some great and some equally horrendous uses of graphic special effects.

You've heard this warning from us before: It is not only our responsibility as computer writers to communicate to you how the tools work, we feel it is also our role to advise against overusing them. Nowhere else in the program—*nowhere*—is this more salient than here with DRAW's corps of special effects.

CHAPTER 14

Appetizers

FOURTEEN

CHAPTER 14

Pâté…crostini…a glass of wine…and maybe some escargots. This chapter looks at the electronic equivalents of these starters and tidbits, from DRAW's bountiful Effects menu.

The Effects Menu

With the exception of fills and outlines, nearly everything you might do (artistic or otherwise) to an object is contained in DRAW's Effects menu. As shown in Figure 14.1, the menu is divided into three sections.

14.1

The Effects menu. Note how easy it would be to binge, with all the hotkeys and roll-ups available.

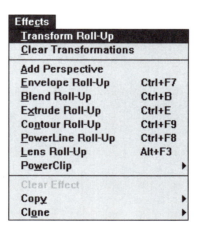

The first menu item is your access to some frequently used but relatively mundane and safe transformations performed on either single or multiple objects, including moving, sizing, rotating, skewing, and flipping them. The entire second section is the Danger Zone, a land of special-effects magic that can quite easily consume you. In the third section you'll find methods to quickly duplicate effects from one object to another, when you are happy with what you've done.

But if you realize you've let yourself be carried away, Clear… offers a measure of damage control, providing an escape for certain operations. And the Clear Transformations item, back up in the first section of the menu, is your steam shovel, useful for quickly digging yourself out of a self-induced trap.

Basic Transformations

NEW FOR 5

> In recognition of how often basic transformations are performed in DRAW, all the fundamental Transform functions—moving, stretching, mirroring, rotating, and skewing—have been placed in a single roll-up that is always available for immediate use. In addition, there is a new Transform function that allows sizing in absolute units rather than stretching by percentages.

The Transform roll-up can be invoked via the Effects menu, or the new Ribbon Bar. Across the top of the roll-up are icons that let you switch among the Transform roll-up pages, or modes. At the lower-right is an arrow button that you can click to reveal a roll-up within the roll-up: the *tic-tac-toe grid* (see Figure 14.2). On all of Transform's pages, this little grid allows you to quickly select one of the nine control points on the imaginary rectangle that encloses a selected object. The role of this grid varies slightly, depending on which Transform mode you are using.

Unlike other roll-ups, each mode of the Transform roll-up is a totally independent function. You cannot specify values in several modes and then apply all transformations at once. Only the values of the selected mode are applied. (As you will see in later chapters, for other Effects roll-ups you are able to specify a number of parameters in various modes, and apply them as one compound effect to an object.)

14.2

The Stretch & Mirror page of the Transform roll-up, with the tic-tac-toe grid displayed

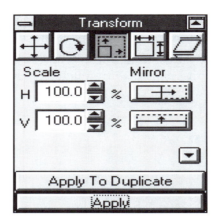

NEW FOR 5

DRAW 5.0 has changed the way all roll-ups appear when first invoked. In previous versions, roll-ups had one standard or default "mode," or group of settings. In DRAW 5.0, however, the page that is visible when any roll-up is invoked will be the page you last used for that roll-up. Some of you will like this change, because you can pick up where you left off in your last DRAW session. We prefer the older method, where the most common mode for that roll-up was always the first one seen.

Here are the five Transform pages, from left to right on the row of icons:

- *Transform / Move* This replaces the Move dialog, formerly accessed from the Arrange menu. It contains all the same functionality, and can still be invoked by the Alt+F7 hotkey.

- *Transform / Rotate* This replaces a portion of the Rotate & Skew dialog, formerly accessed from the Effects menu. Though it's not documented in the CorelDRAW manual, Rotate can be invoked by the Alt+F8 hotkey that was formerly used for Rotate & Skew.

- *Transform / Stretch & Mirror* The functions found here used to be accessed by selecting Effects / Stretch & Mirror. As with Rotate, you can still get to this page with the old Stretch & Mirror hotkey, Alt+F9.

- *Transform / Size* This new function produces results equivalent to stretches, but you get to specify final size values, rather than stretch percentages.

- *Transform / Skew* This replaces the other part of the old Effects / Rotate & Skew dialog.

The Transform modes offer similar types of operations. You can perform some fairly simple transformations on single objects, multiple objects, and grouped objects. In all cases, you can use the roll-up pages' controls, or you can work directly with the objects on screen.

AUTHOR'S NOTE

The units available for moving and sizing in the Transform roll-up have been linked to the Ruler settings in version 5.0. We are unhappy with Corel's decision to do this. Now, whatever units you use for the rulers are the only units available in the Transform roll-up. In prior versions of DRAW, you were free to select other units of measurement when in the Move dialog, and we prefer that flexibility. Typically, a page layout is defined in inches, but text is better expressed in typographic units. Now, to switch, you must access the ruler and change the units there first. This is a step backward in the productivity department.

Stretch & Mirror

You already know how to use the mouse to stretch an object. Simply select one or more objects with the Pick tool, and you'll see the familiar eight sizing handles. Here is a short review of resizing using the mouse.

By dragging one of the corner handles, you stretch the object(s) proportionately in both the horizontal and vertical directions. Drag a side-center handle, and you stretch the object horizontally; drag a top- or bottom-center handle and you stretch the object vertically. Notice that the handle opposite the one you grab remains stationary; you stretch *away* from that anchor point. If you move *toward* the anchor point, you shrink the object. Continue moving toward and eventually past the anchor point, and the object flips, or *mirrors*.

In addition to the normal stretching, you can *constrain* a stretch by using either or both the Ctrl and Shift keys, as follows:

- Holding down the Ctrl key while dragging a handle constrains the stretch to increments of 100%. This includes negative values (dragging across the anchored handle). A constrained stretch with a value of −100% exactly mirrors an object horizontally, vertically, or both.

- The Shift key causes stretching to happen symmetrically from the center, rather than be anchored at the opposite handle.

- You can also use Ctrl and Shift in conjunction, to stretch from the center, and in 100% increments.

A trick we frequently use when mirroring with the Ctrl+click method is to click the secondary mouse button (SMB) just before releasing the primary mouse button, causing the object to be mirrored and duplicated. For example, to quickly create a grid of boxes, you might draw a rectangle, mirror it horizontally, and duplicate it using the SMB technique. Then use the Ctrl+R hotkey to repeat the operation, creating as many boxes as you need in that row. Finally, select the whole row and repeat the mirror process vertically, to create an instant grid. Figure 14.3 shows an example of this technique.

Do We Really Need Transform / Stretch & Mirror?

You might be wondering, "If stretching and mirroring operations are so easily accomplished with the mouse, why would I ever use the roll-up?" But take another, closer look at Figure 14.2. Using Transform / Stretch & Mirror, you can *precisely* enter the percentage of stretch in either or both directions. The key word is *precisely*. If you need to stretch an object in specific

14.3

Beat the clock! This 5-by-5-box grid was created in 63 seconds, using four mouse actions and six simple keystrokes.

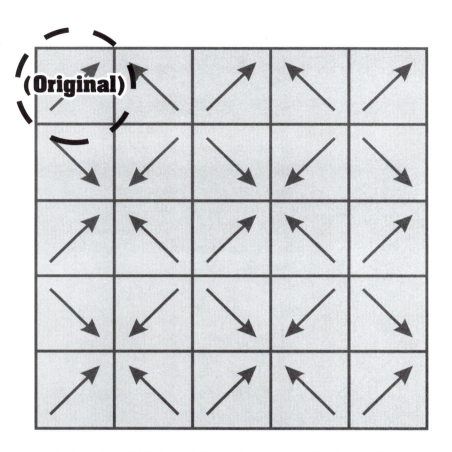

increments (other than 100%, which can be done easily via the Ctrl key), the roll-up is the better choice for executing your stretch operation. You can specify values accurate to 1%. If you try to enter a value such as 50.6%, it will be rounded to 51%.

WATCH OUT!

Be aware that if you have already stretched an object, the percentages you enter in Transform / Stretch & Mirror are designating how much MORE you want to stretch the object, not the TOTAL percentage of stretch the object will undergo.

In DRAW versions 3 and 4.0, the principal reason to stretch an object using the menu rather than the mouse was to achieve accuracy. The new roll-up provides other incentives for using it. Try this short exercise to create an instant telescope:

1. Draw a square, about 2 inches long and wide (remember the Ctrl key), and fill it with a linear fountain fill that is white on the top and black on the bottom.
2. Open the Transform roll-up, click the little arrow button in the lower-right of the roll-up, and click the Stretch & Mirror icon at the top. Your roll-up should look like Figure 14.2.
3. Select the square. Then set the vertical stretch to 75%, and leave the horizontal stretch at 100%. Click on the horizontal (upper) Mirror button.
4. In the tic-tac-toe grid, click the center-right control point. Then click the Apply to Duplicate button three times.

This silly exercise should give you a feel for a few of the myriad combinations of settings and techniques for using Stretch & Mirror. Remember the grid shown in Figure 14.3? We got our time down to 26 seconds using the roll-up. See if you can beat that time.

Rules of Thumb for Stretch & Mirror

- Use Transform / Stretch & Mirror when accuracy is important.
- The roll-up is usually the fastest way to repeat a specific sequence of transformations.

Outlines: To Scale or Not to Scale…

When stretching objects, there are two things that can happen to any outlines you may have applied. The first of these things is…absolutely nothing. In the Outline Pen dialog, you can set an outline to either scale with the image or not. If you don't enable Scale With Image, the object's outline stays set at the original thickness applied, regardless of how much you stretch or shrink the object itself.

When you do select Scale With Image, the outline scales with the image, but only in the directions you stretch. This can be a problem if you stretch an object in only one direction or stretch it more in one direction than another, because you will be left with an outline of uneven thickness. More than likely, this is not what you would have intended.

If, however, you are going to proportionately scale objects, then you probably do want to scale your outlines with the image. This is especially true when you intend to make numerous versions of the same objects at wide-ranging sizes, as one might do in preparing a sheet of camera-ready logos.

Here is a short exercise to demonstrate this point:

1. Create your name using a bold font, set at about 200 points, and filled with a light color.
2. Apply a black outline of about 5 points.

So far it looks pretty good, right? Now imagine that you are creating a camera stat sheet that reproduces this same object in a variety of sizes.

3. Make sure Scale With Image is *not* selected in the Outline Pen dialog.
4. Shrink the text proportionally to about 10 percent of its original size.

Can you still read your name? No? Try zooming in. Still can't read it? This example should make it clear that you need to pay attention to how outlines behave as you stretch and shrink objects. Now repeat the above exercise, but this time turn on Scale With Image. You will be able to scale the object correctly to any size you wish.

If you have Scale With Image turned on and get an undesirable distorted outline after stretching an object disproportionately, here's how to fix it. First, in the Outline Pen dialog, notice that the Nib Shape has changed. Click the Default button to regain an outline of uniform thickness, and enter a new Width value if you wish.

Absolute Sizing

We mentioned earlier that in version 5.0 you can now specify new dimensions for an object, rather than a percentage of stretch. This is accomplished in the Size page of the Transform roll-up, as opposed to Stretch & Mirror. (Open the Size page by clicking the fourth icon from the left in the Transform roll-up.) The end results are the same as Stretch & Mirror would yield. The difference is that you are choosing the specific values to which you want the object scaled, rather than having to calculate the percentage of stretch needed, or trying to watch the status line. It's just two different means to the same end.

WATCH OUT!

If you stretch an object in only one direction, you create a "distorted object." We have already commented on the effect of nonproportional object scaling on scaleable outlines, but this is a more serious problem with rounded rectangles and compound objects that contain holes and walls. For these, there is no way to correct the distortion. Your only recourse is to redraw the object with the correct proportions. You can proportionately stretch with no adverse results, but if you stretch disproportionately, walls meant to be uniform in thickness will vary in the same way as distorted scaled outlines. Unfortunately, to scale an object proportionally using either Stretch & Mirror or Absolute Sizing, you must calculate the proportions yourself. And the only way to automatically scale proportionally is to use the mouse, dragging only corner handles.

Rotate and Skew

Applying rotations and skews with the mouse is similar to applying stretches and mirroring, except for one thing: With the mouse, you first select one or more objects; then—and this is the difference—click one more time on one of the objects already selected. (If you're working in Wireframe view, you must click on an object's border.) With that second click, the selection handles turn into rotation handles at the corners and skew handles along the sides, as shown in Figure 14.4.

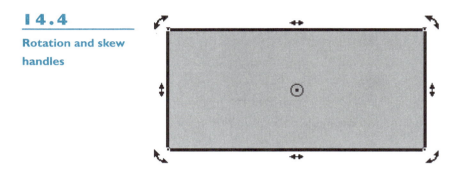

14.4

Rotation and skew handles

Rotations Using the Mouse

To rotate an object, simply click and drag one of the four rotation handles at the corners. It doesn't matter which handle you select to control the rotation; they all do the same thing. But notice the little target in the center of the object—that also is a rotation control. Initially positioned in the object's center, the target can be dragged anywhere, even outside the object. The target is the center of rotation, like a thumbtack around which the object will rotate as you click and drag any of the four handles.

Figure 14.5 shows the results of rotating a rectangle with the target in its initial position, and then with the target moved out to one corner. Once moved, the target stays where you last left it.

As with stretching, the Ctrl key performs a constraining function when you are rotating an object with the mouse. Press Ctrl while dragging a rotation handle, and you force rotations in increments of 15 degrees

14.5

How the target location affects rotations

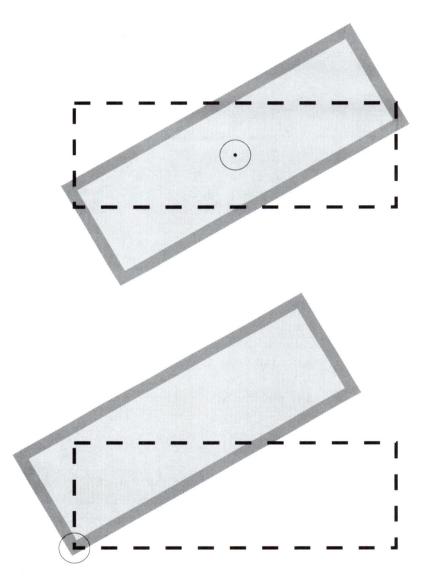

(this default 15-degree setting can be changed via Special / Preferences / General / Constrain Angle). The Shift key does not perform any function for rotations.

INSIDE INFO

 To move the rotation target back to the object's exact center, hold down the Ctrl key while dragging the target. You can also hold down Ctrl to align the target to any one of the eight rotation handles.

Skews Using the Mouse

Skewing can best be visualized with a rectangle. It is comparable to taking a cardboard box with its flaps open, and slowly collapsing the box over to one side. The sides don't bend; the corners just change angles as the box flattens like a pancake.

To skew an object, simply drag one of the skewing handles (the ones in the center of each *side* of the object) in the direction you want the object skewed. The side handles are for vertical skewing; the top and bottom handles control horizontal skewing. As with stretching, the side opposite the handle you drag is the anchored side.

Figure 14.6 shows examples of rectangles and text skewed vertically and horizontally. Normally, you will skew something in one direction or the other, but seldom in both (though there is nothing to prevent you from doing so).

Using the Roll-up to Rotate and Skew

As with the Stretch & Mirror functions, much of the time it is just as easy to accomplish rotations and skews directly on the object as it is, via the roll-up. Similarly, the principal reason to choose the roll-up technique rather than the mouse is for precision and/or repetition. Using the Rotate and Skew pages of the roll-up, you can specify the exact rotation or skew angle, to one-tenth of a degree. You can also specify the exact center of rotation, and whether it is measured relative to the object center or relative to the page.

14.6

Objects that are all askew—vertically (top) and horizontally (bottom)

WATCH OUT!

The same caution applies for rotating and skewing as for stretching and mirroring: If you do them more than once, DRAW doesn't total the degree of change. It starts over from zero each time, making it very difficult to return an object to its original shape or position.

If you use Transform / Rotate, the object will still rotate about the control point. The tic-tac-toe grid allows you to quickly specify any of the nine control points as the center of rotational.

On the Transform / Skew page, the tic-tac-toe grid is used to control which side is anchored when a skew takes place. Click on any of three grid points that are on the side you want anchored.

NEW FOR 5

> Here is a small enhancement that may save you steps realigning objects in certain instances: You can now specify the center of an object as the anchor point for skewing. This can only be done via Transform / Skew. For direct skewing with the mouse you will always use one of the sides of an object as the anchor.

If you plan to stretch an object as well as rotate or skew it, do the stretching first. This is especially important when you're working with text. As an example, try the following:

1. Create a few words of artistic text in a simple sans serif font, such as Arial.
2. Rotate the text 30 degrees, and then stretch it vertically about 50 percent.
3. Create the same text again.
4. This time, stretch it vertically first, and then rotate it 30 degrees.

Did the first method give acceptable results? Probably not. This is because the horizontal and vertical stretches affect whatever is inside the selection handles, in purely vertical or horizontal directions. DRAW ignores the actual length and width axes of the object itself.

AUTHOR'S NOTE

> **UPGRADING FROM VERSION 3?:** Although imported bitmap images could be rotated and printed before DRAW 4.0, they could not be displayed when rotated. DRAW 4.0 and 5.0 have addressed the problem, but not satisfactorily: they can display rotated bitmaps in a pinch—but very crudely in edit mode, and very slowly in full-color preview and print preview. Therefore, whenever possible, it is preferable to rotate and save the bitmap file before importing into DRAW.

Rules of Thumb for Rotate and Skew

- Always stretch objects *first*, and *then* rotate or skew them.
- Skews should usually be either horizontal or vertical, but not both. If you find yourself doing both, it is likely you are trying to achieve a result that would be better accomplished with other tools (such as Envelope, discussed in Chapter 15).

Putting It All into Perspective

The Add Perspective effect represents something of a transition between the simpler transformations we've already described and other, more complex special effects yet to come. Unlike blends and extrusions, which will actually add new elements to your drawings, adding perspective is really just another form of distortion. In that sense it is analogous to the Rotate, Skew, and Stretch & Mirror functions of Transform—the difference being that Perspective is designed specifically to create a sense of depth or dimension relative to a viewpoint. This is something that cannot be accomplished directly with the other distortion tools on the Effects menu.

To add a perspective, first select an object or group with the Pick tool. Then select Add Perspective from the Effects menu. At first it will look as though you have merely switched to the Shape tool. In fact, the Shape tool becomes highlighted, and you will see what appear to be nodes at the four corners of a selection box around your object. They are not normal nodes, however. They are handles that you will drag to create the perspective effect you desire.

WATCH OUT!

 **You cannot select several objects at once and apply a perspective to them. They must be grouped first.**

Now let's examine the two basic types of perspective: one-point and two-point. The type of perspective created depends on how you drag the perspective handles.

One-Point Perspective

Once you've selected Add Perspective from the Effects menu, dragging the perspective handles vertically *or* horizontally (but not both) creates a *one-point perspective.* This gives the impression that the object is receding from view in a single direction. Figure 14.7 shows a billboard, and in Figure 14.8 we have applied a one-point perspective to it. To do this, we dragged the lower-right handle up a bit, and then the upper-right handle down a bit.

14.7
This billboard is viewed straight on; it is lacking in perspective.

Not visible in Figure 14.8 is a hypothetical *vanishing point* that appears as an X on your screen while you are editing a perspective. Because this

14.8

The same billboard with one-point perspective added

point represents the theoretical spot toward which the object is receding, it is normally very far away from the actual object. To see it, you will usually have to zoom out several times. Once it is visible, you will see the vanishing point move as you drag the handles. You can also move the vanishing point itself, as an alternative to moving the handles.

INSIDE INFO

For help creating one-point perspective, hold the Ctrl key while dragging a handle. This constrains movement to solely vertical or horizontal. Hold the Shift key at the same time, and the movement of the opposite handle will symmetrically mirror the movement of the handle you are dragging. If you drag a handle vertically, the opposite handle that moves is the upper or lower counterpart. If you drag horizontally, it is the left or right counterpart.

Two-Point Perspective

Remember that one-point perspective is maintained only if all handle dragging is confined to either horizontal or vertical movements. You will still have a one-point perspective even if you move all four handles, *if* they have all been moved *along the same axis*—which brings us to how to create two-point perspective. From what we have said so far, you might conclude that this is done by moving any of the perspective handles in combinations of *both* vertical and horizontal directions, and you would be right. This can happen in two ways: You can take two different handles and drag them separately, or you can drag a single handle in a diagonal direction. Dragging toward the center of the object pushes the object into the screen, and dragging away from the center pulls the object toward you.

WATCH OUT!

Before you apply any perspectives, make sure your object is already shaped the way you want it. In other words, any node editing done with the Shape tool must be done before perspective is added. Once you have applied a perspective to an object, the normal Shape tool functions are not available for that object.

So what exactly is a two-point perspective? It means that the object appears to be receding in two directions at once. In Figure 14.9 we have an exaggerated two-point perspective—sort of a mole's-eye view of our Burma Shave billboard. In the figure, notice that there are two vanishing points.

14.9

A mole's eye view of two-point perspective

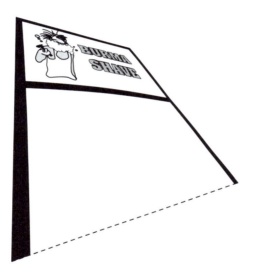

If the difference between one-point and two-point is still not quite clear, imagine that you are working with a movie camera, filming our billboard from one of those nifty mobile camera cranes. If you swing around the sign in either purely horizontal or purely vertical motions, your film will have a one-point perspective. But swing around wildly, in all directions at once, and you'll get a two-point perspective (along with a queasy stomach).

Following is a short exercise in creating a perspective.

1. Draw a white rectangle in roughly the center of the page.
2. Open the Symbols roll-up, and drag any symbol (an animal symbol works well) into the center of your rectangle. Size it as if you were creating a flag. Fill it with any color you prefer.
3. Group the symbol and rectangle.
4. With the group selected, go the Effects menu and Add Perspective.
5. Drag the upper-right corner handle about one-third of the distance towards the center of the rectangle.
6. Zoom out, if necessary (use the hotkey F3), until both vanishing points are visible.
7. Experiment by moving each of the vanishing points in various directions.

You have just created a two-point perspective. When the vanishing points are visible, you can manipulate the perspective by either continuing to drag the handles or by dragging the vanishing points. Most of the time, it is more convenient to move the handles, because you must zoom too far out to see the vanishing points.

WATCH OUT!

Perspective can be a useful effect, but there is one limitation to note: Applying perspective does not scale object outlines, even if you enable Scale With Image in the Outline Pen dialog. If you use a thick outline as a border on an object, don't expect it to scale realistically when you add perspective. In our billboard example, the sign's frame scales realistically only because the sign itself is made up of two solid, filled objects that have been grouped along with the text and cartoon, before perspective was added to the group. By the way, pattern fills do not scale according to the perspective, either.

Copying Perspectives

Let's jump ahead for a moment to the lower portion of the Effects menu. The Copy flyout allows you to copy a number of special effects from one object to another. Copying a perspective sounds like it might be a valuable operation, and you might expect that you could create nice three-dimensional scenes using it. Actually, however, this command simply copies the same relative distortion from one object to another. If you are trying to achieve depth and a sense of perspective for an entire scene, you will probably have to apply perspectives individually to objects, rather than using the Copy Perspective option. You may even find that the Envelope tool, introduced in the next chapter, is frequently a more flexible tool for achieving what you want. Of course, a requisite skill is the ability to visualize three dimensions and translate them to a two-dimensional environment—one thing that separates the skilled artists from the rest of us.

While we are on the topic of marginally useful features, take note of another option available to you. You can take an object to which you have already applied a perspective and add perspective to it again. This creates a brand-new selection box with perspective handles on top of the distortions you have previously applied. We honestly can't think of a particularly sound reason for doing this, but the option is available. If your intention is to add a totally different perspective to an object, use the Effects / Clear Perspective command to clear the existing perspective and then add a new perspective. If you have added several perspectives on top of one another, Clear Perspective will clear them in the reverse order in which they were applied.

By the way, notice that the Clear Perspective option is a chameleon. Until you select an object that has a special effect applied to it, the option reads Clear Effect and is unavailable (grayed out) on the menu. Once you do select an object, the menu option will describe and clear whatever effect was the most recently applied to that particular object.

Bring On the Steam Shovels

As we approach our discussions on the heavyweights of DRAW's special effects in upcoming chapters, keep the following helpful escape and clean-up commands in mind.

Sometimes, you'll need some heavy equipment to clean up a mess you've made when your urge to transform everything on the page has gone haywire. You can clear the most recent special effect applied to an object with the Effects / Clear… command. But for industrial-strength jobs, there is the Effects / Clear Transformations command. This item clears any rotations, skews, and stretches that have been applied to an object, and it does so in one step. It also clears any perspectives and envelopes. In other words, it clears all basic transformations that have been applied to an object, in one operation.

With Effects / Clear…, Effects / Clear Transformations, and the Undo command, you have enough equipment to dig yourself out of all but the deepest traps. Knowing this, you can charge ahead now, experiment, and…what the heck?…let yourself get a little out of control.

This chapter has been your warm-up. Next stop: The Special Effects Danger Zone…

CHAPTER 15

The Envelope, Please

FIFTEEN

CHAPTER 15

Although DRAW's Envelope command is similar in some respects to Perspective, discussed in Chapter 14, we think Envelope is far more interesting and versatile. Enveloping is a tool for distorting objects, and does not actually add any new elements to your drawing. Essentially, when you apply an envelope to an object, it becomes "elastic," allowing you to stretch the object to fit the outline of the envelope.

Envelopes can be applied to any object or group—even to open curves and text. Shaping text is probably one of the most common applications of envelopes (as done to the GO FOR IT! text in Chapter 5). Artistic text that has been enveloped can still be edited, though you cannot select individual strings and change their attributes. Beginning with version 4.0, you can also apply an envelope to paragraph text. Unlike enveloped artistic text, this does not distort the text itself. Instead, the envelope distorts the text frame, causing the text to wrap differently. Examples coming soon.

Creating an Envelope

As with Perspective, the first thing you do to apply an envelope is to select an object or group. (For enveloping, multiple objects must be grouped or combined.) Then choose the Envelope roll-up from the Effects menu, or use Ctrl+F7. This roll-up, shown below, was first introduced in version 4.0 and is unchanged in 5.0. Version 3.0 has envelopes as a feature, but no roll-up—you must continually access an Envelope command from the Effects menu to create new envelopes. Also, more envelope features were added in version 4.0.

With an object or group selected and the roll-up open, you will select from one of four envelope-editing modes, available on the icons in the

center section of the roll-up. Your choice determines the basic form your envelope will take. The first three modes—Straight Line, Single Arc, and Two Curves—all behave similarly, creating envelope shapes similar to those depicted by their icons. Let's take a look at these three first (before we explore the fourth one, Unconstrained).

Enveloping Fundamentals

After you select a mode, click Add New to place an envelope outline around the selected object or group. Nothing has actually happened yet to the object. You will see the Shape tool become active (as it does with Perspective). And, as you did with Perspective, you shape your envelope using the handles or nodes that appear on the outline (with an Envelope you get eight of them).

Drag the handles to create an envelope. You'll see the changing shape of the outline only; nothing will actually happen to the selected object until you click Apply. This gives you an opportunity to make numerous adjustments to the envelope using the handles, before actually applying it to the object. You can even bail out and start over completely by clicking on Reset Envelope.

When you're shaping an envelope in the Straight Line, Single Arc, or Two Curves modes, you move the center handles either directly toward or away from the object's center. (These nodes will not move laterally.)

Corner handles can be moved either up/down or left/right; the User's Manual says "up/down & left/right," but this is misleading. You cannot initially move these handles diagonally as you can Perspective handles. They will move horizontally and *then* vertically.

To get a feel for creating a simple envelope, try the following exercise. It looks longer than it really is, and you'll learn a lot.

1. Draw a rectangle.
2. Invoke the Envelope roll-up (Ctrl+F7).
3. Select the Pick tool, and make sure your rectangle is selected.
4. In the roll-up, click the first icon, for the Straight Line mode.
5. Click Add New, and you'll see a group of small selection handles around the rectangle's periphery.
6. Grab the top-center handle, and try dragging it left and right. You'll find that it won't move.
7. Drag the handle up, creating a "tent" shape.

As you drag handles, notice that the envelope outline's shape changes, but nothing has happened to your rectangle yet. If you were to click the Reset Envelope button, the eight handles disappear, and you would be back to square one.

8. Now select the top-left corner handle and try moving it in a diagonal direction. Won't budge? Try dragging it up first, stop, and then drag left.
9. Click Apply and watch carefully—remember what happens to your object. We'll discuss the result shortly.
10. To clear this envelope, go to the Effects menu and select Clear Envelope.
11. Click Add New again.
12. Grab the top-center handle, and hold the Shift key as you drag up and down.
13. Try the same thing holding the Ctrl key.
14. Try it one more time, holding both Ctrl and Shift.

15. Try the same sequence (steps 10 through 14), with a corner handle.

The foregoing steps have shown you how the Ctrl and Shift keys add considerable control over shaping envelopes. Holding the Ctrl key forces opposite handles to move in the same direction; holding the Shift key forces opposite handles to move in opposite directions; and using both in conjunction moves all four corners or sides toward or away from the center.

Now let's get back to what happened in step 9. You may wonder why your rectangle didn't follow the envelope shape exactly when you applied it. DRAW tries to force an object to fit as well as possible to an envelope, but is affected by three factors:

- The *mapping option* you choose (we'll talk about mapping options shortly)
- Whether you choose to maintain straight lines
- The number of nodes the object has

A rectangle is an object with only four nodes and constructed of straight lines. In the exercise you just completed, the envelope tried to force a single straight line to bend in the middle. In cases like this, DRAW curves the line for an approximate fit. This is a good time to discuss...

The Keep Lines Check Box

Keep Lines was introduced in version 4.0. In version 3.0, all edges are converted to curves automatically as required to approximate the envelope shape. Now, by turning on Keep Lines, you can tell DRAW to keep line segments straight, and create the best fit possible subject to that constraint. Sometimes this proves useful, and sometimes not.

Keep Lines tells DRAW to maintain all straight lines that exist in an object. In the last exercise, the rectangle is composed entirely of straight lines. So, had you enabled Keep Lines, pulling on a center handle would have done absolutely nothing—you would in effect be giving conflicting commands. One says "Try to make the rectangle tent-shaped," and the other says "Okay fine, but don't bend any of my straight lines!"—an impossible task.

Take a look at Figure 15.1. On the left, we have enveloped a rectangle as it would have looked in your exercise, and have depicted the object's actual nodes. In the middle we took the same rectangle, converted it to a curve, and added four more nodes (center nodes on each side) before applying the envelope. Doing this provides "hinges" in the correct places, so the rectangle can exactly fit our Straight Line envelope.

In the center object of Figure 15.1, the Keep Lines option is irrelevant for the envelope mode we chose. On the other hand, if we were using Single Arc mode, the status of Keep Lines makes a significant difference. In the third object, we converted one of the top two segments to a curve, while keeping the other as a line. Then we applied a Single Arc

15.1

This shows how an object's nodes and the Keep Lines option can affect the Envelope function

envelope, with Keep Lines turned on. You can see how the curve segment conforms more closely to the envelope shape, but the line segment does not.

These examples may seem trivial, but by playing with simple objects and trying different combinations of settings, it is much easier to see how the settings interact. Then, when you wish to apply envelopes to more complex objects, you will be better armed to get predictable results.

Before moving on, we suggest that you create a rectangle and a short artistic text string. Experiment on them using the Straight Line, Single Arc, and Two Curve envelope modes. For now, do this with the mapping option left at the default, Putty. After reading the next section, you can go back and try changing the mapping options, as well.

This form of experimentation is the best way to understand how various combinations of options work. There are so many available to you, and as you create more objects and add effects on top of one another it becomes almost impossible to anticipate precisely what will happen. It's best to develop an intuitive feel for the tools, starting simple and then piecing together more complex combinations.

INSIDE INFO

> We mentioned earlier that you can make several changes to an envelope before you actually apply it. You can also change modes AS YOU CREATE your envelope. For example, you can compose a single envelope using a combination of both Straight Line and Single Arc, enabling you to shape the envelope before ever applying it to an object. Also, you can apply one envelope to an object, and then click Add New and apply a totally new envelope to that object. The result is to compound the shaping done with the first envelope, rather than replace it. On the other hand, if you convert to curves an object that already has an envelope, its shape is retained, but the Shape tool reverts to normal node-editing as if an envelope had never been applied.

All about Mapping Options

We find the DRAW User's Manual explanation of the mapping options quite intelligible… to a rocket scientist, maybe! If you can figure out what they are saying, you probably didn't need an explanation in the first place. In defense of the documentation's authors, explaining these options concisely is a daunting task.

To begin our own attempt at illumination, we'll make the point that mapping, as its name implies, controls *the particular way a selected object is shaped to fit into any given envelope*. It does *not* affect the envelope shape itself. The mapping option only comes into play when you click Apply. Therefore, you will choose only one mapping method per envelope.

Sometimes a picture is, indeed, worth a thousand words, so we have composed a sample that compares the four mapping options applied to the same object. In Figure 15.2, we created a grid with some text sitting on top of it. We grouped these two objects and duplicated the group four times. (Remember, you cannot apply an envelope to multiple objects unless they are first grouped or combined.) In the center is the unenveloped group. Behind it is an outline of the envelope shape, created by using a combination of Straight Line and Single Curve modes.

15.2

How the four mapping options affect enveloped objects (say that fast, four times…)

Original Mapping

Putty Mapping

Group to be enveloped with shape of envelope

Horizontal Mapping

Vertical Mapping

To each of the four duplicates, we applied exactly the same envelope shape, but we selected a different mapping option for each version. The results are, as you can see, dramatically different. In practice, you may see more or less impact from changing mapping options, depending on the shape of the particular envelope and the shape and nature of the object(s) being fit into it.

Here are descriptions of the four mapping options:

Original   Original is the sole mapping method available in DRAW 3.0. In this mode, there is a very literal mapping of the object's nodes to the control points and curvature of the envelope. This can result in some extreme distortion, as shown in Figure 15.2.

Putty   Putty is the new default mapping method, introduced in DRAW 4.0. It attempts to produce a more subtle distortion, by fitting the perimeter and then applying a more relaxed or elastic fit of the rest of the object to the envelope.

Horizontal and Vertical   In the Horizontal and Vertical mapping methods, the object is first stretched uniformly in both axes to fit an imaginary rectangle that encloses the envelope shape. Then the object is shrunk along one axis only (vertical or horizontal) until all elements are within the envelope. Vertical mapping is particularly useful where text is involved, because most text has distinct vertical elements. Substantial horizontal distortions of text are very apparent and often distracting, as shown in Figure 15.2. There are situations where the Horizontal mapping method can be useful as well, and we'll get to this later.

Another Example of Mapping

Now that you have seen the mapping options, we have one more example for you to consider, using a single-curve envelope with vertical mapping. Two examples of the same basic technique are shown in Figure 15.3. Both use the same envelope style, but there is quite a difference in the results. Which looks better to you?

Try creating the first sample, by enveloping a single two-line text string. Hold down the Shift key as you drag the top-center handle away from the center, to produce symmetrical Single Arc curves on the top and bot-

15.3

Two rings created with enveloped text: Which looks better?

tom. This is the easier approach, but the second version is what we want you to achieve, constructing what looks like a ring, set with words instead of gems. The problem in the first example is that the respective bottom and top edges of the two lines stretch away from each other, disrupting the three-dimensional illusion we want.

To create the second version, create two separate text strings and then align them. Apply a separate envelope to each, with only the top side of one and the bottom side of the other curved. This is more what we had in mind.

INSIDE INFO

Here's a little trick to apply identical but mirrored envelopes to objects, as was done in the second sample of Figure 15.3. Create the envelope for one of the objects. Vertically mirror the second object (flip it upside-down), and use Effects / Copy / Envelope From... to apply the same envelope you created for the first object. Then vertically mirror the object again, and align the two objects as needed.

Rules of Thumb for Mapped Envelopes

- If an object doesn't conform well to an envelope you are trying to apply, you will usually need to clear it, add strategically placed nodes that can act as hinges, and try again.
- Vertical mapping usually produces less distracting, more readable artistic text.
- If you plan to envelope multiple lines of text, they should usually be created as separate strings with envelopes applied to each, rather than a single envelope applied to one multiple-line string.

Unconstrained Envelopes

The Unconstrained mode—that fourth icon in the center of the roll-up—provides the greatest versatility to envelopes. It allows you to shape the envelope using all the same techniques you would use to shape or node-edit objects, including selecting and moving several nodes at once, and adjusting control points to change the curvature of the nodes. In versions 4.0 and 5.0, you can use most of the Node Edit roll-up's options while working on an envelope. This includes adding and deleting nodes, and changing the node type to be line or curve, cusp, smooth, or symmetric.

It is important to keep in mind the difference between shaping an envelope and *directly* shaping an object. Try this exercise:

1. If necessary, invoke the Envelope roll-up.
2. Draw a square about 2 inches high near the top of the page.
3. Click the fourth icon in the Envelope roll-up to select Unconstrained mode.
4. Click Add New.
5. Drag the top-left corner handle diagonally away from the object center.
6. Adjust the control points for that handle to make the envelope bulge out a lot on the lower side of the handle, and to curve inward considerably on the upper side.
7. Before applying the envelope, select Single Line mode (remember, you can mix modes in an envelope).
8. Select the opposite corner handle, and drag it horizontally away from the object center.
9. Make sure Putty is the selected mapping option, and click Apply.

Did the rectangle fit precisely to your envelope? Perhaps you need more nodes. Let's add some, and at the same time get more acquainted with another feature on the Effects menu: the Copy flyout. We'll also throw in a couple more tricks that may improve your productivity.

10. With the Pick tool, select the rectangle.
11. Press the + key on your numeric keypad to create an exact duplicate of the object, right on top of the original. Drag the duplicate away from the original until both are completely visible.
12. With the duplicate still selected, select Effects / Clear Envelope.
13. Convert that rectangle to curves by selecting Arrange / Convert to Curves or by pressing Ctrl+Q.
14. Switch to the Shape tool, and marquee-select all four nodes on the rectangular curve. (Remember, it only *looks* like a rectangle now that it's been converted.)

15. Double-click a node to bring up the Node Edit roll-up, and click the Add Nodes button (the one with the plus sign) to create four additional nodes.

16. Select Effects / Copy. On the flyout that appears, select Copy Envelope.

17. When the big black arrow appears, click on the original enveloped rectangle.

You should find that the second version, which was converted to curves with more nodes added, makes a better fit. Sometimes it will be necessary to add more nodes to an object so it can better conform to an envelope. Also keep in mind the mapping option you select; it, too, will affect the fit. In certain instances, the style of nodes *within* the object will also affect the envelope fit.

More Ways to Create Envelopes

DRAW 4.0 added two related features within the Envelope roll-up: Add Preset and Create From…, both of which greatly extend the usefulness of the Unconstrained envelope mode. Both make the job of shaping your envelope much easier.

The Add Preset option allows you to select a predefined shape as your envelope. Just click this button instead of Add New; the mode automatically switches to Unconstrained, and a flyout appears containing predefined shapes. Click to select one, and an envelope outline appears on the currently selected object. The envelope proportions are adjusted according to the proportions of the object. At that point you have a choice of applying it or further editing it, just as you would any other envelope.

An extension of Add Preset is Create From…, which allows you to create an envelope from a single, ungrouped object on your page. Select this option, and you are presented with the familiar big black arrow, used to select the object from which you want to derive the envelope. Unlike the presets, this type envelope will exactly match the original object's size and shape.

The Envelope presets are certainly useful, but this new Create From… option is really hot. Figure 15.4 shows how a simple logo was composed using Create From…, and also demonstrates a practical application for Horizontal mapping. At the top is a series of identical objects. The first was created with the Freehand Drawing tool, with Snap To Grid turned

15.4

Cloning an envelope from another object

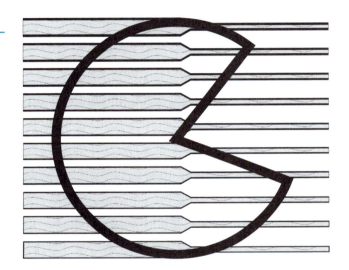

on, and then filled with one of the two-color pattern fills to suggest a wood-grain look. This object was duplicated a number of times using the drag-and-duplicate technique and then the Repeat command. The collection of objects was then grouped. Next, we created the Pacman shape from a circle, and modified it with the Shape tool.

Once the envelope shape and group were created, we used Create From… with Horizontal mapping set, to apply the pattern as an envelope to our collection of boards. As you can see, with relatively few steps you can create some very interesting objects.

INSIDE INFO

> **The CorelDRAW User's Manual doesn't mention this, but the object you select as the guide for an envelope must be a single shape. It cannot be part of a group or a combined object. If, for example, you want to use a complex letter as an envelope, such as a B, you must convert the B to curves, break it apart, and select the object that forms the perimeter shape as your envelope.**

Envelopes and Paragraph Text

We mentioned earlier that envelopes can be applied to paragraph text in DRAW 4.0 and 5.0. This is one of the most practical uses for the Create From… option. Applying an envelope to paragraph text enables you to essentially "pour" text into a shape.

When you select paragraph text, the mapping option in the Envelope roll-up automatically changes to Text, the only mapping option available. You apply an envelope to paragraph text just as you would to any other object, using any of the techniques we have already described (the three standard envelope modes, the Unconstrained option, Add Preset, and Create From…).

After you click Apply, your text flows (wraps) as if it had been poured into the envelope. The text itself is not altered or distorted. Unlike other objects, only one envelope can be applied to paragraph text. If you apply a new envelope, it replaces the old one, rather than compounding the effect of the first envelope.

As an example of using envelopes with text, take a look at Figure 15.5. We started with a gorilla shape, culled from the Animals category in the Symbols library. To fit the word *GORILLA* (as artistic text) inside of the shape, we used Create From…, with Vertical mapping applied. We then centered the text on the original gorilla shape. This did not quite give us what we wanted; some of the text strayed outside the actual envelope boundaries, and the *G* was distorted too much. But by switching to the Shape tool we were able to make adjustments to the envelope until the text fitted just as we wanted it.

15.5

Monkeying around with envelopes and text

The banana bunch is a group of objects, so to flow paragraph text within it, we had to first ungroup it. We selected the main curve that forms the overall shape of the bananas and copied this shape as our envelope to the paragraph text. Next, we regrouped the bananas and centered the enveloped text on top of them.

The word *PRODUCTIONS* is a bit of a teaser, to keep you tuned in for special effects still to come. We applied an unconstrained envelope to this artistic text, shaping it so that the weight of the gorilla appears to be flexing the letters. After applying the envelope, we used the Extrude command (coming up in Chapter 17) to produce three-dimensional text. We also applied a blend to the globe behind the gorilla, to give it a little more dimension.

Text Wrap

A common desktop-publishing technique is to have a column of text flow around a graphic object. This can be done in DRAW using nearly the same technique as is used to flow text within a shape. Figure 15.6 shows an example. It is merely a matter of shaping any envelope applied to paragraph text so that it avoids the other object. We have added a dotted outline to show more clearly the envelope that has been applied to the text.

Chapter 11 offers a step-by-step account of paragraph text being shaped inside and around objects.

INSIDE INFO

In version 5.0, envelopes shaped with inside turns like the one shown in Figure 15.6 can be easily created via the Create From... feature, rather than manually shaping the envelope. You can also do this in version 4.0, but there aren't as many tools available for creating an appropriately shaped object. In 5.0, using the new Trim command in the Arrange menu makes creating shapes like this a piece of cake.

15.6
That's a (text) wrap!

Gorilla Productions, the King Kong of theme party planning. Have an important event coming up? Let us make it one to remember.

Take our Tarzan and Jane wedding, for example. Why do the tired old wedding march when you can swing in on our authentic grapevines. Don't have a big enough tree? We'll handle that as well. We supply the bride and groom with environmentally correct simulated leopard-skin ensembles, and we will even provide a cute little Cheeta costume for the ring bearer.

So, for your next party, call the city's top banana:

GORILLA PRODUCTIONS!
Phone: (123) BIG-FOOT.

The next chapter features two commands, Blend and Contour, that don't merely warp, twist, or spindle selected objects. Each performs its own form of computer wizardry to add new elements to your artwork.

CHAPTER 16

Metamorphoses

SIXTEEN

CHAPTER 16

In the movie industry, the hot new special effect is *morphing*. To morph means to change from one shape to another (remember *Terminator 2?*). CorelDRAW has its own set of tools for metamorphoses, and though they might not be quite worthy of Arnold and the Big Screen, they can produce stunning effects on your computer's video monitor. This chapter focuses on DRAW's powerful Blend tool, as well as the newer Contour tool.

Blending Objects

Blending is deceptively easy to explain and visualize, but will prove to be one of the more entertaining and powerful features you use in DRAW. A blend contains two *control objects,* which we refer to as the *start* and *end objects*. When you apply a blend, a series of intermediate objects or steps are created that represent a transformation of the start object into the end object.

The transformation comprises changes to the shape, fill, and outline, from the first object into the other object. Each of these three aspects is modified by a certain percentage in each step of the blend, based on the number of *steps* or spacing you specify for the blend. With more steps, the amount of change per individual step is smaller, usually resulting in a smoother, less obvious transition—and a more complex drawing.

Blending can be done even with two objects that are quite dissimilar. For example, an object with no outline and a pattern fill can be blended with an object that has an outline and a uniform fill. Although there are almost no limits to the types of objects that can be blended, some combinations are more effective than others. In fact, some make no visual sense whatsoever.

You can access the Blend roll-up, shown just below, via Effects / Blend, or you can press Ctrl+B (this is one of the few Effects hotkeys that actually makes mnemonic sense). The Blend roll-up is used not only to create new blends, but to edit or manipulate existing ones.

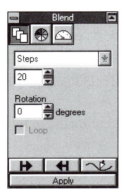

There are three pages built into the roll-up, identified by the three buttons across the top. The button with little tiled rectangles selects the default mode, which controls the geometry or layout of a blend, letting you specify steps, spacing, and rotations. The next button, the color wheel, gives you options for applying color to intermediate steps in a blend. The last button, which looks like a speedometer, contains a potpourri of controls to modify standard blends. The four buttons at the bottom of the roll-up, described later, are always visible, regardless of what mode is active.

Blending 101

After a brief explanation of a few basic laws of blending, we'll have you jump right into some exercises. As stated earlier, DRAW's Blend tools are functionally easy to understand, but they have far too many possibilities to cover verbally. Experimentation is the key to success.

Successful blending of two objects requires that you first make sure they meet the criteria for blending; and those criteria are… just about anything. Seriously! Unlike some other special effects, there are very few restrictions imposed for blending. You are free to blend nearly any two objects you wish, including grouped objects and complex curves (text being a good example). The only objects that cannot be blended are paragraph text, extrusions, and contour groups.

Blended groups are dynamic in nature. Once you have created a blend between two objects, you can transform the control objects, and the entire blend will automatically adjust.

Explore some of the basics in the following exercise:

1. Draw a red rectangle about 2 inches by 1 inch, in the upper-left corner of the page.
2. Apply a black, medium-thickness outline to the rectangle.
3. Switch to the Pick tool, making sure your rectangle is still selected.
4. Drag the rectangle to the lower-right corner of the page, and before releasing the primary mouse button, tap the secondary mouse button once to leave a copy of the original.
5. Change the fill of the second rectangle to yellow.
6. Display the Blend roll-up, with Effects / Blend Roll-up or by pressing Ctrl+B. (Notice that the Apply button is initially unavailable.)
7. Select both rectangles and notice that the Apply button now becomes available. Click it.

You should now have 22 equally spaced rectangles, representing 20 steps (the default number of steps) plus the start and end control objects. They should gradually change from the red start object to the yellow end object, with all other aspects remaining constant. Notice that the status line shows that you have a blend group selected. When you select a blend group, you are free to modify it, using the roll-up options as well as direct transformations of the two original objects. In the following steps, you will modify the blend group and see what effects these changes have:

8. In the Blend roll-up, change the number of Steps from 20 to 3. Nothing happens, right?

9. Click Apply. Now something happens: five equally spaced rectangles.
10. Click the first of the two large horizontal arrow buttons in the Blend roll-up, and then click Show Start in the drop-down menu that appears.

The two arrow buttons in the Blend roll-up make it easy to select the control objects—an otherwise tedious task. Use these buttons to specify a new (different) start or end object for the blend. Okay, back to business:

11. Change the fill color of the starting rectangle to a gradient fill (choose whatever colors and style you want).
12. With the start rectangle still selected, remove its outline.
13. Drag the start rectangle to the right a few inches, and click it again to reach the on-screen rotation controls.
14. Rotate the start object about 45 degrees.
15. Finally, click the Shape tool and drag a corner node of the start object to create a rounded rectangle.

Let's review what you should notice in the foregoing steps. As you modified either or both of the control objects, the blend group was automatically updated. Anything you do to a control object in a dynamic blend group immediately updates the entire group. Any options selected from the roll-up, on the other hand, are not applied until you click the Apply button. This allows you to set several options from the roll-up and then apply all of them at once.

In step 11 you verified one of DRAW's rules about fills that is listed in the User's Manual: If you blend a fountain-filled object with a uniform/solid-filled object, the intermediate steps are fountain fills of changing base colors.

When you removed the outline in step 12, you saw another important rule demonstrated: If one object has an outline and the other does not, then the intermediate steps will not have an outline. On the other hand, if both have outlines but of differing thickness and style, the outlines are blended just like other aspects of the blend group.

Going Deeper with Blends

When you rotated the start object, you got a result that probably wasn't very startling and hopefully looked pretty decent. The end result, after rounding the start rectangle, was probably more surprising, and did not look very good. Blending from one shape to another can be very effective, but it can also be troublesome. This is because the two objects may often contain unequal numbers of nodes, the mapping of which determines the shape of intermediate steps.

In the previous exercise, the end rectangle had four nodes; but when you rounded the start rectangle, each corner node split in two, forming eight nodes. This caused problems in blending from one rectangle to the other. Often, to achieve a better-looking blend, you will have to add nodes to get the two objects to blend more appropriately.

INSIDE INFO

In the above exercise, if you were to try and fix the node mismatch, your first inclination might be to convert the end rectangle to a curve and manually add nodes. A better and quicker solution is to zoom way in on one corner of the end rectangle. Switch to the Shape tool, move the corner node just enough so that two nodes and a minimal radius are visible. Now you have matching nodes, but when you zoom back out, the tiny radius won't be noticeable.

Unequal numbers of nodes in control objects can sometimes be overcome by changing the starting nodes of each object. The Blend roll-up provides a tool for doing this: Map Nodes. Bear in mind, however, that remapping the nodes may or may not produce better-looking results. By default, DRAW maps the first node of one object to the first node of the second object, but this doesn't always yield the best outcome, or the payoff you expect.

You can produce some interesting effects by purposely changing the node mapping. For example, try the following exercise:

1. In a new drawing, draw a rectangle at the top, dragging the cursor from upper-left to lower-right to create the rectangle.
2. Draw another rectangle in the lower portion of the page, but this time create it by dragging from lower-right to upper-left.
3. Invoke the Blend roll-up and apply the blend. Was the result what you expected? Probably not. Can it be fixed? But of course!
4. If necessary, reselect the entire blend group, by clicking on any of the intermediate steps.
5. Select the speedometer button in the roll-up, and then select the Map Nodes button.
6. Using the curved arrow cursor that appears, click on the upper-left handle of the bottom rectangle.
7. Next, click on the upper-left handle of the top rectangle.
8. Click Apply, and the blend will straighten itself out.

WATCH OUT!

Node mismatching can sometimes happen accidentally, even with two objects with comparable nodes, as the previous exercise demonstrated. It happened when you drew the rectangles differently. If you create two shapes by dragging in different directions for each, you will get results similar to that in Figure 16.1.

Rules of Thumb for Blending

- To ensure consistency—especially for blending purposes—get in the habit of drawing shapes in the same direction every time. Most common is to draw from the upper-left corner to the lower-right.
- For best results, blend objects that have an equal number of nodes. If you don't have an equal number, try adding some.

16.1
Here is what can happen when you mismatch nodes.

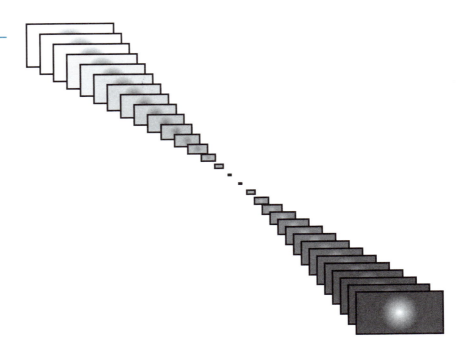

Fringe Players

In this next exercise you will get familiar with other options available using the buttons at the bottom of the Blend roll-up.

1. In the upper-left corner of the page, draw a blue ellipse.
2. In the upper-right corner, draw a green ellipse.
3. In the lower-left corner, draw a red ellipse.
4. Select the blue ellipse and the green ellipse, and blend them.
5. Click the first (left) arrow button in the roll-up, and select New Start. A large arrow cursor appears.
6. Click the red ellipse, and you will get an error message. Answer No.
7. Try clicking the second arrow button, and choosing New End. Then select the red ellipse, and click Apply.

The error message in step 6 was telling you that a start object has to be behind, or stacked earlier in the drawing than the end object. Since the red ellipse was the most recently drawn object, it is the topmost object, and therefore can't be the start object for a blend ending at the green ellipse. It could, however, be the end object. If you needed it to be the start object, you'll have to move it to the back, and then choose New Start.

This brings up an important issue not discussed previously: It is the stacking order of the individual objects that determines the start and end objects of a blend. The object that is positioned further back in the drawing will always be the start object. If you select a blend group and then choose Arrange / Reverse Order, you cause the start and end objects to swap places, because you are changing their relative stacking order. The intermediate steps are automatically updated accordingly.

WATCH OUT!

If you are using multiple layers in a project, be aware that in order for you to blend two objects, they must reside on the same layer. If they don't, you must move them to the same layer before attempting to blend them. The Apply button will be unavailable unless two selected objects are on the same layer.

Figure 16.2 shows how a rectangle and ellipse blend initially. We have left the outlines on so you can more easily see the rotation that takes place. In the right-hand image, we have remapped the nodes so that the rotation has disappeared. We want to reemphasize that when you blend objects of different shapes, it may be necessary to add *and/or* remap nodes to get a better-looking transition.

WATCH OUT!

A bigger challenge exists when the objects differ substantially in the number of subpaths they include. Some of the intermediate steps may appear only as outlines, or not appear at all. If this is the situation, the best advice we can give you is that tired old cliché: Experiment, experiment, and then experiment some more.

16.2
A blend with a twist, and one straight up

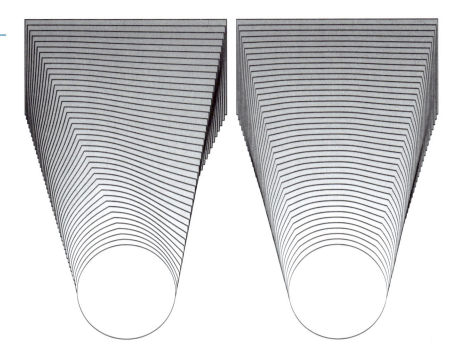

Colors, Colors, Colors

You may be curious about the little color wheel icon on the Blend roll-up, and this next exercise shows you how to use this control. (Fear not, we'll also explore further among the options of the other sets of controls in this roll-up, but in this chapter we are working our way from the simple to the complex.)

1. Clear any mess you made in the last exercises, by starting a new drawing. From Layout / Page Setup, choose letter-size and portrait orientation.
2. Type the word **Wow** in the upper-left corner of the page, using a heavy typeface set at 24 points.
3. Make sure your text object has no outline, and color it blue.
4. Duplicate the Wow and move the copy to the lower-right corner.
5. Change the duplicate Wow to a 60-point typeface and color it cyan.
6. Select both Wows and apply an eight-step blend.

7. Click the color wheel icon in the Blend roll-up.

Notice the color wheel that is displayed, and the black line running from cyan to blue. This indicates the path of color transition that your blend will take. By default, a blend changes colors along a linear path on the color wheel, but you have the option of changing that path, using the Rainbow option in the roll-up.

8. With the blend group still selected, click the Rainbow check box. Observe how the color path changes from a line to an arc.
9. Click Apply.

With Rainbow selected, you might expect to see a broader range of colors applied to your blend. (An arc is a longer path than a straight line, so you'd expect it would traverse through more colors.) In this exercise, however, you will not see a very dramatic change. Notice the two arrows indicating clockwise and counterclockwise below the color wheel. Counterclockwise is the default direction in your example, and in this case is still a very short path.

10. Click the clockwise button, and notice the arc now swings through a much broader range of colors in the color wheel.
11. Click Apply, and you will see a true rainbow of colors.

INSIDE INFO

To maximize the effect of a rainbow, make the two control objects the same color. If you apply a gradient fill to one or both control objects, Rainbow will still work. The end points of the arc will be the gradient's starting color.

Blends That Do Cartwheels: The Rotation and Loop Controls

Okay, so "cartwheels" is a slight exaggeration… but the Rotation and Loop controls can cause some nifty acrobatics. The Rotation setting is functional on its own, but it is really designed to be used in conjunction with the Loop field. Let's try these out.

1. In a new drawing, create the word **Loopy** in 24-point blue type, in the upper-left corner.
2. Duplicate the text string, and place it in the lower-right corner, changing its color to red.
3. Select both objects and invoke the Blend roll-up.
4. Set the steps to 10, and the rotation angle to 45 degrees.
5. Click Apply.

It should now be pretty obvious what Rotation does to your blend. By itself, Rotation would be a useful tool, except that only the intermediate steps of a blend rotate. This makes for a rather abrupt end to the blend. You might be thinking you could just delete the end object; but then the whole blend would disappear because they are dynamically linked.

A way around this is to use a command that is not on the Effects menu but that you will often find useful with special-effects groups. It's the Separate choice on the Arrange menu, and it can be used to break the link in dynamic groups such as blends and extrusions. If you separate a blend group, you end up with three objects: the two control objects, and a simple group composed of the intermediate steps. You can then either rotate the control objects to match the group rotation interval, or delete them.

You can experiment more with rotations later, but while you still have the blend group selected, try working with the Loop function. Select the blend group, click the Loop check box, and then click Apply. Loop essentially forces the blend to follow an arc from its start object to its end object, rather than a straight line. The Rotation angle controls both the amount of rotation of the intermediate steps and the curvature of the loop — but there is no simple explanation of the relationship between the two. Experimentation is the best way to figure it out. The larger the angle, the larger the curvature, until you reach 180 degrees. At that point, the curvature decreases, but the loop will look like it contains an extra coil.

Figure 16.3 contains examples of blend groups that were looped. As both the start and end objects, we used an object composed of a combined circle and rectangle. Using a combined object means there is a hole in it, making it easier to see exactly what's happening in each step of the looped blend. The six samples are all identical except for the rotation angle.

16.3

Some looped blends

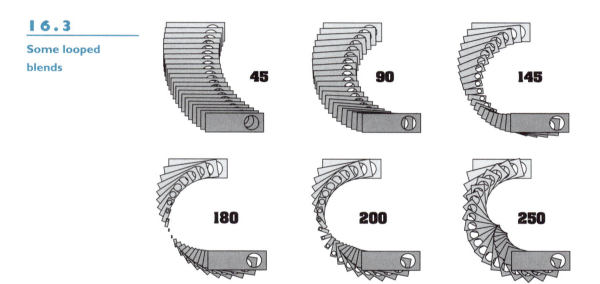

The loop passes through the *rotational centers* of the two control objects, but these are not necessarily the centers of the objects. Recall from the work you did on rotation and skewing that you can move the center of rotation for an object anywhere you want.

The CorelDRAW User's Manual casually mentions that moving the centers of rotation, then rotating the start and end objects, can cause some interesting effects. This statement is deliberately vague because it is next to impossible to detail what will happen in all situations. In Figure 16.4, we have taken the 90-degree blend group from Figure 16.3 and provided a few samples of this variation. The upper-left group is the original; the upper-right and lower-left groups have only the end object rotated; and the lower-right group has both objects rotated.

16.4

Some really loopy blends

Taking a Different Path

It's fine using Loop to fit a blend to an arc, but what if you want to fit the blend to a specific or more complex path? You're in luck: DRAW provides a convenient avenue for doing just that. It's that icon in the Blend roll-up that you may have been eyeing, the one on the lower-right with an arrow and a curve on it: the Blend to Path button.

You can fit blend groups to open paths, to closed paths, or even to objects with multiple subpaths, such as the letter *B*. Blend to Path can be a productivity enhancement as well as a way to accomplish some very interesting and artistic effects. The following exercise shows you the basics of blending to a path, while demonstrating a nifty technique that might be applied to creating certain types of forms, such as organizational charts.

1. Create a new drawing that is letter size and with landscape orientation.
2. Draw a straight horizontal line, centered on the page, about 9 inches long. (Use Snap To Grid or the Ctrl key to force a perfectly horizontal line.)
3. Draw a rectangle about 1 inch by 0.75 inch, anywhere on the page.
4. Fill the rectangle white, give it a black outline, and duplicate it (Ctrl+D).
5. Open the Blend roll-up (Ctrl+B), if it isn't already visible.
6. Select both rectangles with the Pick tool.
7. In the roll-up, set Steps to **3**, and click the Blend to Path icon.
8. In the flyout, select New Path; a large arrow cursor appears.
9. Click the straight line you drew, and then click Apply.

Your results probably do not look very uniform, and in fact probably overlap, depending on how your two objects were originally positioned. When you first blend to a path, the spacing between the control objects is maintained, as it was before the blend-to-path occurred. You can then drag the control objects to any point along the path, and the intermediate steps will space themselves accordingly.

10. Select the blend group, click the Full Path check box, and then click Apply.

Full Path spreads the objects evenly, from the start to the end of the blend path. Notice that the control objects are centered on the end points of the line.

Blending in Reverse Until now you have always set the number of blend steps, and DRAW has determined the correct, uniform spacing based on that. When you blend to a path, however, you can take the process in reverse: You can specify the spacing and DRAW will determine the number of steps.

1. If necessary, reselect the blend group on your screen.
2. Turn off Full Path and click the arrow next to the word Steps in the roll-up.
3. Click Spacing, set the spacing to **2.7** inches, and click Apply.
4. Change the spacing to **1.2** inches and click Apply.

The reason you turned off Full Path is because using both Full Path and Spacing is contradictory. Unless a Spacing value can be evenly divided into the path length, there is no way to both achieve a set spacing and exactly fill the path. The first attempt at spacing (step 3) worked quite well. The second attempt (step 4) resulted in several evenly spaced boxes, but the ending one was probably not spaced correctly. It stayed in the same spot as when the Spacing value was 2.7 inches. This can be corrected, however.

The foregoing problem happens frequently, but there is an easy solution. Select the end object of a blend-to-path group, drag it slightly *toward* the other objects, and then release it. This action causes the spacing to be adjusted automatically. If you drag *away from* the other objects, you will maintain the spacing but add more boxes to the group, as well. Remember, now that you specified the spacing, the roll-up tells DRAW to create as many intermediate steps as necessary to maintain that spacing between the start and end groups. Any time you change spacing, you will need to drag either the start or the end object, to update the spacing correctly.

Experiment with dragging the end object toward and away from the start object. Spacing is automatically adjusted, and a box is either added or deleted to the blend group. You will also find that the end object will never align with the exact end of your path, unless you change the Spacing value.

Composing Organization Charts

Using Blend to Path with either the step or spacing method can make short work of projects such as organization charts. You can easily create one set of boxes, duplicate the whole blend group as many times as needed for the various levels of hierarchy in the chart, and simply adjust the steps and/or line length for each level. Perhaps yet another middle manager was recently added to your staff. No problem—just change the number of steps in the blend group. Easy modification is the advantage to constructing organizational charts in this way.

Figure 16.5 shows an organization chart we constructed using Blend to Path. The whole chart, including drop shadows, was created using about 15 separate steps, total. Drop shadows were created by selecting the entire blend group at once, selecting Edit / Clone, and pressing Shift+PgDn to move the new set to the back. While still selected, the group was given a black fill and no outline (to hide the connecting or blend-to-path lines), and dragged to the proper position. Now, if we need to add or delete a position, we can easily change the steps of the box blend; and the drop shadow, being a clone, will follow suit.

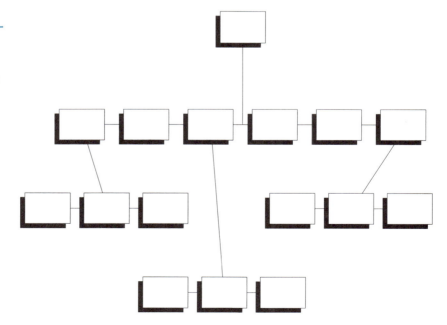

16.5

A quick-and-easy org chart created using Blend to Path (total number of steps: 15)

Blend to Path has a wide array of uses. You can also use it to produce some interesting artistic effects. In Figure 16.6, we have created a nameplate for the Banque du Bob. The nameplate was designed to convey the power, security, and sophistication of the institution.

We began by creating a large letter *B* to use as our path. We then blended a series of circles to the path, representing rivets. We chose the Full Path option for this, and adjusted the number of steps until we got the appropriate spacing of the spheres. (You may have to do some experimentation to get the fit you want in situations like this, adjusting

16.6

A power nameplate, apropos to the Banque du Bob

the number of steps and the locations of the start or end point, and perhaps even resizing the path itself somewhat.) The *B* and the rivets, by the way, all have a conical fountain, giving them a metallic look.

The Subtler Side of Blending

Up to this point, we have deliberately restricted our blends to those with distinctly visible steps. We have done so mainly to let you see how they actually behave. If you were to re-create any of the samples in Figure 16.3, a screen refresh would look almost like a simple animation, making it very clear how the blend proceeds. Blends of distinct steps are useful as explanatory tools and, like the org chart, they also have considerable utility in the field. More often, however, the Blend feature is used to create subtle color/shape transitions that are not readily apparent to the viewer as discrete steps (hence the name, Blend).

As one example, look again at Figure 16.6, where we created the "embossed" look for the bank title text by applying one of the more subtle forms of blending. To get this effect, we outlined the text and filled it with a light shade of gray, making the outline very large (12-point) in relation to the type size (60-point). Next, we duplicated the text, removed the fill, and changed to a black thin outline (0.5-point). Finally, we blended these two objects in 10 steps, offsetting the start object very slightly to give just a hint of dimension to the blend.

Blending is frequently used as a method to add shading and dimension to objects. Sometimes similar effects can be produced with gradient fills, but blending allows more variety and control. The key aspect of this technique is to create a start object that has no outline and the same fill as the object being shaded/highlighted. To shade, you then blend to an end object with a darker tint or black; to highlight, you use an end object with a lighter tint or white.

In Figure 16.7, we have created an eight ball, using a combination of a blend and some radial fills. At the top, we show the various components, so that you can more readily see the blend applied to the ball itself. You might think that creating a shaded ball like this would be accomplished more easily with the fountain fill tool, and to some extent that is true. In the middle of Figure 16.7, we have created a similar ball using a simple radial fountain fill. It looks pretty good but doesn't have quite the intensity we were looking for. So, we used a blend to more closely control the way the ball is highlighted. This was accomplished using simple circles as the blend objects, with the shade/highlight method just described. We decided radial fountain fills with offset

16.7

In front of the eight ball

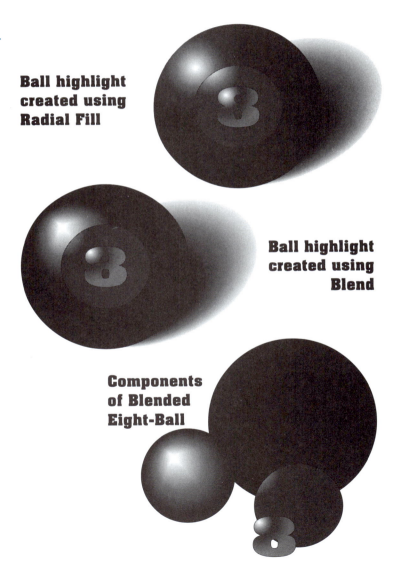

Ball highlight created using Radial Fill

Ball highlight created using Blend

Components of Blended Eight-Ball

centers and edge padding would suffice for the numeral 8 and the circle that contains it. These matched the flow of the blend closely enough to yield a composition that is looks fairly realistic.

By the way, if you look closely at this figure, you may notice another effect in use. We applied a slight envelope to the circle and the 8, making them bulge horizontally at the center, thus adding more dimension to the ball.

We were getting hungry while writing this section, so our next example, Figure 16.8, offers our rendition of an ice-cream cone, along with a map that makes use of a similar blend. The ice-cream cone may not be the most artistic rendering, but it provides examples of lighting/shading effects that would be nearly impossible to achieve without the blends.

> **Being Smart with Steps**
>
> Reducing the number of steps in a blend to a minimum is a very good technique to use while you are developing your masterpieces. It speeds up redraws and allows you to shape the control objects more clearly. Once you have it the way you like, reselect the blend group and increase the number of steps.
>
> More steps produce smoother blends, but they also make a drawing more complex. Certain blends will require more steps than others to produce a smooth transition, so be prepared to experiment. The maximum number of steps that will still improve the smoothness of transitions will be limited by the output device you are using.
>
> A 300-dpi laser printer can print relatively few shades of gray, so a blend of 100 steps would be a waste of time, except for being able to admire it on your monitor. For a high-resolution imagesetter or other output device capable of producing many gray levels, 100 steps is not an unreasonable number at all. The number of steps actually required will also depend on the distance spanned by the blend, and the range of shades involved.

428 CH. 16 METAMORPHOSES

16.8

The anatomy of a melting ice-cream cone

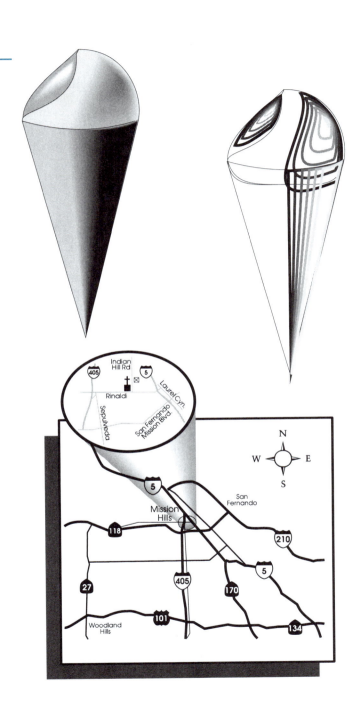

The wireframe cone on the right shows how our real one was constructed. We removed all fills, outlined all the blend steps, and also reduced the number of blend steps from 40 to 4; so that you can more easily see what is going on. You can see we weren't especially precise in the shaping of some objects, knowing they were going to be obscured by other objects.

The map in Figure 16.8 makes unique use of a blend similar to the one applied on the ice-cream cone. The cone leading to the map inset is made to appear transparent by placing all the objects it intersects on top of it. By using appropriate fills for shading, it seems that the cone is in the foreground and you are looking through it.

Compounding, Splitting and (Con)Fusing Blends

In all versions of DRAW, it's possible to use the end of one blend group as the start of another. In the User's Manual, this is referred to as *chaining blends*. Although the explanation indicates that you can select any step within a blend to chain, this is not true. You *can* do something similar, using the Blend roll-up's Split Blend option (new to 4.0), but you cannot simply click an intermediate step of an existing blend to blend with another object. End points are the only objects that can be used this way.

When you do use the end of one blend as the start of another, you create a *compound blend.* Another form of compound blend results from attaching two blend groups to the same path. This second option can be quite helpful, but, frankly, we had a difficult time finding a use for the first type of compound blend.

Then, inspiration hit us—Figure 16.9 is an abstract objet d'art that we initially titled Volcanic Reflection, but because we were still suffering hunger pangs (ah, the agony of the starving artist), we renamed it Sliced Bagel. The main elements are each composed of three ellipses, as shown to the right. The large gray ellipse was blended to the white ellipse; then the white ellipse was selected and blended to the smaller black ellipse. The whole compound blend group was duplicated, vertically mirrored, and placed on the filled rectangle. Voilà! Instant masterpiece!

16.9
The Sliced Bagel

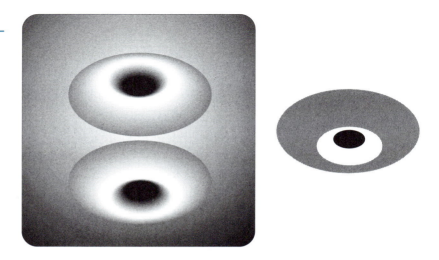

Art Mirroring Life   A somewhat more practical application for compound blends is for achieving shading that is more realistic and less computerish. Blends and gradient fills both have uniform steps, making it difficult to render the real-life random scattering and reflecting of light. By compounding blends, using different numbers and sizes of steps, this subtlety can be attained. In some cases, custom gradient fills—introduced in version 4.0—can be used in the same way.

Figure 16.10 depicts two versions of Corel's newly acquired and highly fictitious blimp. The version at the top was shaded with a simple gray-to-white blend. The one on the bottom employs a compound blend from gray to white, and then to black. Which looks more realistic and vibrant to you? (It's a rhetorical question—hopefully, you said the one on the bottom.)

If, after creating either form of compound blend, you need to make modifications to an individual blend group, you must follow a slightly different selection sequence to get at individual elements. Hold down the Ctrl key while you click on one of the two (or more) blends that the object contains. The status line will read "Blend Group" rather than "Compound Object of X Elements." Once you have a particular blend selected, the normal procedures apply for modifying it.

16.10
The Corel Blimp

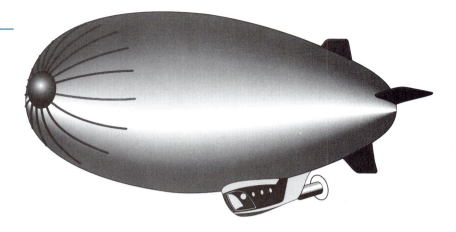

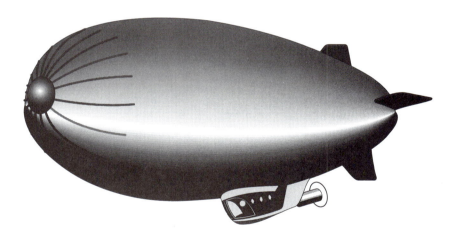

Figure 16.11 shows a compound blend to path. Each leaf is a group made up of an open curve, with a Calligraphic Pen applied to form the stem, and a closed curve forming the leafy shape. Only one group was created and duplicated for the top side of the branch, and a similar set for the bottom side. Each set was then blended to the same path: the branch (which is also an open curve with a Calligraphic Pen applied).

16.11

A branch and leaves constructed using blend to path

INSIDE INFO

If you have a compound object composed of several blend groups, and the blends in turn contain control objects that are groups, you can still select individual elements of the group for modification by the following procedure: Ctrl+click on one of the blend groups. Then click the Start or End arrow button at the bottom of the roll-up, and from the menu choose Show Start or Show End. If the control objects are easy to get to, you can Ctrl+click directly on them. To select individual elements of the start or end group, use Ctrl+Tab until the one you need to modify is highlighted.

There are a few additional steps required to get the look we wanted for the branch. First, to make it appear to recede into the page, we shrank the end object of each blend group. (This can be done either before or after blending to the path.) More importantly, recall our earlier discussion under "Blends That Do Cartwheels" about moving the centers of rotation. At the time, it may have seemed of little consequence, but in blending to path, the center of rotation is of major import. The rotation target is the point through which the path passes. So, even if you don't need to rotate either the start or end object, the rotation target still may need to be moved, to get the correct position of the blend objects relative to the path. In Figure 16.11, the target is moved to the very base of the stem of each control leaf, so that the leaves properly blend along the branch.

Once the lower branch was created, we duplicated it (the entire compound object), rotated it a bit, and then reshaped the branch itself somewhat with the Shape tool. Then we simply reduced the number of steps for each blend group attached to that branch, and we had the beginnings of an entire tree.

Taking Apart and Putting Together Version 4.0 added the ability to split and fuse blends. The buttons for these operations are found in Blend / Speedometer. Splitting a blend is somewhat like creating a compound blend, except that it allows you to select an intermediate step as the split point. The blend is split into two blend groups that become linked parts of a compound object. Once defined, the step you choose as the split point acts as both the end point of the first blend, and the start point of the second blend. You are free to keep splitting a blend as many times as there are steps available. Once split, you can move any of the control objects in your compound object, and each blend group containing it will rearrange according to the control object's new position.

If you wish to undo a split, you can utilize the Fuse command, also found in Blend / Speedometer. First, select the compound object; then, with the Ctrl key pressed, click anywhere on the particular blend you wish to fuse.

As nifty as this fusing capability seems, we honestly have never seen any artwork that makes practical use of it. We're sure some Corel user out there has found this to be an invaluable function… We just haven't heard from you yet.

NEW FOR 5

 Chapter 14 discusses effects that can be either copied or cloned. Blend is included on both the Copy and Clone flyouts. What's the difference? Copying a blend involves selecting two objects and copying the blend attributes from an existing blend. All the specific settings you apply within the Blend roll-up itself get copied, but the new blend is an independent group. In contrast, cloning maintains a link to the parent (control) blend group. Any modifications you make to the parent blend are reflected in any cloned blend groups. You cannot directly modify the attributes of a cloned blend; you must modify the control blend.

More Rules of Thumb for Blending

- Blends are usually a better choice than fountain fills to achieve realistic and dramatic highlight/shading effects. They are more flexible, and are less likely to cause PostScript *limitcheck* errors at print time.

- If a highlight/shading effect needs to be repeated on several objects within a drawing, and can be created satisfactorily with a simple or custom fountain fill, the fill is the better choice. Once you have created the right fill for one object, you can use the Fill roll-up to lift the fill from that object, modify its angle and center to account for changes in position, and then easily apply it to another object. (See the branch example in Figure 16.11.)

- Keep the number of blend steps to a minimum while creating complex drawings. Then, when you have the desired shape and relationship between control elements, increase the steps to the number you need.

- It is usually a waste to use more than 25 blend steps for a 300-dpi laser printer. The 600-dpi printers can utilize 50 to 60 steps, and high-resolution imagesetters handle 100 or more effectively.

And now, on to Blend's next of kin: Contours.

Contours: The Lay of the Land

Contours are second cousins to blends. They consist of a series of discrete steps, usually traversing a range of colors. Unlike blends, however, the steps of a contour are solely based on a single start object, rather than a metamorphosis from one object to another. Each contour step maintains the same general shape as the start object. The Steps value gets either larger or smaller by an amount you define, but maintains the shape of the start object as closely as possible. The name *contour* comes from topographic maps that use contour lines to represent elevation changes.

The Contour roll-up, shown just below, can be accessed from the Effects menu or by typing Ctrl+F9. Use of the roll-up and application of contours is fairly straightforward. The following exercise will familiarize you with the various options.

1. Start a new drawing.
2. Create a yellow-filled rectangle about 2 inches by 4 inches.
3. Apply a 2-point red outline to the rectangle.
4. Invoke the Contour roll-up (Ctrl+F9), and click Apply.

You will end up with what looks like three new rectangles centered inside your original rectangle, each having a progressively darker fill and outline. The roll-up's default settings are to create three dynamically linked contours, each with a perimeter that is .1 inch smaller than that of the previous object or step (this is the Offset value). The Inside option is what causes the steps to be smaller.

The default end fill color is black, as is the outline color. (These are controlled by the two buttons at the bottom of the roll-up.) The intermediate step colors are determined by the colors of the start object. If it has no outline, the contours will not have outlines—regardless of the end color setting. Outline width is also determined by the original object.

Notice that the status line now reads "Contour Group." As with other dynamic groups, you can use Arrange / Separate to break the group into unlinked components that can then be manipulated individually.

5. With the object still selected, click the Outside option in the roll-up.
6. Change the number of Steps to 4, the Offset value to **0.3**, the ending fill color to red, and the outline end color to blue.
7. Click Apply.
8. Click the To Center option in the roll-up, and change Offset to **0.07**. Click Apply.
9. Click the X icon in the Outline Pen flyout to remove the control object's outline.

You have no doubt noticed that the Outside option adds steps that are progressively bigger than the original, increasing in size by the Offset amount. To Center is similar to Inside, except that To Center creates as many steps as are necessary, based on the selected Offset size, to fill the original (control) object. When you reduced the Offset value in the foregoing exercise, thus forcing more steps to be created, and removed the outline, the result looked a lot like something created with a blend. In fact, there are frequent instances where a blend can be used instead of a contour, with identical results.

In Figure 16.12 we have taken the letter *B* and applied each of the three types of contours to it. The bottom-right figure represents an outline blend. The blended outlines make it somewhat similar to the Outside Contours effect. It is the other two Contour options, Inside and To Center, that are hard to achieve using any other tools. Both can be used to produce distinctive neonlike and three-dimensional objects.

16.12

Shapely B's

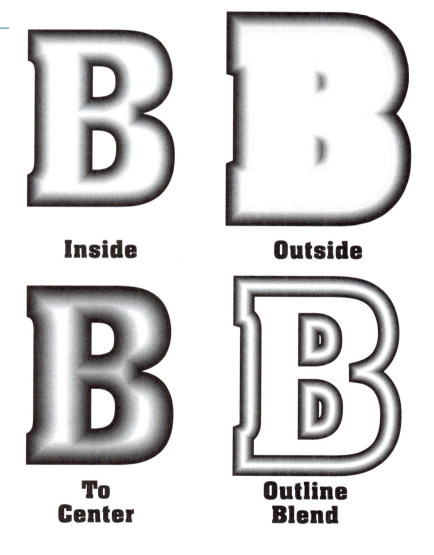

NEW FOR 5

You can use Effects / Clone to copy the contour settings from one object to another, just as you can use Effects / Copy for duplicating blends. Cloning a contour reproduces all the attributes set in the Contour roll-up, and maintains a dynamic link to the original object. Update the original, and the clones come along for the ride. Lest you become overly enamored with this capability, please read our cautionary sidebar about Contours.

If you are not in possession of a superfast computer—or even if you are, but plan to apply contours to large numbers of curvy objects (i.e. a text string)—a good approach is to experiment with a dummy object made up solely of straight lines. Figure 16.13 gives you an example of what we mean. The object on the left can be modified far more quickly than the letter *B* on the right.

INSIDE INFO

Once you have an object contoured to your liking, group it. We know it sounds weird to "group a dynamic group," but by doing so, you can resize the object without forcing DRAW to rebuild the contours, thus saving loads of time. DRAW will scale the contours along with the original control object, which is probably what you want anyway. If you need to change the contour settings, you can ungroup the object and apply the new settings.

You can even apply a contour to an open curve, and this can yield some impressive results. When you select an open curve, there will, logically, be only one Contour option available, Outside. After you apply the contour, set the outline to none and experiment with the fill options. Your best bet is to fill the control curve with white, and then set the ending contour to another color. (Don't worry if it doesn't make sense to be filling an open curve; it works.) Figure 16.14 is an example of this technique.

Create a Contour, Take a Coffee Break

If you're impressed with the results shown in Figure 16.12 and are ready to charge off and try more complex samples than the silly rectangles we had you create earlier, *wait!!!* As simple as the contour concept is, the CPU processing it requires is enormous. DRAW's contour function can handle straight lines easily, but when curves are introduced, watch out!

We ran a few time trials, using a 386/33MHz system with 8MB RAM as our test system. A simple rectangle with 4 contour steps took about 2 seconds to generate; 20 steps took 5 seconds; and 60 steps took 11 seconds. We then tried this with a rounded rectangle—not a terribly complex object, one would think. To create 4 contour steps took 2 minutes, and a 20-stepper took a whopping 6 minutes! Needless to say, we didn't bother with 60 steps. On a 486/66MHz, the same rounded rectangles took 10, 18, and 20 seconds, respectively.

So your options are to get a very fast system if you don't already have one, or have a large pot of coffee handy. Even with a fast system, applying the contour to a string of text results in lengthy wait times. Be aware, too, that resizing a contour group causes the contours to be generated all over again. They are a dynamic group based on the roll-up settings, and these must be maintained when the object is resized.

Keep in mind that curves are what chew up the time. Experiment with dummy objects made up entirely of straight lines, of approximately the same size and proportions as the objects that you plan to contour. Then, once you have the settings you like, apply the contour to the real objects…and go have a cup of coffee. Figure 16.13 is an example of the process. We created two rectangles and combined them (on the left) to create an object similar to the *B*. Applying the contours shown took about 10 seconds. Applying the same contours to the *B* took over 5 minutes.

16.13

Save time; experiment with a dummy

16.14

The lead author's initials in contour

Note how we avoided any curves that would slow things down. To the left is the original curve used to create the effect on the right. (It is a combined curve containing two subpaths.)

Next up in our journey through DRAW's special effects: Extrusions.

CHAPTER 17

Energizing with Extrude

SEVENTEEN

CHAPTER 17

The Extrude effect is one of our favorites. It is very powerful and, when used wisely, extruding allows even the artistically inept to produce impressive art. We make a distinction, however, between artistic ineptitude, as in "incapable of drawing straight lines and circles," and aesthetic insensitivity. When it's used indiscriminately, Extrude is one of the major contributors to horrific computer art. And if what you lack is good taste rather than a modest degree of skill, extrusions will only help you dig a deeper grave.

Extrusions Add Depth and Breadth

Extruding is one of DRAW's most clever functions, allowing you to select any simple object and easily turn it into something three-dimensional. By three-dimensional we don't mean a subtle suggestion of depth, resulting from shading or highlights, as you might produce with the Blend and Fountain Fill tools. Extrude is more explicit. It creates new surfaces that are dynamically linked to the original object and are specifically meant to produce a 3-D appearance. This is done by projecting significant points of your control object towards a hypothetical *vanishing point*, and then connecting those points to form closed surfaces.

Both open and closed curves can be extruded, including multipath curves and text. Text that is extruded is still editable, and the extrusion will update automatically to reflect the edits. Similarly, other control objects can be stretched, skewed, rotated, and so forth, and the extrusion will be updated following the changes.

WATCH OUT!

Be sure of your reasons for applying an extrusion. Don't apply one just for the sake of showing off your software. Unless a drawing is meant to be a three-dimensional rendered scene, you should usually limit the use of extrusions to one or two elements. This is especially true with artistic text elements. Add too many, and the drawing loses its anchor; things appear to be floating randomly in space.

The Extrude Roll-up

As with most other special effects, Extrude has its own roll-up (see Figure 17.1). To access it, choose Effects / Extrude or press Ctrl+E (hooray, another one that's easy to memorize). In the figure, the roll-up is shown

17.1

The Extrude roll-up, showing the page of geometry settings

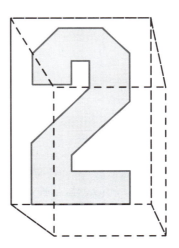

along with a large number 2 that is about to be extruded. You can see the outlines projecting out, showing how the 2 will be extruded. Notice that the roll-up has five icons across the top, each of which represents a separate page of controls.

In Figure 17.1, the Extrude roll-up is open to the Depth page—the controls that let you govern the basic nature and shape of your extrusions. This page, accessed by the second icon from the left at the top of the roll-up, is the page you will probably use most frequently. And don't worry if, like us, you are lousy at geometry or have trouble visualizing spatial relationships. An extrusion is just another dynamically linked effect, and thus is easy to edit until what you see is really what you want. The settings on all Extrusion roll-up pages can be adjusted before applying an extrusion—or after, if you didn't like what you got the first time.

The small **X** in Figure 17.1 represents the hypothetical vanishing point of the object. If this screen shot showed the entire page, you would see that the **X** is in the center of the page. This is the vanishing point's default location when you first invoke the Roll-up, but you are free to move it anywhere you like.

Putting Extrusions in Perspective

First, we'll define the types of extrusions available and then explain what role the vanishing point plays for them. In Figure 17.1, you see the default extrusion type, called Small Back, being applied to the 2. In Figure 17.2, we have edited the extrusion by opening the drop-down list of available extrusion types and selecting a different type, Big Back. Notice the outline showing how the new extrusion will project, once it is applied.

The first four extrusion types all add perspective; they make the object appear to be either receding into or coming out of the page. The back face of the object will be either smaller or bigger than the front, depending on the option chosen. The last two, Back Parallel and Front Parallel, are sometimes called *orthogonal projections*. The front and back faces in these shapes are always exactly the same size. This type of projection is typically used in engineering drawings, less frequently in artistic renderings.

17.2

The list of available extrusion types

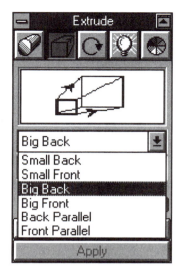

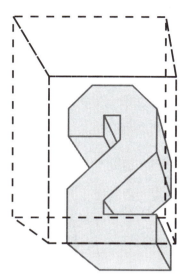

In Figures 17.1 and 17.2, notice the outlines indicating how the object will extrude. Sometimes these outlines are difficult to see and interpret, which is why the roll-up shows you a little graphic representation of each type (just above the drop-down list box). You can see what will happen before you apply the extrusion.

Wondering what the difference is between Big Front and Small Back? Look closely at the little graphics in the roll-up. The thicker outlines indicate where the control object is located, with the arrows showing the direction it is extruded. In Figure 17.3 we have placed a 2, with square holes in it, right on top of another 2 of the same size and font and filled with polka dots. We extruded the rear 2 using Small Back, and the front one, with the holes in it, using Big Front. The control faces of the characters are right on top of each other, in the middle of our extrusion sandwich. On the lower-right, we slid the 2s apart, to help you see what is going on.

17.3

These two deuces (placed together top-left, and moved apart lower-right) are extruded using Big Front and Small Back, so that they connect smoothly.

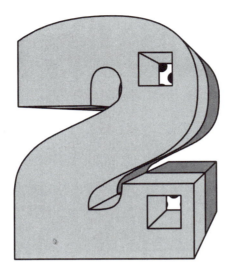

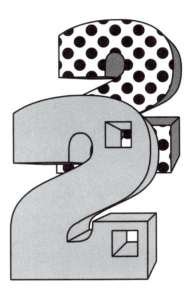

The Vanishing Point   The vanishing point performs one function for perspective extrusions, and a somewhat different function for the two parallel forms (described just below). If you watched cartoons as a kid (or if you still do), imagine the typical scene where Wile E. Coyote is trying to outrun an oncoming train. The railroad tracks recede, appearing to vanish into the horizon. The point on the cartoonist's page where they disappear is comparable to the vanishing point on the DRAW page.

The train must appear to recede toward the vanishing point, but it doesn't vanish. It has a set length or depth, which is obviously less than the tracks. This is what the Depth setting controls: how far toward or away from the vanishing point an object actually projects. The Depth setting can range from 1 to 99, with 99 being the equivalent of infinity. In other words, a very high setting makes the object appear extremely long. Conversely, a very small number indicates minimal thickness for the extruded object.

Most perspective extrusions you create will use the default form, Small Back, in which case the previous description of the vanishing point is perfectly applicable. But for two of the perspective forms, Big Back and Small Front, the vanishing point will appear to be coming out of the drawing rather than receding into it. Big Front and Small Front extrusions start at the control face and extrude toward the viewer (the control object is in back and is usually hidden from view); but Big Back and Small Back extrusions extend away from the viewer.

If you think all these combinations seem confusing, you are not alone. We can barely decipher it—and we wrote it. There is no simple way to describe, in words, what all these options do. Fortunately, you will probably be sticking to Small Back extrusions most of the time, and you can always experiment with the other settings to *see* how they work.

Parallel Extrusions

The Depth option is unavailable for the parallel extrusions. For these, the vanishing point functions as nothing more than a marker defining the center of the extruded face. It has nothing to do with horizons, since no perspective is implied. Positioning the vanishing point determines both the direction and the apparent length of the extruded object, which is why the depth setting is not used.

Figure 17.4 shows two examples of parallel extrusions, with the second one in the process of modification. The extrusion lines are all parallel; there is no attempt to convey perspective. The extrusion in process emphasizes how the vanishing point controls the length and direction of the extrusion.

17.4

Parallel extrusions do not have perspective, appearing as large shadows.

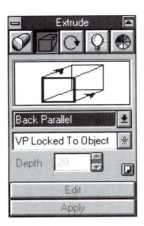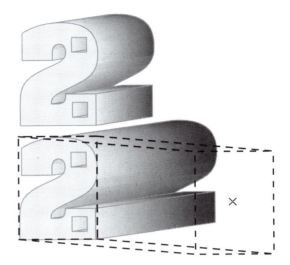

In Figure 17.5, we produced samples of each parallel extrusion and, going a step further, cut away a surface of each so you can see where the control objects are—they are darker than the rest of the extrusion. We also marked where the vanishing point would be for each extrusion. Remember that for parallel extrusions, the so-called vanishing point is a misnomer; it is simply the center of the extruded face.

There is something you should notice in the first extrusion at the top of Figure 17.5. Recall that we said the vanishing point controls the position of the extruded face. If the extruded face happens to be the back surface, however, in our world it would be invisible to us. Therefore, DRAW does not bother creating it.

Getting Down to Business

We're sure you're getting anxious to start doing your own 3-D rendering. The next few exercises will take you on a tour of most options in the Extrude roll-up. At the same time, we will use a few features introduced in earlier sections, and some hotkeys to get you accustomed to the available shortcuts.

1. Create a new letter-size drawing, in landscape orientation.

Getting Down to Business **449**

17.5
Deuces running wild

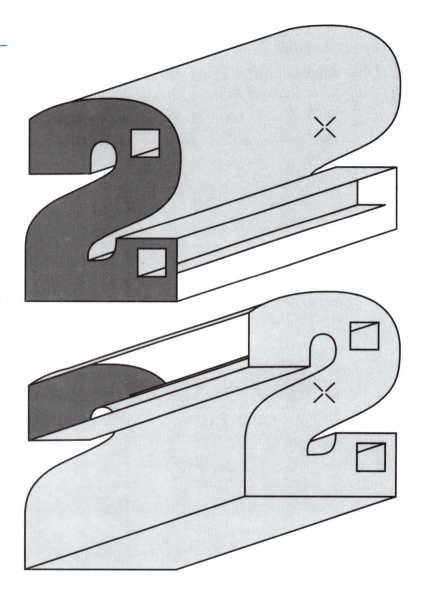

2. Draw a light-colored square about 2 inches wide anywhere on the page. (Remember, holding Ctrl while dragging forces a square; watch the status line for size.) Apply a 2-point black outline to the square.

3. Draw another square (color doesn't matter) about 1 inch wide anywhere on the page.

4. With the Pick tool, select both rectangles. Press Ctrl+A (Arrange / Align), click Align to Center of Page, and then OK.

5. Rotate the smaller rectangle only, by 45 degrees.

6. Reselect both rectangles, and press Ctrl+L (Arrange / Combine) to create an object with a hole in it.

7. Press Ctrl+E to invoke the Extrude roll-up, switch to the Depth settings (if necessary), and immediately click Apply.

Not very exciting, is it? So far, you should have something that looks like Figure 17.6: a square with a diamond-shaped hole in it. Pay particular attention to the default settings in the Extrude roll-up. Notice that the standard extrusion is Small Back, with a depth of 20. The vanishing point is always placed at the center of the page when the roll-up is first invoked. That is why it shows up in the center of your object, since you

17.6

Extruding a box with a hole in it

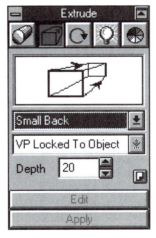
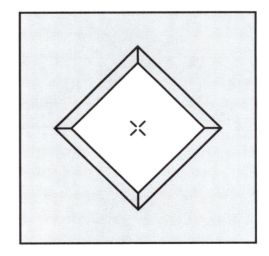

centered the object on the page. The rather bland result of this extrusion is because the perspective (controlled by the vanishing point) is set as if you are looking at the object straight on, so not a lot of dimension is evident. (At least you can see the sides of the hole through the box.)

Okay, so you weren't impressed with your first extrusion. Let's make it more interesting. Notice that the roll-up and your object are still in edit mode (the vanishing point is still visible and the Edit button is grayed out), so you can immediately start modifying the extrusion. If you were to deselect this object and come back to it later, you would have to first select it and then click the Edit button in the roll-up.

WATCH OUT!

When you reselect any dynamic linked groups such as extrusions, pay attention to the status line. It will tell you whether the group object or the control object is selected. It doesn't matter which one you select when you are editing an extrusion via the roll-up; but when you move, resize, or duplicate objects, it does matter. For example, if you select only the control object of an extrusion and duplicate it, only that object is duplicated and is not part of any extrusion. If you select the extrude group, then the entire dynamic group gets duplicated. In the case of extruded text, in order to edit it, you must select the control object only, not the entire extrude group.

So, to continue our exercise,

8. Make sure the vanishing point is still visible. If not, click Edit in the Extrude roll-up. Then, click and drag the vanishing point diagonally up and to the right roughly 2 inches, but don't click Apply yet.

9. Click the little paging icon in the lower-right corner of the roll-up, and choose Measured from Object Center. Adjust both values to read exactly 2 inches. Now, click Apply.

10. Click twice somewhere off the object, to deselect it.

11. Click the control face itself, and make sure that the status line reads "Control Curve."
12. Use the Fill tool flyout or Fill roll-up to apply a linear fountain fill of your choice to the control curve.

Does that look better? You should now have a more distinctly three-dimensional object, as depicted in Figure 17.7. When you changed the fill of the control curve, the fill of the entire object changed accordingly. We had you choose a fountain fill just so you would be aware that you are not limited to solid-color fills for extrusions. You can fill them just about any way you wish.

Editing the Vanishing Point

When you click on the paging icon in the lower-right corner of the Depth page, the roll-up changes to display a set of options for precise positioning of the vanishing point. You can either drag the vanishing point and watch the values change in the boxes, or enter the exact values in the roll-up to position the vanishing point. Positioning can be set relative to either the page origin—usually its lower-left corner—or the control object's center. (This was the option you chose in the foregoing exercise.)

Color, Shading, and Lights

The default method of filling extruded surfaces, as you may have already figured out, is to match the control curve's fill. If that changes, the rest of the object changes, without any further action required. But, are there alternative ways to fill the extruded faces?

Use Object Fill

Click on the color wheel icon at the top of the Extrude roll-up, and you switch to Extrude's Color settings page. There are three basic options for colorizing. The default is Use Object Fill. This means that whenever you select either the control object or the whole extrusion, and assign any sort of fill, all faces in that extrusion will automatically change to

Color, Shading, and Lights   453

17.7

This extruded box provides a feeling of depth.

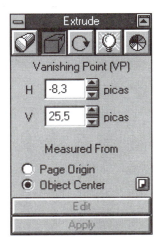

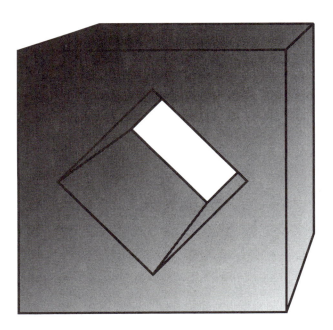

the fill you selected. (The roll-up does not play a part in updating the color, once this option has been applied.)

NEW FOR 5

In the Extrude / Color settings, notice an option called **Drape Fills**. This is a new feature to version 5.0. By default, it is turned on. Only applicable for the first fill option, Use Object Fill, Drape Fills treats the extrusion as a whole when filling it. In prior DRAW versions, each surface of the extruded object was treated as a separate object when a fill was applied. This is irrelevant for solid color fills, but wasn't always satisfactory for fountain fills. Take a look at Figure 17.8. Though the same linear fountain fill was applied to both objects, they look quite different. The block on the left has the Drape Fills option turned on; the block on the right does not. As a quick-and-dirty way of shading a solid, applying a draped fountain fill can come in very handy.

17.8

Draped and undraped extrusion fills

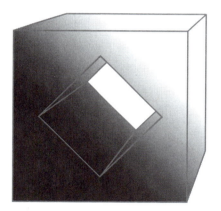 

Solid Fills

Turning back to the Color settings, let's take a look at Color / Solid Fill. As its name implies, this option allows you to select a solid color from a flyout palette to apply to the extruded faces. Once it's chosen, the faces will retain that color, independent of how you choose to fill the control object.

The palette that appears always matches whatever custom pallete you currently have loaded. You can click on the More button to mix or select any solid color from whatever color model you prefer.

Once Solid Fill has been chosen, if you need to change the extruded surfaces' fill, you must do it through the Extrude roll-up. If you select the extrude group and choose a fill the normal way, from the Fill dialogs or palettes, you will only change the control object's fill.

Adding Realism through Shading

Shade, the last Extrude / Color option, was designed to yield a more realistic shaded appearance to the surfaces of the extrusion. You can use Shade in that role—or you can ignore that and instead generate your own attention-grabbing color effects that have absolutely nothing to do with reality.

DRAW assumes that shading should naturally flow from the control object's fill color to black—a reasonable assumption in most instances. But you are free to change both the starting and ending colors of the shade. When you apply the Shade option, DRAW creates fountain fills for each extruded surface, based on the two colors you choose. Like Solid Fill, you get flyout palettes for selecting both start and end colors.

In the following exercise, you will create a simple shaded object.

1. Create a new drawing, and type your initials in a 72-point, bold sans serif font, such as Avant Garde Medium.
2. Draw a rectangle large enough to enclose your initials, and center the two objects.
3. Combine the objects, and fill the resulting object yellow, with a 2-point black outline.
4. Invoke the Extrude roll-up. Adjust the vanishing point of your object so that you can easily see the upper-right faces of the block.
5. Switch to the Color settings and select the Shade option. Click Apply.

6. Try selecting some other From and To colors, and apply them to see the results.

7. With the object still selected, select another fill color for the control object.

You can change the colors used for shading the extruded parts, yet the dynamic link of an extrude group is still in effect.

INSIDE INFO

Because they are composed of fountain fills, shaded extrusions can take a fair amount of time to display. The more complex they are, the longer they will take. If you want to speed up redraws for any fountain fill, decrease the number of fountain steps displayed. This is done via Special / Preferences / View. Bear in mind that this setting does not affect how fountain fills are printed.

Lighting Effects

Shading can produce added realism in your objects, but it is not very flexible. The fourth page of the Extrude roll-up (its icon is a light bulb) gives you the Light Source controls. These settings allow you to simulate light falling on your extruded object from various directions.

DRAW 3 and 4.0 both had a Light Source option, but it has proven to be of limited value. You had access to a single light source that could be placed in one of 16 positions relative to the extrusion. There was an intensity control, but its coarse tuning rendered it virtually useless. In version 5.0, there are now three separate light sources that can be applied in any combination (see Figure 17.9). The intensity controls offer finer scaling for more subtle adjustments to the intensity of all three sources.

To select the origin and direction for a light source, click one of the three "light switches" on the left of the roll-up. As each switch is turned on, a numbered spot will appear at one of the 16 points on the grid at the right, surrounding the shaded sphere. To change the position of any light source, you simply drag it to a different grid point.

17.9
Shedding more realistic light on the subject

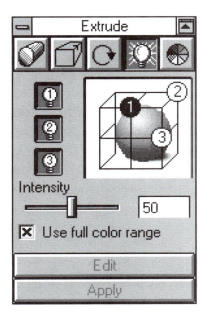
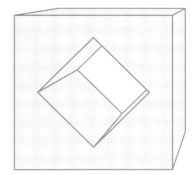

The Intensity slider adjusts the currently selected light source (the numbered spot for the one that is selected will be black rather than gray). Thus, each source can be in one of 16 positions, and each can have its own intensity.

WATCH OUT!

Be prepared to do a lot of experimentation with the Extrude light source controls. You will soon discover that turning on the light will often darken object faces, unless the intensity is 100 and the light source is facing the surface directly. You may have to change the object fill to a lighter color to start with, in order to get the effect you ultimately want.

Applying a light source is fairly simple. Predicting the results is something of a hat trick. You'll want to experiment with the light sources on your own. We've provided a few samples in Figure 17.10 to help you visualize the effects. In this figure are eight samples, each with different lighting effects. The center object is the original, with no lighting applied. For each sample, we have indicated the intensity of the light source by a number, and its origin by the number's position. The top row of samples all use a single light source; the two in the middle row use two; and the ones in the bottom row all use three.

The light sources provided in DRAW 5.0 are certainly an improvement over previous versions. Still, as is evident in Figure 17.10, the effects are

17.10

The effects of various light-source combinations on an extrusion

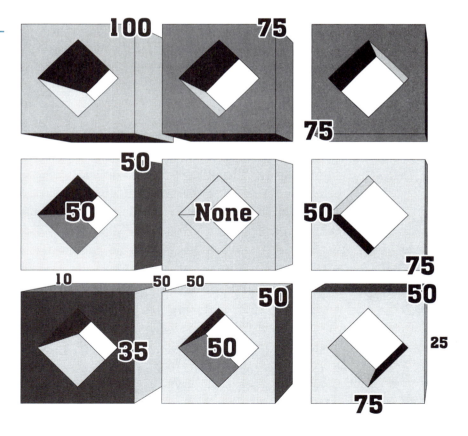

not very subtle when used with solid filled objects. To get more impressive results, you can combine Extrude's Shade option with the light sources. In Figure 17.11 you'll find the same blocks from Figure 17.10, this time with Shade turned on for each one. (We've also added our own special Earthquake Effect to them as well. You'll learn how that was done shortly.)

17.11

A reprise of Figure 17.10—the same light sources, but with shading and tremors added

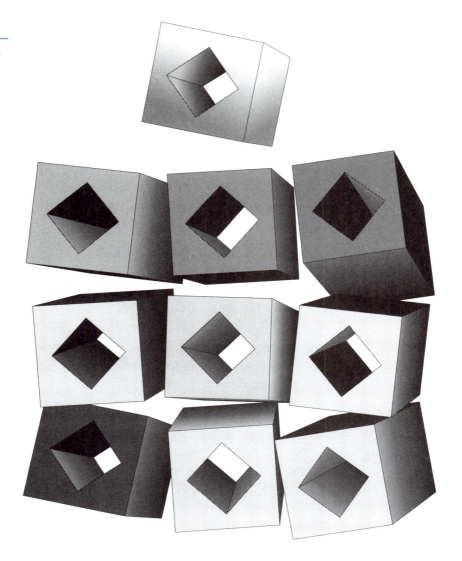

Creating Cutaways and Other Tricks

Now we'll share the secret of creating the cutaway views you saw in Figure 17.5. Version 4.0 introduced the technique of using the Ctrl key to select individual objects within groups. Once they're selected, you are free to move them, apply various fills and outlines, or even resize individual objects—without breaking the group apart. We used this capability to quickly create the cutaway.

We simply held the Ctrl key down as we selected the desired face. The status line read "Child Curve," to which we assigned no fill, thus creating a transparent surface. Once one child curve is selected, you can press Ctrl+Tab to cycle through all the child curves of a group. This allows you to select surfaces that may not be fully visible. (This technique works for other dynamic groups, as well, such as compound blends.)

You can do just about anything you want to child curves, but bear in mind that any time you return to the Extrude roll-up to make a modification, you clear any modifications made to independent child curves. So if you are going to use this technique, make sure you have applied all desired roll-up settings first, before tweaking various child curves.

Beyond Extrude's Lighting Tools

Even combining Extrude's light source and Shade options may not give you the flexibility you would like for shading extrusions just so. As an alternative, you can select individual child curves and apply various fountain fills to them to get the shading you want. The top cube in Figure 17.11 was shaded using this technique. We think it's a more realistic-looking shaded object. Again, the only hazard with this technique is that updating any extrusion settings (or even the control curve's fill) will undo all your manual fills.

INSIDE INFO

If you've used the Shade option, and you then apply a fountain fill to one or more child curves, changing the control curve's fill color will change the colors on the child curve, as well, but the fill type (radial, conical, and so on) will be retained. We're not certain how useful this would be, but it was an interesting discovery.

Using the Separate Command   If you want to manually fill an extrusion, and wish to make sure the changes are permanent to individual elements of an extruded object, you should separate and perhaps even ungroup the extrusion once you have it shaped the way you wish. It is then no longer a dynamic group, so all changes made to individual faces are independent of one another. The Arrange / Separate command can be used with any dynamic link group, to break the link. When applied to extrusions, the command breaks the extrusion into two objects: the original control object, and a conventional group made up of all the surfaces generated by the Extrude command. You can further ungroup all the objects, so they are all directly selectable.

The downside of this is that you can no longer edit the object as an extrusion. So, before breaking the link, make sure it's the way you want it. If you use this technique, we suggest you ungroup the extrude surfaces, and regroup the entire set of objects. You can then select each child curve in the same way as usual to do your custom colorizing. Should you accidentally refill the entire group, Undo will recover what you had before. This way, you keep the geometric integrity of the extrusion and can still color it any way you want.

Rules of Thumb for Extruding

- More often than not, the light sources and shading effects provided in the Extrude roll-up are too inflexible to get the proper lighting/shading on an extruded object. The light sources take time and experimentation to get suitable results. It is usually easier to reach for the Fill roll-up and apply fountain fills at various angles to child curves of the object.
- If you decide to separate an extrusion, make a copy of it first, just in case you decide you want to modify it later.

Vanishing Points Revisited

Before we move on to the "Rotating Extrusions" section, which is how the tumbling blocks of Figure 17.11 were created, let's return to our old friend the vanishing point for a moment. Take another look back at Figure 17.10. Although lit differently, all the blocks have the proper spatial relationship to one another. This was not a fortuitous accident; we accomplished it by making sure each object has the same vanishing point. DRAW 3 and 4.0 have indirect ways of accomplishing this, and in the previous edition of this book we mentioned them as odds and ends. Version 5.0, however, has a better set of tools to offer you.

NEW FOR 5

Apparently Corel realized that matching vanishing points was more than a cute parlor trick. DRAW 5.0 provides several new options for controlling relationships between the page, the extruded object, and its vanishing point.

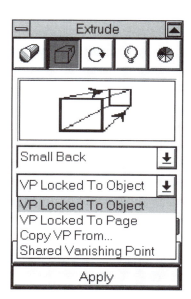

Selecting the first option in the drop-down list of vanishing points, Locked to Object, is equivalent to how vanishing points were maintained in versions 3 and 4.0. Once a vanishing point is set relative to the control face, it stays that way even if the extrusion is moved. In other words, the viewer's perspective changes with the object movement. With this option selected, if you copy an extrusion and move it to another part of the page, you will have two different vanishing points or two different viewer perspectives—not very realistic.

By choosing the Locked to Page option for an extrusion, you can move the object around the page without changing the viewer perspective of the object. In this case, you could duplicate an object and move it to another portion of the page, and have a realistic looking collection of objects. The Copy Extrude From… and Clone Extrude From… commands in the Effects menu work very well in tandem with this option. Creating objects this way ensures they all have the same vanishing point for realistic viewer perspective.

The third option, Copy VP From…, is your afterthought option: It allows you to match vanishing points after extrude objects have already been created. It doesn't create any link between extruded objects, nor does it change any other Extrude options that are set. It simply causes the vanishing point of one extrusion to be matched to any other extrusion you select—similar to copying a fill outline from one object to another.

The last option, Shared Vanishing Point, creates a dynamic link of the vanishing points of two or more extrusions. With this option set, if you change the vanishing point of one object, all others that share that vanishing point are also automatically updated. This one is similar to a cloned extrusion. When you clone, you duplicate all extrusion settings, including depth and fill options. Shared Vanishing Point just ensures a common vanishing point.

Rules of Thumb for Vanishing Points

- Cloning extrusions can be useful, but in very limited circumstances. Bear in mind that you cannot directly modify a cloned extrusion. Also, the difficulty of keeping track of the "master" extrusion makes extrusion cloning a dubious undertaking.

■ It is likely that you will be more interested in establishing common vanishing points (and other settings) among extrusions, than in duplicating all the extrusion settings from one object to another. A more practical approach is to make use of the Shared Vanishing Point option and the Copy Extrude From… command, because it leaves you the flexibility to modify specific settings (fills, depth, and so on) for each extrusion, while maintaining a common viewer perspective.

Rotating Extrusions

Now we'll show you how we created our tumbling blocks in Figure 17.11. The Extrude / Rotation settings (Figure 17.12) are accessed via the center icon, the one with an arrow circling clockwise. Clicking the paging icon in the lower-right corner displays the settings shown in Figure 17.13, allowing you to rotate by number instead of by sight. This type of rotation

17.12

Rotating by sight

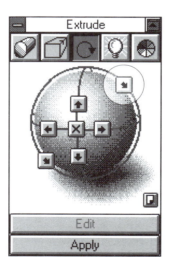

17.13

Rotating by the numbers

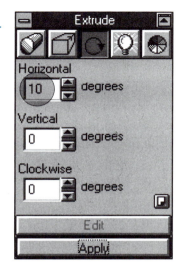
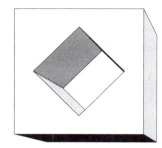
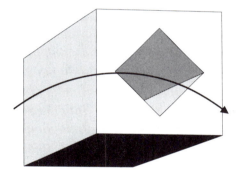

is entirely different from simply selecting the object and rotating it, as you would a two-dimensional object. The roll-up does allow clockwise and counterclockwise rotations, which are the equivalents of simple object rotations—but it also allows you to rotate in two other theoretical axes (horizontal and vertical). Further, you can combine rotations of varying degrees in all three axes.

Figure 17.12 shows a simple clockwise rotation of an object (see the highlighted circle on the particular rotation arrow). The cube on top is before the rotation; the cube on the bottom is after rotation, and the arrow confirms the type of rotation. In Figure 17.13, we did two things: First, we clicked on the paging icon to reach the rotation-by-number controls. Second, we executed a Horizontal rotation, causing the object to swivel on its axis.

To get some practice working with the Extrude / Rotation controls, try the following exercise:

1. Start a new drawing.
2. Draw a light-blue, 2-inch square, with a thin black outline.
3. Using the Scaling page of the Transform roll-up (the middle icon of the five), add a duplicate that is scaled to 80% in both axes.
4. Marquee-select both rectangles and press Ctrl+L to combine them.
5. If it is not displayed, invoke the Extrude roll-up (Ctrl+E). In the Depth page, choose Small Back and Depth 30. Set the vanishing point at 0,0 relative to Object Center, and choose Locked to Object.
6. Click the color wheel icon and choose the Shade option. Then click Apply.
7. Click the Rotation icon and click the Edit button (if you're not already in edit mode).
8. On the sphere, click the left arrow twice, the counterclockwise arrow once, and the up arrow once. (The big X in the middle clears all rotations.) Then click Apply.

NEW FOR 5

If you need to rotate objects by specific amounts, the numeric controls (Figure 17.13) enable you to enter specific positive or negative values.

These steps have taken you from an extruded object like the one at the top of Figure 17.14 to something like the second object in that figure. To get the bottom image, we took it a few steps further. Each click of an

17.14
Rotations made easy

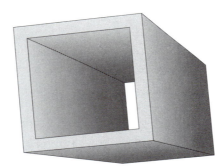

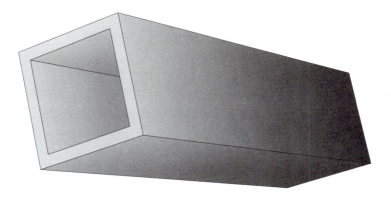

arrow on the sphere is equal to 5 degrees. At each stage of the rotation, DRAW shows a wireframe of how the rotated object will look when you actually apply the effect.

WATCH OUT!

> You cannot use Extrude's Rotation controls unless you have selected Locked to Object as the type of vanishing point. Once you have applied a rotation, you cannot select the vanishing point and move it. If you try to grab it, you will be thrown out of Extrude's editing mode. When you DO need to change the vanishing point, you must reset the rotations (use the center X on the sphere), adjust the vanishing point, and reapply the rotations.

Rules of Thumb for Rotating

- Make sure your vanishing point is set *before* you rotate.

- You can move a rotated extrusion, but its vanishing point will move with it (it's locked to the object). If you are trying to maintain matching vanishing points, clear the rotations, move the extrusion, copy the vanishing point of another extrusion, and then reapply the rotations.

Miscellany

Following are a few odds and ends concerning extruded objects.

The Extrude Roll-up Remembers

An important facet of the Extrude roll-up is that it retains the settings of the most recently applied extrusion. Along with all of Extrude's new copying, cloning, preset (see below), and vanishing point matching capabilities, the roll-up's memory provides another means for quickly producing several related extrusions. If you created some extruded text, for example, with a depth of 15, shading, and a particular light source, the next extruded object you create will take on those same settings, unless you specifically change them.

Color Gallery, Illustration 1

Instant art with CorelDRAW. Even our artistically crippled lead author can produce nice work with the running start that DRAW provides. The image of Big Ben came from the clip art library, and the background is courtesy of DRAW's texture fill patterns. You will find the .CDR file for this and the other illustrations in the GALLERY directory on the Companion CD.

Color Gallery, Illustration 2

If you followed the exercises in Chapter 5, this is the drawing that you created. While it contains a lot of elements, when broken down into bite-size pieces it can be tackled by new and veteran users alike.

Color Gallery, Illustration 3

Georgina Curry's Best of Show entry in the 1993 Corel Design Contest. Curry shares her experiences in producing *The Huntress*, commemorating silent film star Clara Bow, in Chapter 20.

Color Gallery, Illustration 4

David Brickley's *The Diver*, Best of Show in 1990, remains to this day one of the most recognizeable works of CorelDRAW art. Brickley discusses this drawing's humble beginnings in Chapter 21.

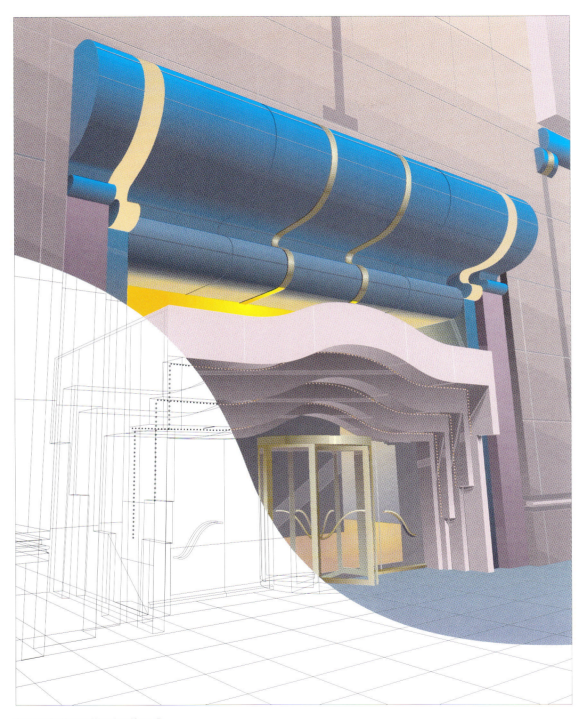

Color Gallery, Illustration 5

Another from David Brickley's collection, this architectural study won an award in 1993 and also earned Brickley a spot on the cover of *Architecture* magazine. Read all about it in Chapter 22.

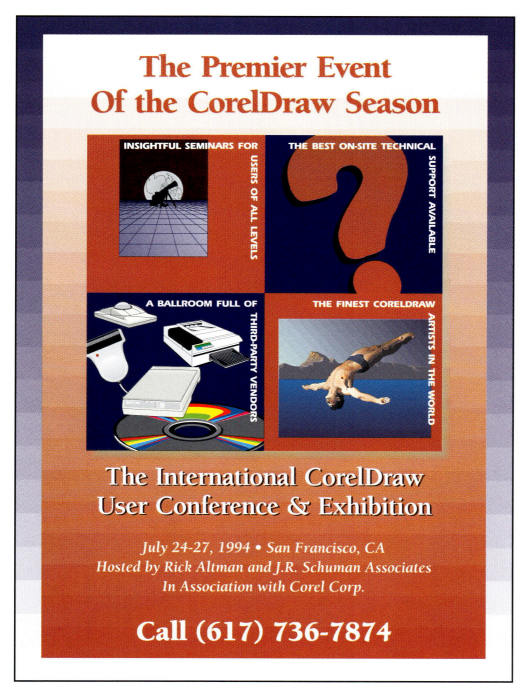

Color Gallery, Illustration 6

An advertisement for the International CorelDRAW User Conference. In Chapter 24, your lead author discusses how he produced this piece by borrowing from another, more talented, artist.

Color Gallery, Illustration 7

Another from the Georgina Curry collection, *Faces* won a Goodwill award from Corel for its efforts to call attention to the HIV crisis facing all of humankind.

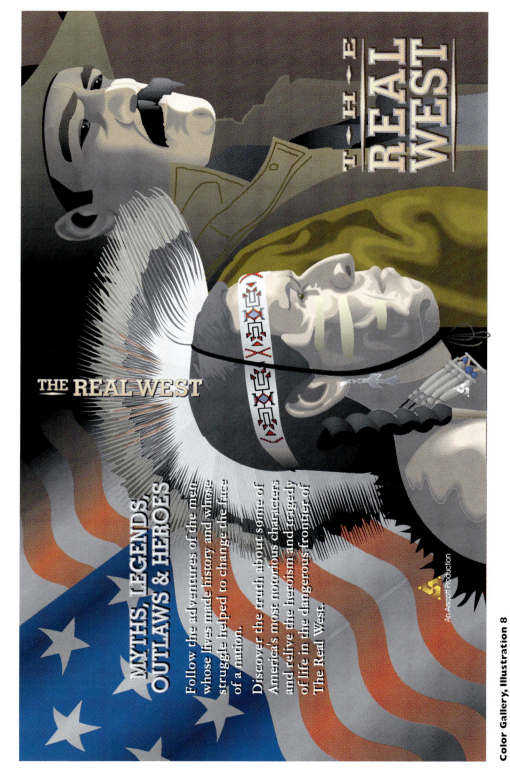

Color Gallery, Illustration 8

Stephen Arscott's *The Wild West* was awarded Best of Show in Corel's 1994 Annual Design Contest.

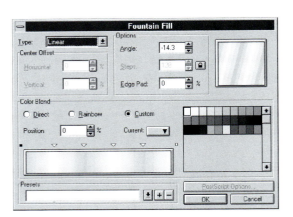

Color Gallery, Illustration 9

In order to give the wheel of this sports car a shiny gold chrome look, we used a fountain fill that alternates between gold and white.

Color Gallery, Illustration 10

The Spoon Forest is the coup de grâce from Chapters 14 through 19, with various special effects used. The sun is a blend, the spoons are PowerLines with fountain fills, the title of the piece is an extrusion, and the whole thing is PowerClipped into the background rectangle.

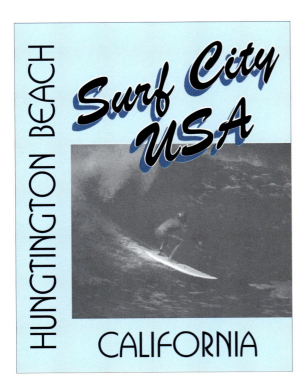

Color Gallery, Illustration 11

What can lenses do to photographs? The low-quality photo of a surfer in a curl (top) wouldn't normally be anyone's choice for a professional advertisement, but thanks to the Tinted Grayscale lens (left) and the Heat Map lens (right), the photo becomes an effective part of these two posters.

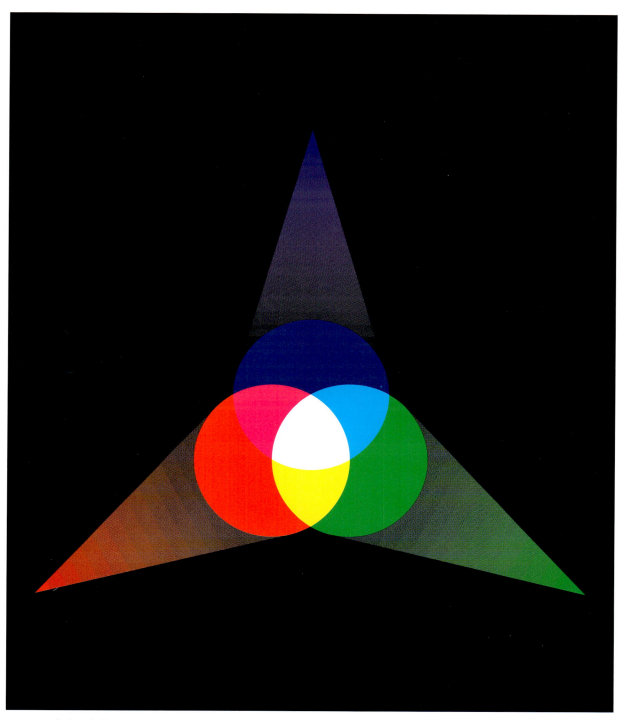

Color Gallery, Illustration 12

The RGB color model in action. Red and Green combine to form *Yellow*; Green and Blue combine to form *Cyan*; Blue and Red combine to form *Magenta*; and all three colors combine to form *White*.

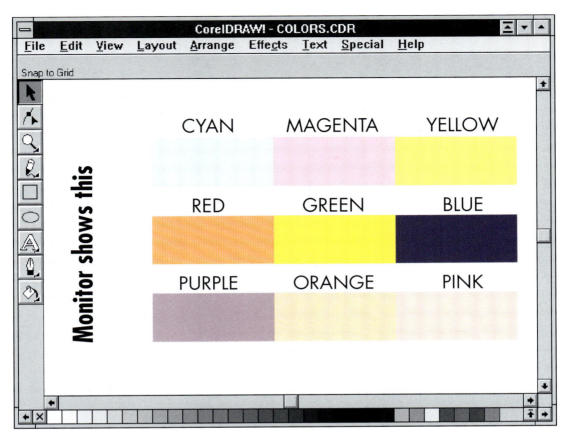

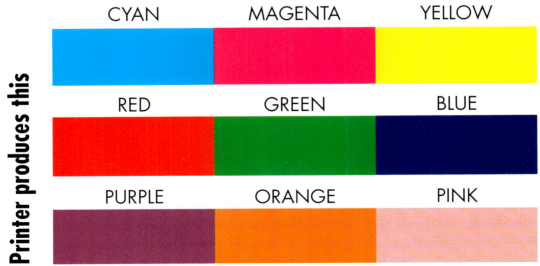

Color Gallery, Illustration 13

Don't trust your monitor to show you accurate colors. As discussed in Chapter 26, your monitor uses a completely different method of producing light and color than does printed material.

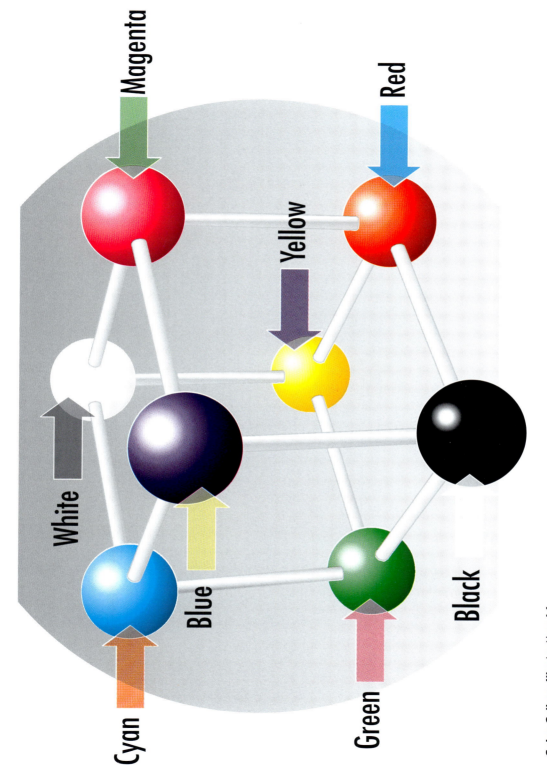

Color Gallery, Illustration 14

The traditional color cube, used to show the relationship between the Red/Green/Blue model and the Cyan/Magenta/Yellow model.

Color Gallery, Illustration 15

How accurate are your scanner, monitor, and color printer? You can follow instructions in Chapter 28 to test your color components. Here you see the difference between a photo and its appearance after being scanned and imported into PHOTO-PAINT.   *photography by Steve Bain*

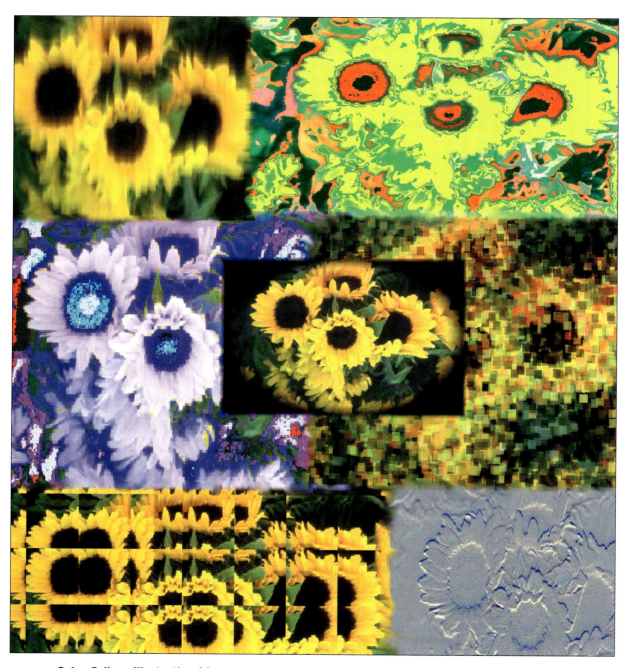

Color Gallery, Illustration 16

Chapter 31's *Sunflowers* image, in the center of this collage, is the basis of the following alterations (clockwise from upper left): Motion Blur, Psychedelic, Pointillism, Emboss, Glass Blocks, and Solarize.

Version 5.0 Has Extrusion Presets

The next time you create some really fantastic extrusion and want to save its settings for posterity, DRAW 5.0 will let you. Select the extrusion, click the first icon to switch to the Presets page of the Extrusion roll-up, and click on Save as…. Name your preset, and it can be applied to any extrudable object or even to an existing extrusion. If applied to an existing extrusion, the preset's attributes supersede the previous settings of the existing extrusion.

Extrusion presets can be accessed via either the Extrude roll-up or the Presets roll-up (see Chapter 9).

There is nothing to stop you from modifying an extrusion generated from a preset. Any or all of the predefined extrusion settings can be modified after you apply the preset. If you really like your modifications, you can save those as a preset, too, or use them to replace the old preset by saving them under the same name.

Experiment with creating and using presets. Even within a single project, a preset can be a valuable starting point for the creation of multiple extrusions. You can always delete the preset, if you don't plan to use it in the future.

Taking Advantage of Common Vanishing Points

Figure 17.15 shows a trophy designed for Corel's Annual Virtual Tennis Tournament. This is an ideal example of how to utilize matching vanishing points. Each element is an extrusion that shares a common vanishing point, but with varied extrusion depths and fills employed.

For the base cube, we used a linear fountain fill. The larger cube and circular shape have conical fills. We weren't content with using the Shade feature, so we filled each child curve independently. The circular emblem was another story. Using the Shade feature produced a group composed of 108 separate objects. So we gave the extrusion a solid fill, and the result was a group of just three objects. We were then able to use fountain fills to get the shading we wanted.

17.15
Using common vanishing points to create complex objects

Getting the text to sit inside the circle shape required a few tricks. First we placed the text in front of the circular extrusion, and extruded the text itself using shaded fills and a shallower depth than the circular object. The result looked silly: On the left side, everything looked fine, but on the right the text solid sat in front of the circular solid (wrong…). To fix this, we copied the control object of the circular extrude, and moved the duplicate curve to the front. The last step was to copy the control text, break it apart, and re-combine the *O* and the *R*. Then each separate letter could be filled with a custom conical fountain fill to get the metallic highlights.

Warping Objects

The next example also makes use of common vanishing points, in this case to create the illusion of a warped fish tank (Figure 17.16). The trick

17.16

Extrusions are fraught with danger—at least for this poor fellow.

to creating the tank is drawing two rectangles of equal width, one taller than the other, and centering them horizontally. (Using Snap To Grid makes short work of such tasks.) Next, we grouped the two rectangles and applied an envelope to create the warp. Grouping allowed them to both be shaped to the same overall envelope.

WATCH OUT!

The technique of grouping and then applying a common envelope is useful, but has limits. If you distort too far, the perimeters of the objects that are supposed to match begin to deviate from one another. You can improve the results by adding nodes to the objects before you group and apply the envelope.

After their common warp was applied, we ungrouped the rectangles; then we added a separate envelope to the rectangle destined to be the water in the tank, to add the slight wave to the surface. We gave the larger rectangle a fairly thick outline and made it hollow (no fill). We then extruded it using Small Back with a depth of about 50. This became the frame of the tank. We used the same extrusion settings for the water, except we applied a linear fountain fill. Using Object Fill would not have produced the correct shading results, so we selected the child curves and applied appropriate linear fountain fills, angled differently from the control curve's fill.

Our bubbles are simply circles with off-center radial fills. We enveloped each text string individually, so they appear to wrap around their particular bubbles. We applied radial fills to the text, to match each bubble's shading. As a last step, we copied the control rectangle of the tank frame, using the + key on the numeric keypad, and moved it forward until it was in front of the bubble floating just above the surface of the water.

Extrusions Don't Have to Be Fancy

Finally, Figure 17.17 shows how an extrusion can breathe life into a simple figure such as this floor plan. Just because the tool is powerful doesn't mean you can't use it for simple stuff. The key to creating a floor plan is to make sure all elements composing the frame have no fill when you extrude them. You need it to be hollow; otherwise, you wouldn't be able to see inside. The walls derive their fill from the Extrude / Color / Shade setting.

17.17

An extrusion makes the floor plan come alive.

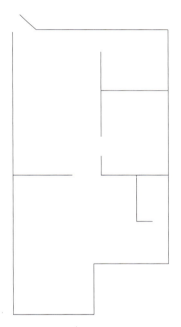
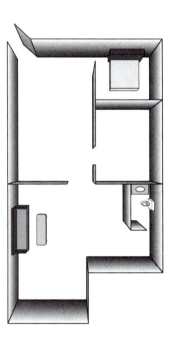

This chapter focused on how the Extrude roll-up's controls can create depth from solid objects. In the next chapter, we'll look at how PowerLines can add depth to simple lines.

CHAPTER 18

The Power of the Line

EIGHTEEN

The standard knock against vector drawing programs, especially from users with a traditional arts background, is the distinctly computerish look of the artwork these programs produce. Even highly detailed work by top-notch computer artists usually has a certain geometric edge to it. Look at the various clip art images supplied with DRAW; as nice as they are, in most you can see their computer origins.

In traditional hand-drawn artwork, edges are usually much softer, and shading more subtle, because elements can be blurred or smudged together. The artist can affect the characteristics of curves by applying varying pressure with various drawing/painting tools. Image-editing (bitmap-based) programs have been getting better at mimicking traditional artistic techniques. For drawing programs, however, it is inherently more difficult to accomplish techniques such as smudging edges, applying transparent fills to objects, cropping portions of an image, and some of the other more "painterly" things that bitmap-based programs can do. In fact, in the previous version of this book, we said vector-based programs would never be able to do any of these things.

We've learned never to say "never" (especially in print!). PowerLines, introduced in DRAW 4.0, provided a significant, though sometimes awkward first step towards mimicking the traditional artist's pens, brushes, and pressure variations. And in Chapter 19 we will introduce some features new to version 5.0 that add even *more* painterly capabilities—and that definitely put us out of the prognostication business.

Making Heads or Tails of PowerLines

To both new and veteran DRAW users, PowerLines might be one of the more arcane and least intuitive tools in the program. If you read the User's Manual, you might assume PowerLines to be an extension of the

Calligraphic Pen controls in the Outline Pen. Actually, PowerLines does extend the effects that users have tried to accomplish with Calligraphic Pen—but with a wholly different approach.

PowerLines are usually applied to open curves, but rather than changing only the outline shape, as Calligraphic Pen does, the PowerLine actually transforms the open curve into a closed curve with its own fill and outline. To further complicate matters, PowerLines can also be applied to closed (filled) objects and even multipath curves, such as text characters. However, this tool is primarily intended for use with open curves.

If this concept is confusing to you, recall that an open curve can also be extruded, and the resulting object always contains at least one closed filled curve. Think of a PowerLine as a shape that can be applied to a path. The CorelDRAW User's Manual shows a set of ready-made shapes available for your use; these can also be used as the basis for creating your own customized PowerLines.

The PowerLine roll-up, shown below, is available from the Effects menu (surprise!) or by pressing Ctrl+F8. The roll-up contains several sets of controls, accessed via the icons at the top.

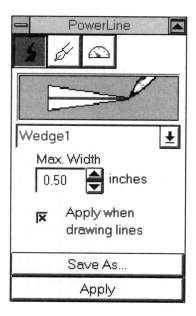

The controls for PowerLines include a collection of presets, a pressure gauge, and the facility for creating and storing your own custom PowerLines. Below the drop-down list box is the Max Width setting, where you can dial or type in the maximum width for the PowerLine shape. The default Max Width setting, when the roll-up is first opened, is 0.50 inch. The Apply When Drawing Lines check box actually means "Apply when drawing any freehand curves," telling DRAW to create PowerLines as you draw a curve. This option is turned on by default, so a PowerLine is applied the minute you draw something with the Pencil tool. It won't automatically apply PowerLines to closed shapes, however. You must do that via the Apply button.

WATCH OUT!

Don't forget that Apply When Drawing Lines is on by default. You will usually want to turn this off, for two reasons. First, it's easier and faster to edit and shape a curve BEFORE a PowerLine has been applied to it. Second, PowerLines take some time to generate, and they will regenerate for EACH AND EVERY CHANGE you make to a curve, no matter how insignificant. If you have a slower computer, if you draw and shape fairly complex curves, or if you draw a lot of curves, be prepared to stare at the hourglass frequently.

An Exercise with PowerLines

This next exercise will give you a sense of the hows and whys of PowerLines. You will first create four practice objects, as shown in Figure 18.1.

1. Create a new, letter-size, landscape drawing.

2. Draw a single vertical line about 3 inches long, with a 2-point black outline.

3. Next to the vertical line, draw a dogleg composed of two straight lines, also with 2-point outlines. Don't try to use Ctrl to make the first line perfectly vertical. Just click, move down, and click to end the first line. Without moving the mouse, click again to start the second line, move diagonally, and click to end the line.

18.1
Your PowerLine practice objects

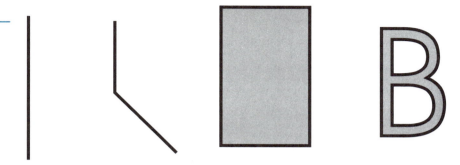

4. To verify that you have drawn the dogleg correctly as a single curve, select the object with the Pick tool; the selection box should enclose both line segments.

5. Further to the right, draw a light-blue rectangle, about 3 inches by 2 inches, with a 2-point black outline.

6. At the far right, create a capital letter using a simple block typeface, about 3 inches high, and with the same fill and outline as the rectangle. Convert the text to curves (Ctrl+Q). Your page should look something like Figure 18.1.

7. Invoke the PowerLine roll-up, via Effects / PowerLine or by pressing Ctrl+F8.

8. Select all the objects (Edit / Select All).

9. Select the first PowerLine preset, Wedge1, and click Apply.

You should now have something like Figure 18.2. Notice what a PowerLine looks like as applied to the various objects: open curves, a simple closed shape, and a shape with multiple subpaths.

INSIDE INFO

It's important to remember that PowerLines can be applied to more than one object at a time. You can save a lot of time by applying the PowerLines as the final step to a collection of curves, rather than as you draw each individual element.

18.2
The practice objects have been zapped with PowerLines.

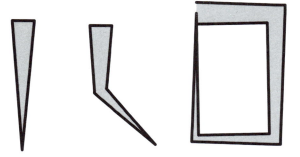

It is likely that the PowerLines you created from the two open curves had a different fill from the other objects, or possibly no fill at all. Ordinarily, you wouldn't think of applying a fill to an open curve, but DRAW keeps track of one anyway. When you initially draw an open curve, your default object fill is used. If your default is none, then no fill is applied.

10. Ensure that all four objects are still selected. Then drag the bottom-center sizing handle downward until the status line indicates about 150%, and release. (Be patient…unless you have a very fast computer, this will probably take a while. If you were applying PowerLines as you drew individual elements, and then modifying each of those objects, you would probably quickly lose patience.)

11. In the roll-up, change the Max Width to .25 inch, and select the Trumpet3 PowerLine. Click Apply.

In addition to demonstrating another preset PowerLine and the effect of a different maximum width, the above exercise shows that you can change a PowerLine after one has already been applied. The new PowerLine replaces, rather than compounds, the original.

INSIDE INFO

When you have several changes planned for a curve that has been PowerLined, you will save a fair amount of time by clearing the PowerLine first, making all necessary curve modifications, and then reapplying the PowerLine.

Watch Those Nodes

Here is a simple exercise to show the consequences of creating Power-Lines with excess nodes in the original curve.

1. Create a new drawing, and invoke the PowerLine roll-up.
2. Change the preset to Teardrop2, but leave the Max Width at 0.5 inches.
3. Make sure Apply When Drawing Lines is checked.
4. With the Pencil tool, draw an S-shape, roughly like the one at the far left in Figure 18.3.

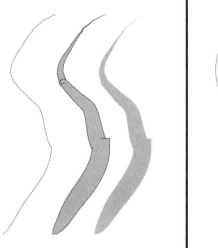

18.3

A PowerLined S-curve, the hard way and the easy way

Drawn with freehand tool (after two cups of coffee)

Drawn as straight lines and then converted to curves and shaped

5. Now hold Ctrl and draw a strictly vertical line.
6. Choose the Shape tool, and double-click the line. On the Node Edit roll-up, select To Curve.
7. Using the control handles, shape the curve like the one at the far right in Figure 18.3.

You can see how long it took to generate the PowerLine, and how messy it looks. Drawing freehand inherently creates many nodes in a curve. The steadier your hand, the smoother the curve and fewer the nodes, but there are nevertheless usually far more nodes than necessary. As with other special effects, PowerLines take longer when there are more nodes. The curve on the right not only looks better, but the PowerLine was generated much more quickly. An alternative to drawing straight lines and converting to curves is to use the Bezier drawing mode. This will have the same advantage of fewer nodes and faster PowerLine creation.

Rules of Thumb for PowerLines

- Regardless of your method for drawing curves, it is usually better to draw the curve *without* applying the PowerLine as you draw. Shape the curve, delete any unwanted nodes, and *then* apply the PowerLine. Remember, the PowerLine is regenerated for every little operation you do to the curve to which it is applied.

- Use "efficiency of scale." Draw and edit all curves that will share a common PowerLine *before* applying it. Select all the curves and apply the PowerLine to them all in one step. It will still take time to generate, but you have saved all the regeneration that would take place for each step along the way.

Speed and Spread

As in other roll-ups, the various PowerLine features are accessed by clicking on icons at the top of the roll-up. The CorelDRAW User's Manual makes a game attempt at explaining the more sophisticated controls, but it probably won't make a lot of sense on your first, second, or even third reading. The results of using these controls are hard to pinpoint, because they vary with the type of curves drawn and the type of PowerLine chosen.

Figure 18.4 demonstrates how the Speed and Spread controls are used. (Both these controls are accessed via the speedometer icon; see the roll-up below.) We drew a shape consisting of straight lines that made some sharp turns, with one gently curved section (shape #1). Moving to shape #2, you see the same curve with a Bullet1 PowerLine applied. Notice how sharp the corners are.

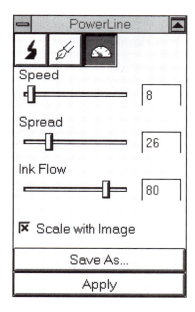

In shape #3, we have added a Speed setting of 30 and used the minimum Spread setting of 1. The Speed control has rounded the sharp turns of the PowerLine, but has also made the object somewhat lumpy. This is where the Spread control comes in. Shape #4 has the same Speed setting, but Spread was increased to 60. This smoothes out the unsightly lumps in the curve.

What's a Nib, Anyway?

In the PowerLines roll-up, the icon that looks like a fountain pen offers controls over the Nib angle, ratio, and intensity. We still don't know the precise definition of a nib, but its behavior for PowerLines is similar to

18.4

How to use Speed and Spread to get rid of unsightly lumps

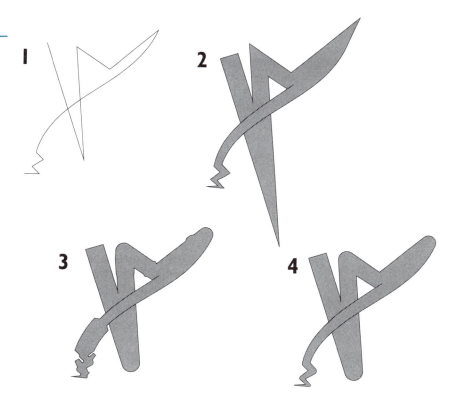

the Outline Pen's Nib. Visualizing changes to the Nib itself is easy. In Figure 18.5 you see both pages of controls for changing the Nib; the paging icon toggles you between the two. You can adjust the Nib numerically or by clicking and dragging it directly.

Rather than try to explain what the Nib controls actually do, and instead of referring you to the User's Manual for a generally unhelpful explanation, we offer you a few specific examples in Figure 18.6. We started with an ellipse and applied the Trumpet3 PowerLine. The next three objects are the same shape, with various Nib adjustments added. Remember that Nib changes, like any other changes, convert a preset PowerLine to a custom PowerLine.

18.5

The Nib controls

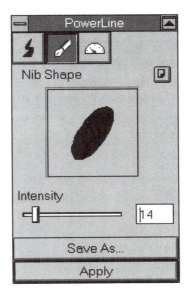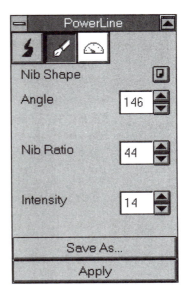

18.6

Concept sketches for Batman's Secret Decoder Ring

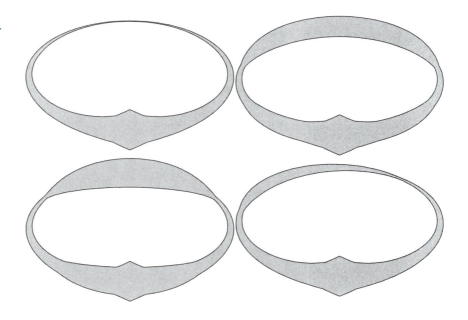

The Problem with Pressure

Pressure sensitivity in a PowerLine seems like a great concept: As you drag the mouse to create a curve, you can, in theory, press the Up Arrow or Down Arrow on your keyboard to increase or decrease the PowerLine width. Sounds wonderful, but it flies in the face of our advice to avoid freehand curve drawing at all costs (too many nodes, too little skill). Unfortunately, freehand drawing is the only way you can use pressure PowerLines; you cannot use this option with line-segment drawing.

Even if we were not predisposed to avoid freehand drawing, we find it next to impossible to synchronize the Up Arrow and Down Arrow keystrokes with a smoothly drawn curve. Perhaps with a pressure-sensitive stylus, this option is more useful, but even in that case we think it easier to create a custom PowerLine using all the options discussed so far—plus one very powerful option that we'll introduce next.

Shaping PowerLines with Pressure Edit

We have already demonstrated that you can use the Shape tool (in the Node Edit roll-up) to modify a curve with a PowerLine applied. But there is an additional option available in the Node Edit roll-up that is specifically for PowerLine shaping: the Pressure Edit check box. This option allows you to customize a preset PowerLine, shaping it in almost any way you like. The following exercise shows you how:

1. Start with a new drawing and, if it isn't already visible, invoke the PowerLine roll-up (Ctrl+F8).
2. Draw a vertical line about 5 inches long, with a 2-point outline.
3. From the PowerLine presets, choose Max Width. (The Max Width preset is probably the one you will use most frequently to create your own customized PowerLines.)
4. Set the Max Width value to **1.00** inch, and click Apply.
5. Apply a red fill to your PowerLine. You should now have what looks like a red rectangle with a black outline.
6. Select the Shape tool.

7. Double-click the original line running through the center of your PowerLine to bring up the Node Edit roll-up. Click the Pressure Edit box.

At this point you will see a rectangle with four flat little circles at the corners, called *pressure handles,* as shown in Figure 18.7. Each node in a curve will have two of these handles associated with it. These handles can be slid in or out along a path running perpendicular to the path of the curve. In your case, you have only two nodes at the moment, and hence four handles total. The next few steps show you how to manipulate the handles.

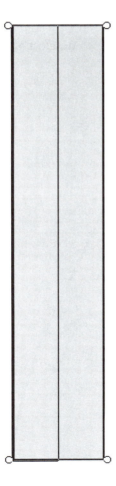

18.7
This curve can be fattened up or slimmed down, thanks to Pressure Edit.

8. Click the top-left handle, and drag it about $1/2$ inch to the left. Notice that the handle itself will only move on a perpendicular path to the curve.

9. Click the upper-right handle and move it to the left, about $1/4$ inch.

10. Select the lower-left handle, hold down Shift, and select the lower-right handle. Once they are both selected, release the Shift key.

11. Drag the lower-left handle to the left about 1 inch.

What you've created should look about as ridiculous as Figure 18.8. And it will look even more ridiculous after the next few steps.

12. Click somewhere off the object to deselect all handles.

18.8

Using Pressure Edit to create quite an ugly PowerLine

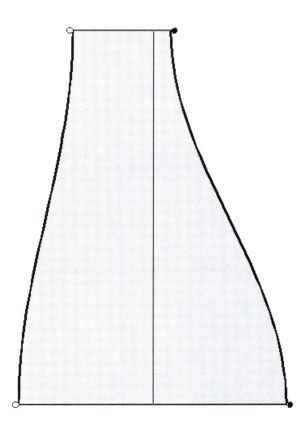

13. Hold down Ctrl, and select the lower-right handle. Notice that the upper-right handle is selected, as well. Drag the lower-right handle all the way to the left.
14. Hold down Ctrl and Shift, and select the lower-left handle. All handles should now be selected. Drag the lower-left handle about $1/2$ inch to the right. Notice that when you select all the handles and drag any one of them, all four move.
15. About a third of the way from the top, click on the control curve. Then, click the + button in the Node Edit roll-up.
16. Click somewhere off the PowerLine to deselect all handles.
17. Click and hold on the left line leading from the new node, and drag the left handle down about an inch. (You click on the line, not the handle.)
18. Select the lower-left handle, and click the Concave button in the Node Edit roll-up.
19. Click the middle-left button, and click the To Line button in the Node Edit roll-up.
20. Select the top- and bottom-left handles only, using the Shift+click method. Drag either handle to the left about 1 inch.
21. Select the middle-right handle, and click the Convex button in the Node Edit roll-up.
22. Drag the handle about 1 inch to the right.

Congratulations! You have created a fine mess that probably looks a lot like ours in Figure 18.9. Your next logical step would normally be to use the Save As… button in the PowerLine roll-up so you could apply this shapely shape to other curves. We have a feeling you will probably skip that, though.

The real point behind this exercise was to introduce you to all the various options you can use in creating your own custom PowerLines. You are free to add as many handles as you like, allowing you to create some substantially complex shapes. Generally, though, PowerLines are designed to be used with fairly simple forms for application to curves of various lengths and shapes. The example in the User's Manual, pages

18.9
A fine mess of a PowerLine

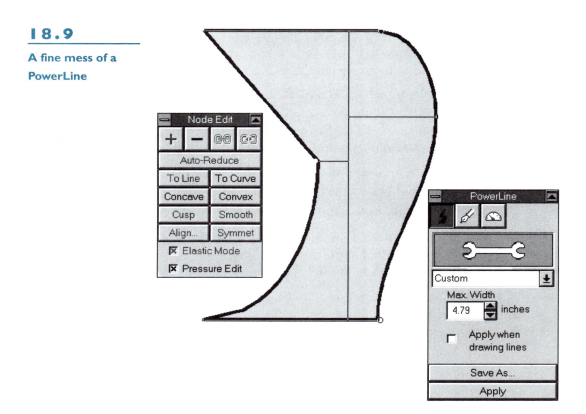

272 and 273, bears studying. The contour of the woman's dress is an ideal application for PowerLines.

Saving Your Own PowerLines

If you were to reproduce the foregoing examples yourself and then switch back to the main PowerLine controls, you would find the Bullet1 PowerLine gone. The list box would read "Custom." Once you modify a preset PowerLine in any way, it becomes a custom PowerLine. This brings us to the Save As... button in the roll-up. When you create a custom PowerLine, you can give the settings a name and save them. Don't worry about overwriting the presets, because DRAW won't let you.

INSIDE INFO

If you save a custom PowerLine under an existing name, DRAW warns you; you can choose to overwrite the existing custom PowerLine or enter a new name. Within the Save As... options is a button for deleting unwanted custom PowerLines that you don't need anymore. But you don't have to save custom PowerLine settings to use them. Just keep the roll-up open, and continue applying the settings to new objects. Or you can copy the PowerLine attributes via the Effects menu.

NEW FOR 5

There were ways to copy PowerLines in version 4.0, but now you can do so with the Copy flyout on the Effects menu. You can also clone PowerLines, just as other effects can be cloned. Again, we recommend saving the copying and cloning as a last step for a collection of curves, rather than applying as you go. The advantage: You can select the original, modify its PowerLine, and all others will get updated in the same way. The problem: If you have more than a few curves, finding your original object can be tough.

What Cost, PowerLines?

If you work at all with complex shapes, you will discover that custom PowerLines take a long time to generate when applied to a curve, and they often do not give you the results you expected. For elaborate shapes, it is sometimes better to create them the old-fashioned way: by drawing closed freehand curves and shaping them.

In addition to the time they take to generate, PowerLines create complex objects with far too many nodes. Consider the Teardrop1 PowerLine applied to a straight line; re-create it in freehand drawing mode, and the equivalent could be done with a curve having just two nodes. Break a PowerLine down into curves, using the Arrange / Separate command; you will end up with the original control curve and not one, but at least two other curves. Select one of these curves with the Shape tool, and you will find it may have upwards of 100 nodes! All those nodes mean more complex files and longer print times.

This is not meant to deter you from creating your own custom PowerLines. Just don't be taken in by the glitter of PowerLines without being aware of the consequences of using them. PowerLines are excellent for developing simple shapes to be used over and over to give the impression of something, such as the tall grass in the User's Manual example, or the shaded pleats of the dress.

More Rules of Thumb for PowerLines

- If you're only going to use a shape a few times in a drawing, it's better to create it the old-fashioned way, drawing closed curves with the freehand drawing tools.
- Use PowerLines when you have many similar, simple shapes to create, such as leaves of grass or the strands of a horse's mane.
- Beware of overly complex custom PowerLines. For each node on the control curve, there are many more on the PowerLine.

The Kitchen Sink

As we leave this section, we can't resist one more example that uses a potpourri of the effects you've seen so far: the Spoon Forest in Figure 18.10 (it's also Illustration 10 of the Color Gallery).

The central elements of the drawing are the spoons. We first created a custom PowerLine for this (Figure 18.11), and then applied it to a few curves of varying shape to create our forest. For the forest floor, we drew

18.10
The Spoon Forest

an ellipse and added a Parallel Back extrusion. We then selected the control ellipse, duplicated it, shrank the duplicate, and blended the two copies to shade the surface the way we wanted. The sun was created with a blend, to make the edges fuzzy.

We produced the title by applying a straight-line, vertically constrained envelope to the text, and then extruded the enveloped text with the light source turned on. Last, we created the shadows by duplicating the spoons using the + key on the numeric keypad, grouping the copies, and applying a black fill. We then did a flip-and-squash stretch of the group by dragging the top-center sizing handle downward. A small amount of skew was added to match the lighting angle coming from the sun. As a final touch we applied a perspective to the shadows to make them appear to be extending toward the viewer.

494 CH. 18 THE POWER OF THE LINE

18.11

The custom Power-Line to create the spoons

AUTHOR'S NOTE

You will find the spoons image as file 18-10.CDR on the Companion CD, along with many other files used to create the effects shown in Chapters 14 through 19. Look for them all in the PICTURES directory, with file names that match their figure numbers in the chapter.

CHAPTER 19

Through the Looking Glass

NINETEEN

This final chapter on our tour of the Effects menu focuses on two exciting new features added to DRAW 5.0's special effects repertoire: PowerClip and Lenses. PowerClip has been long awaited and is a welcome addition. The new Lens roll-up, however, was a pleasant surprise. With Lens, DRAW now has capabilities that are commonplace in paint programs, but unexpected in a vector drawing program.

It happens that both PowerClip and Lenses are fairly easy to use. As always, there are a few technical things to get accustomed to, but you won't have to learn such a multitude of styles, settings, and modes as are found in the Envelope, Blend, and Extrude roll-ups. Our primary challenge with Lens and PowerClip will be to provide you with inspiration for creatively employing them. Until they acquire some mileage with users, they will be features waiting for specific uses. Unlike blends (which are always used to shade objects or to create evenly spaced sets of objects) and unlike extrusions (which are always employed to give dimension), PowerClip and Lenses don't have such definitive roles, at least not at first glance.

PowerClips

We've already given you a peek at the value of PowerClipping, in Chapter 11. PowerClip is a fancy cropping tool. Where an envelope allows you to distort an object's shape or mold it to another object's shape, PowerClipping *trims* the object to fit *within* a shape. The shape is not distorted; rather, anything that falls outside the boundaries of the PowerClip *container* is simply hidden. (We'll explain containers shortly.)

Free-form cropping has long been a feature of painting and image-editing programs such as PHOTO-PAINT. What took DRAW so long to add it, you ask? In paint programs, it is fairly easy to program a routine that simply erases all pixels or dots that fall outside of a masking guideline. In a vector-based program, on the other hand, in which drawings are composed of multitudes of separate objects, each defined mathematically and consisting of open and/or closed curves, the program can't simply erase to crop. If you have ever tried to use node editing to manually trim even a simple element to make it fit inside another object, you can appreciate how complex the programming is for this operation. By the same token, you will also have an inkling of how useful such a tool can be. The new Arrange / Trim command flirts with this capability, but Effects / PowerClip really does it.

PowerClip may be new, but it's already quite powerful. Figure 19.1 shows you the PowerClip flyout. You can place nearly any collection of objects within a container, and you can edit the PowerClip, as well—either by changing the attributes of the objects to be clipped, or by repositioning them relative to the container. You can even nest one PowerClip within another. Further, if you decide you don't like a PowerClip, just extract the contents, and it is as if nothing had ever happened to them.

PowerClip Basics

Creating a PowerClip is simple. Just select one or more objects, and then select Place Inside Container from the PowerClip flyout. You are then presented with an arrow that you use to select the container.

19.1

The short list of PowerClip commands is long on talent.

What's a container? It can be a simple object; a complex, multipath object; a group of objects; text; even an extrusion. A PowerClip can be a container, too; you can nest up to five sets of PowerClips. Bitmaps can be used as contents for a PowerClip, but not as the container.

AUTHOR'S NOTE

 DRAW's online Help continues to improve, and the section on PowerClipping is a good example of truly helpful Help. Explore Help's various hypertext links for the PowerClip topic, and you will find out quite a lot. Also, you can open up a Help topic and toggle back and forth between it and your drawing, using Alt+Tab.

Here is a very simple exercise to give you a feel for the basics of Power-Clipping:

1. Create a new drawing, and open the Symbols roll-up. Set the symbol size at 3 inches. From Plants, drag symbol #33 (the palm tree) onto the page. From Animals1, drag symbol #52 (an elephant) onto the page.
2. Fill the palm tree with dark green, and the elephant with a 30% gray. Position them on the page as shown in Figure 19.2 and then group them.
3. Draw a hollow circle (use the Ctrl key to make it perfect) around the group, as shown in the figure.
4. Reselect the group, and select Effects / PowerClip / Place Inside Container.
5. When the large arrow cursor appears, click on the circle to select it as your container.

Congratulations! You have created your first PowerClip; take note of what the status line calls your new object. Your PowerClip will look something like the unembellished center portion of Figure 19.3, but we've taken it a bit further in this illustration and constructed a decal design with a corny slogan for a travel agency.

19.2

The raw materials for a PowerClip

In Chapter 11, we discussed the similarities between using a PowerClip and using the Arrange / Combine command to produce a hollow mask around a drawing. Prior to DRAW 5.0, the only way to produce the effect in Figure 19.3 would have been by combining the circle with a large white rectangle. This mask would then be placed on top of the elephant and palm tree to crop them. No contest—this is a much easier task with a PowerClip.

The circle PowerClip in Figure 19.2 was hollow, and we filled it for the decal in Figure 19.3. You can apply any sort of fill you like to a PowerClip container, either before or after the PowerClip has been applied.

19.3

The elephant and palm tree have been PowerClipped within this African safari travel decal.

The applied fill will be visible at any point where there is a gap in the PowerClip—that is, an area not filled by the objects contained within it. (Imagine that the PowerClip's contents are sitting *in front of* the container's fill.)

Editing PowerClips

Your group probably wasn't positioned within the PowerClip exactly as ours was in Figure 19.3, even if you positioned them this way before applying the PowerClip. By default, objects are centered within the Power-Clip container. But if the objects in a PowerClip container are not positioned where you want, you can select Effects / PowerClip / Edit Contents and change their location and other attributes as desired.

Following are some things to keep in mind as you edit PowerClips.

Avoid Auto-Centering

Toward the end of the DRAW 5.0 development cycle, Corel received a number of requests for an option to turn off the automatic centering of PowerClips. Most users prefer to situate the objects themselves, rather than have DRAW arbitrarily center everything within the container. Corel added this option, but buried it on the General page of the Preferences dialog. Look for a check box that says Auto-Center Place Inside. It is turned on by default, so all your objects will be centered within the PowerClip when first applied. We suggest you turn it off and keep it off.

Using the Lock Contents Option

Another useful PowerClip element that is somewhat hidden is the Lock Contents to PowerClip option on the Object menu. Whenever you create a PowerClip, the contents are initially locked to the container, so that the whole PowerClip is treated as a single object. That means the contents move, rotate, and scale along with the container. Most of the time you will want to keep a PowerClip's contents locked to the container, but not always. For quick edits of the container and/or repositioning the container relative to the contents, you may want to unlock the contents. Once your edits are done, you can turn the lock back on. To unlock an existing PowerClip, select it and invoke the Object menu (holding the SMB down). Uncheck the Lock Contents to PowerClip option, which is checked by default. By disabling this lock, the contents become fixed to the page, and you can move, rotate, or scale the container without affecting them.

Grouping While Editing

In the first PowerClip exercise of this chapter, you grouped the elements before placing them in the PowerClip container. You could have just as easily marquee-selected the two objects and PowerClipped without grouping. We had you group them to show you that groups, even complex groups of objects, can be placed in a PowerClip. Just as with most drawings, grouping often simplifies your work once you have arranged a set of objects the way you want.

When you choose Edit Contents on the PowerClip flyout, you will see only the contents of the PowerClip, and a wireframe display of the container. This arrangement makes it easier to isolate the work you are doing within the PowerClip, but complicates things if you need to position elements relative to objects outside the container. Turning off auto-centering and making use of the unlocking feature, as described above, usually remedies this problem.

There is nothing to stop you from ungrouping, regrouping, combining, and deleting elements, or changing fills, or doing anything else to the contents of a PowerClip. When you use PowerClip / Edit Contents, think of the contents as a separate drawing that eventually will be cropped by the container outline. Nearly anything you would normally do to objects in a drawing can be done at this point. Then, when you select Finish Editing This Level from the flyout, the PowerClip is reapplied to the contents. The one thing you cannot do in the Edit Contents mode is reposition the container itself. That must be done either before or after editing contents. We have occasionally had a few problems when drawing a new object while in Edit Contents mode, though it usually works. You can play it safe by creating any new objects in normal drawing mode, and then adding them to the PowerClip just as if you were creating a brand-new PowerClip.

Extrusions as PowerClips

Figure 19.4 shows another example of a PowerClip, this time using an extrusion as the container. At the top you see the elements that were placed inside the PowerClip, and on the bottom is the end result. Here are the steps for creating this mock-up of a product package:

1. In a new drawing, create a yellow rectangle about 5 inches wide by 6 inches tall, with a black outline of 0.5 point.

2. Create a small circle and a rectangle, and Arrange / Weld them to form the "keyhole" slot for the shelf rack (look above the *E* in the top image of Figure 19.4 to see how this should appear).

19.4

Extrusions, too, can be PowerClip containers.

Place the slot near the top of the large rectangle, and Arrange / Combine the slot and rectangle.

3. Extrude the shape using Small Back and a depth setting of 5. Fill it with either a solid color or shading (but *don't* select Use Object Fill on the Extrude / Color page).

WATCH OUT!

The Use Object Fill option does not work properly with extrusions as PowerClips, because the entire extrusion gets treated as the PowerClip, not just the control object. This would be an interesting feature if the contents would bend around the corners of an extrusion, but they don't, so it's not. Instead, you end up with a visually confusing object.

4. Drag a 9-inch elephant (#52 in the Animals1 symbol set) anywhere on the page, and fill it 30% gray with no outline.

5. Create the words **L.E. Fonts** as shown in Figure 19.4; use two centered lines and about 150-point type in any font you wish. For now, don't worry about rotating or placement.

6. Select both the text and the elephant, and choose Effects / PowerClip / Place Inside Container. Choose the extrusion as the container.

7. You now need to edit the contents of the PowerClip. Place the elephant approximately as shown in the bottom image of Figure 19.4. Rotate the text about 30 degrees, and place it as shown in the figure. If you like, change the color of the text and add an outline. Then select Finish Editing This Level.

Besides demonstrating how extrusions can be used as PowerClip containers, the foregoing exercise reinforces a point made earlier about PowerClip / Edit Contents. The sequence followed in the exercise left most of the object editing to be done *after* you placed the objects in the container. Remember that you can scale, shape, rotate, fill and even blend objects either before placing them in a PowerClip container or after. The end result should be the same, so you have quite a bit of flexibility.

We didn't include this in the exercise, but to spice up our design, we created a 20-step blend from a black elephant shape that we had distorted with an envelope, to a 30% gray elephant shape slightly reduced in scale.

Making PowerClips Jump through Hoops

If you're still not impressed with PowerClips, take a look at Figure 19.5. Here we used a PowerClip to create an image that would be very difficult to create otherwise: a dolphin jumping through a hoop. In the two-dimensional world of graphics software, this image simply cannot be created without some sort of illusion. A PowerClip provides the illusion.

19.5

Can you make a dolphin jump through a hoop? It's not so easy… unless you turn to a PowerClip.

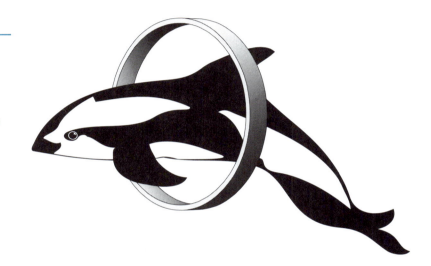

Figure 19.6 shows the steps we took. We found the dolphin in Corel's clip art library. We drew a circle, extruded it, and shaded it to create the hoop. The top image in Figure 19.6 shows that simple starting point; notice that the hoop is in front of the dolphin. In the second image, we selected the dolphin and made a quick copy using the + key, and then we moved it in front of the other two objects. Our choice of duplicating methods was important because the new dolphin had to be directly on top of the old one.

The third image shows the rectangle that we drew to act as the PowerClip container. It encloses the part of the dolphin that will appear to be already through the hoop. We took the duplicated dolphin and Power-Clipped it into this rectangle, so we had a dolphin behind the hoop

19.6

The four steps we took to make this dolphin jump through the hoop. A second dolphin is placed in front of the hoop and clipped into an invisible rectangle.

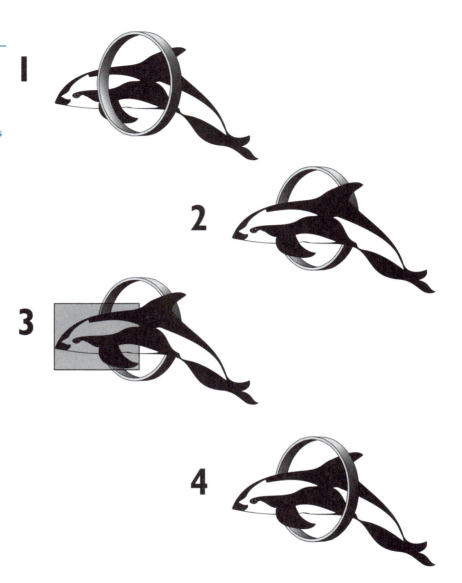

(the original one) and half of a dolphin in front of the hoop (the Power-Clipped one). As the last image shows, once we removed the fill and outline from the PowerClip rectangle, the two dolphins appear to be just one that is halfway through the hoop.

Rules of Thumb for PowerClipping

- For nearly all PowerClipping situations, it is better to leave the Preferences / General / Auto-Center Place Inside setting turned off.
- If you want to position and PowerClip objects in a drawing relative to other objects, position them first and clip them second. You can rearrange objects once they are PowerClipped, using PowerClip / Edit Contents, but when you are editing a PowerClip, DRAW hides all objects that are not part of the PowerClip.

Envelopes and PowerClips

PowerClips give you a lot of illustrative power, and sometimes it can go to your head. We got a tad sadistic with Figure 19.7, sticking this hapless soul's head inside a fish bowl. It was a mean thing to do, but it was, after all, in the interest of science.

Our cartoon employs essentially the same alignment techniques described for Figure 19.6. The only difference was applying a freehand envelope to the contents of the PowerClip, in order to warp this poor bird's head. We needed a reference so that the head inside the bowl wouldn't be too out of whack relative to the body that is outside the bowl. One way would be to duplicate the character, and do all the enveloping first. The bowl is the PowerClip container. Two copies of the bird exist—one is left outside, and one is placed in the container with an envelope applied. By placing an enveloped copy in the fish bowl as the container, the head looks distorted due to the refraction of the bowl, and the bowl crops the rest of the body, so the original undistorted version appears underneath.

19.7

Don't let Power-Clips go to your head!

Using PowerClips to Incorporate Bitmaps

One area where PowerClips can dramatically improve functionality is when you're incorporating a bitmap into a drawing. DRAW has always allowed bitmaps to be placed in a drawing, but in prior versions you had to work with a rectangular image. Even if you created an elliptical portrait by cropping the image in an image editor, the imported image would still be bound by a rectangular area, and that area would be solid white, not hollow. You could also crop images using the Shape tool, but this only allowed rectangular cropping—not much help when you're trying to crop to an elliptical shape.

The solution in past versions of DRAW, described in Chapter 11, was to create a mask from combined objects and place it in front of the bitmap. This technique, however, limits your flexibility in assembling other elements in relation to the bitmap; and editing—even a simple move or scaling operation—was a major headache.

It's better in DRAW 5.0. Figure 19.8, a postcard mailer for a fictional athletic gym, demonstrates how a bitmap can be placed in a PowerClip, as well as the technique of nesting one PowerClip within another.

NEW FOR 5

> The bitmap tiger image we used for Figure 19.8 is from one of Corel's Photo CD albums (Wild Animals). We accomplished this import quite easily with DRAW's new MOSAIC roll-up (see Chapter 33). With MOSAIC, we browsed the Photo CD images in Corel's library, selected the one we liked, and simply dragged it onto the page. An intervening dialog let us determine color or gray-scale, resolution, and whether to apply color correction.

After the tiger image was imported, we drew a hollow ellipse over it. Then we created a duplicate of the ellipse and sized it by adding .2 inch vertically and horizontally, to serve as a white backdrop. Next, we selected the bitmap, invoked Place Inside Container on the PowerClip flyout, and selected the hollow ellipse as the container.

PowerClips can really expand the potential ways in which bitmaps are incorporated into drawings. Now you can use PowerClips to assemble a montage of bitmaps, along with vector elements such as backgrounds and text. You can even rotate PowerClipped bitmaps. Ordinarily, our

19.8

The body of the illustration is PowerClipped within the outer rectangle, and the picture of the tiger is PowerClipped within that.

advice is to rotate bitmaps in image-editing software first, before importing to DRAW, but with PowerClipped bitmaps it's more inviting to rotate bitmaps within DRAW. Just remember that you will see a low-resolution version of the rotated bitmap on the screen. It will print just fine, however.

Nesting PowerClips

Now let's talk about nesting PowerClips, to which we have referred a couple of times in this chapter. Although nesting PowerClips complicates editing, sometimes nesting is the best strategy to take. In our Tiger Gym example, we have several PowerClips nested within one large one. The drop-shadowed text is clipped inside the gray triangle. These elements, plus the white text at an angle, are clipped inside the black rectangle. Finally, the black rectangle PowerClip and the clip art image of the cat and branch are clipped inside the larger gray rectangle. The end result is a pretty nifty assembly.

This collage probably could have been created in DRAW 4.0, through an elaborate scheme of masking and modifying objects, but it wouldn't have been pretty. And with all of those masks lying around the page, any fine-tuning to the individual elements would have been a nightmare. On the other hand, PowerClips are not without penalty when it comes to editing, either. You pay the price in speed and efficiency every time you want to edit the relative sizes or positions of objects within a PowerClip. This is especially true with nested PowerClips. Let's say, for example, that we decide to readjust the drop-shadowed text. To do this, we would have to use PowerClips / Edit Contents for the top-level Power*Clip, then select the black rectangle and go to Edit Contents again, and finally select the triangle and return to Edit Contents once more. We would then make the changes and choose Finish Editing This Level three times.

Before moving on to Lenses, we have one more example of nested PowerClips for you. We liked the effect in Figure 19.5 so much that we couldn't resist building something more elaborate with it. In Figure 19.9 you see the result. This commemorative marble plaque utilizes a two-level nested PowerClip: The PowerClipped dolphin, along with some imported clip art and two rectangles filled with fractal textures, were all PowerClipped inside a circle. You'll find this illustration and many of the others in this chapter on the Companion CD in the PICTURES directory. They are named according to their figure numbers here.

19.9

Another example of a PowerClip inside a PowerClip

Rules of Thumb for Nesting PowerClips

- Think carefully before applying nested PowerClips. Can you accomplish the same thing with a collection of objects in a single PowerClip, or several separate PowerClips? The fewer levels nested, the easier it is to edit them.

- Don't totally abandon the Arrange / Combine masking technique. True, masks created by combining objects are usually less flexible, but in some instances they are the better choice. The mask itself might be difficult to edit, but readjusting how objects are framed by it can often be faster than going in and out of PowerClip editing.

- PowerClips give you the luxury of editing or totally undoing your crops. If you anticipate changing your mind about cropping something, or you need to resize, change the amount of crop, or the like, PowerClip is a better tool than Arrange / Trim, node editing, and related techniques.

Lenses, Lenses, and More Lenses

Lens is a particularly apt word for what this new roll-up, shown in Figure 19.10, accomplishes. The Lens roll-up provides access to eight different cameralike lenses that can be applied to an object. When you apply one of these lens types, the object becomes the lens, filtering your view of all objects that are behind it.

19.10

The Lens roll-up

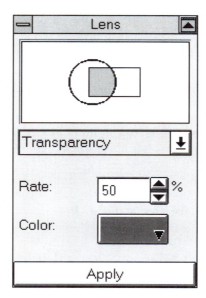

For an object to be a lens, it must be a single, closed element. It can have multiple paths, but it must be a single object. Groups, extrudes, blends, and so forth cannot be lenses, but an artistic text string is considered a single element, so it qualifies.

Before you move on to the next sections, where you'll learn about what each lens does, work through the following exercise. Some of the lens functions are more obvious than others, and the best way to learn about them is to experiment.

1. Start a new drawing, letter-size and with portrait orientation.
2. Near the top of the page, draw a blue-filled rectangle about 2.0 inches wide by 0.5 inch high, with a black outline.
3. Create a duplicate of the blue rectangle, 8 inches below the original. (Try using the Transform roll-up to do this.)
4. Select both rectangles, open the Blend roll-up, and apply 8 steps. Switch to the Colors page of the Blend roll-up, choose the Rainbow option, and click Apply. You should now have 10 rectangles running the gamut of the color spectrum.
5. Make a copy of the Blend group, and place it 2.5 inches to the right of the original group, so that there is a half-inch gap between the groups. For the right-hand blend group, change the start object fill to black, and its end object to white.
6. Draw a yellow ellipse that covers at least a portion of each rectangle, as shown in Figure 19.11. You now have a versatile sample for testing the various lens styles. The ellipse will become the lens through which you will view the rectangles underneath.
7. Invoke the Lens roll-up, from the Effects menu or by typing Alt+F3. Make sure the ellipse is selected, and apply a transparent lens (select Transparency in the drop-down list).

Now go ahead and experiment as much as you like. Try applying each style of lens, and if you need to, refer to the descriptions in the following sections. When a particular lens has additional settings for rate, color, and so on, try varying them over a wide range to see their effect.

In the PICTURES directory, we have provided a file called PHOTOS.CDR that demonstrates the application of all DRAW's lenses. Notice the subtle differences between how a color image and a grayscale image are influenced by the same lens.

19.11
The Official Mastering CorelDRAW Lens Test Pattern

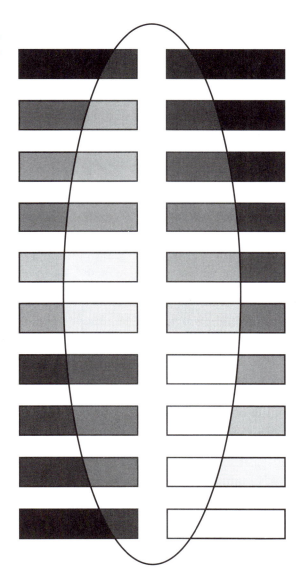

Transparency Likely to be the favorite of the bunch, Transparency causes the colors of the objects under the lens to mix with the lens object's color, creating the illusion that you've placed a piece of transparent film over the object. In the Rate box, you enter a transparency rate from 1% to 100%. The greater this value, the more transparent the lens object; at 100%, the lens fill disappears.

Magnify   Another fun one, this lens causes the objects under the lens to be magnified by the factor you specify in the Amount box, so it looks like you've placed a magnifying glass over the drawing. The maximum magnification factor is 10. Be careful when using this lens with bitmaps; at twice or three times the magnification, most bitmaps will look very jagged.

Brighten   This lens brightens the colors under it by the factor you specify in the Rate box, between −100% and 100%. At 100%, the colors are nearly white; at 0%, the lens has no effect at all; and at −100%, the colors approach black.

Invert   With Invert you can switch the colors under the lens to their complementary colors, based on the CMYK color wheel. For example, red becomes cyan, green becomes magenta, and yellow becomes blue.

Color Limit   Color Limit works much like a color filter on a camera, filtering out all colors under the lens except the one you specify in the Color box. For example, if you place a green lens over an object, all colors except green will be filtered out within the lens area. You can also control the strength of the filter by specifying a value in the Rate box. For the green filter, a rate of 100% will allow only green to show through; a lower setting will allow other colors to show through.

Color Add   The Color Add lens mixes the colors of overlapping objects. This lens has no effect where it overlays white objects, because white already contains 100% of every color.

INSIDE INFO

Once a lens is applied, you can select colors from the on-screen color palette or the Fill roll-up to change the lens tint. This may not seem to be a big deal, but when you're first experimenting with lenses on a drawing, it does save having to constantly access the Lens roll-up and the Apply button.

Tinted Grayscale Objects under this lens appear to have had a tonal scale setting applied. Colors under the lens are mapped from the lens color to an equivalent tone of the color of that lens. For example, a blue lens over a light-colored object creates light blue; the same lens over a dark-colored object creates dark blue.

Heat Map This lens maps colors to other colors in a predefined palette, creating a *heat map* or infrared look. Bright (or hot) colors are mapped to other hot colors (yellow, orange, and so on), and dark (or cool) colors are mapped to cooler colors (blue, cyan, and purple). The palette Rotation value determines where the color mapping begins. For example, a value of 0% or 100% causes mapping to begin at the start of the palette (at white) and move to the right (through cyan, blue, and so on). A value of 50% causes mapping to begin halfway through the palette (at red) and move to the right, and then back to the start of the palette.

None Selecting None removes the lens from the selected object. Note that this is the principal way to remove a lens and return the lens object to a normal solid-filled object. To find out how to replace one lens with another, read on.

Combining Lenses

As you experimented with DRAW's lenses and our Official Lens Test Pattern, you may have wondered about combining the effects of two lens styles. For example, you might want to both magnify and brighten what is under the lens. When you apply a new lens, you replace any existing lens; they are not added together. There is, however, a way to combine the effects of more than one lens: by stacking lens objects on top of one another.

Remember the ellipse you created in the previous exercise? If you were to duplicate it right on top of the original, you would initially double whatever effect had been applied with the single lens. Change the style of one of the duplicates, and you have created a compound lens effect.

In Figure 19.12 we have stacked two lenses to demonstrate a compound lens. One lens magnifies; the other inverts colors. We've rotated each of them just a bit; where they overlap, that's where the lens effects are compounded. Where they do not overlap, only one or the other lens applies. You can stack any number of lenses, but you will find that each additional lens will considerably slow down redraw time, especially when the stacked lenses overlap.

19.12

You can stack lenses to combine their effects.

WATCH OUT!

Artistic text can be used as a lens object, and it performs adequately with all lenses—except Magnify. If you convert the text to curves, however, the Magnify lens will work correctly.

Learning to Use the Lenses

Now that you've experimented with the effects produced by each lens style, let's take a look at some other aspects of applying lenses. You've probably already thought of a number of uses for Transparency and Magnify, but what about some of the others?

Using Tinted Grayscale for that Duo-Tone Look

In the earlier exercise, the steps you took to create a set of black-to-white and then rainbow-colored rectangles were to help clarify the use of the Tinted Grayscale lens. In various (and especially computer) magazines, we have noticed an increased use of what are called *duo-tone photographs*. These are gray-scale images that are printed with a second color tint added to black. If you have a limited budget for commercial printing, you probably aren't producing four-color process work, but you may be doing some two-color printing. Adding a tint to a black-and-white image adds drama to it, yet can be accomplished using just one additional ink besides black.

The Tinted Grayscale lens allows you to create duo-tones from gray-scale images. If you are starting with full-color clip art, you would first convert the color image to a single color and then add the Tinted Grayscale lens. Want to use some clip art as a background or watermark? No problem—just apply a very light gray Tinted Grayscale lens.

WATCH OUT!

Before you get too excited about using Tinted Grayscale as we've described just above, bear in mind one important fact: You cannot use PANTONE spot colors for this technique. If you apply a PANTONE color, it will be converted to CMYK at print time, whether you like it or not. This doesn't mean you can't use the duo-tone technique; it just means you will have to substitute a pure process color for the intended PANTONE color as you are constructing the drawing. Once you have your separations, you can tell your print shop exactly which PANTONE color to use for each plate.

Heat Map

Like Tinted Grayscale, Heat Map is most effective when used with grayscale photographic images. Try importing a photo and applying this lens. The result is an effect that has become very popular in some publications. If you are planning to publish a magazine dedicated to heavy-metal music, this is definitely the lens for you. Illustration 11 in the Color Gallery presents two poster designs, both based on the same grayscale photo. In the more traditional poster, a Tinted Grayscale lens was used. The other, more radical design was created with a Heat Map lens.

Color Limit and Color Add

For its most dramatic effect, use Color Limit as you would a color filter for a camera. For an imported colored photographic bitmap, you can use Color Limit much as a photographer uses different filters to achieve certain tones for a photo. For a gray-scale image, the result of Color Limit looks pretty much the same as what you get with Tinted Grayscale.

Color Add contributes a specific color to the image, rather than filtering it. It tends to brighten.

Using Brighten to Create Text Backdrops

Another popular technique used in many publications is to brighten or "wash out" part of an image in order to place text over it. The Brighten lens makes it easy to accomplish this. Look ahead to Figure 19.15 for an example.

Using Lenses as Windows

How would you create a transparent lens that acts as a window through an otherwise opaque object? To accomplish this, our first idea was to try to put a lens inside a PowerClip. But a transparent lens placed within a PowerClip will not reveal anything placed behind the PowerClip container, unless the container is hollow in the first place. You can place a lens and objects behind it together into a PowerClip container and thus simulate a window.

The best way, however, to create a window, is demonstrated in Figure 19.13. We first created a rectangle with a pattern fill, to serve as a wall. We drew a second rectangle and combined it with the wall to create a hole through the wall. Then we extruded the wall to give the window frame some depth. Finally, we drew two rectangles, transformed them into 60% Transparency lenses, and overlapped them. The result was this look of a partially open glass window.

The key to creating a window like this is to create a hole first, using Arrange / Combine. The magnifying glass in Figure 19.14 is another example of this technique. There, we combined two circles to form the lens ring with a large hole in it, and assigned the Magnify lens to a duplicate of the smaller circle.

Putting Lenses to the Test

We created the image in Figure 19.14 to find out what happens if you use several lenses together. The butterfly is a piece of clip art, which originally had opaque, not translucent wings. We converted most of the major components of the wings into lenses, some overlapping. We also threw in a Magnify lens to add further complexity.

19.13

This western critter really appears to be grazing behind a window shade.

One key lesson learned was that applying lots of lenses really slows things down. Each lens area is redrawn, lens by lens. If you have compound lenses, the effect of the first lens is redrawn, then the next lens, and so on. You can get bogged down in a hurry.

In Figure 19.14, you have several different objects, all using the same lens style and settings. You can often combine these lenses so that they are treated as a single curve. For example, there are eight little spots at the ends of each large butterfly wing; each spot is a lens. By combining all 16 of them, they became a single lens. The advantage is that you modify the effect to all of them at once. The Lens roll-up doesn't allow multiple objects to be selected when a lens is applied, but you can use Combine to get around that.

19.14

This butterfly is made up of four separate lenses.

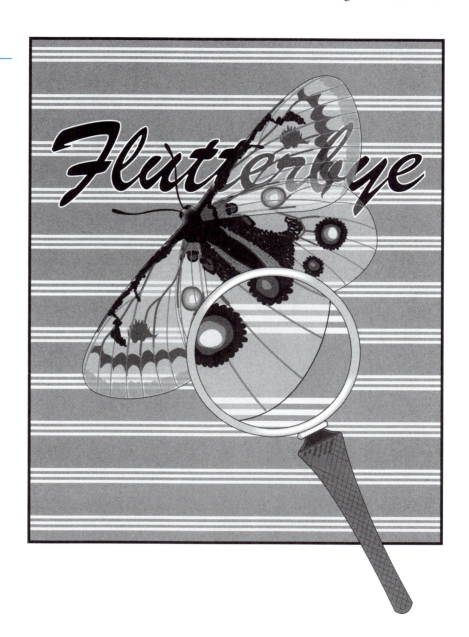

WATCH OUT!

The background for the butterfly illustration is a two-color pattern, and it nicely accentuates the translucency of the wings and the effect of the Magnify lens. We had originally intended to use a full-color pattern for the background—but we crashed big-time when we tried to print it, so complex was the instruction set. Only when we reduced the number of fountain steps did we print successfully, but the quality of the image suffered greatly. The moral of this story? Be careful not only about how many lenses you use, but also what you have behind them.

Putting It All Together

Figure 19.15 shows our first attempt at a new vocation: ornithological trading cards. For this composite image we made extensive use of Power-Clipped bitmaps, some of which were rotated in DRAW and then overlapped over others. The text was placed over an enveloped rectangular, white lens with 60% Transparency. We also added a dash of highlight to two of the bitmaps, using the Brighten lens. You'll find this illustration in the PICTURES directory, but cross your fingers if you try to print it. On our systems, it created almost 10MB of code and sent our printer to its knees more than once.

This concludes our tour of the Effects menu, but we'll leave techno-land with...

One Last Thought about Special Effects

Our last piece of advice for you is this: As you continue to develop your proficiency with special effects, try to think a little like an artist and a little like a computer programmer. If you start as the artist, with as clear a vision as possible of what you want to achieve, you can then ask your alter ego, the Special Effects Expert, to find the best way to go about delivering it. Sometimes this will take imagination and a bit of

19.15

This compound image includes PowerClips, lenses, enveloped text, and rotated bitmaps.

inventiveness, and the magic ingredient may be a somewhat unorthodox use of DRAW's tools.

From our experience with DRAW users, we conclude that artists learning about computers often don't think enough about how the tools actually work and the concepts that support them, choosing tools and techniques that most closely mimic traditional artistic methods. Conversely, computer users learning about art have a tendency to make the method more important than the result. They pick an effect and then try to find an excuse to use it. Whatever type you are (and there is undoubtedly a little of both in all of us), keep to the best sequence of events: First allow your artistic side to define what is needed, and then ask your technical side to help achieve it.

And now, in Part V, we allow the artistic side of our award-winning designers to take center stage.

PART V

DOING IT!

This section of the book has two central themes: How to create beautiful work and how to avoid awful work.

We are well aware that, for a majority of CorelDRAW users, the absence of ugliness is often a primary goal. In fact, it may totally overshadow the pursuit of learning how to create art that is better to begin with. However, we are equally sure that a bit of inspiration goes a long way toward helping you create realistic images, however simple they may be, so we think it in your best interests as computer artists to read these five chapters.

You don't have to be sitting at your computer to get everything out of these chapters. You may be more comfortable on the patio, in your living room, or perhaps another room in the house in which you often do your daily reading…

CHAPTER 20

The Huntress

TWENTY

Georgina Curry, a graphic designer and illustrator in Phoenix, Arizona, developed The Huntress on a 486/33MHz computer with 20MB of RAM, a 210MB SCSI hard disk, and a 24-bit Genoa video card. Claiming that she created the work during her "spare time," she acknowledges that it took approximately three months to complete the project.

Inspired at the Movies

My inspiration for *The Huntress* came from the silent film star Clara Bow. When I saw the elegant beauty in her face, I knew that was the image I wanted to create with DRAW. Specifically, I wanted to capture the essence of her eyes and lips, and I centered the piece around these two elements. *The Huntress* did not begin as a contest piece, but as she developed I saw something unique in her, and felt pleased with the finished project (Figure 20.1).

I would not describe *The Huntress* as complex to produce, but rather a piece that required a tremendous eye for detail that I acquired through my training in the fine arts. *The Huntress* is a testimony to the creative freedom that DRAW's tools and features give to illustrators and designers. DRAW contains all the tools I needed to create this piece. Combining these powerful tools with my education gave me the ability to make *The Huntress* a reality, and the project was quite fun to do.

The most intricate portions of *The Huntress*—her headwear and beadwork—were accomplished by creating radial-filled ellipses, and then using the enveloping and mirroring tools to achieve the visual effect. This was the most time-consuming section of the piece and required tremendous attention to detail.

20.1
Best of Show, 1993:
The Huntress

Virtually all the elements of *The Huntress* were created using a combination of the Blend, Mirror, Extrude, Envelope, Combine, and Add Perspective functions. These tools took the complexity out of the production process and gave me the freedom to experiment with various effects. All I had to do was determine the effect I wanted for a particular section of the piece; DRAW always seemed to have just the right tool to accomplish my objective.

The Feathers

The feathers adorning the head and shoulders of *The Huntress* all evolved from a single "master feather," which was duplicated to produce all the feathers in the finished product. I developed the master feather in halves: I initially created the left side of the feather and then used the horizontal Mirror function to produce the right side. I used the Freehand Drawing tool to create the basic shapes for the tip and shaft of the left side of the feather, and then used the Shape tool to develop their final outline.

I wanted the holes on the tip and shaft to appear transparent, so I used Arrange / Combine to combine the holes with the tip and the shaft.

When the left side was complete, I grouped all of the objects and applied the horizontal Mirror function to create the right side. I then grouped both sides of the feather to create my master feather. Figure 20.2 shows the feather on the drawing boards.

All of the feathers within the image are products of this master feather. The feathers on the headdress were duplicated and manually positioned along the contour of the headdress. I used black and gray for this section of the headdress because I felt this combination was a nice contrast and would provide color balance to the rest of the image.

The shoulder feathers, too, were created from the master feather. Again, I created the left side of the shoulder arrangement first and used the Mirror function to duplicate it for the right side. I used the Add Perspective and Envelope functions from the Effects menu to render the various angles of the individual shoulder feathers. For this section of the image, I chose colors that I felt were more dynamic.

20.2

Producing the feathers is a simple "group-and-dupe" procedure: Create the basic shape, group the objects, and then duplicate them.

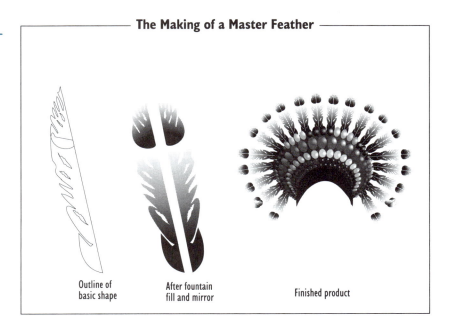

The Making of a Master Feather

Outline of basic shape

After fountain fill and mirror

Finished product

The Face and Hair

The face is a combination of freehand and Bezier drawing. As Figure 20.3 shows, the eyes are the most detailed part of the face, with highlights and shadows separately drawn with subtle changes in grays. The lips consist of two large areas, a dark portion on the upper and lower lips and a lighter red on the lower lip. Highlights were added to the lower lip using the trusty Blend tool.

The main oval of the face is light gray; the contours of the forehead, nose, and chin are defined by the darkened portion of the left side of the face. Again using the Blend tool, I created the shadow beneath the right cheek and the highlight on the left cheek.

The hair was created by using the tool now called the Freehand Drawing tool and varying the widths of the lines. Highlights were drawn on top of these lines and radial-filled. The individual loose strands, added for realism, were created with the Freehand Drawing tool. The wraps on the hair were developed by drawing an ellipse and extruding it to various lengths, depending on the color. The turquoise spiral designs on the braided portion of the hair were drawn as curves, with highlights added

20.3

Killer eyes

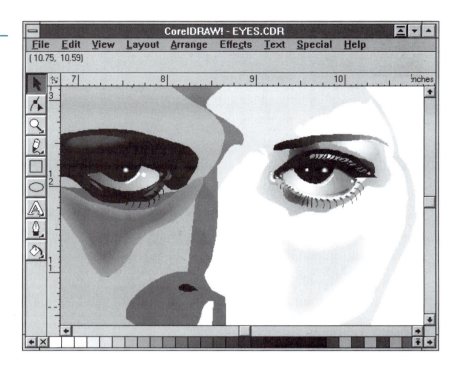

to the top. The smaller highlights in these objects were created with the Blend tool. The beadwork at the end of the hair is a combination of straight lines and radial-filled ellipses.

The Medallion

I constructed the medallion in the center of the headband (Figure 20.4) by developing a series of ellipses. The base of the medallion consists of two ellipses, with radial fills applied in opposite directions. The second and third levels of the medallion were created by duplicating and scaling down the base level.

The metallic beads on the medallion were produced by creating radial-filled ellipses, with darker ellipses used to produce the shadowing effect.

Once I completed the medallion, I incorporated it several times within the illustration. With the help of the Duplicate command and Add Perspective tool, I used it for the earrings and also as elements in the necklace.

20.4

Lots and lots of ellipses went into this medallion.

The Large Beads of the Headdress

I created the large beads on the headdress with the Ellipse tool, duplicating and scaling down each bead to add perspective. I manually placed each bead along the contour of the headdress. After completing each row, I grouped the row and altered the group using Effects / Envelope. To the individual beads I added subtle changes in the hue and intensity of the radial fills, to reinforce the atmospheric perspective of the headdress. Each row of beads was individually created—I did not duplicate one row to create another because each row had to have its own subtle uniqueness.

The Small Beads of the Headdress

The small beads that make up the lower portion of the headdress are the least technical elements of the entire piece. I created a pile of colored beads in an imaginary "bowl" off to the side of the drawing. Then I began to experiment, pulling beads out of this bowl. Since I had no preconceived notion of how I wanted this section to look, this approach turned into a rather time-consuming process. However, after several days an idea began to emerge, which ultimately became this part of the finished piece.

Again, I initially created the left side of this part of the headdress and then used the Mirror function to complete the design, adjusting the colors of the individual beads to create the appropriate shadows and highlights.

The Jeweled Headband

The jeweled headband beneath the smaller beaded portion of the headdress is made up of two components: the gray beads and the emerald jewels.

The gray beads were constructed of five ellipses grouped as one object. The largest ellipse represented the basic form of the bead, two other ellipses were added to produce the black rings circling the bead, and two more ellipses were added to create highlights within each bead. Once the first bead was completed, I then duplicated and resized it to create a column of four beads. With the Ellipse tool, I created two additional hanging beads and added these to the column. I then grouped the column and duplicated it to form additional columns for the final spacing between the emerald jewels.

The emerald jewels were created by developing one jewel composed of a series of seven rectangles and three ellipses. The first rectangle I created was the gray housing or base of the jewel; six additional rectangles provide the basic form, depth, and highlights of the emerald. Three white ellipses were placed in various sections of the emerald for additional highlighting.

Next the basic group (the gray beads and the emerald jewel) was assembled, and I duplicated them to create the entire composition of the headband. I initially created the headband as a straight line and used the Envelope tool to fit it around the forehead. After I had the basic shape and envelope of the headband, I then altered the hue and intensity of the color in various sections to produce my light source.

The Choker

The choker and necklace below the face were the easiest parts to design. The turquoise choker is simply a series of small rectangles. I used Rotate & Skew and Stretch & Mirror from the Transform menu (the Effects menu in 4.0) to give an illusion of perspective to this section of the illustration. I used lighter fills for the highlights and darker fills for the shadows. Effects / Extrude helped me create the rectangular beads beneath the choker. As mentioned earlier, I duplicated the medallion and used it throughout the necklace. To these basic elements I added round beads and clusters of beads, created by constructing radial-filled ellipses.

After the necklace was completed, I duplicated it and filled the new object with gray, which became the shadow that appears on her chest. I used enveloping on this shadow to give her breasts soft curves.

The Scarf

The scarf is composed of four shapes that represent four folds. The design for the last two folds was enveloped. To cut off the design in places where it would fold under, I merely overlapped the folds of fabric. The gold border was created using both radial and linear fills. The colors used are red, brown, and yellow. The highlights in this area were created using a yellow object blending into a white object.

You will find HUNTRESS.CDR included on the Companion CD. (Be patient when opening it—it's a 2MB file!) She also graces the Color Gallery, as Illustration 4.

CHAPTER 21

The Diver

TWENTY-ONE

CHAPTER 21

David Brickley won Best of Show at Corel's inaugural annual design contest, and is arguably the most prolific of all CorelDRAW artists. Since then, not a year has passed that David's work has not been profiled by Corel and other commercial vendors. This and the following two chapters showcase three of his most significant efforts.

A Work in Progress

What strikes me most about *The Diver* is that it's still around. And although I created this piece in 1989, people seem to talk about it almost as though it were new. The original title was *Swimming in the Deep End*, and frankly, I prefer that one. But the people at Corel were very excited about the drawing, and I knew that holding firm on this would be like putting a hand out to stop a speeding locomotive. Oh well, *The Diver* works, and I'm pleased with the way the drawing came out. It's shown here in Figure 21.1, and also in the Color Gallery, Illustration 5.

Still, for me, *The Diver* drawing is really nothing more than a sketch. Should I ever have the time, I will finish it, so that the drawing will stand up to close examination. Figure 21.2 shows, at close range, what looks very much like a computer sketch, instead of the fine craft of a skilled traditional artist. The "finish" in my work has improved since 1989, as I have learned more about DRAW and acquired more capable hardware. Artisanship is not a requisite for producing good art, but most designers strive for it. I want people to walk right up close to my work, as they would a big statue, and see art and design in the details as well as in the work as a whole. The current technology makes that level of "finish" possible now as never before.

21.1

The Diver, winner of the 1990 Corel International Design Contest

21.2

One day, the artist hopes to refine some of these rough edges (at least, for him they're rough).

The Genesis of The Diver

The story of this drawing is one for the grandkids. In April 1989, I was starting a computer graphics freelance venture and was looking for both clients and good software. My strengths were advertising and illustration. I saw the ad for version 1.1 of CorelDRAW and was reasonably impressed with the program's features. But what struck me most was how bad the advertisement itself was. Here was a great product that was underrepresented in its advertising—aha, a potential client.

I called Corel and spoke with the DRAW product manager. DRAW looked like a great product, I said, one with which I might be able to produce something interesting. I proposed a trade: Corel would send me a copy of the program, and I would create an image for its advertising. After I hung up the phone, a little voice whispered, "Yeah, right—fat chance." But the next morning, Federal Express was at the door wanting my signature for a package from Canada. The same little voice said, "I'll be darned, it worked."

Doing It!

I installed DRAW into a no-name 386/16MHz with 1MB of RAM. I had 70MB total hard drive space, being supervised by DOS 3.1 and Windows 2.11. The video display was 13-inch, driven by a standard VGA adapter. At the time, Windows allowed only 8 of the 16 VGA colors to be used. Whatever art DRAW displayed in preview was made up of 8 severely dithered colors; the rest were reserved for the system. For a pointer, I used (and still do use) a Microsoft mouse. This, by the way, was a pretty hot system back in '89.

The original idea for the drawing was a sailboat on a lake near the mountains—thus the body of water with a rugged coastline in the background that still remains in *The Diver*. I started by drawing two wide rectangles to establish the horizon. The rectangle on top was colored as a sky might look with the sun low in the late afternoon. The water was colored to reflect the look of the sky, with a shift to a slightly cooler hue. Figure 21.3 shows these very humble beginnings.

21.3

Award-winning art often starts with the simplest of shapes—in this case, two rectangles.

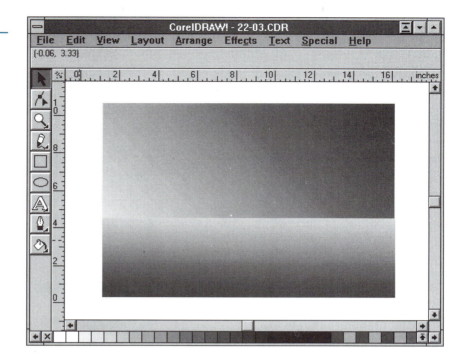

AUTHOR'S NOTE

We confess to being less than 100% accurate with these screen images. We really did try to use a copy of DRAW 1.1 for this chapter. We even found one, but it wouldn't run under Windows 3.11. The prospect of retrofitting one of our systems with Windows 2.11 is where we gave up!

Filling In the Landscape

Next I needed a shape for the mountains. As a rule, I try to use a photograph or other realistic reference when illustrating any real thing. I never try to compete with reality. At this point, however, I wanted to just "rough" something in and look for adequate reference later. The mountains were colored with a graded fill to support the idea of afternoon light.

As you look from left to right across the background, you see the light's intensity fall off (Figure 21.4).

21.4

One of the most important elements of realism is accurate depiction of light source.

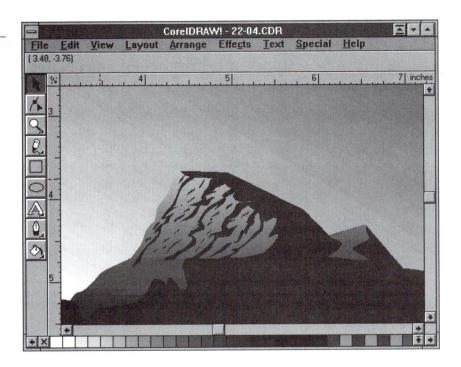

The clouds were created by forming a single cloud shape and duplicating and modifying it many times. Once again, I started very simply: I drew a circle. After converting it to a curve, I used the Shape tool, selected all nodes in the curve, and double-clicked one of them to invoke the Node Edit roll-up. By clicking the + icon in the roll-up, I instantly added 4 more nodes around the circle; I did it again for 8, again to make 16, and yet again for 32. Once I had the nodes created, I converted them to cusps for more editing control (see Chapter 6). As shown in Figure 21.5, after creating the 32 nodes, I billowed the path of each one to create the look of a cloud.

I gave each cloud a different look by pulling groups of nodes away from the center and making some of the billows different sizes. Applying a

21.5

What started as a circle became 32 little wisps and billows of a cloud.

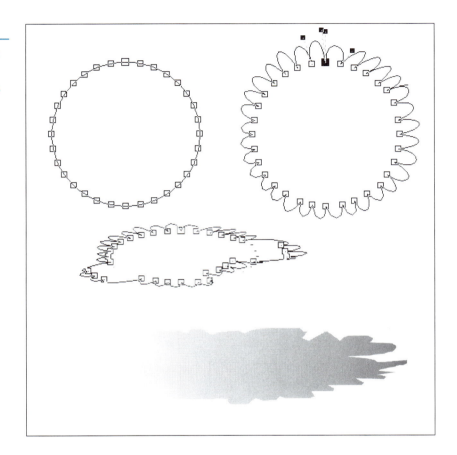

radial fill was quite a challenge in version 1.1—nothing like it is today. In the first versions of DRAW, the radial fill command would start only from the center of an object. To offset the center of a radial, I had to create a small line segment and place it away from the object. This increased the size of the selection area, meaning that the radial fill covered more ground—essentially changing what DRAW thought the center to be.

Finding the Leading Character

I found a picture of a sailboat that would fit nicely into the scene I had just created, and started to draw it into place. For a reality check, I stood back and imagined how the drawing might look finished. What came to mind as

I pictured a sailboat on the water in front of those mountains and clouds was a typical, so-what, no-big-deal, my-Grandma-did-one-just-like-that picture—in other words, pedestrian and ordinary. Certainly nothing that should be in an advertisement. I scuttled the boat immediately, and began a week-long search for a different idea.

I came upon a photo of Greg Louganis in a backward swan off the high-dive, shown in the top half of Figure 21.6. He was so "out there," in his element, calmly throwing himself off that treacherously high place. I kept coming back to the photo and could see it working in the drawing. I knew that it would require a tremendous amount of work to succeed,

21.6

All those hours in art school paid off, as the artist was able to extend his vision beyond the reference of a small photograph.

but I also knew that was part of what would make it special.

Once I settled on the photo of the diver, I needed a way to get it into the drawing. I enlarged the photo onto a piece of acetate (clear plastic). I sized the image to about 10 inches and, using a technical pen, carefully traced the profile and a few major visual features. Then I simply taped the plastic to the front of my display—the poor person's equivalent of the old Autotrace (the TRACE module in version 4.0). In the photo, Greg is going in the opposite direction from the final image. To change that, I flipped the acetate over. From here, I used the Freehand Drawing tool (back then it didn't have a Bezier drawing mode) to draw a line that followed the contours of the lines on the acetate.

INSIDE INFO

When tracing an image manually, it is important to have a known magnification level as a reference. Before you begin, press Shift+F4, the hotkey to view the entire page. Then you will always have a reference to return to, should you zoom in or move the screen while drawing.

When I had completed the profile of the diver, I added a graded, skin-tone-colored fill that set the base for how he would be rendered. It's important to note that only later did I learn this one object would be the source of significant printing problems. The combination of complex outline and fountain fill gave the Linotronic imagesetter a pretty hard time. While printing, the imagesetter would reach a particular point in the file and suddenly gag, sputter, and choke. In later versions, this profile was split in two across the waist to work around that problem.

The most critical area of this drawing is the face. It's a visual hook for the artist; everything else hangs from that. Once the face is done and the likeness works, everything else that follows falls into place a lot easier. As I worked, I scanned my eyes from the face down across the area I drew; doing so helped keep the level of finish consistent.

The process of actually drawing the diver was, I'll admit, arduous. The original photo I worked from was about 3 inches square. I held the photo in my left hand and the mouse in the right. I drew objects that followed the contours of shadows, color changes, highlights, and so on. Most often, I drew the largest objects first to establish a base, and then added smaller color objects on top. If this had been a traditional art medium, I would now be describing these objects as brush strokes.

The key word in that last sentence is *if*. This is not a traditional medium, and that fact makes itself known to me every day I use the software. I'll admit that I sometimes miss the pleasure of taking pencil or pen to paper to produce final drawings. I still get to sketch a lot—nothing replaces sketching and doodling when developing ideas—but these days I turn the final work over to DRAW. There is one all-compelling reason for this: CorelDRAW lets you change your mind! Electronic drawing software always provides you with recourse. There are undo and clear commands, backup files, and multiple versions of a drawing. There are fill tools that can instantly change an object's color, and tremendous flexibility in outline styles and pen thicknesses.

I remember all too well a few major-league disasters in which drawings were ruined by one slip of the charcoal. Obviously, we all have our favorite horror stories with DRAW as well. But on balance, DRAW provides one of the greatest gifts an artist could ask for: the freedom to experiment, to change one's mind.

As an artist, I have spent a great deal of time drawing the human anatomy. This made it possible for me to compensate for features that were not clear in the photo. As the lower half of Figure 21.6 shows, I drew the diver flipped over so that he was right-side-up. This orientation was much more natural and easier to work with.

Today, as I study the drawing using modern tools—such as a 1024 × 768 display rendering 256 colors—I see many things I would do differently. *The Diver* is full of instances where I tried to "seam-stitch" objects. Instead of drawing objects one on top of another, often I drew them side-by-side, making them meet along the edges. For example, Figure 21.7 is a close-up of the diver's right thigh. The top part of the leg was drawn using shapes stacked on top of one another (preferred method). But the muscle on the lower leg was drawn using objects that touched only at the edges. If there is even a whisper of an opening between the objects, background color (or white space) bleeds through; this becomes especially apparent when this file is printed at high resolution to a film recorder or imagesetter. Drawing objects side-by-side is not only more risky, it's more difficult, because any adjustment you make to one object must be followed by an adjustment to the object it touches. Also, PostScript is designed to deal with objects that are stacked. Today I draw everything that way.

DRAW 1.1 did not have an interruptible display (and of course, no layers); therefore, I was forced to separate the large parts of the drawing so the background was not behind the diver. Otherwise, I would have had to endure interminable delays as the background painted and repainted.

21.7

No more side-by-side drawing for this artist—from now on, it's layers upon layers.

Also missing from DRAW's list of features then was a color preview; to see a full-screen color preview (if you can call 13 inches a full screen), I had to issue the command and wait…and wait…and wait….

Looking Back

The question I am asked the most often today is, how long did it take me? That's hard to quantify. I worked on it from April through June 1989. Forced to proffer a number, I would say about 300 hours, but now that PCs are so much faster, there is a different time-to-effort ratio. Of those 300 hours, many were taken up with my watching the screen redraw.

The other difficulties were the small display and the extremely dithered colors. I had to redo a good deal of work when I saw how the file looked when printed by an HP PaintJet. Getting that color proof, however, was no easy matter. I had no color printer, nor access to one. Up to this point, all I had for feedback was the little 13-inch, 8-color display (it's amazing how backward we were just five years ago!). Then Corel agreed to output the drawing for me on a PaintJet, so I set out to create a print file. I loaded the PaintJet driver and issued the command for DRAW to print the drawing to a disk file. That was about 9:30 in the evening. I retired for the night with the "Printing File" message still flashing and the hard drive grinding away. *It finished at 9:30 the following morning*—all that activity for a 350K print file that took only two minutes to print!

I am told that, when the floppy disk arrived at Corel, a few dozen copies of my diver were circulated around the offices. Until that time, the engineers and executives had only seen simple things created with DRAW, and they were very excited by this first real example of the program's capability.

Meanwhile, back at the ranch, I received my copy of the printout. Everyone at Corel might have been thrilled, but I was horrified. The water was way too blue, the sky seemed all wrong, the clouds looked like popcorn, and the diver himself was far from done. I continued to work on the drawing, making adjustments according to what I saw in the printout. To me, this was very much a "work in progress." Unbeknownst to me, however, the stir at Corel was a de facto endorsement of the work, and the drawing was considered done. That set into motion a series of events that culminated in the idea of an annual design contest, in which *The Diver* was entered and subsequently the victor.

An interesting piece of trivia from these events: There is no .CDR file that represents the winning entry back in 1989. Corel used the print file I sent them, while I continued to refine and change the drawing. The finished product you will find on the Companion CD is much more refined than the images printed in Corel's Art Show books.

Nonetheless, the visual theme of the drawing remains the same—namely, the fall of sunlight across the clouds, the mountains, and the diver's form. You can see that these elements have a large illuminated area on the left, with the sunlight trailing off toward the right. You also may notice that the clouds billow large above the mountains. This feeling is mirrored by the diver and, in a similar way, by the mountains. In other words, there are simple relationships between these elements that make them belong together.

I haven't set forth on any other pieces like *The Diver*, largely because of the amount of time I'm forced to sit watching the screen redraw. With today's faster computers, that is becoming less of a concern and more of an excuse. There are a number of images I plan to illustrate once I get one of those faster machines hooked to the other end of my mouse. Stay tuned—it's all work-in-progress…

CHAPTER 22

The Entrance

TWENTY-TWO

CHAPTER 22

I created *The Entrance* as an assignment for CalComp, which manufactures large-scale color raster printers and plotters. CalComp wanted to demonstrate to its target market of architects that they do not need to give up the benefits of a pen plotter when buying the new color raster plotter. They can have rich color as well as sharp, clean lines with CalComp's product.

The idea was to illustrate something whose design and technical merits would appeal to architects. The image we decided to produce was an elaborate entrance to a contemporary building. CalComp intended to present the drawing on the cover of *Architecture* magazine. Figure 22.1 shows the finished work. You can also see it as Illustration 6 of the Color Gallery.

In Search of Reference

This story will demonstrate that much of the work to produce *The Entrance* was done before I ever took hand to mouse. As I explained in the foregoing chapter about *The Diver,* whenever I illustrate a tangible item found in the real world, I try to use a good reference; I never attempt to compete with reality, as the quality of my work would inevitably suffer if I did. With that in mind, I began a search for a photo of an elaborate and contemporary entrance. After about a week of poring through book stores and libraries, looking for something that was both interesting and appropriate to the task, I came up with nothing—not every interesting photograph will make an equally interesting illustration. Only one thing left to do: Create my own reference.

Looking around downtown San Francisco, I came upon a building in the financial district that was perfect for this project: long, graceful curves punctuated with crisp accents and repeating shapes (Figure 22.2).

22.1

The Entrance, as it appeared on the cover of *Architecture* magazine.

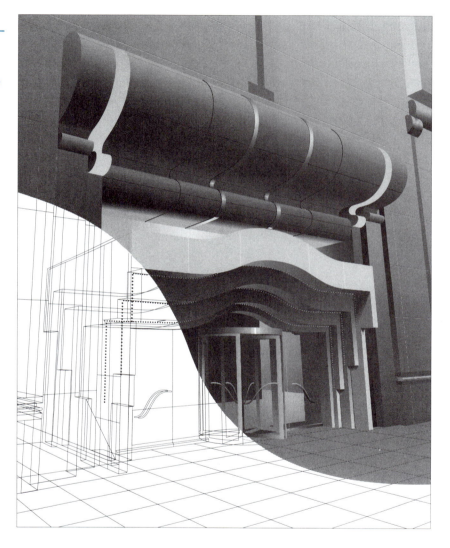

I photographed the building at a time of day when the sun was well up but still at an angle (10:00 a.m. in winter). Using a 28mm lens, I shot about three rolls of 36-exposure print film, taking a series of pictures that accentuated the height and scale of the entrance. I stood to the left of the entrance, and whether I moved in close for details or far away for long shots, I walked toward or away from the building along that same angle.

2.2

The artist could not find a good reference, so he created one himself, taking this photo of a San Francisco building.

From Camera to Computer

I selected a print from the stack of photos and scanned it at 120 dpi and 8 bits of color (in other words, low resolution and with crude colors). I saved this scan as a .PCX file, imported it into DRAW, and manually traced only the major elements of the entrance. You're probably wondering right about now, "Why didn't he just use TRACE?" I avoid tracing complex images because I generally find myself with just as much work to do cleaning up the trace as is required to draw the lines manually in the first place. Besides, I prefer to "know" the objects in my drawings, as opposed to having a bunch of objects land on my work from the TRACE program. Though I recognize the value of TRACE (and refer you to Chapter 40 for notes on its use), I would rather get my hands dirty and create the elements myself.

I established three-point perspective guidelines (see Figure 22.3) to help me correctly place objects wherever they belonged. The perspective of the building (determined by where I stood while taking the photo) required a very long vertical guideline. The left and right guidelines were not very long, but to allow enough room for the top perspective line, the drawing itself had to be moved to the extreme bottom of the drawing area. The perspective lines all have one of their ends anchored at a vanishing point (the point where all things seem to converge to a dot when moved along the plane toward the horizon or the zenith). Study the building's lines in Figure 22.2, and you'll see that they all follow one of the three perspective lines created in Figure 22.3. Every single line I created for this drawing (and I created a lot!) adhered to one of these three perspectives.

Setting the Tone

My approach to illustrating complicated images such as this is to first set the color and lighting direction with the largest object, and then

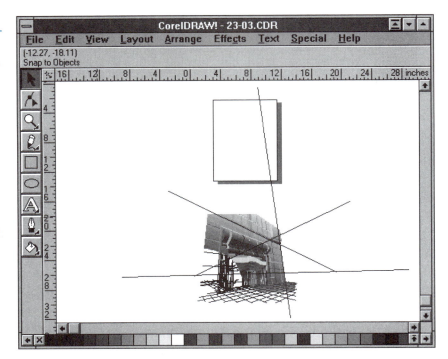

22.3

To achieve the proper vertical perspective, the artist needed to use every spare inch of the drawing area. You can see how far off the standard page he went in order to set the proper perspective.

build on that by drawing objects that support the color and lighting direction. All the features of *The Entrance* drawing are colored and drawn to suggest a light source high and to the right. All the shadows are deep but softened, and suggest a wide, bright, tempered light source such as a partly cloudy sky.

Notice that all the exterior features were rendered according to the light source. This gives the entire drawing a sense of time and place, with each element fitted realistically into the whole. Figure 22.4 shows the shape I drew to set this lighting tone. This simple object became the cornerstone for all that followed it, and the colors I chose for the gradient were planned to ripple through all of the other elements.

22.4

This one curve sets the tone for the entire drawing.

Exercising Artist's License

In the photo, the color of the building's entrance is a blend of dark grays and burgundies. To stay with this color scheme would not have shown off the color plotter's best capabilities, so I decided to take some liberties with the building's color scheme. (I said I work *from* a reference, not that I hold it as gospel!) I added blues and aquas to the facade, which turned up the energy on the interior lights and created a visual focus over the entrance. I also pumped up the color on the exterior surface to help emphasize the range from highlight into shadow.

Drawing programs are not very forgiving; if you are not exacting in your work, it will become apparent when you print. The most helpful tool for doing this type of precise work is the Snap To Objects command (Layout / Snap To Objects). Snap To Objects helps you align objects by their nodes, so that corners match, lines meet exactly at their ends, and so forth. Using the Node Edit tool, I selected a node in an object and dragged that node near a node in another object (Snap To Objects only works between two separate objects). As I approached the other object, the node virtually leaped from my cursor and attached itself to the nearby node.

Snap To Objects is very helpful when objects share a corner—you don't have to zoom way in to be precise, and you don't have to worry about trying to set up an elaborate grid and snap to it. Instead, just snap to the object, and you're done. If the first node is in the correct spot, all the others will fall into place as you drag them nearby.

Peeling the Corner

To create the "peeled" effect in the lower-left corner, I drew an object that followed the lower-left profile of the exterior wall. I drew it with a gracefully curved inside edge, as shown in image 1 of Figure 22.5. I colored this object white so it gave the appearance that the drawing was cleanly cut off with a swash.

On top of the white corner object, I drew black lines that appeared to connect with features and objects that were colored on the other side of the swash. Despite how it looks in image 2 of Figure 22.5, none of the

22.5

Nothing crosses over the curve— the 3-D lines on the left and the filled objects on the right both stop at the boundary of the curve.

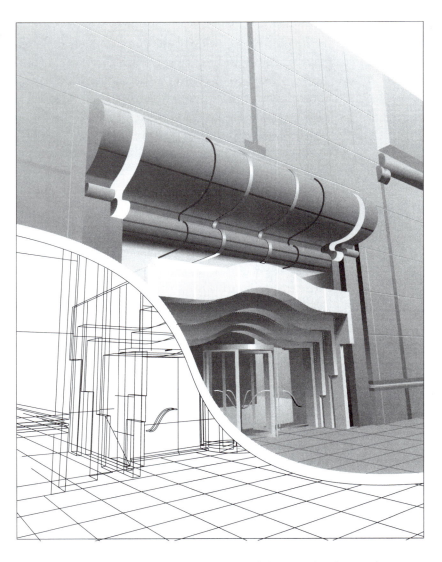

objects extends from one side to the other of the swash; they are separate. All the black lines end right on the edge of the white object.

You can see the effect of referring to the perspective guidelines for correct angles by examining the line work in this area of the drawing. Many lines seem oriented directly toward the vanishing point. I did not bother to finish those loose ends because they were to be masked off later. (Recall from Chapter 5 how the snowboarder drawing was also framed on all four sides.)

Doing It!

The curved awning was perhaps the most difficult part of this drawing. I needed to create a credible reference system to ensure that the curves were right. The awning is a composite masonry or cement construction with seams. It also sports a pair of decorative brass straps and illuminated trim, to emphasize and repeat the curve theme of the entrance as a whole. Visually, in the drawing, these elements had to work together in perspective as an integral set of repeating, modulating shapes. If one curve or shape was not drawn correctly in perspective, the integrity of the piece would suffer.

I decided to make a new layer, called Ellipse, and set the override color to magenta. (The Layers roll-up allows you to create a global color for all objects on a layer.) I drew a circle and shaped it into an ellipse to fit the large (closest) end of the awning, and created another ellipse to fit the other end of the awning. Using the Blend roll up, I blended 40 ellipses for a smooth transition of shapes in perspective. (I used that large a number of steps so that whenever I needed to refer to a curve, one would be very close by.) I separated and then ungrouped the blend so I could eliminate the ellipses that were not needed (which was most of them).

Using this set of ellipses, I found I could adjust each curve on the awning so they all worked well together. There was a lot of tweaking to make this part of the drawing right, but it would have been very hard without the ellipse guides. Figure 22.6 shows both the process of creating the blend of 40 (image 1) and the final number of ellipses used (image 2).

The twinkling lights under the arches were created using asterisks from the Arial typeface. I simply held the * key down to generate a long string of asterisks. Real scientific, eh? I sized them at about 5.5 points and fitted them to a path that closely followed the curve of the arch.

22.6

To create the awning, the artist engaged in some planned overkill. He blended two ellipses together to make 40 (image 1), then separated and deleted all those he didn't need (image 2).

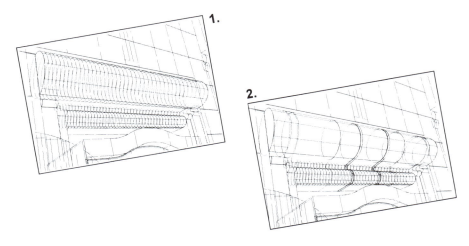

Then I spaced them out using Node Edit. I set the color to a yellow-orange combination to resemble small filaments of a light bulb. The star shape of the asterisks makes the lights twinkle; even the black-and-white image in Figure 22.7 shows that off.

You may notice that the drawing itself doesn't have a clearly defined, standard outside shape (such as a square or rectangle). I designed the drawing to have a matte or mask that hides all but the part of the

22.7

This string of "twinkling" lights is resourcefully created from Arial asterisks.

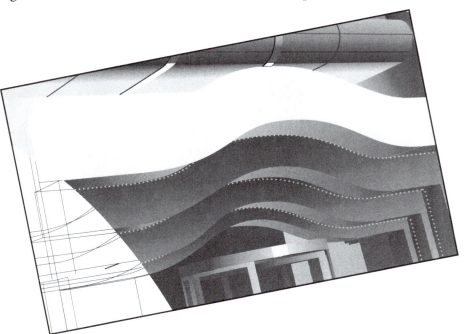

drawing intended to be seen. This is the more traditional way of creating art, allowing an artist to create the work free of constraints and then mask the finished work so it presents cleanly. As explained in Chapter 11, to create this mask I drew a large rectangle covering the entire piece and then created another one the size of the finished view. Then I combined the two rectangles. This step makes a window in the first rectangle the size of the second rectangle. (Remember the cookie-cutter analogy discussed in Chapters 4 and 11?) Then I colored the mask solid white and placed it on its own layer in front of the drawing.

The Entrance was a challenging drawing, and I was pleased with how it turned out. As with *The Diver* (Chapter 21), part of the appeal of *The Entrance* is how it describes the light. Though it's a contemporary building, rather than having the typical cold and sterile look, it seems to invite you to come in. I must admit, part of that is due to the way I altered reality and took license with the colors. Thank goodness for that artist's license....

CHAPTER 23

Eagle

TWENTY-THREE

CHAPTER 23

The illustration shown in Figure 23.1 began as an assignment from CalComp, just as *The Entrance* did (see Chapter 22). The company was in the planning stages of announcing a new large-format ink-jet product called TechJET Designer™ and asked me to create a promotional poster for it. This poster would be printed by the plotter itself while on display at trade shows and showrooms. Everything in this promotional effort was directed at their target market for this plotter: engineers, architects, and an assortment of designers.

First Steps: Defining the Project

The most important step when beginning a project of any scope is to clearly define the problem. In this case, defining the problem was simple. I needed to create a poster whose design was so interesting that people would want to keep it after they left the trade show or dealer. The poster's "keepsake" value was essential to its success as a promotional tool.

The plotter's name suggested some possibilities. Designing an illustration around such an unfamiliar term as TechJET Designer meant there would be a few limits to how the idea would be expressed. After playing with several ideas, I decided on one that really pushed the visual representation of the TechJET part of the product name. I wanted to design a "jet" that was "technical," with extravagant color and personality. I avoided the obvious visual: a jet. No matter how good the drawing of a jet might be, it would still be a jet, and the idea would not be unique.

Instead, I wanted something else that would fly—perhaps a bird, a big bird, maybe an eagle. Better yet, I'd give it a twist to tie it into the product name, and make it a jet-powered eagle, screaming down out of the sky. I'd add design personality with art deco and Buck Rogers-style design elements (such as a jet-engine backpack and metal armor). When I

First Steps: Defining the Project **569**

23.1
Artist David Brickley created *Eagle* **to show off the capabilities of a client's ink-jet plotter.**

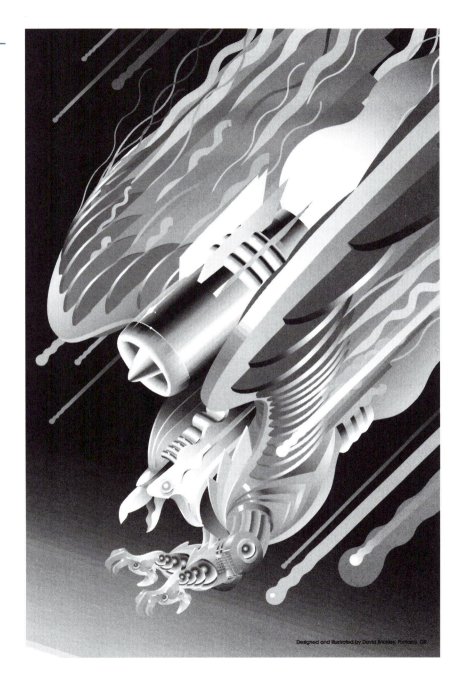

described my idea to the client, they were hesitant. A poster showing a jet-powered eagle had more personality than they were accustomed to, but they liked the possibility that something so unusual would be captivating and memorable.

Finding a Good Reference

I began *Eagle* with the most rudimentary requirement: good reference material. I needed pictures of eagles. I went to libraries, book stores, and rummaged through my own picture files, and gathered many images of eagles in flight. From these I would come to know the bird's proportions, body language, and expressions. I was looking for an eagle flying from right to left and reaching out with extended claws. I found one picture of an eagle in that pose, but it was small and the eagle was flying in the wrong direction and in dark silhouette. I was stuck. None of the other images I found had what I needed. So I traced the one I had, filled in some detail on my own, flipped the paper over, and enlarged it using an opaque projector.

Beginning the Sketch

With the enlarged outline of a diving eagle in hand, I began making attempts at stylized drawings of the eagle, using exaggerated mechanical elements. The direction in which I was heading is reminiscent of the way artists about 50 years ago were seeing the future. In their work, these artists expressed the machine age as heroic. Using mechanical elements such as sleek aerodynamic shapes, powerful engines, and accents such as large fins and manifolds, these artists gave validity to an era created with larger-than-life machines.

Experimentation was important here. I needed to explore and discover what elements within this genre would give my piece movement and personality. I spent a week drawing freehand in pencil, creating nearly 20 different versions of diving eagles before I arrived at a design I liked. I think it's important to do your "thinking" away from the computer, without software or hardware to influence or distract. Working in pencil frees me to do what I want and what is right for the solution, without being limited to whatever the computer allows.

Another reason for spending this much time in the beginning was that I had never before worked in this genre. I had to explore its potential and invent ways to describe the eagle in flight, diving at high speed. The eagle's movement and posture suggested a number of possible approaches—all of which had to be kept in context with the action, describe the moment, and develop the appropriate spirit. For example, an eagle perched instead of flying would have features altogether different from my bird-in-flight. The bird-at-rest would have exhibited another presence and another side of its personality, and I would have needed to tell a different story altogether with my illustration.

During my explorations, I saw another interesting connection between the eagle and the plotter. The ink-jet plotter creates an image by spraying microscopic droplets of ink on paper. To help make that connection, I added droplets to the drawing—streaks of ink droplets alongside the eagle. The streaks are ostensibly "flying" from the ink-jet head to the paper; they add drama and action to the drawing. I changed the body of the eagle to the same droplet shape, and he began to truly personify the ink-jet technology.

Getting Down to Business

Having arrived at a final design on paper, I scanned it to a 1-bit .PCX bitmap at about 72 dpi. The single level of color (black or white pixels) meant the bitmap would have a small file size yet retain an acceptable amount of detail. This was important; as one works to trace over a bitmap in CorelDRAW, small bitmap files redraw faster than large ones. The cumulative time spent waiting for the screen to redraw was thus significantly reduced.

Using XYZ Reference Lines

Now that I was working in DRAW, the first thing I drew over the bitmap was an XYZ reference system, consisting of three lines as shown in Figure 23.2. These helped keep the objects in my drawing in a consistent orientation. All objects having features that shared these angles were drawn with reference to these lines.

23.2

XYZ reference lines were used to help draw in three dimensions.

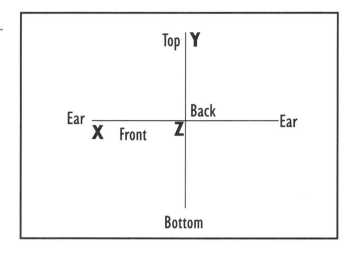

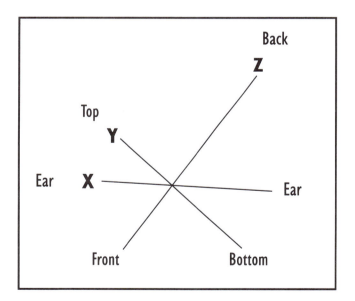

Reference lines help whenever you are illustrating in perspective or mechanical shapes. There are many books that make a science of perspective and mechanical drawing, and I do not make any claims about my expertise. But this is what I did: I established a three-axis reference based on the height, width, and depth indicated by the final pencil drawing. In other words, I drew a line down the length of the eagle. This was the main axis of the drawing—the z-axis, from the front (head) to the back (tail) of the eagle. I then drew a line from left to right—ear to ear—for the x-axis. Last, as the y-axis, I drew a line from the top to the bottom of the eagle. I used these axes for almost every object I drew; for example, all the droplet streaks followed the z-axis.

At the top of Figure 23.2 is a set of XYZ reference lines looking straight down the z-axis. This is equivalent to looking at the eagle head on. At the bottom of the figure is the actual axis setup for *Eagle.*

Doing It

I started the drawing at the eagle's head and shoulder. With the help of a group of reference ellipses, I easily shaped and placed the circular tubes on the neck. In mechanical drawing, a single reference system is necessary for a group of objects whose shapes and placement must be aligned. For example, each of the tail fins on the jet engine needs the others to be correct visually. To make that possible, I created a reference system to locate the corners of each fin shape; this system is shown in Figure 23.3. If you use this technique correctly, drawing a group of related objects can be as easy as "connecting the dots." Despite the software and hardware involved, this is traditional two-dimensional drawing that relies on a reference system to correctly place, scale, and shape elements to visually represent a three-dimensional image.

I take two different approaches to vector illustration. If I am drawing objects to describe color—for example, a highlight on a face in a portrait—then I color all the objects as I draw them. If, however, I am drawing objects to describe shape, as in *Eagle,* I draw the objects so that their shape is correct, and color them later. For *Eagle,* I had progressed to the fifth drawing before I started to add color.

I continued making adjustments and changes to almost every part of the design, knowing the drawing would evolve as I worked. New possibilities continued to appear as I worked, and I acted on them whenever

23.3

The early stages of the Eagle illustration; no color was added until drawing #5 (bottom-right).

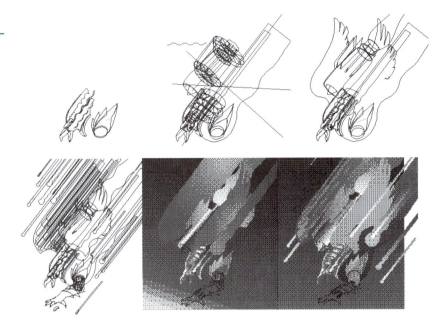

I could. Although this illustration is by nature interpretive (meaning I can do whatever I want), I am still beholden to a number of fundamental principals. Most important are all the considerations of composition and color, action and gesture, personality and concept, and so forth.

The feet and claws were a problem. They didn't seem to "belong." I let them be and continued to work on the rest of the drawing, trusting that the answer would present itself as the drawing evolved. I left the feet roughly indicated so I could sense their size and position and went ahead to the rest of the eagle.

Refining the Wings

The area of the illustration I changed most significantly was the wings, starting with the one in the back. Once I started adding color, the original design of the wings did not seem to sufficiently describe the eagle's character and its diving action. To better emphasize both, I returned to the pencil drawings and revised the elements I was using to describe the wing. To get more action and interest, I devised a wing design that sported long, colorful, straight lines contrasting with wavy streamers of different lengths and weights. To help convey the look of an actual wing, I created a series of disc-shaped ellipses and placed them along the wings' curved leading edge.

The new wing design helped the illustration in another important area: range. All the elements in the wing are composed of simple building blocks from the more complex shapes and features seen in the body. The whimsy of the streamers contrasted with the eagle's overall aggressive posture and helped present a range of persona. Every good story has at least one character who changes or is changed by the events. Although it is easier to show range in a story, you should take every opportunity to show a range of persona in an illustration, as well.

The colors used in the back wing are muted to help define a different kind of range: contrast. Depth is reinforced by the "faded-by-atmosphere" color scheme. Distant colors (as in faraway mountains) are, by nature, softer and less pure. This phenomenon is often exploited and emphasized in illustrations to help separate foreground, midrange, and background. The wing's muted colors contrast with the richer colors in the body, to give the eagle a range of color and depth.

In yet another fashion, range is demonstrated by the level of detail in this illustration. As you look from the upper-right (where the eagle came from) to the lower-left (where he's going), the level of detail increases. The legs and talons are the focal point of the action and are made important by the heightened detail. The wings, on the other hand, are less important and simpler in design, made of larger repeating shapes.

Fine-Tuning the Claws: Back to the Drawing Board

Eventually, it was time to resolve the issue of the feet and claws seeming foreign to this eagle. Once again, I returned to pencil and paper and started drawing claws—all kinds. I then understood what bothered me about the original design (the left-hand image in Figure 23.4). I looked at what made the face of the eagle and realized the claw design was not true to the eagle's character, because I was using the wrong shapes. I switched to blocked shapes like those in the eagle's face and… Presto! Feet that fit.

The redesigned feet are shown on the right in Figure 23.4. Because the feet are duplicates of each other (at least in my drawing) I only had to illustrate one complete leg and foot. The last thing I did to finish the drawing (when all else was done) was duplicate the entire leg with its talons and move it behind the body, in a position offset from the one in front.

23.4
Feet that feel right

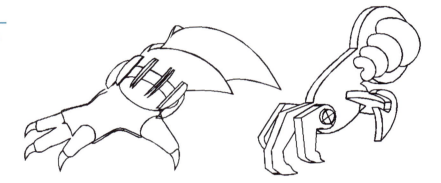

Blending Multiple Colors

The DRAW feature that ultimately made *Eagle* possible was the Custom option in the Fountain Fill dialog box. This feature allows you to assign multiple-color gradient fills to a closed object, as shown in Figure 23.5. It may take six or more colors to properly render a smooth, rounded shape, and there are many round shapes in *Eagle*. Custom fountain fills made it possible to effectively render these shapes, by helping me to control the application of multiple-color gradients in each object.

Custom fountain fills result in complicated color schemes that do not work well with some other DRAW 5.0 features. For example, if you were to create two objects, assign different sets of multiple colors to each, then Blend the two objects together, the Blend tool would ignore some of the color values when making the in-between objects. Blend would create the shapes correctly, but some color transitions would be abrupt. Too bad.

23.5

This dialog box allows you to blend multiple colors easily.

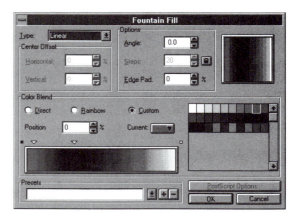

To see what you can do with custom fountain fills, try this:

1. Create a long rectangle.
2. Convert it to curves, making the long sides parallel curves.

3. Open the Fountain Fill dialog, and change the Angle of the fill to 0.
4. Click the Custom option to get a set of color gradient controls.

On the lower-left is a sample scale for designing your gradient fill. Above that is a position control and a current color button. On the right is a scrollable palette. At each end of the sample scale there is a small square button. Double-click on the button at the left end of the scale, and a small triangle appears next to it. This triangle is assigned whatever color value is on the left end of the scale—in this case, black. Click and drag the triangle across the scale. Where you place the triangle determines the end point of a new color gradient. You set the color at that point by clicking on the palette.

5. To create the gradient shown in Figure 23.5, start with the triangle positioned all the way to the left. Drag it one-third of the way toward the right until the position control reads 33%. In the palette, click on black to make that the color at the position you just designated (it may be black already).
6. Click on the small square button on the left end of the sample scale, and then click on a medium gray in the palette.
7. Double-click on the small black square on the right end of the sample scale, and click on light gray in the palette on the right. Click and drag the new triangle across the scale, almost all the way to the left. The position control should read 5%. Click on OK.

The rectangle object should now look more metallic, with a highlight and a soft fill light. This gives it a three-dimensional appearance and thus more realism.

I use the Fountain Fill / Custom option extensively because it offers the most control over where colors appear in objects. See Chapter 8 for more details on how to use this feature.

Drawing Three-Dimensional Objects to Make the Jet Engine

The most difficult area to render was the intake of the jet engine. It was difficult because I needed to render a highlighted shape with a surface rounded in two directions: from inside the engine intake to outside, and also around the lip of the opening. After several rather lame attempts, I decided on the direct but labor-intensive method. I created narrow strips that wrapped around the inside-to-outside contour, as shown in Figure 23.6. These strips roughly followed a pattern that divided the intake symmetrically around the z-axis. Precision wasn't important to their shape, because when finished, their colors would make them appear all blended together into one solid shape. Still, there were hours of fussing to get this one area finished.

23.6

Rendering the jet engine intake

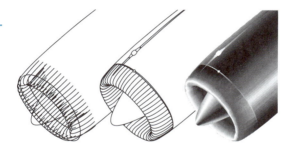

Each of the 40 objects in this arrangement has a very complicated blend of fountain fill colors to help indicate its part of the engine's intake. Each object has blended fountain fill colors that work in concert with colors of the adjacent objects. Together, these objects carry several blended colors around the many contours of the intake's reflective surface. As your eye scans across the group of objects, all you see is the front end of the jet engine.

This part of the drawing would have been much easier with a three-dimensional modeling program, but I had to simulate 3-D using a carefully designed reference system. Drawing three-dimensional objects using a two-dimensional program is similar to what drafters have had to do for centuries. Such a reference system, shown in various stages of development in Figure 23.7, is required to effectively draw 3-D objects such as this intake and the fins. That I was able to render something this complex with DRAW speaks well of the software.

23.7

Using a reference system to create the jet engine's fins

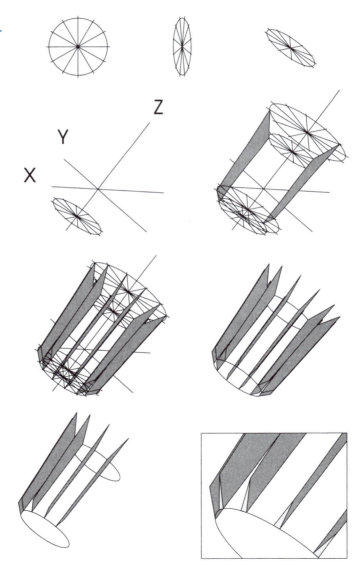

To create the reference system for the fins, I followed these steps:

1. I created a perfect circle on the page and then drew a straight line across the circle. Using the Transform roll-up, I rotated the line 30 degrees, clicking on Apply to Duplicate five times. I now had seven objects: one circle and six lines.

2. I selected all seven objects with the Pick tool. Using the Align dialog (press Ctrl+A), I centered all lines vertically and horizontally and then grouped everything by pressing Ctrl+G.

3. I clicked on the group again to display the rotate/skew handles and rotated the group clockwise 15 degrees. I clicked again to return to the sizing handles, and squeezed the whole group horizontally to 30% of its original width.

4. I rotated the group again, this time 45 degrees counterclockwise.

At this point I needed to use the XYZ reference system I created for this project. The three lines of this reference system together represent the three dimensions: height, width, and depth. Whenever the orientation of the view of this space was changed, the orientation of all lines changed together, helping to organize and guide the drawing so that it remained accurate dimensionally.

5. I aligned the center of the circle/lines group (where all six lines intersect) to the z-axis on the XYZ reference lines, as shown in Figure 23.7.

6. I duplicated the group and enlarged the copy to 130%. I moved the enlarged group a short distance up the z-axis. (This distance determines the angle of the front edge of the fin, and it was important to make sure that both groups were centered on the z-axis.)

7. I duplicated both groups and moved the duplicates up the z-axis a distance roughly equivalent to the length of the large ellipse. I selected the copy of the big group only, enlarged it 125%, and moved it a bit farther up the z-axis. The size and placement of this group determines the length and angle of the fins.

At this point I had four ellipses (really circles) rotated to correspond to the position of the jet engine. The two smaller ellipses lay in the surface of the engine, indicating the base corners of the fins. The larger ellipses were the outer corners of the fins. The lines radiating from the centers of the ellipses indicated the position of the fins. Each fin would be created by connecting the dots—that is, the intersections of four corresponding lines with their respective ellipses.

8. To draw each fin, I used the Pencil tool in Bezier mode to connect similar intersections (where parallel lines cross their respective ellipses).

9. I continued to connect similar intersections to make the five needed for the actual drawing.

10. To create the thick front edge of the fins, I enabled Layout / Snap To Objects and used the Bezier Drawing tool to create a simple triangle. I created a triangle with three clicks of the Bezier tool; the objects are so small that precise thickness is not necessary.

11. I moved the reference system to an invisible layer by selecting the objects and choosing Move To from the Layers roll-up's flyout. The circles at the front and back of the fins were left in this example for your visual reference.

Some Rules of Thumb for Artists and Designers

- Design your work away from the computer. Do your thinking without any technology involved.

- Even if you can't draw, you can still get the essential idea down on paper first. You will likely find your work improves immediately.

- If you are illustrating a recognizable "thing," you must work from good reference pictures. Otherwise, you'll be trying to pit your memory against reality. It's harder, and reality usually wins this contest anyway…hands down.

- Good design does not have to respect a budget or a schedule. People who examine your work will not say, "You know, the best thing about this piece is that it was done under budget and on time." All they will know is whether they like what they see.

- To stay creative, you must grow. Push your skills against your own limits, not against your clients'. Improve your work by making your reach exceed your grasp. If you surpass your clients' taste or insight, get different clients. You owe it to yourself.

I hope you find my work and thoughts useful. If you take only one message with you from this chapter, it should be this: What is most important is the process, not the end result. A well-tended creative process is like rich soil in a garden; the ideas you plant there will grow and bear fruit. Enjoy!

CHAPTER 24

Avoiding Design Tragedies

TWENTY-FOUR

CHAPTER 24

This chapter adopts the voice of first person singular, representing the views of your lead author but not necessarily those of the rest of the team. My teammates might share my *views,* but not my *point of view,* because many of them don't have the same perspective as I do: that of an unabashed amateur. I lack the skills, the vision, and probably the judgment required to produce professional artwork with CorelDRAW, and this is certainly not true of some of the award-winning illustrators on my team. Perhaps one of the smartest things I have done as a desktop publisher is to acknowledge my amateur status every single day I go to work.

Even with this qualification, I still almost didn't write this chapter, because I was afraid of lapsing into a tedious repetition of trite advice about producing good desktop design. I may still do that, as difficult as it is to be original with this topic, but my intention is to deliver one prevailing message:

The computer is a tool for *enhancing* imagination and creative thought. It can never *replace* those qualities.

There are no shortcuts to good design. It takes years of training, experience, and practice. There is no comparison between a professional designer's polished output and an amateur's quick fix, yet many amateurs believe the marketing hype that, yes, they too can produce professional work if they buy CorelDRAW and products like it. Desktop design has given millions of computer users the power to create bad design—no wonder so many traditional artists still avoid the computer and continue to watch its evolution with disdain and apprehension.

If you absorb nothing else from this chapter, remember this: Becoming proficient with CorelDRAW does not make you a good designer—only a prolific one… maybe only a prolific *bad* one. I named this chapter very carefully; it won't tell you how to produce beautiful design, but rather how to avoid bad design. I won't burden you with long dissertations about how to think like a designer, and I won't bore you with so-called page makeovers—in which a nice, friendly page is turned into a paradigm of electronic publishing with ultra-high-tech, futuristic design elements. I'll leave those for the magazines.

My intention is to make you aware of some critical red flags in desktop design; if heeded, they can help you on the road to becoming a capable desktop designer. In keeping with my belief that the message in your work is of paramount importance, this chapter's emphasis is on text-based projects.

The Look at Me! Syndrome

I have a friend who works at a photocopy store that recently added a desktop publishing department, and he now produces résumés for drop-in customers. He acknowledges that he doesn't know the first thing about making a résumé look good, but his customers are usually so tickled by the laser-printed output that they leave happy. "Fonts!" he exclaims. "That's all they care about."

My friend's customers have been seduced by the Look at Me! approach to design, in which the appearance of an illustration takes on an artificially inflated significance. The Look at Me! syndrome is characterized by the designer's (perpetrator's?) tendency to utilize in one project every single effect offered within a software program, regardless of its appropriateness to the task. Look at Me! is one of the major contributors to "laser sludge," as traditional designers like to refer to the less-than-brilliant efforts from today's desktop publishing community.

It's only natural that desktop design would spawn such a syndrome; after all, its primary focus is the *presentation* of ideas, rather than the ideas themselves. You can see examples of Look at Me! everywhere. A product's order form used to have a bit of bold in it, maybe a few hairlines. Now it has rounded rectangles, gray shading everywhere, bold and italic all over the place, fancy borders, and little hands pointing to all the important things. The only embellishments in yesterday's newsletters were page numbers; now they have little clip-art people holding signs with the page numbers on them. Technical manuals had bold headlines, maybe set a few points larger than the body text; now they have drop caps, small caps, and white type in black boxes—*yes, all at the same time.*

Diagnosing and Treating Look at Me!

Do you suffer from Look at Me! syndrome? Take the following quiz and find out:

- Do you routinely set headlines in sizes above 36-point? Above 48-point?
- If a headline can't be read from across the room, does that mean it isn't big enough?
- Do you use color in documents just because it looks good on your new monitor?
- If one typeface looks good, does that mean two will look better? How about three? How about forty?
- If bold isn't strong enough, would all caps be better?
- Is an underline better than no underline?
- Is a double-underline twice as good as a single underline?
- Do you ever add a background shade to text just because you feel like it?
- Do you set white type on a black background to make it more dramatic?

And the special bonus question:

- Do you ever start producing an illustration before you have decided what you are going to say?

If you answered Yes to more than a couple of these questions, you show symptoms of the syndrome. It means you make a habit of overembellishing your work—even if it's just a study on the refrigerator life of a box of baking soda. It means you look for ways to grab your readers before they read the first sentence. You try to make your documents say, "Look at Me!"

You can cure yourself of the syndrome by remembering that it's not necessarily the *design* of your work that needs to say "look at me," it's the *ideas*. If only I had a nickel for every time I have proclaimed in seminars or consulting sessions: Let the content determine the form. Only use the big headline when the idea merits it. Don't italicize a passage unless it is truly significant. When you highlight too many passages of text, you don't present a clear sense of priority to your readers, and they have little motivation to continue reading. In short, when you make everything bold, you make nothing bold.

Those of you suffering from Look at Me! syndrome should ponder the following arguments.

The Message Is Everything!

If you spend 10 minutes making a headline look fancy, spend 20 minutes making sure it says the perfect thing. It's so easy to get carried away formatting text in DRAW, because so many elements can be attached: space above, below, to the left and to the right; rules, bullets, and boxes; shading, dingbats, and all of the special effects discussed in Part IV. You have many, many opportunities to louse up a perfectly good line of text, so at the very least, make sure its message is strong enough to survive if you do overdesign. My rule of thumb: For every minute spent using the Pick or Shape tool and the Effects menu, spend two with the Text tool. Make sure your text conveys the precise message you intend.

Bigger Is Not Better

If a headline stands out sufficiently when set in 24-point, don't set it larger "just to be sure." I still remember a client of mine in 1989 who had been using her trusty HP LaserJet II printer, the one for which font support generally consisted of about two or three sizes and weights of Dutch and Swiss. Then one day she added to her printer a PostScript interpreter, providing lots of typefaces and built-in scaleable fonts. The laser sludge she began cranking out was proof positive of her new love for the technology.

"What size are your headlines?" I asked.

"Forty-five points."

"How'd you arrive at that figure?"

"Forty-four didn't quite fill the entire column."

Looking at her work, I always had the feeling she'd produced it while at a rock concert.

Then one day, a miracle occurred: The PostScript board in her printer went out and she was forced to use it as a plain old HP LaserJet. It was the most important step she ever took toward capable design. Instead of automatically making her headlines huge to focus attention, she began manipulating the space around them. She complained the whole way about not having all the choices with which she had become so infatuated, but having her choices limited was a positive constraint and a definite boon to her projects' design.

Easy on the Attributes

Don't apply text attributes to more than one passage of text per column or page. You've all seen those "YOU MAY HAVE ALREADY WON…" sweepstakes letters that pile up in your mailbox, usually with Ed McMahon's face on the envelope. Open one, and you have no idea what to read first. Wait, I'd better take that back… your name is set red in 128-point Garamond Ultra, so you probably read that first. After that, every third paragraph is either bold, italic, underlined, or maybe all three. This isn't even laser sludge; it's generally produced on a high-resolution imagesetter. That, of course, doesn't save it from the Desktop Publishing Hall of Shame.

As I said earlier, when you highlight everything, you highlight nothing. Your readers don't know where to begin, and if they somehow make it through the rough terrain of your artwork, their psychological reaction to its look will probably overshadow any ideas you intended to convey.

The next time you want to highlight a passage, try just using white space

like this.

It will be easier on your readers' eyes, it will accomplish the same purpose, and it will demonstrate both your sense of design and your sensibilities in general. It will probably be easier to produce, too.

Be Brilliant!

Write something that's so good, it truly merits special attention. I have no magic strategies here, except to say that writers struggle with the same tendency toward overproduction that illustrators do (you should have seen this manuscript before three editors pared it down).

For example, suppose you lead off your advertisement with the words, *Finally, the product you've been waiting for!* True, it's an attention-grabber, but if you set it in a 48-point bold typeface with an extrusion behind it, you end up with instant laser sludge. Or you could begin with two simple words: *It's here.* (No exclamation mark.) Now your headline conveys a clarity of thought and purpose, and if you can't resist setting it in big type, it won't look so bad because it's only two words. It may take you hours to hone your prose down to its simplest, most effective form, but it will be worth it. Good writing is only part art and inspiration; it's also craft and perspiration.

Figure 24.1, though it may not look like it at first glance, is actually quite carefully prepared. The image on the left, which we'll call "Ugly," is taken straight from an advertisement in a recent Sunday newspaper (except for the name of the product and its description which I sort of made up). The rounded rectangles, the ultrabold headline, the boldface letters, the tight margins, the exclamation marks—they all contribute to make this a shining example of desktop design at its worst. (I can't say for sure that this was produced on the desktop, but the rounded rectangles and the plain Helvetica push that probability to about 95 percent.)

24.1
Form vs. content: Ugly vs. Not So Ugly

> **The Miracle That You Have Been Waiting For!!**
>
> Yes, you, for a limited time only, can finally unlock the key to longevity. For the first time ever in the Western World come the deep, dark secrets of the WALA WALA PLANT, featuring a special, scientifically tested and certified herb that actually *slows down the aging process.*
>
> And it can be yours for the low, low price of $39.95 per month. But wait—there's more! The price drops to $37.95 once you pass your 80th birthday, and then drops by a dollar every five years after that!
>
> Operators are standing by, so pick up the phone and order your lifetime supply of the WALA WALA ageless wonder. Not available in any stores!!

> **The Secret is out**
>
> For centuries, humans have searched for magical potions that will increase their life spans—the mythical fountains of youth. Silver-haired Americans have spent an estimated $13 billion on various "if you act now" schemes that claim never-ending youth.
>
> But now the secret is out.
>
> If you want to live longer, you don't need to pay anyone, eat exotic herbs, or chant unrecognizable hymns. If you want to live longer, do this:
>
> **Stop smoking, eat good foods, and exercise regularly.**
>
> That's the secret. That will be $150, please...

The image on the right, which we'll call "Not So Ugly," has only one objective: to deliver its message. I forced myself to produce it in less than ten minutes, and limited myself to nothing fancier than the single gray bar at the bottom. The white space around the entire piece makes it much more inviting than its counterpart, and the white space around the essential message ("Stop smoking, eat good foods…") calls it gently to your attention. I was tempted to set it in italic, but resisted. I did allow the move from Brittanic Light to Medium.

The Not So Ugly rendition has one sustaining virtue: It is not so ugly. It does not detract from its message, nor does it try to be more than it should be. An accomplished artist might take Not So Ugly and produce wonderful things with it. Could you? If the answer is no, perhaps you shouldn't try.

Small Is Beautiful

A first cousin to the Look at Me! syndrome is Pompousitis—the uncontrollable compulsion to use graphic and text elements. We've already touched on some of its symptoms in the previous sections, but the Look at Me! syndrome usually has a purpose: to call attention. Pompousitis, on the other hand, is an aimless attempt to cram as many elements onto an electronic page as possible. It's kind of like eating potato chips in front of the television—you do it because they're there and because you want to.

The suggestions in the paragraphs that follow might not be appropriate for every DRAW project, but the minimalist approach is a good, safe starting point for many illustrations. Not only will it yield cleaner-looking work, it will be easier on your schedule: Bad design usually takes longer to produce than good, simple design.

Diagnosing and Treating Pompousitis

Let's find out if you have Pompousitis.

- If everything on your page is in regular type, do you feel compelled to italicize something?

- Do you create headlines that are mostly boldface *and* italic? How about boldface, italic, and all caps?

- If a section of your page is empty, does that mean that you've done something wrong?

In your next project, try subscribing to the belief that Small is Beautiful, and Less is More. Consider the suggestions in the following sections.

No Lines Allowed

Create a document with no rules, hairlines, or underlines at all. When I lecture before Ventura Publisher or PageMaker users, I approach the subject of ruling lines with great trepidation, because I know they are going to be abused—especially shaded lines, which never look as good when laser-printed as they do on your screen. When I see newsletters or technical manuals with lines running in all directions, I am reminded of childhood summer vacations: We would go to the park and throw tanbark at one another because we couldn't think of anything better to do.

I think many desktop publishers use ruling lines the way I used to use tanbark. Take those ruling lines out, and don't feel compelled to replace them with anything.

Take the Two-Typeface Challenge

For one entire project, try using only one or two type families. Here again, some of the more attractive text-based work that I have seen produced on the desktop came from the old HP LaserJets, which did not give their owners 35 different typefaces with which to hang themselves. There is nothing wrong with mixing, say, a sans serif headline with serif body text, but many desktop publishers don't know where to draw the line. It's far better to use too few faces than too many.

Somebody forgot to tell that to the well-intentioned editor of the newsletter shown in Figure 24.2. This is a page from a computer user group's monthly bulletin; it is obvious that the editor owns CorelDRAW and is luxuriating in all of its typefaces. Let's count them:

1. First deck of headline
2. Second deck of headline
3. Standing cap
4. Body copy
5. Text in left-hand box
6. A Big Welcome… and Thanks… in top-right box
7. Names of members
8. NEXT MEETING in bottom-right box
9. Date/place of next meeting
10. Invitation to attend

Yes, ladies and gentlemen, ten different typefaces have found their way onto this page. Irrespective of the fact that many of this newsletter's forgiving readers probably liked it, this is the classic case of Pompousitis—use of typefaces as determined by possession. You have 'em, so you use 'em.

24.2

Oh, god of fonts, how do I love thee? Let me count the ways...

The President's Piece

Word processing in Windows has never been better than with the newest version of Ami Pro, Release 4.0. It packs impressive new features that ensure real ease of use for the product and a smooth learning curve for users who are making the transition from the text-based word processors to the graphical user interface. Lotus has continued to hold the leadership position by implementing features that are relevant, the ones that facilitate the day-to-day work users care about. With release 4.0, Ami Pro now has Object Linking and Embedding (OLE), as well as efficient drag and drop features for moving and copying text.

When compared with release 3.0, this new version is not more complicated, even though it's been made a lot more powerful. Compared to other Windows word processors, users will find Ami Pro has distinct advantages in formatting commands, when preparing tables, and especially when needing to merge documents. Lotus has made a logical extension of the SmartIcon technology that was introduced earlier, but it's exciting, nonetheless.

This consistent look and feel will be found in upcoming releases of 1-2-3 for Windows and Freelance Graphics for Windows, too. Called their "Working Together" strategy, Lotus will standardize the menu bar, SmartIcons, and the active status bar along the bottom of the screen for the other applications. Completing this strategy, Ami Pro users will also be able to access Lotus Notes and cc:mail without leaving the program. A special SmartIcon group can be selected for the Working Together group.

Just the experience of opening a document in the new release gives the user a big clue that this is going to be a great experience. There's a preview option that shows any document that has been highlighted in true WYSIWYG. It's possible to copy from the preview without finishing the loading of the document. How often have you opened a document just for an address or short section of text? Ami Pro gives users the option of putting information onto the Clipboard with very little hassle.

Lotus has delivered a cure for the fear and loathing that many users felt for Mail Merge. The Merge screen is a guided tutorial on how to create the data file and how to compose the merge document. Data files can be created or edited, as can be the merge files. The data records appear as card file entries with each entry in an identified field. There's no guessing and the names of the fields are used, rather than arbitrary numbers.

When it's time to use the data in a letter or to make labels, a dialog box lists the field names in the data file. They can then be highlighted and inserted into the merge file without retyping the names.

The club would like to thank:

Practical Peripherals of Westlake Village, CA for supplying a V32/42 modem for our BBS

and

Octave Systems of Campbell for providing the hard drive for our BBS

A Big Welcome to the Following New Members...

Tom Day	Mountain View
K. Peter Dyer	Milpitas
Shirley Lambelet	Foster City
Betty Lee	Stanford
Jon Lindsay	Stanford
Bob Moberg	Palo Alto
Thomas Morgan	Campbell
Jim Patton	Mountain View
Jerome Teixeira	Palo Alto

...and Thanks to Renewing Members

Becky Ridgemont	Cupertino
Fred Ridgemont	Cupertino
Don Baird	Redwood City
Bob Bottini	Redwood City
Nancy Helmy	Palo Alto
Matt Lehmann	Cupertino
Ron Nicholas	Los Altos

NEXT MEETING

August 2, 7:30pm
1760 Oak Avenue, Menlo Park

Help us to make decisions about the club. All members are welcome. You don't have to be a club officer to get your views heard.

It's best to pick just one or two typefaces for a complete job. Figure 24.3 shows the same newsletter page, but with two typefaces instead of ten. The main article is set entirely in Garamond, and the text in the left margin and in the box is set entirely in two weights of Eras; both are from the CorelDRAW typeface library. The only redesigning done here is a small amount of text editing, the addition of four bullets, and the removal of boxes and rules. Notice the dramatic difference made just by streamlining the typeface selection.

This is as much an exercise in willpower as it is sound typographic advice. Do you know why professional typographers have type libraries consisting of thousands of faces? It's not so they can use them all for all of their projects; it's so they can pick the right *one or two* for a given project. Once they make those choices, they leave the rest for another day.

24.3

This page, redone with only two typefaces, will offend neither your eyes nor your sensibilities.

Letter From The Prez…

Word processing in Windows has never been better than with the newest version of Ami Pro, Release 4.0. It packs impressive new features that ensure real ease of use for the product and a smooth learning curve for users who are making the transition from the text-based word processors to the graphical user interface. Lotus has continued to hold the leadership position by implementing features that are relevant, the ones that facilitate the day-to-day work users care about. With release 4.0, Ami Pro now has Object Linking and Embedding (OLE), as well as efficient drag and drop features for moving and copying text.

When compared with release 3.0, this new version is not more complicated, even though it's been made a lot more powerful. Compared to other Windows word processors, users will find Ami Pro has distinct advantages in formatting commands, when preparing tables, and especially when needing to merge documents. Lotus has made a logical extension of the SmartIcon technology that was introduced earlier, but it's exciting, nonetheless.

This consistent look and feel will be found in upcoming releases of 1-2-3 for Windows and Freelance Graphics for Windows, too. Called their "Working Together" strategy, Lotus will standardize the menu bar, SmartIcons, and the active status bar along the bottom of the screen for the other applications. Completing this strategy, Ami Pro users will also be able to access Lotus Notes and cc:mail without leaving the program. A special SmartIcon group can be selected for the Working Together group.

Just the experience of opening a document in the new release gives the user a big clue that this is going to be a great experience. There's a preview option that shows any document that has been highlighted in true WYSIWYG. It's possible to copy from the preview without finishing the loading of the document. How often have you opened a document just for an address or short section of text? Ami Pro gives users the option of putting information onto the Clipboard with very little hassle.

Lotus has delivered a cure for the fear and loathing that many users felt for Mail Merge. The Merge screen is a guided tutorial on how to create the data file and how to compose the merge document. Data files can be created or edited, as can be the merge files. The data records appear as card file entries with each entry in an identified field. There's no guessing and the names of the fields are used, rather than arbitrary numbers.

When it's time to use the data in a letter or to make labels, a dialog box lists the field names in the data file. They can then be highlighted and inserted into the merge file without retyping the names. When it comes time to merge the files and get output, the user has the option of viewing first and then printing, or going straight to the printer. Another option is to save to file. Merging can take place after sorting and conditional selection of the data in the file according to criteria set by the user.

The user can call up custom groups of icons appropriate to the situation, such as editing, proofing, graphics, working together, or tables. If none of these groups meet the users needs, icons can be saved in groups and added to the choices that Ami Pro offers. For quick customizing, drag-and-drop can be applied to the icons to rearrange them.

Thanks to

- Practical Peripherals of Westlake Village, for supplying a V32/42 modem for our BBS and
- Octave Systems of Campbell for providing the hard drive for our BBS

Next Meeting

- December 2, 7:30pm at 1760 Oak Avenue in Menlo Park.
- Help us to make decisions about the club. All members are welcome. You don't have to be a club officer to get your views heard.

A Big Welcome to the Following New Members

Tom Day	Mountain View
K. Peter Dyer	Milpitas
Shirley Lambelet	Foster City
Betty Lee	Stanford
Jon Lindsay	Stanford
Bob Moberg	Palo Alto
Thomas Morgan	Campbell
Jim Patton	Mountain View
Jerome Teixeira	Palo Alto

And Thanks to Renewing Members

Becky Ridgemont	Cupertino
Fred Ridgemont	Cupertino
Don Baird	Redwood City
Bob Bottini	Redwood City
Nancy Helmy	Palo Alto
Matt Lehmann	Cupertino
Ron Nicholas	Los Altos

Most well-conceived CorelDRAW projects use one or two type families with various weights, styles, and sizes. There are illustrators who can use more typefaces with deft discretion, but I think those who fit that profile constitute the minority. Most of us should take the Two-Typeface Test when we produce work in and out of DRAW. We should force ourselves to make do with just two, or even one typeface (or type families, to be precise) for an entire project.

Use White Space

Create an illustration that has more white space than text. When I was the editor of *Inside Tennis* magazine several years ago, I found head designer Thomas Burns to be a master of white space. The magazine was a jam-packed tabloid, and Thomas was usually shackled with far too many elements for each article. But every so often he would be given a bit of breathing room, and beautiful things would happen. For instance, he might leave the top two-thirds of a page completely blank, save for a single line of type. Once, he threw the headline out entirely, opting for a very large drop cap to bring the page into focus. Everything he tried seemed to work with such elegant simplicity (this despite the fact that he didn't know beans about tennis).

Try creating a drawing where the white space prevails. Then try creating entire columns of white space, or large top and bottom margins. (Is Figure 24.3 any worse for wear because half of its left column is white? Doubt it…) As you experiment, make sure to print many samples, or at least toggle into full-screen preview often. It is difficult to visualize white space on the screen, what with DRAW's page border, rulers, guidelines, and grid points taking up space.

Relax Your Posture

Many desktop designers exhibit a knee-jerk reaction to setting type: They justify all text, whether or not there is a legitimate reason for it. There are times when the formality of a document makes justified type appropriate, but all too often it just makes your work look rigid and boxy. Also, centered headlines are often effective, but they can become dreadfully boring if you employ them all the time.

If you're in the centered headline/justified text rut, break out of it by left-aligning everything and avoiding hyphenation, especially if you are producing documents with wider columns (narrow, multicolumn pages might need to be hyphenated). At first, this new practice may seem odd—give it a chance, though; it will grow on you. Did you notice that the Not so Ugly rendition of Figure 24.1 included a right-aligned headline? It's subtle enough to elude the attention of many.

"Borrow" Good Design

Imitation is not only the highest form of flattery; it is often good business. No, I'm not suggesting that you republish the September issue of *Rolling Stone,* articles and all—just that you keep an eye out for advertisements, articles, newsletters, and graphics that you think are presented well.

The next time you pick up a magazine, skim it for more than just a good article to read. And when you find a well-presented piece, there is hardly better practice than to try re-creating it in CorelDRAW or your preferred page-layout program. Use a bit of dummy text and a few fake headlines, and try to recapture the style and the design. Notice the following:

- The use of call-out text
- The size of subheads
- The use of white space around headlines
- How drop shadows are created
- The colors used for spot elements
- How photos are integrated into the layout
- How backgrounds are created
- The use of illustrations to communicate

Don't look just at the desktop publishing magazines—they usually try too hard to be noticed. Choose an established, national monthly magazine whose priority is a particular message, not the medium for delivering that message.

This "borrowing" is completely legal; you can't get sued for look-and-feel infringement on a publication's design. Good design belongs to the public domain. There is nothing wrong with adapting an existing design that you find appealing, as long as you don't clone a trademarked logo or copyrighted slogan.

I recently had occasion to borrow. I had to prepare a full-page advertisement for the 1994 International CorelDraw Conference but only had 24 hours in which to do it. While browsing Corel's *ArtShow 4,* a compendium of 1993 entrants in Corel's annual design contest, I came upon a piece that struck a respondent chord in me. Shown in Figure 24.4, this piece by well-known CorelDRAW artist Chris Purcell touts a technical support system for COMPAQ computers, in which four features are highlighted. I had intended to highlight four features of the Conference, as well, and decided that Chris's basic design would be a good starting point. I didn't dare try to incorporate the flair that he shows in his piece—I'd surely fall on my face.

Figure 24.5 shows my finished effort, and Illustration No. 6 in the Color Gallery shows it in color. I stole the background of the double fountain fills going in opposite directions, but didn't try the extra shadowing or the squiggles employed in Chris's design. My four squares use the same 90-degree type technique, and the large question mark was just right in advertising our own technical support.

I knew that the dark type at the top would have good contrast against the light portion of the inner rectangle, but I had no idea if the white type near the middle ("The International CorelDraw…") would show up against the medium-colored part of the fountain. I had no time to make an accurate color proof, so I took the easy way out and placed a black shadow behind the type. One of those type strings—the white one or the black one—would surely show!

24.4

Chris Purcell's QuickSource illustration was a good candidate to "borrow" from.

Chris likely created all of his elements from scratch, or from raw materials such as clip art shapes. I, on the other hand, used complete pictures from other sources, such as the stargazer in the top-left square, the computer components in the lower-left square, and David Brickley's *The Diver* on the lower-right. Chris won an award for his work; mine can claim only that it succeeds in advertising the main features of the Conference and achieving an absence of ugliness.

24.5

The result of your lead author's thievery

Trying to replicate well-designed work is an excellent way to practice with DRAW's tools and develop your own sense of design.

Steal from Yourself, Too

And while you're at it, don't forget to borrow from yourself. If you've done something that works, do it again. All successful designers do this. Think of two or three publications that you find to be particularly well designed, perhaps *Newsweek, Life, The Atlantic Monthly,* or *Sports Illustrated.* As you visualize them, certain characteristics will come to mind, such as *Life*'s use of large type, or *Sports Illustrated*'s catchy headlines burned into full-page photos, or *Newsweek*'s section heads of white type on red bars.

These magazines are all well designed, not because they do something fabulously different every month, but because they do the same good things over and over again. They all have found a design that works, and have stayed with it for years at a time. That is what makes them distinctive.

Similarly, you need not think that every one of your projects has to be a perfect original—even the most skilled designers and illustrators don't try to do that. Once you produce a nice logo, cover page for a brochure, or some other work you particularly like, "bottle" it—create a template from it and use it for your next similar project. You'll surely decide to vary the theme, but you can at least start with a well-tested design. When something works, *get as much mileage out of it as you can.*

Have a Plan

I promised no dissertations, so I'll make this short. Everybody has a plan when starting a project, right? Would that that were true! All too often, amateur designers sit down in front of the CorelDRAW controls with no idea at all of where they want to go. "If I play around long enough, something will come to me," is how one client of mine described this phenomenon. There is absolutely nothing wrong with that—it's the electronic equivalent of doodling on a cocktail napkin—but it's the *first* step in design, not the final one.

What it all boils down to is a question of process, of how you approach a publishing project. Humor aside, here is an effective plan of attack:

1. Decide what you want to do.
2. Do it.

This may sound trite, but you'd be surprised by how many inexperienced DRAW users do *the exact opposite.* They become totally enamored with the tools, they start to play around, they begin to build, and build, and build, and then, "*Oh…what was it that I wanted to say in all of this?*" They lose sight of their message; suddenly, their objective has been reduced to visual razzle-dazzle.

I see it over and over again. And you might argue that the experts are the culprits, authoring books like this one, writing magazine articles, and giving seminars—all devoted to the use of this software. Indeed, I'm partly responsible for the unusual attention given to the creative process. If you stopped reading after the chapters in Part IV about DRAW's special effects, you might walk away believing that those fancy effects are a substitute for sound judgment in design, technical skills, and a trained eye. However, until DRAW offers a command called "Paste Brilliant Design Idea," nothing could be further from the truth.

Here is how I see the possible outcomes of form versus content:

Best Case:	Your use of fancy graphics fits the message
Still Okay:	Graphics are weak, but message is strong
In Trouble:	Graphics and message are both weak
Worst Case:	Fancy graphics with weak message

If you have succumbed to the Worst Case scenario, you are the electronic equivalent of the stereotypical dumb blonde: You are telling your readers: "I don't have anything to say, but I'm nice to look at."

You can't just live the Nike commercial; you can't "Just do it." You must first decide what you want to do. Then you can go do it.

Typography and the Fine Art of Restraint

If you are reading this section with the expectation that it is going to turn you into an inspired connoisseur of the art of typography, you're liable to be disappointed. In fact (and don't let the publishers hear me saying this), if you're reading this *book* with that hope, well, sorry. Even if I were one of those brilliant typographers (and I'm not), the very idea that I could impart that wisdom to you within a few book-sized pages would be an insult to the profession.

No, when it comes to typography, my skills fall clearly on the other side of the fence. I grunt and groan, scratch and claw, try and fail, and through it all occasionally happen upon typographic efforts that fall somewhere between acceptable and effective—once in a long while, they're even good. And that makes me ideally suited to write this final section. I know all too well the pitfalls that await the unsuspecting and unseasoned DRAW user, and I know intimately the risk of trying for too much. I also know the value of playing it safe. If I have perfected anything when it comes to type, it is the fine art of restraint.

Coupled with a good understanding of the mechanics of DRAW's typesetting engine, a conservative approach to type usage can lead to good mileage and tremendous satisfaction. Here are a few topics to ponder along your journey.

Resist the Temptation to Install All Five Jillion Typefaces

Let's set aside for a moment the incredibly high fire danger of having too many typefaces at your disposal. Indeed, in the hands of the typographically challenged, too many choices can lead to disasters of unspeakable proportion.

There is also a pragmatic argument against permitting CorelDRAW to drop upon you its entire typographic load, and that is the hit on performance. Excessive numbers of fonts in your system will produce a drain on virtually every area of Windows-based computing. The chart in Figure 24.6 provides the damning evidence.

Before you install your next copy of CorelDRAW, my advice is to spend a few minutes with the type samples provided in the clip art book, pick out a few dozen, and see if you can't survive on that. If you have already installed the Canadian kitchen sink, then it might be time to get friendly with the Font section of the Windows Control Panel. There you will find a window full of typeface names and a button called Remove. Get the picture?

NEW FOR 5

It doesn't show up on the menu during the DRAW 5.0 installation, but buried on the CD is a free copy of FontMinder, the popular font management utility from Ares Software. It will help you significantly in your quest to tame your typefaces. See the discussion in Chapter 33.

24.6

Are all those typefaces worth it? Maybe not...

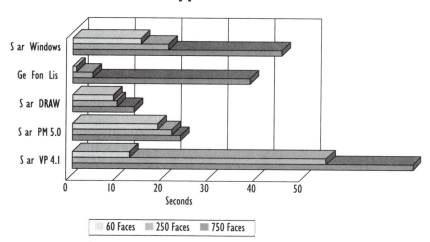

Choose the Right Category of Typefaces

I place almost all of DRAW's typefaces into two distinct categories: serious and absurd, the latter term used lovingly, of course. The absurd faces most definitely have their place in the publishing arena; wonderful logos, fliers, T-shirts, and other media are designed with them every day. But the potential for overuse is great, and they often find their way into drawings that would be better served by the straight-and-narrow. And then they look…well, absurd.

The reverse is certainly true, also, as nothing promises to cure insomnia like an invitation to a surprise party done up entirely in Helvetica.

At home, the arrival of our first daughter a couple of years ago was a good excuse to roll out DRAW for a birth announcement, complete with a scanned photo and a "California Sleeping License." The whole thing was full of whimsy, but the inside needed a straight-laced typeface to pass as a mock serious driver's license. We chose Corel's Castle for that. The outside of the announcement needed to look more like a cartoon, for which we used a fun typeface called Marker that you'll find on the Companion CD. Figure 24.7 shows both the inside and outside of the finished product, and Figure 24.8 shows the dreadful results of choosing from the wrong category—oy vey.

To Every Face—Kern, Kern, Kern

I don't care if you bought the most expensive Type 1 face that Adobe offers. I don't care if you have personally added 5,000 kerning pairs to your typefaces. I don't care—you must still scrutinize your display faces if you want quality output.

Figure 24.9 shows a headline set in Adobe Garamond, one of the most refined typefaces available. Yet, when set in large type like this, even a properly kerned typeface shows excess space between letters. The example in the middle has been kerned in DRAW by −3%, and that closes up most of the gaps. Still, in order to make this headline look its best, you must manually kern many of the character pairs.

24.7

The front of this birth announcement is the perfect place for an "absurd" typeface, while the spoof of the driver's license must be serious.

Notice the words *combine* and *insomniac*. Here are the steps to manually kern the letters in these words:

1. Set a Nudge value of .5 point.
2. Switch to the Shape tool.
3. Find the character that needs to move left, and select it *and every character to its right*.

24.8

Front of the announcement in a straight typeface: **BORING**. Inside in an absurd typeface: **ABSURD!**

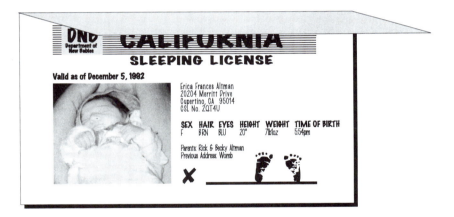

When you manually kern, you move only the selected characters. If you don't select all characters to the right of the one you want to move, you will be creating one gap while closing up another.

4. Using the Left Arrow key, nudge the characters to the left until the gap closes.

5. Look to the right for the next character that needs to be kerned. Hold the Shift key and deselect each character in between.

24.9

Always look for opportunities to kern, and carefully examine the results.

UNKERNED

What do you get when you combine an insomniac, an agnostic, and a dyslexic?

GLOBALLY KERNED -3%

What do you get when you combine an insomniac, an agnostic, and a dyslexic?

GLOBALLY KERNED AND MANUALLY KERNED

What do you get when you combine an insomniac, an agnostic, and a dyslexic?

For this exercise, it will help if you consult Figure 24.10. In *insomniac*, there are two letters that clearly need to be moved left: the *s* and the second *n*. To move the *s* to the left, you select it and all characters to its right and then nudge them all to the left. Once that is done to your satisfaction, deselect the *s* (hold Shift and click that letter's node) and inspect the rest of the letters. The *o* is fine: Shift+click its node and move on. The *m* is fine: Shift+click. The *n* is not, so start nudging (all of the other characters that need to move left are still selected). Then deselect the *n* and keep going down the line. Tedious, perhaps; worth the effort, definitely.

In the next chapter, we… What? You want to know what you get when you do what? Oh, the answer to the riddle—it's easy. What you get when you combine an insomniac, an agnostic, and a dyslexic is someone who lies awake at night wondering if there really is a dog.

24.10

To kern the s, you must move to the left not just the s, but every character to its right.

in.som.niac,

Moving back from the ridiculous, Part VI throws a blanket on DRAW's print engine, its color capabilities, and its fortunes with importing and exporting.

PART VI

THE CORELDRAW FREEWAY

There isn't really a stretch of road called the Corel Freeway, but it's not hard to imagine this piece of software being patterned after a busy freeway during rush hour: Used by dozens of different vehicles…lots of entrances and exits…rules that govern usage…lots of ways to break the rules…and, of course, a few good crashes along the way…some of them fatal.

This part of the book looks at CorelDRAW as the giant freeway that it is. We explore how data comes and goes, how color and quality black-and-white images are produced, how professionals prepare for printing, how files are passed to and from, and how to choose the right fuel (spelled f-o-r-m-a-t) for the trip. We start with the largest artery of the freeway—the print engine—and then move from there into color theory and to importing and exporting.

Chapter 25

Print, Darn You!

TWENTY-FIVE

CHAPTER 25

We don't remember where we heard it first, but the saying has become somewhat legendary in CorelDRAW circles: "If you can't get your drawings to print, then the whole thing is nothing more than a fancy video game." So if it's time to print your project, this chapter is for you, and we hope you'll get more out of it than you would a game of Space Invaders…

This chapter is essentially a guided tour of DRAW's Print dialogs, of which there are a multitude. Rest assured that once you understand where you're going and what all of the options do, you'll quickly become comfortable with DRAW's printing functions. You'll also be able to take control over your printing operations to a degree you might not have thought possible.

Understanding the Print dialogs is the key to controlling DRAW's printing power. Our grand tour follows the same route you will take when you prepare your drawings for printing and then actually print them. This discussion is heavy on PostScript emphasis, as most of DRAW's more ticklish printing issues involve PostScript printers in some way. But even if you use another kind of printer, you have most of the same options and capabilities available to you; if anything, printing to HP LaserJets and other non-PostScript printers is more straightforward than using PostScript.

If you've used DRAW 4.0, most of the options you see here will be familiar, but in version 5.0 you'll find some of them in different places. DRAW 5.0's new dialogs that have "pages" give you access to options without the subterranean labyrinth of dialogs we had in DRAW 4.0. You can move from page to page with the mouse or the arrow keys on your keyboard. And if you're moving up from DRAW 3, you're in for a lot of new sights.

Figure 25.1 presents the set of dialogs you will use when printing from DRAW 5.0. As you can see, there is an awful lot going on, so let's start from the beginning.

Printing with DRAW entails three important steps: selecting a printer, setting up the page, and choosing the appropriate print options.

25.1

The dialogs used for printing and page setup with DRAW 5.0

Print Setup Dialog

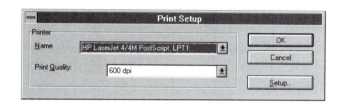

Page Setup Options

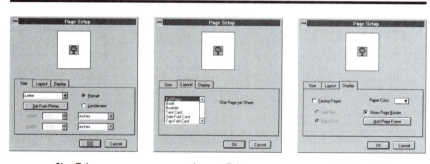

Size Tab　　　　　　Layout Tab　　　　　　Display Tab

Selecting a Printer

Our first stop on the tour is the Print Setup dialog (Figure 25.2). Here is where you choose the printer and resolution you'll use for your drawing. Click the Setup button and you'll get another dialog where you can set page orientation, paper size, and paper source. If this dialog looks familiar, there is good reason: You've probably seen it in all of the other Windows applications you've used. DRAW borrows this dialog from the Printers section of the Windows Control Panel.

25.2

The DRAW 5.0 Print Setup dialog

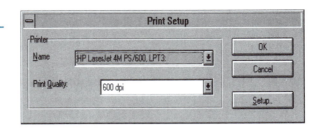

Your printer choice here is not irrevocable; in DRAW's Print dialog (described later in this chapter), you get a drop-down list of all installed printers, allowing you to switch just before printing if you need to. In that dialog, too, there's a Setup button that takes you right to Control Panel's setup options.

AUTHOR'S NOTE

We will refer frequently to Control Panel, the Windows one-stop shop for installing and configuring output devices for use with applications running under Windows. If you haven't seen it for yourself, open up the Main group on the Windows desktop, double-click Control Panel, and then double-click Printers.

You don't need to own a printer in order to "print" to it. As long as you have installed it under Windows, you can use it as your target printer. This lets you prepare output to take to a service bureau, so you don't have to actually purchase one of those $40,000 imagesetters.

As you'll soon see, DRAW makes several critical printing decisions based on the printer chosen in this dialog, so it's important to pick the correct one before you create any final output.

Setting Up the Page

Our next stop is the Page Setup dialog. Before you begin work on your drawing, always use Layout / Page Setup to display this dialog and tell DRAW what paper size and orientation you want, as demonstrated in

Figure 25.3. You can also double-click the page border to get to Page Setup quickly.

25.3

Proper printing requires proper paper sizes. DRAW can support paper sizes as large as 30 inches square.

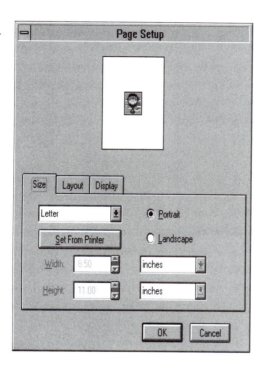

Page Setup, Size Options

On this page of the Page Setup dialog, you tell DRAW what size drawing you want to create and whether you want Portrait or Landscape orientation.

Note that there are paper size settings in the Control Panel's Printers Setup, as well as in DRAW's Page Setup / Size page. Once you set the Control Panel paper size, Windows relays that information to all of your Windows programs, including DRAW, but DRAW's paper size is independent of the printer's. Think of it this way: DRAW's Page Setup dialog sets the drawing size, and Control Panel sets the paper size on which you'll print the drawing.

You can override the printer's paper size settings, and later in this chapter we'll show you how you can print larger drawings than what your printer supports—up to approximately 30 inches. DRAW lets you create a drawing of pretty much any size you like, regardless of your printer's capabilities. It's not unusual to create drawings that are too large for your own printer if your ultimate goal is to produce output on an imagesetter or other high-end device.

You can use the Fit to Page option (in Print Options / Layout) when you print to accommodate drawings that are too large for your printer, but if your aim is to produce a drawing that is sized specifically for your printer, the Set From Printer button will help. It automatically sets your drawing to the page size you specify in Control Panel. Be sure to allow for your printer's margins.

Page Setup, Layout Options

In the Layout page, shown in Figure 25.4, you can choose one of several predefined standard page layouts. You'll see later, in the "Print Options" section, how these layouts interact with the Print dialogs.

Page Setup, Display Options

As its name suggests, on this page (Figure 25.5) you'll find options that control the way DRAW displays your drawing.

Facing Pages   Since version 4.0, DRAW has supported multiple pages in one file. Facing Pages lets you control how DRAW displays your multipage projects. If you check Facing Pages, DRAW displays two side-by-side pages at once—handy for work that includes graphics spanning more than one page. Use the Left First and Right First buttons to determine whether your layout displays with the first page on the left (as it might in a brochure) or with the first page on the right (as in most booklets and other bound materials).

Add Page Frame   The Add Page Frame button adds an instant background to your drawing. It places a rectangle on the drawing, sized to match your selected Paper Size. Once you OK the dialog, the new

25.4
The Page Setup dialog's Layout page

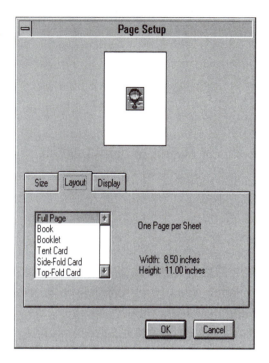

rectangle will be selected, so you can immediately apply any of DRAW's fills. Because the rectangle is always sent to the back of the drawing, behind any objects you may already have drawn, you can easily add a Page Frame to your drawing at any time.

Paper Color The Paper Color setting works something like Add Page Frame, but the results are quite different. When you specify a paper color, DRAW displays your drawing as though it were printed on paper of that color, without actually printing the color. Paper Color is useful if you print on colored paper, because it gives you a screen preview of what the printed drawing will look like. You get a chance to make sure that your colored objects contrast well with the paper color, and you can quickly test the effect of various colors without having to make endless trial printouts.

25.5

The Page Setup dialog's Display page

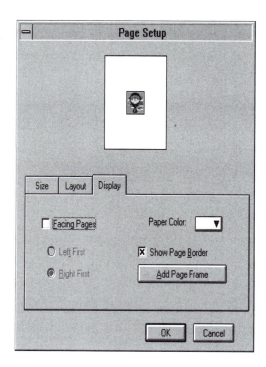

WATCH OUT!

DRAW does not take into account the show-through of the paper color. So if you create a rectangle and specify colored paper, and give the rectangle a black tint (30%), the rectangle appears gray, instead of a darker version of the paper color, as it should.

Paper Color is also handy when you create graphics for export to another program that provides its own background (for instance, presentation programs such as Persuasion, PowerPoint, Freelance, and Corel's SHOW module). By using Paper Color to approximate the color you'll be using later, you get a good idea what the final presentation will look like. Since the paper color doesn't actually print or export, it won't interfere with the background provided by the presentation program.

Paper Color or Page Frame—which to use? It's a simple choice: If you want to lock in the background no matter where your drawing prints or exports, use Add Page Frame and set the fill to whatever background you like. If you simply want to get an idea what the drawing will look like on a background that will be supplied elsewhere (on colored paper from your printer, for example, or from another program), use Paper Color.

Show Page Border   Show Page Border lets you choose whether or not you want to see a box on screen representing the dimensions of the page size you've set up in DRAW. When you're designing for a particular page size, it's handy to leave this option on, so you don't accidentally draw off the page. If you're working on graphics that will be exported (where page size and paper size are not at issue), you may prefer the extra uncluttered working area you get when you turn off the page border. The choice is yours.

A word to the wise: If you turn off Page Border, there won't be any page border to double-click when you want to call up the Page Setup dialog quickly.

DRAW's Page Border setting doesn't indicate the actual printable area of your printer. Laser printers cannot print to the very edge of the paper, so be sure to allow for this when creating your drawings.

INSIDE INFO

Here is how to find out just how close to the paper edge your laser printer can print. In Page Setup / Size, set the correct paper size, then click Add Page Frame in the Display page, and then click OK. Fill the page frame with a light shade of gray and then print (making sure in Print Options / Layout that Width and Height are set to 100% and Fit to Page is not enabled). The white margins on your printout represent your printer's dead zone. Any drawing elements that must print should be kept inside these margins when you design your pages.

The Print Dialog

Having set the various Print Setup and Page Setup options the way you want them, you're ready to go to work on your drawing. Sooner or later, you'll want to print your work, and that's when you'll turn to the Print Dialog, Figure 25.6.

When you issue the Print command (File / Print or Ctrl+P) you'll see the dialog shown in Figure 25.7. In many cases, all you have to do to

25.6

Your road map for printing with DRAW 5.0

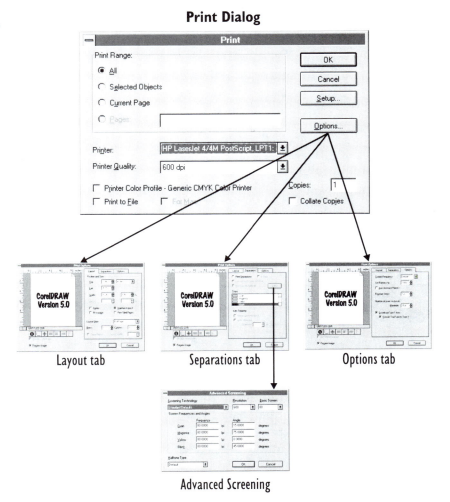

print your work is click OK. But, as with most of DRAW's functions, a truckload of options awaits you just below the surface.

25.7

DRAW 5.0's new Print dialog

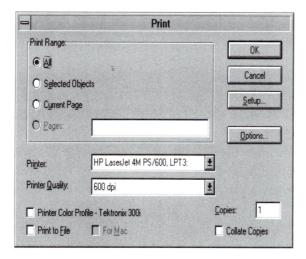

Print Range

Using the Print Range buttons, you can be selective about exactly what will print when you click OK.

- **All** prints it all… every object on every page of the current drawing.

- **Selected Objects** prints only the currently selected object. If you're fine-tuning a particular object or working on a small portion of your drawing, you can accelerate proof printing dramatically by using this option. It's only available when objects are selected in your drawing; otherwise, DRAW assumes you want to print everything.

- **Current Page** prints the entire current page (the page you're currently viewing).

- **Pages** is not available unless your document contains more than one page. You can specify a particular page or range of pages to print.

Printer and Printer Quality

By selecting from the Printer drop-down list, you can override your earlier printer choices in Control Panel or DRAW's Print Setup dialog. You can select any printer you have installed in Windows. For Printer Quality, DRAW determines what resolution settings the selected printer supports and lets you choose the one you want.

Printer Color Profile

This reminds you which Printer Color Profile you've selected and allows you to turn DRAW's color correction on and off. (You will read all about CorelDRAW's new Color Manager in Chapter 28.)

Print to File and For Mac

Check this option if you want to capture your output to a disk file instead of sending it directly to a printer—for example, when preparing PostScript print files to be taken to a service bureau. When you OK the Print dialog, DRAW presents a window for you to provide a file name and path for your output.

To the right of the Print to File option you'll find the For Mac check box. If you check this option when you print to file, DRAW makes a file suitable for Macintosh-equipped service bureaus. In normal Print to File operations, the Windows PostScript driver puts a special character (Ctrl+D or hex 04, to be precise) at the beginning and end of each file. This causes trouble for service bureaus that run their printers and imagesetters from Macs. A knowledgeable service bureau will know how to remove these extraneous characters, but why make extra work? If your service bureau uses Macs, click the For Mac box when you print to file.

Another Use for Print to File
Print files are useful for more than just sending files to a service bureau. You can create a print file for use with any device that is not attached directly to your computer. Let's say you have a color thermal printer at the office, but DRAW is installed on your machine at home. You can create your drawing at home, choose the color printer in the Print dialog (assuming the printer is installed),

and create the print file. Write it to a diskette, take it to the office, and use the DOS COPY command to send the file to the printer. The syntax for the COPY command is

> COPY *filename port* /B

where *filename* is the name of your DRAW file, and *port* is the port where your printer is attached (LPT1, COM2, or the like). The /B tells DOS to expect binary information, not necessarily ASCII.

Copies and Collate Copies

Want extra printouts of your drawing? This is the place to ask for them. This setting overrides the Copies settings that may be present in one of the Control Panel's Printer dialogs (depending upon your printer).

On PostScript printers, it's considerably faster to get multiple copies from DRAW's Copies setting than it is to print multiple times. PostScript printers may take quite a while to process any one page, but once they have done so, they keep the page in memory, quickly churning out additional copies at the speed of the printer engine. Other printer drivers may or may not support multiple copies, forcing DRAW to send the complete drawing once for each copy, in which case there's very little time savings.

To test whether your printer and its driver support DRAW's Copies option, pick a relatively simple drawing and print it with Copies set to 2. If the printer pauses a bit and then prints two copies, one right after the other, you're in the duplicating business. If the printer pauses, then prints, then pauses, then prints again, Copies is not supported.

For all the improvements, there's one little nuisance that might sneak up on you if you're not on the lookout: Changes you make in the Print Options dialog do not take effect until you OK both Print Options *and* the Print dialog itself. You must actually print a page before all your options will "take." If you OK Print Options but Cancel out of Print, your selections in Print Options won't be saved.

The Print Preview Area

Click the Options button in the Print dialog, and the first thing you'll notice is the large print preview area on the left side of the Print Options window. It shows you the page size you have selected in Control Panel / Printers / Setup, and the printable area of the page. If you check the Preview Image check box, you'll see a preview of your drawing, positioned as it will print on paper.

WATCH OUT!

> DRAW is no speed demon when it comes to previewing your image in the Print dialog, taking as long or longer to render your drawing there as it does in DRAW's main screen. If you want to turn the preview off by unchecking the Preview Image check box, DRAW 5.0 remembers this setting; the preview stays off until you turn it on again. Of course, Preview Image is interruptible—you can turn it off and halt the rendering of a drawing in midstream.

Those Mysterious Buttons under the Print Preview Area

The buttons under the print preview area let you enable and disable instructions to DRAW to place additional information on your printouts, such as file names, crop marks, and register marks. These elements are most useful when you're printing separations, so we'll discuss them later, in "Printing Color Separations."

Print Options, Layout Page

The Layout page of the Print Options dialog (Figure 25.8) is where you take control over how DRAW positions your drawing on the final printed page.

Position and Size Settings Use the Position and Size settings to change the location and dimensions of your drawing when it prints

25.8
The Print Options dialog's Layout page

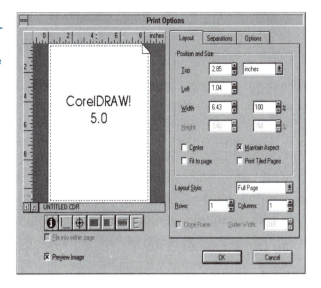

on the current printer page area. Unlike DRAW 4.0, in 5.0 you do it strictly by the numbers, using Left, Top, Width, and Height dial-up controls. For Width and Height you can specify either absolute sizes or a scaling percentage.

If you're worried about distorting your drawing by entering nonproportional scaling factors, you'll save wear and tear on your calculator if you check Maintain Aspect. DRAW will dim the Height boxes and, as you change Width, it will calculate the correct Height needed to scale your drawing without distortion.

Center No mystery here—check this and DRAW centers your drawing on the printer page, regardless of how you have sized it. Of course, if your drawing is too big for your printer, centered or not, you have a problem. The solution is…

Fit to Page Check Fit to Page before you print, and DRAW will automatically scale your printout to fill the printer page. If you have selected objects, you can check Selected Objects Only in the Print dialog and Fit to Page here, and you'll get a "zoomed" printout of your objects. DRAW prints only the selected objects, scaled to full-page size.

Conversely, if you're working on an oversize drawing, check Fit to Page, and DRAW will scale the printout to fit your printer's maximum page size. DRAW alters just the printout, not your drawing.

Print Tiled Pages If your drawing is larger than the printer's paper size or contains objects that are off the edges of the page (or if you scale it off the page), you can use Tile to print the drawing at actual size across multiple pages. DRAW uses as many pages as it needs to print the entire image. You can then tape the printout together see what it will look like when you print it on a printer capable of the larger page size. Depending on the nature of your drawing, you might be able to use your tiled printouts, carefully spliced, as final output.

Splitting the Drawing into Tiles Determining where DRAW will split objects between pages can be tricky. For PostScript printers, DRAW searches for the lower-leftmost object in the image and prints it at the lower-left of the printable area of the first page. As it encounters objects that won't fit on this page, it adds new pages as needed. This works the same for non-PostScript printers, with one twist: DRAW starts in the upper-left corner rather than the lower-left.

The top image in Figure 25.9 shows how DRAW tiles an oversized image to a PostScript printer. The large gray rectangle extends beyond a standard page, so DRAW creates a second page to accommodate it. As you can see, however, during the tiling process DRAW moves all of the objects toward the bottom-left of the page. To avoid this, you can fool DRAW by placing an *invisible* object in the lower-leftmost corner of your drawing, as shown in the image at the bottom of Figure 25.9. (To make an object invisible, just set both its fill and outline to None.) When DRAW is ready to tile, it finds that invisible object at the bottom and places it at the bottom—in other words, no change at all is made.

Layout Style Settings Have you ever drawn something and then longed for a way to have the computer automatically fit multiple copies of it on one page? Long no longer: DRAW's new Layout Style settings do exactly that.

25.9

Two ways to tell DRAW to tile—the normal way and the inventive way

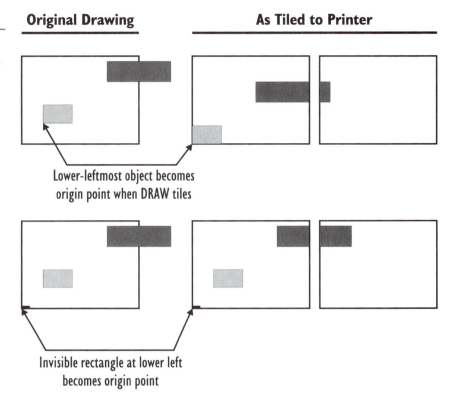

Let's take a 2-by-3-inch business card as an example. Using pre-5.0 DRAW, you'd create the card and then group, dupe, and position additional copies to fill the page. Tedious. Boring. Worse, it makes for very slow redraws. And it's almost certain that, once you've done all the grouping and duping, somebody will want to make just a teensy-weensy little change, and there goes all your work. Things are different, thank goodness, with DRAW 5.0. You create the drawing, after specifying the actual size of the card in Page Layout, and DRAW does the tedious grouping 'n duping for you automatically at print time. No need to wait on redraws of multicopies, and if there's a change, you make it once and once only.

How does it work? With Layout Style set to Full Page, change Rows and Columns to set the number of rows and columns of copies you want on the page. Check Clone Frame, and DRAW will automatically duplicate your drawing as many times as required to fill the matrix you've specified. You can control the spacing between the copies with Gutter Width. Naturally, the results are displayed in the live preview area to the left.

WATCH OUT!

DRAW will attempt to maintain your drawing at its original size, but there are limits. If you ask for more rows and columns than will fit on the page (four columns worth of 3-inch-wide business cards, for instance) DRAW 5.0 will shrink your drawing to accommodate you. But you'll get no warning, other than what you see in the preview area, so keep an eye on that preview as you change Rows and Columns settings.

DRAW also understands that there are special Layout Styles that want special treatment. You can have DRAW automatically handle these by matching your selection in Layout Styles to the style you chose in Page Setup.

Options, Schmoptions

It forever perplexes us why a software developer will choose to place one group of options on a main dialog, and others in a subdialog called Options. Aren't they all options? What makes the Options options any better than the others? Why do they get singled out? We will leave these earth-moving questions for another day. Following are descriptions of the options that DRAW deems worthy of placement in the Options page of the Print Options dialog shown in Figure 25.10. We'll cover the Separations page a little further along.

Screen Frequency   Examined in depth in Chapter 27, "Turning Gray with Dignity," the Screen Frequency field together with the resolution of your printer determine the number of gray shades you can produce on a PostScript printer or imagesetter. The lower you set Screen Frequency, the more gray shades you can print, but the coarser the

25.10

The Options page in the Print Options dialog, where you set the optional options

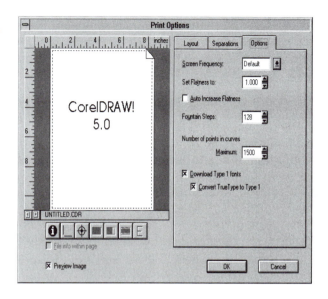

image will look. Conversely, higher Screen Frequency settings allow you to produce fine grays, even on a 300-dpi laser printer, but not many of them.

To get a feel for how this works, draw a large rectangle, fill it with a black-to-white linear fountain fill, and then print it several times at various screen settings. Until you change it, DRAW will use your laser printer's default screen frequency of 53 or 60. This will produce about 30 gray values, and the result will be visibly banded. By reducing the screen frequency to 30 or so, you can nearly eliminate banding, but the fill will look like it's printed with BBs instead of 300-dpi laser printer dots.

It's a straight trade-off: the size of the screen dot vs. the number of printable grays. You don't get a lot of maneuvering room on a 300-dpi printer, but move up to a 1,270-dpi imagesetter, and you have considerably more flexibility. By setting the Screen Frequency field correctly, you can have 256 different gray values, smooth fountain fills, and still keep the dot size from growing to obnoxious proportions. Chapter 27 has all of the details.

Set Flatness To   PostScript printers don't really draw curves; they break curves into tiny line segments. The Set Flatness To value governs the number of line segments that are printed per curve. The more segments a PostScript printer has to calculate, the longer the curve will take to print.

To speed up your printouts, you can increase the Set Flatness To value from its default of 1. Your curves will look a little rough if you raise the value too high, but you can always reduce the number later when you're doing your final printout. On a 300-dpi laser printer, values up to 10 will have only a marginally visible effect, but may dramatically accelerate printing of complex drawings.

Figure 25.11 shows the effect of changing the Flatness setting. Our sample object, made of simple curves, is printed using an extremely high (#1) and then using an extremely low (#2) flatness setting. The difference in print quality is obvious, and the printing time is cut in half. At higher printing resolutions, you can set fairly high flatness values without such an extreme effect on print quality, as example #3, printed at 600 dpi, shows.

Remember the Set Flatness To setting if you run into a PostScript *limitcheck* error when printing. Changing Flatness is one of the techniques most likely to solve this sticky problem. We'll tell you more about this and other problem-solving strategies later, in the "Troubleshooting" section of this chapter.

Fountain Steps   How many steps does it take to print a smooth fountain fill? That depends on the drawing and the output device, but the Fountain Steps option is where you make sure the job is done right. This setting determines the number of steps used to create a fountain fill, where one color gradually turns into another.

Just as you can control the number of steps DRAW uses to draw fountain fills on screen, you can adjust the number of steps (or stripes) used when it prints. The more fountain steps you specify at print time, the smoother your image will look, and the longer it will take to print. No free lunches here—all those extra stripes have to be calculated and rendered, and that takes time. It's more efficient to set a fairly low value

25.11
Different settings for Set Flatness To will produce varying print speeds and quality

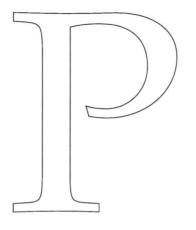
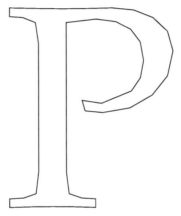
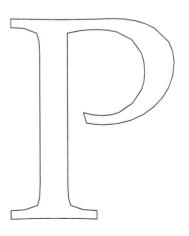

during the early stages of a complex drawing, and then bump up the value when you fine-tune the nearly finished work and need to see a more accurate printout.

INSIDE INFO

> **Fountain Steps affects all fountain fills that you left "locked" in the Fountain Fill dialog. It does not affect the ones that you unlocked in order to set a new Steps value. Use the Fills dialog to specify a large number of fountain steps for only those objects that really need them. You can then set a low value for Fountain Steps in Print Options, and thus speed up your print times considerably.**

By the way, on 300-dpi PostScript printers, setting Fountain Steps to anything over about 30 is a waste of time. Without adjusting the screen frequency, 33 is the maximum number of gray shades you can print. Higher settings for Fountain Steps won't produce smoother fountain fills, but they will slow printing. If you decrease the screen frequency, you can get a smoother fountain, but you'll have a much coarser dot. Figure 25.12 shows the effect of changing the screen.

Number of Points in Curves   The setting for Maximum Number of Points in Curves allows you to take control of the complexity of DRAW's curves at print time. The more points in any curve, the more likely it will produce PostScript printing errors. DRAW will automatically break curves over the Maximum number into shorter curves with fewer points. We explain this further in the "Troubleshooting" section of this chapter.

At Last! DRAW Downloads Fonts!   The last two check boxes on the Options page—Download Type 1 Fonts and Convert TrueType to Type 1—will make a lot of long-term DRAW users very happy indeed. In short, DRAW 5.0 now handles PostScript printer font downloading just like other Windows programs. For the long explanation, turn to

25.12

Lowering the value for Screen Frequency produces a smoother but coarser pattern.

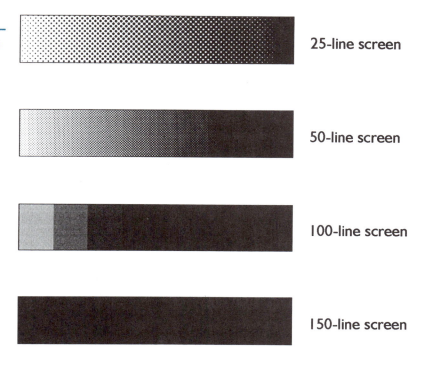

Appendix A, where DRAW's new font-handling capabilities are discussed in detail.

Printing Color Separations

DRAW can print color separations of your artwork for use on four-color printing presses. However, we must make one thing very clear. *Printing presses can only produce two colors at a time: the color of the ink that is being used, or no color at all.* That's it—either ink or no ink. Printing presses cannot produce blue, yellow, purple, or any other colors simultaneously.

Four-color printing is done in four separate printing passes, each time with a different color ink. As discussed in Chapter 26, those four colors are **C**yan, **M**agenta, **Y**ellow, and blac**K**—CMYK—the four composite process colors from which all others are created.

Let's say you have a drawing consisting of three rectangles, one filled red, one blue, and one green, and all with black outlines. When you tell DRAW to print color separations, it creates a separate page for each of the colors it finds in the drawing. If you are using specific spot colors, as defined in Chapter 26, DRAW creates one page for each spot color. When you use process colors, DRAW prints four pages—one each for cyan, magenta, yellow, and black. Each page represents a piece of film that will ultimately be used by the printing press.

According to the CMYK color model, red is made up of magenta and yellow, so the red rectangle in your drawing will be represented on both the yellow and magenta films. The green rectangle will appear on both the cyan and yellow separations, and the blue one will turn up on the cyan and magenta films. Since the rectangles all had a black outline in the original, the outlines show up on the black film.

You create the PostScript print file, consisting of four pages, one each for the four colors. Your service bureau then produces four pieces of film, one for each color. From the film, your print shop creates the plates, and the press transfers the image onto paper four times, each time with a different ink. The drawing 4COLOR.CDR in the PRACTICE directory shows this process.

Your real-life drawings are probably more complex than the three little rectangles in the example above, and so is the actual printing process. For instance, you probably don't limit yourself to solid colors that can be reproduced with 100% blocks of the primary printing inks. And you probably don't limit yourself to nice, neat rectangles, with no overlap. Therefore, some potential decisions await you. Several of these issues are addressed when you check Print Separations in the Separations page of the Print Options dialog.

To print shades of a particular color (instead of just pure colors), you need the image converted to dots—the kind of dots discussed in Chapter 27. If the colors are a mixture of the printing primaries (CMYK), that means you'll need two (or more) dot-screened areas to print one atop the other in perfect registration. If one dot-screened area is the least bit off when it prints over another, you get moiré patterns in the final print run, which can degrade the quality of your finished work. Figure 25.13 shows a moiré pattern in effect.

Expecting perfect registration from a printing press is not realistic, so rather than wage a futile war against moiré patterns, printers overlay the screens at different angles. Somewhere, somehow, somebody figured out that moirés are least likely to occur when each screen prints at an angle of 30 degrees to the previous one. DRAW automatically applies these screen angles when you print separations.

So much for the basic theory. How does DRAW handle color separations? You start by checking Print Separations in the Separations page of the Print Options dialog (Figure 25.14). As for the rest of the settings on this page, it's beyond the scope of any book—even this one with its four-color Color Gallery—to fully describe all the color and prepress bells and whistles. Nonetheless, here is an overview.

25.13

When screen patterns line up perfectly (above), everything is wonderful. When they don't (below), everything is miserable.

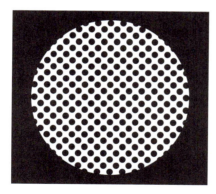

Perfect registration: All the dots align on top of one another

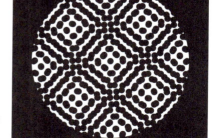

Flawed registration: Dots do not align exactly, causing dreaded moiré effect

25.14

Print Options Separations Page

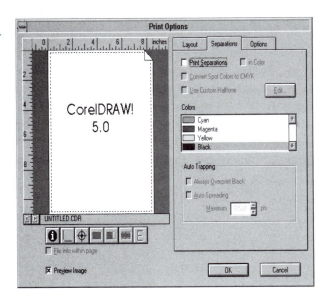

In Color If you have a color printer, check this In Color box beside Print Separations to have DRAW print each separation page in its actual color rather than black. The cyan separation will print in cyan, the magenta separation in magenta, and so on, each color on a separate page. Load transparencies into your printer to get a quick-and-dirty color-key proof of your separations. They won't be color-accurate, but you may find them useful for analyzing your drawing or for checking trap (more on that shortly).

Convert Spot Colors to CMYK This option forces DRAW to convert spot colors in your drawing to CMYK and print them on the appropriate separations, rather than printing each spot color on its own page as DRAW would normally do. There are potentially significant implications here for those who work with PANTONE spot colors:

- If you enable the Convert option, don't expect perfection. When DRAW breaks down a spot color and divvies out the portions to each of the CMYK colors, it does so according to a formula that is inherently flawed. Don't blame DRAW, though—some spot colors simply don't have CMYK equivalents.

- If you don't enable the Convert option, DRAW creates a page for each spot color in your drawing. If your drawing has process colors also, then you're talking about a lot of pages, a lot of films and plates, a lot of print runs, and a lot of dollars. Two spot colors plus process colors equals six separate color plates.

Use Custom Halftone By default, DRAW prints separations using screen rulings and angles appropriate for the output device and resolution you selected in Control Panel / Printers / Setup. By checking Use Custom Halftone and clicking the Edit button, you get the Advanced Screening dialog (Figure 25.15), which allows you to take total control of this technically complex aspect of making color separations. And "technically complex" is a subtle hint that unless you're armed with very specific instructions from your service bureau, you'll do well to leave the values in the Advanced Screening dialog at their defaults. If you know what you're doing, however, DRAW won't stand in the way of your doing it.

Colors This is where you choose which separation pages you want to print: cyan, magenta, yellow, black, and any spot colors you've used in your drawing, or none of them. Well, okay—you need to pick at least one.

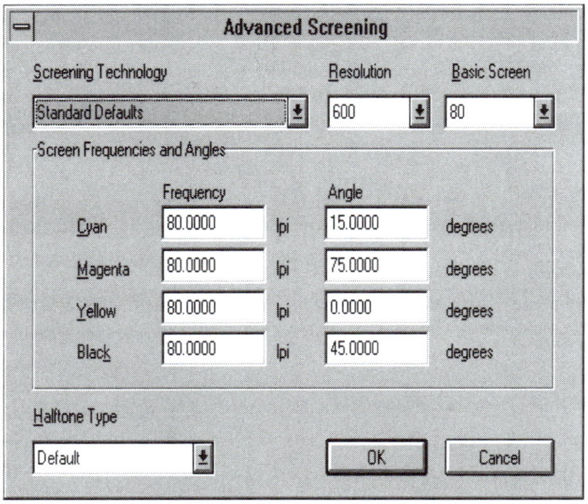

25.15

The power user can have a field day in the Advanced Screening dialog.

It's always a good idea to check this part of the dialog carefully before you OK a separations printout. It's all too easy to accidentally use a spot color instead of a process color. The Colors window in the Separations page displays each color used in your drawing. If you have used spot colors in your drawing and are working on a four-color project, make sure to check the Convert Spot Colors to CMYK check box; otherwise, you may wind up creating a lot more than just four separation plates.

INSIDE INFO

Color separations can turn into huge files when you print them to disk. It's unlikely that a whole set of separations will fit onto a floppy disk, so how are you going to get them to your service bureau? It'll help a lot if you select and print one color at a time using the Colors box. One color, one file, one floppy.

Auto-Trapping DRAW's Auto-Trapping feature is a simple (and simplistic) method of adding trap to colors. *Trapping* is covered in detail in Chapter 26, and the manual method of trapping described there usually proves more versatile and reliable. The CorelDRAW User's Manual discusses the Auto-Trapping feature as well as the issue of trapping in general.

Now, About Those Buttons...

Underneath the preview area (and illustrated in Figure 25.16) there's a row of buttons that control some additional printing features. All of these elements will print in the margin, beyond the page size you chose in Page Setup / Size. If your printer is set for the same size as your page, these elements won't appear (except for File Information, which has an option to Print Within Page). Here are descriptions of these buttons, left to right.

File Info Click the File Info button, and DRAW will add the following elements to your printout: the drawing's file name, the date and time, line screen, current color profile, and the color plate identifier.

25.16

The buttons under the preview area in the Print Options screen

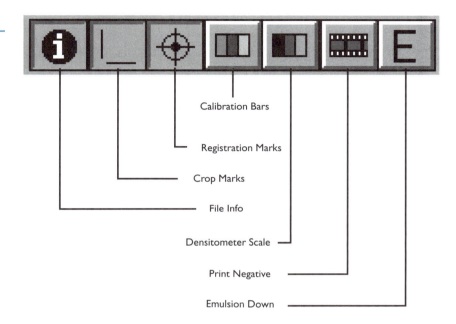

Check the File Info Within Page check box to get DRAW to make sure all this information falls within the printable area of your page.

Though File Info is useful for black-and-white work, it's absolutely essential for color separations. Imagine what fun it would be if the annual report came rolling off the press with all the yellow ink printing from the cyan plate and vice versa. As long as you tell DRAW to label the separations via the File Info button, at least it won't be your head that rolls if this kind of mix-up occurs.

Crop Marks and Registration Marks In DRAW 5.0, crop marks and registration marks are separate options, and for good reason. Crop marks are useful whenever you need to define the boundaries of an image. When you print with the Crop Marks option turned on, DRAW adds marks on the edges of the page to define the outer margins of the page size you selected in Print / Setup / Paper Size.

You can get crop marks only if you are printing your image to a page larger than the size you've specified under Layout / Page Setup / Size. A laser printer can't print to the edge of the page (and even if it could, the crop marks would be really on the edge). Using the Print dialog's Fit to Page option won't help, because DRAW does not consider crop marks to be part of the drawing that it fits to the page size. When you print to an imagesetter, however, you can choose special page sizes that solve this problem neatly. You'll want to print your letter-size pages to the imagesetter's Letter-Extra page size, whose oversized $9\frac{1}{2}$-by-12-inch dimensions provide room for both crop and registration marks.

Registration marks aren't needed normally, but for color separations they are essential. Without registration marks, it would be virtually impossible to line up the plates on the printing press (more about this later, in "Printing Color Separations").

Calibration Bars and Densitometer Scale   Calibration bars (color bars) and the densitometer scale pertain to printing color separations, and are only available if you've checked Print Separations in the Print Options / Separations page. When you enable these bars, DRAW will print, respectively, a series of rectangles in the primary printing colors, and a black-to-white step wedge. These are useful for checking four-color proofs and isolating printing press problems.

Print Negative and Emulsion Down   It's common for printers to specify their film requirements using terms such as "Right reading / emulsion down / film negatives." This simply means that with the film held with the emulsion side away from you, the image will read normally, and black and white will be reversed.

Emulsion refers to the light-sensitive coating applied to the photographic film and paper used by imagesetters. Normally, imagesetter output is "emulsion up," meaning that it prints a normal (or "right-reading") image onto the emulsion side of the paper or film. Printing with Emulsion Down enabled flops your image end for end so that it "reads right" from the nonemulsion side of the resulting film.

Clicking the Print Negative button instructs DRAW to print your drawing with blacks and whites reversed. This is useful if your printer requires film negatives instead of paper positives for making printing plates.

Figure 25.17 shows the result of enabling Print Negative and Emulsion Down in various combinations.

Most service bureaus will do the positive/negative and emulsion up/down conversions if you ask them. It's generally best to print normally, tell them what you want, and let them handle it. If you prefer to take care of it yourself or just want to make proof prints on your laser printer, use the Print Negative and Emulsion Down buttons as required.

25.17

The result of enabling Print Negative and Emulsion Down

Printed normally

Printed negative

Printed emulsion down

Printed negative *and* emulsion down

INSIDE INFO

> If you want to try out these options but don't have a printer that handles extra-large page sizes, use Page Setup to create a custom page size smaller than your printer's page size. We find that 5 by 7 inches is convenient. You can turn on all the crop and registration marks and other goodies, and they'll show up on your letter-size printouts.

This concludes our tour of DRAW's printing dialogs. By now, you should have all the options set exactly the way you want them. OK the Print dialog and let the fun begin.

What happens, though, when you click OK and nothing happens?

Troubleshooting Guide for PostScript Printing

DRAW has earned a reputation with some service bureaus as something of a troublemaker, and every DRAW user has favorite stories about the drawing that took eleventy-something hours to print, or caused the printer to erupt in a nonstop stream of gibberish. Here are a few of the most common gotchas, and their solutions.

Hardware Problems

The first thing to do when you have problems printing a file is to simply turn the printer off and then back on. The printer might be confused by a previous file, or some fonts that you downloaded earlier might be using memory that the printer needs to print your page. Turning the power off and on again is the fastest, most reliable way to clear the printer's head.

It's also possible for the PostScript data to get corrupted on its way to the printer and cause errors. PostScript printers are not at all forgiving of bad data…one bad byte can cause a whole page to fail.

If you print to a serial port, there can be handshaking problems (between computer and printer) that cause maddeningly intermittent problems. Some files will print, others won't, or the printer will skip a page here and there. If you're experiencing this kind of problem, check the port settings in Control Panel / Printers / Setup. Make sure they match those recommended in your printer's manual.

Slow Print or No Print At All

The same set of problems can cause a page to print slowly or not at all. Many printing problems can be traced to one cause: complexity. It's all too easy to create files in DRAW that are all but unprintable. The trouble is not with DRAW's PostScript output, as is sometimes alleged. It's that DRAW offers so many cool effects that its users sometimes get carried away. Once you learn what makes an image complex from the PostScript printer's point of view, you'll be able to work out strategies for printing challenging files and, better yet, avoid those challenges in the first place.

So what makes life miserable for a PostScript printer? What does it think of as "complex"? And what can you do to make its job easier?

The most obvious source of complexity is complexity itself. A drawing with a thousand rectangles is naturally going to take longer to print. The more stuff you pile into your file, the longer you'll wait for your printout. PostScript is remarkably robust at handling huge numbers of relatively simple objects, so the penalty you pay is mostly one of printing speed.

If you really do need all those objects in your drawing, then have at it. Just be prepared to wait for your printouts. You can speed up interim proofs by selecting just the objects you're currently working with and clicking Selected Objects in the Print dialog. Only the objects you've selected will print.

You can also use DRAW's layering tools to turn whole sections of your drawing off as far as the printer is concerned.

Complex Curves

Every PostScript printer has a limit to the number of segments it can calculate for a curve. Sooner or later, one of your drawings may fail to print due to a *limitcheck* error. This means one of the curves in your drawing has exceeded the printer's limit. The higher the output resolution, the more segments used, so you're more likely to run into this error from your service bureau's imagesetter than from your own laser printer. If this happens, you have several options:

- Simplify the curve in your drawing. Remove unnecessary nodes; use straight-line segments instead of curves where possible. (The Auto-Reduce command in the Node Edit roll-up can be a big help.)

- Break the curve into several segments. PostScript limitations apply on a per-curve basis. If you convert one curve into two, it shouldn't change your drawing, but it may enable you to print where you couldn't before.

INSIDE INFO

If it sounds like too much trouble to subdivide your curve, let DRAW do the work for you. The Maximum Number of Points in Curves setting in the Print Options / Options page determines how complex a curve must be before DRAW steps in and breaks it into multiple segments automatically. This setting can be reduced to as low as 20 for problem drawings.

- Increase the Set Flatness To value in Print Options / Options. The higher you set it, the fewer line segments PostScript will use in drawing the curve. Try increasing the value a little at a time (Corel suggests jumps of 4 or 5) until your drawing prints. Keep in mind that a Flatness setting that produces noticeable flat spots on your laser-printed curves may print beautifully on an imagesetter because of its higher resolution.

- Before printing, check Auto Increase Flatness in Print Options / Options. This activates special code in DRAW's PostScript output that makes the Flatness value increase gradually until the curve prints. Auto Increase Flatness only increases the setting until it gets to 10 higher than the value you specified in the Set Flatness To field, so you can ensure that your curves don't get flattened too much. If the curve hasn't printed by the time the Auto Increase operation gets to 10 beyond the value in the Flatness field, the printer will skip the curve altogether.
- If none of these suggestions helps, try printing to a different printer or imagesetter that might have fewer limitations. Try to find one with Level 2 PostScript, which is far less susceptible to the *limitcheck* problem.

INSIDE INFO

If you're worried about whether your drawing will print on an imagesetter, use a Set Flatness To value of .20 and print to your laser printer. This will force the printer to produce as many line segments per curve as the imagesetter will produce at 1,270 dpi. If the drawing doesn't print, it probably won't on the imagesetter either. If you'll be printing to the imagesetter at 2,450 dpi, use .10, instead.

Bitmaps

Bitmap images, though not particularly complex for a PostScript printer to process, tend to be large files. And since PostScript isn't very efficient at representing bitmap data, the file gets even bigger when it's sent out as part of a PostScript print job. As a result, getting all the data to the printer can take a long time.

Speeding up bitmap printing is mostly a matter of using every trick you can think of to minimize the amount of data DRAW sends out. The biggest time savings comes from converting your bitmap images to the lowest common denominator that will still print the level of color or gray tones you need. For instance, a 5-by-7-inch piece of line art scanned at 300 dpi as a monochrome bitmap will weigh in at about 400K uncompressed. The same image converted to 256-level gray-scale will be eight times as big, about 3MB. The same image in 24-bit color will be another three times larger, or about 9.5MB. Guess which prints the fastest.

Level 1 PostScript printers tend to choke on color bitmap images—yet another reason to convert your color bitmaps to gray-scale before printing whenever you can.

Speaking of big, how big should a bitmap file be to get the best output? For simple monochrome images, you'll get the best results if the pixels in the image map directly to the pixels in your printer. For example, you'd want to scan that 5-by-7-inch piece of line art at 300 dpi if you plan to print it at 5 by 7. That way, each pixel in the image can be represented by one pixel on the 300-dpi laser printer.

If you need to print the same image at 50% of its original size, you'll be better off scanning it at 150 dpi in the first place than shrinking a higher-resolution image down to fit. Conversely, scan at 600 dpi if you'll be printing at 200% of the original size (or at 100% on a 600-dpi printer). Use the following formula to calculate the appropriate scanner dpi setting:

> scan dpi = (printer resolution X reproduced size) / original size

The situation gets more complex for gray and color images. Because of the way gray values get screened to dots in PostScript, the rule of thumb is to scan your original art so that the printed image represents somewhere between 1.4 and 2 times the screen frequency at which you'll be printing.

Returning to the example of a 5-by-7-inch photo, now our mission is to reproduce it as a 2.5-by-3.5-inch halftone image. Our printing company tells us that they want a 120-line screen, so that's how we'll set Screen Frequency when we print later. The formula for calculating the minimum resolution for the scan is as follows:

> scan dpi = (Screen Frequency X reproduced size X 1.4) / original size

Note that Screen Frequency is measured in lpi (lines per inch), and the image itself is measured in inches.

The Screen Frequency is a given (from the printing company), so pick corresponding dimensions of the photo (original and as printed), and run the numbers:

120 lpi X 3.5 X 1.4 / 7 inches = 84 dpi scanning resolution

Remember that all these calculations hinge on using the 1.4 "fudge factor" we started with. This represents the minimum resolution that will produce acceptable results on most PostScript output devices. Feel free to bump that number up for the sake of a little extra quality insurance, but don't go much higher than 2. Higher factors will only produce extra data that the printer or imagesetter can't use and will only have to throw away (which adds to printing time). Scanning at a bit more than the minimum also gives you a safety margin in case you unexpectedly need to enlarge the image a little.

If you need to crop a bitmap image, do it in your scanner software or in PHOTO-PAINT before you import it into DRAW. It will redraw more quickly on your screen and will print faster, as well.

You can also prerotate your bitmaps in PHOTO-PAINT to save printing time. The speed gain isn't quite so dramatic as it is with precropping, but it's still noticeable.

| **Making Slides? The Resolution Rules Are Different** | All the normal line screen and resolution formulas go out the window when you output to color slides. Slides are shot on a film recorder, which may or may not use PostScript files. Unlike printers and imagesetters, which only print black and white and must resort to trickery even to get gray-scale, film recorders are true, continuous-tone color devices. Any pixel on the slide can be any of 16-plus million colors. Because of this, you don't need to worry with the Screen Frequency setting. |

With bitmaps, however, to get the best results you do have to give some thought to the size of the image, just as with other output devices. Start with the resolution your service bureau uses for slide output. Generally, it'll be expressed as "4K" or "4,000-line" or some similar designation. Here are the actual image sizes these figures represent:

Film Recorder Resolution	Image Size in Pixels
2K (2,000-line)	2,048 × 1,366
4K (4,000-line)	4,096 × 2,732
8K (8,000-line)	8,192 × 5,464
16K (16,000-line)	16,384 × 10,928

If you want the absolute best, no-compromise, sacrifice-everything-for-the-sake-of-quality images possible, you'll have to use bitmap images that match the film recorder resolution, pixel for pixel. For instance, for a full-frame bitmap shot at 4K, you'll want to start with a 4,096 × 2,732-pixel scan. But before you decide to go all out, know this: Full-color scans at that size will be approximately 33MB of data. You'll grow old and gray trying to manipulate them, and develop ulcers trying to figure out how to get the files to your service bureau.

Naturally, if the image is less than full frame, you can reduce the size of your scan proportionally. Reducing the image to 50 percent of full-frame means that you can reduce the scan dpi by half, resulting in a file one-fourth as large.

We've found that lower resolutions will do the job just fine; as little as one-quarter of the "pixel-for-pixel" resolution will produce perfectly adequate slides. You can scan a 512-pixel-wide image, pop it into your drawing at half the 11-inch width of the slide page size, output at 4K, and be quite pleased with the results.

Fills

We recently conducted some time trials of various DRAW fills by clocking a PostScript printer as it crunched on the word ART set in Times Bold at 144 points and filled in various ways. Here are the results:

Fill	Relative Print Time
Linear fountain fills at 0°, 45°, and 90°	1.2 to 1.3 times longer than solid black
Radial fountain fill	2.3 times longer than solid black
PostScript fill (Crystal Lattice)	3.1 times longer than solid black
Two-color bitmap pattern fill (small $ signs)	4.7 times longer than solid black
Fractal fill	6.1 times longer than solid black
Color bitmap pattern fill	85.5 times longer than solid black

The sleeper in the group was the fractal fill pattern; we expected it to be an extremely slow performers, but it turned in quite a respectable time. On the other hand, at 1/85 the normal text print speed, we certainly won't choose color bitmap pattern fills for rush jobs…

Note that all of these drawings did print (eventually), shooting down the "Corel Produces Bad PostScript" theory. At the same time, if your service bureau charges for excess print time (and most do, it seems) you can run up some heart-stopping imagesetter bills if you give in to the urge to bitmap-fill everything in sight.

Embedded .EPS Files

When DRAW imports an Adobe Illustrator .EPS file, DRAW converts the graphics into its own proprietary format. The objects contained in the .EPS file won't be any more or less likely to cause printing problems than if you'd drawn the same graphic in DRAW originally.

DRAW 5.0's EPS (Placeable) import feature is another story altogether. When DRAW imports a Placeable EPS, it doesn't convert the graphics at all. It shows you a simplified preview of the image for placement only. Other than that, the only control DRAW has over an .EPS file is the ability to scale and move it about the drawing page.

At print time, DRAW issues a few setup commands, and then inserts the .EPS file, virtually unaltered, into the PostScript output. Since this is the standard way programs are supposed to handle "placed" (as opposed to imported) .EPS files, there's no problem so far. What can happen, though, is that something in the .EPS file may conflict with what DRAW is doing in the rest of the drawing, causing the page to fail. This is easy to diagnose: Remove the placed .EPS file from your drawing (or move it to a nonprinting layer) and print again. If it prints, the .EPS file was the problem.

First, check to see if the .EPS file itself contains another .EPS image. These "nested" .EPS images are notorious for causing printing problems. Multiple .EPS images in one DRAW file should cause few if any problems, however, so if you can reimport the images as separate .EPS files, you can probably solve your printing problem.

Apart from that, there's no direct solution. Try experimenting with the .EPS export options in the source program, assuming that it's available to you, or try moving the graphic into DRAW using another export format, such as .CGM. If that doesn't work and you have a deadline approaching, it may be time to punt. You may be able to save the game by adding a rectangle to your drawing in place of the .EPS file, and printing conventionally. Then print the .EPS from another program that can handle it (possibly a desktop publishing program or high-end word processor), and marry the two images via paste-up or on the printer's stripping table. One hundred percent electronic production may be an attractive notion, but there's no law preventing you from mixing in traditional production methods.

If It Still Won't Print

If you've done everything suggested here and still can't get your drawing through your laser printer or the imagesetter at the service bureau, there are still a few tricks to try.

CorelDRAW ships with a PostScript error handler program. An error handler is software that you send to your printer, where it sits quietly in the background waiting for something to trigger an error condition in the printer. When that happens, the error handler intercepts the printer's error messages, records several other bits of information, and prints it all out in a report that can be helpful in tracking down the source of PostScript problems.

The error handler is named EHANDLER.PS and is installed in the \DRAW\EHANDLER subdirectory of your CorelDRAW directory. That subdirectory also contains several other useful files and an instruction file. To send the EHANDLER.PS to your printer, issue the command

    COPY C:\COREL50\DRAW\EHANDLER\EHANDLER.PS *port*

substituting the correct path and supplying the port (LPT1, for example) for your computer.

Print your problem file again. This time, when the file gets to the point where the error occurs, EHANDLER will print a simple report that tells you the type of error that occurred, the specific PostScript command that provoked the error, and the values on the PostScript stack, which is a kind of holding area for parameters.

If you know a little about PostScript, these few bits of information can sometimes point you in the direction of a solution. And if you don't know PostScript from the Post Office, the error report will be helpful to have in front of you when you report the problem to Corel Technical Support.

A whole book chapter just to learn how to print?? Yes—CorelDRAW's printing engine is arguably the most involved, feature-laden, complex, and resource-hungry aspect of the entire program. And it's also the most powerful. You needn't think back more than a few years in the electronic graphics business to recall a time when the features discussed here were strictly the province of multimillion-dollar proprietary graphics workstations that ran only on mainframe computers. Today DRAW's print engine puts that power on your desktop computer.

Next up: DRAW's powerful but oh-so-scary system for managing colors.

Working with Color

CHAPTER TWENTY-SIX

CHAPTER 26

The thing about color publishing? You can't do it halfway. To engage in it at all requires that you learn more about it than you ever wanted to know.

Since the color revolution came to the PC in early 1992, a truckload of new technical terms and requirements has been dumped on our desktops. As soon as we seized the power of 16 million colors, on screen and on paper, the repercussions began to resound through the rest of the industry—in unsuspecting service bureaus, color prepress houses, print shops, and most of all (or is that worst of all?), for readers. The industry has never been the same, for better or for worse.

Some of the material in this chapter deals with topics you've already encountered if you read Chapter 8, "Fill 'er Up," in which you learned how to use DRAW's fill options, and in Chapter 25, "Print, Darn You!" What we'll explore here is the beautiful, mysterious, and often scary world of color publishing. Our goal, however—as it has been throughout the book—is to provide a nuts-and-bolts overview for those who must develop a good overall understanding. Ambitious users will want to make a second stop on the Corel Freeway at Chapter 28, "Preparing for Press."

The Theory of Color

What is color? That may seem an unnecessary question to many people, but successful use of color—be it for traditional four-color printing or for output to a slide recorder as transparencies—requires some consideration of color theory and how it influences the use of your tools. In this case, of course, the tool is CorelDRAW.

Color is powerful because it acts on all of our senses. Color touches our emotions, it arouses, it demands interpretation. In the colder, physical world, however, the key to all discussion of color is how our eyes perceive it.

In the absence of light, no color perception is possible; everything is black. The simplest example of this is when you walk through the living room at night and smack your shins on the coffee table. But once there is light present, the eye can perceive color—as *reflected and/or transmitted light*. Figure 26.1 shows an example of each of these three possibilities.

26.1

Light strikes an object; the object absorbs part of the spectrum and reflects and/or transmits the rest.

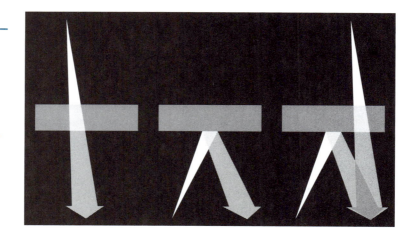

AUTHOR'S NOTE

We know that it's a dicey proposition to report on issues of color in a book printed in black and white. Therefore, you'll find most of the illustrations for this chapter contained on the Companion CD in the PICTURES directory. They are named according to their figure numbers here—except for one small difference. We thought this was going to be Chapter 27 when we created the images, so they're all called 27-01.CDR, 27-02.CDR, etc. Sorry about that...

Colors behave differently depending on whether they are produced by transmitted light or reflected light. Transmitted light is light coming through *from behind* an object; its color is determined by how much and what kind of light is allowed to pass through the object. Reflected light is that which bounces off the *front* of an object; its color depends on how much and what kind of light is reflected, and what is absorbed by the surface.

Why is this transmit/reflect business important? Because printed matter and computer monitors represent light in these two very different ways. Video displays *transmit* light, and our eyes see the images as they appear emanating from the screen. The paper (or other surface) on which material is printed *reflects* light. To complicate matters further, the *ink* used to print in process color (CMYK) is transparent, and thus *transmits* light; but spot color inks are generally opaque, and thus *reflect* light.

The difference between transmitted and reflected light can be dramatic—ask anyone who chose a color because it looked good on screen, only to be surprised (and usually disappointed) by the printed result.

Components of Light

Light, itself, is composed of a spectrum of colors, which you've seen for yourself in rainbows. When all the colors of the spectrum are present in equal quantity, your eye perceives the color as white. This is not immediately intuitive, and many people would guess just the opposite (that when all the colors are present, you see black). An object is perceived as being a certain color because of the way it reflects and/or transmits some of the visible spectrum and absorbs the rest. When any portion of that spectrum is missing, your eye perceives the remaining portions of the spectrum as a specific color.

An object appears black, not because it is the result of all colors combined, but because that object (be it black paper or black ink on paper) is actually absorbing all or most of the light spectrum, and reflecting very little back to your eye. There is an easy proof of this absence-of-light-equals-black theory—just reach up there and turn off the light switch (and watch out for that coffee table).

Additive Primary Colors

In terms of color theory, white light is composed of three primary bands of the visible spectrum (all other perceived colors being combinations of these three): red, green, and blue, which are referred to as *additive primary colors*. They are so named because, when added together, these three colors of light produce the perception of white light (again, contrary to what your intuition might lead you to believe). Figure 26.2 shows a stylized version of the traditional prismatic separation of white light into these three bands of primary colors.

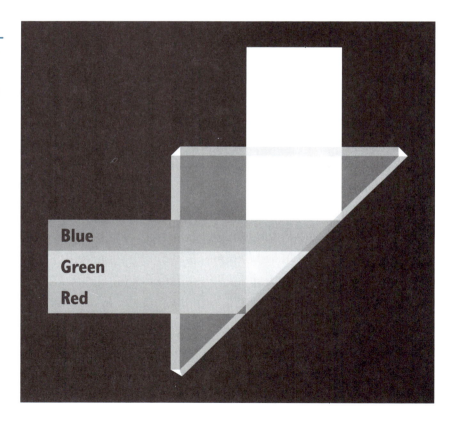

26.2

White light is composed of three primary colors: red, green, and blue.

The human eye is sensitive to these three primary colors, interpreting other colors from these three, according to the amount of each—much the way a computer monitor or television screen recreates a color image.

In fact, the initials of these three colors, RGB, are used as the name of one of the color models—namely, the one used by computer displays. (If you took a magnifying glass to a white area of your color monitor, you would see small dots or thin lines of red, green, and blue.)

A piece of white paper appears white because it reflects these three component colors. On the other hand, a piece of black velvet absorbs nearly all the visible spectrum, reflecting back little or none of the light, thus appearing black. A piece of clear glass absorbs hardly any of the three components, and so white light passing through appears white to your eye. Figure 26.3 shows the effect of white, black, and transparent objects on white light.

26.3

White light components—red, green, and blue—as they are reflected by white, absorbed by black, and transmitted by transparent objects

It is important (well, somewhat important… OK, so it's trivial) to note that there is really no such thing as a purely reflective object. If there were, you wouldn't be able to see it. The same goes for purely transparent objects; they would be invisible. Purely black objects don't exist, either. Even in deep space, small particles of matter reflect light (we know, we've been there…).

Subtractive Primary Colors

The primary colors with which you are probably more familiar are cyan, magenta, and yellow, the *subtractive primary colors.* They are so named because they are blends of two, not three, of the additive primary colors; one color has been subtracted. For example, the color magenta (red plus blue) is the result of the additive primary color green being subtracted from white light.

Color Models

Enough already with the addition and subtraction. The important point is that there is more than one way to describe colors, just as there is more than one way to perceive colors (transmitted or reflected). Different descriptions of color are appropriate to various media, based on how each medium creates color. This has brought the advent of *color models,* which are quantifiable and measurable formulas for depicting hues, tints, and shades. These color models have their own associated terminology, and, just as meanings often get lost in the translations of spoken languages, color model terminology can be confusing. Nonetheless, these models are essential for our sanity; without them, we'd have no hope of communicating our color needs.

When working with color in DRAW, you have three choices of color models. There are other choices for applying color in the list box that shows the color models, but they are not *models*, per se. They're more like swatch books—you pick a color and if you don't like it, you pick another. Color *models*, on the other hand, are specifically designed to provide you with the components to mix and match your own custom colors:

- HSB: Hue/Saturation/Brightness
- RGB: Red/Green/Blue
- CMYK: Cyan/Magenta/Yellow/Black

HSB: Hue/Saturation/Brightness

The Hue/Saturation/Brightness (HSB) model is probably the least used, least useful, and least understood of the color models. Ironically enough, however, it most closely represents how we humans perceive color. Figure 26.4 shows all of the dynamics of the HSB model; we'll cover them one by one in the paragraphs that follow.

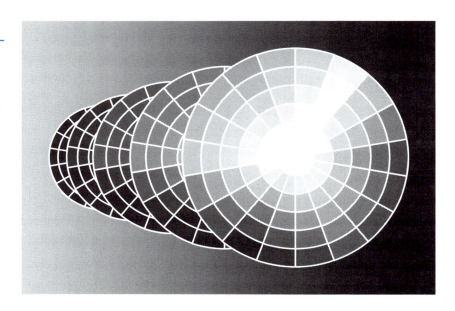

26.4

Each part of these HSB wheels represents a 20% difference from any adjacent part, either in hue or saturation. Each wheel has a 20% difference in brightness from the wheel below or above it.

Hue refers to the type of color being described, and it runs the gamut of red, orange, yellow, green, cyan, blue, violet, magenta, and then back to red. Simply put, think of Hue as the color itself, as you progress around the wheel. In CorelDRAW, each number that you select for Hue represents a different color. Figure 26.5 shows this concept of "hue on a wheel."

Think of Saturation as intensity, or how much there is of the color. A Saturation value of 100 represents a solid color, and a value of 5 represents a 5% tint of that color. The lower the value of Saturation, the more white has been added. Figure 26.6 shows the spectrum of Saturation values as they move toward the center of the wheel.

Brightness is determined by either the dimming of light (it gets darker), or simply the addition of black. The lower the Brightness number, the

26.5

Hue is color around the circle, represented here by the wedges of color.

closer to black the color appears. Each of the HSB wheels shown in Figure 26.4 represents a different Brightness level.

RGB: Red/Green/Blue

The Red/Green/Blue (RGB) color model describes the color spectrum as it is rendered by your video monitor. Red, green, and blue are the colors transmitted by the phosphors of your display. Color aficionados often refer to a three-dimensional cube to describe the dynamics of the RGB model. Virtually any color can be described by its Red/Green/Blue components—mixing red and green, for instance, produces yellow.

Figure 26.7 shows how the RGB model relates to the CMYK model (discussed next), which is used in commercial printing. As mentioned earlier, white is produced when the Red, Green, and Blue components are all set at 100%; black comes from RGB all set at 0%; and grays

26.6

Saturation is the quantity of the specific hue that is used, represented by the position between the circle's edge and its center.

26.7

The traditional "color cube" used to show the relationship between the Red/Green/Blue model and the Cyan/Magenta/Yellow model

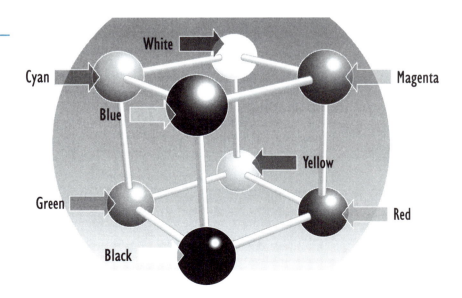

result from setting the three RGB values at equal percentages somewhere in between 0 and 100 (low numbers for dark grays, high numbers for light grays).

You can see this for yourself just by opening the Uniform Fill dialog, choosing the RGB Color Model from the Show drop-down list, and dialing up different percentages for Red, Green, and Blue. By varying these percentages, you can describe practically any color. Figure 26.8 shows the color relationships with somewhat more flair; you can find this illustration in color in the Color Gallery, Illustration 12.

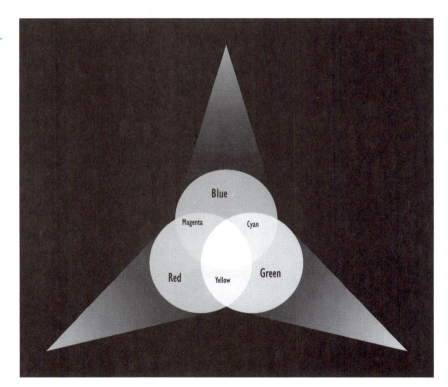

26.8

All three additive primary colors combine to form white; red and green form yellow; green and blue form cyan; and blue and red form magenta.

CMYK: Cyan/Magenta/Yellow/Black

CMYK is the standard color model used by commercial printers, representing the four colors of ink used to describe the color spectrum. Most DRAW users who produce four-color work (process color) use this model—it pays to speak the same language as your print shop. (By the way, the *K* is used to represent Black because *B* could also stand for Blue.)

Think of Cyan, Magenta, and Yellow as the flip sides of Red, Green, and Blue. For instance, mixing red and green produces yellow; mixing yellow and cyan produces green. Figure 26.9 shows the four CMYK colors and the colors that result from their combinations.

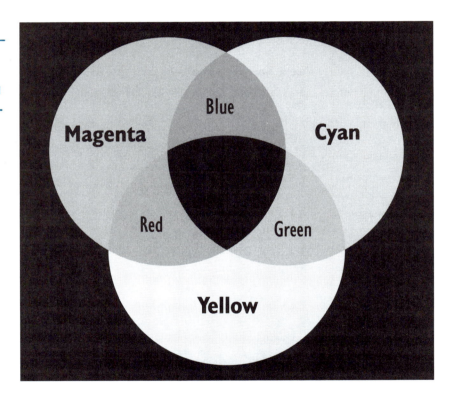

26.9

Cyan, yellow, and magenta meet to form red, green, and blue, as well as virtually every other color imaginable.

The important distinction between the CMYK and RGB models gets a bit technical, but it all has to do with reflected and transmitted light. The CMYK model defines the result of white light reflecting from an object that contains the specific color. A yellow object absorbs blue light only, and appears to your eye as yellow because both green and red light are reflected. As you recall from our discussion of the RGB color model, green and red light combine to form yellow.

You don't need to understand the nuances of these relationships, but you must remember this: Your perception of color on the screen (transmitted light) is totally different from your perception of color on printed material (reflected light). Colors that you assign to objects in DRAW will usually appear darker once they are printed, because reflected light is not as brilliant as transmitted light. Illustration 13 in the Color Gallery shows an example of colors in a DRAW screen that look very different from the same colors when printed.

The moral of this story? If you need to really nail a color for use in a drawing, don't trust what you see on your screen. (See the sidebar later in the chapter, "How Your Monitor Lies to You.") Always work with a color swatch book—either the TruMatch Colorfinder, which shows over 2,000 colors generated from the CMYK model, or the PANTONE Color Formula Guide, which offers thousands of spot colors (discussed next).

As with RGB, the CMYK model can be represented as a cube, as shown in Figure 26.10. Though this cube has only a few gradations of color, and the actual color model has an infinite variety, in DRAW you are limited to 100 gradations between any two or three primary colors.

To conclude this part of the discussion, we will resist the technical jargon about how subtractive colors absorb components of the visible spectrum, and instead refer you to Figure 26.11, a depiction of white light traveling through transparent objects. On the left, the cyan-colored

26.10

The CMYK cube of colors. The view on the right shows the back sides and bottom of the cube on the left.

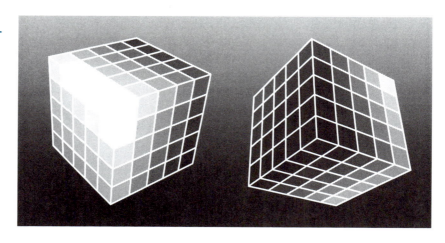

26.11

Transparent objects absorb, or filter out, components of the visible spectrum from the light passing through.

glass absorbs all of the red component of white light, allowing only blue and green to pass through. In the middle, it's the yellow glass absorbing all of the blue component; and on the right, the magenta glass absorbs the green.

In each case in Figure 26.11, the color on the opposite side of the spectrum, known as the *complementary color,* is absorbed. Refer back to Figure 26.7 and you'll see that red and cyan are on opposite sides of the cube, and if you check Figure 26.8, you'll see that blue and green light combine to form cyan. Sure enough, the left image of Figure 26.11 bears this out: Red is absorbed by cyan, and blue and green are transmitted.

Other Color Options

If you don't feel up to creating your own custom colors with the aforementioned models, you can choose prebuilt colors from CorelDRAW's built-in "swatch-book" options:

- Grayscale
- Uniform Colors
- FOCOLTONE Colors

- PANTONE Spot Colors
- PANTONE Process Colors
- TruMatch Colors

Spot Color

No, Spot Color is not the hue of your dog, but rather a way of designating colors that is totally different from the models discussed so far. When you print in four colors, everything is separated out into its CMYK components, and you deliver four pieces of film to your printer. Spot colors, on the other hand, describe specific ink colors that do not get separated into four components. If your work contains only one or two colors (in addition to black), you can define these colors as spot colors. Each spot color gets its own piece of film, and your printer is directed to use a specific ink color, perhaps one from the PANTONE Matching System, which is the most widely used color-matching system in the world.

Why use spot color instead of process color? Here are a few reasons:

- You may not have the budget for process color printing, which typically requires a four-color press and the expense of creating and printing from four negatives and plates. By using one or two spot colors, in addition to or instead of black, you can substantially reduce the cost of a project yet still add color to your work.

- Spot color can achieve colors that cannot be produced with process colors. If you compare a swatch book showing PANTONE colors and one showing TruMatch colors (the latter showing colors created with CMYK combinations), you'll note that there are many colors in the PANTONE book that do not have equivalents in the TruMatch book.

- Spot color allows you to use PANTONE inks that are, at least in part, fluorescent. (These can also be used in addition to process color, to make colors "pop out.")

- Spot color can be used to place actual white ink on colored paper, behind other images such as color photographs. This effect can make a big difference in the clarity of the photograph.

- Spot color can be used for application of matte and/or gloss varnish, for adding special effects.

The best way to define spot colors is to use the PANTONE color model, accepted as a worldwide standard by commercial printers. PANTONE inks are pure and unmixed, yielding consistent results. You can define PANTONE colors in DRAW either by name or by sight. (However, you'd better read the upcoming sidebar, "How Your Monitor Lies to You," before doing the latter.) Figure 26.12 shows the Uniform Fill dialog displaying its library of PANTONE colors.

26.12

You can choose PANTONE colors by sight or by name.

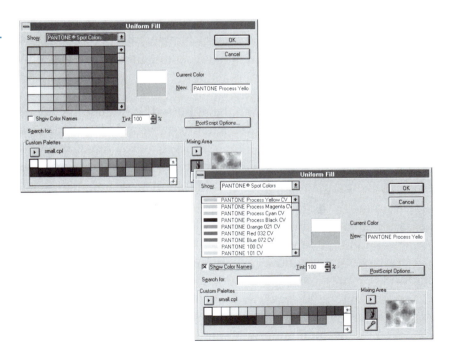

INSIDE INFO

Color purists might be interested to note that, in reality, most commercial printers do mix their own PANTONE inks according to a recipe provided by PANTONE. Though they are not mixed in the fashion of process colors directly on the paper, the printer may very well come up with a mix that does not match the intended color, either by not strictly following the recipe or by following a recipe that is out of date.

When you work with spot colors, you don't have the same flexibility as when you are printing with process colors; however, you can still get substantial diversity by varying the *tint* of a color. The two dialogs in Figure 26.12 both offer a Tint % field, in which you can vary the intensity of the color without introducing any new colors. There is nothing stopping you from introducing a second or a third spot color into your work—but you'll pay for it.

How Your Monitor Lies to You

Your printer speaks the language of CMYK; your monitor speaks RGB. Getting them to communicate could be more hilarious than the game of Telephone you used to play as a child. Except for one thing: This comedy of errors could cost you a few thousand dollars.

Set aside for the moment the fact that RGB colors don't map exactly to CMYK colors. That's a minor matter. Far more important is the issue of transmitted versus reflected light, discussed in "The Theory of Color" earlier in this chapter. Your video monitor *transmits* light directly from its phosphors, but the inks used by your printer *reflect* light. The upshot: Color on your screen can look radically different from the color in your project's final output. Trusting your monitor could be a huge and expensive mistake.

The solution is to purchase a color swatch book from either PANTONE or TruMatch. Yes, they cost a lot (between $50 and $100), but if you work with color, they are as critical to the desktop publishing process as your RAM chips and your hard drive. With these books, you can choose exactly the right color, ask DRAW for it by its precise name, and be assured of the end result—regardless of what DRAW shows you on screen.

Illustration 13 in the Color Gallery is a simulation of the difference between on-screen color and printed color. (To show you the actual effect, we would have had to supply a video monitor with every book...maybe next time.) You can see in the illustration how the inaccuracy ranges from subtle to ridiculous. Perhaps an even better way to see this is to compare one of the Color Gallery illustrations with what you see on screen when you load the corresponding file from the GALLERY directory of the Companion CD. For instance, open HUNTRESS.CDR or DIVER.CDR, and compare the on-screen colors with those in the Color Gallery.

If you are producing work for on-screen presentations, of course you can confidently choose colors by sight; in DRAW, what you see is what you'll get in your slide show. But for color work going out to a printing press, remember: Monitors lie.

INSIDE INFO

If you ever think you need to produce a drawing with four spot colors (or three spot colors and black), you might want to return to square one. If you're going to be producing four sheets of film anyway, it might be better to use process color and have access to the entire CMYK spectrum.

Color Trapping

Producing professional-quality color illustrations requires more skill and knowledge than for black-and-white printing. And even a program as sophisticated and powerful as CorelDRAW can't do it all for you. Just as you need to move the mouse on a pad or the stylus on a tablet to do your design work, you need to know about color from the printer's point of view.

Printers do their best to make sure that a sheet of paper running through a high-speed press will come out with all four color layers accurately placed on top of one another. (The degree of accuracy in this process is called *registration*, and the guides used by printers to keep the printing plates and the paper aligned are *registration marks*.) However, the images on the plates don't always align perfectly; in fact, they rarely do—and if the error is significant, there may be visible gaps between adjoining colors. In these gaps, the paper color shows through.

As a desktop designer, it's your responsibility to minimize such errors. You do this by applying *trapping* (you trap the registration errors that might occur during the printing process). Trapping is the process of overlapping, very slightly, two adjacent colors. This overlap insures against the white gaps that can appear from registration errors.

INSIDE INFO

 Color trapping is not required when printing to a color laser printer, slide processor, or other single-pass output device. Trapping is only required for printing on a printing press, when distinct pieces of film and/or printing plates are used to represent the colors used.

You don't always need to trap adjacent colors. If they share a component process color, the adjacent colors don't require any trap. For an illustration of this concept, consult Figure 26.13. The simple figure at the top is composed of red, green, and blue. When separated for color printing, cyan, magenta, and yellow are represented; the three pieces of film you send to your print shop will look like the images in Figure 26.13.

The green circle and the blue quadrangle both contain the color cyan. And you'll notice that the first piece of film, representing cyan, covers the entire area. Therefore, there is no way the paper can show through the area between the green and the blue, and you don't need to apply any trap to that area. Likewise, the blue and red quadrangles each contain magenta, and they don't need to be trapped, either.

26.13

The picture at the top need not be trapped, because each pair of adjacent elements (ones that share a common side) includes a shared process color.

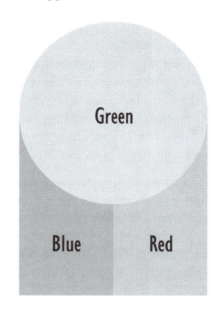

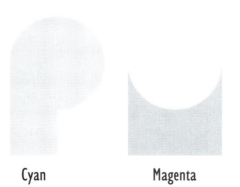

Color Trapping **677**

There is only one potential trouble spot, and that is the junction of all three colors. Conceivably, a speck of white could peek through there, but it would not be significant enough to consider.

The image shown in Figure 26.14 *does* need to be trapped, however, in two different places. The orange ball and the cyan quadrangle share no

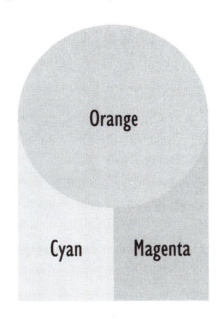

26.14

This object needs trapping between the orange and cyan, and between the cyan and magenta, because neither of the edges is covered by a shared component color.

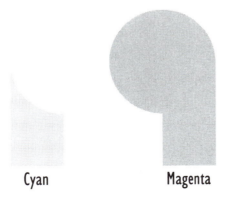

Cyan　　　　　Magenta　　　　　Yellow

CMYK color between them; the cyan and magenta quadrangles, too, are distinct. (The orange and magenta areas share magenta, and therefore need no trap.)

How to Apply Trapping

In its simplest form, trapping is an outline. You apply an outline to one of the adjacent objects, so that it fills the gap that might occur during printing. That's the simple part. But deciding which color to use, and which object to add it to, are not so simple.

Bear in mind these two concepts involved in trapping:

- **Spreads** are used to trap a lighter-colored foreground object on a dark background; the lighter color is spread outward to overlap the darker background color.

- **Chokes** are used to trap a darker-colored foreground object on a light background; the lighter background color is constricted (choked) inward to overlap the darker foreground color.

If you don't feel like learning these new terms, that's okay. Just remember this: As a general rule, you apply the trap to the lighter color.

Though DRAW provides an Auto-Trapping feature in its network of printing dialogs, it is important to know how trap is created, since you will occasionally need to apply it manually. Figure 26.15 shows three examples of trapping. We have taken some liberties with these examples, because trapping doesn't show on screen, only on the film that is made.

26.15

Three ways to trap color

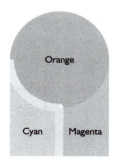  

So to illustrate the point in this figure, we have set the outlines representing the traps much thicker than needed.

The leftmost example shows the trapping that is necessary: an outline to the lighter color (cyan) at the cyan/orange and cyan/magenta boundary. (The outline is shown as a thick, light-gray outline for illustration purposes; the actual outline would be the same color as the object, and thus not visible.) Unfortunately, there is no way to clip the end of the line at the outer edge of the object, so the outline hangs over the edge.

In the middle object, the orange circle has an outline applied to trap both the cyan and magenta, but now the orange circle is wider than the other objects, and it hangs over the edge.

The rightmost object solves the overhang problem by applying outlines to all objects. Now the overall image is distorted somewhat, but the width is the same all around.

Normally, you would use much thinner lines than the ones shown here—no more than half a point—so the disparity in object dimensions wouldn't be nearly as noticeable. You can usually get away with choosing the first (and easiest) method in Figure 26.15.

After you have added the outline to provide the trap, you must assign the appropriate color to it, using the Outline Color dialog. Then you choose Overprint Outline from the Object menu, telling DRAW to *overprint* the object. DRAW will lay down both colors completely, instead of *knocking out* one color where it overlays another. (Remember, to get to the Object menu, use the secondary mouse button.)

AUTHOR'S NOTE

Not to take all the wind out of the sail here, but if you're at all uncomfortable with applying trap, either automatically or manually, then don't do it. Good print and prepress shops are well equipped to apply trap to your work—they've been doing it for years. Don't be embarrassed to ask for help with trapping; thousands of illustrators and publishers do so regularly.

The Aesthetics of Color

You should be just as careful when you're applying color in your DRAW work as when you're decorating your living room or kitchen. OK, bad example. How about your wardrobe? Your car? Surely there must be some analogy that works here…

One of the fundamental principles of creating pleasing arrangements of color is *contrast—the contrast between dark and light colors, the contrast between complementary colors, or both.*

Color with Text

Remember your complementary colors when mixing text with a background. You need contrast, and complementary colors provide it. But if the colors are highly saturated, the contrast can be too great and may look psychedelic. In Figure 26.16, yellow text works well against the dark-blue background, providing good contrast (the example on the left), but not nearly so well against a red background (on the right). The black-and-white rendition here doesn't illustrate the point as well as the original file, and you can open it and see for yourself—it's file 26-16.CDR in the PICTURES directory on the Companion CD. On the other hand, printing your color files to a black-and-white version such as this one is often a good test of contrast, even though the specific colors don't show.

It will help you decide on the colors you need if you view your illustration under the conditions you expect others will encounter. Try reading a color-laser printout of your project under a weak lamp at night. If you're creating something large, make a smaller version of it and hold it at arm's length, or view it from across the room.

Color for Realism

Ever notice how the mountains in the distance seem to be bleached of their color? You know there's color there—if you were standing on the mountain, you wouldn't see just grays and muted purples. You'd see green trees and yellow wild mustard and straw-colored dried grass and brown dirt.

26.16

For text readability, choose your background color on the basis of contrast.

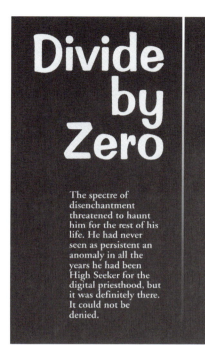

What causes that? Remember our discussion about how red, green, and blue light combine to form white light. When you're seeing an object from a distance, the light reflecting off the object is re-combining to white light (because the eye can't distinguish the individual objects) and getting further filtered by the air and the particles in the air. As a result, things that are farther away appear to have less color, or seem gray.

You can achieve this same effect for objects that are supposed to be in the distance, by adding just a touch of the complementary color and backing off the original color ever so slightly. The overall result is a grayish form of the original color. To see this in action, open DISTANCE.CDR from the PICTURES directory.

In the next chapter, we put away the crayons and pick up the charcoal…

CHAPTER 27

Turning Gray with Dignity

TWENTY-SEVEN

CHAPTER 27

If you think that working in color is complicated and working in black and white is simple, you're only half-right. Color *is* complicated. But so, too, is black and white, and everything in between—especially the in-between part, otherwise known as grays.

True, to understand grays you don't need to concern yourself with color trapping, PMS numbers, complementary colors, or CMYK values, but you must know your dots and lines, to which an entire special lingo is devoted. And if that weren't enough, to really master black-and-white printing, you need a refresher course in algebra and geometry.

Most of this chapter is light on the math, qualitative in its approach, and heavy on simple illustrations. It finishes, however, with a bit of number crunching, for those who need to know the intricacies of gray-scale printing.

Dots All, Folks

You probably already know about print resolution—that's the easy part. The *resolution* of your output device is a measure of how many dots it can squeeze into a small space. Standard laser printers can print 300 × 300 of them in a square inch, newer printers get 600 × 600 into that same inch, and the high-resolution imagesetters pack in 1,200 dots or more.

You don't need to know rocket science to figure out that in order to fit 1,200 dots across one inch, the dots must be considerably smaller than the ones that fit 300 to an inch. So if your dot is smaller, your blacks are blacker and your curves are curvier. Indeed, the smaller the dot, the finer the resolution, and the better the results of your design efforts. Figure 27.1 shows the bottom part of a lowercase italic *t,* printed at 300 dots per inch (dpi) and 1,200 dpi. At this magnification, the difference is obvious.

27.1

This blow-up of part of an italic serif *t* shows how dots at 1,200 dpi (on the right) turn corners better than dots at 300 dpi.

300 dots per inch   1200 dots per inch

When your task is simply to fill a space with black dots, the formula is simple: Cram in as many as you possibly can. But when you introduce the element of gray dots, the landscape changes significantly—primarily because *there is no such thing as a gray dot* in black-and-white printing. If you really do want a gray dot, then choose PANTONE Warm Gray 7, or perhaps Cool Gray 3. Ah, but now you're working with a second color, and that's cheating.

What's important to understand in all of this is how gray is created from black ink on a printing press. This is done by the not-so-simple process of printing small black dots in a regular pattern; the eye blends them into gray (if you don't look too closely). The array of dots is called a screen. This screen has nothing whatever to do with a video screen; in fact, it has more in common with a window screen. Usually, the dots are arranged in straight rows, and the fineness of the screen is indicated as the number of rows (or lines) of dots per inch. This may be stated, for example, as "85 lines per inch" or simply "an 85-line screen."

The number of lines per inch (lpi) only indicates the fineness of the screen, however, not how dark or light it appears. That is determined by the size of the dots. On a "10% screen," ten percent of the paper area is covered by ink, giving the appearance of a light gray. An "80% screen," on the other hand, is nearly black. Figure 27.2 is a simple illustration of this concept: The screens with smaller dots give the appearance of light gray, and the patterns with larger, overlapping dots produce the illusion of dark gray.

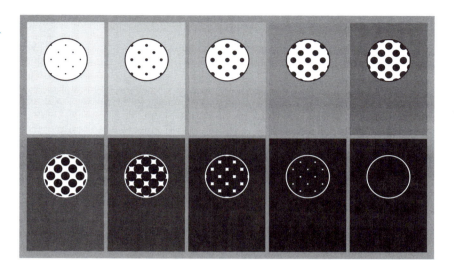

27.2

An enlarged view of the gray illusion. Smaller dots and more white space equal light gray; larger dots and less white space equal dark gray.

Now let's return to your laser printer: Another factor in the concept of grays is that the laser printer or imagesetter can produce dots of only one size. It cannot directly reproduce the various dot sizes used to create various shades of gray on a printing press. What the laser printer can (and does) do is create each dot of a screen as a group of the printer's own smaller dots. To avoid confusing these two types of dots, we will give them different names: screen dots (the ones illustrated in Figure 27.2) and printer dots (the much smaller dots used by the laser printer to create both text and graphics).

Your printer creates screens by grouping its tiny printer dots to form the larger dots of the screen pattern. The smaller the dot your printer can create (that is, the higher its resolution), the more variety is possible in the pattern. You might think, then, that your goal would be to use as high a line screen as possible. Indeed, a higher frequency can produce finer grays and sharper images; unfortunately, it can also produce mud. You can only use a higher line screen if the printer dots are small enough; if you create a screen with too many lines per inch, you lose the ability to render gray.

When you print a scanned photograph containing 256 shades of gray, if the output device is of sufficiently high resolution, it produces 256 distinctly different screen patterns. Each dot pattern is slightly different, with dots and white space rearranged to produce varying illusions of gray. In order to render each shade of gray effectively, the output device needs to have sufficient elbow room—in other words, higher resolution.

This brings up an issue often misunderstood by many novice and not-so-novice users: Pushing a printer or a scanner to its maximum resolution won't by itself get you better gray tones. Higher resolution is of benefit only if you take advantage of it by using an effective arrangement of screen dots. It's not your job to tell the printer exactly how to create the matrix—the printer knows how to do that. It *is* your job, however, to ensure that the printer does *its* job, by knowing the resolution of your output device and checking the setting for line screen (discussed later in the chapter).

Getting Gray from the Grid

Standard laser printers produce larger dots than higher-resolution devices do. This does not mean that standard laser printers cannot produce gray tones, but there is a trade-off: You can get either higher resolution, or more gray tones, but not both. The smallest dot at 300 dpi is not small enough to give you the best of both worlds, leaving you with two choices. You can increase the line screen (which will improve detail but limit the number of gray tones rendered), or you can settle for a coarser line screen (which will sacrifice detail but increase the range of grays).

To quantify this, in order to get decent gray tones at 300 dpi, you will have to print with a line screen of about 60, as opposed to the 120- to 133-line screen supported by higher-resolution devices. If you tell DRAW to print to your 300-dpi laser printer with a very high line screen, you'll force the printer to use a smaller screen dot, thus providing fewer gray levels. The output samples later in the chapter illustrate this.

Figure 27.3 is the first in a series of various screen dot sizes. This 2 × 2 matrix provides just three gradations of gray (not counting solid black and solid white). With this pattern, you can produce 25%, 50%, and 75% gray images—that's all. Other patterns are possible, such as two vertical dots or a single dot on the lower-left, but then you are only changing the angle of the matrix, not the actual percentages of black and white. With only four printer dots per screen dot, there is very little opportunity for gray tones.

Figure 27.4 shows the gray tones that can be achieved with a screen dot composed of a 3 × 3 matrix of printer dots. Figure 27.5 shows the grays possible with a 4 × 4 matrix; and Figure 27.6 shows the possibilities of a 5 × 5 matrix. You can achieve these tonal qualities at any resolution. You can get 24 shades of gray even from a 300-dpi laser printer, but that 5 × 5 matrix would require a low line-screen number (60 lines to an inch, to be precise).

27.3

A 2 × 2 matrix of printer dots provides just three levels of gray.

27.4

A 3 × 3 matrix of printer dots gives 8 gradations of gray: 11%, 22%, 33%, 44%, 56%, 67%, 78%, and 89%, plus solid black.

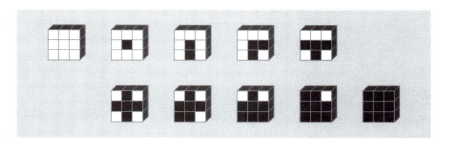

27.5

A 4 × 4 matrix of printer dots gives 15 gradations of gray, from 6.67% through 93.33% in 6.67% increments, plus solid black and solid white.

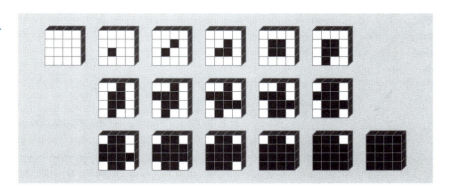

27.6

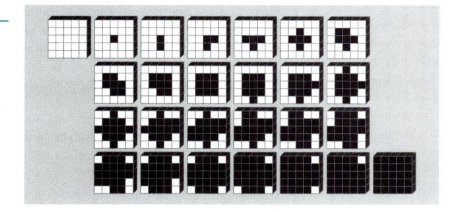

A 5 × 5 matrix of printer dots gives 24 gradations of gray, from 4% through 96% in 4% increments, plus solid black and solid white.

Think of it this way: You have a large sheet of graph paper, with squares that are 1/4 inch apart. Congratulations—you are the proud owner of a 4-dpi output device (4 squares to each inch). Your mission is to create the appearance of 50% gray, using only a felt pen. You are not allowed to write in between the squares; your only option is to fill in every other square in a checkerboard pattern, as shown in Figure 27.7. In this figure, the matrix is a group of 4 squares, with 2 dots on and 2 dots off.

27.7

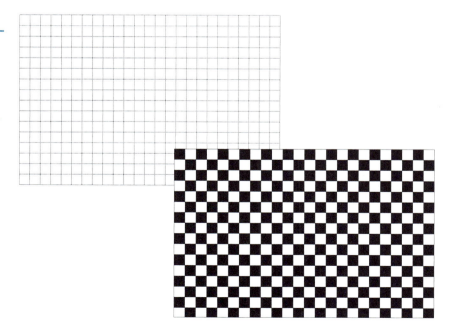

With squares of 1/4 inch and a 2-line-per-inch screen, this graph paper can only produce coarse gray tones.

Figure 27.8 shows the same checkerboard pattern, but this time the squares on the graph paper are 1/8 inch apart. Ah, 8 dpi—you're moving up in the world. With the smaller matrix, this rendition of 50% gray looks more like gray (although, granted, these are very coarse resolutions). Compare a region of Figure 27.8 that is the same size as a matrix in Figure 27.7 (4 squares, 2 on and 2 off), and you'll see that there are many more dots in that area. The higher the resolution, the higher the frequency possible in the matrix—resulting in more gray tones.

27.8

Better with a 1/8-inch matrix

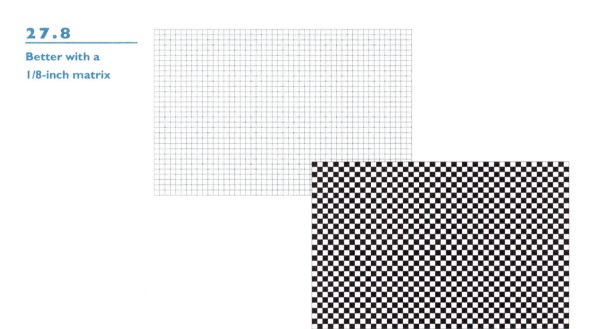

Figure 27.9, with its 16-dpi resolution, can produce a denser pattern. The graph paper gives you an idea of how the resolution affects your matrix, which in turn plays a vital role in the representation of gray.

We've already fudged a little on our promise to keep the first part of this discussion qualitative and not too scientific (it gets much worse, you'll see). Unless you really need to know the inner workings of gray-scale

27.9
Better still with a 1/16-inch matrix

theory, you'll get by if you just remember this: The illusion of gray is produced by the *pattern* between black dots and white space. If the pattern is too dense, the illusion of gray is lost. At lower resolutions, therefore, you need to use *fewer* dots, not more.

Figures 25.10, 25.11, and 25.12 illustrate the relationship between dots per inch (the size of the dot), and lines per inch (the frequency of the matrix). We use simple rectangles and text to show when clarity and readability are at their best and their worst.

As Figure 27.10 shows, 300-dpi output cannot withstand much beyond a 60-line screen. If you have a new toner cartridge with even distribution, you can use denser patterns for boxes that don't have any text inside, provided that your laser printer output is intended to be the final product. If you take your laser originals to a photocopy center and ask them to reproduce your 85-line screen output, you'll get mud. Best to play it safe and stay at 60 lines for 300-dpi output.

27.10

300 dots per inch

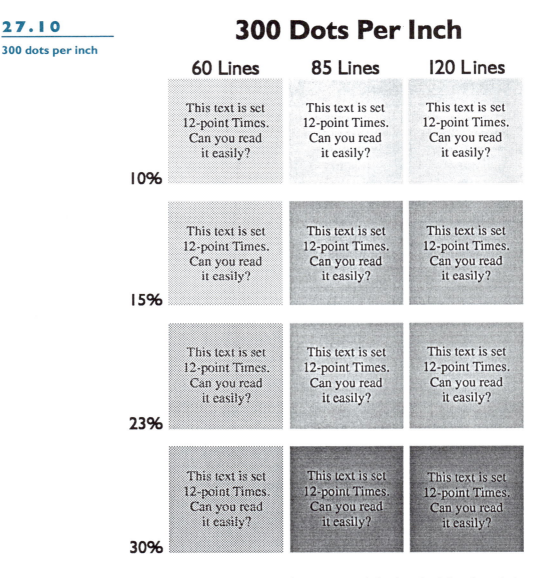

According to Figure 27.11, 85 lines per inch looks ideal for 600-dpi output, as from an HP LaserJet 4M. And Figure 27.12 shows how the 1,200-dpi output can support an even higher density of lines. When ordering film at your service bureau, you can ask for 133-line screens, even 150 in some cases, if your print shop can handle such fine screens.

27.11
600 dots per inch

600 Dots Per Inch

	60 Lines	85 Lines	120 Lines
10%	This text is set 12-point Times. Can you read it easily?	This text is set 12-point Times. Can you read it easily?	This text is set 12-point Times. Can you read it easily?
15%	This text is set 12-point Times. Can you read it easily?	This text is set 12-point Times. Can you read it easily?	This text is set 12-point Times. Can you read it easily?
23%	This text is set 12-point Times. Can you read it easily?	This text is set 12-point Times. Can you read it easily?	This text is set 12-point Times. Can you read it easily?
30%	This text is set 12-point Times. Can you read it easily?	This text is set 12-point Times. Can you read it easily?	This text is set 12-point Times. Can you read it easily?

Setting Line Screens in DRAW

Whether or not you understand the intricacies of lines, dots, screen dots, and grays, you can still take measures to ensure good output with your black-and-white drawings. Using Figures 25.10 through 25.12 as

27.12

1,200 dots per inch

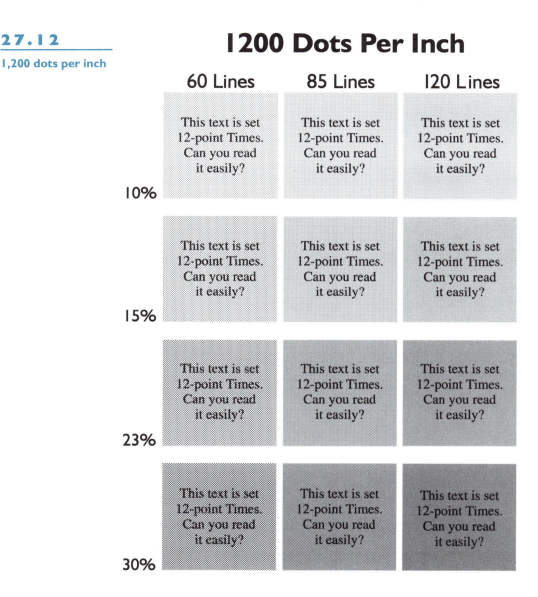

your guide, you can establish proper settings for line screens and pass those settings on to DRAW.

The first thing to be said about this task is that line screens are a PostScript phenomenon, and only relevant when printing to a PostScript laser printer or creating print files to be taken to your service bureau. Other printers, such as non-PostScript HP LaserJets, have their own controls for adjusting dot patterns, accessible through the Windows Control Panel / Printers section.

Creating Print Files

Let's say that you are sending your work to your service bureau, and you determine that a screen of 120 lines will best produce the gray tones that you have incorporated into your work. Assuming that all of the objects are to be set at 120 lines, your course of action is clear and simple:

1. Select File / Print / Options.
2. In the Screen Frequency drop-down list on the Options page of the dialog, choose 120. ("Screen Frequency" means the same thing as line screen.)
3. OK this dialog and then OK the main Print dialog, and you're ready to issue the Print command.

Whether you are printing to a local printer or creating a PostScript print file (both of which are discussed in Chapter 25), all objects on the page will have a line screen of 120 lines. (This includes solid objects as well as gray tones, even though this setting doesn't matter with solids. When there is total coverage of dots in a given space, the screen density becomes irrelevant.)

INSIDE INFO

If you do not set the line screen before printing, you might still get the correct value. When Options / Screen Frequency is set to Default, DRAW consults the PostScript printer driver for the line screen value, using its current setting.

Creating Encapsulated PostScript Files

If your drawings are designed to be placed into another application, then you will want to create, rather than a print file, an *encapsulated PostScript* (.EPS) file. DRAW's .EPS export command does not have controls for setting the screen density, but that doesn't mean you cannot control it. An .EPS file is designed to be incorporated into another document, perhaps one that has been created by a different program altogether. You set the screen when you print from that application. In PageMaker 5.0, for instance, you click the Color button on the Print dialog and then enter the value in the lpi box.

Many programs, including DRAW and PageMaker, have a control for the line screen. Then again, many programs don't. However, practically every program provides access to the Windows PostScript printer driver, where you *can* adjust the line screen. To get there, use File / Print Setup, or click Setup from within the Print dialog (every Windows program offers one or both of those avenues). Then click Options, Advanced, and find the field called Halftone Frequency (yet another synonym for screen density).

One Print Job, Many Screens

The two methods for setting screens discussed above are global operations; they establish the screen that will prevail for all objects in a drawing. You can also set an individual line screen for a selected object in a drawing, as long as you observe one rule: You must be using a spot color model, not a process color model. Rather than dialing up the percentage of black and leaving the other three CMYK values at 0%, you would use a spot color model (such as PANTONE). From there, you would choose the color black and set a tint for it, as shown in the Uniform Fill dialog in Figure 27.13.

Once that's done, the PostScript Options button becomes available, and clicking it brings you to the dialog of settings shown on the right of Figure 27.13. For the Halftone Screen type, select Dot; then enter the desired screen density in the Frequency field. The value of 87 shown in the figure is a bit absurd (increments of 5 are barely noticeable at higher resolutions), but we wanted to show you that you can indeed dial up any value at all for the line screen.

27.13

Each object can have its own line screen setting.

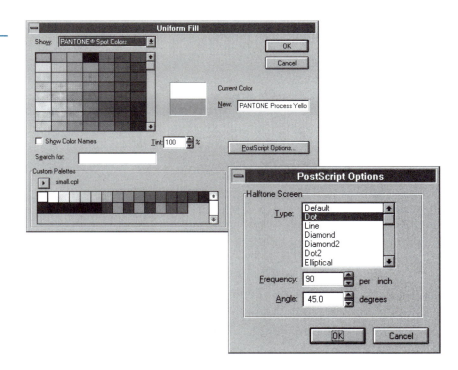

By giving an object its own personalized line screen, you are overruling any line screen value you set for the whole image. If you set the Screen Frequency value in the DRAW Print dialogs to 100, it will prevail over all objects, *except* those to which you have assigned a custom line screen. The same thing applies to an .EPS file: When you place it in and print it from another document, the line screen settings when you print will act on all objects, except the ones to which you have manually assigned individual line screens.

Creative Screens

Most users set screens by adjusting the frequency of the dot matrix, but there are several other options that DRAW provides for you, with which you can create text effects that are particularly well suited for lower-resolution output. Figure 27.14 shows several of these, alongside the settings that produced them. These settings are all contained within the PostScript Options dialog available from any of the Fill dialogs. Remember, though,

27.14

Who says fountain fills are only good at high resolution? Here are settings that produce effective patterns at 300 dpi.

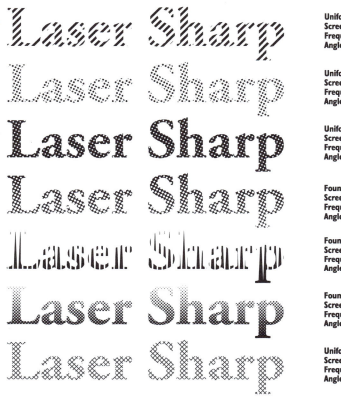

that these screens can only be seen when printed from a PostScript printer; they will not show on your screen.

By the Numbers (Ugh)

Just in case you haven't noticed the mathematical pattern emerging here, the number of gray levels can be figured by squaring the matrix size and adding 1. Say what? As we warned you, the following discussion is somewhat technical. Casual users may want to pass on this.

Here is the formula for determining the number of gray levels. It is determined by adding 1 to the square of the output device's resolution, divided by the specified line screen resolution.

$(dpi / line\ screen)^2 + 1 = number\ of\ gray\ levels$

When you instruct DRAW to use a 100-line screen for a gray tone on your 300-dpi laser printer, what you're going to get is 10 possible gradations (8 grays plus white and solid black). In other words, you're instructing your printer to start a new matrix of dots every one-hundredth of an inch. But if the printer only gets 300 dots in an inch, it can only get 3 in one-hundredth of an inch. That means your printer will use a 3 × 3 matrix to represent grays, like the matrix shown in Figure 27.4. So you get a relatively high resolution (100 lpi) at the expense of gradations.

On the opposite extreme, were you to specify a line screen of 30 on the same laser printer, you could achieve 101 gray levels:

```
300 / 30 = 10
10² = 100
100 + 1 = 101
```

This would give you a line screen of very low resolution, but many more gray levels—probably more than you would care to use.

When you print a fountain fill to a 300-dpi printer, in many cases you will get visible banding unless you use a line screen of very low resolution. What value you use depends greatly on the values of your fountain fill and the distance it will span. If the distance spanned by the gradient is small, the banding may not be noticeable. A gradient progressing from solid black to white across a 1/4-inch span, with a line screen of 60 on a 300-dpi printer, would create 26 bands—not distinguishable in that distance.

On the other hand, the same fountain settings to the same printer, but with a line screen of 75 spanning 17 inches, will be noticeably banded with 17 bands averaging about an inch wide. This gradient, output to a Linotronic at 2,540 dpi, will provide a much nicer gradation, even at 100 lpi. This gradient provides 646 gray levels, which, divided into the 17-inch span, yield bands of approximately 2.5/100 inch.

Next stop on the freeway: the Prepress exit.

28

CHAPTER

Preparing for Press

TWENTY-EIGHT

If you think that preparing for a commercial print job or a full-color printing project is only a little more complicated than whipping out a flier on your LaserJet, then this chapter is for you. You might not like what you're about to find out, but it's required reading, nonetheless. CorelDRAW, with all of its modules, is a wonderful front-end for professional publishing and printing, but it is crucial that you understand what happens to your artwork after you deliver it to your service bureau or print shop.

If this chapter reads a bit like an essay or a magazine article, that's no coincidence. It was originally written by Steve Bain for *Corel Magazine*, and has been updated, revised, and reprinted here with permission. All of the original photography in this chapter is by Bain, also. (With ten issues annually, *Corel Magazine* has rapidly become the voice of the CorelDRAW community. You can get subscription information by calling 800-856-0062.)

Some of the language contained here was introduced in Chapter 26, "Working with Color," and we assume that you are familiar with the terms introduced there. This chapter is for advanced users and users who want to become advanced.

Monitoring Your Monitor

Here's the situation: You are asked to prepare a wonderfully complex, full-color illustration or brochure, in as short a time as possible and with as small a budget as imaginable. Hey, no problem, you say to yourself. You've got years of training, a bundle of original ideas, and you're pretty savvy with CorelDRAW. After surviving several weeks of skipped lunches and a couple of all-nighters, you're done. The laser-printer proofs look out-of-this-world, the boss likes what you've created, and the client loves it. Now all you have to do is drop the proofs off at a service bureau and have them printed.

A few days later when the color proofs come back from the film people, everything looks "off," somehow. The blues aren't blue anymore; they're purple. Your reds are more like orange, and your browns have turned yellow. What began as a work of beauty has turned into a candidate for *The Amateur Hour.* Was the film processing off, or was it your colors? Your office has turned into a merry-go-round of finger pointing, and the boss wants to "take you out for a drink." The client wants your head on a stick. It's all over.

Has this nightmare happened to you yet? It will—if you dive headlong into full-color publishing without first making sure your color system is telling you the truth. In the world of color production there are almost as many variables in the process as there are reproducible colors. The keys to achieving proper color are controlling all these variables and knowing your equipment. But with color technology changing almost weekly, it's a challenge to keep up.

Desktop color production requires a color scanner, a desktop color proofing device, a color monitor, and several pairs of eyes in addition to yours. To follow along with this discussion, you will need to have a color monitor, a quality video card capable of at least 256 colors, and hopefully, a sense of humor.

Calibrating Your Monitor

If you read Chapter 26 and its accompanying sidebar, you already know that your monitor rarely tells you the truth when you ask it to display colors. Some monitors come with a calibration software utility, and CorelDRAW 5.0 has its own Color Manager (discussed later in the chapter). Regardless of the tools you use to calibrate, however, there is work to do beforehand. Following these steps will ensure a controlled environment for viewing colors on your monitor, as well as on your hardcopy original.

Warm Up Your Monitor—and Your Swatches   First, get your hands on a color swatch book that matches the color model you intend to use (CMYK, PANTONE, TruMatch, or the like). Make sure your swatch book is fairly new; over time, swatches fade if left in bright sunlight or even bright office lighting. Armed with your up-to-date swatches, turn on your monitor and let it warm up for at least half an hour to make sure the color display has stabilized.

Control the Lighting   Set the lighting in your work area so that it's close to typical levels. Controlled lighting is ideal; pull the shades to keep natural light from entering the room. Let's face it—the sun rises and sets and we keep working. As the light changes during the day, so does the spectrum of light your eyes let in, and so does the appearance of the colors on your monitor.

Establish Comfort Levels   Set the brightness and contrast controls on your monitor to comfortable levels, and then leave them alone. If you share a machine with other workers, put a little Don't Mess With Me sign on the monitor. You don't want to work for hours to perfect a full-color illustration and find out at the final stage that your colors are all wrong because myopic Bob down the hall likes to borrow your machine after you've gone home.

Set the Background Color   Set the background color of your monitor to a neutral gray. The background color can influence the way you view other colors on screen. A red background, for instance, will make all other colors look less red in comparison.

Choose Your Calibration Weapon   Select your weapon of choice: either an independent calibration software package that you trust, or the features built into CorelDRAW.

Using the CorelDRAW Color Manager

In CorelDRAW 5.0, the engineers have finally got it right. The fundamental concept underlying DRAW 5.0's Color Manager (integrated across all the CorelDRAW applications) is that the user should make the display look like the output, rather than the other way around. The range of colors your monitor can display, known as the *gamut,* is much wider than that of any output device you might use. Trying to print all the colors you can see on your screen would be an exercise in frustration. Therefore, you must throttle the monitor back to what your output device—whether printer, film recorder, or imagesetter—can provide.

Corel also earns kudos for supplying preset controls for many popular output devices. There are profiles for 24 monitors, including generic and NTSC standard; 19 printers, including generic CMYK, generic RGB, and SWOP; and 7 scanners. There is no distinction between coated and uncoated stock under SWOP, and no other offset specifications such as Toyo or Eurostandard. (Of course, when we went to calibrate one of *our* color printers, an EFI RIP driving a Xerox 5775, we found no profile available for it.)

A *device color profile* (DVP) is a data file used by color management systems, containing a description of the color-handling properties of a specific device. The DVP takes into account such variables as phosphor type, gamma, and white point temperature for monitors; tonal response curve and dot gain for printers; and the color reproduction characteristics of scanners. This data is used to adjust the way an image is displayed on your monitor, so you see the truest possible representation of your output. However straightforward and definitive this may sound, the theories of device color profiles and color management systems are something of a black art. You should set aside an afternoon for this task if you want to ensure good results. (We calibrated one of our systems in a couple of hours on a Saturday; we also installed CorelDRAW, optimized the hard drive, and updated a video driver…the ideal way to spend a day off.)

Your first step is to locate the scanner target that came with CorelDRAW (the picture of the woman surrounded by a table of fruit). Take good care of this target; it and the accompanying color swatch together are the sample image used throughout the calibration process. The picture is also found as MONCALIB.BMP, in the COLOR subdirectory of your main Corel directory.

If your video card allows you to establish systemwide settings for gamma and color balance, we recommend resetting them to their factory defaults. Most especially, the gamma should be set at 1.00. Otherwise, any adjustments you make in DRAW will be nearly meaningless and very frustrating.

Get yourself settled into a good viewing environment. Then, from either DRAW or PHOTO-PAINT, select File / Color Manager. The first dialog you will encounter, the System Color Profile shown in Figure 28.1, is a listing of the devices eligible for calibration. The first time you open this dialog, the profile is called _DEFAULT.CCS (the .CCS stands for Color Calibration System); henceforth, the profile displayed will be the last one you selected. The same profile is used across all Corel applications installed on your computer.

In the middle of the dialog, three drop-down list boxes indicate the current monitor, printer, and scanner. Scroll through these lists to see if

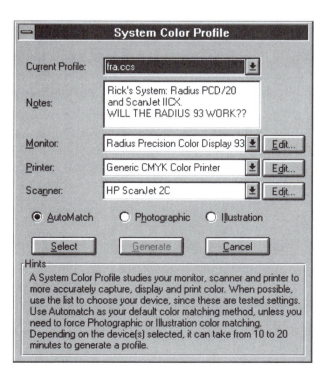

28.1

A completed system color profile, based on the preset controls built into the Color Manager

your devices are listed. If they are, you're home free. Maybe. (See the upcoming section on "Rolling Your Own..." for what to do if they aren't.) You will need to designate a separate profile for each combination of monitor, printer, and scanner you use, so you hardware hounds in the audience might be in for a long day of calibrating.

Once the devices in your system have been selected in the system color profile, it is simplicity itself to generate the actual .CCS file. Simply click on the Generate button, and go for coffee. On one of our systems, a 60MHz Pentium, it took less than two minutes to generate a profile; on a 486 DX2, it took about six minutes, and on a 486-25 notebook, it took the better part of an episode of *Murder, She Wrote*.

Because the only way to test-drive a color profile is to put it in action and produce some screen and printer output, you may find yourself generating several profiles before you are happy with the results. Name the experimental profiles appropriately, so you can follow the sequence in which they were generated. Using the Notes box in the dialog, keep track of what you changed or included in each profile. In the profile in Figure 28.1, our lead author has recorded a reminder to himself to see whether a different Radius display will produce acceptable results.

Rolling Your Own... Profile, That Is

If you cannot find your devices in the lists supplied in the System Color Profile dialog, you must manually generate a profile for them. This is not difficult, but it is tedious.

Your monitor will be the easiest to calibrate: All you need do is make the woman on your screen look like the one in the picture. From within Color Manager, click on the Edit button next to the Monitor list box. You will be assaulted by another dialog with a lot of numbers in little boxes. Unless you are technically savvy or especially adventurous, you will not want to adjust your display from here. Instead, click on the Interactive button to find a picture of the soon-to-be-famous woman, flanked by myriad buttons, sliders, value boxes, and other terrifying things.

Your chief concern is the Cool/Warm slider, which sets the monitor's white-point temperature and gamma. You could muck about with the Chromaticity settings, but it's unlikely you'll see significant effects. Your default settings will probably be a gamma of 2.2 and a white point of between 7,000 and 9,000 degrees Kelvin. Compare the original photo with the image on screen, and if it looks acceptable (or if you are not very picky), then call it a day. If not, you will need to get intimate with some of the more esoteric controls.

AUTHOR'S NOTE

Ever wonder what a Kelvin is? British mathematician and physicist William Thomson Kelvin, First Baron (1824–1907), was one of the leading physical scientists and greatest teachers of his time. In 1848, Lord Kelvin proposed the absolute scale of temperature that still bears his name. Kelvin measures the number of Celsius degrees above absolute zero.

In general, the "cooler" an image—that is, the lower the white point—the bluer it will look. Study the color of the woman's blouse, the coffee cup, and the whipped cream on the sundae. Slide the Cool/Warm slider up and down, clicking Preview periodically until you get something that looks right. The most common white points for monitors are at the 500 degree marks (5,500, 6,000, 6,500, 7,000, and 7,500). Your white point will also be influenced somewhat by your viewing conditions; the brighter your ambient light, the higher your white point will need to be to compensate.

The gamma controls affect the red, green, and blue components of an image. There is some interplay between the gamma controls and the Cool/Warm slider, so here, too, you will need to fiddle to get the desired results. Sit back from your monitor, far enough for the lines on the left side of the gamma adjustment panel to blend into a uniform gray. Figure 28.2 compares the result of using the default color profile (top image) and the result of applying a profile with significantly different settings. Even in black and white, you can see the difference on screen. Illustration No. 15 in the second section of the Color Gallery demonstrates with even more clarity how different screen images can be from an original photo.

28.2

Two different system color profiles produce two very different images on screen.

WATCH OUT!

In the Interactive Monitor Calibration dialog, make sure that the Identical option is enabled before you begin experimenting with the gamma setting, or you may disrupt the balance of your display. If you do not get a neutral gray while adjusting the master gamma, then your monitor's color balance is out of whack. You can adjust this to a limited extent by fiddling with the gamma of the RGB channels individually, but the results will almost certainly be off elsewhere. If good color is important to you, do NOT adjust the color balance; buy a new monitor. If your monitor cannot hold a good color balance, it may not be long for this world.

It is important that you understand one thing: System color profiles do not change how the image will print. Figure 28.2 has captured how an image appears *on screen*, not in print. Both these images will print exactly the same. The goal of monitor calibration is to change your display so that it will more accurately depict the printout. Taking these calibration measures on one of our monitors helped us to see that our cyan was way off, looking more like sky blue. Screen tints of cyan were almost invisible, but the calibration process corrected that.

NEW FOR 5

Once you have created your system color profile and placed it into active duty, you can still decide whether to use it or not on a case-by-case basis. From View / Color Correction, you have four choices: None uses no color correction and gives the fastest screen draw; Fast offers a minimal level of color correction without unduly reducing your screen response time; Accurate uses all the profile settings you created and thus gives measurably slower bitmap rendering; and Simulate Printer studies your printer settings in the system color profile and attempts to match your monitor with the expected printed output.

Monitoring Your Scanner

You've finally convinced your boss that a scanner is the way to go. You've put your reputation on the line by promising that the scanner will greatly streamline your color separation efforts, eliminate having to pay for manual halftones, and give you unlimited creative resources. The boss buys your convincing argument, with only one catch: "Don't ask for anything else!"

Your shiny new color scanner arrives. You hook up a few cables and load some software, and the boss grins as you power it up. Let's put those rush jobs on hold for a few minutes while you scan in a beautiful picture of your company president. It appears on the screen and, frankly, looks a bit… well… repulsive. Not to be discouraged by what you assume is just a monitor glitch, you send the file to your color bubble-jet or laser printer. The result sends chills up your spine: It's even darker than the screen image.

Your first fear may be that your scanner is defective or, worse, that you've entered a wilderness of scanner problems with lingo understood only by the most sophisticated of computer art specialists. Your next thought is, "Where can I hide so the boss won't find me?" But relax. Keep in mind that your scanner is just a recording device. As with a stereo amplifier, you may have to adjust the bass and treble a bit to get all of the effects.

Aiming for WYSIWYG

When you scan an image, there are a number of decisions you will need to make concerning resolution, compression type (if any), and format (TIFF, BMP, TGA, EPS, or PCX). These decisions will be determined by the image's intended use. Most of the time, the role of a desktop flatbed scan—especially with color—is as a proof, to define the position of a picture that will later be inserted manually or electronically. Or the scan may be intended as a design element or artistic image, in which the image is intentionally portrayed with an added effect. Either way, you can't go wrong with TIFF files, which are widely accepted and compatible with virtually all graphics, layout, and word processing programs.

Let's say that you have decided on TIFF files for your images, and that you scanned the photo at a very low resolution of 72 dpi. During scanning, all RGB color information will be recorded for each of those 72 dots residing in each linear inch. (Most scanners record in RGB, the same method by which monitors transmit their images to your eyes.)

WATCH OUT!

> Before going any further, be sure that you have calibrated your monitor as described in the previous section: Adjust the room lighting, fix monitor settings such as brightness and contrast, and create a color-accurate profile. Doing all this ensures a firmly controlled medium from which to measure the scanned image results.

Scanner calibration can follow one of several paths, all detailed in the CorelDRAW manual, beginning on page 495. Here we'll take a look at some tricks that can make the process easier for you.

To calibrate your scanner, you will need to make a scan (stop the presses!) and use it as a reference. The picture of the woman you used to calibrate the monitor will work just fine. Save the image (the COLOR subdirectory is a good place to put it), and call it REFERENC.TIF. Return to the System Color Profile dialog, but this time click on the Edit button next to Scanner. Then choose Image under Scanned Target; click on the Browse button next to Scanned Target and find the TIFF file; then click on the Scanned Target button. So, let's see, here... There's an option called Scanned Target, a text window called Scanned Target, and a button called Scanned Target. Go figure...

Once you navigate this maze of scanned targets, your TIFF file will appear within a special marquee, with right-angled marks called *fiducial marks* (we have no idea what the CorelDRAW User's Manual means by this). Stretch each corner of the marquee to the edge of the picture itself. The purpose here is to allow the standard reference file to be aligned with your scan, so that the color swatches can be compared.

Some calculation is done by the program, and the results are saved as your scanner's color profile. Neat trick, we think. OK the dialog with the scanned image in it, and wait once again while the calculations are done. OK the special dialog and, once you are back at the System Color Profile dialog, click the Generate button to put the final touches on your system profile.

Printer Calibration

Printer calibration is possible, but it is not easy, and we don't really recommend it. The path of least resistance is to select system color profiles closest to your actual output and move on.

WATCH OUT!

> **Should you insist on adjusting printer calibration, the means to experiment are in the Printer Characterization dialogs (reached via Color Manager / Printer Edit / Color Match). The adjustments available are quite complete, but be forewarned: You experiment at considerable risk to your wallet, because test output can be very expensive. To our knowledge, no one has ever formulated universal criteria for these settings; they can only be determined by the tedious process of measuring, cutting, fitting, using a spectrophotometer or colorimeter, and printing miles of film or reams of laser paper. These are sophisticated and expensive devices and not for use by amateurs, beginners, or the faint of heart.**

The Straight and Narrow

Before beginning the printer calibration process, you must first make sure that at least your monitor has been calibrated, according to the foregoing discussion. The next step is to get your hands on a color swatch (preferably, one printed in the last six months) that will give you an accurate comparison to your color printer's output. We normally use PANTONE swatches, but a process color swatch will also do.

Create a document consisting of the colors you use most often; an example is shown in Figure 28.3. The easiest way to do this is to create one square, with a label such as "PANTONE *nnn*." Center the label under the box, and then group and copy several times. Set a color fill for each of your squares according to the colors you use most often, and label each square with its color name. For process colors, label the CMYK

28.3

An example of your own personal color swatch

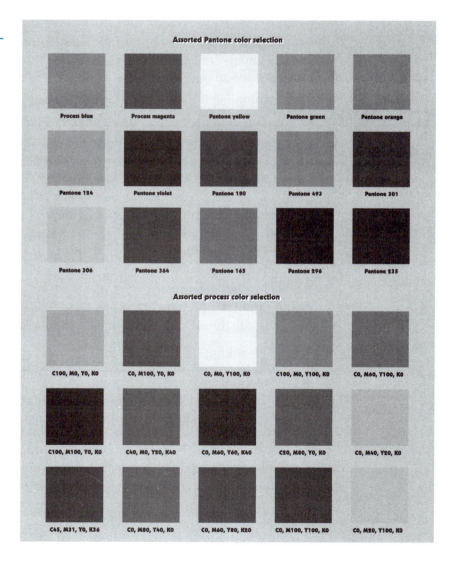

values as letters followed by the screen percentage. In Figure 28.3 we have arranged squares for 15 PANTONE colors and 15 process colors. Most print shops use this same coding method for identifying process color screen values at the film stripping stage.

You'll want to include colors from items commonly used in your work environment, such as your company logo. Concentrate on the brighter side of the color wheel, and avoid very dark colors like dark brown, violet, and dark blues, which look almost black. Make sure to include samples of cyan, magenta, yellow, and black, each at 100%. For the background, place a neutral, 20% screen tint of black. This will reduce the amount of contrast between the colors you are viewing and the white of the paper on which they will be printed.

After printing this file to your color printer, compare the results of the output to the colors of your on-screen swatch and then to your swatch book. The next step in the calibration process depends on whether or not you can adjust the color of your printer's output.

PostScript Color Printers These printers have color PostScript algorithms, which cannot be altered, written into their drivers. The accuracy of PostScript printers depends on how well their drivers read the color information from the print engine of your software. Because the algorithms can't be adjusted, you will either have accurate color or you won't. If you don't, you will have to get to know the quirks of your particular printer in order to choose colors from a swatch book and get those same colors from your printer.

Non-PostScript Color Printers These printers use drivers that interpret the color from your print engine but usually have some type of utility to control RGB, intensity, and gamma settings. This will become a hit-or-miss affair for you, but if your aim is precision color, it will be worth the work.

To save time and costly print materials, try cropping the samples to a specific area using the cropping tool: Select the bitmap image and move the middle handles on the bitmap with the Shape tool. Once you have determined just the right combination of commands to match your original, you can make the same changes to any image from that particular scanner and be assured your color proofing device will provide accurate color.

WATCH OUT!

> Keep in mind the experts' warning: If you are planning to have your film color separated for reproduction on a traditional printing press, you must remove your for-position-only image before sending the file to the service bureau. It must be replaced either with mechanical film separations produced in the traditional way or with a professionally scanned image from a bureau's ultra-high-resolution drum scanner. It's best not to rely on flatbed scanners to produce high-resolution color images.

Cancel Hawaii: The Colors Are All Wrong

Has this ever happened to you? Your megadesign project for your firm's most difficult but highest-paying client is finally out the door, completed. You wisely bit your tongue through all their last-minute, obsessive little changes. Only 12 sets of revisions! So what—they're worth it. And besides, as soon as the files are imaged, you're off to Maui to bake under lofty palms and spend your life savings on a few of those drinks with little umbrellas. You can relax now; there's nothing to worry about. The service bureau will take care of the rest.

Then the phone rings. It's the printer… and it's for you. From the phone you hear the four words from hell: "Your film's all wrong." The statement itself causes the hair on your neck to stand up. What went wrong? Who's to blame? Where's the color key? Doesn't anybody check these things anymore? What does "all wrong" mean, anyway?

All indicators point to the fact that your process colors are, in fact, wrong. Now that's impossible, because you've completely calibrated your system—monitor, scanner, and color printer—using a professional color swatch. Your colors *can't* be wrong. Did you screw up or can you blame someone else? In a business such as desktop publishing, which involves so many processes and so many different and ever-changing trades and technologies, it can seem nearly impossible to pinpoint answers to questions like these.

Throughout this chapter, we've looked at everything within the limits of our own systems. There's one final but critical process we haven't looked at yet, however: interaction of the imagesetter and the film processor. These machines perform at the final and most critical stages of any electronic publishing, and even though they are usually owned and operated by someone else, it is important that you understand their roles. Just like the rest of your system, if the imagesetter and film processor aren't tuned and operating correctly, all is lost.

The problem is that most of us are good little consumers and will entrust months of layout or illustration work to the people who operate these machines. We assume that they've done everything they're supposed to do in terms of system maintenance and calibration.

For an insider's perspective, we contacted Allan Larson, imagesetter operator at Laser's Edge in Vancouver. Allan watches over imagesetters and film processors for a living; it's his job to check the calibration of the imaging equipment and ensure everything is operating within professionally established standards. The company's setup includes a Linotronic model 500 exclusively for paper output, a model 330 for film output up to spot-color registration, and an AGFA SelectSet 7000 for large-sized film output and process color registration. Their color-proofing devices are a Canon CLC 500 controlled by a Fiery raster image processor (RIP) for continuous tone, and two Lasermaster Display Makers for large-sized color output (up to 3 feet wide, and any length). Needless to say, Larson is well equipped. And with all that data flying to and from the imagesetters, and all that film streaming out, something is bound to go out of sync.

Following Through

Larson recommends, once you have gone to the trouble of calibrating your monitor, scanner, and color-proofing device to ensure accurate color, that you also develop a good working knowledge of the film and printing stages. When you have a properly imaged set of film, the next step is to make a *laminate proof*, or what the experts call a *match print*. This match print is made with a specialized process in which each film separation is exposed to a micro-thin color carrier sheet. Then all the carrier sheets are bonded together onto a white backing, to simulate the actual printing on a press. A color overlay proof, or color key, is not sufficient to accurately represent the results of the film output.

Now you can return to your PC and calibrate your system to match the actual film. Look closely at the even screen tints, the graduated fills, and the scanned images. Check your colors carefully. By matching your proof to what will actually print on the press, you can now trust your monitor's colors. And because you have a fully calibrated system, every stage will reflect the proper colors.

Sending the files off to be imaged is a stage of the process that is almost never in the hands of the "electronic artist" and so may be one of the most difficult to understand and control. How can you trust your film if you're not the one who produced it? How can you recognize inferior film versus correctly created film?

The first step is to find a reputable service bureau. Visit one and ask for a tour. In fact, once you're there, don't stop asking questions until they push you out the door. Most service bureau operators are proud of their operations and will tell you what you need to know. We don't expect you to become an expert on the service bureau industry, but if you've been wondering exactly how they do what they do, read on.

Basic Imagesetter Operation

"The PostScript code generated by your printer and by Windows drivers tells a story of what is on your page and how it was built," Larson says. "When you send that story down to the RIP, it builds the page into memory and from there instructs a laser to begin exposing the film, usually by way of a highly focused light source and a spinning mirror arrangement." The accuracy at the highest resolution possible on the AGFA SelectSet 7000 is 3,600 dpi, which means the laser has to focus on a point 1/3,600 inch wide. It's accurate to within 1 or 2 microns over four or five plates of film—far exceeding the registration most printing presses can hold.

There are two main types of imagesetter film processes in use: the *capstan system* and the *drum model*. The capstan system is a roll-fed model; a 200-foot roll of film is loaded at one end, much as it is loaded into a 35-mm camera. It's fed over the area where the laser exposes it, into a take-up cassette. Tiny rollers coax the film through the machine and pinch it so that it is perfectly taut. Theoretically, you could create a document the width of the roll (usually 12 or 18 inches) and extending the entire length of the roll (200 to 250 feet), but you would want to keep a fire extinguisher handy for the RIP's explosion. The operator determines when the cassette is full and removes it for film processing, just as you would when your 35-mm camera gets to the end of its film.

With the drum model, the film is cut into a 22-by-26-inch sheet and vacuum-sealed to the inside of an area shaped like a half-barrel. The laser mechanism is mounted above this area and moves back and forth across the film to expose it. Once the film imaging is complete, the exposed sheet is moved into a take-up cassette, and an unexposed sheet takes its place.

There is one significant difference in the way these two types of imagesetters operate: In the capstan, the film moves and the laser doesn't; in the drum, the laser moves and the film is stationary. Incidentally, the drum model sells for about $200,000. According to Larson, "the SelectSet 7000 has a 300-pound weight inside it to prevent vibration. It's a much more accurate method of imaging."

A Calibration a Day

Larson tells us "there are a number of variables that will all affect the quality of your film. Every morning our entire system is calibrated. What you should try to do is maintain consistency so that no matter which day you run film through your system, you always get the same quality. And it only takes one changed variable to ruin your whole day."

Film processors automatically process, fix, wash, and dry the film by pulling it through a series of rubber and steel rollers. The variables influencing this process can greatly change the quality of your output. Film processor speed, water temperature and filtration, chemical replenishment rate, and regular, complete cleanings are all important factors.

"A well-set-up processing system should have a fresh and constant supply of filtered water controlled by a temperature regulator," warns Larson. "Never try to run one of these processors from a water supply fed from a pail. You'll never achieve consistent results this way." Apparently, even the quality of the city water supply can be factor. In some areas where the water is more acidic than usual, some adjustment to the chemistry may be required. In areas where excessive rainfall can flood the water supply, the water may become muddier than usual, lowering water purity.

"To test our system we have a control strip [similar to a gray-scale] that we image and process each day, which includes various screen percentages including solid black," Larson said. "By using a densitometer, we measure each area on the strip. The solid will tell us our D-max measure, which is our blackest black. This measure is for obtaining nice black type that doesn't fill and doesn't let light through. Then we look at our screen percentages of 5, 50, and 95 percent. Our goal is to stay within 2 percent. Performing this densitometer test enables us to judge how much we'll adjust the imagesetter's density values."

Other factors affecting the film include its age, the ambient air temperature, how and where the film is stored, and from what point on the roll it originates. "At the end of a roll, the film is wound much tighter, and if it's tight enough, the film will actually stretch," Larson said. "So you should never try to image color separations near the end of a roll. For the same reason, you should never try to image separations split by the end of one roll and the beginning of another."

In the case of calibrating color imagesetters, such as the Fiery RIP-controlled Canon CLC 500, which operates on a principle different from film imagesetters, other factors come into play. "Our Canon is really sensitive to humidity," Larson tells us. "During calibration each morning, the printer takes a humidity reading of the air in the room and applies a specific magnetic charge to the paper as it's going through the machine. The more humid it is, the better the paper will hold a charge, and the better your colors will be. So, on hot and humid summer days your color proofs will look great, and a little more washed out on cold, dry, sunny winter days."

Watching for Poor Output

Occasionally you may receive output from a service bureau that doesn't look quite right to you. Sometimes your worries are justified, and sometimes not. Here are some things to watch for:

- If your film comes back looking bluish or greenish where it should be clear, it may be because it was packaged too soon after processing. This won't affect the quality of the finished piece, but if it bothers you, just leave the film out in the open for a while.

- What if you see a 2-inch-wide haze on your film that looks like a poorly exposed area? It may be dust on the mirrors of the imagesetter. If you can hold your film up and see light through the black areas, then the film isn't dark enough. If the film looks smudged or gray, it probably has been processed too quickly.

- What about scratches? They're a sign of a dirty processor. These scratches will show up as tiny hairs when the printing plate is made, and this kind of output from the service bureau should be refused.

- Banding appears as visible stripes or steps in graduated screens generated by the software. The higher the screen frequency, or lines per inch (lpi), of the output, the more visible the steps will be. (You can avoid this by setting Print / Options / Options / Fountain Steps to the maximum of 250 steps.)

- Moirés are the result of incorrect screen angle (angle of the rows of dots), generated by either the software or the imagesetter. In process color film output, angles should be as follows: cyan, 15°; magenta, 75°; yellow, 0°; black, 45°. In some cases, the imagesetter may have other software controlling the RIP, which will tweak or nudge the angles to better match the screen frequency you have requested.

- If you have requested paper output and you see gray smudges on it, these are usually silver deposits, also caused by a dirty processor. If the marks are anywhere near your images, they may affect the quality of your project or require adding extra opacity to the film at the stripping stage. Return such output to the service bureau.

The color calibration process of your system can take weeks to complete and may not be accurate the first time around. And system calibration often falls victim to changing variables, so don't forget any of the steps you took to achieve your ideal calibration—it's almost a given that you'll be doing it again sometime soon. Hopefully, technology will continue to improve, and soon we'll never have to worry about it. Until then, though, the adjustments made toward perfecting your color system will be well worth the effort. Everyone involved—from your clients to your printers—will appreciate your efforts, and it may just give you the advantage you need to succeed in this increasingly competitive industry.

CHAPTER 29

Importing to DRAW

TWENTY-NINE

CHAPTER 29

This brief chapter is not a tutorial on how to import files into DRAW. If you want that, go back to Chapter 4, which contains a detailed, step-by-step approach to the mechanics of importing. This chapter assumes you know how to import, but want more insight and strategy concerning the different methods and formats available to you.

This is rush hour on the Corel Freeway—there are lots of on-ramps for you to choose…

Why Import?

A dumb question? We think not. The usual reason—to bring in a piece of clip art—is not the only one. There are three reasons to import graphics into DRAW, and three distinct ways to do it.

1. **To edit an existing graphic.** A graphic that is in a standard vector format—such as AI, CGM, or WMF—can be imported into DRAW and then edited. Once you import it into DRAW, you can then change it and integrate it into a larger drawing. A finished drawing can be imported and made to be one small component of a more complex project. For example, check out Illustration No. 6 in the Color Gallery. There, your lead author imported small pieces of clip art as well as full, robust drawings to produce the composite drawing.

2. **To incorporate an existing graphic.** We've chosen our words carefully: *edit* in #1 above, and *incorporate* here in #2. There are graphic formats that cannot be taken apart and edited by DRAW, but they can still be imported and printed by DRAW. These include all of the bitmap formats, and .EPS files (although this changes in 5.0; discussion forthcoming). You'll see

an example shortly of a bitmap graphic imported to DRAW and used as part of a drawing.

3. **To create a hot-link.** DRAW is a willing party to the Object Linking and Embedding phenomenon (you know it as OLE), in which graphics travel across the Clipboard and are able to retrace their steps back to the original program that created them. We'll explore OLE in detail in this chapter and the next one.

Importing linked or embedded objects is not done through the File / Import command, but rather with the Edit / Paste Special command. Nonetheless, this operation qualifies as an import, and we consider it as such. If you wanted to use broad categories, you could get away with thinking of incoming graphics as being in vector or bitmap format. Imported vector art can be taken apart and edited; bitmap art cannot.

NEW FOR 5

DRAW 5.0 includes a PostScript interpreter that can take PostScript print files and .EPS files and actually replicate them on screen. How well does it work? Stay tuned...

What Happens When You Import?

Importing (or pasting) graphics is not a one-size-fits-all proposition, although in all cases DRAW uses a *filter* to perform the task. A filter acts as a translator, enabling DRAW to convert vector art into its own internal language, and bitmap art into printable images. The key word here is *translate,* and it has implications for you: If DRAW has to translate graphic information, how do you know whether DRAW has got it right?

As recently as 1992, the answer to this question would have been "Cross your fingers, don't forget your mantra, and only import on Tuesday nights, when atmospheric conditions seem to be more favorable." Before today's file format standards were adopted and placed into service, exchanging graphics information was all too often one big crapshoot. It required both parties, the exporting program and the importing program, to be on the same wavelength; and even then, elements such as hairlines, typeface names, and color mixes carried long odds of being interpreted correctly.

Today your prospects of accurate graphics exchange are much brighter, with the Windows Metafile (WMF) format taking hold and being recognized as an accurate and reliable format for translating graphic information. This bodes well for users of non-PostScript devices, as well as for those who want to take advantage of OLE.

Importing Clip Art

Getting clip art files remains the No. 1 reason that DRAW users reach for the Import command. Whether from an external source or from Corel's vast library of clip art, DRAW's defining characteristic for tens of thousands of users is its ability to ingest and digest clip art images from many different sources.

Our surveys show that most clip art is used for applications no more complicated than in Figure 29.1, which shows several cartoon figures, originally in CGM format, integrated into one composite drawing. Remember, also, that the drawing you produced in Chapter 5 used as its central figure a piece of clip art.

The clip art images that make up Figure 29.1 were not changed in any way, except for the addition of a slight skew to the man peeking over the desk. But most vector art that is imported into DRAW can be taken apart and edited, *just as if you had created the objects there initially.* This last point is important: When it imports vector art, DRAW uses its filter to translate all objects into elements that it understands. Therefore, all objects are of a type that *you* understand—curves, lines, and text characters, with and without fills and outlines. Figure 29.2 shows Frosty, a longtime resident of Corel's clip art library, suffering from a breakdown—decidedly worse than a meltdown—at the hands of the Arrange / Ungroup command.

Some graphic formats tax DRAW's filtering to the max. The CGM and GEM file types are notorious for being unruly with fills and outlines; and .AI files often get typeface names wrong. In some cases, you feel

29.1

These pieces of clip art can be easily integrated into a single drawing.

fortunate just to have enough data to work with.

Other formats need very little translating. In fact, Frosty needs no translating at all, as he is stored in DRAW's own format. Importing him involves the same process as using the File / Open command to open him

29.2

Disaster strikes Frosty the Snowman in the form of the Ungroup command.

directly, with one important distinction: If you use File / Open to get FROSTY, you retrieve it at the expense of anything else on the page. DRAW asks you if you want to save and then closes down the current file. Further, you cannot make any changes to Frosty without first copying him to your hard drive (you can't write to a CD). In contrast, the Import command *adds* Frosty to your current drawing. File / Open replaces one file with another; File / Import adds one file to another.

Imported vector art always arrives on the page as one group of objects. We're not sure if this is an engineering requirement or just a decision on the part of the developers, but we like it. Generally, the first thing you want to do to imported art is move it and resize it, and these two operations are eminently easier to do with a group. Once you have incorporated it into your drawing, then you can ungroup it and adjust its individual parts as needed.

AUTHOR'S NOTE

UPGRADING FROM VERSION 3? Your need to ungroup imported art will decrease significantly, as of version 4.0. Now you can select individual pieces of a group and make changes to them without having to reach for the Ungroup command. Hold Ctrl as you select objects within a group; the selection handles will show up as dots instead of squares.

Because vector art can be disassembled and edited, it remains the most versatile form of clip art. The following paragraphs offer brief descriptions of the more popular vector flavors. For further notes on these and the other vector-based formats, consult online Help. Search for the individual format name, or search for Import and choose subtopics from there.

Adobe Illustrator Files

Few things are more frustrating for us while teaching or lecturing on these topics than having to stop and explain how .EPS files created by Adobe Illustrator are different from standard .EPS files (even though it was Adobe that created the EPS format in the first place).

Adobe Illustrator uses a special type of encapsulated PostScript format as its native file format. Illustrator (.AI) files look like .EPS files—they are stored in ASCII, and you can find in them a lot of the same unintelligible syntax as in standard .EPS files (*gsave, annotatepage, grestore,* and *packedarray,* for instance). Unlike standard .EPS files, however, Illustrator files can be imported, converted, and placed in a drawing as a group of editable objects. Though they generally produce highly refined, extremely accurate art, Illustrator files confuse the heck out of unsuspecting users who are led to believe that *all* .EPS files can be imported and edited the way that .AI files can.

To make matters even more interesting, DRAW now *can* import standard .EPS files, but not in the way it imports other vector formats (more on this shortly). To minimize confusion, in this chapter we will refer to Adobe's special flavor of EPS as *Illustrator format*, or as *.AI files*. For your own sake, think of this format as completely distinct from standard .EPS files.

AutoCAD

AutoCAD's .DXF files can be imported into DRAW with relatively little back talk. Like Illustrator files, AutoCAD files are stored in ASCII format, making for an easier conversion. However, there are numerous features of AutoCAD that have no equivalents in DRAW, not the least of which is three-dimensionality. DRAW lives in only two dimensions and will force an incoming .DXF file into the same narrow confines.

For a complete discussion on the AutoCAD/CorelDRAW connection, use DRAW's online Help. Press F1, choose Search, type **AUTOCAD**, and select Notes on Importing.

CorelDRAW's CDR Format

The CDR file format and the new CMX format will forever be your friendliest, as they need no filtering or interpreting whatsoever. Whatever is in the desired file—fountain fills, blends, unique typefaces, and so forth—will survive unscathed the trip into your current drawing (assuming you have installed the typefaces required by the incoming .CDR file). Version 2.0 and 3.0 .CDR files might show excess character and word spacing, requiring a trip to the Text roll-up or the Object menu (to apply a different style).

Computer Graphics Metafile

The CGM format has come a long way, yet still has a ways to go. Commercial clip art stored in CGM format is usually simple enough to be low risk; trouble arises when you are forced to import a complex chart or image as a .CGM file, perhaps because the originating program offers no other export choices. It takes two to tango here—DRAW's ability to *import* a .CGM file will be no better than the originating program's ability to *export* a .CGM file.

Compare Figure 29.3, a chart produced in Harvard Graphics, with the charts in Figure 29.4, which show (a) the same chart exported to CGM and imported to DRAW, and (b) the same chart exported to WMF and imported to DRAW.

The original chart (Figure 29.3) features a smooth fountain-fill background and crisp text set in various weights of Eras, a classic Adobe Type 1 face. In the .CGM file that Harvard exported and DRAW imported, the fountain has been replaced by a 25% shade, the text is now all set in Arial, and the labels running up the y-axis are misaligned. Also, there are many duplicate lines drawn on top of one another.

We're not sure what to blame here—DRAW's import filter or Harvard's export filter—and we're not sure if blame is necessarily warranted. After

29.3

This chart, produced in Harvard Graphics, will be our guinea pig for importing into DRAW.

Original Harvard Graphics chart

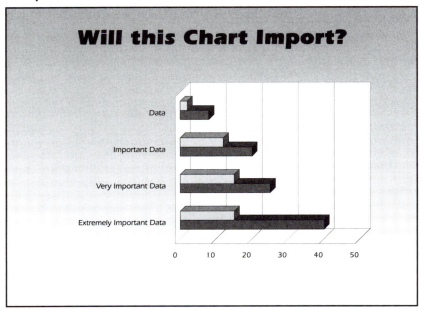

29.4

Importing .CGM files to DRAW often produces less-than-perfect results (compare to Figure 29.3), but .WMF files usually fare much better.

Chart imported to DRAW as .CGM file

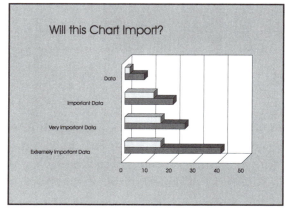

Chart imported to DRAW as .WMF file

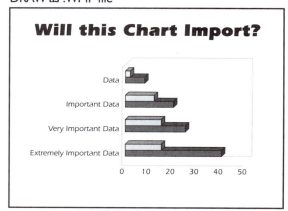

all, no objects disappeared during the transfer, the bars and the frame of the chart are all there, and the text came in as text, not a collection of uneditable curves. The discrepancies can all be fixed in about 10 minutes. We would deem this an acceptable transfer, given the limitations we have encountered with the CGM format. (We have certainly seen worse. In fact, the first time our lead author wrote about this topic in a CorelDRAW book, he showed a .CGM file that came into DRAW upside-down and mirrored!)

Windows Metafile

The WMF format has enjoyed the most significant advances of any format, as more and more developers jump on this bandwagon. Though we don't know beans about the inner workings of file formats and how they are created, we can observe that WMF has become clean, accurate, and very compact. The lower chart in Figure 29.4 shows the .WMF file imported into DRAW. The only imperfections are that the fountain fill background came in solid white (a 30-second fix), and we got some duplicate lines (although not nearly as many as with the CGM import).

As you'll see in Chapter 30, the WMF formats receive high marks in our Annual Export Torture Test, now in its third year.

Importing .EPS Files

As of version 4.0, DRAW added .EPS files to its list of importable files, and 5.0 adds yet another wrinkle to the export game. The capability of importing .EPS files means DRAW can now import data in what is generally regarded as the most accurate and reliable format available today: encapsulated PostScript. Assuming you have a PostScript driver installed under Windows, you can now import into DRAW data created from any Windows program that prints. Allow us two paragraphs of background.

PostScript is a set of instructions, stored in plain ASCII text, that make sense to printers and other output devices having the ability to interpret them. PostScript instructions have one common objective: to describe a page. In fact, PostScript is referred to as a *page description language*. PostScript is not unlike other programming languages, such as Pascal, Turbo C, and the various flavors of BASIC, but there is one big difference. With few exceptions, PostScript doesn't live inside your computer; it lives inside your printer. When PostScript instructions are sent to a PostScript printer, it begins building an image of the page. To communicate with your service bureau, you deliver a file full of PostScript instructions, and your service bureau's imagesetter interprets, describes, and produces your pages.

Encapsulated PostScript is a subtle variation of PostScript. An .EPS file is not designed to be sent directly to the printer (although you often can do it), but rather is intended to be incorporated into another document and then sent to the printer from there. An .EPS file can be scaled up and down like any other graphic (that's what is meant by "encapsulated"). All of the output samples in this book (including Figures 29.3 and 29.4 earlier) were produced as .EPS files and imported into Ventura Publisher for final publishing and printing.

Now here is the wrinkle: In addition to what DRAW calls Placeable EPS (in other words, DRAW places the file on the page but doesn't try to convert it, and doesn't let you edit it), DRAW 5.0 also offers an import called Interpreted PostScript. When using this filter, DRAW will try to do what your printer does—interpret the data and construct the image, using DRAW's native elements. In this case, the key word is *try*. Interpreted PostScript has proven to be good for little more than compiling an electronic stockpile.

Though we had no problems at all placing our Harvard Graphics chart as an .EPS file (and getting a perfect printout from it), we didn't do well at all with the Interpreted version. When we tried to import a PostScript print file, we experienced a spectacular and complete system crash. We did succeed in importing an .EPS file made from the chart, but as Figure 29.5 shows, the results are quite flawed. Typefaces are all off, letter spacing is a joke, and many parts of the chart are simply missing. This result would serve us if, and only if we were without the original file that produced the .EPS file and desperately needed just a clue about what the image looked like. Our tests indicate that the new Interpreted import choice cannot be counted on for any type of high-fidelity work. Think of it as an emergency measure.

29.5

Results from the PostScript (Interpreted) filter are radically inferior to those of the EPS (Placeable) filter.

Chart imported to DRAW as Placeable .EPS file

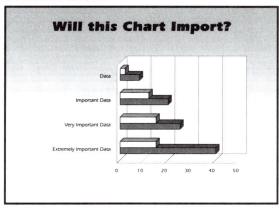

Chart imported to DRAW as Interpreted PostScript file

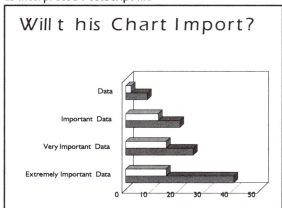

An EPS Test

If you have a PostScript printer, you can see how the two kinds of PostScript importing work by following these steps:

1. Start DRAW and create a drawing. Anything will do, including that blob you created in Chapter 9. We created a gray oval with some text inside.

2. Use File / Export to create an .EPS file. Check the Include Header option and set a Resolution of 72. Make note of the name and location of the file.

WATCH OUT!

Can't find EPS Export? Maybe you didn't install the filter when you installed CorelDRAW. Run Setup again, uncheck everything except Filters, click Customize, and then add EPS from the window of export filters (and any others you might want).

3. Go to File / Import, and choose EPS (Placeable).
4. Find the file you just created and double-click it. A representation of your drawing will appear as a single, uneditable object.
5. Return to File / Import, choose PostScript (Interpreted) as the format, and double-click on the same file. Cross your fingers and hope that you don't crash.
6. A replication of your original—though we can't predict how accurate it will be—will appear on your screen.

You'll notice right away that the placed EPS graphic looks different from the original object. (Actually, it looks a lot like an imported bitmap, and for a very good reason, which we'll explain shortly.) Don't bother reaching for the Ungroup command; this graphic cannot be ungrouped, taken apart, or edited in any way. Why? Because DRAW's Placeable EPS filter doesn't speak PostScript; in fact, it doesn't really apply a filter to the file at all. When you import the file, DRAW says to itself, "Yup, that's an .EPS file, all right—I'll just drop it on the page and let the printer worry about it." And when it comes time to print, DRAW does just that: It includes the .EPS file in the PostScript data stream, and the printer interprets it and prints it.

You may wonder, if DRAW doesn't try to read the file, how come it can display the image on screen? First off, it hardly does. The image you see on the screen is a low-rent rendition of the way your image will look when actually printed, and nothing at all like the fidelity you are used to seeing from DRAW. Second, DRAW won't always show you your image; sometimes it will just display a computer screen with a line drawn through it.

Programs that include an export filter for creating Placeable EPS files usually have a provision for including a bitmap image—a TIFF file, to be specific—in the file itself. When you export an .EPS file, DRAW asks you for a Header Resolution. (Other programs call these "screen previews" or "image headers.") When you ask to have one included in an .EPS file, the program creating the .EPS file whips up a quick TIFF rendition of the drawing and tucks it away at the bottom of the .EPS file. Thanks to that image header, programs that receive .EPS files have something to show you. The header serves only as a positioner, and generally contains little detail. But that is of no consequence to the end result, since the PostScript printer ignores the image header completely, concentrating instead on the good stuff.

So the reason .EPS files look like imported bitmap images is because that is exactly what DRAW shows you. Figure 29.6 shows the original image (top), a placed .EPS file taken from the original (middle), and an interpreted PostScript file from the original (bottom). The figure illustrates the poor quality of the Placeable EPS file on screen. The Interpreted PostScript file doesn't appear to have fared too badly, but upon closer inspection you'll see that the text is badly spaced, having been converted to strings of overlapping artistic text.

In the printout shown in Figure 29.7, you can see that the Placeable EPS file prints beautifully, indistinguishable from the source. But the Interpreted file has lost its text entirely. Indeed, we noticed some very strange behavior when trying to adjust the text created from the Interpreted file. We got ghost images back where the text was originally created, almost as if—to get technical for a moment—the text was still holding on to its original bounding box information.

29.6

Looks can be deceiving: The Placeable EPS file doesn't look too healthy in this on-screen image…

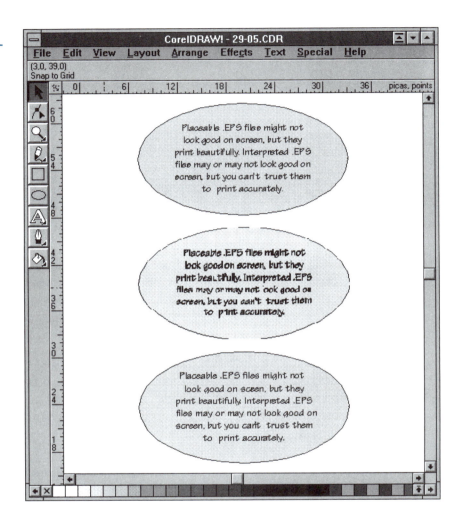

WATCH OUT!

As good as Placeable EPS files are, they're not worth much more than their image headers if you intend to print them to a non-PostScript printer. The printer will just ignore all of the PostScript code and print only the image header.

29.7

...but it's really the Interpreted PostScript file that's sick.

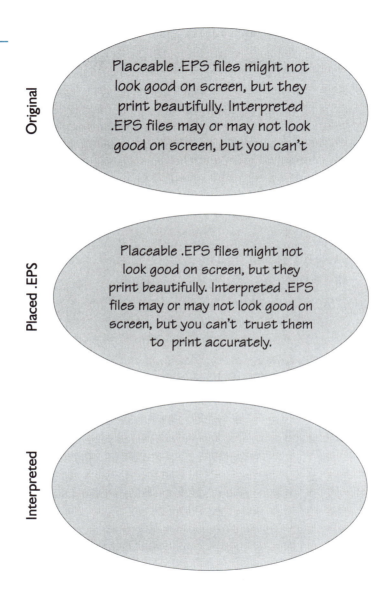

Although you cannot take apart and edit the objects in a Placeable EPS file, you can rotate, skew, stretch, and/or mirror them without loss of fidelity. The only exception to this is if your .EPS file contains a bitmap image; scaling or stretching a bitmap image could be hazardous to your career.

Importing Bitmap Images

DRAW can import many different bitmap formats, including the heavyweights TIFF and PCX. Color, black and white, gray—DRAW doesn't care. To a large degree, DRAW treats these as it does .EPS files, simply passing them on to the printer.

However, DRAW does speak bitmap to some extent. It can show you your imported bitmap images in considerable detail. If an imported bitmap contains 16 million colors, DRAW will show you an image of near television quality. Figure 29.8 shows off DRAW's screen rendering and printing prowess with bitmaps of sufficient color (or gray). The printout from the 16-million color image is virtually lifelike.

You can't do much to bitmap images in DRAW, and what you can do, you do at your own risk. For instance:

- **You can scale a bitmap, but...** Bitmap images that contain gray or color are made up of dot matrices, which are extremely size

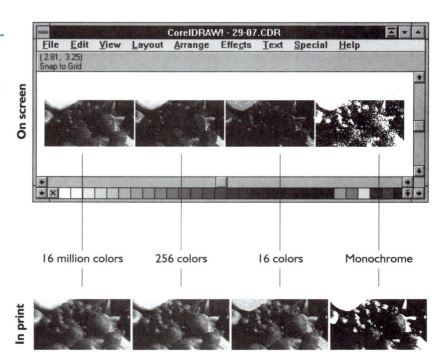

29.8

If your bitmap image has the detail, DRAW will show it.

sensitive. Skewing a gray-scale or color bitmap is certain death; scaling it proportionally is also risky.

- **You can rotate a bitmap, but…** DRAW insists on showing you as much detail as it can, making for v-e-r-y s-l-o-w drawing times. So it's better to rotate the image before importing it. You can quell DRAW's high-resolution ways by toggling View / Bitmaps / High Resolution, and the results of doing this are clear in Figure 29.9. Most DRAW users prefer to keep their display of bitmaps at high resolution and have their bitmaps rotated before they reach DRAW.

- **You can overlay objects on bitmaps, but…** DRAW is not a paint program; it doesn't support transparent objects. Anything you place on top of a bitmap image covers that part of the image completely.

Unless you have substantial field experience with color and gray-scale printing, your best bet is to use bitmap images as backdrops to your drawings. Figure 29.10 shows a perfect use for a bitmap image in this calendar featuring an animal of the month. The artist, Billie Gist of Houston, Texas, scanned this image to fit the space precisely; therefore, no excess fiddling was required in DRAW. Where bitmap images are concerned, the less fiddling, the better.

Bitmaps and Pieces

Here are a few odds and ends concerning bitmap images.

Lots of Dots, Lots of Data   Imported bitmaps can get big—in a hurry. Even if the file size isn't large, DRAW might need to move a mountain or two to import and display certain bitmap images. For instance, a TIFF file stored in the now-common compressed format might take up no more than 100K on your hard drive. But when you import it, DRAW uncompresses it, and the space requirements balloon to as much as four times the original size. The .CDR file containing this bitmap will grow quite large, and DRAW will swipe an equally large chunk of space from your Windows TEMP directory.

29.9

If you ask DRAW to show you rotated bitmaps in high resolution, you should know the trade-off.

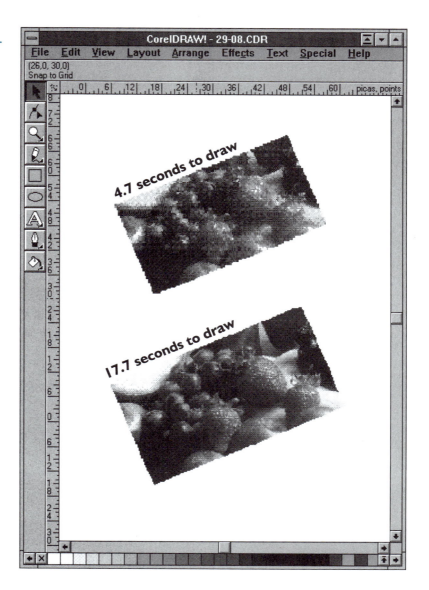

Crop with the Shape Tool Bitmap images can be cropped in DRAW with no loss of fidelity. To crop a bitmap, select it and then choose the Shape tool. The selection handles around the image become cropping handles; by moving any one of them toward the middle of the image, you are essentially pulling a white window shade over the image.

29.10

An effective use of a bitmap incorporated into a drawing

Cropping does not rescale the image; it only limits the portion that is visible.

Also, remember that you can apply a PowerClip to a bitmap, essentially stuffing it inside any other object.

Cropping and clipping images in DRAW is convenient, but not efficient. It's not as if you have removed that part of the image—DRAW still must hold it in memory and keep track of all those dots. If you are working with large images, it would be better to crop the image in your image-editing program and then import the newly shorn image to DRAW. The value of cropping is realized when you haven't yet decided how much image to use and are experimenting with different appearances. As we said, cropping is a tool of convenience.

Support for Separations   As of version 4.0, DRAW can import TIFF files that contain color-separation information. These so-called CMYK TIFF files are like ready-to-roll color files, with all process-color information already separated. These special TIFF files used to be persona non grata with DRAW, but since 4.0, DRAW understands them and imports them.

Importing Linked Data

You have already had a taste of OLE in Chapter 11, when you saw the behavior of three different types of imported text, including an embedded Word for Windows object. Most of the discussion about OLE takes place in Chapter 30, but here is a preview, and a look at how DRAW functions on the receiving end of the OLE operation.

It used to be simple: You copy from one program and paste into another. That was all there was to the story—the data was perfectly content to travel hither and yon and drop itself into any program willing to accept it. Once it reached its destination, it completely forgot where it came from.

Not anymore. Today, data remembers its roots and is able to automatically return to its nest for a bit of rework. Data that remembers its source is the essence of OLE. Now things are more complicated, but also more powerful.

Servers and Clients

When a software manufacturer proclaims that its program is "OLE-compliant," that means the program is able to function either as the source or the destination in an OLE exchange. In other words, it can supply data out across the Clipboard and be on call should the data need revising, or it can receive data from across the Clipboard and be able to make the call to the source program. Programs that can act as the source for linked data are called *servers;* these programs serve data to other programs. Programs that receive linked data are called *clients*; they are the programs to which data is served.

DRAW can function as a client or a server. It can be the source of hot-linked data, or it can receive the data. The dead giveaway of a program that is an OLE client is the Edit menu: If it offers a Paste Special command, then it is OLE-capable.

Creating an OLE Link

Creating an OLE link between two applications involves little more than a copy-and-paste across the Clipboard. To follow along with this procedure, you'll need to have PHOTO-PAINT installed on your system, and access to a bitmap file. If you can't readily locate one, you can use ROSE.PCX from the PRACTICE directory.

1. Start PHOTO-PAINT and open an image.

2. Using the Rectangular Masking tool (the tool second from the top in the PHOTO-PAINT toolbox), select a portion, any size, of the file.

3. Go to Edit / Copy to copy the selected part of the image to the Clipboard.

4. Close the image with File / Close, but don't exit PHOTO-PAINT. (This step isn't required, but it helps illustrate the OLE process; specifically, that the file is no longer open in PHOTO-PAINT.)

5. Switch to Program Manager and start DRAW (or switch to DRAW if it is already running).

6. Go to Edit / Paste Special. You will see the dialog shown in Figure 29.11. (If Paste Special is unavailable on your Edit menu, return to PHOTO-PAINT and repeat the first three steps of this procedure.)

7. Set the Paste Special options to match Figure 29.11 and OK the dialog.

Notice first that your image is shining out at you from DRAW, and second, that the status line refers to the image as a "PHOTO-PAINT image." In other words, DRAW understands that this object came from someplace else and, if necessary, knows how to get back there.

29.11

Establishing the link

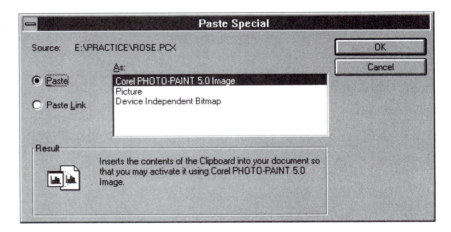

Editing a Linked Object

Once the link is established, setting OLE in motion involves nothing more than a double-click. If you decide that you need to make a change to your image, you don't have to bother reopening the file in PHOTO-PAINT and then reimporting it. Do this instead:

1. In DRAW, double-click the image. PHOTO-PAINT immediately swings into active duty and opens the file. Notice the name of the file—it's the name of the .CDR file (or UNTITLED.CDR

if you haven't saved yet). PHOTO-PAINT knows that this object belongs to DRAW and that the request to edit it came from DRAW.

2. Make a change to the image, any change at all—even a big white eraser mark through it.

3. Go to File / Update. The Update command isn't normally on the File menu, but PHOTO-PAINT knows that it is in the middle of an OLE operation. PHOTO-PAINT isn't interested in saving the file, but rather in *updating the object that is stored in the DRAW file* (a subtle distinction, we agree, but an important one to the OLE procedure).

4. Return to DRAW, and notice that the change to the image is already reflected.

Linked Files and Embedded Objects

There are two distinct types of data that an OLE client can receive: *linked files* and *embedded objects*. When DRAW received the image from PHOTO-PAINT in the foregoing exercise, DRAW gave you a choice (via the Paste Special dialog) of how it would treat the incoming data. DRAW can either swallow up a copy of the image for itself and be completely self-sufficient in handling this file, or it can link itself to the original file. Most programs call these two choices Paste Object and Paste Link; DRAW calls them Paste and Paste Link. (If you paste with Edit / Paste or Ctrl+V instead of Edit / Paste Special, DRAW defaults to Paste Object.)

To understand OLE, you must first understand this: When an OLE server copies a picture to the Clipboard, it copies more than just the graphical information required by the client for printing. It also copies

- The name of the program that produced the graphic
- The name and full path to the graphic file
- And even the data that makes up the original file

On the receiving end, an OLE client provides you with several choices of how to accept the data (listed in the Paste Special dialog). You can always ask to paste just the picture with no link information at all, usually referred to in Paste Special as just "Metafile" or "Bitmap." If you select the Paste Link choice, you create a *link* between the image in DRAW and the original file. The default choice of Paste embeds an *object* into DRAW. These two OLE choices are quite different, and their differences become especially apparent when you want to edit the image later.

If you paste the graphic image as a standard metafile, the image comes in cold and limp, with no idea of its source. You can double-click on that graphic until the next solar eclipse and you won't get back to the source. But the two OLE choices both spring into action, each in its own way, when you double-click the imported object.

Editing a Linked File

When you double-click on an image that was pasted as a linked file, you trigger a series of events for which Windows plays referee. Your double-click acts as an announcement.

DRAW (client): "Hey Windows, I need to do some editing. Take care of this for me, will you?"

Windows: "I'm checking my big black book, and I see here that the image you want to edit was pasted as a linked file. The file name is SCAN.TIF, it was produced in PHOTO-PAINT, and it was stored in your D:\IMAGES directory. I see that you have PHOTO-PAINT already in memory, so I don't need to launch it—I'll just switch to it and open SCAN.TIF. When you're done editing, issue a Save command, and the image in your drawing will update immediately."

This is really no different from going through the motions yourself, but being spared those motions is a great convenience. When you are done editing the original file in the source program, a Save command performs the equivalent of your copying the image to the Clipboard, switching to DRAW, and pasting the image. OLE takes care of all of that for you automatically.

Editing an Embedded Object

This one is different. An embedded object doesn't need an original file—everything needed to view, print, *and edit* the file is contained in the object: It's like a minioriginal file. In this case your double-click initiates the following dialog:

DRAW (client): "Hey Windows, I need to do some editing. Take care of this for me, will you?"

Windows: "I'm checking my big black book, and I see here that the image you want to edit was pasted as an embedded object. Therefore, I won't try to find an original file; I just need to make sure I can open the program that created it. I'm opening PHOTO-PAINT right now and dumping the object into it. There. When you're done, choose File / Update to update the image in your drawing."

We like to think of it this way: With a linked file, PHOTO-PAINT still owns the image. Its fate is tied to that original file. But with an embedded object, DRAW owns the image. Everything necessary to view, print, and edit it is contained in the object.

INSIDE INFO

Regardless of your choice in Paste Special—embedded object, linked file, or boring old picture—you get the same image quality. Windows uses the WMF format for transferring vector art across the Clipboard, and BMP for bitmap images. The two OLE choices add convenience, but not at the expense of quality.

Rules of Thumb for Linked vs. Embedded

Although both methods of using OLE offer you the editing convenience of the double-click, the rules of thumb for usage of the two techniques are different.

- Use linked files when you want to maintain control of an original file. Perhaps you have a chart that you have pasted from CHART into several drawings. The chart might change, and if it does, it's important that the change be reflected across all of the drawings that use it. If you have pasted the chart as a linked file, changing that original will automatically change every occurrence of it throughout your drawings.

- Use embedded objects when you want independent control over an image. If you're going to paste 25 charts from CHART and you want each one to have its own destiny, then paste them as objects. In this case there is no original file—changing one pasted image has no impact on any of the others, as each one is an independent object.

- Also, it's a good idea to use an embedded object when you are sending a drawing to users on different systems. If you gave a drawing with a linked file to a colleague, he or she would not be able to edit the linked image without also having the source file. But, as emphasized earlier, the embedded object needs no original file; everything that is required for editing is contained in the object. Your colleague would have to have the original application that created the object, but that's all.

DRAW's Role in OLE

You won't often need DRAW to act as the client in an OLE operation. Most graphics imported into DRAW can be changed from within DRAW, obviating the need for DRAW to trace a graphic back to its source for changes. Just above, you stepped through the most common scenario under which DRAW plays client: when an imported *bitmap* image needs to go back for rework.

DRAW really shines as an OLE partner when it acts as *server*, not client. After all, one of DRAW's missions in life is to supply graphics to documents in other programs. That will be the highlight of the next freeway exit, "Exporting from DRAW."

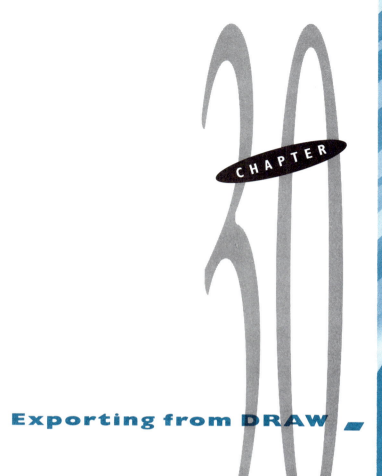

Exporting from DRAW

CHAPTER THIRTY

CHAPTER 30

At long last, we've come to the final chapter in the CorelDRAW section of this book. Our guess is that after 29 chapters and some five gazillion pages, the last thing you want to read is a long, exhaustive, and heavy treatise covering far more than you might care to know about exporting files. And after *writing* five gazillion pages, we don't particularly feel like throwing anything heavy at you, either.

That means we have chosen the perfect topic to end this book, because we think the best way to cover the topic of exporting is to show you, rather than just tell you. If you want to learn about the science of file filters, come to one of our conferences and corner an engineer. If you want to actually write a filter, you have our deepest sympathies. If you simply want to determine which format works best, read on.

Those of you who produce and print your artwork entirely within DRAW won't be interested in this chapter. Thank you for coming, and please leave by the exits. The other 99% of you regularly, perhaps constantly, produce work that is designed to be incorporated into something else—a letter in your word processor, a brochure in PageMaker, a logo in Ventura Publisher, a background for a chart, or one of hundreds of other types of drawings that will find their way into other documents. The export questions you face are among the most salient of all. This chapter is for you.

Choose Your Weapon

The first question you must face: What format should you use to export your work? At the risk of oversimplification, we intend to clean up this landscape considerably. If you're producing art designed to be used in another Windows program, we recommend you limit your choices to three:

- Encapsulated PostScript (EPS)

- Windows Metafile (WMF)
- The Clipboard

We maintain that there are few exceptions to this rule. If you have a PostScript printer, you can't go wrong with EPS. In our tests, EPS came in at or near the top in all categories: output quality, speed of export, size of file, time needed to spool to the printer, and time to print. Because of its flexibility in accommodating halftones, EPS is also the best equipped to handle such demanding elements as bitmap images, fine grays, fountain fills, and blends. If you read no further in this chapter—if you stop here and conclude that you will export all of your work as Encapsulated PostScript—then you will do just fine.

If you don't have a PostScript printer, there is still hope for you. In fact, DRAW 5.0 restores a significant measure of hope that was killed off in 4.0. The WMF format as well as the various Clipboard options all produce good results, each with its own benefits and drawbacks.

In general, use of all the other formats should be limited to specialty assignments—for example, CGM for sending files to some slide services, HPGL for creating work destined for a plotter, DXF for work going into Auto-CAD, and PCX or TIFF for sending artwork as bitmap images.

The Third Annual Export Torture Test

Submitted for your approval, the following illustration was created for our now-famous annual test of DRAW's exporting prowess. This is the third one; the first test was performed in late 1992 with DRAW 3.0, and the second one in the DRAW 4.0 edition of this book in 1993.

We borrowed the calendar idea (you saw it first in Chapter 29) from artist Billie Gist and produced several elements that we think are indicative of a file filter's accuracy:

- We blended the outlines around the month and date, to give them a glowing look. If an export format can't handle shifts in tone of at least 5 percent, the effect will be lost.

■ For the days of the month, we changed to Geometric 231, a typeface with very fine lines and loopy curves—both potentially taxing on some file formats.

- Behind the calendar we placed a conical fountain fill with several transitions between white and 20% black. These transitions are challenging to all file formats.
- The wheel is composed of .25-point hairlines. How well will they be rendered?
- The cube has two sides with graded shadows; and the top side has an extremely subtle shade that may be too subtle for many formats.
- The jet is an imported bitmap image; most formats simply ignore it.
- Finally, all these elements have been placed inside a PowerClip. Will the various file formats honor the clipping path?

If you would like to conduct your own tests, you will find TORTURE.CDR in the PICTURES directory. It is a 450K file, and requires that you install the Geometric 231 type family from Corel's library (or you'll need to set the calendar days and dates in a different face).

We exported this composite drawing from DRAW in ten different formats, including across the Clipboard, and recorded the size of the file and how long it took DRAW to create it. Then we printed each one from PageMaker 5.0 and from Ventura Publisher 4.2 (unless otherwise noted, all output samples in this chapter are from PageMaker). Of course, we wanted to also use Ventura 5.0 for these tests, but couldn't because of Corel's initial shipping delays for its new acquisition.

For each export, we recorded the time needed to send the print job to Print Manager, as well as the time elapsed until the printer started up. To be consistent, we switched to Print Manager as it spooled to the printer and made sure there were no background tasks in operation. Most importantly, of course, we evaluated the quality of the output. Table 30.1 lists the time and size statistics for each format.

When copying across the Clipboard, we determined file size by saving the data as a .CLP file, using the Clipboard utility supplied with Windows. All testing was performed on a Hewlett-Packard LaserJet 4M running in PostScript mode. Here is our report.

Table 30.1: Export Formats and Their Performance Records

FORMAT	EXPORT TIME	FILE SIZE	TIME TO SPOOL	SIZE OF PRINTER DATA	TIME TO PRINT
CGM	:12	53K	:04	125K	:45
AutoCAD†	:04	308K	:03	101K	:18
EPS	:18	2.6MB	:30	2.6MB	2:03
GEM†	:14	70K	1:14	8.5MB	8:27:50
GEM‡	:14	70K	:05	110K	:25
HPGL	:03	70K	:18	340K	1:45
PCX†	3:12	273K	:41	4.7MB	2:22
PCX‡	3:12	273K	4:52	14.3MB	12:05
TIF†	2:43	7.1MB	:35	1.2MB	1:17
TIF‡	2:43	7.1MB	4:52	14.3MB	12:05
WMF	:08	291K	1:13	950K	4:30
OLE	:05	1.6MB	:23	950K	4:30

† In PageMaker
‡ In Ventura

CGM

The first thing you'll notice about the .CGM file, shown in Figure 30.1, is that it is missing the picture of the jet. Most vector formats are unable to integrate bitmap images, so we were not particularly alarmed or shocked by the jet's absence. Though there is visible banding in the conical fill and the cube's shade, it is well within our definition of reasonable. We have come to expect inaccurate outlines with .CGM files, and our expectations were met: The blend effect on the month and year came out completely black. In the Ventura printout, the month and year were missing altogether, and the hairline wheel printed white instead of black.

30.1

This .CGM file printed from PageMaker produces acceptable fountain fills but distorted outlines.

Our conclusion: CGM survives the torture test, and in fact performs better than it did in 1992 or 1993. On the other hand, there is no longer much use for this format. Most professional slide services now work with PostScript files or original application files. The only use we see for CGM is if you're communicating with an older slide shop that uses out-of-date equipment, or sending art to a non-Windows program that has limited import options.

DXF

This well-known AutoCAD flavor produced a very small image size, surrounded by a very large invisible box (see Figure 30.2). All fills and blends are hollowed out.

We won't spend too much time harping on these imperfections, because in all fairness, the DXF filter is not designed for this type of use. Choose it only when you want to send a DRAW image directly into AutoCAD or a compatible program. Clearly, DXF is not designed for conventional work. Ventura wouldn't even load the file.

EPS

It's a three-peat for Encapsulated PostScript, and we won't be surprised if by the year 2000 it has stretched its string of victories to nine. The EPS filter produced 2.6MB of code in just 18 seconds, and the resultant file was equally efficient when making its way through Print Manager and to the laser printer.

Output was crisp and superb from both programs, and as Figure 30.3 shows, the .EPS file handled everything we threw at it, including the jet. It is the only vector-based format to accept bitmaps.

As discussed in Chapter 29, applications such as PageMaker and Ventura cannot read an .EPS file and produce an image from it; instead, they rely on a bitmap image that is commonly embedded within the EPS code. DRAW calls it an image header, and including one can have a significant effect on export time. The times and sizes shown in Table 30.1 are for just the PostScript code. Here is what happens if you include an image header:

Header	Time to Export	Size of File
Black and white	0:50 min.	2.6MB
72-dpi header	1:05 min.	2.7MB

Header	Time to Export	Size of File
72dpi / 8-bit color	1:05 min.	2.8MB
150-dpi header	2:00 min.	3.2MB

30.2

The AutoCAD DXF format is not designed for exporting from DRAW to standard applications.

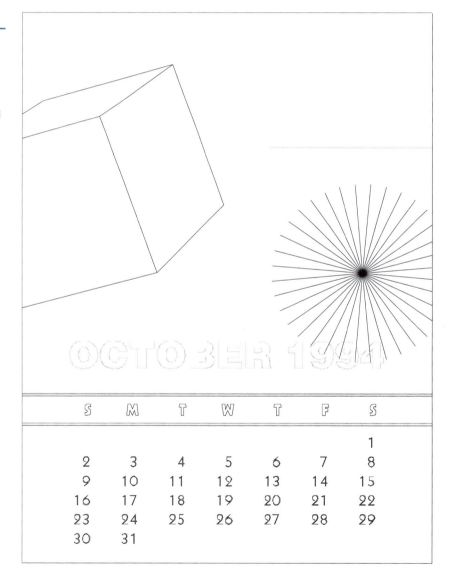

30.3
The winner and still champion: Encapsulated PostScript

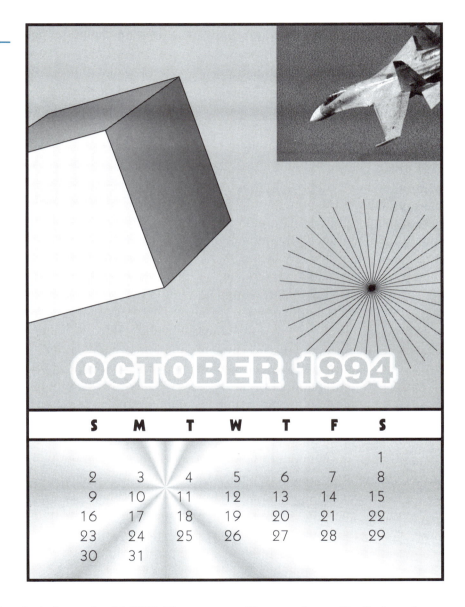

So what's the catch with EPS? There are two: You must have a PostScript printer in order to print these files; and screen clarity will be poor. In fact, EPS ranks among the worst in terms of screen image quality. Ventura users, be sure to use 8-bit image headers, or all you will get is mud, as Figure 30.4 demonstrates.

30.4

Though they print well, .EPS files don't look so hot on screen, especially when using low-resolution headers in Ventura.

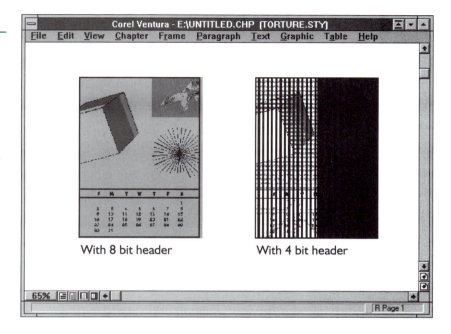

Our conclusion: PostScript printer owners should use .EPS files for all conventional exporting to other applications. The only exception might be to take advantage of the convenience of OLE, discussed later in the chapter.

GEM

Our tests with the virtually obsolete GEM format were the most intriguing of all. In just 14 seconds, DRAW's GEM export filter produced a file of a paltry 70K. With such a small amount of data, we expected little more than what Figure 30.5 shows—a rendering with very few shades. Now here's the strange part: Ventura sent only 110K of data to Print Manager, which in turn spat this out in just over 1 minute. Page-Maker, on the other hand, committed the electronic equivalent of a filibuster. It read the entire telephone book to Print Manager, sending it over 8.5MB of data. Poor Print Manager needed almost 4 minutes just to reach the 1% mark, and another 9.5 minutes to reach 2% completion. It delivered the final drawing to us... *8.5 hours later!* The final printout was virtually identical to the one from Ventura, so we spared our production staff the torture of another day-long print job—Figure 30.5 is from Ventura.

But we couldn't just leave it at that, so we sent the image to the printer again, this time using the driver for the non-PostScript HP LaserJet 4.

30.5

Not too many gray shades are supported by the old GEM format.

Ready for this? It created a mere 231K of code and produced identical output in barely 30 seconds.

The GEM file did work fine when used with the old GEM version of Ventura, but even in that situation EPS would be a better choice. We don't think you should have to wait eight hours for anything, so we recommend that you think of GEM, like CGM, as an export format whose day is done.

HPGL

As with DXF, the HPGL format is for specialty jobs, and the fact that the output from PageMaker and Ventura is unacceptable carries extenuating circumstances. As Figure 30.6 shows, all objects are rendered as outlines—there are no fill patterns at all. HPGL files are designed to be sent to plotters, and producing lines is exactly what a plotter is designed to do.

In other words, we can't blame the messenger for this bad news; the messenger was given a wrong street address and told to deliver the wrong package. Our torture test is simply not representative of the type of work one would send to a plotter. Plotters don't do fills, and they certainly don't do bitmaps. Therefore, we exonerate the HPGL format from all charges brought against it and, in conclusion, recommend you use HPGL files only when sending work directly to a plotter.

PCX and TIFF

We have heard stories of users exporting all of their work in bitmapped format, just to avoid using the more complex printer commands and instructions that have been known to produce printer errors. We understand that cutting off your nose to spite your face is also an option. Sorry, but the thought of producing vector images by describing every single dot that occurs on a page is too much for us to imagine.

Figure 30.7 shows the result of exporting a 256-color .PCX file and printing it from PageMaker or Ventura. Ventura took its sweet time with it, over 12 minutes, but PageMaker pumped it out in two.

30.6

Use HPGL files when seeking output from a plotter.

However, both of them fell down miserably in the shading department, and the fine type of the calendar does not hold up to even moderate scrutiny. This is the result of a print file that is fixed at 300 dpi. When we created a 600-dpi bitmap instead, PageMaker spooled over 33MB of data to Print Manager!

30.7

As with all bitmaps, .PCX files are of finite resolution and number of colors. In this case, both sets of numbers are found lacking.

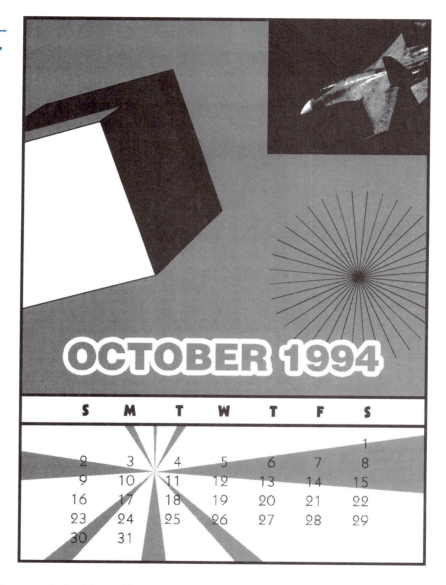

We created the TIFF file with 16 million colors instead of 256, and the 7.1MB file that DRAW churned out gave us a hint that something voluminous was developing. Indeed, Figure 30.8 shows the dramatically better shading achieved by adding all of those colors, but alas, the text still looks like something a 300-dpi printer dragged in. We shudder to think

30.8

This TIFF image has better tonal value than the PCX, but resolution is unimproved. The fine text cannot survive a close inspection.

of the file size had we created the image at 16 million colors *and* 600 dpi. Even then, the more curved parts of the drawing would not be much competition for the crisp 1,200-dpi (or even 2,500-dpi) output possible from the vector formats.

Our conclusion is that these two formats are best used for producing bitmap images that can then be brought into a paint program (not a page-layout program) for modification. There is no other legitimate value in converting high-resolution vector objects into fixed-resolution bitmap images.

WMF

Though it's been around for a while, the Windows Metafile format has only recently been given legitimacy as an export format. In 1993, it was our rookie of the year; it appears, however, that WMF might be suffering through its sophomore slump.

But wait—we're getting ahead of ourselves. We must first point out that we prefer WMF over all other formats discussed so far (except EPS). Metafile is clean, compact, well supported, and widely embraced. Figure 30.9 is an example of what it can do. And if you don't have a PostScript printer, .WMF files will help keep you from feeling like a second-class citizen.

Our primary disappointment with WMF this year was the loss of bitmap support that we were delighted to find in 1993; as you can see in Figure 30.9, WMF, like the other vector formats, offers up only the gray box. We also had to carefully navigate the dialog box of choices that DRAW presents before beginning the file export process.

When we designated that text be rendered as text (instead of curves) and imported into PageMaker, all of the tabs in the days of the week were lost (but not, curiously, in the days of the month). We re-exported and chose curves and got correct results, but in both cases, PageMaker did not show us a very good screen rendering. It was much poorer than in the two previous contests.

We had to make two copies of the file—one with the "placeable header" for PageMaker, and one without it for Ventura. And, still up to its old tricks with .WMF files, Ventura squashed the image in the frame, requiring a trip to Sizing & Scaling to fill it out over the entire frame. We had carefully created our frame in Ventura to the exact dimensions of the drawing; if we hadn't, it would have resulted in certain distortion.

30.9

Output from the .WMF file is very good, but not as good as it was last year and the year before.

Despite these quirks, our conclusion is that you not hesitate to rely on WMF as your export format if you do not have a PostScript printer or you don't want to use the Clipboard. Overall, WMF passes our tests here with high marks.

The Promise of
Object Linking and Embedding

In 1993, we wrote the following:

> The major disappointment for us has been the poor showing by DRAW in sending out information across the Clipboard. When pasted from DRAW, PageMaker refused to print the test file, and Ventura printed only the large lettering and a black box where the [bitmap] is supposed to go.
>
> Corel committed to using the new OLE 2.0 technology, but Microsoft's drivers were late and unstable. That is why pieces of text often turn up missing when pasted from DRAW. It's the reason DRAW's Clipboard performance has gone from excellent to poor. And it's the reason we can no longer recommend that you use it.
>
> When we meet here again next year for the Third Annual Torture Test, one of the burning questions will be: Has DRAW improved its Clipboard performance as a result of improved OLE 2.0 specifications?

We are delighted to report that the answer is yes. Corel had to go through the entire DRAW 4.0 season with unstable and inadequate Clipboard services, but now these problems appear to be completely resolved. We had outstanding success moving our drawing back and forth between DRAW and PageMaker, Ventura, Word for Windows, and other applications, maintaining full editability and getting precisely the behavior we expected each time.

Figure 30.10 illustrates the crisp and clean output possible with Clipboard transfers, although the absence of the jet indicates that the lack of bitmap support has become fundamental to the Windows Metafile format, which is used by both .WMF files and the Clipboard. Whether we pasted a static Metafile, embedded an object, or created a link to a file, output results were unswervingly accurate and consistent: 12 seconds to spool from PageMaker, 995K of print data created, 4.5 minutes to print.

30.10

Good news for OLE enthusiasts: DRAW 5.0 shines in sending graphical data out to others. This printout was the result of a copy-and-paste between DRAW and PageMaker.

The fact that these numbers are so consistent indicates that the output quality of the image was not affected by the way we used OLE. This was a huge issue last year: Embedded objects would print without all of the characters intact, linked files would frequently crash when imported, and static pastes were subject to distortions. It appears that DRAW 5.0 is rock solid when it comes to delivering clean, reliable graphical data across the Clipboard. Screen images are quite good, too.

Furthermore, we were astonished by the performance. If you have upgraded from DRAW 4.0, you probably remember all too well how slow the Clipboard was. It would sometimes take 5 or 10 seconds just to copy one simple rectangle. By contrast, DRAW 5.0 copied our entire test drawing to the Clipboard—1.6MB of data—in 5 seconds. Compare that with the .CGM filter's 12 seconds to produce 53K of code, and it is clear that the data pathway under OLE 2.0 is quite vast.

Figure 30.11 demonstrates one of the enduring values of object embedding. Here is an actual letter from our lead author to one of his contributors.

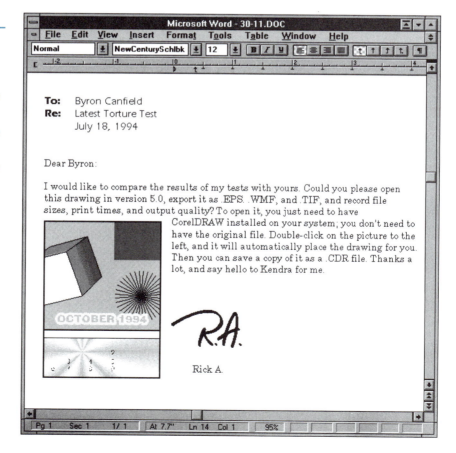

30.11

Thanks to object embedding, one file delivers our lead author's letter and the drawing. A double-click on the image automatically starts DRAW and opens the drawing.

He has embedded the torture test drawing right into his letter and has asked one of his contributors to open it. Because the drawing is an embedded object, Byron doesn't need an original file. All he needs are Word for Windows (so he can open the letter) and CorelDRAW. To open the drawing in DRAW, he need only double-click on it. The OLE engine takes care of all the rest.

We noticed one area that needs a caveat: embedding objects that contain paragraph text. Paragraph text is the only element under the CorelDRAW sphere of influence that cannot be interactively scaled by DRAW. All other objects have selection handles, allowing them to be made bigger or smaller, but with paragraph text, only the frame size changes. Therefore, if you size or stretch an embedded object in another application and then double-click to edit it in DRAW, DRAW will perform the same scaling operation as it places the image on screen—but if any paragraph text is included, the text will not resize; only the frame will. This is only relevant with embedded objects and paragraph text, not with linked files or artistic text. And it is hardly fatal, since the text can still be easily adjusted. Because TORTURE.CDR on the Companion CD has paragraph text in it, you can experiment with this for yourself.

This glitch is a far cry from the text problems exhibited by the previous version of OLE. To see if we could find the breaking point of text across the Clipboard, we conducted a second, more rigorous, torture test. First we surveyed our lineup of programs already in memory:

    Word for Windows 2.0

    CorelDRAW 5.0

    CorelDRAW 4.0

    Fax Manager

    Tiffany (a screen-shot utility)

    Norton Commander

    Print Manager

A good start, we figured. After loading both PageMaker 5.0 and Ventura 4.2 (the latter with breath held), we then switched to DRAW 5.0, and typed as artistic text **Now is the time for all good men to come to the aid of their Clipboard.**

and copied it down the page ten times. DRAW 4.0 wouldn't even let us create that much text as one artistic string; DRAW 5.0 not only eagerly gobbled it up, but also quickly sent it out across the Clipboard. We then

> Switched to PageMaker and pasted the text as an object
>
> Switched to Ventura and copied it as a linked file
>
> Moved to Word and copied it as an object

With version 4.0, we would by now have surely seen a paste of truncated text. Having met with no such problems to this point in 5.0, we began editing. We double-clicked all over the place, each time being returned to DRAW 5.0 and receiving the text, exactly as it appeared originally. Some of our double-clicks required that yet another copy of DRAW be loaded. We formatted, we added, we enveloped, we Power-Clipped, we added lenses—and we sent it back out to all of the OLE receptacles. (We wondered the entire time if DRAW 4.0 would get it in the way, but it sat quietly in the background, only speaking when spoken to. We did switch to it a few times and pasted various pieces to it, without incident.) In Figure 30.12 you see this second torture test in midsession.

Finally, Word choked and died (GPF: WINWORD.EXE). Like a football coach whose star running back is injured, we substituted Microsoft Write, and then we pasted to it, copied from it, and generally picked up right where we left off. The other players on the team remained oblivious, and all continued to function in perfect form. Microsoft itself couldn't have staged a more effective OLE demonstration than what took place here (except for Word biting the dust!).

Will it be as good for you? Who knows—hardware and software configurations are a dark art. We conducted this torture test on a PC with 16MB of RAM and an equal amount of swap file space. However, we think it's safe to say your OLE operations with DRAW 5.0 will be a much more fruitful and enjoyable experience than in any time in DRAW's history.

30.12

No problems with the new OLE, as DRAW elements go flying in all directions.

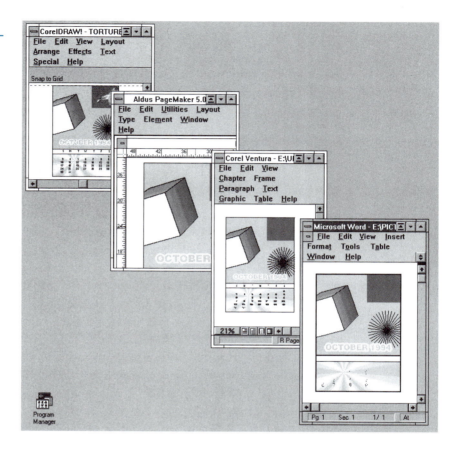

Summarizing the Torture Test

The safest, most reliable, and highest-fidelity method of transferring data from DRAW to other applications is via an encapsulated PostScript file. None of our celebration over OLE can mitigate that. If you have a PostScript printer and you want to make sure you are working with peak accuracy, use EPS files—end of discussion.

If you do not have a PostScript printer, however, or if you have several copies of DRAW-based art that need to be managed carefully, or if you want to distribute documents that contain DRAW files, or if you simply enjoy working with live links, then you should give OLE a try. It is ready to earn your confidence.

What the Heck Is a .CMX File?

Corel is trying to create its own little information highway among the CorelDRAW applications, and the vehicles that will travel this expressway will be called Presentation Exchange Data. In the initial release of DRAW 5.0 only a portion of the infrastructure had been built for these carriers. It included the file name extension, which logic would dictate would be .PED, but instead is .CMX.

A .CMX file resembles an efficient, compressed .CDR file. It contains only the information necessary to render a drawing, without any of the styles, layers, grid information, or other elements that are not crucial to the drawing. You may have noticed that all of the clip art on the CorelDRAW CD is stored in .CMX format. You may have also noticed the Save Presentation Exchange Data button at the lower-left of the Save As dialog.

Corel hopes to use .CMX as the universal file exchange language within CorelDRAW applications and, ideally, beyond. As the theory goes, if you include this extra Presentation Exchange Data in your drawing, then other Corel applications will be able to import your .CDR files directly, pick out the essential graphical information, and produce a high-fidelity copy of your work. At the time of this writing, however, adding this Presentation Data to your drawings only serves to produce larger .CDR files.

Fact is, no one is quite sure yet what Corel has in mind for this Presentation Exchange business yet. There was rampant speculation among beta testers as to future implementation. One of them, Chayim Lando, even discovered that an ambitious user could add a line to the [ExportFilters] section of the CORELFLT.INI file:

```
CMX=EXPCDR,"Corel Presentation Exchange",*.cmx,21
```

> that allowed creation of .CMX files. Corel engineers insist that .CMX files you make now might not be usable in later releases, but you can try this for yourself by adding that line to CORELFLT.INI and noting that "Corel Presentation Exchange" becomes a choice among the export formats. Indeed, the resulting file can be imported into any other CorelDRAW application. When we took our 454K TORTURE.CDR file and exported it to .CMX, the resulting file was only 344K, and it loaded perfectly back into DRAW, PHOTO-PAINT, and the other applications in the box.
>
> It would be wise for you to heed Corel's warning about not using .CMX yet for real work, and remember that, as of summer 1994, the ultimate plans for this private format were not yet revealed. All we know is that Corel engineers have yet another trick up their sleeves...

We certainly appreciate being able to finish the DRAW section of this book on a more upbeat note than in our 1993 book, in which we had to report on the dreadful goings-on with the early stages of OLE 2.0. DRAW will always have its detractors, and Corel its critics for its ambitious and sometimes overaggressive upgrades, but nobody can say that the program isn't a good Windows neighbor. As of 5.0, DRAW's ability to communicate with the rest of the Windows community should earn it a good citizen award.

Next up: CorelDRAW's other program modules.

PART VII

THE SUPPORTING CAST

We knew that this part would be the source of much discussion and debate—among us authors, and between us and the publishers. The central question: What to do with the other modules in the CorelDRAW package—PHOTO-PAINT, CHART, SHOW, MOVE, etc., etc., et al. (We're already reserving all of Part VIII for VENTURA.) How much space do we devote to a collection of programs that see significantly less use than DRAW? (Some DRAW users have barely heard of VENTURA, while others know it inside and out.)

Should we encourage Corel users to learn the other modules? Is that our responsibility, or it a bit unseemly? If it is outside the scope of this book to cover the other modules completely, then how do we handle them? Tutorial? Overview? Coverage of new features? There were lots of questions...

This part attempts to give a little bit to everyone. With a bit of tutorial, a solid overview, and close attention to new features as of 5.0, we hope to deliver to you an informed perspective of how these modules operate, who might use them, and how you might use them.

CHAPTER 31

PHOTO-PAINT

THIRTY-ONE

CHAPTER 31

You are about to enter a world where images are not defined by lines, curves, and nodes. In this world, images are defined by something smaller: the pixel. Welcome to the wonderful world of bitmaps and bitmap editing. That's what Corel PHOTO-PAINT is all about—manipulating bitmap images.

Unlike CorelDRAW's vector images, which are made of lines and curves, the images you work with in PHOTO-PAINT consist of millions of pixels. For the most part, these images are photographs that have been converted to digital form by a scanner. In fact, if you have a scanner, you can use PHOTO-PAINT to convert your old paper photos into editable digital images. But that's getting ahead of the story.

Digital photos come in several varieties. Black-and-white, 1-bit images look more like line art than photos. Sixteen-color, 4-bit images look very splotchy and cartoonish. The next step up is 256-color or 256-shade gray-scale, 8-bit images; these are adequate for use in desktop presentations, but they're not quite natural looking. At the top of the scale are images capable of 16.8 million colors, or 24-bit images, also referred to as *true-color images* because they capture the maximum number of colors the eye can see. These 24-bit images present the continuous tones necessary for photographic quality most accurately, and these are the images we'll be modifying here in PHOTO-PAINT.

PHOTO-PAINT's Tools

PHOTO-PAINT earns its name by providing tools for photo manipulation and creation, as well as for painting. Both types of tools operate exclusively on the pixel level. And both sets of tools are so plentiful that we can't begin to discuss all of them here. PHOTO-PAINT is a deep and powerful program that's a good choice for any image-editing task. With this bounty of tools, you can

- Scan and retouch photos
- Create composite photos made up of multiple images
- Paint with tools that mimic natural media
- Create photo "paintings" consisting of photos, special effects, and paint

All of these capabilities existed in previous versions of PHOTO-PAINT, and many new additions to version 5.0 make the utility a bitmap powerhouse. PHOTO-PAINT is now faster, more capable, and easier to use than ever before. For increased productivity, Corel has added

- Improved memory management
- The ability to open just a piece of an image
- The ability to crop or resample an image
- The ability to enter text directly on the image
- Support for OLE 2.0, so you can drag and drop across applications

And Corel's engineers know that all work and no play makes PHOTO-PAINT a dull application, so they've made it more creative, too. You'll find

- Better masking, including the ability to save and reuse masks, and to node-edit, merge, move, and invert masks
- Color masking
- Independent floating bitmap objects and a file format that supports them
- Support for industry-standard Photoshop plug-in filters
- New funky filters
- New brush styles
- A universal Fill roll-up that provides access to all CorelDRAW fills

PHOTO-PAINT's painting tools are powerful, too, but they can't compete with stand-alone natural media paint programs. For this reason, we'll focus our attention in this chapter on the image-editing tools. As you read, keep in mind that there's enough power and complexity in PHOTO-PAINT to warrant an entire book. This chapter only scratches the surface.

Getting Comfortable with PHOTO-PAINT

Before you can begin to create better-looking photos, photo collages, and painted images, you'll need to learn a bit about the tools and conventions used by PHOTO-PAINT. No matter what you do in this program, you'll need to know how to work the Tool Settings roll-up, the Zoom tools, the Color roll-up, and the Undo tools. There's no better time than the present, so let's jump in and start exploring.

The Tool Settings Roll-up

The Tool Settings roll-up (Figure 31.1) is a bit like NASA's Mission Control. You'll use the options on this roll-up to adjust and customize PHOTO-PAINT's many paint tools. The settings present in the roll-up will depend upon which tool you're using. And because the settings are specific to the selected tool, you don't have to worry that the changes you make will affect other tools.

Follow these steps to explore the Tool Settings roll-up:

1. Click on the Paintbrush tool in the toolbar at the side of the PHOTO-PAINT window.

2. To open the Tool Settings roll-up, click on the View menu and choose Tool Settings Roll-Up (or just press F8).

3. Notice the three icons across the top part of the roll-up; these icons let you select the shape of your tool (ellipse, square, or special).

31.1

Think of the Tool Settings roll-up as PHOTO-PAINT's Mission Control.

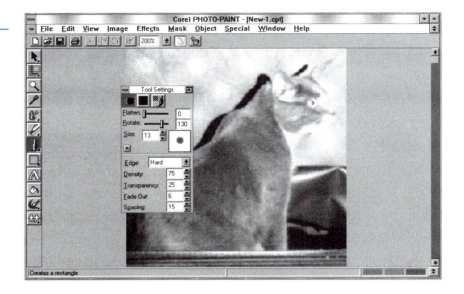

4. Grab the Flatten slider and adjust it. Lower numbers create a rounder, thicker brush, and higher numbers produce a flatter, more linear brush.

5. Grab the Rotate slider and move it to angle your brush. Positive numbers rotate to the left, negative to the right.

6. In the Size box, type in a number or click on the arrows to adjust the size of the brush.

7. In the Edge box, select a brush edge, which determines the quality of the edges of your strokes. Soft gives you a smooth, almost blended edge; Hard keeps the edges sharp.

8. Try adjusting Density. Higher numbers produce bolder, stronger strokes, and lower numbers produce finer, more delicate strokes.

9. Fiddle with Fade Out. This controls how quickly your brush strokes disappear. Higher numbers yield faster fade-out (or the appearance of shorter strokes). In traditional painting terms, Fade-Out is similar to loading less paint on your brush and gradually decreasing its pressure.

10. Try adjusting the Transparency and Spacing. Transparency determines the opacity of your paint application; the higher the number, the more transparent the stroke. Spacing determines how often in a stroke the paint is applied. Try a Spacing setting of 1 or 2 for a smooth stroke; the higher numbers give strokes a dotted or stepped appearance.

When you've had your fill of fiddling, paint with the brush. Go back and readjust some of the settings to see the changes they produce.

The Zoom Tools

Because you're working with individual pixels in PHOTO-PAINT, the success of a complex operation may hinge upon your ability to zoom. Sometimes, it's a matter of zoom or die. If you think we're overstating the case, try to create or fine-tune a mask without zooming the image first. It will look horrible, trust us.

Fortunately, all you need to know to be a zoom star is how to point and click. PHOTO-PAINT gives you three Zoom tools to make it easier to work with magnified images. The main tool is the magnifying glass, and there are two companion tools (the Hand and the Locator, which looks like a compass). All of them are stored in the Zoom flyout menu (Figure 31.2).

Here are a few tricks for working with the Zoom tools:

- To zoom in on an image, click on the left mouse button. To zoom out, click the right mouse button.
- Use the Hand tool to pan across a zoomed image. It's easier than using the slider bars.
- Use the Locator tool to find where you are in a duplicate zoomed image.

Getting Comfortable with PHOTO-PAINT 787

31.2

If you can't zoom, you can't paint.

The Color Roll-up

Think of the Color roll-up (Figure 31.3) as your personal paint box. Here is where you can

- Choose the color model you want to work in
- Choose the color of the paper (or background) for a new paint image
- Choose the color you want to paint with
- Load, save, and create color palettes
- Load a bitmap image to use as a color palette.

Bear in mind that the colors you choose here will have no impact on fill colors. To select colors for a gradient, texture, or flood fill, you'll use the Fill roll-up.

31.3

The Color roll-up is a mix master's paradise.

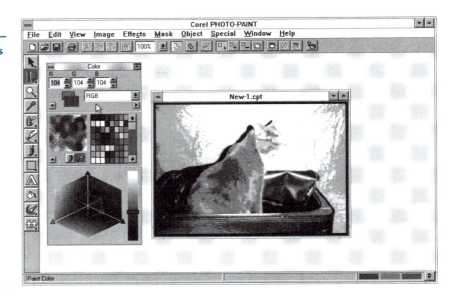

The Undo Tools

Because nobody's perfect, PHOTO-PAINT gives you several different ways to undo your slip-ups. What you're doing and how much of a mistake you've made will determine which Undo tool works best. So which Oops do you use? The Undo flyout is shown in Figure 31.4; here are some tips for using it.

If you've painted a line, applied an effect, or done something else you wish you hadn't, and you haven't yet unselected the offending tool or taken another step, choose Edit / Undo. Or double-click the Local Undo tool—it's the one that looks like a bottle of typing correction fluid.

The other option for reversing an action while a tool is still selected is to click the Local Undo tool, and then paint over the parts of the image you've botched. Like Edit / Undo, the Local Undo tool only corrects the mistakes you've made since the last time you chose a command or tool.

If you'd just as soon eliminate an entire section of your picture, click on the first Eraser tool (the middle one). It looks just like what it is, and works much the same way. Drag the eraser over the ugly bits, and they'll

31.4

To err is human, so you'll probably find a use for each of these Undo tools.

disappear completely. Remember though, that all you'll be left with is the underlying paper; so if you have drawn a not-so-straight line over a beautiful, satisfying background, don't use the Eraser.

Maybe you hate the whole image and just want to start over. Just double-click the (first) Eraser on your picture, and you get a nice clean page to work on.

If you want to change one color in a given area to another color, use the second Eraser tool (the one at the end). This one isn't really an eraser, but rather a color replacer. It acts as a nifty little "search-and-replace" tool (like the one in your word processor, but for colors, not text). "Rub" this tool over an area in the image, and all instances of one color are replaced with the color you specify in the Color roll-up.

AUTHOR'S NOTE

For the ultimate in Oops! protection, experiment with the Checkpoints option on the File menu.

Creating an Image

Now that you're familiar with the tools, let's explore some of the more difficult aspects of working with PHOTO-PAINT to manipulate images. In this section, we'll be working directly with images, in order to better understand what it is you can do to make photos look better and how you go about doing it. When you've finished working through the exercises, you'll know how to retouch, revamp and re-create images—and you'll have some masterpieces of your own to show your friends. All of the images we refer to in the exercises can be found in the PRACTICE directory on the Companion CD.

When a Whole Image Is Too Much

Bitmap images like the true-color (16.8 million colors) photos we'll be working with can get to be enormous in a hurry. The sheer size of the images and the number of pixels your computer must shuttle around to complete an operation makes working with bitmaps a memory- and time-consuming process. To eliminate some of the headaches inherent to working with this amount of data, Corel has added some new File / Open options to the current version of PHOTO-PAINT. Take a look at the drop-down list in the lower-right of the Open an Image dialog in Figure 31.5

31.5

Opening a file is more complicated but more efficient than it used to be.

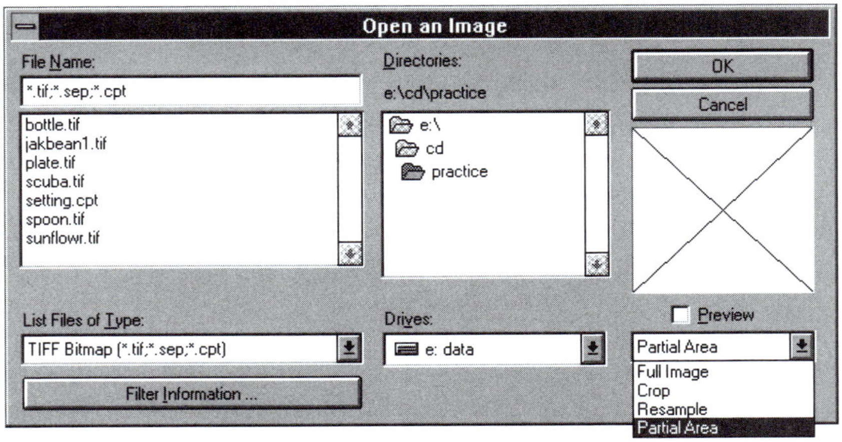

Full Image   Loading a full image is the best choice only when it's a small image, a gray-scale image (which is smaller in file size than a true-color image), or an image to which you want to make one global change.

Crop   Select Crop when you only need a piece of a larger image, for instance, one person out of a group shot. You can physically position the crop box over the image portion you need, or you can enter its screen coordinates or the preferred height and width. Don't worry that you might later decide you want more of the image. PHOTO-PAINT will take the area you mark for cropping and save it as a new file. The original image remains untouched.

Resample   Because resampling allows you to reduce the overall size and/or resolution in dpi (dots per inch) of an image, Resample is the best choice when image quality isn't a primary issue, when space is at a premium, or when your output device doesn't support the image's original resolution.

Before you choose this option, consider where you're going to use the altered image. If you only have a 2-by-2-inch space for a photo in your newsletter, and the original image is 5 by 7 inches, by all means reduce its size. By the same token, if you're going to print that newsletter on a black-and-white laser printer, which has a maximum resolution of 300 dpi, attempting anything above that resolution is futile.

Partial Area   As shown in Figure 31.6, the Partial Area option allows you to open a segment of an image, work on it, and then save that section back into the main image. You can then open another segment and continue your work.

This is the best choice when you're working with a large, high-resolution, full-color image, or if you're experimenting with memory-intensive operations such as applying a motion blur (or other filter), cloning part of the image, or using the Magic Wand selection tool (discussed shortly). Partial Area is also a good choice if memory is at a premium in your setup and you want to be able to Undo a complex action. For example,

31.6

The Partial Area option is indispensable when you're working with large images.

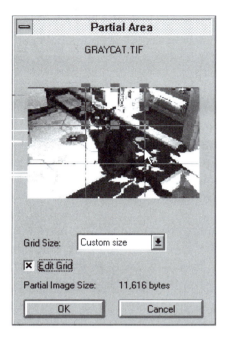

suppose you've adjusted the brightness on a full-color photo of a landscape and then decide it's too bright. You may find that the program can't Undo such a major alteration.

Here's an exercise to practice using the Partial Area option:

1. Choose File/Open from the File Menu.
2. From the File List, choose SUNFLWR.TIF in the PRACTICE directory. Make sure Preview is selected, so you can see a thumbnail of the image.
3. Choose Partial Area from the drop-down list under the Preview window, and click OK. The sunflower gets a 3-by-3 grid overlay. One section of the grid will be flashing to indicate that it's the active selection.
4. From the Grid Size drop-down list, choose 2 x 2. Click on the upper-right corner of the sunflower image to select it, and then click OK.

When the image opens, you'll notice a grid in its upper-right corner; this tells you you're working on only part of the image. When you do something to this piece and then save it, your changes are automatically incorporated with the rest of the image. However, if you open another piece of the image without saving the current piece, your changes will be gone for good.

Working with Masks

Now that you've learned how to open a large file, let's get busy and make some changes to an image, using a mask. A mask is a selection you create around part of an image, to shield that part from changes made or effects applied to the rest of the photograph. You use a mask when you want to change only part of an image. For instance, you might want to blur just the car in a racing scene, so that it looks like it was speeding along a roadway, or change the color of just the roses in a mixed bouquet of flowers.

Creating a mask is a simple, if exacting process. Your biggest allies here are a steady mouse and lots of patience.

Using the Mask Flyout

The tools you need for masking are located on a flyout from the Mask tool on the side toolbar (see Figure 31.7).

By the way, the Object Picker tool (the arrow icon on the side toolbar) holds tools for selecting and creating objects. These tools look and work very much like the masking tools, but they cannot be used to shield part of an image.

Rules of Thumb   *You can use the Mask tools separately or in combination, as desired, to create just the shape you need. In most cases, any of the masking tools is almost as good a choice as another. Let the shape you're trying to mask determine which tool you choose. Here are some rules of thumb.*

31.7

The masking tools flyout from the Mask tool

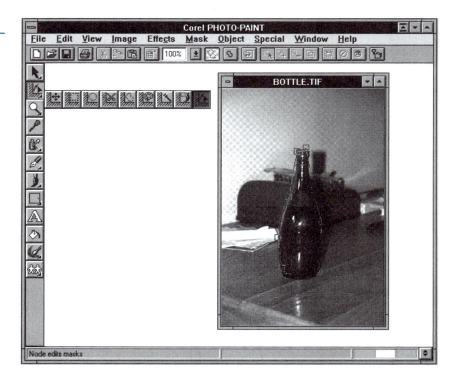

Use the Rectangle, Circle/Ellipse, and Polygon tools to create simple masks, or as a starting point for more complex masks. These tools work just like their counterparts in DRAW's toolbox. Just click, hold, and drag, or use a series of clicks to create the shape you want.

To use them effectively for masking, the Freehand and Lasso tools require a lot of patience and a well-zoomed image. You can use either tool for creating an irregularly shaped mask, but the Lasso is better suited to masking distinctively colored areas, because it snaps to the masked area that differs in color from the surrounding area.

Use the Magic Wand when you want to mask all the areas in an image that have a similar color. The important thing to remember when using this tool is that the color of the object to be masked must be significantly different from the colors in the rest of the image. So, the Magic Wand will work well when you want to mask, say, an apple out of a basket of bananas; but the Wand would probably be useless for masking an apple out of a field of red poppies. Bear in mind, too, that this is a memory-intensive tool, so use it sparingly.

Creating a Mask

You can name, save, and reuse your masks, but first you need to create them. So let's get started.

1. Open the image SPOON.TIF from the PRACTICE directory, using File / Open with the Partial Area option selected. Customize the grid so the spoon fits in one square.
2. Zoom in so the spoon fills the image area, but doesn't extend beyond it.
3. Choose the Polygon tool (the scissors) on the Mask flyout.
4. Click on the bottom edge of the spoon handle, and drag to the point where the handle meets the bowl of the spoon. Click again to place another node.
5. Continue to add nodes until the mask surrounds the entire spoon, and then double-click to close the mask polygon. Don't worry if your mask isn't precisely on the edge of the spoon. You will begin to fine-tune it in the next step.
6. Click on the Node Edit tool. In a second or two, PHOTO-PAINT will convert the mask into an editable vector outline, as shown in Figure 31.8.
7. Now shape the mask so that it surrounds exactly the portion of the image you want masked. Click on any of the nodes, and drag it to a better-fitting place, just as you would any vector point. Continue until the mask is perfect.
8. Now that your mask is complete, switch back to the Pick tool, and use the Mask menu to name and save the mask. We'll be using it again later on, in "Working with Objects."
9. Once you've saved the mask, go to Mask / Remove to remove the mask from the image.

31.8

A mask in node-editing mode

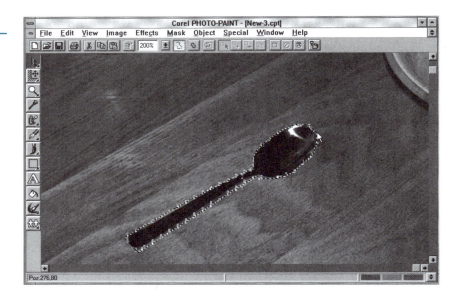

Using the Color Mask Roll-Up

You may have noticed that in addition to the masking tools flyout, there is a Mask command on the PHOTO-PAINT menu. This menu contains the more sophisticated masking techniques and tools. One of the most important is the Color Mask roll-up (Figure 31.9), which is particularly useful when you to want to alter or protect a single color or range of colors throughout an image. Think of it as the ultimate colorizing tool—if only you had one for those days when your shirt doesn't match your pants!

Let's try using Color Mask to change the colors of an object.

1. Open the image PLATE.TIF in the PRACTICE directory. This time, select Full Image in the Open an Image dialog.

2. Open the Color Mask roll-up from the Mask menu, or by pressing F4. Make sure the function box shows Modify Selected Colors.

Now you need to select the colors you want to change. Start by clicking on the first color bar in the roll-up, and then click the Eyedropper tool over part of one of the edges of the plate. Notice that when you click

31.9

The Color Mask roll-up

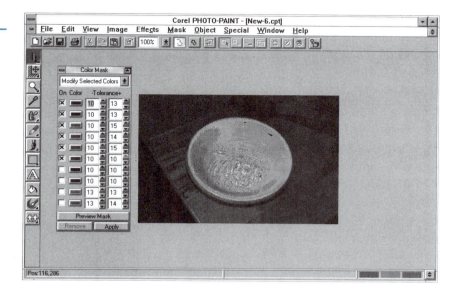

the Eyedropper, the color bar changes to reflect that color. Use this as a guide for adding more colors.

3. Move down the chart of color bars in the roll-up, assigning colors to all the bars, choosing colors from the plate until they're all represented. Start from an edge of the plate, and work your way inward to be sure you capture the full range of colors.

4. Click the On check box before each color bar, or all that work you just did will go to waste.

5. When you're done, click Preview Mask at the bottom of the roll-up to see how well the color selection works.

If parts of the image remain unmasked, try again. You might also try fiddling with the Tolerance controls beside each color bar, which dictate how close to the selected color a pixel must be in order to fall into the realm of the mask.

6. When you're satisfied with the mask, click Apply.

7. To make use of all your work creating that mask let's change the color of the plate to a bright yellow. Select the paintbrush and drag it over the plate. Notice that if you extend the paintbrush onto a color that's not part of the mask, nothing happens.

You can save this masterpiece, if you like.

Working with Objects

Maybe you're thinking, after reading the above section title, "Oh, I read all about objects in the CorelDRAW chapters. I can skip this part." Well, forget it. Why? Because those were vector objects you were working with in CorelDRAW—and now we're talking bitmaps. Bitmap objects. So what's the difference? A bitmap object, like a vector object, is an independent entity that can be moved, altered, or deleted without affecting the rest of the image. Unlike a vector object, however, a bitmap object must be specifically created as an object. In other words, you must select a piece of a bitmap image and convert it to an object, in order for that object to function independently of the underlying image.

Is this added work worth it? Yes—because objects let you act upon specific pieces of an image. Though they add a couple of steps to your composition time, objects can make your life easier when you're creating *composite images* (images composed of parts of other images). You can take, say, a spoon from one picture and a bottle from another, and combine them with a plate to produce—drum roll, please—a place setting. (Guess what you're going to do in a moment…)

Before we start creating objects, let's take a look at how they behave.

1. Open the file SETTING.CPT, located in the PRACTICE directory.
2. Click on the bottle or the spoon and try to move either one. Notice how you can pick up that piece of the photo and drag it anywhere on the image without affecting anything else.
3. Click on the plate to select it.

Nothing happened, right? That's because the plate is not an object; it's a regular old bitmap that's part of the underlying image. Close this image now (without saving it) and let's start making objects.

There are a couple of ways to create objects. For one you use an existing mask, and for the other you use PHOTO-PAINT's object selection tools (on the Pick tool flyout) to define a selection. Both types of objects are controlled by the Layers / Objects roll-up, which you can see in Figure 31.10. Here you can hide or view an object, choose its layer order, and adjust its transparency and edge quality.

Let's start by creating an object the easy way—working from an existing mask.

1. Open the file SPOON.TIF, with which we worked earlier. Select Mask / Load and choose the name you assigned to your mask. (If you didn't remember to save your mask earlier, just create a simple mask now using the Rectangle tool. Be sure to get all of the spoon and as little of the background as possible. Hurry up, we're waiting.)
2. Now use Edit / Copy to copy the mask to the Clipboard.

31.10

Use the Layers / Objects roll-up to control objects.

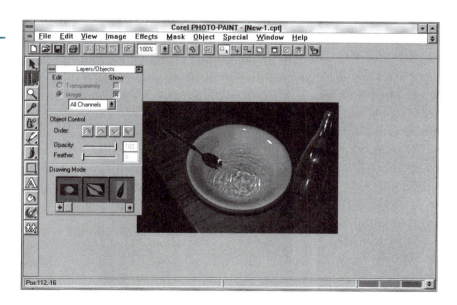

3. Open the plate image (PLATE.TIF), and choose Paste from the Clipboard.

4. Grab that spoon and move it over next to the plate. Move the corners to resize the spoon so it doesn't dwarf the plate.

WATCH OUT!

When you want to save an image with its objects intact, you must use PHOTO-PAINT's native CPT format. If you use any other format, the objects lose their superpowers and become just part of the background.

5. Save the new composite image as STILIFE.CPT.

Next, let's assume you don't already have a mask of your intended object, and try creating an object from scratch.

1. Open BOTTLE.TIF from the PRACTICE directory.

2. Open the Pick tool flyout and use one of the selection tools to select the bottle. Fine-tune your selection as we did the mask earlier.

3. Click on the Object Create button on the top toolbar (it's the one with a free-form shape over a rectangle). You can also choose Create Object from the Object menu.

Voilà! You've made an object. Now let's add that object into the place setting.

4. Open STILIFE.CPT and tile the two images. If you didn't save the composite earlier, open SETTING.CPT and work with that.

5. Click and hold the mouse on the bottle object, and drag it over to STILIFE. Release the mouse, and the bottle becomes part of the place setting.

6. To finish your masterpiece, resize the bottle, rotate it (using the Object / Rotate command), and place it alongside the plate. Adjust its opacity and feathering to make it blend into the composite.

7. Save this new image, and celebrate; you've created your first composite image.

Enhancing the Image

Once you've created a basic image, it's time to clean it up and make it more exciting. You can do this using any or all of PHOTO-PAINT's retouching and painting tools and special effects filters. There are far too many of these tools and filters to describe in detail here, but we'll try to cover a couple of the most important and commonly used ones. You'll want to do some experimenting with all of them on your own. It's the only way to get a feel for what they can do and when you might want to use them.

Even if you never expect to do anything more than work with a simple scanned-in photo, it's vital that you learn to use these enhancement tools. No scan is perfect, and no image so complete that it can't use a little help.

Using the Retouching Tools

The retouching tools encompass the indispensable filters (such as Color Map, Gamma, Brightness, and Contrast) as well as the painting tools (including Clone, Paintbrush, and Bucket Fill). The filters are best for adjusting a too-dark or too-light image. The painting tools are perfect for correcting photos with composition problems such as tears, stains, and empty spots.

Equalizing   Since most scanned images start off either too light or too dark, let's try using the Equalize effect; we'll decrease the range of some shadows and increase the range of some light areas, to brighten and sharpen a muddy image. In Figure 31.11 you can see the histogram of the tonal range for the Sunflowers image.

31.11

Sunflowers before and after equalizing the histogram to enhance the light tones and decrease the dark tones.

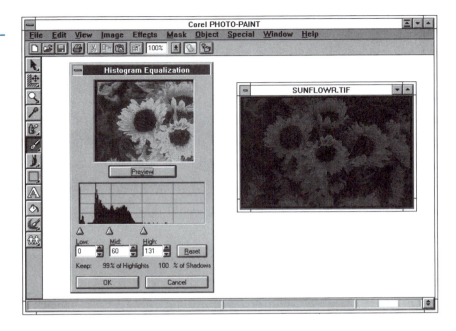

Note that you could also use the Brightness/Contrast controls in conjunction with the Sharpen filter to brighten up this image. This is generally the case with retouching tools: There are at least two ways to do just about anything you can think of.

1. Open SUNFLWR.TIF from the PRACTICE directory.
2. Select Effects / Tone / Equalize.
3. Using the sliders on the bottom of the tone histogram, bring the low slider in toward the midtones. Experiment by adjusting the various sliders till you have a pleasing, clear image.

The foregoing technique maintains the highlights in the image while decreasing some of the shadows. The result will be brighter yellows and greater detail in the shadows. You'll find that most of the effects are easier to use than Equalize (with the possible exception of gamma correction, which uses a curve representing the tones in the image). To adjust Brightness and Contrast, for instance, you simply move a couple of sliders.

Cloning   Let's try using another useful retouching technique: cloning. In cloning, you're using one part of an image as a paintbrush to replace another part. For instance, in the still-life we created earlier, you could add another plate by cloning the one that's already on the table into another part of the image. Use cloning for correcting images with visible flaws such as creases, or for improving poor composition. Since you already have the Sunflowers open, let's work with that image and add another flower to the upper-left corner.

1. Click on the Clone tool (the twins at the bottom of the side toolbar).
2. Shift+click on the flower you want to duplicate. This anchors the source-point crosshairs.
3. Position the brush (it will look like whatever brush you last used) in the spot where you want the new flower to go. Use the Tool Settings roll-up to make your brush larger, so you pick up more of the flower in a single stroke.
4. Click and drag to start cloning, and keep painting until your new flower is full-grown.

Once you've created your sunflower field of two, try your hand at some of the more exotic filters and effects, such as Impressionist and Glass Blocks. These can turn your images from standard photos to works of art. Be warned, though: Fiddling with filters can be addictive! For that matter, so can playing with PHOTO-PAINT.

CHAPTER 32

Creating a Presentation

THIRTY-TWO

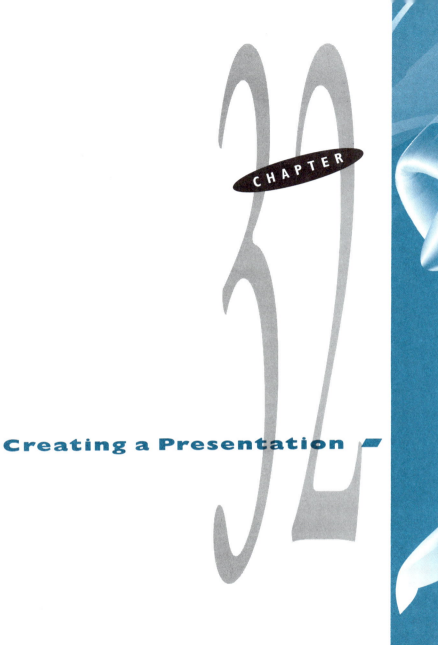

CHAPTER 32

Corel's strategy concerning presentation software is unique in the industry: Instead of offering you one do-it-all program, it gives you five separate applications. Indeed, CHART, MOVE, PHOTO-PAINT, and DRAW can all act as contributors to a presentation. Charts and graphs can be furnished by CHART, animation courtesy of MOVE, screen shots and other bitmap images from PHOTO-PAINT, and of course, vector drawings from DRAW. The Grand Central Station for your presentation is SHOW. Think of SHOW as one big OLE holding tank for the elements that make up your presentation. Each element is hot-linked back to its source; just double-click it and you can edit it in the original program.

Though this novel approach has a certain elegance, with each program playing its specific role, it has not yet proven to be a comfortable choice among users. Both versions 3.0 and 4.0 of CHART and SHOW have been too slow and buggy, and both display a definite proclivity for producing massive amounts of data. MOVE, which made its debut in version 4.0, is a solid performer in its second release. Up to now, however, most users of presentation software seem to prefer the coupling of at least the presentation and charting engines into one application.

Step One: The Chart

CHART has improved considerably since version 4.0. The frequency of "General Protection Faults" that users experienced while using that version has been greatly reduced. There are several new chart types available, including bubble, Gantt, polar, and radar charts, and over 250 new spreadsheet functions. Editing charts is easy with the 3D, Fill, Pen, Pictograph, and MOSAIC roll-ups; and context-sensitive menus are available by clicking on the right mouse button.

Figure 32.1 shows a simple chart, produced in CHART, advertising a body-building beverage. You can open this file, DYNO.CCH in the PRACTICE directory, and examine it inside and out as you like. You'll need to install the Franklin Gothic Heavy Italic typeface from Corel's typeface library in order to view the chart the way it was created.

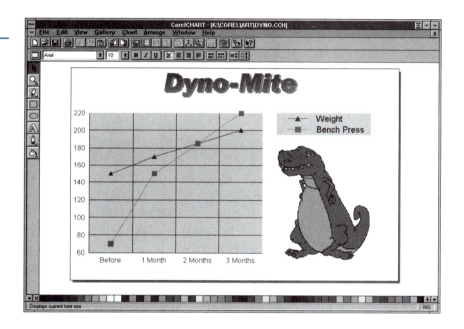

32.1

This simple chart was easy to make using CHART's drop-down list of chart formats.

Though we don't offer a step-by-step tutorial on how we created this chart, we can tell you this:

- When you select File / New, you're presented with an extensive list of chart formats. Pick the format you want, and CHART inserts a sample chart in that format. All you have to do is change the sample data.

- Importing objects from other Corel products is easy. For instance, the T-Rex is an actor from MOVE, and the title is courtesy of DRAW.

- Be careful: Any change to a chart forces an entire screen redraw—a maddening prospect when working with virtually any type of chart. If you have a particularly complex chart, you may want to simplify things by selecting the Wireframe option in the View menu (or from the Ribbon Bar) to see only the chart's outlines.

- Certain standard menu options missing in CHART can be annoying. The program lacks a list of previously accessed charts under the File menu, for instance, and there's no Edit / Repeat command.

Despite the last two points, this chart was relatively easy to put together.

WATCH OUT!

Though changing chart types is simple using the drop-down menus, you're asking for trouble if you try to change the chart type too many times before saving the file to disk. It's a sure-fire way to trigger a General Protection Fault. We also had considerable trouble opening a chart that was produced with CHART 4.0, usually ending with a GPF.

CHART offers some of the best fine-tuning tools of any charting program we have worked with, as well as full spreadsheet capabilities, and the ability to import database information using Corel's QUERY utility. The interface has improved since version 4.0. All in all, however, CHART still has a ways to go to be taken seriously as an upper-tier charting program.

Step Two: The Animation

Corel's animation module, MOVE, hasn't changed much since version 4.0. It remains both a solid utility and a source of endless fun, for the curious user as well as the semiserious animator. Loaded with prebuilt elements for you to use and take apart, the program abounds with running starts for those who want to build animated sequences. Some of the new features in MOVE 5.0 include improved import and export capabilities and a new morphing utility.

You can use the *actors* (the things or creatures that move) supplied with MOVE, or use DRAW to produce your own, or import them from other animation or image file formats. A sample library of actors is provided in the \MOVE\SAMPLES directory on the CorelDRAW CD. You can use the Clipboard to add files from DRAW or PHOTO-PAINT, or use File / Import to bring in actors of another file format.

Figure 32.2 shows one of the frames of an animation sequence in which an unsuspecting little dinosaur runs into our prehistoric friend, T-Rex. We pulled both dinosaurs from MOVE's online library of actors and put them together on screen. To provide the shocked expression on our little dino buddy, we used the Edit Actor option (see "Morphing Around," just below).

32.2

This poor little dino is about to hit an unexpected obstacle.

To replay the dino's surprise, find DYNOREX.CMV in the PRACTICE directory, and open it in MOVE. Even if you have never used the program, you'll have no trouble working the VCR-like controls on the bottom of the screen.

We enjoyed our time in MOVE, but we anticipate little relevance for this program in most DRAW users' work. We see MOVE as appealing to a different audience, reaffirming our belief that MOVE should be unbundled from DRAW and sold separately.

Morphing Around

You can have even more fun with MOVE's new Effects / Morph Cel command. Morphing is like DRAW's blending—one object becomes another. Though MOVE's morphing utility isn't as sophisticated as the ones used in those big special-effects movies, it's still a useful and fun way to create a smooth transition from one cel to the next.

To get to the Edit Actor screen, double-click an actor and then click the Edit Actor button. From there, go to the first of the two cels you want to morph, and select Effects / Morph Cel. In the Morph window, you'll see the cel you just selected, along with the one immediately following it. If you just click on OK at this point, you'll get a single-cel morph that is halfway between the two in the Morph window. If you want the morph to occupy more time, just increase the number of cels in the Cels to Create box.

The Effects / Morph Cel operation takes into account color, shape, location, and size when creating transitional cels. So, if you just do a plain morph from one cel to the next, the effect is essentially a fade between the first and second cels. Figures 32.3 and 32.4 show a morph in progress. You can open and experiment with the morphed animation if you like; it's POW.CMV in the PRACTICE directory.

You can control how the morphing takes place by using control points; these tell the morphing utility how to move from point A to point B. You can use up to 1,000 pairs of control points for each morph. If you're dealing with a complex or colorful object, you'll probably want to use as many control points as possible. But be warned: Adding control points can be a tedious, time-consuming, and frustrating process. The Pick tool in this utility is not as precise as we would like.

32.3

Morphing lets you transition from one cel to the next.

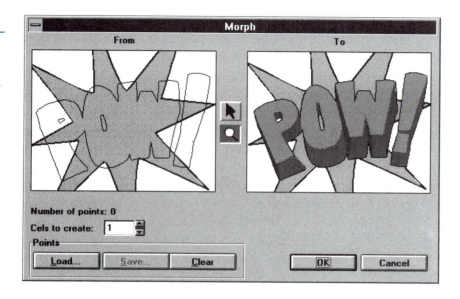

32.4

The morphed, or rather faded, result

To save your control points as you go, just click on Save from the Morph window. Then, if you want to check your work, you can click OK to start the morphing process. If you don't like the result, just delete the morphed cel, reload your control points from the Morph window, and try again.

Step Three: The Presentation

Corel's SHOW module has improved over version 4.0 in terms of its basic capabilities and performance. You can now directly add text to presentations, although without the sophisticated text manipulation features of DRAW. For the most part, however, SHOW is still intended to be a staging ground for elements created elsewhere. It provides a full complement of presentation options and a well-implemented time-line tool for fast and efficient integration of elements.

In Figure 32.5 you can see the simple six-slide presentation that we assembled using bits and pieces from DRAW, CHART, and MOVE. We particularly appreciated the ability to stage slide elements one by one,

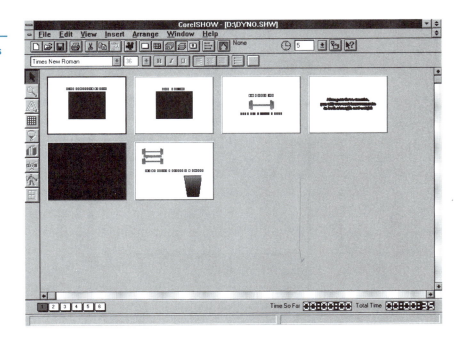

32.5

All of the elements come together in SHOW.

as though each were in a separate slide. We used this feature to control how the text and graphics are displayed. In slides 1 and 2, the animations begin before the text appears. In both cases, the text created in DRAW and the animations from MOVE reside on the same slides, but can be controlled individually using the Timelines roll-up. Slides 3 and 6 feature text and graphics from DRAW. Slide 4 is the chart created in CHART, discussed earlier.

You can run this infomercial for yourself. It's called DYNO.SHW (in the PRACTICE directory, of course), and you don't need any special hardware—although we could easily have added sound to our presentation.

SHOW's Weaknesses

SHOW has some problems, some of them merely annoying, others potentially disastrous:

Go Easy with Dissolve   In general, SHOW's slide transition effects work quite well. However, we recommend avoiding dissolves on any slide with imported animations. The dissolve affects the entire cel, not just the actors in it, resulting in a rather bizarre screen effect. There is still no easy way to change the global default transition effects. You can control the transition from any one slide, or element of a slide, to another, but the only way to change the default that controls the entire presentation is to select each slide and make the change. This limitation is made slightly less painful by the Slide Sorter view, which lets you select all slides at once; nonetheless, we are disappointed now, as we were in SHOW 4.0, by the absence of a tool that controls default transitions.

SHOW Needs a Diet...   SHOW is not terribly stable, and is somewhat of a system resource hog. The program needs huge amounts of disk and swap-file space, memory, and all the CPU power you can throw at it. For instance, though DYNO.SHW has only six relatively simple slides, the file is nearly 1MB file.

...and a Few More Horsepower   In our previous edition, we complained about the speed, or rather the lack of it, in SHOW's ability to prepare slides for presentation. SHOW is still a bit on the slow side, but it has improved considerably. When we gave the word to run DYNO, we had to wait over a minute for it to start.

To remedy this, there is a runtime version of SHOW, but you need to save your .SHW file as an .SHR (SHOW Runtime) file before you can play it. The runtime version works quite well, and it only takes a few seconds to load and begin playing the slide show. If you're making a presentation in front of an audience and don't want them to wait for the slide show to generate, you'll probably want to save the file in SHR format and run it with the runtime version.

CHAPTER 33

The Utilities

THIRTY-THREE

CHAPTER 33

Y ou could create a pretty good software product just by taking all of the ancillary programs that Corel stuffs into the CorelDRAW box and releasing them on their own. In this chapter we'll discuss the capabilities of TRACE and MOSAIC, the font management skills of Ares FontMinder, and KERN, which is new to version 5.0. Let's see—bitmap-to-vector conversion, image cataloging, font management, typeface kerning control—we could call it The Corel Utilities and sell it for $149! And after our attorney bails us out of jail for product theft, we will release this chapter as a booklet covering those utilities…

Tracing Your Way

Because much of the attention goes to Corel's flashier applications, TRACE has been largely ignored, its icon sitting quietly on the Windows desktop. In fact, if you performed a custom installation of CorelDRAW, you might have left TRACE out entirely. In Version 5.0, however, TRACE deserves a better fate. With a redesigned interface, optical character recognition, and built-in scanning, TRACE is now a much more useful tool for the CorelDRAW user.

One of the best things about the current version of TRACE is its simplicity. Although there is enough flexibility for artistic flair, most users will get workable results using the default settings and without having to fiddle too much.

Our purpose here is to show you the controls, set an example or two, and then encourage you to play. After all, it seems that the philosophy behind all of the CorelDRAW applications is that working with these tools can be fun.

Why TRACE?

If you are new to drawing programs, this is the first question you might ask. The answer lies in the differences between the two types of graphic images—bitmap and vector—created by software. These images are made up of either digital dots (bits) or mathematical instructions for drawing lines and curves (vectors). Paint programs (such as PHOTO-PAINT) manipulate pixels and bits, and their graphics are called bitmaps. Drawing programs (such as CorelDRAW) work with points of reference to draw lines and curves (vectors), and their graphics are called vector graphics. (If you've read the discussion in Chapter 1, then this paragraph is review.)

DRAW is able to import and display bitmap images, but it cannot edit or manipulate them. TRACE, on the other hand, takes bitmapped graphics and converts them to lines and curves that *are* understood by DRAW. This is the essential role of TRACE: automatic conversion of bitmap images into vector objects.

A Tour of TRACE

Figure 33.1 shows TRACE's opening screen. It has the general appearance of all of Corel's applications and its layout follows CorelDRAW's interface. Icons for quick access to many of the most-used functions are located on the Ribbon Bar below the menu, saving you the time and trouble of plowing through menu selections. As is often the case with icons, however, you may not be able to immediately divine their functions. To help you out, every function that you activate as you move your mouse around screen is detailed in a status line at the lower-left of the screen.

NEW FOR 5

The Eyedropper, used to quickly pick up a color from the original image, has been promoted to a full-fledged tool and is now in the toolbox along the left edge of the screen.

33.1

A place for everything and everything in the usual place: DRAW users will feel comfortable with the TRACE screen.

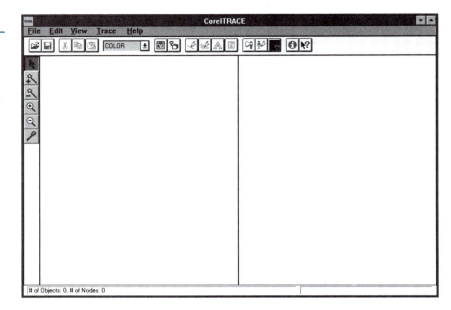

The toolbox along the left side of the screen gives you access to the Selection Arrow, Magic Wand, Magnifying Glass, and Eyedropper. These let you pick and choose specific parts of an image to trace, as well as enlarge the view and make the task easier. Take some time to get to know the location and role of these tools. As you move your cursor over or select each one, a brief description of its function appears in the status line.

The Ribbon Bar along the top of the screen (under the menu bar) offers quick access to TRACE's commands and functions. You must still manage the settings of the tracing options through menu selections, however. The Tracing Options dialog has five pages of settings, identified by the tabs across the top. Each of the tracing methods is customizable, but the beauty of TRACE is its ability to produce good results from the default settings. In other words, you can start tracing images before you know the first thing about anything. You do need to remember that there is a very specific criterion for traceable images: Simple line art and well-defined elements trace well; complex curves with lots of overlapping elements do not.

WATCH OUT!

Because of inconsistencies in TWAIN scanner drivers, some of you will find that your scans appear in TRACE with the colors reversed or inverted. To bring them back to normal, go to the Tracing Options dialog and look on the Image page (Figure 33.2) for the Invert Colors option. Click this check box before or after the scan is made.

33.2

The Tracing Options dialog's Image page—one of five pages of options for tracing

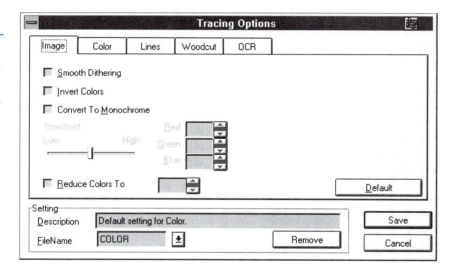

The Mechanics of Tracing

To put TRACE to use, you must first give it a bitmap image to work with. There are two ways to do this: Open a file that you already have on disk, or use a scanner to digitize a piece of art. Both these actions are performed from the File menu, Figure 33.3. (Also shown in this figure is the Batch Files roll-up.)

If you use a scanner, your sources for images are almost limitless. No longer must you rely on others to provide you with bitmap files, or have to create them yourself in a paint program. Now you can scan directly

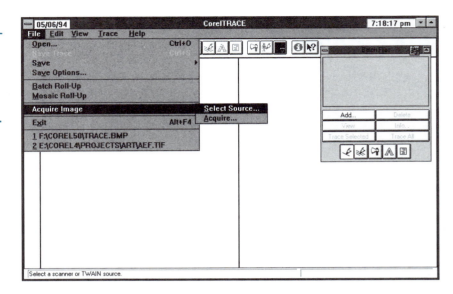

33.3

The methods of bringing a bitmap image into TRACE: Open an existing file; and Acquire Image to scan in an image. The Batch roll-up is for multiple images.

into TRACE, convert the image to vector, and send it to DRAW—without ever having a file on disk. (It is good practice, however, to keep backup files of your artwork.)

TRACE can handle files in several formats—BMP, TIFF, PCX, TGA, and Photo CD—but converts them to Windows BMP format before tracing. If you scan an image and then save it within TRACE, it will be saved in BMP format.

When you're scanning an image, the File / Acquire Image dialog is specific to the scanner that you have connected. Detailed instructions on the use of this dialog and the care and feeding of your scanner will come from the scanner manufacturer. The purpose of TWAIN is to allow device manufacturers to write a single driver that will work with any Windows-based program that contains the TWAIN interface. (Rumor has it that TWAIN stands for Technology Without An Interesting Name, because it was developed by a committee and no one could agree on a name that wasn't already in use.)

One of the reasons for converting bitmaps into vector images is because bitmaps are constructed of dots and look grainy and gritty. If you enlarge a bitmap, it just worsens this gritty appearance. Once converted to a vector image, though, it looks much smoother, can be sized up or down with no loss in image quality, and can be printed at the highest possible resolution of your output device.

Figure 33.4 shows a typical application for TRACE: an image to be used as a company logo. This image consists of only black and white, although TRACE is perfectly capable of rendering in color. This piece of clip art was scanned from an image about 3 inches tall. You can scan the image from this book or use SCUBA.TIF in the PRACTICE directory.

INSIDE INFO

With small images, scan at a resolution one-half of the maximum your scanner allows (300 dpi instead of 600 dpi, for example), and scale to 200%.

Scanning images can be confusing. For example, scanning at high resolutions may be a waste of effort if the image is ultimately destined to be imported and printed as a bitmap. Often, the extra resolution goes unused in the final output, causing the scanned files to be unnecessarily large.

When scanning images for tracing, however, the rules are completely different. Every dot you can cram into a given area will be useful during tracing, to get the most accurate representation. To see this graphically, scan an image into PHOTO-PAINT at both 300 and 600 dpi, and then enlarge both images. The 300-dpi scan quickly becomes jagged and then unrecognizable, but the 600-dpi scan can be enlarged to almost 200% before losing detail. Eliminating this jaggedness is the primary reason for tracing images and converting them to vector images in the first place. The rougher and more jagged the image, the more manual clean-up work will be required, so making the image less jagged before the trace will improve the accuracy and quality of the trace.

On the other hand, it is even more important to work with an image large enough to allow TRACE to adequately turn corners. And because most scanning programs won't allow you to enlarge the image when

3 3 . 4

This piece of clip art is an ideal candidate to be traced.

scanning at the highest resolution of the scanner, it is often better to scan at a lower resolution and then set the scanner to scale the image to 200%.

Figure 33.5 shows the diver image after it has been opened in TRACE.

33.5

This image is ready to be traced.

INSIDE INFO

If you are starting with a small piece of original black-and-white art, use a copy machine to enlarge it as much as possible before scanning.

Presto, Change-o

Ironically, the actual tracing is perhaps the easiest part of all: Just click the Outline Trace button, or select it from the Trace menu. Depending on the speed of your PC, you will get a finished vector image in the right-hand window in a minute or two. More complex images might require fiddling with the Line Attribute controls or doing some other types of fine-tuning, but we recommend that you start by just clicking the Trace button. In many cases, that will be all you'll need.

INSIDE INFO

If you haven't done it already, enlarge the TRACE window to fill your screen. (Don't forget, though—this is just a low-resolution screen image.) Enlarging the window makes it easier to select a part of the image if that's all you need to trace, as well as to determine if the trace result is acceptable.

Figure 33.6 shows the completed trace of the diver (on the right) alongside the original bitmapped image (on the left). As you examine your traced image, two things will be obvious if the original image was not straight when scanned: Horizontal and vertical lines will be jagged, and any text portion of the scan will be rough. You'll either need to clean up these imperfections in DRAW, or overlook them. An ounce of scanning prevention is definitely worth a pound of clean-up.

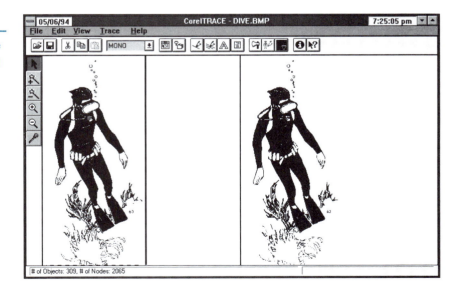

33.6

TRACE studies the original bitmapped image (left) and produces a collection of vector curves to replicate it (right).

Cleaning Up

There is one other check you can make before issuing your seal of approval on the trace operation. Click the Info button on the Ribbon Bar to get information about the number of paths and nodes TRACE used to reproduce the object. Bear in mind that a complex drawing can bring a printer or imagesetter to its knees—not to mention slow down both the computer and printer, cost you time and money at the service bureau, and above all, indicate sloppy work on your part.

NEW FOR 5

The number of nodes and paths in the traced image show on the bottom status line while the image is displayed.

Most tracing programs, TRACE included, have a tendency to create too many paths and too many nodes. There are several techniques that you can use, at different stages of your project and using various programs, to produce the cleanest and most precise results.

Begin with the highest resolution possible on the largest image possible, and (usually) the more contrast the better.

Keep it simple. Sometimes it's easier to fix the bitmap *before* tracing. Take another look at Figure 33.6; in that trace of the original image there are hundreds of paths and thousands of nodes. Figure 33.7 shows how erasing the seaweed (in PHOTO-PAINT) made the final image much simpler. Simplicity can mean the difference between a dream job or a nightmare at the printer's.

Fiddling with the Tracing Option Settings   Though it is true that the default settings for the Tracing Options will serve for most images, if you find that your trace comes out with an unwieldy number of paths and nodes, it's time to start fiddling. Because the images you trace will be unique, there are no hard-and-fast fiddling rules to apply; generally, however, increasing curved lines and decreasing the tightness of the trace will reduce the complexity of the trace.

33.7

A much simpler and more effective trace of the diver

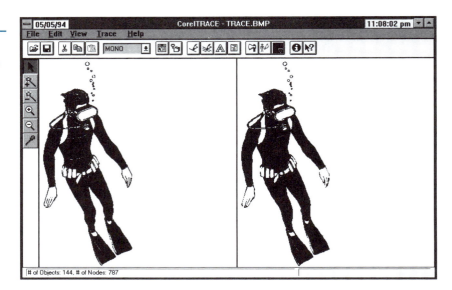

Figure 33.8 shows the ever-critical settings on the Lines page of the Tracing Options dialog (Trace / Edit Options). These settings will often play a big role in your traces.

- *Curve Precision* tells TRACE how tightly to follow curves in an image. The better the precision, the more nodes in the final output.

33.8

Correct line attributes are key to correct traces.

- *Line Precision* tells TRACE whether to render a particular line as straight or a curve. The looser the setting, the fewer curved lines and nodes there will be.

- *Target Curve Length* tells TRACE how to connect the various paths. The longer the curve, the fewer paths and nodes.

- *Sample Rate* averages the nodes within a path; this lets you smooth out stair-steps and reduce the total number of nodes. In many cases this will compensate for a bitmap with lots of jaggies.

- *Minimum Object Size* tells TRACE to ignore objects made up of a quantity of pixels that is less than this setting. When you're tracing gray-scale images that consist of many disconnected dots, you'll want to use Minimum Object Size with caution, but this setting can be invaluable in cleaning up line drawings.

- *Outline Filtering* determines the smoothness of outlined objects, and its effects are more noticeable when tracing images of 150 dpi or less. To smooth the jaggies, choose Smooth Points or Medium. If fine lines in the traced image appear broken or don't show up at all, set Outline Filtering to None.

Remember that for every Tracing Options adjustment you make, there will be compromises and trade-offs. Quite often, loosening the trace will make the result look sloppy and require still more clean-up. Changing the settings to Very Good can make for long tracing times and curves with many nodes.

Once you find settings that are optimum for specific work, you can permanently record them. In the Setting fields at the bottom of the Tracing Options dialog, type in a file name and description (to help you remember what it's for). Even though these fields appear on every page of the dialog, all the settings are saved at once. The drop-down list box on the Ribbon Bar gives you quick access to these settings, by file name.

Moving Uptown

Now that you have your traced image, you must save it to a file so it can be brought into DRAW and/or incorporated into other projects. The easiest method for doing this is clicking the Diskette button on the Ribbon Bar. TRACE will use the same file name as the original image, with the extension .EPS. If you want more file-naming options, choose File / Save As, which lets you save the original image or the traced image with any file name and in any location on your drives.

WATCH OUT!

Though it is possible to simply paste the traced image into DRAW across the Clipboard without ever saving it to disk, we recommend against this for two reasons: When copying across the Clipboard, Windows converts the file to WMF format, which is not quite as accurate as EPS. Also, until you save the image in a .CDR file, you don't have a backup in case of disaster.

Mopping Up with DRAW

Your traced image is saved in Adobe Illustrator format, a special flavor of EPS that can be converted and edited (as distinct from standard EPS , which cannot be converted by most programs). To work in DRAW with your traced image, choose File / Import, and select Corel TRACE!, *.EPS.

Before you can do any editing of this image, first ungroup it (select the group and choose Arrange / Ungroup). Then use the Shape tool and the Node Edit roll-up to clean up the objects as necessary.

INSIDE INFO

Unless the typeface is so unusual that there is no equivalent in your type library, don't waste your time trying to straighten out scanned text. In most cases you can match the typeface from among the vast array included with DRAW. If you can't, then you must either use the scanned text or find a similar typeface, convert the text to curves, and reshape the text as well as you can. Either way, it's a tedious job, to say the least.

By selecting lines and filled objects in the drawing, you can see how TRACE goes about its business of creating paths, curves, and fills to replicate a bitmapped image. You will probably notice that there are many more nodes than necessary. Here is where DRAW 5's new Auto-Reduce command, discussed in Chapter 6, can be a lifesaver.

The Finished Work

The remainder of your work on the traced image should be pretty routine at this point, including moving nodes to straighten and reshape lines, and moving control handles to smooth and reshape curves. (For a refresher on curve shaping and node editing, review Chapter 6, "As the Curve Turns.")

Figure 33.9 shows the original bitmapped image. Figure 33.10 shows the finished work.

33.9

Before: the enlarged bitmap image before the trace

33.10
After: the high-quality vector drawing after the trace

Cataloging Art with MOSAIC

MOSAIC is a useful tool for viewing virtually any type of file. Think of it as a visual version of File Manager. As Figure 33.11 shows, you can open multiple directories and get a listing of all the files in each directory—DRAW files, graphics files, document files—any file in that directory. As long as there is an association established through Windows

33.11

MOSAIC can double as your file manager.

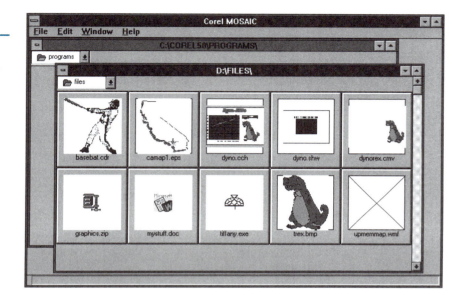

(for instance, .DOC files to be opened by Word for Windows), then you can open the file from MOSAIC with a simple double-click.

With version 5.0, a number of different file formats are now supported. In addition to the native Corel formats of CDR, CPT, CCH, and CMV, MOSAIC will display thumbnail images of files in a number of other formats, including EPS, TIF, BMP, PCX, GIF, and AI. For files in other formats, MOSAIC notifies you of the association established. In Figure 33.11, a double-click on the MYSTUFF.DOC file will launch Word for Windows and open that file. The GRAPHICS.ZIP file can even be opened by MOSAIC, thanks to the WINZIP utility to which the file is associated. Notice MOSAIC's icon for the UPMEMMAP.WMF file, which tells you that MOSAIC knows of no such association for that file. Were a program installed on this system that could read .WMF files, such as Hijaak for Windows, the association would exist. (In any event, because DRAW can import .WMF files, you can choose MOSAIC's Edit / Import into CorelDRAW command, which automatically launches DRAW and issues the appropriate import command.)

With MOSAIC, you can also create libraries that hold files in compressed form. This is handy for archiving purposes, and is doubly beneficial because MOSAIC can open these libraries and provide access to the individual files, without your having to manually decompress them.

You can also create catalogs that do not contain any actual files, but rather references to files stored anywhere on your system. Catalogs can be very handy if you want to group together files that you normally store in different directories. For example, if you keep all of your clip art files in a directory called CLIPART, but you want to reference those files in your DOCS directory, you can create a catalog in your DOCS directory that points to the files you want to use in the CLIPART directory, without actually copying the files over. This can be especially useful if you have a limited amount of disk space, and don't want multiple copies of the same file.

We did discover a few annoying problems with MOSAIC:

- If you double-click on an .EPS file, MOSAIC tries to open the file in DRAW, causing a General Protection Fault. If you use the Edit / Import into CorelDRAW option, MOSAIC imports the file just fine.
- The Directory drop-down list can be frustrating. It only allows you to change one level in either direction when moving through directories. Since the directory tree only goes back to the root directory list, you can't change drives using this list. If you want to change to a different drive, you have to use File / New Collection, instead.
- You can't copy a graphics file from one .CLB file to another.
- If you move a .CLB file to another location on your hard disk, MOSAIC can't open it.

If you have difficult file-management tasks, we encourage you to take a close look at the new MOSAIC. Its interface is very friendly, its mission in life is clear, and it performs quickly and reliably. For more information on MOSAIC operation, see the comprehensive how-to section in MOSAIC's online Help.

NEW FOR 5

New in Version 5.0, a scaled-down version of MOSAIC is available as a roll-up in DRAW, PHOTO-PAINT, TRACE, SHOW, MOVE, CHART, and Ventura Publisher, and is shown in Figure 33.12. This roll-up version is really just intended to be a read-only utility, and so does not have any of the menu bar options available in the standard version of MOSAIC. But even though you can't use it to create catalogs or libraries, the MOSAIC roll-up does provide an easy way to view and open files.

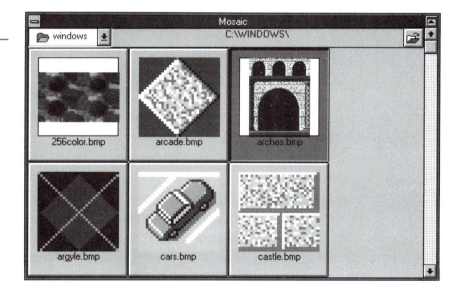

33.12

The MOSAIC roll-up version makes it easy to search for and open files in most Corel programs.

Font Management Made Easy, with Ares FontMinder

FontMinder from Ares Software is a drag-and-drop font management utility that makes it easy to install and remove fonts. For font junkies like us, it's a great little utility to keep track of all the typefaces we have lying about. What with the 825+ typefaces that ship with CorelDRAW, we are absolutely giddy over Corel's agreement with Ares to include a streamlined version of FontMinder in the version 5.0 box.

AUTHOR'S NOTE

 **FontMinder isn't installed automatically by CorelDRAW Setup. You need to install it separately from the FONTMNDR directory on the CD-ROM, Disk 1.**

The first time you run FontMinder, it creates a Master Library of the fonts on your system. You tell it which directories to search by dragging and dropping them into the list of directories, and FontMinder generates a library of all the fonts it finds in those directories. If it finds duplicate copies of the same font, it asks you which one you want to use, and gives you the option of deleting the duplicate font file.

When the Master Library is complete, FontMinder gives you a list of all your fonts, making it easy to see which fonts you have and which ones are currently installed. FontMinder uses a tree structure similar to that of the Windows File Manager. For example, if you double-click on Arial in the Install Fonts list, you'll see a list of all the Arial variations you have installed.

Installing and removing fonts is simple. If you want to install a new font, just drag it from the Font Library list over to the Install Fonts list, and it's done (see Figure 33.13). If you want to remove a currently installed font, just drag it over to the Disposal icon, and it's gone.

If you've ever been frustrated by font names like tt0141m_.ttf, you'll appreciate the way FontMinder lets you preview new fonts before you install them, as shown in Figure 33.14. Just select File / Preview New Fonts, and choose the font name whose mystery you want to reveal.

But perhaps the most useful feature of FontMinder is its ability to create *font packs*—groups of fonts that you can easily shuttle in and out of active duty. Say, for example, you use a group of five fonts for a newsletter you produce once a month, and you never use those fonts for anything

33.13

With FontMinder, you can install fonts at the drop of a mouse.

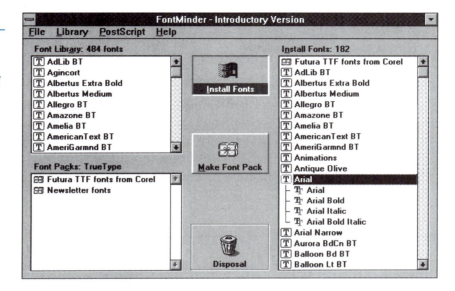

33.14

The truth about the mysterious tt0141m_.ttf is uncovered by FontMinder's Preview New Fonts command.

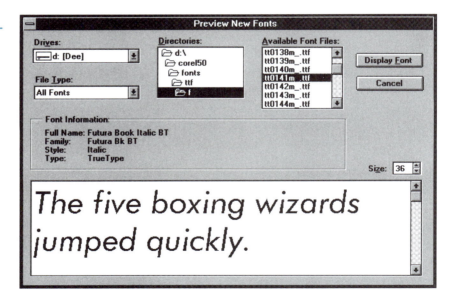

else. FontMinder lets you package those five fonts together, so you can install and uninstall them as a group. When you don't need them, just remove the font pack from the list of Install Fonts (see Figure 33.13). To create a new font pack, just click on the Make Font Pack icon, and drag the fonts from the Font Library list over to the Font Packs list. When you're done selecting fonts, double-click on the Make Font Pack icon, and the new pack is added. If you want, you can then remove the fonts you just packed from the list of Install Fonts.

The version of FontMinder that comes in the CorelDRAW box is an introductory version. The full version, which costs an additional $29.95, lets you preview and manage TrueType and PostScript fonts together, associate font packs with specific documents, print font samples before installing them, and download PostScript Type 1 fonts to your printer. For more information, call Ares Software Corp. at 800-783-2737.

Adjusting Font Kerning with KERN

KERN is a new utility in version 5.0 that helps you adjust the kerning of letter pairs in Postscript Type 1 fonts. KERN alters the font metrics (.PFM) file, which is where the height, width, and kerning for the font is stored. It does not alter the .PFB file, which is where the font itself lives.

KERN is very easy to use. When you launch it, KERN asks you to select a PFM file to adjust. After you select a font, it displays a selection of letter pairs (see Figure 33.15). All you do is select the letter pair you want to adjust, and slide the scroll bar forward or backward to change the kerning between the two letters.

33.15

KERN lets you easily adjust the kerning for PostScript Type 1 font letter pairs.

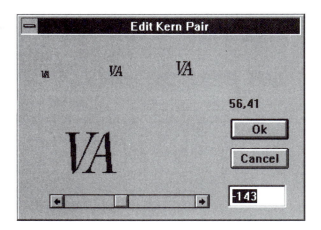

If you want to change the kerning for a letter pair that isn't displayed, use Update / Add to enter the new letter pair. To see what the new kerning looks like on your printer, select File / Print. After you save the file, Windows and your PostScript interpreter will use the new font metrics saved in the .PFM file to create the font.

WATCH OUT!

Although TrueType font users won't find this utility very useful, for PostScript users it can be an easy way to adjust letter-pair kerning. Be careful, though: If you decide later on that you want to change back to the default kerning, you'll need to reinstall the font. Therefore, it's wise to make backup copies of your PFM fonts before adjusting them with KERN.

If you purchased the initial release of CorelDRAW 5.0 in the early summer of 1994, then you didn't get KERN in the box. It shipped with Ventura, which was slipped into the box in midsummer. When we asked Corel officials about that, we found it curious that they anticipated KERN would be a Ventura-specific utility. KERN makes changes to the actual font metrics of PostScript typefaces, so those changes will be seen not just by Ventura and not just by the CorelDRAW applications, but across *all* Windows applications.

PART VIII
THE WORLD OF VENTURA

In these two extensive chapters, we offer an overview of the tremendously successful and powerful Ventura desktop publishing program, newly acquired and renovated by Corel. After learning this program's unique approach to establishing and managing the style and the layout of art and text elements, you will discover just how much greater DRAW can be when combined with a first-rate desktop publishing program.

CHAPTER 34

Publishing Basics

THIRTY-FOUR

CHAPTER 34

esktop publishing is a funny term. People publish books, magazines, catalogs, newsletters, and brochures, but we've yet to meet anyone who publishes desktops. And for most serious computer-based publishers, the concept of fitting all their equipment on a desktop is pretty far fetched. In France, desktop publishing is called PAO (Publication Assistée par Ordinateur), which translates to "computer-assisted publishing." And that's really what we're talking about here: Desktop publishing (DTP) is using a desktop computer to assemble a finished publication from pieces that are most often developed in other, more specialized programs. These pieces are then combined into a document that is beyond the scope of any of the original programs.

How to "Publish a Desktop"

The basic concept is simple enough. Word processors process words, drawing programs create drawings, scanners scan, and bitmap editors edit bitmaps. Then a DTP program formats them and puts them all together in a final publication, often adding additional elements such as indexes, footnotes, cross-references, and a table of contents.

Although most DTP programs include at least some of the same features as the other types of applications that contribute to the final product, each of these tools has its own specific role. Here are some of the classic distinctions between drawing, word processing, and desktop publishing programs.

Drawing Programs These programs are able to

- Create and manipulate complex graphics
- Manage text as a graphics element

- Provide graphics-oriented special features (such as sophisticated editing tools, color management, and special visual effects)
- Import and export a wide variety of graphics file formats
- Integrate with paint and image-manipulation programs

The primary market for drawing programs is among graphic artists.

Word Processors Word processing programs have only limited ability to work with graphics elements. These programs

- Help you create and manipulate text
- Offer intuitive entry and quick processing of text
- Flow text automatically from one line, column, or page to the next one
- Provide text-oriented special features (such as search and replace, spelling and grammar checking, outline generation, and mail merge)
- Integrate with other office applications (such as spreadsheets, e-mail, and presentation programs)

The primary market for word processors is among business professionals.

Desktop Publishing These programs offer

- On-screen layout and formatting of text and graphics
- Integration of elements from diverse sources
- Precision control of text and graphics placement
- Strict typographic controls
- Format-oriented special features (such as powerful styles, automated formatting, and data-driven publishing)
- Features for managing long documents (such as tables of contents, indexes, cross-references, and flexible numbering and pagination)
- Consistent, repeatable styles and layout in long structured documents

Choosing Your Weapon

The lines between the three types of applications discussed above have become increasingly blurred. More and more graphics and formatting features are cropping up in high-end (and even not-so-high-end) word processors. Drawing programs now have multipage layout capability. And desktop publishing programs can perform many tasks that were previously the exclusive province of other applications.

Nonetheless, although FrameMaker's drawing tools, for instance, have grown in sophistication, they'll never match CorelDRAW's. Ventura Publisher's editor and spell checker still don't compare to WordPerfect's. You can produce a full-length book in Word for Windows, and many people do (especially if they happen to work for a certain company in Redmond, Washington)—but there are much easier ways to do the job, and with much better results.

So choosing the best tool for a project is often a question of emphasis and degree. If you're working primarily with words but need some graphics and layout features, a good word processor is most likely your best bet. For graphics combined with some text that needs formatting, you'll probably want to use a drawing program (see Figure 34.1). Though Ventura 5.0 now has access to many of CorelDRAW's graphics capabilities, only a determined masochist would attempt to design a

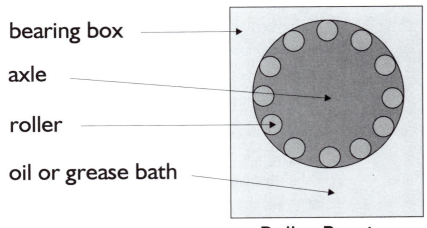

34.1

This technical drawing is created quite easily in DRAW, but would be much more difficult with Ventura's less-sophisticated drawing tools.

complex ad or poster in Ventura rather than in DRAW, and since the two programs operate at opposite ends of the publishing spectrum, they complement each other very well.

Ventura Publisher: Not a Swiss Army Knife

All DTP programs exist to create and format finished documents, although the ways in which they accomplish this task can be markedly different. Unlike some other desktop publishing programs, Ventura neither claims nor tries to be an all-in-one publishing solution. Although you can produce a document entirely within Ventura, its built-in text and graphics features have limited functionality and are not designed to be substitutes for full-blown word processing and drawing programs. Usually, you don't write the words and draw the drawings with Ventura itself; rather, Ventura helps you establish and manage the style and the layout of these elements that you have created in other programs.

You can still edit imported text and graphics in their original applications, even after they have become part of a Ventura document. When you're working with text, whether before or after you've incorporated it into a Ventura chapter, why not use the more powerful editing capabilities and spelling/grammar checkers built into your favorite word processor? And when you need anything more than a very simple illustration, you would do well to create it in DRAW and then import or link it to your Ventura document. For example, in Ventura there's simply no way you could have created and edited a drawing with blends and extruded text like the one in Figure 34.2.

What is unique about Ventura is its ability to help you manage all the elements of a document. When you need to take your words and pictures and create a composite publication that includes additional formatting and features; when you need to ensure stylistic consistency throughout a complex document or series of documents; and when you need automatically applied formatting or precise typographic control in a document of any length—that's when it's time to turn to Ventura.

34.2

This was easy to create in DRAW; it would have been impossible in Ventura.

We don't need to put a figure on this page to show you the type of project best suited for Ventura—because you're holding one in your hands. Though it's true that CorelDRAW could *produce* this page for you, could it automatically number the figures across all of Chapter 34? Could DRAW place running heads across the top of each page, heads that pick up specific headlines from the text of the page? Could DRAW number all the chapters and the pages of this book automatically? No, no, and no.

Sometimes the choice of application for final output is obvious; other times it is less so. The old stereotype is that DRAW is best suited for short, free-form, design-intensive documents, and Ventura's forté is longer, structured, content-intensive documents such as technical manuals, product catalogs, and books like this one. But appearances can be deceiving.

The menu illustrated in Figure 34.3 was initially created in DRAW. After the client's third revision of the format, however, it became apparent that this would be a much better project for Ventura. It took only a few minutes to define and create the style sheet, and once done, it was easy to make global format changes as the layout was being finalized. We created brunch, lunch, and dinner versions of the menu by simply loading different text files; future revisions to accommodate alternating menu selections will also be easy to make, by simply editing or replacing the text files.

34.3

This menu was an excellent candidate for Ventura.

Brunch

Aperitivi

Bellini
Sparkling wine and peach nectar 5.00

Mimosa
Sparkling wine and fresh orange juice 4.75

Virgin Bloody Mary 3.00

Prosecco
Glass of sparkling wine 4.50

Fresh squeezed Orange or Grapefruit Juice 2.75

Antipasti

Antipasti Misti
Assorted Appetizer Plate from our antipasti table
6.95 for one   11.95 for two

Prosciutto e Frutta
Prosciutto di Parma and fresh seasonal fruit 7.50

Salmone Marinato
House cured salmon with mixed greens and radishes 8.95

Frutta Fresca
Fresh seasonal fruit platter served with fresh fruit yogurt 4.25

Bruschetta
Grilled Tuscan bread topped with grilled eggplant and black olives 3.95

Insalate

Caesar
Crisp romaine lettuce, classic Caesar anchovy dressing 5.75

Arancia
Mixed baby greens with a citrus vinaigrette,
candied walnuts, and basil infused olive oil 5.25

Funghi e Ricotta Salata
Mixed baby greens, grilled Portabella mushrooms,
pinenuts, ricotta salata, thyme and garlic infused olive oil 5.50

Specialitas

Frittata con Granchi
Rolled Italian omelette with fresh Dungeness crabmeat,
roasted red bell peppers, mascarpone and whole grained mustard 12.50

Salsiccia e Polenta
Homemade Sicilian sausage served over
soft polenta with tomatoes, roasted peppers 7.50

Salmone Bollito
Poached salmon fillet, served with pickled
vegetables, lemon aioli, and salsa verde 14.50

Insalata di Pollo
Grilled chicken salad with roasted garlic, bell peppers,
Portabella mushrooms, baby greens, with balsamic vinaigrette 9.95

Linguine Carbonara
Pancetta sauteed with garlic, tossed with eggs, reggiano
parmigiano, pecorino romano, and housemade linguine 8.95

Insalata di Tonno
Grilled Ahi tuna, mixed greens, fresh artichoke hearts, olives,
capers, hard boiled egg, red wine vinaigrette and roasted pepper aioli 10.95

Uove e Verdure al Forno
Roasted celery, carrots, fennel, fresh tomatoes,
oregano, and topped with two poached eggs 8.50

Pane Fritto
"French Toast" – Filone bread dipped in orange batter
and sauteed. Served with fresh strawberries and mascarpone 7.95

Contorni (Side Dishes)
Tuscan roasted potatoes 2.25
Applewood smoked bacon 3.95
One egg – poached, scrambled, or fried 1.50
Grilled homemade Sicilian or Tuscan sausage 2.75

*Please refrain from smoking
Not responsible for personal property*

Although it certainly would have been possible to complete this project in DRAW, it also would have been much more difficult. DRAW's styles fall well short of Ventura's paragraph tags in speed and flexibility, and DRAW has no real provision for swapping text files (its Merge Back command is light years behind Ventura's text-shuffling capabilities).

Workgroup Publishing

Often, when you are working alone, there may be several different ways to approach document production, and desktop publishing may or may not be the best way to go. But as soon as a project involves more than one person, desktop publishing is often the *only* way to go.

To many people, the term *workgroup publishing* conjures up the image of a corporate hive of worker bees, each one buzzing around a terminal, toiling away on one particular contribution to the company's next humongous publication. Some publishing operations are actually like that, and FrameMaker actively markets itself to fill that particular niche. Large companies such as Boeing and Ford, and even Frame Technology itself may have hundreds of people logged on to a network working on various parts of the same manual at the same time. In that case, a DTP program is obviously the best tool for putting together all the pieces of the project.

But the book you are reading now is also a good example of Ventura's ability to integrate diverse elements in non-network workgroup publishing. Several authors contributed various parts to this volume, from several different locations across the United States and Canada. We used Word for Windows, WordPerfect, Ami Pro, Microsoft Write, and even Word on a Macintosh. Because Ventura keeps imported text in its original files and formats, revisions and edits of these various contributions were easily made by the writers and the editors later in the publishing process.

Most of the illustrations for this book were created in DRAW, of course. Like the text, however, it was easy to integrate the DRAW pictures, as well as other graphics from various sources and formats, and to update them later as needed.

Different Strokes for Different Desktops

The requirements for publishing a newsletter and a 1,000-page technical manual are radically different. This is why many publishers who produce a variety of documents own and use two or perhaps even three different desktop publishing programs, just as graphic artists often use Freehand or Illustrator as well as CorelDRAW.

DTP programs fall into two basic categories. *Page layout programs* include applications such as QuarkXPress or the aptly named PageMaker. Although you can use them to produce longer documents, they are designed especially for producing individual pages. You work with elements on the page much as a graphic artist does with elements on a pasteboard, formatting them and moving them around until you've found the layout that you like. It's an ideal way to create loosely formatted, one-of-a-kind items such as fliers and brochures.

But creativity isn't the only skill required when you need 20 identically formatted chapters for a book, or newsletter issues with exactly the same look and layout from month to month, or a series of company documents that have *precisely* the same style of text and graphics elements. For these projects you need to be able to reproduce an existing format reliably, without having to re-create it each and every time. This is when you should turn to the second type of DTP application—one with a more structured, *publication-centered* approach. With this type of program, of which Ventura is a prime example, the formats of and relationships among elements can be strictly defined and then applied to as many different publications as you need.

As you'll soon discover, Ventura is as much a document *format* builder as it is a *document* builder. In the next chapter, we'll look at what makes Ventura Publisher unique and why it is especially well suited to certain types of publishing.

CHAPTER 35

How Ventura Thinks

THIRTY-FIVE

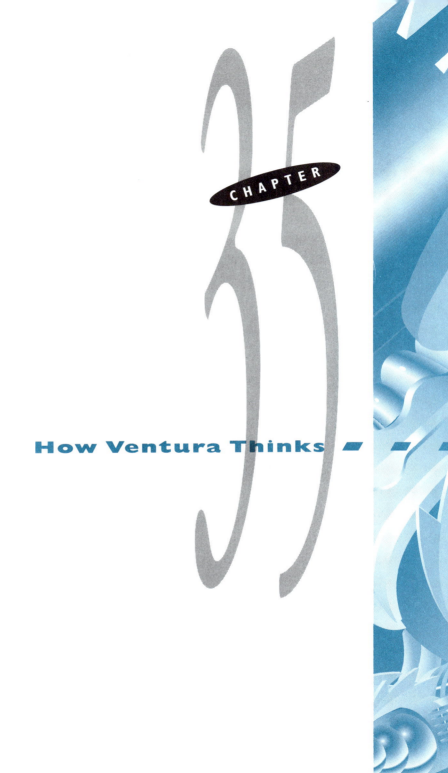

Chapter 35

Pity the poor Cro-Magnon publisher. It wasn't easy chipping away at the wall of that cave until each mastodon looked just so and the pictures told exactly the right story. One false slip of the flint, and the whole thing was ruined. No wonder they call it "carved in stone."

The Roots of Desktop Publishing

Luckily, things changed considerably. On medieval scrolls the artwork and text may have been just as permanent as on stone, but at least parchment and bark were a little easier to work with. And a few centuries later, Gutenberg would introduce movable type to the Western world, initiating a revolution in the craft of putting words on paper.

What we think of today as desktop publishing has origins in two totally different traditions: graphic design and traditional typesetting. On the computer, these two skills were at first pretty much mutually exclusive, just as in the non-computer world. Graphic design was the province of drawing programs and, later, of design-oriented publishing of free-form documents in the WYSIWYG (What You See Is What You Get) graphical environment of the Macintosh. Tag-based typesetting systems, on the other hand, were developed for longer or more structured documents such as books and periodicals. In these systems, instead of developing a page layout interactively, typesetting codes ("tags") for formatting and pagination were embedded in the text and later translated into instructions about how the document would be formatted. Because the tags were strictly defined, so was the format of the resulting document.

Enter Ventura

In 1986, a small start-up company in Salinas, California, released version 1.0 of Ventura Publisher. Ventura ran under Digital Research's GEM graphical environment, and people were amazed at how Mac-like it looked. Something very different was going on under Ventura's hood, though.

Ventura Publisher was not only the first desktop publishing program for the PC, it was also the first computer publishing program to really merge the page-layout and typesetting approaches. For the first time, it was possible to create highly structured documents in a WYSIWYG environment. Moreover, unlike other desktop publishing programs, effective use of Ventura required the user's understanding of how the program itself functions. Although it was possible (albeit inefficient) to produce a Ventura document entirely by entering or importing all the elements and then working with them interactively, you could also do virtually all of your layout, editing, and formatting outside of Ventura, using templates, macros, and advanced preformatting techniques. Regular Ventura users soon learned that the way to unleash the full power of the program was through a combination of the two approaches: thinking and working like a programmer as well as an artist.

This idea may seem intimidating to you at first, especially if you've never used styles or tags before. If you're accustomed to drawing programs or to the pasteboard metaphor of PageMaker, there's nothing very intuitive about using Ventura. It's hard to visualize the effect of changing formatting instructions in a text file, the same way you can immediately see the result of changing a graphical element on the screen.

Ventura may also be confusing to you at first if you're not used to working with file pointers and directory structures, because Ventura does not bring all the parts of a document together into the same file. Instead, it simply keeps track of the sources of all the pieces of a chapter and adds its own formatting codes to the original text documents. Another separate file is used to store paragraph formatting information, and an additional chapter-specific file is generated for some of the text elements created inside Ventura.

At first glance, this may seem to be a crazy way of doing things, and your initial reaction may well be "What a curious way for a program to operate, leaving all those different files out there." But there's a method to Ventura's madness. Once you've learned the basic ideas behind how Ventura thinks, and once you've started to think like Ventura does, everything will start to fit together.

Ventura 101

Most of how Ventura thinks comes down to these three basic concepts:

- A multiple-file format
- Frame-based documents
- Modular components

Lumped vs. Unlumped Files

Perhaps it's fitting that a Canadian company now owns Ventura. Americans have historically taken pride in their country as a "melting pot" of combined nationalities and cultures. Canadians, on the other hand, talk of creating a "cultural mosaic" of elements that work together but still retain their distinct identities—one is no less Armenian or Vietnamese or Somali for also being Canadian. And this is precisely the way Ventura operates, producing chapters and larger publications from files that also retain their own separate identities.

Single-File Format Most desktop publishing and drawing programs use what might be called the Lumped File format, which we have deftly illustrated in Figure 35.1. With this format, all text, graphics, and formatting information for a document are included in a single publication file. For instance, anything you add to a DRAW document ends up in the final .CDR file (except for OLE-linked elements). Prior to PageMaker 4.0, everything included in a PageMaker document also was incorporated into the final publication, and that remains the default for PageMaker 5.0.

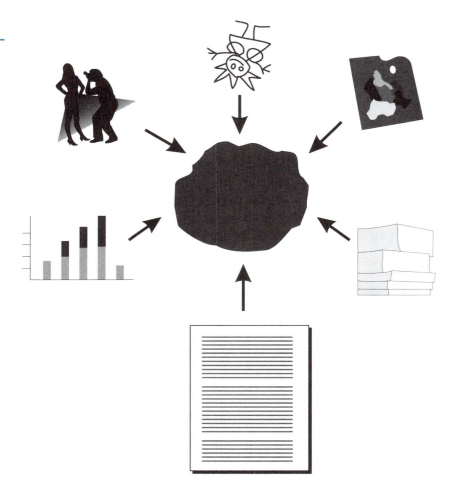

35.1

In the Lumped File format, all elements combine to form the final document.

Once something has been tossed into that melting-pot document, its source doesn't matter, because from that point on you work with a copy of the original item. Changes you make affect only the contents of the final document, and unless you're using OLE links, you can copy or move that single file and have everything necessary to re-create the entire document.

Multiple Files with Pointers Ventura Publisher is different from PageMaker and CorelDRAW and applications like them. Ventura is not an *integrator,* but rather an *organizer* of separate elements. And those elements remain separate, just like the individual tiles in a mosaic. For example, when you edit imported text within Ventura, you are actually working with the original source file. Any changes you make in Ventura will be there the next time you open that file in your word processor, and any changes you make in your word processor will appear the next time you open any Ventura chapter that uses the file.

A Ventura *chapter* (.CHP) file is not the document itself, but rather a blueprint—a list of what is contained in the chapter and a set of instructions to Ventura about how to assemble the document from the component parts (see Figure 35.2). With very few exceptions, the .CHP file does not contain any of the chapter's actual content. Instead, it contains *pointers* (full DOS path names) to the location of the other files that store the content. Each chapter file also has a pointer to a separate style sheet file, which contains chapter and paragraph formatting information.

35.2

A Ventura .CHP file doesn't contain the component parts of a chapter; instead, it just points to the style sheet and the text and graphics files.

As shown in Figure 35.3, pointers in multichapter publications (.PUB files) work the same way as they do in a single chapter file. Just as each chapter contains a list of text and graphics files, each publication contains a list of chapters. Using that list, you can create a table of contents or index and then add it to the publication.

35.3

Chapters and pointers in a Ventura .PUB file, which contains a list of chapters that you can use to generate an index or table of contents.

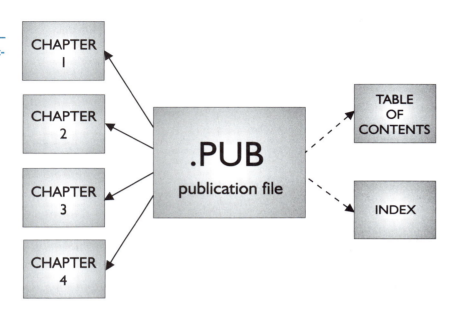

NEW FOR 5

Ventura chapter and publication management has always been somewhat of a challenge because multiple files were often located in different directories or even on different drives. The Ventura 5.0 Publication Manager allows you to view and print a list of all the files included in any chapter or multichapter publication. Figure 35.4 shows how Ventura views a chapter and Figure 35.5 shows how it views a publication. The Publication Manager also has Smart Copy, Smart Move, and Smart Delete functions for managing chapters and their associated files.

The Frame Is the Key

Unlike many other DTP and graphics programs, Ventura requires that you place all text and graphics in frames. The contents of each frame are tracked with references to an external text file or graphics file, or to internal chapter elements.

35.4

The Publication Manager's list of chapters

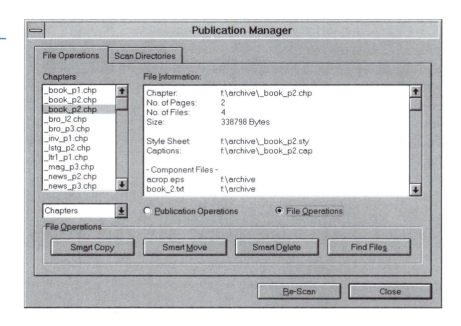

35.5

The Publication Manager's list of publications

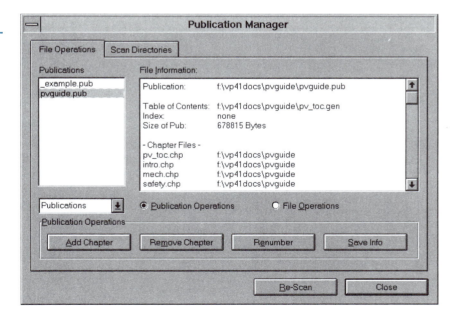

Ventura's frames are a requirement, not an option—*every* element must be in a frame. Unlike DRAW or PageMaker, to move an object in Ventura you must move the frame in which it resides. Ventura even considers the base page as just another frame, and headers and footers, as well. You can add additional frames to a page, and these added frames can be moved, copied, and resized. Any frame can be formatted, and the formatting information for most frames can be saved in *frame tags,* which can then be applied to other frames in the chapter.

Modular Components

One of Ventura's greatest strengths is its ability to mix and match component pieces. With Ventura's pointers, it's easy to change the style sheet, text, and graphics files associated with a chapter, or the chapters included in a publication. Since there's no limit to the number of pointers that can point to a given file:

- Text and graphics files can be shared between any number of chapters
- Style sheets can be shared between any number of chapters
- A chapter can be included in any number of publications

In fact, about the only things that cannot be shared in this way are text and graphics elements created inside Ventura itself for a specific chapter. Before we explore the potential power of this modular approach, let's look closer at some of the individual pieces of a Ventura document.

Ventura Productions

Earlier, we compared the text and graphics elements in a Ventura chapter to the tiles in a mosaic, but a theatrical production is probably a better analogy to use for understanding how the chapter elements work together.

The Director

If a Ventura chapter were a stage play, the chapter (.CHP) file would be the director, who organizes and orchestrates the show. The chapter file's job is to locate the cast, stage the production, and direct the action. A .CHP file contains

- General chapter layout and typography
- Chapter-level elements such as page headers and footers
- A list of external text and graphics files used in the chapter
- Size, position, and formatting for each frame
- Where to find the contents of each frame
- A pointer to the style sheet used by the chapter

Every time you open a Ventura chapter, Ventura first loads the style sheet called for in the .CHP file. Then the program goes out across your system and locates all of the other files that are part of that chapter. Finally, it re-creates the overall chapter layout, reconstructs each frame, loads their contents, and applies the proper formatting defined by the style sheet.

It's important to remember that all this happens *every time you open a chapter.* Therefore, although the list of files and the instructions for assembling them will not have changed since you last worked on the chapter, it's quite possible that you or someone else will have changed one or more of the files in the list. And if this is the case, the contents or formatting of your chapter will no longer be the same. Ventura has taken criticism in the press for this methodology. Most of Ventura's users, however, don't consider this a bug; they see it as a feature, and a very useful one at that.

The Costume Designer

Ever seen a waiter in an elegant restaurant working in blue jeans and sneakers, or a diva on stage in a bikini? It's just as unlikely that you'll ever see a banner headline set in 10-point Times Roman or receive a formal engraved invitation set in Courier.

Every professional theater needs a good costume designer, and at Ventura Productions that's the job of the style sheet. A style sheet contains formatting tags that can be applied to paragraphs anywhere in the document, whether in an imported text file, text typed directly into a frame, headers and footers, or picture captions and callouts. Some of the formats you can specify in a paragraph tag include the following:

- Type specifications: typeface, point size, color, and style (normal, bold, or italic)
- Bullets and drop caps
- Overscoring, strikethrough, and underlining
- Ruling lines above, below, or around paragraphs
- Tab settings
- Hyphenation rules, including which language's rules to apply
- Horizontal and vertical alignment
- Text rotation
- Indents and outdents
- Spacing between lines, paragraphs, and words
- Whether lines of text span a column or the entire frame
- Line, column, and page breaks

Figure 35.6 shows the Character tab of Ventura's Paragraph Settings dialog. At the top, under the title bar, you can see the tabs for all five categories of paragraph settings—Alignment, Spacing, Defaults, and Typography, in addition to Character.

Suppose a paragraph tag called Headline calls for 40-point Helvetica bold, green color, double-underlining, a half-inch outdent into the margin, with a red pointing hand as a bullet. Pretty ugly, but it's sure to get people's attention. As soon as you apply that Headline tag to another paragraph in your chapter, it will instantly become just as ugly. (You can use any name you like for a paragraph tag, including "Ugly Green Head.") If you later come to your senses and change the tag attributes to something a little easier on the eye, all Headline paragraphs will instantly follow suit.

35.6

The Paragraph Settings dialog has five tabs of settings

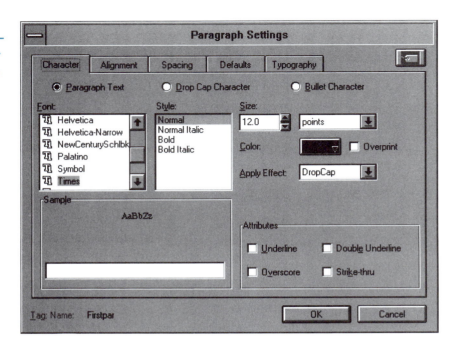

As you see, paragraph tags are powerful formatting elements, and so are the style sheets that store them. Just as no designer wants to spend days or weeks re-creating another set of costumes that have already been designed and beautifully coordinated, you certainly don't want to have to set up the same paragraph tags over and over again. A style sheet handily stores your collection of tags so you can use it in other chapters, now or later. You can also copy individual tags among style sheets.

The Cast

In most Ventura chapters, the major players are text and graphics files that have been created in other programs, and the only thing about them that's actually a part of the chapter itself is their pointer in the .CHP file. Here's an example of a file list for a Ventura 4.2 chapter with text and graphics files located on several different drives and in several formats:

```
#T 01 E:\MANUAL\INTRO\BOOK1.TXT 0001 * *
#G 06 F:\ARCHIVE\GRAPHICS\WIDGET.CGM * * *
```

```
#G 07 E:\MANUAL\PICS\LOGO12.EPS 0040 00A0 00D9
#T 22 D:\WINWORD\REFGUIDE\SAFETY.DOC * * *
```

where the #T or #G indicate whether it's a text or a graphics file; the two-digit number is a Ventura-specific code to identify the format; and the path and file name tell Ventura where to find the file.

Ventura doesn't know or care what's *in* any of the chapter files. It only knows what their names are, where they are located on your hard disk or network, and what filter should be used to import them. For instance, the line

```
#T 22 d:\samples\boring.doc * * *
```

in a .CHP file tells Ventura to import the text file \SAMPLES\BORING.DOC on drive D, through the Word for Windows 2.0 filter (represented by the 22). Perhaps since you last opened this chapter you've edited BORING.DOC to make it less boring, or even rewritten it completely. Ventura neither knows nor cares; the program obediently fetches what it assumes is the same old boring BORING.DOC, from the same location on your system.

Sometimes this kind of blind trust comes in very handy. Suppose you've prepared hundreds of documents that all include pointers to LOGO.EPS, your company logo, and the new vice president of marketing has decided it's time for a different corporate image. As long as the new logo, too, is in .EPS format, all you need to do is overwrite LOGO.EPS with the revised artwork, and that's what will appear the next time you open any of the documents that have the logo.

There are two important differences between imported text and graphics files. First, a text file can be edited from within Ventura; a graphics file cannot. This is because Ventura is working with a copy in memory of the graphics file, rather than with the original file. You can size and crop it in Ventura, but that won't affect the original; to change that, you'll need to return to the program that originally created the graphic. The second difference is that you can load the same graphics file into as many frames as you like in the same chapter; but only one copy of a text file can be placed in a given chapter.

NEW FOR 5

 Earlier versions of Ventura relied on the original GEM graphics engine, which could only handle .GEM vector files and .IMG bitmap files. When a graphic in any other format was loaded into a Ventura chapter, a duplicate .GEM or .IMG file was created. In Ventura 5.0, all graphics formats are imported directly, and these duplicate files are no longer required.

The Extras

Often you'll add to your Ventura chapters text elements that are not part of another file. Perhaps you need to type text directly into an empty frame. Or maybe you want to add a caption to a figure, or create a few picture callouts like those shown in Figure 35.7. Ventura creates a new file in which to store these elements. No pointers are required for

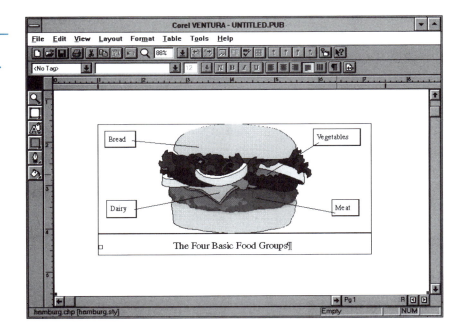

35.7

An imported graphic with a caption and callouts added in Ventura

this so-called caption file, because it is always in the same directory as the .CHP file and has the same name with a .CAP file name extension.

NEW FOR 5

Prior to version 5.0, Ventura stashed all of a chapter's graphics that were created with Ventura's own drawing tools in a similar, chapter-specific file with a .VGR extension. With version 5.0, Ventura graphics are now incorporated into the .CHP file.

Exporting .CAP Text Frame text (text typed directly into a frame) can be exported from the .CAP file and saved in separate external files in any format that Ventura recognizes. Text typed directly onto an inserted page normally goes into the .CAP file, but, as with frame text, you can choose to save it in a separately named file instead. Text typed directly onto the base page *must* be saved into a named file. The default is an ASCII file with the same name as the chapter plus a .TXT file name extension, but you can specify another file name or format as needed. The following table summarizes where Ventura stores or locates the text and graphics elements of a chapter.

Chapter Element	Origin	Where Stored or Referenced
Imported text	External file	Pointer in .CHP file to the original file
Imported graphics	External file	Pointer in .CHP file to the original file
Ventura graphics	Created in Ventura	*Pre-5.0:* chapter-specific .VGR file; *Ver. 5.0:* .CHP file
Text entered on base page	Entered in Ventura	Stored in an external named file
Text entered on a new page	Entered in Ventura	.CAP file (default) or external file

Chapter Element	Origin	Where Stored or Referenced
Text entered in a frame	Entered in Ventura	.CAP file (default) or external file
Figure captions	Entered in Ventura	.CAP file
Graphic "box text"	Entered in Ventura	.CAP file
Headers and footers	Entered in Ventura	.CHP file

Infinite (Almost) Diversity

"Infinite diversity in infinite combinations"—you *Star Trek* fans may remember this Vulcan motto to describe the range of possible life forms in the universe. Ventura's possible combinations aren't quite infinite and aren't nearly as diverse as the universe, but the Vulcan motto is a pretty good description of how independent files allow just about any combination imaginable.

Probably the most obvious example of such combinations is sharing text or graphics files between chapters, but the most powerful one is…

Sharing Style Sheets

If you use CorelDRAW, or a word processor such as Word for Windows or WordPerfect, you're probably already familiar with the concepts of styles, which are collections of format attributes, and templates, which are collections of styles. But how many times has DRAW asked you whether you want to save the changes to a template when you didn't even know you'd been *using* one, let alone changed it? Or asked you if you wanted to update your drawing by applying a changed style, when you had no idea what the changes were? And how often have you wondered whether Subhead Text means the same thing in two different Word documents that were both based on the same template? Well, in Ventura, there's never any question about it—you're *always* using a style sheet, and the latest version is *always* applied to every chapter because it's reloaded each time you open the chapter.

Here's where you can see the importance of having pointers to external style information; any change you make to a style sheet is instantly reflected in every chapter using that style sheet. This makes updating the appearance of hundreds of manuals or data sheets almost as easy as changing a single graphic or piece of boilerplate text.

Tag, You're It   Figure 35.8 shows a series of players (pages) who have visited the costume designer in the wardrobe department. These wholesale changes were made with one operation: We changed from one wardrobe (style sheet) to another and to another and then back again. Each style sheet has different costumes (sets of formatting instructions) for the tags used in the chapter. When one set of costumes is replaced by another, the look of the scene (chapter) changes instantly and, in some cases, dramatically.

Let's carry this idea a little further. Suppose one of the services your company provides is customized resumes…well, semicustomized. You're certainly not about to design the resume layout from scratch each time. That's what style sheets are for, right? But the same format probably won't work equally well for a plumber and a college professor. So why not set up three or four style sheets that all use the same paragraph tag names but with different formatting for those tags? Then it will be easy to offer your clients a choice of formats, by simply showing them an example of a resume created with each style sheet. The same idea can be easily adapted to flyers and other types of documents.

Presto, Change-o

Now let's consider the opposite approach: leaving the style sheet alone but changing the other elements in the chapter that use it. Suppose you are producing a monthly newsletter in which the only changes from issue to issue are in the content of some of the text and graphics files. The layout is pretty much the same from month to month: On page 1 there's always a lead story with one photo, and the story is continued in the right-hand column of page 3. There's always a monthly calendar of events on the back page. The president's column always appears in exactly the same spot on page 2, as does a profile of one of the group's members on page three. Sure, you can set up a document template with

35.8

These documents use the same chapter file and the same text. Only the style sheet has changed.

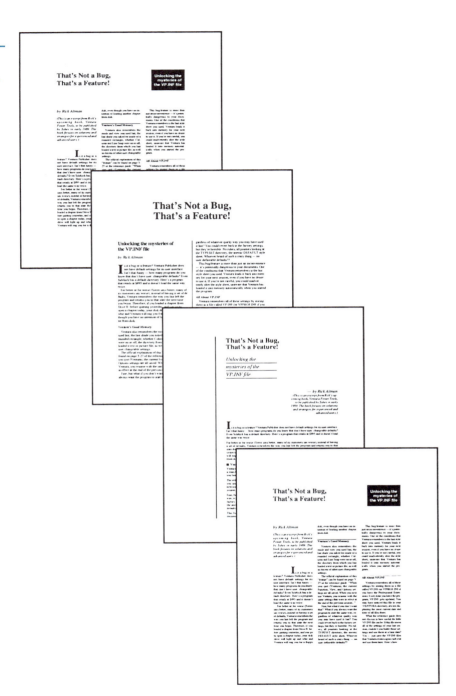

placeholder frames into which you can pour the text and pictures each month, but with Ventura you can take this one step further.

As we did earlier to update our company logo, we can do the same for the stories and pictures in each month's newsletter: We simply overwrite the old files. Of course, we'll probably still need to do a little rearranging and retagging afterwards, but we're already most of the way there. Here's the game plan:

1. Create a template chapter for your newsletter, which includes all fixed design elements and placeholder frames for the stories and pictures.
2. Load "dummy" files into the placeholder frames, giving them file names that identify how or where the file is used, rather than what it contains (story1, story2, calendar, contents, profile, photo1, and so forth).
3. When you are ready to produce an actual edition of the newsletter, copy the current month's stories and pictures over your dummy files, using the same file names that you used in the template.
4. When you next open your chapter, all the new files will be in place.

A Rose by Any Other Name…

You've just received several text files for your next project—and they're all in different formats. Word for Windows, Word for the Mac, WordPerfect, Ami Pro, ASCII—they're all represented. No problem. Ventura can import all of them. But suppose after you've begun the chapter, you realize working with it would be much easier if all text was in WordPerfect, because that's the word processor you normally use for revisions. That's no problem, either. Simply save your text files in a different format *from within Ventura,* and then save the chapter again. The chapter pointers will be rewritten for the correct file names and formats, and you'll be able to edit all of the files in WordPerfect as well as in Ventura.

It's HOW Many Pages?

Byron Canfield's contributions to this book are the chapters on DRAW's color features, but he has two other claims to fame in the Ventura community: He recently produced an 8,000-page document, and he makes extensive and often very creative use of keyboard macros (which helped make it possible to tackle that long document). As you work with Ventura, you'll soon develop your own favorite techniques for managing "monster" documents, but here's a quick tour of some of Ventura's long document and automation features.

Long Document Features

Ventura offers a few features that may not be terribly useful when you're putting together a brochure, but are invaluable in long publications and technical or academic documents.

Table of Contents   Ventura will automatically create a table of contents or similar list for an entire publication, with up to ten levels of entries. These entries are created by extracting text to which you have assigned paragraph tags specified for each level of the list. The list is produced as a separate file that you can then format and add as a chapter to your publication.

Indexes   Ventura will automatically create an index from the text associated with index markers. The list of index entries is sorted alphabetically and saved, with corresponding page and/or chapter numbers, to a text file. The index can include main entries and subentries, as well as cross-references to other entries.

Auto-Numbering   Using a variety of numbering formats, Ventura will automatically insert consecutive numbers or letters before similarly-tagged paragraphs in a document. You can also use this feature to insert specified text before every paragraph with the same tag, with or without the automatic numbers.

Cross-References   Cross-references are used to direct readers to a page, chapter, figure, caption, table, or section in the same document.

You can insert a cross-reference anywhere in your document except in a header, footer, or footnote. This long-document feature can be very useful in shorter documents, too—for example, in the "Continued on" and "Continued from" page references in newsletter articles. You can also use a cross-reference to refer to a placeholder for "variable text." When the definition of a variable text item is changed, so are all the related cross-references in the text. Cross-references are automatically updated whenever you renumber the document.

Footnotes Ventura's footnotes are placed in a separate frame at the bottom of the page. They can be numbered in several different formats, with numbering restarting at either the beginning of the chapter or on each page. You can format footnotes and footnote frames just as you can any other Ventura frame or paragraph.

Ventura on Auto-Pilot

Ventura is an automation maniac. It lets you establish elaborate and incredibly powerful strategies for raising your production potential. Here are a few of the many ways you can tap into the Ventura automation engine.

Preformatting Text Files All of Ventura's paragraph and local text-formatting codes are stored as part of the text itself. When you tag a paragraph in a Ventura document with, say, Bullet2, Ventura inserts

```
@Bullet2 =
```

at the beginning of the paragraph. This tells Ventura to format that paragraph according to the specifications of the Bullet2 tag in the current style sheet. If the current style sheet has no such tag, Ventura will automatically create the tag, which you can then define as you wish. Finally, if there is no tag name at all at the beginning of a paragraph, that paragraph is automatically assigned the default tag of Body Text. Thus "regular" text, doesn't need a tag name; it automatically becomes Body Text in Ventura.

Local character-formatting is handled in a similar way. When you select some text and change its text attributes, the information that tells

Ventura what changes to make is also written into the text file, in the form of codes between angle brackets. These codes include not only local text-formatting but also index entries, footnotes, cross-references, and frame anchors to anchor pictures to the text flow.

So if you know the correct codes for tags and local formatting, why can't you just enter them with your word processor and thus "pre-tag" files so they'll be properly formatted when you bring them into Ventura? The answer, of course, is that you can, and thousands of Ventura users do. Preformatting files is a very powerful tool in automated publishing operations. And because the text files are still accessible outside of Ventura after they become part of a chapter, you can edit the paragraph tag and formatting codes as well as the text. Seemingly minor changes to embedded formatting codes in a text file can have dramatic—and often disastrous—effects on a Ventura document. So if you ever want to experiment with this, be sure to back up all of your files first.

Automation with Macros Ventura does not have its own scripting language (at least, not yet) but you can use the Windows macro recorder to automate repetitive operations both inside and outside of Ventura. Resourceful users have also used Word and WordPerfect macros to convert word processing codes and footnotes into a form that Ventura understands, to update cross-reference or index entries in text files, and to perform many more specialized tasks.

Although it takes time to initially set up the macros (and, perhaps, to learn how to write them), these tools will save you significant effort later, in long documents and repetitive projects.

File Management

When you work on long documents, it's very easy for Ventura files to get scattered all around your hard disk, and before you know it document and project management has become a real nightmare. As soon as a chapter or publication grows beyond half a dozen or so files, that's when it's time to establish a system of file management that will still make sense to you six months or a year from now. You know, the day when your boss walks in the door and says, "Remember that catalog you did last November? We need an updated version by the end of the week."…

What's New in Ventura 5.0

Ever since the acquisition of Ventura Publisher by Corel in the fall of 1993, feelings have been mixed in the Ventura community. Some believe this is the best thing that could have happened to the program. Others fear it's just a matter of time before Corel phases out the features that make Ventura unique, turning it into a faceless "desktop publishing" module in the CorelDRAW box. But just about everyone agrees that, for Ventura to survive at all, some kind of change was necessary.

The Game Plan…

Corel had several publicly stated goals for Ventura 5.0.

- Integration into the CorelDRAW suite of applications, with shared graphics, printing, and color-management technology
- Reorganization of tools and menus to improve efficiency, accessibility, and ease of use, especially for new users
- Adoption of Windows conventions, most notably the ANSI character set and standard Windows editing shortcut keys
- Addition of long-requested new features, such as text wrap around irregular objects, free rotation of text and graphics, and .CDR file importing capability
- Improved font and file management

And the Outcome…

At the time of its acquisition, Ventura Publisher was undergoing what was supposed to be a total rewrite of its code, which would allow for expansion of features and capabilities as well as easier porting to other platforms and operating systems. What has surfaced as Ventura 5.0 falls well short of that "from-the-ground-up" rewrite. On the other hand, major changes in the program hint at more dramatic changes in the future.

The most significant changes to Ventura are probably the direct or indirect result of the program's incorporation into the CorelDRAW suite of applications. This was far more than just a marketing move. It also meant a fundamental alteration of how the program operates, due to shared printing, graphics, and color-management engines—"shared" quite literally, since when Ventura is installed along with other Corel applications, they actually use the same files to perform common functions.

Thus Ventura now has the same color separation, trapping and (though admittedly limited) imposition capability as DRAW itself. Ventura also shares DRAW's graphics import filters, which finally releases Ventura from having to create duplicate .IMG or .GEM files for all other graphics formats.

A New "Look and Feel"

Although the changes under Ventura's hood are the most significant, the changes in the user interface will be most evident. When you start Ventura 5.0, you'll immediately notice the addition of a DRAW-style toolbox, including flyout menus for Zoom, Line, and Fill tools. Figure 35.9 shows an example of the Fill tool's work.

Also new to Ventura are the helpful roll-ups that are now familiar to users of the rest of the CorelDRAW suite. Ventura 5.0 sports a total of nine roll-ups: Files, Tags, Cross-References, Index Entries, Placement, Node Editing (of text wraps), Quick Format, a Character roll-up for inserting characters at the cursor, and a Mosaic roll-up (Figure 35.10) with "drag-and-drop" graphics import capability. Many of these roll-ups perform functions that can also be accessed in other ways, reflecting Corel's commitment to the philosophy that it should be as easy as possible to work from wherever you happen to be in the program interface.

In keeping with this approach, Ventura 5.0's menus have been completely rearranged. In past versions, the menu structure was based on the various tools for working on chapters, frames, paragraphs, text, tables, and graphics. In version 5.0, the emphasis has changed from tools to functions. The Chapter, Frame, Paragraph, Text, and Graphics menus have been consolidated into two new Layout and Format menus. The new

35.9

Line and Fill tools allow DRAW-style fills and outlines to be applied to Ventura graphics.

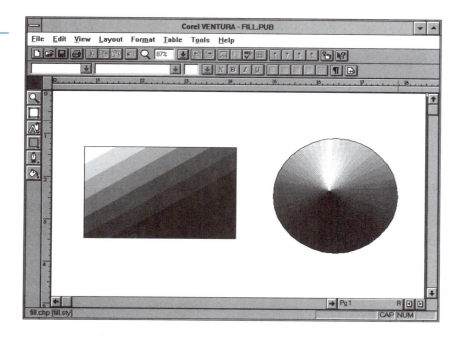

35.10

The Mosaic roll-up lets you import graphics by "dragging" them onto the page.

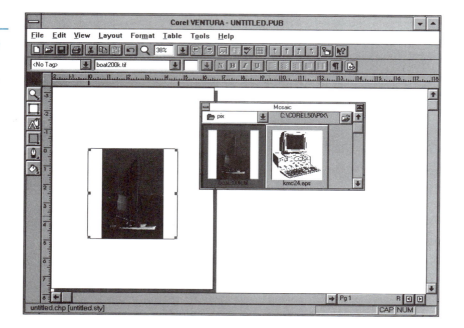

Format menu (Figure 35.11) allows formatting of frames, paragraphs, selected text, graphics, and tables; the Layout menu contains chapter-level layout and style-sheet functions. As with the roll-ups, in nearly all cases you can also reach these menu functions via other avenues.

35.11

The Format menu

Paragraph...	Ctrl+T
Selected Text...	Ctrl+T
Frame...	F6
Graphic...	
Table...	Ctrl+F9
Manage Tag List...	Shift+F9
Manage Overrides...	Shift+F10
Override Counter...	
Re-Anchor Frames...	
Renumber Publication	
Update Auto Numbering	Ctrl+F2
Ruling Lines...	Ctrl+F8
Breaks...	
TOC & Index...	

WATCH OUT!

Ventura 5.0's new ability to access various functions without changing tools is a mixed blessing for users, because one person's ease of use can be another's confusion. The new interface will definitely require a period of adjustment for current users.

Ventura veterans will need some time to get used to a plethora of new keyboard commands, too. It is unlikely, however, that there will be many complaints about the adoption of standard Windows text-editing keys, or of DRAW's F2/F3/F4 Zoom shortcuts. Another welcome change is Ventura 5.0's almost total conversion to the Windows ANSI character set. Now, the only time Ventura's old character codes will be required is when you need to enter embedded characters in ASCII files.

New File Formats

With Corel's acquisition of Ventura came rumors of conversion to a single-file architecture, but it did not come to pass (welcome news to Ventura Publisher loyalists). What did occur, however, were some significant changes in Ventura's file formats, so that it is no longer possible to save Ventura 5.0 documents in earlier formats.

Documents, Chapters, and Publications

The most significant change is a move from chapter-based toward publication-based documents. All Ventura 5.0 documents, even those consisting of a single chapter, will now be publications; and most file-management functions are now based (at least by default) on the .PUB rather than the .CHP. As before, chapter files (including those from previous versions) can be shared between any number of publications, but Corel definitely wants us to start thinking of a chapter as an element in a publication, just as text and graphics files are elements in a chapter. Ventura 5.0 allows you to move easily between the chapters of an open publication—and no extra steps are required to generate publication-level tables of contents, cross-references, and indexes.

The chapter file format itself has also undergone major changes. Ventura 5.0's .CHP files are now binary instead of editable ASCII, and these .CHP files now incorporate information about the chapter's frame tags and graphic elements that was previously stored in separate chapter-specific .FRM and .VGR files.

Where's the .WID?

Width tables are a thing of the past, to the dismay of some users and the relief of others. And Ventura is finally moving to font identification by name rather than ID number. Unfortunately, because of the limitations of the old font ID system, in some cases fonts used in older documents are being mapped incorrectly. Once the conversion to Ventura 5.0 has been completed, these problems should disappear.

New Features

What else is new in Ventura 5.0? Here's a list. You'll find some of the "biggies" we've all been waiting for, as well as a few unexpected surprises.

- Text wrap around irregular objects, with a Bezier tool for editing the path (see Figure 35.12)
- Free rotation of frames and their contents
- A text editor for text-mode editing of files in a chapter
- A Thesaurus, and multiple personal spell-check dictionaries
- Automatic correction of text input errors, called Type Assist
- Additional text and graphics filters, including Microsoft Word and WordPerfect 6, SGML (using the included TagWrite utility), and .CDR import
- The PANOSE font-matching system
- Frame position locking
- A pasteboard outside the printed page area

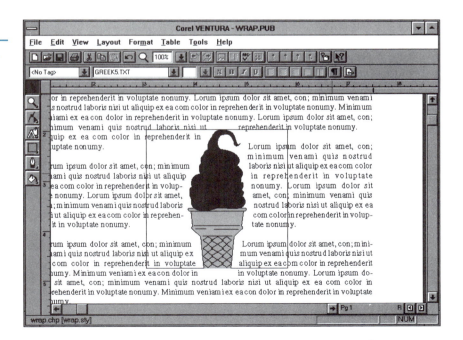

35.12

Ventura 5.0 allows you to flow text around irregularly shaped objects.

- A Publication Manager, with Smart Copy, Smart Move, and Smart Delete functions
- CorelKERN—a stand-alone utility for editing font kerning pairs (see Chapter 33)

Two new features are worthy of particular attention:

Local Formatting Local paragraph formatting, or tag overrides, is a concept very familiar to PageMaker users. This allows you to change the format of individual paragraphs, as well as to make global changes to paragraph tags. Local paragraph formatting information will be stored in the text file, just as local character formatting is.

Quick Format This feature is aimed squarely at new users, to help you get up to speed with Ventura. Quick Format provides several efficient default formats for common types of documents. Another aid for new users and existing ones, as well, is a series of default paragraph Tag Types that can be used as starting points for creating basic categories of tags. You don't have to use the Tag Types—any paragraph tag can still be based on any other existing tag, as in previous versions of Ventura.

Associated Programs

Associated Programs…or, whatever happened to Ventura Separator, Scan, and Database Publisher?

The first question is easy to answer: In place of Separator, Ventura now uses the much more sophisticated color separation capabilities of the CorelDRAW printing engine.

Many users would like the ability to scan directly into a Ventura frame, which the old Scan program made possible only to a very limited degree. Ventura 5.0 does not have direct TWAIN support, so even this limited functionality is no longer available. PHOTO-PAINT, however, which is bundled with the stand-alone edition of Ventura as well as the CorelDRAW suite, is TWAIN compliant, and offers bitmap editing as well as scanned image importing.

Replacing Ventura Database Publisher (part of Corel's Ventura Publisher 4.2 package), CorelQUERY takes a different approach to the publication of data-intensive documents, accessing other applications to import or link tabular data directly into Ventura.

And Still on the Wish List...

Corel may have added the kitchen sink to Ventura, but after so many years of neglect, there are still quite a few features that remain on our Grand Wish List. Among them are

- Ability to open more than one document or more than one Ventura session at a time
- Mixed portrait and landscape pages in a chapter
- Parent/child tag relationships
- Character tags
- Multiple indexes and tables of contents
- Built-in macro or scripting language
- Tabs in justified text
- Multiple-paragraph footnotes and table cells
- A choice of footnotes or endnotes
- More than six repeating frames in a chapter
- The end of arbitrary limits to the number of tags in a style sheet, files in a chapter, and characters in a paragraph

Ventura users may not have to wait too long for some of these, because we're now living in Corel Standard Time—and that means Ventura 6.0 is right around the corner.

Advanced Font Management

APPENDIX A

We know that there are some users who based their decision to upgrade to CorelDRAW 5.0 solely on the improvements made to the engine that governs typeface management. If you are among that group, this appendix may be more salient to you than the other 35 chapters combined.

DRAW's method of delivering fonts to your PostScript printer or service bureau has historically been an unorthodox, awkward, and confusing affair. You had to either accept the fact that DRAW was going to convert your nice clean typefaces to curves, or learn far more about the CORELFNT.INI file than you would have ever wanted to know. The previous edition of this appendix, written for DRAW 4.0, represented one of the most involved and complex writing tasks we have ever faced. All that changed entirely with CorelDRAW 5.0, and this appendix covers in detail how the new DRAW goes about the business of delivering typefaces to PostScript printing devices.

As you work through this appendix, bear in mind that whenever we refer to DRAW we mean CorelDRAW 5.0, and that we assume that by now you already have a good working knowledge of DRAW, Windows, and Windows font management.

AUTHOR'S NOTE

 We considered republishing the Font Management appendix from our previous book in addition to this updated one, with the thought that you could share the older one with colleagues who still use DRAW 3.0 or 4.0. This book is already too fat, thank you; however, you can find the entire discussion from the previous appendix on the Companion CD (in the NOTES directory). Called TYPE.EXE, it is a self-executing electronic document that can be opened and read on any Windows system. You can distribute TYPE.EXE without restriction, to anyone who might benefit from it (as long as you don't charge a fee for it).

Three Things Typographical

We'll start with the general and work our way in. There are three ways in which DRAW can deliver type to your laser printer, imagesetter, or film recorder. (From now on, we'll refer to all PostScript output devices simply as "printers.")

1. It can study each letterform and break it down into Bezier curves, as if you had drawn each character with the Bezier tool, or had used the Convert to Curves command. You have probably heard this referred to as *sending your text as curves*.

2. It can place in the stream of PostScript code the entire character set for a given typeface. Once done, that typeface remains in memory for the rest of the print job, making it easy for printers to call for it. You know this as *downloading a typeface*.

3. It can assume that a certain typeface is already resident in printer memory, either because the printer was built that way, or because you downloaded the typeface to the printer yourself. If DRAW believes a typeface to be already resident, it won't send any typeface information in the PostScript code at all, except to call for the typeface by name. You know this as *using resident typefaces*.

DRAW used to make only two of the above deliveries: sending type as curves or using resident typefaces. And although it has added a third delivery method, DRAW 5.0's methods and operations are far, far simpler and easier to understand than before. No longer must you go behind the scenes to edit the CORELFNT.INI file in order to instruct DRAW how to handle typefaces. (That file still exists and can be used, but has been pretty much rendered moot.) Now there are two places where you can go to tell DRAW how to manage typefaces:

- When creating a PostScript print file, go to Print / Options / Options and find the two check boxes labeled Download Type 1 Fonts and Convert TrueType to Type 1.

- When exporting your work as Encapsulated PostScript files, in the Export EPS dialog find the two radio buttons labeled As Curves and As Text, and the check box labeled Include Fonts.

Sending Text as Curves

We call this the "Leave me alone—don't bother me" option. If you want to bypass altogether the issues surrounding typefaces, you can ask DRAW to send your text as curves. This is analogous to using the Arrange / Convert to Curves command, although not as drastic, because your text is still text when you return from printing and resume editing on screen.

To send text as curves, you simply uncheck the Download Type 1 Fonts box in Print / Options / Options. When you disable that option, you essentially tell DRAW: "Don't concern yourself with WIN.INI, don't check for resident fonts, don't do anything—just shut up and make curves."

Figure A.1 is a composite illustration showing a simple drawing in DRAW, and a snippet of the pertinent PostScript code that represents it. This is the code produced when you ask DRAW to send your text as curves. As you can see, each character is represented by a series of numbers and letters. This is DRAW's way of defining each node, path, line segment, and curve that makes up a character.

A.1

When you tell DRAW to send your text as curves, you give it permission to break up your text into little component parts. All these numbers represent the twists and turns of "Fonts!"

```
%CHAR: 0 0 (F) @t
40 0 m
40 358 L
282 358 L
282 316 L
88 316 L
88 204 L
@c
F
%CHAR: 305 0 (o) @t
321 130 m
321 178 334 214 360 237 c
382 256 410 266 442 266 c
477 266 507 254 529 231 c
551 207 563 174 563 133 c
563 100 558 73 548 54 c
@c
F
%CHAR: 583 0 (n) @t
617 0 m
617 260 L
657 260 L
657 223 L
675 251 703 266 738 266 c
754 266 769 263 781 258 c
794 252 804 244 810 235 c
816 226 822 214 824 202 c
826 194 827 179 827 159 c
@c
F
```

WATCH OUT!

The Download Type 1 Fonts option is a bit misleading, because it gives the impression that it addresses only PostScript Type 1 faces. If you uncheck that box, ALL text—TrueType or Type 1—is sent as curves.

To Curve or Not to Curve?

There is one good reason for, and one against, sending your text as curves. When you set text as curves, DRAW is concerned only with rendering the particular characters it needs; but when you download a typeface, DRAW sends the entire character set (as do all Windows applications). That can take up a fair amount of real estate in a PostScript file, and it's certainly worth it if you go on to set several paragraphs of text in that face. But if you are only setting a word or two, it's not very efficient. For a drawing that involves lots of typeface changes, and small amounts of text for each face, you might be better off sending your text as curves.

As an example, we took the ransom note in Figure A.2 (refer to Chapter 10 to see how we created it) and created two PostScript print files from it. Rendered as curves, this was a fairly easy chore for DRAW: to describe the 45 characters as curves is not much more complex than if the characters were all one typeface. But when sent as text, this job became a paragon of waste: 45 typefaces were downloaded just to set one character in each of them.

A.2

45 characters from 45 fonts. Sent as curves: 65 K. Sent as text: 445K!

Buy 500 books froM uS or we wiLl form✿t your hard drive.

We have used an extreme example here—most of the time, the difference in file consumption will not be so dramatic. On the other hand, the reason *against* sending text as curves is rather absolute: The text simply doesn't look as good, especially from laser printers.

Figure A.3 shows lines of text printed at 600 dpi from an HP LaserJet 4. The lower line (with text rendered as curves) suffers noticeably. The characters are heavier and often distorted; this is particularly clear with the *e* and *g*. You can expect this drop-off in quality to be even more noticeable at 300 dpi.

A.3

At laser printer resolutions, text printed as curves does not stack up well against the real McCoy.

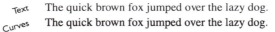

The quick brown fox jumped over the lazy dog.
The quick brown fox jumped over the lazy dog.

The quick brown fox jumped over
The quick brown fox jumped over

Text as curves fares much better at higher resolutions. Imagesetter output will show these lines to be indistinguishable from one another; and that holds true, as well, for the WinJet 1200 (LaserMaster's printer enhancement that brings virtual 1200-dpi printing to the LaserJet 4).

Unless you are experiencing significant printing problems or severely slow output, our recommendation is that you keep the Download Type 1 Fonts option enabled. This is not like the old All Fonts Resident option, which entailed high risk of the dreaded "Courier Output" substitution. Download Type 1 Fonts is just telling DRAW to use real, live typefaces whenever possible. Your text-based work will be the better for it.

Downloading Typefaces

Let's start with what this option does *not* do: The Download Type 1 Fonts option does not download your Type 1 fonts…not necessarily, anyway. We really wish that Corel would have given this option a different name—it is sure to confuse more than a few users. Here is how it works:

If You Are Using TrueType Fonts   In this case, enabling Download Type 1 Fonts has no effect whatsoever, unless you also enable Convert TrueType to Type 1 (more on that shortly). DRAW will render all text set in TrueType faces as curves, just as before.

If You Are Using Type 1 Fonts   In this case, enabling Download Type 1 Fonts issues the following instruction: "Hey, DRAW, this user does not want you to send the text as curves. Instead, you are to use the actual typeface. In order to determine how to use it, check with the WIN.INI file."

And here we get to the heart of the matter. DRAW now consults WIN.INI for its typeface management instructions, just as all the other Windows applications do. It looks for those magic WIN.INI instructions that tell it whether to download a typeface with the print job, or to assume the face is already resident in the printer. We wish that DRAW had named the option "Check WIN.INI" instead of "Download Type 1 Fonts," because the typefaces will only be downloaded if WIN.INI says so.

Many of you are already familiar with the typeface encoding that takes place in WIN.INI, but if you are not, go to DRAW's online Help and search for WIN.INI to get a focused explanation. The *Reader's Digest* version goes like this: Typefaces are referenced in WIN.INI by their file names (complete with paths). The reference that is required in all circumstances is the one that points to the *printer font metric* (.PFM) file. That is the file that keeps track of character spacing, kerning, and other critical information needed by applications to render text on screen and prepare it for printing.

When you install, say, Eras Light into the environment, Windows (or Adobe Type Manager, to be precise) places the following line in WIN.INI for each of the PostScript printers you have installed:

    softfontxx=d:\psfonts\pfm\erl_____.pfm

If you know that your service bureau always keeps Eras Light resident in its imagesetters, then this line of code will produce PostScript files that correctly call for Eras Light during print time. But if you are printing to your laser printer, or you know that your service bureau does *not* keep Eras Light resident, you would then want the typeface to be included (downloaded) with the print job. Windows notifies its printer driver of this by adding a second part to the line in WIN.INI:

    softfontxx=d:\psfonts\pfm\erl_____.pfm,**d:\psfonts\erl_____.pfb**

The second part (in boldface above for clarity) shows the path to the actual *printer font binary* (.PFB) file. That is what tells DRAW to download the typeface.

To reiterate: Enabling the Download Type 1 Fonts box *does not* arbitrarily force DRAW to download your typefaces. It only gives DRAW permission to check WIN.INI. It is WIN.INI that says yea or nay to downloading. Figures A.4 and A.5 show the kind of code that is produced in either case. If your printer already has Eras Light resident in printer memory, then the code needed to render text is barely more than the text itself. Both of these figures are abbreviated for demonstration purposes, but the point is still clear: In Figure A.4, DRAW essentially says, "Use the typeface you already have; here is the text—go do it." In Figure A.5, on the other hand, DRAW has to download the entire character set before it can set any text, saying, "As far as I know, you might need to set every single character that the typeface has before this job is out, so I'm going to deliver the entire set to you now." (We had to abbreviate Figure A.5 severely. The letters and numbers go on about 20 times longer than what is shown.)

A.4

When DRAW doesn't have to download a typeface, the code it creates is lean and mean.

```
CorelDrawReencodeVect
/ItcEras-Light Z
%StartPage
[0.07200 0.00000
0.00000 0.07200
2077.19991 2359.22390]
@tm
/_R64-ItcEras-Light
500.00 z
0 0 (Fonts!) @t
%EndPage
```

There is no difference whatsoever in output quality between these two scenarios. It doesn't matter how the typeface got there—by downloading during printing, by downloading prior to any print jobs, or by divine presence, having been built in to the printer—the typeface is treated the same once it's there. The only possible exception is when you have a typeface on your system that is somehow different from the one your service bureau has (perhaps an older version or a different manufacturer).

A.5

Downloading typefaces is no small job, requiring lots of elbow room in a PostScript file. This is just the first of about twenty pages' worth of code.

```
%%BeginResource: font
ItcEras-Light
%!PS-AdobeFont-1.0: ItcEras-
Light 001.000%%CreationDate:
Fri Jun 24 17:02:40
1988%%VMusage: 27857 30325%
Eras is a registered
trademark of International
Typeface Corporation.11 dict
begin/FontInfo 10 dict dup
begin/version (001.000)
readonly def/Notice
(Copyright (c) 1988 Adobe
Systems Incorporated.
CD5A1ED1AFDCAE92B83F3245EB6335D64E8A2971FFF0E577C060957F944202DE9E44
5C98BEA377D1B66D7E9A4EB2F296AEDBE86A3BEE0F47D18FC460CAA5AE21
0F945C9E9747763BD004998F09A20B5E9D3013321877E5D6FCB257D2B8D514F8853D
6AF21B8521E6A554C42386156DA840417DDA2A08A72719DB1E2E2F275F02
6F519E9F9F466BCCCBF7970BF3613EBE5B5F6787082060EE9702BD3B2CDD83CFB82F
51FD1140F8FB3C938B7E4D5364A0A2C3F07153F4F0F90D478A7D0E14573C
00000000000000000000000000000000000000000000000000000000
00000000000000000000000000000000000000000000000000000000
00000000000000000000000000000000000000000000000000000000
00000000000000000000000000000000000000000000000000000000
0000000000000000000000000000000000cleartomark
%%EndResource
[ 0 0 0 0 0 0 0 0 0 0 0 0 0 0 0 0 0 0 0 0 0 0 0 0 0 0 0 0 0 0
293 237 356 587 587 847 688 205 305 305 534 587 293 249 293 405 587
587 587 587 587 587 587 587 587 587 293 293 587 587 587 466 795 619
595 627 730 562 532 742 732 244 388 567 474 840 752 803 536 803 560
587 205 587 356 1000 534 534 587 1205 478 271 1031 587 587 587 587
CorelDrawReencodeVect /_R66-ItcEras-Light /ItcEras-Light Z
%%EndSetup

/_R66-ItcEras-Light 500.00 z
0 0 (Fonts!) @t
```

Converting TrueType Faces

If you enable the Download Type 1 Fonts option, another option becomes available: Convert TrueType to Type 1. We had to study this one a bit, because we really didn't know what was meant by "converting" a

TrueType face to Type 1. We normally associate language like that with a font conversion utility that can read .TTF files and create .PFBs, or something like that.

In this context, the conversion takes place on the fly, authored by the PostScript printer driver while it is preparing to create the PostScript code. The TrueType format is an entirely different language from PostScript, but it has many common elements—not the least of which is the internal intelligence known as *hinting*, which allows typefaces to adjust their letterforms slightly to print better at 300 and 600 dpi.

Without the conversion, TrueType faces are sent into the PostScript stream as curves; with the conversion, they are sent as typefaces, with their intelligence maintained. Our printing tests produced output similar to Figure A.3. Text as curves was inferior to text as text (in this case, text that had been converted to Type 1 format).

Rules of Thumb

With DRAW 5.0, our recommendations are not nearly as convoluted as in previous years. We recommend that you

- Turn on the Download Type 1 Fonts option
- And then turn on Convert TrueType to Type 1

As discussed, there are times when it might be more prudent to send text as curves—especially to imagesetters, where the loss of typeface fidelity won't be noticeable—but we suggest that you consider the preceding two settings as your defaults. We predict that, a vast majority of the time, you will want your Type 1 handling decisions to be made by WIN.INI and your TrueType faces to be converted to Type 1.

These are also the factory defaults that Corel has instituted. Should you want to change these settings, DRAW will remember that you made the change for the duration of the current session, but once you close and reopen DRAW, they revert back to their original defaults. In order to permanently change the defaults, you have to make a trip to the CORELPRN.INI file, located with all of the other .INI files in Corel's

CONFIG directory. Find the two lines in the [Config] section that read

```
PSDownloadType1Fonts=1
PSConvertTrueTypeToType1=1
```

Changing the value of either to 0 will permanently change the default.

Making .EPS Files

The Export EPS dialog contains similar controls that handle the questions of curves, typefaces, and downloading. There is one exception: Unlike printing, .EPS files are not made with a particular printer in mind. They are designed to be portable and therefore printable from a wide variety of printers. As a result, they cannot take their marching orders from WIN.INI, whose instructions are tied to particular printers.

Therefore, your choices when making .EPS files are as follows:

- Send as curves
- Send as text, with all typefaces assumed resident
- Send as text, with typefaces always downloaded

Figure A.6 shows the Export EPS dialog settings for these three situations and details the results. Because there are no such things yet as printer-resident TrueType faces, the second choice doesn't apply to TrueType faces. (The As Text option in the dialog is not dimmed because DRAW can't know if you have other text in your drawing, so if you click As Text, your TrueType text is sent as curves, anyway.)

The safest route to take is the third choice: text as text, with fonts included. If you know that you are using only printer-resident Type 1 fonts, you can uncheck the Include Fonts box.

Managing the Backstage Business

No matter how simple all of this has become in 5.0, there is still some housekeeping to do. Happily, Corel has provided tools to simplify that, as well.

A.6

The choices in the Export EPS dialog for exporting your work as EPS files

Both Formats
Text sent to the PostScript stream as curves

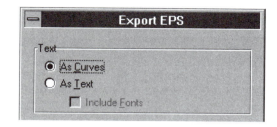

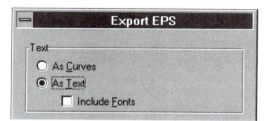

PostScript
Text sent as text; all fonts treated as resident

TrueType
Text sent as curves

Both Formats
Text sent as text; all fonts downloaded

Managing CORELFNT.INI

Good news—you no longer need to mess with this file to get your typefaces to print correctly. The only substitutions listed in the [PSResidentFonts] section are the no-brainers, such as AvantGarde for the old Avalon, Bookman for Brooklyn, and so forth. We haven't come across any bad matches thus far in 5.0, as there were in 4.0 (for instance, when a substituted typeface did not have matching font metrics, resulting in poorly spaced text). Most importantly, you don't need to carefully add lines to this file to register your typefaces. The insatiably curious can tinker with this file if they want to (back it up first); by and large, however, for most work you can ignore this file.

Managing WIN.INI

Because DRAW can now get its instructions from WIN.INI, you need to make sure those instructions are correct. This can get tricky, because you might want separate settings for when you are printing to your laser printer (and certain faces are resident), and for when you are creating PostScript files for your service bureau (where other faces might be resident). WIN.INI can keep separate sets of instructions, based on which printer port is chosen (for example, printing to LPT1 might indicate your laser printer and printing to FILE might indicate your service bureau).

Here is where Ares FontMinder—a version of which is now included with CorelDRAW (see Chapter 33)—comes in handy. FontMinder can keep your font assignments and your port assignments clean and correct. You tell it which typefaces are to be treated as resident when sending data to a particular device. Then FontMinder makes all of the appropriate changes to WIN.INI.

And now, on to your lead author's favorite part of the book: Junk & Miscellany.

Appendix B

Junk & Miscellany

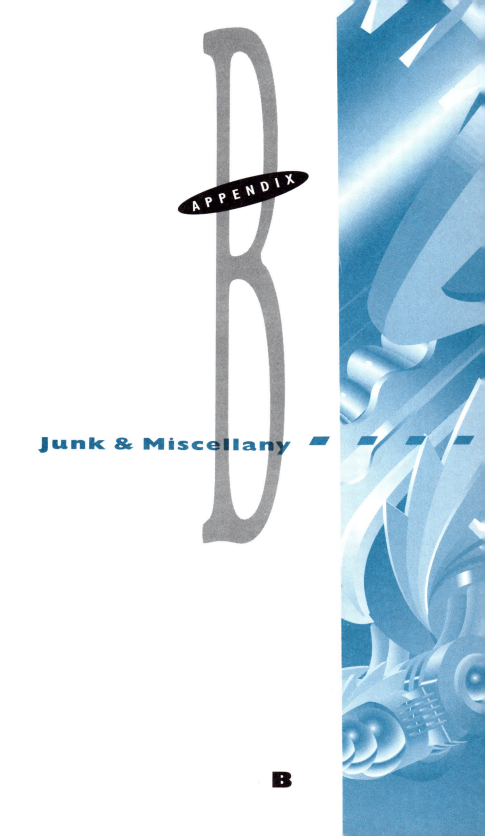

APPENDIX B

Even with 35 chapters and three appendixes, I find it impossible to write a book in which all the topics I want to cover fall neatly into categories. That's why no book of mine goes to the printer without some sort of "Everything Else" chapter. Good thing, too—these potpourri sections are usually the most popular. I always save them for the end, and add to the list of topics as my writing team works though the book. Think of this as a big README file, full of odds and ends, by-the-ways, and late-breaking news. As I sit poised to compile this appendix, I wonder if I shouldn't just wait and save it for an entirely new book. I can see it now on the shelves: *CorelDRAW Junk and Miscellany*, by John Doe. (Would you put *your* name on that book title?)

Without any further ado, here is a loosely organized collection of late-breaking news and miscellaneous tidbits about CorelDRAW.

Keeping Two Versions of DRAW

With Corel's reputation for less-than-perfect initial releases of DRAW, we know that there are quite a few of you who are upgrading to the latest version…but don't want to delete the old one just yet. Also, many service bureaus and consultants need continuing access to DRAW 4.0 and even 3.0 in order to maintain compatibility with existing customers and clients. This is easily done: Upon installation, DRAW asks you to choose a directory, and as long as you don't choose the directory that houses DRAW 4.0 or 3.0, you'll be okay. The WIN.INI file will keep separate entries for each version.

The greater challenge arises when you want to run DRAW 5.0, 4.0, or 3.0 *at the same time.* Each version is run from an executable file called CORELDRW.EXE, so when one is in memory and another is called,

Windows becomes confused. OLE activities would be quite an adventure, also, under these conditions...you'd double-click on an embedded object and there'd be no telling which program would step up to claim it.

The answer is simple: *Rename the .EXE files.* Keep DRAW 5.0 the way it is, but go to your main CORELDRAW 4.0 and/or 3.0 directories and search the DRAW subdirectory for CORELDRW.EXE. Rename it to, say, DRAW4.EXE or DRAW3.EXE. Once that's done, you'll need to edit the properties of the Program Manager icon that launches each application, so that Program Manager knows to look for the appropriate .EXE file.

The only caveat: Load the latest version first. If you start a session with DRAW 5.0, you'll then be able to load 4.0 and/or 3.0. But if you start with 3.0 and then double-click on the 4.0 or 5.0 icon, you are likely to get the wrong copy.

Figure B.1 is the real thing: a snapshot of DRAW 5.0, 4.0, and 3.0, all running at the same time, and even sharing data back and forth. Why would you ever want to do this? Hey, this is Junk & Miscellany—I don't

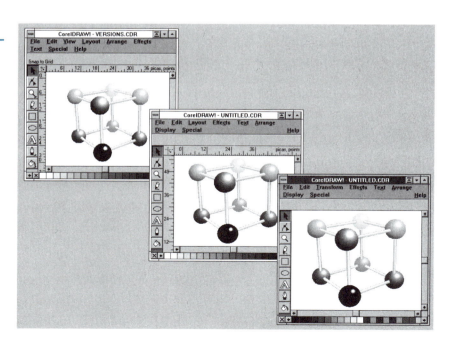

B.1

On a 16MB system, it is possible to run all three versions of DRAW, and even to transfer data among them.

need to justify anything here… Seriously, if you suspect that one version of DRAW has a bug, doesn't work the way you want it to, or handles your artwork incorrectly, running two versions simultaneously is the easiest way to check.

Running Two Copies of DRAW 5.0

This suggestion is a bit more palatable: There are numerous instances when running two copies of DRAW 5.0 would be helpful. In your modern-day word processor, you probably take for granted the capability of opening two files simultaneously. Once that's done, it's easy to take bits and pieces of one file and paste them into another. DRAW, however, does not support the opening of multiple files in one session, so you might not ever think of the graphical equivalent to the multiple cut-and-paste in your word processor. But imagine the possibilities: You are browsing several files for bits and pieces that you want to dump into a new drawing. The ways to do this in DRAW are not terribly pleasant:

- You could open one file, copy, and close; open a new drawing, paste, and close; open another file, copy, and close; open another new one, paste, and so on and so forth, ad infinitum, ad nauseam.

- Or you could open a new drawing and, one by one, import other files and strip away all components that you don't want.

In cases when there's only one element you want to copy from one drawing to another, then DRAW's limitation won't kill you. But if you have many pieces to gather up, the two strategies above point out quite clearly that DRAW is woefully limited in its file-sharing capabilities—all because it doesn't support the notion of opening more than one file at once.

Here's the humorous part: DRAW won't let you open two files, but Windows will let you open two sessions of DRAW. With two sessions going, each showing a different file, rapid and repeated transfer of elements is now as simple as it is in your word processor. Just copy from one and paste to another. Figure B.2 offers a silly example. DRAW-ING1 contains a piece that DRAWING2 needs. If you imported DRAWING2 into DRAWING1, you would get the needed piece, plus four unwanted pieces. If you tried to cut and paste with just one session of DRAW, you would have to gyrate between the two drawings. With two sessions open, however, this becomes a simple cut-and-paste maneuver.

This double-session strategy is not as disk-intensive as you might think, because the second copy of DRAW finds many of its required parts already in memory and uses them from there. The second copy usually loads quickly, with very little disk activity at all.

B.2

What's the simplest route to transferring Ball No. 4 into DRAWING2? The double-session strategy.

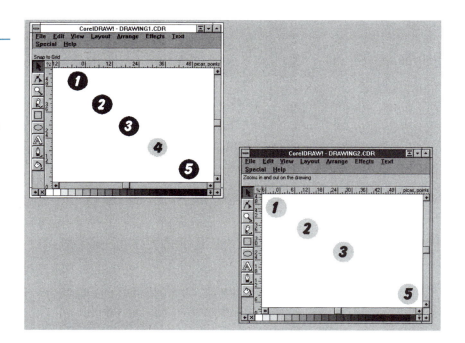

Outies and INIs

There are dozens of behind-the-scenes files in DRAW that affect output and user settings, and with the current architecture, introduced in 4.0, these files can be somewhat hard to locate. Here is a brief tour of DRAW's user-serviceable parts and their locations. As always, before editing these files, be sure to back them up first, or know where to find the originals on the program CD or disks.

The COLOR Directory

This directory contains all of the files needed for color correction and color management. Many of these files are ASCII-based, making them easily browsed. However, we recommend you not try to edit these files.

The CONFIG Directory

This directory houses all of the initialization files—INIs, for short—that control program defaults and hundreds of other settings that determine how DRAW and its associates perform. DRAW 3.0 stores almost all of its settings in CORELDRW.INI; both DRAW 4.0 and 5.0 distribute them across many files. Here is a brief tour.

CORELAPP.INI This file's primary purpose in life is to tell CorelDRAW where to look for things. Fonts…filters…dictionaries…executables… they all have their place in the gigantic CorelDRAW puzzle, and CORELAPP.INI's job is to play traffic cop. If you want to run certain parts of the program from the CD, such as import and export filters, you can edit this file and change the directory entry for FiltersDir.

Your program serial number is also stored in this file.

CORELDRW.INI This file controls many of the meat-and-potatoes settings in the main DRAW module. Here is where DRAW keeps its current settings for whether to make backup files with each save; whether DRAW's window is maximized or not; where to look for template files; how to render objects that are being moved; and several dozen other functions. This file also keeps track of the last four files used—a valuable aid to advanced users who demonstrate DRAW before groups. If your script calls for specific files to be opened sequentially, you can edit CORELDRW.INI with those names, ensuring your ready access to them.

Corel's engineers make a point of warning you away from this file; that's their job. But we make a point of inviting you to experiment—that's *our* job. Just back it up first…

CORELFLT.INI This file determines which file filters show up in the import and export dialogs, the filters' names, and what file name extension is associated with them. As soon as I cracked the seal on the software, I bolted for this file to make two changes.

First, for importing of Word for Windows files, I changed

    MSWW2=W4W44F.DLL,"MS Word for Windows 2.x",*.DOC;*.*,9,1

to

    MSWW2=W4W44F.DLL,"Word for Windows 2.x",*.DOC,9,1

When navigating the drop-down list of file types, I want to be able to press W and go right to Word—I don't like having to remember to press M for Microsoft.

Second, my Word files always have .DOC extensions, and I don't like that the filter wants to show me all files. Removing the *.* near the end of the MSWW2= line did the trick. I also changed CorelMOVE to Move, CorelCHART to Chart, CorelPHOTO-PAINT to Paint…you get the idea. I rarely use all of the file filters, but I'd hate to have to go back to Setup each time I wanted to add one. So I have installed them all and REMarked out the ones I rarely use.

CORELFNT.INI This file has received quite a demotion in DRAW 5.0—happily so. This used to be the major-league important file that records font substitutions and decisions on a font's resident status. Now those tasks are all handled by WIN.INI and the various print settings discussed in Appendix A. The only sections in COREL-FNT.INI of moderate interest now are the listings for the Symbols library, and a substitution map of old .WFN typefaces from 3.0 days and earlier.

CORELPRN.INI A myriad of printing issues are covered in this file, including default screen settings, handling of bitmap images, thresholds for printing complex objects, halftone angles, color separation controls, and so on.

And Finally... The CORELCHT.INI, CORELMOS.INI, CORELMOV.INI, CORELPNT.INI, CORELSHW.INI, and CORELTRC.INI files control the behavior and performance of each of the other six modules in the program.

The CUSTOM Directory

Herein lie a bevy of palettes and patterns. The only user-serviceable file remaining in this directory is CORELDRW.DOT, which controls the dotted and dashed lines that are available in the Outline Pen dialog and roll-up. CORELDRW.DOT speaks a foreign language—with numbers representing the length of, pattern of, and space between each dot—but with a bit of experimentation, you can make good use of this file, should you have a carefully designed pattern that you want to automate. You'll need to close and reopen DRAW for each change to this file.

The PROGRAMS Directory

This is it. This is where the guts of the applications reside. Executable files...data libraries...import and export filters...common engines...help files. The over 20MB of data in this directory make up the heart, soul, and brain of CorelDRAW.

What We Haven't Covered

Though I hate to disillusion anyone who thought that this many pages would be quite enough to cover every aspect of DRAW, it isn't. But I can categorically state that the list of topics *not* covered in this book is shorter than the list of topics that *are* covered. Following are descriptions of some of DRAW's less frequently used tools, and others that simply deserve more ink than they have received so far in this text.

The New Arrange Commands

We didn't mean to give the Arrange menu's new Intersection and Trim commands short shrift—but they're so easy to use, we didn't think a tutorial was necessary. Here are a couple of semi-useless exercises that might be fun. First, for Intersection:

1. Create a long thin rectangle, colored black with a black outline.
2. Make a duplicate of the rectangle on top of itself (+ key) and fill it white.
3. Select both rectangles by double-clicking the Pick tool, and choose Effects / Blend.
4. Set the Steps to 10 and the Rotation to 180.
5. Apply, and check your screen against Figure B.3.
6. Separate the blend and then ungroup the 10 objects.

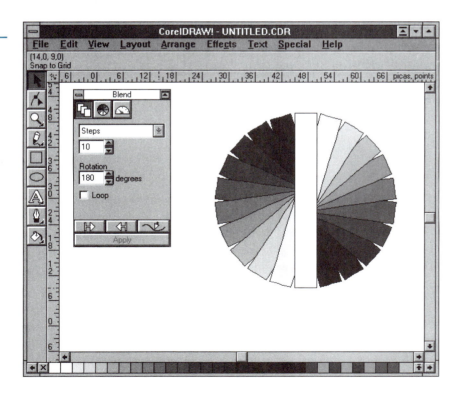

B.3

Can you guess what the intersection of this wheel will be?

7. When all objects are ungrouped, select them all.
8. Now invoke Arrange / Intersection and sit back.

Figure B.4 shows the result of intersecting these rectangles: a little regular polygon (which looks just like a circle) right in the center. Intersection is very literal: It looks for the areas that are overlapped by all selected objects. Because you blended the objects in a 180-degree arc, the intersection object is a regular polygon. (This is a simple method of creating regular polygons with an even number of sides.) As shown in Figure B.5, it's much easier to study this effect in Wireframe view. The shot in the figure was taken before the Intersection command was invoked, but you can clearly see what the intersection looks like. (We can't stress enough how helpful Wireframe view can be for studying the basic essence of objects.)

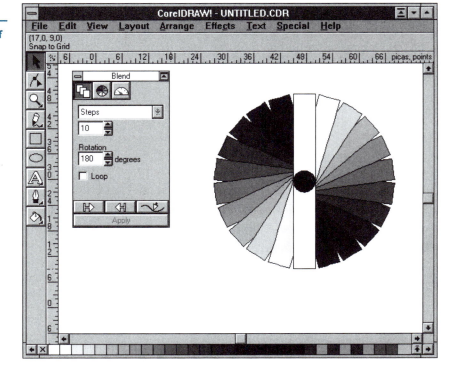

B.4

The intersection of these blends is a regular polygon that looks like a circle.

B.5

Switching to Wireframe view reveals the intersection of the rectangles with complete clarity.

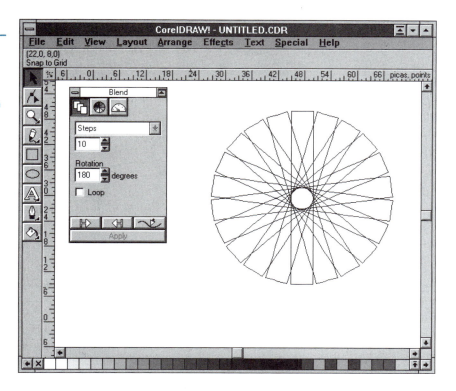

Now let's use Arrange / Trim to quickly create a little sprocket from our intersection.

1. Create a big gray circle and a small circle of any color. Duplicate the small circle. Place them anywhere, as long as you can see all of them at once.
2. Select the two small circles and invoke Blend.
3. Click on the Path tool (the curved line and the pointer), click New Path, and then click on the big circle.
4. Choose Full Path and then Apply.
5. Vary the number of steps until your screen resembles ours in Figure B.6.
6. Separate the blend group and then ungroup the circles.

B.6

The result of blending two objects along a path

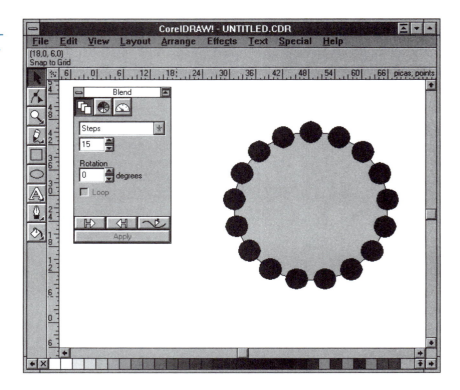

7. Select all of the little circles and Combine them. (The easiest way to do this is to use Edit / Select All, then deselect the big circle, and then Arrange / Combine.)

8. With the combined circles still selected, Shift+select the big circle and choose Arrange / Trim.

9. Delete the combined circles to see the results of your trim, as shown in Figure B.7.

Just for fun, continue:

10. Create another circle and center it horizontally and vertically in your sprocket.

11. Select the circle and the sprocket and Arrange / Combine them.

12. Open Extrude and Apply.

B.7

Arrange / Trim has sliced into the big circles at the precise points where it overlaps with the small circles.

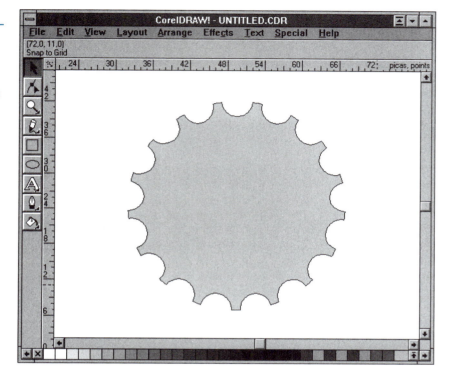

13. Experiment on your own with the Rotation and Light Source controls. Our fiddling led to Figure B.8.

Dimension Lines

Figure B.8 includes a precise measurement of the diameter of our sprocket, and this was produced courtesy of the Dimension Line tool, greatly improved in DRAW 5.0. The User's Guide includes a clear and complete examination of dimension lines (DLs), beginning on page 27.

The most significant improvement is Corel's promotion of dimension lines from dead to alive. In other words, you now can link a dimension line to an object—as we have done with the sprocket—so that when the object is moved or sized, the dimension line will automatically move and update with the object. The key to creating a live dimension line (Corel calls them *linked dimensions*) is to enable Layout / Snap To Objects. Once done, you can snap both ends of the dimension line to

B.8

While the extrusion provides the realism, it is the new Arrange / Trim command that brings true simplicity to the production of this sprocket.

control points and ensure that they remain linked to those points. Here are some random thoughts concerning dimension lines:

Use the Any Angle Tool When you access the Pencil flyout, the third, fourth, and fifth icons are for creating DLs. Use the fifth one, which I like to refer to as the Any Angle tool. There are plenty of ways to constrain this tool to drawing purely vertical or horizontal lines, should you need to—the most likely way is using Ctrl while creating the line.

Snap to Something Don't trust your eyes or your mouse. If you are creating a DL that measures an object already on the page, sprint to the Layout / Snap To Objects toggle to ensure that your lines are accurate and linked.

If you are creating DLs to represent a distance—not necessarily the length of an object—you should either enable Snap To Guideline and use a pair of guidelines, or set a grid and enable Snap To Grid.

Take Control of the Number If the controls in the Dimension roll-up (reached by double-clicking the dimension text) are not sufficient for your text needs, then fire them. If you want to edit, format, or reposition the number of your DL, just select the text and go for it, as you would any other object in DRAW. Version 5.0's controls are much better than 4.0's; there are new options for adding suffixes and prefixes, for instance. But for determining the typeface, size, and alignment of the text, get in there with your Pick tool and do it yourself. This is especially handy if you want distinct prefixes and suffixes for multiple dimension lines, as shown in our absurd collection of holiday Dimension Lines in Figure B.9.

Print Merge

I didn't write at length about this function, because I have never encountered anyone who uses it in DRAW, and don't imagine there are very many who do. Merge printing is a word-processing task; it doesn't seem even remotely relevant to mainstream DRAW usage. Okay, so I wear my bias on my sleeve—what else is new? For those who want to know more, the User's Manual devotes two pages (380–381) to this function.

Snapping Objects

No doubt about it, DRAW's three Snap functions are wonderful tools for precision workers. Though we discuss them throughout the entire book, we don't cover them in precisely one place. If you need more information, DRAW's handy online Help provides an assist once again.

B.9

Dimension lines can do all 12 days of Christmas.

On the Fifth Day of Christmas My True Love Gave to Me...

5 golden rings

4 calling birds

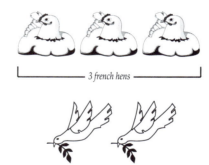
3 french hens

2 turtle doves

And 1 partridge in a pear tree

Press F1 for Help, choose Search, type **SNAP**, and press Enter to see clear and focused discussions of Snap To Grid, Snap To Guidelines, and Snap To Objects.

Layers

We talked quite a bit about layers in Chapter 5, when we guided you through creation of the snowboarder drawing, but there is one aspect of layering for which we haven't yet found the right spot. Thank heavens for Junk and Miscellany…

If you have worked at all with the Layers roll-up, you know that each layer can be made visible and/or printable, for better screen performance and selective printing. Generally overlooked, however, is the fact that this extends to the Guides and Grid layers. Granted, you usually won't want a drawing to print with its guides and grid showing, but there are times when this can be quite helpful. Take the floor plan shown in Figure B.10, for instance. When you need to show this to a colleague, and its scale and proportion are important, then printing it with its guides and grid will be very useful. Just as you do for the conventional layers, double-click on Guides or Grid in the Layers roll-up, and check the Printable field in the Layer Options dialog.

B.10

The Guides and Grid layers are usually just for on-screen work, but you can set them to be printed just as you can any other object on the page.

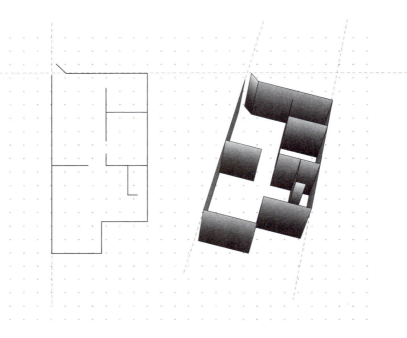

Extract and Merge Back

These two handy, if infrequently used tools can be valuable for those who turn to DRAW for text-heavy work. If you need to do a substantial amount of editing to text stored in DRAW, you can easily accomplish it in your comfortable word processor by using the Special / Extract command to export the text to an ASCII file. After editing, use the Merge Back command to automatically replace the old text with the new. DRAW places a bunch of format codes into the text, which you can largely ignore. As long as you make sure to keep the file in ASCII format, it can safely be merged back into the drawing.

If the text of a drawing needs to be edited by several people, using Extract and Merge Back will allow you to send just the text, not the .CDR file. This might be not only more efficient, but also safer for your drawings, as you eliminate the risk of other users' adversely affecting your designs.

Object Data

This feature, accessible only through the Object menu, acts like a visual database, through which you can assign numbers and labels to elements of a drawing. In the summer of 1993, I sent out a query requesting users to step forward with examples of real-world use of this tool. The only responses I got were from people telling me they never even knew that this was part of DRAW.

My call to the user community is still out there: If you're using the Object Data tool, I'd sure like to know about it. Meanwhile, if you want to explore this interesting idea that hasn't caught on, go to online Help and search for Object Data.

Odds and Ends

As we approach the home stretch, here comes the kitchen sink, in no particular order.

Fast Tool-Switching

Here's the scene: You have just finished typing a string of artistic text and would like to modify it. Perhaps you want to resize it, move it, rotate it, fill it, extrude it, change its font... Those things are all easy to do to text, but you can't do any of them until you select the text with the Pick tool. As you probably know, in DRAW the Spacebar toggles between the Pick tool and the current tool—but not if you're typing text. In that case, the Spacebar enters a space. And clicking inside the text only moves your cursor to another part of the string. According to the User's Manual, your only option is to grab the mouse and make the trek all the way up to the Pick tool and then back.

Try Ctrl+Spacebar. We couldn't find this in any of the documentation, but that quick hotkey takes you out of typing mode and right to the Pick tool. Very handy.

Movable Rulers

If you're lining up text according to precise guidelines, you may not appreciate having the rulers so far away. Hold Shift and you can drag them right onto the page, as shown in Figure B.11.

Instant Nodes

If you are working with the Shape tool, and you need to add a node or two to a curve or line segment, don't think that you have to double-click to get the Node Edit roll-up or (if it's already on screen) mouse over to it. Instead, use the + key on the numeric keypad. Select a node, or a spot on the path where you want to add the node, and press the + key. That's it.

Faking the Quick Copy

Don't you just love the Quick Copy command—pressing the + key on the numeric keypad—to instantly make a duplicate right on top of the original? But do you also use a notebook computer, which makes pressing that + key about as easy as cleaning melted cheese from a toaster oven?

B.11

Your rulers don't need to stay at the top and left. Hold Shift and drag them wherever you want to.

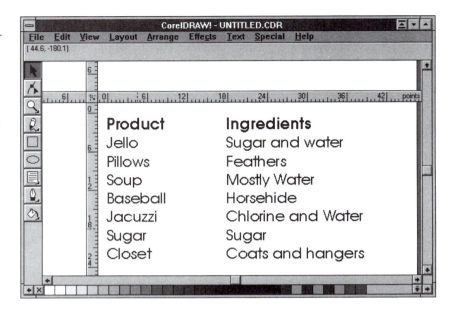

If your numeric-keypad + key has been relegated to some hidden function key, you can create your own alternate Quick Copy. Go to Special / Preferences / General, and under Place Duplicates and Clones, set both Horizontal and Vertical to 0. Now the Duplicate command (Ctrl+D) will work just like Quick Copy, but notebook computer users will have a much easier time getting to it.

Removing Guidelines

DRAW's guidelines are quite powerful, but until now, management of same has been unpleasant. If you have dragged two dozen guidelines onto your page and now want to remove them, good luck. You can ask for guidelines to be invisible, but that's not the same as being able to remove them and start over.

DRAW 5.0 to the rescue. Its new Guidelines Setup dialog has a Delete All button with which you can instantly delete all guidelines. It limits you to removing only horizontal or vertical guidelines at one time, so removing all guidelines is a two-step process. Still beats the heck out of removing them all one by one.

If you do want to remove just one or two guidelines, there is a far easier way than dragging them back to the ruler from whence they came. Instead, just drag them into the *ruler that they intersect*. This is tough to explain—take a look at Figure B.12, a screen with one simple guideline. To remove the guideline, there's an easier way than dragging it back to the vertical ruler. Instead of schlepping it back there, try dragging it into the horizontal ruler. Click on the guideline near the top ruler and just pinch it into the ruler. Done. Much easier than taking the cross-country trip to the other ruler.

I discovered this by accident when I was checking to see if I could remove a paragraph tab by dragging it off the ruler, as I do in my word processor. I mishandled the mouse, clicked at the wrong place, and instead of dragging down, dragged up. Next thing I knew, the guideline for lining up the tab was gone. I had removed it by dragging it up into the ruler. Turns out that this trick is available in version 4.0 and 3.0, also.

B.12

To remove this guideline, don't drag it left, drag it up!

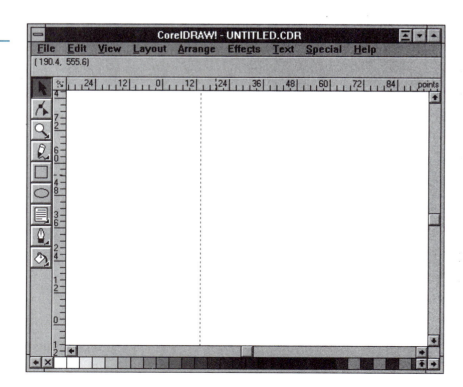

Super-Duper Business Cards

We discussed this in Chapter 25 when we threw a blanket on DRAW's print engine, but it strikes us that DRAW 5.0's ability to print forms will be a real sleeper among its new feature set. Specifically, we refer to its ability to create "two-up" business cards with amazing ease. Here's how it works:

1. Start with a custom page that is precisely fitted to your business card, such as $3\frac{1}{2}$ by 2 inches.
2. Create your card within those confines, as shown in Figure B.13.
3. Issue the Print command, and if asked about automatically adjusting the orientation of the page, say No. This might be the only time where you will want to print a landscape drawing on a portrait page.
4. Go to the Layout page of Options and verify that Layout Style is set to Full Page.

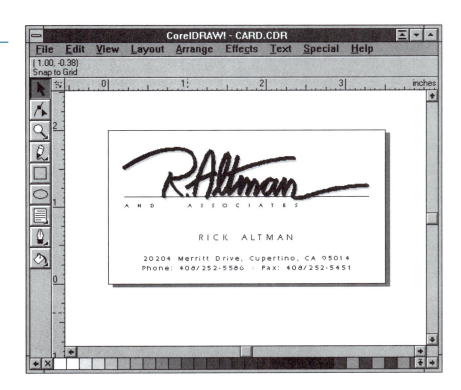

B.13

From one simple business card can come an entire sheet of them, ready for printing.

5. Set Rows to 4, Columns to 2, and enable Clone Frame. It is this last option that turns the one card into eight.

6. Turn on Preview Image and click on the crop marks icon (the second one from the left in the row of seven below the page. Your screen should look like Figure B.14.

7. Print. You should get output that looks like Figure B.15, with precision alignment and perfect crop marks.

This beats the heck out of cloning or duplicating the card to make the composite artwork yourself. Not only does that method introduce the possibility of error, but the file will take much, much longer to load. In contrast, here are the statistics for the card shown in Figure B.15:

Arrangement	Size of File	Time to Load
Single card	89K	0:29
Eight on a page	517K	2:57

Best of all, you don't have to mess with creating crop marks. That alone is worth the price of admission.

B.14

Ready to make camera-ready art...

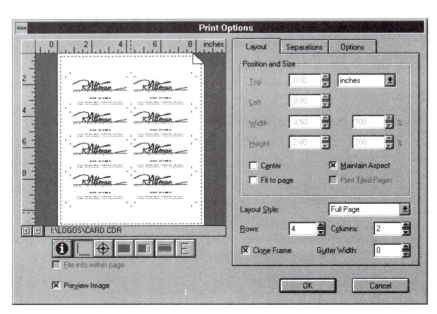

B.15
...and done

Join the CorelDRAW Community

Our last topic is a plug for our continuing and traveling series of seminars and conferences for CorelDRAW users. The 1993 and 1994 International CorelDRAW User Conferences were attended by hundreds of enthusiastic users in Washington, D.C. and San Francisco. These events bring together so many wonderful elements for DRAW users: seminars with expert lecturers, networking opportunities, great parties, and a slew of prizes to be awarded.

On a smaller scale, our two-day seminars offer crash courses in numerous DRAW topics, from novice to expert, all in an affordable and highly digestible form. We will begin a tour of eight West Coast cities, beginning with Seattle and Portland in November, 1994, and head south, finishing with San Diego and Los Angeles in January, 1995.

Our annual three-day Ventura Publisher Summit will enter its sixth year in March 1995. For up-to-date information on all of these events, call our Seminar Hotline at 408-252-5586.

You might also want to contact the Association of Corel Artists and Designers to see if there is a local chapter near you. This user group provides valuable support services to DRAW users seeking to meet their colleagues. You can reach ACAD at 818-563-2223.

That's All, Folks

We would love to hear from you about your favorite and not-so-favorite parts of our book. Call or write:

>Rick Altman
>20204 Merritt Drive
>Cupertino, CA 95014
>Fax: 408-252-5451
>CompuServe: 72341,1714

APPENDIX C

The Companion CD

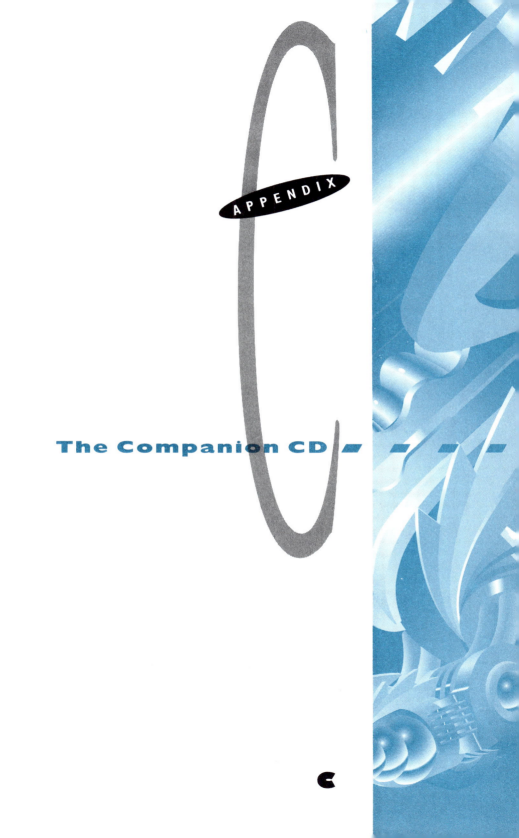

APPENDIX

Including the Companion CD in this book was not a decision that we made lightly. We knew that by doing so we would be leaving some users out in the cold, namely those who do not yet own CD players. Ultimately, there were two factors that helped persuade us in favor of the CD. First and foremost is the incredibly high value that we can provide with a CD. One or two diskettes allow us to deliver about 4 or 5 megabytes of material to you; the CD provides us with much more space. We can include uncompressed programs that you can run straight off the CD, and we can offer programs that are so large they wouldn't fit on any small number of diskettes.

The second factor in our decision was this: If you don't own a CD player, you probably know someone who does, and you are well within your rights to copy what you want from the CD to diskettes. (Even if you don't own a CD player today, we think there's an excellent chance that you will very soon. They are rapidly following the evolutionary path of the 3.5-inch disk drive—remember when you wondered if you would ever have one of those?)

AUTHOR'S NOTE

If you don't have access to a CD player, you can order a diskette with the book's practice files. These files can be very useful to have as you follow along with the exercises in the book. The ordering instructions are at the end of this appendix.

AUTHOR'S NOTE

Some of these programs will not run unless you have the appropriate Visual BASIC.DLL file in your WINDOWS\SYSTEM directory. Although some of the programs that require this file include a setup program that copies that appropriate .DLL files as necessary, others do not. To avoid this issue while trying out these programs, first copy the three files VBRUN100.DLL, VBRUN200.DLL, and VBRUN300.DLL from the VBRUN directory on the CD to your WINDOWS\SYSTEM directory. This will allow you to run any program written in Visual BASIC, regardless of whether it includes the proper .DLL file.

What You'll Find on the Companion CD

The Companion CD contains an assortment of sample images, utilities, practice files, and other information designed to not only increase your productivity in and around CorelDRAW, but also to provide a bit of recreation. It includes

- A directory of Windows and DOS utilities culled from many sources, selected with the goal of making your use of CorelDRAW and related software easier and more productive.

- A Gallery directory containing the works of various artists. These images were all created using CorelDRAW.

- A directory of practice files for following along with the many discussions and exercises throughout the book.

- A multimedia presentation of Corel Corporation's product offerings. Here you can find information on companion products to CorelDRAW such as photo CDs and clip art collections.

- A selection of TrueType fonts that you can put to use in your own projects.

The root directory on the CD contains ten subdirectories, as listed here. The files in each directory are listed at the end of this appendix.

ARCHIVES		The compressed versions of the utility programs found in the UTIL subdirectory
COREL		A multimedia presentation of Corel Corporation's products
FONTS		TrueType fonts
GALLERY		Sample artwork, including the images from this book's Color Galleries
NOTES		Technical information and advice concerning Windows General Protection Faults (GPFs) when running CorelDRAW; also, our previous edition's chapter on Advanced Font Management for DRAW 4.0, in case you can't let go of the old ways
PICTURES		Images presenting special effects with DRAW's PowerClips and Lenses (presented in Chapter 19) and the theory and practice of color printing and image making (Chapter 26)
PRACTICE		The practice files from this book
SOUND		Sound clips discussing the work of the artist who created the award-winning FACES.CDR image (Illustration #7 in our Color Gallery)
UTIL		Windows-based and DOS-based utility programs
VBRUN		Files needed to run some of the programs included on this CD. Copy these files to your WINDOWS\SYSTEM directory before trying to run any of the programs.

AUTHOR'S NOTE

INSTALLATION NOTES: Many of the DOS-based programs in the UTIL subdirectory have varying installation requirements, which are detailed in the program's README file(s). The TrueType fonts in the FONTS directory can be installed from the Fonts section of the Windows Control Panel.

The Utilities

The UTIL directory contains many useful utilities for CorelDRAW. Some of these programs require you to run a setup program located in the program's directory before you can use them. The setup program copies and expands the program on your hard disk. The other utilities you can run straight from the CD. However, you will probably find it easier to use them from your hard disk if you use them frequently, so we suggest copying any of the programs you use regularly.

Each utility is located in its own subdirectory within the UTIL directory. For example, the Professional Capture System is located in UTIL\PCS. An archived copy of each utility can be found in the ARCHIVES directory. These are provided to make installation on other systems easier.

Many of the utility programs included on the CD are *shareware*. Shareware is a method of software distribution that allows you to try out software before you pay for it. Each of the shareware programs on the CD has its own licensing terms. You should refer to the documentation that comes with each program to determine the restrictions on its use and how you can become a registered user. You should also pay as directed for any of the shareware programs that you decide to use on a continual basis.

As mentioned at the top of this appendix, some of these programs will not run unless you have the appropriate Visual BASIC .DLL file in your WINDOWS\SYSTEM directory. Although some of the programs that require this file include a setup program that copies the appropriate files to your WINDOWS\SYSTEM directory, others do not. To avoid this issue while trying out these programs, first copy the three files VBRUN-100.DLL, VBRUN200.DLL, and VBRUN300.DLL from the VBRUN directory on the CD to your WINDOWS\SYSTEM directory. This will allow you to run any program written in Visual BASIC, regardless of whether it includes the proper .DLL file.

Following are brief descriptions of the utilities on the Companion CD; for detailed information on each program, refer to its documentation or its online help. Most of the programs include installation instructions and other basic documentation in .TXT or .DOC files, usually named along the lines of README, README.1ST, READ.ME, or MANUAL, that you can read with Windows Notepad or with Mega Edit (a program that is on the CD). As always with software distributed in this fashion, while all of the programs on the Companion CD have been thoroughly tested for reliability and safety, you do use them at your own risk.

AUTHOR'S NOTE

Some of the documentation in these programs may refer to the necessity for installing the software from drive A. You will not be installing from your A drive—you will instead be installing from your CD-ROM drive. In the installation instructions for any given program, replace any reference to drive A with the drive and the directory that contains the program on the CD.

Alchemy

Image Alchemy is an incredibly comprehensive bitmap conversion and display program. Just about any type of bitmap file can be converted to or from using this application. Alchemy also offers a number of palette manipulation and display options.

CDFont

CDFont peeks into your CorelDRAW 3.0 CDR files, and then tells you the names of the fonts they use. This program is very useful when you need to use CorelDRAW 3.0 files in CorelDRAW 5.0.

Display

Display is a very fast DOS-based bitmap display program, which also supports a number of animation formats. This program normally requires a math coprocessor to speed up image decoding, but if you lack a coprocessor chip you can configure display to work without one. See the included documentation.

DragView

Drag and View lets you view the contents of files without having to run the application (word processor, database, spreadsheet, or other graphics program) that created them. You can also

- View any file in plain ASCII or hexadecimal format.
- Open multiple windows so you can easily compare files.
- Search for text in any file, or for a hexadecimal string in the Hex viewer.
- Go to any cell in a spreadsheet, any record in a database, or any address in the hexadecimal view of a file.

EPSF

With *EPSF*, a program for the manipulation of PC EPS files, you can

- Display information about the contents of an EPS file.
- Extract from an EPS file the pure PostScript section or the TIFF or WMF preview sections.
- Build a DCS (Desktop Color Separation) file.
- Move standard PostScript comments (such as %%BoundingBox) from the end to the start of a pure PostScript EPS file.

You can get instructions for using EPSF by running

    EPSF ?

from the DOS command line.

FontBook

With *Font Book* you can print out typeface specimen sheets in a variety of different designs, each with a different purpose. You can view typefaces on screen in large, clear type, compare up to 100 typefaces, and examine bold, italic, and bold/italic variations.

FontName

FontNamer looks inside the font files you have installed on your machine and finds the names of fonts for you. This is handy because the name of a font is often quite different from its file name. You can view font names on the screen, one at a time, or print a list. You can also use this program to delete font files from your computer.

FPower

Font Power manages all of your fonts with a single program.

GDS

Graphic Display System is another DOS-based bitmap display program. GDS has the interesting capability of creating a catalog that contains thumbnails of many bitmap images. This is a very useful function for creating a database of images that you can browse through quickly.

GhostScr

Ghostscript is a Windows application that allows you to preview and print PostScript (.PS) files on PostScript and non-PostScript compatible printers. Ghostscript comes with an interactive viewer for screen previews and supports color and multipage PostScript documents.

J-Pilot

With *Jet Pilot* you can easily control the settings of your HP LaserJet printer, including page settings (paper size, orientation, and margins) and font characteristics (typeface, pitch, height, and style).

Mac-ette

Mac-ette is a DOS utility that reads Macintosh 1.4MB diskettes on a PC equipped with a $3\frac{1}{2}''$ high-density drive.

MegaEdit

MegaEdit is a powerful ASCII text editor, designed to facilitate complex editing tasks involving multiple and/or large files in situations where such tasks would be difficult or impossible with other editors currently available for Windows.

NeoBookP

NeoBookPro is is a multimedia authoring package. You can use it to script and compile multimedia presentations that include graphics and sound. NeoBook offers an easy interface and comprehensive tools for creating interactive presentations. This program must first be installed to your computer's hard disk. Start by running INSTALL.EXE.

NeoPaint

NeoPaint is a full-featured DOS-based bitmap paint and manipulation program. Although it is DOS-based, it has its own easy-to-use graphical interface. NeoPaint offers comprehensive tool palette for bitmap editing and creation. This program must first be installed to a hard disk before you can use it. Run the INSTALL.EXE in the UTIL\NEOPAINT\ directory.

NeoShow

NeoShow is a slideshow program that allows you to control the display of a series of graphic images. Like the other Neo programs from OSCS software, NeoShow needs to be installed before you can run it.

OKFont

OKFonts performs the tests necessary to find and eliminate bad fonts from your font list. Users who routinely add and remove large volumes of fonts are particularly susceptible to fonts that are either bad or missing. OKFonts will find those fonts and let you delete them.

Pappren

Printer's Apprentice is a font-management utility that helps you manage all your TrueType and Adobe Type 1 fonts by printing inventory sheets (in three styles), character set charts, keyboard layouts, and specimen sheets. This utility was named best Windows font utility by *PC Magazine,* October 27, 1992.

PCS

Professional Capture System is made up of two separate programs: DOS-Capture for the DOS environment, and WinCapture for the Windows environment. These programs allow you to capture screens from DOS and Windows applications and store them in files, and are especially helpful if you are producing software documentation.

PlugIn

Plug-In makes Windows Program Manager better, by adding items to Program Manager's menus and enhancing existing commands. Plug-In's features include:

- An enhancement to the Run command that gives you a history list of the last 25 commands entered
- A powerful icon browser

- A SpeedList feature that gives you instant access to your favorite icons
- Custom cursor replacements for the standard pointer and hourglass
- Detailed information on your system configuration and the memory usage by each application, with system resource displays and alarms
- A QuickRun menu providing easy access to frequently used commands

AUTHOR'S NOTE

Plug-In is for use with Windows Program Manager. You should not use it with Norton Desktop.

PSP

Paint Shop Pro is a powerful image manipulation tool. It allows you to use files in various formats and to prepare files for use on Macintosh computers.

Qpeg486

One of the fastest JPEG decoders around, *Qpeg486* will also display numerous other graphic formats. QPEG's fast preview mode makes it particularly suited for scanning through long lists of images. This program must first be installed to a hard disk before you can run it. Read the included documentation for information on how to configure Qpeg optimally for your graphics adapter.

RenameTT

Rename TrueType is a DOS program for changing the name that Windows uses to identify a TrueType font. RenameTT modifies the actual TrueType font file to change the name of the font. Since very similar typefaces from different vendors usually have different names, it can be helpful to use this utility to change the names to those you are accustomed to using. You determine the new name of the font and include that as a parameter when you run the program. Be advised, however: If you change the names of Corel-supplied typefaces, you risk not being able to reliably share .CDR files with other DRAW users, as typeface names will no longer be consistent from one system to another.

ROMCAT

With *ROMCAT* you can catalog the directory structure of one or more CDs or floppy disks and collect information about CorelDRAW 3.0 and 4.0 drawings. You can also quickly locate clip art stored on the CDs for CorelDRAW 4.0. This last feature has made this program one of the most popular of all CorelDRAW utilities. …Soon to be updated for version 5.0—check for it on the SYBEX Forum on CompuServe.

UC

UltraClip creates and manages its own virtual clipboard (in addition to the Windows Clipboard), allowing you to

- Create mini clipboards that store snapshots of the Windows Clipboard.
- Create OLE objects with embedded or linked data.
- View thumbnail-sized images of what's on the clipboard for quick retrieval.
- Track the contents of the Windows Clipboard.
- Print proof sheets of thumbnails or graphics.
- Save and retrieve the mini-clipboard objects.
- Save and restore the current UltraClip desktop and its objects.
- Edit and manipulate the mini-clipboard objects with text objects.
- Edit OLE objects.

VesaView

VesaView is a comprehensive and easy-to-use bitmap display application.

VuImage

VuImage is a DOS-based program that allows you to display and print .GIF, .TIF, and .PCX files on a wide range of display hardware and printers.

Notes

The NOTES directory contains miscellaneous information related to CorelDraw. A small WRI files contains some information on potential conflicts with older systems and what to do about General Protection Faults in CorelDraw. The larger TYPE.EXE file is an executable text viewer that contains information about the use of type in CorelDraw. Although written for version 4.0 it still contains much pertinent information. Simply run the TYPE.EXE program from Windows.

Corel Corporation Product Demo

This program allows you to examine the Corel Corp's software offerings. This is an interactive multimedia demo, and it allows you to examine the packages that interest you. Among the products displayed are CorelDraw (obviously), Corel Ventura, Corel's various CD-ROM art packages, and Corel's SCSI manager software. To start the presentation go to the COREL\PRODTOUR\ directory and run PRODTOUR.EXE.

AUTHOR'S NOTE

The Corel Product Demo can take a l-o-o-o-o-n-g time to start running, even from the CD. Just give it some time before you despair. It should go eventually.

Practice Files

You will find references frequently throughout the book to files that you can find in the PRACTICE directory. You can use these files as you follow along with the book. We include here files that you need to follow along with exercises, and also files that will help you better understand the function of a tool, command, or effect. Many of the .CDR images were placed here so you can open them up, take them apart, and reverse-engineer the techniques used.

All of the files can be opened straight from the CD, but in order to make changes and save those changes, you will need to first copy the files to your hard drive.

The Art Gallery

This is where you will find professionally created sample images, as well as all the images shown in our Color Galleries (the color pages in the book). These works show the possibilities provided by CorelDraw, and can be good sources of ideas and inspiration. Some of the files in here are winners in Corel's annual international art competition. Check it out.

Sounds

This directory contains a discussion of Georgina Curry's approach to creating the FACES image (Illustration #7 in the Color Gallery, file 07.CDR in the GALLERY directory). These are WAV sample files. The quality of playback will depend in large part on your system hardware and soundcards. At a minimum you need Windows MediaPlayer (part of your regular Windows installation).

TrueType Fonts

The FONTS directory contains a selection of shareware TrueType fonts. Included here you will find:

Calendar Normal   A font for creating calendars

CommScript   A font of scripted letters

ComicsCarToon–Plain Regular   A font designed to look like hand lettering as you might see it in comic books

MarkerFinePoint–Plain Regular   A font that gives your text a simple hand-lettered look

MarkerFeltThin–Plain Regular   Another eye-catching hand-lettered font

MarkerFeltWide–Plain Regular   A heavier, bolder font that is great when you need to get your audience's attention

SnyderSpeed–Plain Regular   A bold, scripted, free-form font that's great in large sizes

Vassallo Regular   A casual, slanted, fun font

The TXT files in the FONTS directory contain information about the creator of each font. Like some of the utilities programs, these fonts are shareware. If you want to keep using a shareware font, you should follow the instructions included with it to register the font with its creator.

AUTHOR'S NOTE

These TrueType fonts are not guaranteed to work on all systems. Some noncommercial typefaces are more temperamental about hardware and software configurations than commercial, fully tested, typefaces. Possible problems include inaccurate display at certain point sizes and inability to print to some printers.

List of Files

Here, to give you an idea before you start copying files to your hard drive, is a list of all the files on the CD, arranged by directory. This information should help you to anticipate just how large individual files are when you are allocating disk space for them.

```
Root Directory of Companion CD
    ARCHIVES      <DIR>
    COREL         <DIR>
    FONTS         <DIR>
    GALLERY       <DIR>
    NOTES         <DIR>
    PICTURES      <DIR>
    PRACTICE      <DIR>
    SOUND         <DIR>
    UTIL          <DIR>
    VBRUN         <DIR>
Directory of \ARCHIVES
    ALCH17    ZIP       478,208
    CDFONT    ZIP        31,201
    DISP181A  ZIP       662,329
    DRAGVU    ZIP       516,254
    EPSF      ZIP        20,746
    FNTNAM    ZIP        18,092
    FONTB3    ZIP       116,060
    FPOWER    ZIP       613,347
    GDS3      EXE       323,856
    GS261INI  ZIP       335,951
    GS261WIN  ZIP       294,460
    GSVIEW    ZIP        91,290
    JP14      ZIP        57,287
    NEOBKP    ZIP       637,170
    NEOPNT    ZIP       649,993
    OKFONT    ZIP        23,875
    PCS       ZIP       139,031
    PLUGIN    ZIP       457,631
    PRNAP     ZIP       630,385
    PSP20     ZIP       477,432
    QPEG14D   ZIP       414,261
    RENAMETT  ZIP        17,364
    ROMCAT    ZIP       189,892
```

```
    UC       ZIP        149,104
    UNZIP    DOC          9,737
    UNZIP    EXE         30,581
    VESAVW65 ZIP        293,176
    VUIMAG   ZIP        119,132
         28 files     7,797,845 bytes

Directory of \COREL
    BOX_SHOT     <DIR>
    DR5PRESS     <DIR>
    DR5SCRNS     <DIR>
    PRODTOUR     <DIR>
    SLIDESHW     <DIR>
          5 files

Directory of \COREL\BOX_SHOT
    DRW5BOX  TIF      2,387,752
    DRW5_B&W TIF        796,076
          2 files     3,183,828 bytes

Directory of \COREL\DR5PRESS
    NEWPROD  DOC         12,288
    PRESS5   DOC         24,576
          2 files        36,864 bytes

Directory of \COREL\DR5SCRNS
    D5SCREEN TIF     51,780,582
          1 files    51,780,582 bytes

Directory of \COREL\PRODTOUR
    ARTSHOW  MMM      3,546,822
    DMPRDCTS MMM      1,466,432
    DRAW3    MMM      4,669,264
    DRAW4    MMM      5,675,702
    DRAW5    MMM      7,593,946
    FLOW     MMM      2,788,016
    GALLERY  MMM      2,590,220
    LINGO    INI            738
    NETMAN   MMM      1,172,488
    POWER    MMM      2,125,416
    PRODTOUR EXE        375,291
    PROPHOTO MMM      3,273,258
```

```
            SCSI2      MMM     1,697,756
            SCSIMAC    MMM     2,373,316
            VENTURA    MMM     2,254,576
                    15 files     41,603,241 bytes

Directory of \COREL\SLIDESHW
            50MIKE     SHW     7,596,916
            SHOW       TXT         1,324
                     2 files      7,598,240 bytes

Directory of \FONTS
            35README   TXT        10,346
            BEEBOP     TTF        28,352
            BLADE      TTF        33,708
            CAL-HINT   TXT         3,516
            CALENDAR   TTF        28,692
            COCT____   TTF        40,492
            COMSC      WRI         5,248
            COMSC___   TTF        69,456
            COOLFACE   TTF        49,504
            CRYPT      TTF        59,168
            CTOONTT    TXT         4,227
            FUNKY      TTF        17,464
            HEIDLBRG   TTF        32,608
            MAFP____   TTF        49,300
            MAFT____   TTF        48,392
            MAFW____   TTF        48,712
            MFFINEPT   TXT         4,350
            MFTHINTT   TXT         3,637
            MFWIDETT   TXT         3,823
            NEWYORK    TTF        24,804
            PEACE___   TTF        24,516
            POLO       TTF        43,728
            SEE35HDS   CRD       278,613
            SHATTER    TTF        63,196
            SNS_____   TTF        38,128
            SSPEEDTT   TXT         3,813
            STICK      TTF        44,524
            SUPER      TTF        27,908
            TERMINAL   TTF        38,780
            VASSALLO   TTF        56,428
            VASSALLO   TXT           957
```

```
              31 files     1,186,390 bytes
Directory of \GALLERY
       01       CDR         797,576
       02       CDR         346,804
       03       CDR       2,243,090
       04       CDR         139,884
       05       CDR         150,654
       06       CDR       1,249,694
       07       CDR       9,066,274
       08       CDR       2,185,170
       09       CDR         770,330
       10       CDR         176,468
       11       CDR         553,772
       12       CDR          21,896
       13       CDR       1,249,674
       14       CDR          27,908
       15       TIF         441,476
       16       TIF       2,769,324
       2CRANES  CDR          58,702
       2MOROCCO CDR         308,778
       3BEAKERS CDR          84,450
       4COLOR   CDR          54,332
       4C_TEXT  CDR          18,140
       58CHEVPU CDR          43,228
       ARCHITEC CDR         109,262
       ARNOLD   CDR          30,486
       BIGBEN   CDR         647,060
       BONSAIC  CDR         306,880
       BOOK     CDR          38,970
       BOOK     CDT           3,434
       BOOK     TXT           4,007
       BOS      CDR          23,558
       CALENDAR CDR          56,622
       CAMERA   CDR         594,858
       CLOWN    CDR          76,178
       CRAYON   CDR         571,040
       CROAK    CCH         155,920
       CROAK    CMV         167,114
       C_HOLDER CDR         304,224
       DISTANCE CDR          13,052
       DIVER    CDR         128,154
```

File	Ext	Size
DMARBLE1	JPG	54,343
DMARBLE2	JPG	191,131
DREAMER	CDR	70,164
DUESENB	CDR	275,224
EASTREG3	CDR	136,644
ELVISNIX	GIF	244,922
EMBOSS	CDR	19,142
ENTRANCE	CDR	122,534
EYE	CDR	53,632
FACTY1	JPG	113,566
FACTY2	JPG	139,336
FLAG	CDR	18,392
FLAGMASK	CDR	18,970
FLOWTEXT	CDR	19,160
FMDESIGN	CDR	43,740
FROG	SHW	1,099,770
GOFORIT!	CDR	394,402
GURL3	JPG	41,316
HANDLOGO	CDR	94,538
HUNTRESS	CDR	2,243,678
LITEHSE5	CDR	43,474
MAN4	JPG	107,150
MASK	CDR	13,988
MEXICO_2	CDR	82,910
MOODROM1	CDR	24,748
MSTRPCE1	CDR	12,488
PARATEXT	CDR	13,312
PLENITUD	CDR	118,262
PLMDESGN	CDR	47,564
PSYLOCHE	JPG	39,719
PULL	JPG	117,316
RACING	CDR	233,102
ROSE	PCX	69,167
SAMPLE1	CDR	400,216
SAMPLE2	CDR	66,250
SAMPLE3	CDR	29,688
SAMPLE4	CDR	15,556
SAMPLE5	CDR	100,962
SEAFOODC	CDR	18,216
SELICO	CDR	22,692
SHADOWS	CDR	85,946
SMAN	JPG	57,874

```
        SNOWBARN CDR         195,068
        SNOWBORD CDR          38,838
        SPOONS   CDR         159,472
        SQUEEZE  CDR          13,840
        SQUEEZE2 CDR          13,790
        STILL    JPG         407,424
        SYMPHONY CDR          50,848
        TEXT_FIT CDR          11,618
        TORTURE  CDR         141,994
        TROLLEY  TIF          40,655
        TROLLY   CDR          22,160
        TXT2CRVS CDR          16,884
        VILLAGE  CDR          54,312
        WOMAN4   JPG         177,134
               95 files   34,447,684 bytes

Directory of \NOTES
        GPFS     WRI           7,680
        TYPE     EXE         295,171
                2 files      302,851 bytes

Directory of \PICTURES
        19-02    CDR          17,764
        19-03    CDR          33,104
        19-04    CDR          65,152
        19-05    CDR          25,280
        19-08    CDR         682,474
        19-09    CDR         694,180
        19-11    CDR          18,432
        19-13    CDR          87,650
        19-15    CDR         392,108
        19-16    CDR       1,842,660
        27-02    CDR          16,714
        27-03    CDR          22,682
        27-04    CDR         208,136
        27-05    CDR          55,390
        27-06    CDR          78,112
        27-07    CDR          22,134
        27-08    CDR          19,598
        27-09    CDR          16,018
        27-10    CDR          64,626
        27-11    CDR          25,852
```

```
27-12      CDR         20,854
27-13      CDR        381,434
27-14      CDR         16,158
BIG_BEN    CDR        797,576
DISTANCE   CDR         54,190
PHOTOS     CDR        546,392
TORTURE    CDR        455,172
        27 files     6,659,842 bytes
```

Directory of \PRACTICE
```
11-09      CDR         23,364
11-14      CDR         14,126
11-22      CDR        202,592
4COLOR     CDR         54,332
8-BALL     CDR        138,592
ALBERT     CDR        174,768
BANQUE     CDR         82,018
BLEND1     CDR         23,064
BLEND2     CDR         44,078
BLOCKS     CDR        134,682
BOOK       CDR         44,198
BOOK       CDT          3,670
BOOK       TXT          4,017
BOTTLE     TIF        295,396
CHILD      CDR          8,402
DYNO       SHW        841,216
DYNO       CCH        313,246
DYNOREX    CMV         79,830
EMBOSS     CDR         22,418
ENVTEXT1   CDR         37,656
ENVTEXT2   CDR         38,386
FITPATH1   CDR         30,680
FITPATH2   CDR         29,778
FLR_PLAN   CDR         38,442
GOFORIT!   CDR        383,510
GORILLA1   CDR        159,104
GORILLA2   CDR         90,926
JAKBEAN1   TIF         91,827
MSTRPCE1   CDR         12,122
PARATEXT   CDR         13,496
PEDASTAL   CDR         50,982
PELICAN    CDR         28,920
```

```
        PLATE     TIF       187,660
        POW       CMV       369,440
        POWERCLP  CDR       315,044
        ROSE      PCX        69,167
        ROTATION  CDR        20,916
        SCUBA     TIF        45,210
        SETTING   CPT       361,238
        SNOWBORD  CDR        37,472
        SPOON     TIF       187,660
        SPOONS    CDR       169,878
        SUNFLOWR  TIF       187,660
        TRAPPED   CDR       129,354
        UNTEXT    CDR        27,400
              45 files    5,617,937 bytes
Directory of \SOUND
        1         WAV       479,588
        2         WAV       523,684
        3         WAV       405,176
        4         WAV       498,880
        5         WAV       518,172
        6         WAV       468,564
        7         WAV       567,780
        8         WAV       281,156
        9         WAV       325,252
        10        WAV       308,716
              10 files    4,376,968 bytes

Directory of \UTIL
        ALCHEMY      <DIR>
        CDFONT       <DIR>
        DISPLAY      <DIR>
        DRAGVIEW     <DIR>
        EPSF         <DIR>
        FONTBOOK     <DIR>
        FONTNAME     <DIR>
        FPOWER       <DIR>
        GDS          <DIR>
        GHOSTSCR     <DIR>
        JPILOT       <DIR>
        MAC-ETTE     <DIR>
        MEGAEDIT     <DIR>
        NEOBOOKP     <DIR>
```

```
              NEOPAINT      <DIR>
              NEOSHOW       <DIR>
              OKFONT        <DIR>
              PAPPREN       <DIR>
              PCS           <DIR>
              PLUGIN        <DIR>
              PSP           <DIR>
              QPEG          <DIR>
              RENAMETT      <DIR>
              ROMCAT        <DIR>
              UC            <DIR>
              VESAVIEW      <DIR>
              VUIMAGE       <DIR>
                    27 files

     Directory of \UTIL\ALCHEMY
              ALCHEMY   EXE      893,103
              MANUAL    EXE       88,914
              ORDER     FRM        2,476
              READ      ME           918
              SAMPLE    JPG       52,767
                    5 files     1,038,178 bytes

     Directory of \UTIL\CDFONT
              CDFONT    EXE       30,208
              CDFONT    WRI      119,680
              README    TXT          857
              REGISTER  TXT        2,466
                    4 files       153,211 bytes

     Directory of \UTIL\DISPLAY
              BRIEF     DOC        4,841
              CHANGE              16,870
              CONFIG    DIS       11,179
              COPY             <DIR>
              DISPLAY   DOC       23,641
              DISPLAY   EXE      809,984
              DRIVER    TXT        4,099
              DRIVER           <DIR>
              DRVSRC           <DIR>
              EMU387              36,864
              FAQ                  1,042
```

```
            FONTS        <DIR>
            FORMAT   TXT         1,378
            GO32     EXE        77,178
            HINT     DOC         1,585
            INSTALL              4,158
            MATCH    DOC         2,646
            RUNME    BAT           390
            UTIL         <DIR>
                19 files       995,855 bytes
```

Directory of \UTIL\DISPLAY\COPY
```
            COPYING  CB          4,360
            COPYING  DJ          2,648
            COPYING  GNU        12,737
            COPYMISC DOC         2,757
                 4 files        22,502 bytes
```

Directory of \UTIL\DISPLAY\DRIVER
```
            ACUMOS   GRN           547
            AHEADA   GRD           287
            AHEADB   GRD           267
            ATI      GRD           375
            ATIGUPRO GRN           513
            ATIULTRA GRN         1,208
            ATIVGA   GRN           565
            CHIPS    GRD           282
            CIRRUS54 GRN           700
            CL5426   GRN           549
            ET3000   GRN           530
            ET4000   GRN           884
            EVEREX   GRD           311
            GENOA    GRD           285
            NEWSS24X GRN           668
            OAK      GRN           499
            PARADISE GRD           263
            REALTEK  GRN           577
            SPARADIS GRN           549
            SS24X    GRN         1,041
            STDVGA   GRN           502
            STEALTH  GRN           617
            TR8900   GRN           578
            VESA111  VDR         3,046
```

```
             VESA_S3   GRN            735
             VIDEO7    GRD            331
             VIPER     GRN            749
             WD90C3X   GRN            624
             WDVANILA  GRN            609
                 29 files       18,691 bytes

    Directory of \UTIL\DISPLAY\DRVSRC
             ACUMOS    ASM         13,857
             AHEADA    ASM          4,253
             AHEADB    ASM          4,055
             ATI       ASM          7,493
             ATIGUPRO  ASM         11,534
             ATIULTRA  ASM         13,068
             ATIVGA    ASM         11,803
             CHIPS     ASM          4,243
             CIRRUS54  ASM         15,716
             CL5426    ASM         11,781
             ET3000    ASM         11,034
             ET4000    ASM         14,743
             EVEREX    ASM          4,289
             GENOA     ASM          5,667
             GRDRIVER  INC          2,769
             IBM8514A  C            6,278
             MAKEFILE               1,288
             NEWSS24X  ASM         14,618
             OAK       ASM         11,181
             PARADISE  ASM          4,038
             REALTEK   ASM         12,455
             REG8514A  H            9,126
             SPARADIS  ASM          8,462
             SS24X     ASM         14,863
             STDVGA    ASM         11,376
             STEALTH   ASM         12,631
             TR8900    ASM         11,363
             VESA_S3   ASM         14,764
             VIDEO7    ASM          4,426
             VIPER     ASM         14,345
             WD90C3X   ASM         11,929
             WDVANILA  ASM         11,599
                 32 files      311,047 bytes
```

```
Directory of \UTIL\DISPLAY\FONTS
COUR11    FNT        2,858
COUR11B   FNT        2,856
COUR11BI  FNT        2,856
COUR11I   FNT        2,858
COUR12    FNT        2,948
COUR12B   FNT        2,946
COUR12BI  FNT        4,086
COUR12I   FNT        2,948
COUR14    FNT        3,145
COUR14B   FNT        3,144
COUR14BI  FNT        4,473
COUR14I   FNT        4,475
COUR16    FNT        4,855
COUR16B   FNT        4,853
COUR16BI  FNT        4,853
COUR16I   FNT        4,855
COUR20    FNT        5,609
COUR20B   FNT        5,614
COUR20BI  FNT        5,614
COUR20I   FNT        5,609
COUR25    FNT        6,559
COUR25B   FNT        6,564
COUR25BI  FNT        8,939
COUR25I   FNT        8,934
COUR34    FNT       11,533
COUR34B   FNT       11,531
COUR34BI  FNT       14,761
COUR34I   FNT       11,533
PC6X14    FNT        3,640
PC6X8     FNT        2,104
PC8X14    FNT        3,640
PC8X14T   FNT        3,640
PC8X16    FNT        4,152
PC8X8     FNT        2,104
PC8X8T    FNT        2,104
XM10X17   FNT        3,286
XM10X17B  FNT        3,286
XM10X20   FNT        3,856
XM10X20B  FNT        3,856
XM12X20   FNT        3,856
XM12X20B  FNT        3,856
```

```
           XM16X25   FNT         4,806
           XM16X25B  FNT         4,806
           XM16X25I  FNT         4,806
           XM4X5     FNT           531
           XM4X6     FNT         1,489
           XM5X8     FNT         1,679
           XM6X10    FNT         1,871
           XM6X10B   FNT         1,869
           XM6X12    FNT         2,061
           XM6X12B   FNT         2,059
           XM6X12I   FNT         2,061
           XM7X13    FNT         1,591
           XM7X13B   FNT         1,589
           XM8X12    FNT         2,061
           XM8X12B   FNT         2,059
           XM8X16    FNT         2,441
           XM8X16B   FNT         2,439
           XM8X16I   FNT         1,576
           XM9X15    FNT         3,771
           XM9X15B   FNT         3,769
                  61 files         254,523 bytes

Directory of \UTIL\DISPLAY\UTIL
     MAKEFILE                707
     PIECES        <DIR>
     VESAINFO  C           5,355
     VESAINFO  COM         7,928
             4 files          13,990 bytes

Directory of \UTIL\DISPLAY\UTIL\PIECES
     VESAINFO  C           5,787
             1 file           5,787 bytes

Directory of \UTIL\DRAGVIEW
     ACCUSOFT  DLL       194,255
     DFCTL     DLL        18,256
     DV        EXE       104,576
     DVA       DLL        10,192
     DVAM      DLL        11,232
     DVCPPAR   DLL        18,144
     DVDB      DLL        17,936
     DVDBPAR   DLL        20,352
```

```
DVG        DLL         14,896
DVH        DLL         20,784
DVHELP     HLP         63,333
DVI        DLL         13,424
DVLZ       DLL         10,832
DVMANUAL   TXT         15,919
DVMANUAL   WRI         18,048
DVMF       DLL         15,648
DVMW3      DLL         24,864
DVPX       DLL         86,224
DVQAW      DLL          9,808
DVQPW      DLL         27,424
DVQW       DLL         10,192
DVSETUP    EXE         72,176
DVSETUP    INI          1,240
DVSITE     WRI         13,056
DVSPPAR    DLL         26,784
DVWAV      DLL          9,456
DVWD       DLL         10,896
DVWDB      DLL         30,720
DVWDB3     DLL         30,656
DVWK       DLL         25,776
DVWK3      DLL         26,720
DVWP       DLL         11,824
DVWP6      DLL         11,648
DVWPPAR    DLL         27,136
DVWPS      DLL         10,608
DVXL       DLL         27,728
DVXL5      DLL         31,216
DVZP       DLL         11,184
FILE_ID    DIZ            375
FML        DLL         20,752
REGFORM    TXT          4,012
REGFORM    WRI          5,376
VENDOR     DOC          3,229
       43 files     1,138,907 bytes
```

Directory of \UTIL\EPSF
```
    EPSF       EXE         40,784
           1 file       40,784 bytes
```

```
Directory of \UTIL\FONTBOOK
FONTBOOK EXE         268,238
FONTBOOK HLP          29,778
FONTBOOK TXT           4,869
TEXT     DAT           3,134
         4 files         306,019 bytes

Directory of \UTIL\FONTNAME
FONTNAME EXE          29,249
FONTNAME WRI          10,496
         2 files          39,745 bytes

Directory of \UTIL\FPOWER
FOP      FON           8,704
FPHELP   HLP          81,693
FPOWER   DLL          25,714
FPOWER   ICO             766
FPOWER   TBK         146,178
FPOWER   WRI           5,888
TBKBASE  DLL         353,824
TBKCOMP  DLL         101,808
TBKFILE  DLL          16,576
TBKNET   EXE           5,360
TBKUTIL  DLL          59,152
TBOOK    EXE         398,880
        12 files       1,204,543 bytes

Directory of \UTIL\GDS
CONFIG                   341
GDS      CFG          30,285
GDS      EXE          83,928
GDS      ICO             766
GDS      OVL         188,380
GDSABOUT TXT           9,134
GDSBUY   TXT           4,332
GDSCAT   TXT           4,109
GDSCMD   TXT           4,712
GDSCONV  TXT           2,636
GDSMODE  TXT           5,151
GDSSHOW  TXT           1,737
GDSTITLE GIF          32,053
GDSUSER  CFG           1,123
```

```
           GDSVIEW  TXT         2,716
           GDSWELCM TXT         8,307
           GDS_TEXT PAL           480
           GETVBIOS EXE         1,341
           QUICKFLI EXE        13,706
           REGISTER PRN        51,529
           REGISTER TXT         2,846
           SAMPLE   GIF        29,122
           VIDEOID  DOC         3,182
           VIDEOID  EXE         7,061
           VIEWHELP GIF        13,783
                  25 files       502,760 bytes

Directory of  \UTIL\GHOSTSCR
           ALPHABET PS          1,495
           BDFTOPS  BAT            62
           BDFTOPS  PS         23,537
           BENCH    PS          2,455
           CHEQ     PS         59,822
           CHESS    PS          3,148
           COLORCIR PS          1,935
           COMMDLG  DLL        90,092
           COMMPROD DOC        10,406
           COPYING             18,321
           CP       BAT            17
           DECRYPT  PS            308
           DEVICES  DOC        14,334
           DRIVERS  DOC        28,929
           EMPTY    PS              0
           ESCHER   PS         10,899
           FONT2C   BAT            79
           FONT2C   PS         14,570
           FONTMAP             11,596
           FONTMAP  ATM         4,620
           FONTS    DOC        12,393
           FONTS            <DIR>
           GOLFER   PS         26,897
           GS2      BAT            39
           GS3      BAT            42
           GSADDMOD BAT            41
           GSBJ     BAT            90
           GSDJ     BAT            89
```

```
GSDJ500    BAT          96
GSGRAPH    ICO         766
GSLJ       BAT          93
GSLP       BAT          90
GSLP       PS       14,378
GSND       BAT          44
GSNDT      BAT          48
GSSETDEV   BAT          53
GSSETMOD   BAT          45
GST        BAT          36
GSTEXT     ICO         766
GSTT       BAT          37
GSVIEW     BAT          88
GSVIEW     DOC      33,624
GSVIEW     EXE     129,040
GSVIEW     HLP      48,036
GSVIEW     HPJ          83
GSWIN      EXE     574,464
GSWIN      RES       1,808
GS_DBT_E   PS        3,016
GS_DPS1    PS       10,186
GS_FONTS   PS       17,583
GS_INIT    PS       29,051
GS_LEV2    PS       11,109
GS_STATD   PS        6,682
GS_SYM_E   PS        3,841
GS_TYPE0   PS        1,861
HELPERS    DOC       6,008
HERSHEY    DOC      11,437
HISTORY              2,903
HISTORY    DOC      47,720
HUMOR      DOC       2,560
IMPATH     PS        5,861
LANDSCAP   PS        1,484
LANGUAGE   DOC      15,620
LEVEL1     PS           57
LIB        DOC       3,801
LINES      PS        2,775
MAKE       DOC      27,350
MARKPATH   PS        2,105
MERGEINI   PS        2,391
MV         BAT          16
```

```
NEWS                  76,815
PACKING   LST          4,889
PCHARSTR  PS           2,135
PPATH     PS           1,849
PRFONT    PS           2,465
PROPERTY  INI          1,600
PS2ASCII  BAT            340
PS2ASCII  PS          12,616
PS2EPSI   BAT            681
PS2EPSI   DOC          2,579
PS2EPSI   PS           6,266
PS2IMAGE  PS           6,371
PSFILES   DOC          5,436
PSTOPPM   PS           7,562
QUIT      PS               6
README                14,016
README    1ST         10,798
README    DOC          3,667
RM        BAT            113
SAVE      PS              10
SCREEN    PS             772
SHELL     DLL         41,953
SHOWCHAR  PS           2,804
SHOWPAGE  PS              10
SNOWFLAK  PS           2,161
TIGER     PS          81,252
TRACEOP   PS           2,538
TYPE1OPS  PS           7,020
UGLYR     GSF         23,137
UNIX-LPR  DOC          5,833
UNPROT    PS           1,868
USE       DOC         25,423
USE       PS          38,434
WATERFAL  PS           2,511
WINMAPS   PS           4,038
WRFONT    PS           9,828
XFONTS    DOC          6,842
         107 files   1,771,866 bytes

Directory of \UTIL\GHOSTSCR\FONTS
  BCHB    AFM         22,262
  BCHB    GSF         53,104
```

```
            BCHBI    GSF      55,900
            BCHR     GSF      54,563
            BCHRI    GSF      55,709
            NCRB     GSF      99,879
            NCRBI    GSF      98,950
            NCRR     GSF      99,270
            NCRRI    GSF      96,734
            PBKD     GSF      37,343
            PBKDI    GSF      37,278
            PBKL     GSF      36,951
            PBKLI    GSF      39,364
            PHVB     GSF      71,902
            PHVBO    GSF      81,807
            PHVR     GSF      73,527
            PHVRO    GSF      82,686
            PHVRRN   GSF      43,662
            PTMB     GSF      79,562
            PTMBI    GSF      87,809
            PTMR     GSF      80,741
            PTMRI    GSF      89,059
            PUTB     GSF      62,181
            PUTBI    GSF      64,983
            PUTRI    GSF      64,363
                 25 files    1,669,589 bytes

Directory of \UTIL\JPILOT
            INVOICE  DOC       4,100
            JP       COM      46,412
            JP       HLP      16,899
            JPCONFIG COM      26,090
            JPCONFIG HLP       6,342
            LJ2      FNT       1,509
            LJ2D     FNT       5,049
            LJ2P     FNT       4,223
            LJ3      FNT       5,049
            LJ3D     FNT       5,049
            LJ3P     FNT       5,049
            LJ3SI    FNT       5,049
            LJ4      FNT       3,869
            MANUAL   DOC      59,542
                 14 files      194,231 bytes
```

```
Directory of \UTIL\MAC-ETTE
    MAC-ETTE DOC         6,725
    MAC-ETTE EXE        28,231
          2 files        34,956 bytes

Directory of \UTIL\MEGAEDIT
    COMMDLG  DLL        89,248
    MEGAED   DLL         3,072
    MEGAEDIT EXE       145,920
    MEGAEDIT HLP        48,234
    READ1ST  TXT         6,751
    README   TXT         5,919
    REGISTER TXT         6,130
    REG_FORM TXT         2,501
    RELEASE  TXT         5,111
    VENDOR   TXT         3,910
         10 files       316,796 bytes

Directory of \UTIL\NEOBOOKP
    FILE_ID  DIZ           434
    INSTALL  EXE        20,995
    NB1      CMP       336,412
    NB2      CMP        43,733
    NB3      CMP       137,504
    NB4      CMP         8,793
    NB5      CMP        78,422
    NB6      CMP        13,528
          8 files       639,821 bytes

Directory of \UTIL\NEOPAINT
    FILE_ID  DIZ           456
    INSTALL  EXE        56,784
    NP1      ZIP       302,595
    NP2      ZIP        87,631
    NP3      ZIP        98,500
    NP4      ZIP        71,403
    NP5      ZIP        53,547
    NP6      ZIP        46,680
          8 files       717,596 bytes

Directory of \UTIL\NEOSHOW
    FILE_ID  DIZ           459
```

```
          INSTALL  EXE      33,232
          NS       ZIP     192,672
          SAMPLE   ZIP     280,873
                  4 files        507,236 bytes

     Directory of \UTIL\OKFONT
          OKFONTS  EXE      45,121
          OKFONTS  WRI      14,720
                  2 files         59,841 bytes

     Directory of \UTIL\PAPPREN
          CBK      VB$      30,385
          CCFCURS  DL$      49,670
          CCMOUSE  VB$       6,810
          CMDIALOG VB$      10,810
          DWSPYDLL DL$      38,052
          GRID     VB$      27,586
          INSTALL  BIN      52,879
          INSTALL  EXE       5,888
          INSTALL  INF       1,305
          KEYSTAT  VB$      10,777
          PA       EX$      94,355
          PA       HL$      63,025
          PACONTRL EX$      20,149
          PASETUP  BMP      14,182
          PICCLIP  VB$       9,920
          README   TXT       4,637
          SS3D2    VB$      43,679
          THREED   VB$      33,378
          VBRUN300 DL$     274,493
                 19 files        791,980 bytes

     Directory of \UTIL\PCS
          FILE_ID  DIZ         431
          PCS      CMP     101,200
          README   TXT      14,547
          SETUP    EXE      61,392
          VENDOR   DOC       3,026
                  5 files        180,596 bytes

     Directory of \UTIL\PLUGIN
          BATON    CUR         326
```

BIGNOSE	CUR	326
BIRDS2	WAV	24,528
CLUCK1	WAV	1,004
COUNT3	WAV	18,124
DIVE1	WAV	10,426
FATARR	CUR	326
FILE_ID	DIZ	445
GCLOCK	CUR	326
GIANTARR	CUR	326
GIRL	CUR	326
GROUP	EXE	17,680
GULL1	WAV	7,365
HAND	CUR	326
HGLASS	CUR	326
HORN1	WAV	12,691
INVARR	CUR	326
LION1	WAV	13,842
MAN	CUR	326
OPEN1	WAV	6,546
PACKING	LST	2,298
PISYS200	DLL	112,662
PLUGIN	EXE	247,672
PLUGIN	HLP	81,915
PLUGIN	QR	1,443
PLUGIN	RA	459
PLUGINQM	BAT	28
PLUGINQM	PIF	545
PLUGINQN	BAT	37
PLUGINQN	PIF	545
POP1	WAV	6,093
README	1ST	739
README	TXT	17,299
SFX1	WAV	5,043
SFX2	WAV	5,295
SFX3	WAV	5,770
SFX4	WAV	15,990
SWATCH	CUR	326
TAP1	WAV	1,219
TAP2	WAV	1,349
TRUCKIN	CUR	326
UNPOP1	WAV	3,394
VENDINFO	DIZ	15,821

```
         VENDOR    DOC               216
         WOMAN     CUR               326
         YAWN      CUR               326
         YAWN1     WAV            34,697
                47 files          677,744 bytes

Directory of \UTIL\PSP
         FILE_ID   DIZ               440
         INSTALL   EX$           103,141
         INSTALL   INS             2,736
         PSP1      CMP           148,057
         PSP2      CMP           322,125
         README    TXT            21,766
         SETUP     EXE            47,616
         VENDOR    DOC             8,607
                 8 files          654,488 bytes

Directory of \UTIL\QPEG
         FILE_ID   DIZ               256
         FILE_ID   GER               288
         INSTALL   DAT           400,505
         INSTALL   EXE            13,642
                 4 files          414,691 bytes

Directory of \UTIL\RENAMETT
         RENAMETT  EXE            18,976
         RENAMETT  TXT            19,212
                 2 files           38,188 bytes

Directory of \UTIL\ROMCAT
         CLIPART   ROM           230,912
         README    TXT             8,093
         ROMCAT    EXE            66,048
         ROMCAT    HLP            18,854
                 4 files          323,907 bytes

Directory of \UTIL\UC
         CTL3D     DLL            14,416
         UC        EXE           177,920
         UC        HLP           115,838
         UC        WRI            60,928
                 4 files          369,102 bytes
```

```
Directory of \UTIL\VESAVIEW
    FILE_ID   DIZ            470
    VESAVIEW  EXE        558,304
    VESAVIEW  LGX          7,693
    VESAVIEW  LGO         30,962
    VESAVIEW  ICO            766
    VESAVIEW  WP         108,564
    VESAVIEW  DOC         89,913
            7 files      796,672 bytes

Directory of \UTIL\VUIMAGE
    D8514AI   VDR          3,904
    D8514AI8  VDR          3,860
    D8514R    VDR          2,049
    DAHEADB   VDR          1,215
    DATIV     VDR          1,024
    DCHT      VDR            898
    DCIRR     VDR          1,537
    DE673     VDR            678
    DE678     VDR          1,617
    DGVGA     VDR          1,088
    DHGS      VDR          1,939
    DNCR      VDR            991
    DNVGA     VDR          1,516
    DOAK      VDR            777
    DORCH     VDR          1,112
    DPV1024   VDR            807
    DPVGA     VDR            812
    DQVISN    VDR          1,054
    DS3911    VDR          1,032
    DSTBPG    VDR          1,251
    DTANDY    VDR          1,235
    DTRID     VDR          1,393
    DTSNG4    VDR          1,251
    DV71024   VDR            821
    DV7FW     VDR            659
    DV7VRAM   VDR          1,050
    DVESA     VDR          4,008
    DVESA1    VDR          2,628
    NINTLACE  EXE         23,109
    ORDERFRM  TXT          3,134
```

```
              PROGRAMS TXT         5,232
              VUIMG    TXT        71,644
              VUIMG    EXE        97,485
                     33 files       242,810 bytes

       Directory of \VBRUN
              VBRUN100 DLL       271,264
              VBRUN200 DLL       356,992
              VBRUN300 DLL       398,416
                      3 files     1,026,672 bytes

       Total files listed:
                    864 files   182,067,596 bytes
```

If You Don't Have a CD Player

While we obviously cannot deliver the entire Companion CD to you on a floppy diskette, we do make available all of the practice files. To receive a 3½" diskette with the practice files, send $7.50 and a stamped, self-addressed disk mailer or envelope to: R. Altman & Associates, 20204 Merritt Drive, Cupertino, CA 95014. Write "Auxiliary Diskette" somewhere on the outer envelope so that our staff can process it correctly.

You don't need to send a blank diskette, but make sure to include the SASE and correct postage. Standard disk mailers require $.52 or $.75 postage, and a No. 10 envelope with a diskette needs $.52.

Index

NOTE TO THE READER: **Boldfaced** numbers indicate pages where you'll find the principal discussion of a topic or a definition of the term. *Italic* numbers indicate pages where the topic is illustrated in a figure.

Numbers and Symbols

3-D rendering. *See* extrusions
… (ellipsis), in menus, 30
+ (plus key)
    adding nodes with, 913
    for Quick Copy command, 913–914

A

absolute sizing, **374**
ACAD (Association of Corel Artists and Designers), **919**
Actual Size option, Zoom tool, 23
Add Page Frame option, Page Setup dialog box, 110, 620–621
Add Perspective command, **380–386**. *See also* Effects menu
    clearing perspective, 386
    copying perspectives, 386
    for multiple objects, 380
    one-point perspective, 381–383, *381*, *382*
    outlines and, 385
    overview of, 380
    pattern fills and, 385
    Shape tool and, 383
    two-point perspective, 383–385, *384*
    vanishing points and, 381–382, 384
Add Preset option, Envelope roll-up, 401
adding
    bitmap images with PowerClips, **508–510**, *510*, 743
    dimension with blends, **425–429**, *426*, *428*
    nodes, 913

    rectangles to pages as frames, 110, 137–142, 620–621
    styles
        to CORELDRW.CDT, 246, *246*
        to templates, 246–248, 254
    typefaces, 339, 356, *356*
additive primary colors, **661–662**, *661*, *662*
address, the author's, **919**, 960
Adobe Illustrator files (.AI), importing, 726, 729–730
Adobe Type Manager (ATM), 351. *See also* typefaces
Advanced Screening dialog box, *624*, 641, *641*
ALBERT.CDR file, 315–322
Alchemy utility, 926, 944
Align command, Arrange menu, **97–99**, *98*, *99*, 318
Align tool, Node Edit roll-up, 172
aligning. *See also* justifying
    nodes, 172
    objects, **97–99**, *98*, *99*
    text, 274
Alt key. *See also* Ctrl key; F keys; hotkeys; Shift key
    + Enter (Undo undo), 19
    + F5 (Presets roll-up), 256
    + F8 (Rotate), 368
    for menu hotkeys, 14–15
Altman, Rick, address of, **919**, 960
Angle option, Fountain Fill dialog box, 218, *220*
animating, with CorelMOVE, 808–810, *809*
Apply When Drawing Lines option, PowerLines roll-up, 478
applying
    color trapping, 678–679, *678*

envelopes, 395
fill patterns, 196–197
graphic styles to another object, 241–243, *243*, *244*
PowerLines, 479, 480, 482
presets, 257–258, *257*
ARCHIVES directory (Companion CD), 924, 925, 936–937
Ares Software, FontMinder software, 605, **833–836**
Arrange menu
    Align command, **97–99**, *98*, *99*, 318
    Break Apart command, 95
    Combine command
        combining objects, *94*, 95
        creating masks, 68, **315–319**, *319*, 322–323, 512
        hotkey, 33
        new features in CorelDRAW 4.0, 58, *59*
    Convert to Curves command, 33, 151, **175–177**, **330–332**, *331*, *332*
    Group command, 94–95, *94*
    Intersection command, 70, *71*, 903–904
    overview of, **32–33**, *32*
    Reverse Order command, 415
    Separate command, 461
    Trim command, 70, *71*, 405, 497, 513, **905–907**, *907*, *908*
    Ungroup command, 726, 728–729, *728*
    Weld command, 58, *59*, *94*, 96, 128–130
arrow keys, text editing with, 290–291
Arrowhead Editor dialog box, 183–184, *184*
arrows, creating, 183–185, *184*, *185*
art. *See* clip art; examples; GALLERY directory
artistic text. *See also* paragraph text; text
    converting to paragraph text, **294**
    in CorelDRAW 5.0, 64, 65
    creating, **279–280**, *280*
    drawing speed, **354–355**, *355*
    envelopes and, 390

exporting across Clipboard, 772–773, *774*
hotkey, 25, 294
justifying, 288–290, *289*, *290*
node editing, **173–175**, *174*
versus paragraph text, 270, **280–282**, 291–294, *293*, **354–355**, *355*
presets for, 259–260
spacing, 274, *274*, 276–278
text styles for, 335, 337
Text tool and, **25**, 270
when to use, **292**
ASCII files, importing, 88
Association of Corel Artists and Designers (ACAD), **919**
ATM (Adobe Type Manager), 351. *See also* typefaces
AutoCAD .DXF files
    exporting, 758, *759*
    importing, 730
Auto-Center Place Inside option, Preferences dialog box, 320, 321–322, 501, 507
Auto-Reduce feature, Node Edit roll-up, 168–169, *169*, *170*, 648
Auto-Trapping options, Print Options dialog box, 642, 678
Avant Garde BT typeface, styles and, 253–254

B

Back Parallel extrusions, **444**
backgrounds, Paper Color setting, 621–623
backing up, CORELDRW.CDT file, 248
Behind Fill option, Outline Pen dialog box, 189, *190*, 313, *314*
Bezier curves. *See also* curves
    creating, **155–156**
    overview of, 7, *8*
    Pencil tool and, 23, 155–156
Big Front extrusions, **445**, *446*
bitmap fill patterns, 50

Bold page numbers: primary discussion of the topic. Italic page numbers: the topic is illustrated in a figure

bitmap images. *See also*
   CorelPHOTO-PAINT; .TIF files
   adding with PowerClips, **508–510**, *510*, 743
   color separations and, 744
   converting to vector art. *See* CorelTRACE
   cropping, 651, 742–744
   exporting, **763–767**, *765*, *766*
   file size of, 741
   importing, **740–744**, *740*, *742*, *743*
   overlaying objects on, 741
   printing, **649–651**
   rotating, 61, *62*, 379, 509–510, 651, 741
   scaling, 740–741
   scanning, 650–651
   versus vector art, **4–8**, *7*, 817
bitmap objects, in CorelPHOTO-PAINT, **798–801**, *799*
Blend roll-up
   Blend to Path option, 420–425
   Color wheel, 416–417
   Loop control, 418–419, *419*, *420*
   Map Nodes option, 412–413
   overview of, 53, *53*, 409, *409*
   Rotation control, 417–418
blends, **408–434**. *See also* contours
   adding dimension with, **425–429**, *426*, *428*
   blending to paths, **420–425**, 431–433
      compound blend to path, 431–433, *432*
      organization charts, 423, *423*
      special effects, 424–425, *424*
      step calculation and, 421–422
   chaining, 429
   coloring, **416–417**
   compound blends, **429–433**, *430*, *431*, *432*
   copying versus cloning, 434
   in fountain fills, **211–213**
   layers and, 415
   node mapping and, **412–413**, *414*, 415
   overview of, **408–411**

Rotation and Loop controls, **417–419**, *419*, *420*
selecting in compound blends, 432
shading with, **425–429**, *426*, *428*, 434
in snowboarder exercise, 114–117, 122–123, 131
splitting and fusing, 433
start and end objects, 408, **414–415**, *416*
steps, 117, 410–411, 421–422, 427, 434
tips, 413, 434
boldface type
   creating, 274
   versus outlined text, 356–359, *357*, *358*
BOOK.TXT file, 337
book's CD. *See* Companion CD
borders. *See* Outline Pen dialog box; outlining
borrowing good design, **598–601**, *600*, *601*
BOTTLE.TIF file, 800
Break Apart command, Arrange menu, 95

breaking, nodes and paths, **170–171**
Brickley, David. *See The Diver*; *Eagle*; *The Entrance*
bullets
   Common Bullets typeface, 253–254
   for paragraph text, 284
   styles and, 253–254
   Zapf Dingbats and, 284
business cards, printing, **630–632**, **916–917**, *917*
buttons in Print Options dialog box, 628, *629*, **642–646**, *643*
   Calibration Bars and Densitometer Scale buttons, 644
   Crop Marks and Registration Marks buttons, 643–644
   File Info button, 642–643
   Print Negative and Emulsion Down buttons, 644–645, *645*

Bold page numbers: primary discussion of the topic. *Italic* page numbers: the topic is illustrated in a figure

C

calculating distances, with dimension lines, 24, *24*, 69–70, **907–909**, *910*
calibrating, **703–721**. *See also* color calibration
    imagesetters and film processors, **716–721**
    monitors, **703–710**
        manually, 707–710, *709*
        overview of, 703–706
        with System Color Profile dialog box, 706–707, *706*
    printers, **713–716**, *714*
    scanners, **711–713**
calibration bars, printing, 644
Calligraphy options, Outline Pen dialog box, 188–189, *189*, 477
caption files (.CAP), Ventura Publisher, 864–866, *864*
cataloging art. *See* CorelMOSAIC
.CCS files, 707
CD, book's. *See* Companion CD
CDFont utility, 927, 944
.CDR files
    versus .CMX files, 775
    importing, 730
    saving styles in, 250–251
.CDT files, 246, 253
Center Offset option, Fountain Fill dialog box, 218, *220*
Center option, Print Options dialog box, 629
.CGM files
    exporting, 756–758, *757*
    importing, 726–727, 730–732, *731*, *732*
chaining, blends, 429
changing. *See also* editing
    color assignments, 78
    default style set, **246–248**, 254
    envelope modes, 395
    node types, 161–162
    units of measurement, 369
chapter files (.CHP), Ventura Publisher, **856–857**, *856*, *857*, *858*, **859–860**, 862–863, 877
Character Attributes dialog box, 271–272, *272*, 274, 291
character formatting, 271–272, *272*, 278–279, *278*
CHART program, 806–808, *807*
Checkpoints command, CorelPHOTO-PAINT, 789
child curves, **460**
chokes, color trapping and, **678**
choosing. *See* selecting
Clear Effect command, Effects menu, 54, 386, 387
Clear Perspective command, Effects menu, 386
Clear Transformations command, Effects menu, 387
clip art
    cataloging. *See* CorelMOSAIC
    importing, **726–729**, *727*, *728*
    table of contents, 76
    ungrouping, 726, 728–729, *728*
Clipboard
    Edit menu and, 31
    exporting across, 753–754, **769–773**, *770*, *771*, *774*
    importing across, **744–750**
    pasting text from, 324–325, *325*
    pasting traced images across, 828
Clone command, Edit menu, 31, 58, 245
Clone tool, CorelPHOTO-PAINT, 803
cloning
    contours, 438
    versus copying blends, 434
    envelopes from objects, 401–403, *402*
    extrusions, 463–464
    printing multiple copies of an image on a page, **630–632**, **916–917**, *917*
clouds. *See* snowboarder exercise

Bold page numbers: primary discussion of the topic. Italic page numbers: the topic is illustrated in a figure

.CMX files
    versus .CDR files, 775
    importing, 730
    overview of, 76, **775–776**
CMYK color model. *See also* color models
    color separations and, 637–638
    converting spot colors to, **640–641**, 642
    on-screen colors and, **673–674**
    overview of, **667–670**
    RGB color model and, 665–667, *666*, *667*, 668, *668*
    Uniform Fill options, **199–201**, *200*
Collate Copies option, Print dialog box, 627

color, **658–681**. *See also* coloring; gray shades
    changing color assignments, 78
    complementary colors, 670, *670*
    design and, **680–681**, *681*
    printing color separations in, 640
    screen representation of, 199, 660, 669, **673–674**
    selecting for fountain fills, 211, *212*, 216–217, *217*
Color Blend options, Fountain Fill dialog box, 211–214, *212*
color calibration, **702–722**. *See also* Color Manager
    calibrating, **703–721**
        imagesetters and film processors, **716–721**
        monitors, **703–710**, *709*
        printers, **713–716**, *714*
        scanners, **711–713**
    device color profiles (DVPs), 705
    overview of, 702–703
    service bureaus and, **721–722**
color correction feature, for printers, 626, 710

COLOR directory (CorelDRAW), 900
Color drop-down list, Outline Pen dialog box, 186
Color Manager, **704–710**. *See also* color calibration
    device color profiles (DVPs), 705
    Interactive Monitor Calibration dialog box, 707–710
    overview of, 704–705
    Printer Characterization dialog box, 713
    scanner target and color swatch, 705, *709*
    System Color Profile dialog box, **706–710**
        manual color profiles, 707–710, *709*
        system generated color profiles, 706–707, *706*
    video card settings, 706
Color Mask roll-up, CorelPHOTO-PAINT, 796–798, *797*
color models, **197–202**, **663–670**. *See also* color; color theory
    CMYK color model
        color separations and, 637–638
        converting spot colors to, 640–641, 642
        on-screen colors and, 673–674
        overview of, **667–670**
        RGB color model and, 665–667, *666*, *667*, 668, *668*
        Uniform Fill options, 199–201, *200*
    HSB color model
        overview of, **664–665**, *664*, *665*, *666*
        Uniform Fill options, 201–202
    overview of, 663
    PANTONE colors
        PANTONE spot color model, 672–673, *672*
        swatch books, 199, 669, **673–674**, 704
        Tinted Grayscale lenses and, 520
    RGB color model
        CMYK color model and, 665–667, *666*, *667*, 668, *668*
        on-screen colors and, 673–674
        overview of, **665–667**, *666*, *667*
        Uniform Fill options, 201–202
    selecting in Uniform Fill dialog box, **197–199**, *198*, 672, *672*
    spot color, **671–673**, *672*, 674

Bold page numbers: primary discussion of the topic. Italic page numbers: the topic is illustrated in a figure

converting to CMYK color model, 640–641, 642
fountain fills and, 216–217, *217*
line screens and, 696–697, *697*
PANTONE spot color model, 672–673, *672*
versus process color, **671–672**
Color page, Extrude roll-up, **452–456**
  Drape Fills option, 454, *454*
  Shade option, 455–456
  Solid Fill option, 454–455
  Use Object Fill option, 452–453, 504
Color Palette submenu, Custom Colors command, 205
color palettes
  in CorelDRAW 4.0, 60
  in CorelDRAW 5.0, 201
  overview of, 16
  in Uniform Fill dialog box, 201, **202–206**
    creating custom colors, 202–205, *204*, *205*
    custom palettes, 202
    searching for colors, 205–206
color profiles. *See* color calibration; Color Manager
Color roll-up, CorelPHOTO-PAINT, 787, *788*
color separations
  bitmap images and, 744
  fountain fills and, 216–217, *217*
  printing, **637–642**, *639*
    Auto-Trapping feature, 642
    in color, 640
    converting spot colors to CMYK, 640–641, 642
    custom halftone options, 641
    overview of, 637–639
    printing calibration bars and densitometer scale, 644
    registration and moiré patterns, 638–639, *639*
    selecting separation pages to print, 641–642
  scanners and, 716
  Ventura Publisher and, 879
color swatch books, 199, 669, **673–674**, 704
color theory, **658–663**. *See also* color; color models
  additive primary colors, 661–662, *661*, *662*
  light and, 659–660, *659*
  overview of, 658–659
  subtractive primary colors, 663
color trapping, **675–679**
  applying, **678–679**, *678*
  defined, **675**
  knockouts and, 679
  overprinting objects and, 679
  registration marks and, 675
  spreads and chokes and, 678
  when to use, **675–678**, *676*, *677*
Color wheel, Blend roll-up, 416–417
coloring
  blends, 416–417
  extrusions, **452–456**, 460, 461
    Drape Fills option, 454, *454*
    Shade option, 455–456, 460, 461
    Solid Fill option, 454–455
    Use Object Fill option, 452–453, 504
Colors options, Print Options dialog box, 641–642
columns of paragraph text, 285
Combine command, Arrange menu
  changes in CorelDRAW 4.0, 58, *59*
  combining objects, *94*, 95
  creating text masks, 68, **315–319**, *319*, 322–323, 512
  hotkey, 33
combining
  blends, 433
  envelopes and combined objects, 403
  objects, *94*, **95**, 403

special effects, **524**, *525*
text with objects, 95
commands. *See also* menus
  dimmed commands, 30
Common Bullets typeface, styles and, 253–254
common vanishing points, 461–464, 469–472, *470, 471*
Companion CD, **922–960**
  ARCHIVES directory, 924, 925, 936–937
  COREL directory
    Corel Product Demo program, 933
    overview of, 924, 937–938
  diskette version (Practice files only), 960
  FONTS directory, 924, 938–939
    TrueType typefaces in, 925, 935
  GALLERY directory, 924, **934**, **939–942**
    BOOK.TXT file, 337
    DIVER.CDR file, 674
    FACES file (07.CDR), 924, 934
    HUNTRESS.CDR file, 539, 674
  GRAY.PAL file, 202
  NOTES directory
    overview of, 924, 933, 941
    TYPE.EXE file, 883
  overview of, **922–925**
  PICTURES directory, **924**, **941–942**
    Chapter 26 examples, 659
    combined special effects example, 524, *525*
    DIVER.CDR file, 674
    HUNTRESS.CDR file, 674
    PHOTOS.CDR file, 514, *515*
    PowerClip example, 511, *512*
    TORTURE.CDR file, 755
  PRACTICE directory, 924, 934, **942–943**
    ALBERT.CDR file, 315–322
    BOTTLE.TIF file, 800
    diskette version of, **960**
    DYNO.CCH file, 807, *807*
    DYNO.SHW file, *812*, 813
    DYNOREX.CMV file, 809, *809*
    EMBOSS.CDR file, 307
    ENVTEXT1.CDR file, 299
    ENVTEXT2.CDR file, 299
    PLATE.TIF file, 796, *797*
    POW.CMV file, 810, *811*
    SCUBA.TIF file, 821
    SETTING.CPT file, 798–799, *799*, 800
    SPOON.TIF file, 795, *796*, 799
  SMALL.PAL file, 202
  SOUND directory, 924, 934, **943**
  UTIL directory, 924, **925–933**, **943–960**
    Alchemy, 926, 944
    CDFont, 927, 944
    Display, 927, 944–948
    DragView, 927, 948–949
    EPSF, 927–928, 949
    FontBook, 928, 950
    FontNamer, 928, 950
    FontPower, 928, 950
    Ghostscript, 928, 951–954
    Graphic Display System (GDS), 928, 950–951
    J-Pilot, 929, 954
    Mac-ette, 929, 955
    MegaEdit, 929, 955
    NeoBookPro, 929, 955
    NeoPaint, 929, 955
    NeoShow, 930, 955–956
    OKFonts, 930, 956
    overview of, 925–926
    Paint Shop Pro (PSP), 931, 958
    PlugIn, 930–931, 956–958
    Printer's Apprentice (Papren), 930, 956
    Professional Capture System (PCS), 930, 956
    Qpeg486, 931, 958
    RenameTrueType, 931–932, 958
    ROMCAT, 932, 958
    UltraClip (UC), 932, 958
    VesaView, 933, 958
    VuImage, 933, 959–960

Bold page numbers: primary discussion of the topic. Italic page numbers: the topic is illustrated in a figure

VBRUN directory, 923, 924, 926, 960
warranty, vii
complementary colors, **670**, *670*
compound blends, **429–433**, *430*, *431*, *432*
CONFIG directory (CorelDRAW), 900–902
conical fountain fills, 50, *51*, 208–211, *208*, *209*, *220*
constraining
    fountain fill center offset, 218
    and moving objects, 84
    rotation, 375–376
    stretches, 370
containers, PowerClip, **498**
contours, 54, **435–440**, *437*, *440*. *See also* blends
Convert Spot Colors to CMYK option, Print Options dialog box, 640–641, 642
Convert to Curves command, Arrange menu, 33, 151, **175–177**, **330–332**, *331*, *332*
Convert TrueType to Type 1 option, Print Options dialog box, 636–637, 890–891
converting
    artistic text to paragraph text, 294
    bitmap images to vector art. *See* CorelTRACE
    CorelDRAW 3.0 text spacing to 4.0 and 5.0, 276–278
    objects to curves, 33, 151, **175–177**, *176*, *177*
    spot colors to CMYK colors, 640–641, 642
    text to curves, 330–332, *331*, *332*
    typefaces and, 883, **884–887**, *885*, *886*, *887*
    TrueType typefaces to Type 1 typefaces, 636–637, 890–891
copies, printing, 627
Copy Attributes From dialog box, 100
COPY command, DOS, 627

Copy Effects command, 54
Copy Extrude From option, Extrude roll-up, 464
Copy VP From option, Extrude roll-up, 463
copying
    attributes of objects, 100
    versus cloning blends, 434
    extrusions, 463–464
    perspectives, 386
    Quick Copy command, 913–914
COREL directory (Companion CD)
    Corel Product Demo program, 933
    overview of, 924, 937–938
Corel International Design Contest. *See* examples; GALLERY directory
Corel Magazine, 702
Corel Product Demo program, 933
CORELAPP.INI file, 900
CorelCHART, 806–808, *807*
CORELCHT.INI file, 902
CorelDRAW
    Association of Corel Artists and Designers (ACAD), **919**
    AutoCAD and, 730
    versus CorelPHOTO-PAINT, **4–8**, *7*, *8*
    directories, **899–902**. *See also* Companion CD
        COLOR, 900
        CONFIG, 900–902
        CUSTOM, 902
        PROGRAMS, 902
    as a drawing program, 4–8, *7*, *8*
    editing traced images in, 828–829, *829*, *830*
    versus FrameMaker, 40
    Object Linking and Embedding and, 750
    versus PageMaker, 39, 46, 238, 359
    running multiple versions of, **896–898**, *897*
    seminars, **918–919**

Bold page numbers: primary discussion of the topic. Italic page numbers: the topic is illustrated in a figure

versus Ventura Publisher, 845–848, *846, 847*
versus word processors, 359
versus Xpress, 40
CorelDRAW 3.0
　changing text attributes, 335
　rotated bitmaps, 61, *62*, 379
　running with versions 4.0 and 5.0, **896–898**, *897*
　selecting objects in groups, 95
　text spacing, 276
CorelDRAW 4.0, **39–63**. *See also entries for specific features*
　behind the scenes changes, **57–58**, *57*
　drawing features, **47–52**
　　bitmap fill patterns, 50
　　conical fountain fills, 50, *51*
　　Dimension Line tool, 24
　　fill steps, 51, *52*
　　multiple fills, 50, *52*
　　node editing, 48
　　PowerLines, 49–50, *49*
　　preset fountain fills, 51
　File menu, **54–55**
　limitations, **60–63**
　　performance, 61
　　price, 62–63
　　reference guide, 61
　　revisions, 63
　　rotated bitmaps, 61, *62*, 379
　miscellaneous changes, **58–60**
　　cloning, 58
　　color palettes, 60
　　Combine command, 58, *59*
　　floating toolbox, 60
　　graphic object styles, 41
　　roll-up control, 60, *60*
　　selecting inside groups, 58, *59*
　　Undo command, 58
　　Weld command, 58, *59*
　multiple page support, **39–40**
　Object Data Manager roll-up, **55–56**, *56*
　Object menu, 55–56
　overview of, **39–41**
　Print dialog box, **55**, *55*
　running with versions 3.0 and 5.0, **896–898**, *897*
　special effects, **53–54**
　　Blend tool, 53, *53*
　　Clear Effect command, 54, 386, 387
　　contours, 54
　　Copy Effects command, 54
　　envelopes, 53
　　extrusions, 53–54
　　Rotate & Skew tool, 54
　　Stretch & Mirror tool, 54
　styles, **40–41**, *41*
　templates, 43
　text features, **40–47**
　　defaults, 43–44
　　Edit Text dialog box, 44–45
　　Paragraph dialog box, 44, *44*
　　paragraph text, 46–47
　　text envelopes for wrapping text, 46–47, *47*
　　text flow, 46, *47*
　　text inside objects, 47
　　Text roll-up, 45–46, *45*
　　text styles, 40, *41*
　　typefaces, 42, *43*
　　word processing features, 44–45
　text spacing, 276–277
CorelDRAW 5.0, **63–80**. *See also entries for specific features*; Ventura Publisher
　color palettes, 201
　interface changes, **71–74**
　　drag and drop importing, 73–74, *75*
　　Mosaic roll-up, 73
　　presets (macros), 72
　　Ribbon Bar, 71–72
　　square fountain fills, 72, *74*
　　Uniform Fill dialog box, 72, *73*
　limitations, **77–80**
　　changing color assignments, 78
　　distributing copies of objects, 78
　　no multiple document support, 77

Bold page numbers: primary discussion of the topic. Italic page numbers: the topic is illustrated in a figure

no roll-up hotkeys, 77–78
no uninstall procedure, 77
Save option, 78
text features, 79–80, *79*
miscellaneous changes, **75–76**
    clip art guide, 76
    .CMX file format, 76
    importing PostScript files (.EPS), 75
    pop-up tool help, 75–76
    roll-up controls, 76, *76*
new tools, **66–71**
    Dimension Line tool, 24, 69–70
    Intersection tool, 70, *71*
    Lens roll-up, 67, *67*
    PowerClip tool, 68, *68*, *69*
    Trim tool, 70, *71*
performance, **64**
printing features, 74–75
roll-ups, **368**
rotated bitmaps, 61, *62*, 379
running two copies of, **898–899**
running with versions 3.0 and 4.0, **896–898**, *897*
text features, **64–66**, **79–80**
    artistic text, 64, 65
    limitations, 79–80, *79*
    paragraph text, 64
    text flow, 46
    Text roll-up, 64–65, *65*
    typefaces, 42
text spacing, 277
Ventura Publisher, **63**
View menu, 31, *31*
CORELDRW.CDT file, 246–248, 254
CORELDRW.CPL file, 202
CORELDRW.DOT file, 186, 902
CORELDRW.INI file, 900–901
CORELFLT.INI file, 88, 775–776, 901
CORELFNT.INI file, 884, 893–894, 901
CorelKERN, 836–837
CORELMOS.INI file, 902
CorelMOSAIC, **830–833**, *831*
creating libraries and catalogs, 832
file formats supported, 831
importing bitmaps with, 509
limitations, 832
roll-up version, 73, 833, *833*
CORELMOV.INI file, 902
CorelMOVE, 806, **808–812**
animating with, 808–810, *809*
morphing feature, 810–812, *811*
CorelPHOTO-PAINT, **782–803**
bitmap objects, **798–801**, *799*
Color roll-up, 787, *788*
versus CorelDRAW, 4–8, *7*, *8*
File / Checkpoints command, 789
masks, **793–798**
    Color Mask roll-up, 796–798, *797*
    creating masks, 795, *796*
    Mask tools, 793–795, *794*
Node Edit tool, 795, *796*
Object Picker tool, 793
Open an Image dialog box, **790–793**, *790*
    Crop option, 791
    Full Image option, 791
    Partial Area option, 791–793, *792*
    Resample option, 791
overview of, 782–784
as a paint program, 4–8, *7*, *8*
pasting objects from, 89
retouching tools, **801–803**
    Clone tool, 803
    Equalize tool, 801–802, *802*
Tool Settings roll-up, 784–786, *785*
Undo tools, 788–789, *789*
Zoom tools, 786, *787*
CORELPNT.INI file, 902
CORELPRN.INI file, 891–892, 901–902
CorelSHOW, **812–814**
limitations, 813–814
running presentations, 812–813, *812*
CORELSHW.INI file, 902
CorelTRACE, **816–829**

Bold page numbers: primary discussion of the topic. Italic page numbers: the topic is illustrated in a figure

editing traced images in CorelDRAW, 828–829, *829*, *830*
overview of, 816–819, *818*, *819*
paths and nodes and, 825, *826*
saving traced images, 827–828
scanning images into, 819–823, *820*, *823*
tracing, 823–824, *824*
versus drawing curves, **168**
Tracing Options dialog box, 819, *819*, 825–827, *826*
TWAIN scanner drivers and, 819, 820
CORELTRC.INI file, 902
Corners options, Outline Pen dialog box, 186, *187*
Create Arrow command, Special menu, 184–185, *185*
Create From option, Envelope roll-up, 401–403, *402*
creating. *See also* designing
arrows, 183–185, *185*
artistic text, 279–280, *280*
Bezier curves, 155–156
boldface type, 274
catalogs with CorelMOSAIC, 832
curves, 151–154, *152*, *153*, 166
envelopes, 390–393, 401–403
fountain fills, 206–208, *207*, 214, *215*
graphic styles, 239–241
libraries with CorelMOSAIC, 832
lines, 151–154, *154*
masks in CorelPHOTO-PAINT, 795, *796*
objects, 82–83
objects for graphic styles, 238–239, *239*
OLE links, 745–746, *746*
PostScript files (.EPS)
for gray shades, 696, *697*
typefaces and, 884, 892, *893*
PowerClips, 497–500, *499*, *500*
presets, 256–257, *256*
for artistic text, 259–260
objects during recording, 258
print files for gray shades, 695
templates, 248–251

text masks
with Combine command, 68, **315–319**, *319*, 322–323
with PowerClip tool, **319–323**, *322*
text styles, **334–335**, 339–342
crop marks, printing, 643–644
cropping. *See also* PowerClips
bitmap images, 651, 742–744
in CorelPHOTO-PAINT, 791
cross-references, in Ventura Publisher, 870–871
Ctrl key. *See also* Alt key; F keys; hotkeys; Shift key
+ B (Blend), 409
+ E (Extrude), 443
+ F3 (Layers roll-up), 108
+ F5 (Styles roll-up), 248
+ F7 (Envelope roll-up), 390
+ F8 (PowerLines), 477
+ F9 (Contour), 435
+ F11 (Symbols roll-up), 90
+ G (Group), 95
+ J (Preferences), 19
+ P (Print), 624
+ R (Repeat), 101
+ S (Save), 97
+ Spacebar (Pick tool toggle), 913
+ U (Ungroup), 95
+ W (redraw screen), 31
+ Y (Snap To Grid), 102
+ Z (Undo), 19
constraining with
fountain fill center offset, 218
and moving objects, 84
one-point perspective, 383
rotation, 375–376
stretches, 370
envelopes and, 393
kerning with, 175
moving rotation target with, 377
selecting objects inside groups, 58
text editing with, 290–291
Curry, Georgina. *See The Huntress* example

Bold page numbers: primary discussion of the topic. Italic page numbers: the topic is illustrated in a figure

curves, **151–156**. *See also* nodes; paths
  Bezier curves
    creating, **155–156**
    overview of, 7, *8*
    Pencil tool and, 23, 155–156
  child curves, **460**
  converting objects to, 33, 151, **175–177**, *176, 177*
  converting text to, **330–332**, *331, 332*
    typefaces and, 883, **884–887**, *885, 886, 887*
  creating, **151–154**, *152, 153,* 166
  drawing programs and, 6–7, *7, 8*
  inflection of, 156–157, *157*
  printing, **634**, *635,* 636, **648–649**
  reshaping, 166
  setting number of points in, 636, 648
  strategies for drawing, **162–166**
    creating curves, 166
    defining basic shape, 162–165
    reshaping curves, 166
    TRACE and, **168**
  typefaces and, 883, **884–887**, *885, 886, 887*
cusp nodes
  defined, **159–160**, *161*
  Preferences settings, 154
Custom Colors command, Color Palette submenu, 205
CUSTOM directory (CorelDRAW), 902
Custom option, Fountain Fill dialog box, 578
cutaway views of extrusions, *449,* **460**
Cyan/Magenta/Yellow/Black color model. *See* CMYK color model

D

Database Publisher program, Ventura Publisher, 880
defaults
  changing default style set, **246–248**, 254
  Default Graphic style, 247, 250
  default text styles, 334–335
  Outline Pen dialog box, **191**
  text defaults in CorelDRAW 4.0, 43–44
deleting guidelines, 914–915, *915*
densitometer scale, printing, 644
Depth page, Extrude roll-up, *443,* 444
design, **582–583, 586–610**. *See also* examples
  borrowing good design, **598–601**, *600, 601*
  color and, **680–681**, *681*
  headline design, **589–590, 591–592**
    bigger is not better, 589–590
    justification, 598
    the message is senior to formatting, 589, 591–592, *592,* 603
  justifying text, 597–598
  Look at Me! syndrome, **587–589**
  overusing graphic and text elements, **592–593**
  planning, **602–603**
  Pompousitis, **592–593**
  reusing designs, 602
  ruling lines, 593–594
  text attributes, 590–591
  tips, **582–583, 586–587**
  typefaces and, **594–597, 604–610**
    installing too many, 604–605, *605*
    kerning, 606–610, *609, 610*
    limiting use of, 594–597, *595, 596*
    selecting categories of, 606, *607, 608*
  using white space, 591, 597
designing. *See also* creating
  objects for graphic styles, 238–239, *239*
desktop publishing programs, **842–849**. *See also* Ventura Publisher
  versus drawing programs and word processors, 842–843
  page layout versus publication-centered programs, 849
  Ventura Publisher and, **844–849**, 852
  workgroup publishing, 848

Bold page numbers: primary discussion of the topic. Italic page numbers: the topic is illustrated in a figure

device color profiles (DVPs), **705**
dialog boxes, **16–20**, *18*
dimension, adding with blends, **425–429**, *426*, *428*
Dimension Line tool, 24, *24*, 69–70, **907–909**, *910*
dimmed commands, 30
directories (CorelDRAW), **899–902**. *See also* Companion CD
    COLOR, 900
    CONFIG, 900–902
    CUSTOM, 902
    PROGRAMS, 902
Display menu. *See* View menu
Display page, Page Setup dialog box, **620–623**, *622*
    Add Page Frame option, 110, 620–621
    Facing Pages option, 620
    Paper Color option, 621–623
    Show Page Border option, 23, 623
Display utility, 927, 944–948
displaying. *See also* hiding
    guidelines, 914–915, *915*
    paper size on-screen, 623
    screen elements, **16**, *17*
distances, calculating with dimension lines, 24, *24*, 69–70, **907–909**, *910*
distributing, copies of objects, 78
DIVER.CDR file, 674
The Diver example, **542–553**, *543*. *See also* examples
    the background, 544, *545*
    the diver image, 547–552, *548*, *551*
    filling in the landscape, 545–547, *546*, *547*
    on-screen versus printed colors and, 674
    origin of, 544
    overview of, 542, 552–553
DLLs (Dynamic Link Libraries), 57
document-centered desktop publishing programs, 849
documents
    long documents in Ventura Publisher, **870–871**
    support for multiple, 77
dolphin jumping through hoop example, 505–507, *505*, *506*
DOS COPY command, 627
dots per inch (dpi). *See also* line screens
    gray shades and, 684–692, *685*, *686*, *692*, *693*, *694*
downloading typefaces, 636–637, 883, **887–890**
DragView utility, 927, 948–949
Drape Fills option, Extrude roll-up, 454, *454*
DRAW. *See* CorelDRAW
drawing. *See also* curves; lines
    freehand drawing
        Pencil tool and, 23
        PowerLines and, 478, 482
    strategies for, **162–166**
        creating curves, 166
        defining basic shape, 162–165
        reshaping curves, 166
        TRACE and, **168**
drawing programs. *See also* CorelDRAW
    curves and, 6–7, *7*, *8*
    versus desktop publishing programs and word processors, 842–843
    versus paint programs, **4–8**, *7*, *8*, 817
drawing speed. *See also* performance; screens
    artistic text versus paragraph text, 282, 354–355, *355*
    bitmaps and, 31, 61, *62*, 379
    bold text versus outlined text, 356–359, *357*, *358*
    extrusions and, 456
    for fountain fills, 210, *210*
    paragraph text and, 282
    PostScript versus TrueType typefaces, 352–354, *353*
drawings. *See also* graphic objects
    positioning for printing, 628–629
    printing in tiles, **630**, *631*
DTP. *See* desktop publishing

Duplicate command, 914
DVPs (device color profiles), **705**
.DXF files
    exporting, 758, *759*
    importing, 730
Dynamic Link Libraries (DLLs), 57
DYNO.CCH file, 807, *807*
DYNO.SHW file, *812*, 813
DYNOREX.CMV file, 809, *809*

E

Eagle example, **568–582**, *569*
    beginning the sketch, 570–571
    blending multiple colors, 576–578, *577*
    the claws, 575–576, *576*
    defining the project, 568–570
    the jet engine, 579–582, *579*, *580*
    sketching the eagle, 573–574
    using XYZ reference lines, 571–573, *572*, 579–581, *580*
    the wings, 574–575 *Eagle*
Edge Pad option, Fountain Fill dialog box, 221–222, *221*
Edit Contents command, PowerClip submenu, 500–502
Edit Kern Pair dialog box, 836, *836*
Edit menu
    Clone command, 31, 58, 245
    Copy Attributes From command, 100
    overview of, **30–31**, *30*
    Paste Special command, 746
    Repeat command, 101
    Select All command, 93
Edit Preset dialog box, 256, *256*
Edit Text dialog box
    hotkeys, 44–45, 291
    overview of, 44–45, 271, *273*
Edit Wireframe command, View menu, 92

editing. *See also* changing; node editing
    embedded objects, 749
    importing and, 724
    linked files, 748

PowerClips, **500–502**
    Auto-Center Place Inside option and, 501, 507
    grouping and, 501–502
    Lock Contents to PowerClip option and, 501
    traced images in CorelDRAW, 828–829, *829*, *830*
    vanishing points, 452
Effects menu, **33–34**, **366–387**. *See also* blends; contours; extrusions; PowerClips; PowerLines; special effects; wrapping text
    Add Perspective command, **380–386**
        clearing perspective, **386**
        copying perspectives, **386**
        for multiple objects, 380
        one-point perspective, **381–383**, *381*, *382*
        outlines and, 385
        overview of, 380
        pattern fills and, 385
        Shape tool and, 383
        two-point perspective, **383–385**, *384*
        vanishing points and, 381–382, 384
    Blend command, 409
    Clear Effect command, 54, 386, 387
    Clear Perspective command, 386
    Clear Transformations command, 387
    Contour command, 435
    Envelope command, 390
    Extrude command, 443
    overview of, **33–34**, *33*, **366–367**, *366*
    PowerClip submenu, 497, *497*
        Edit Contents command, 500–502
        Extract Contents command, 300, 322
        Place Inside Container command, 306, 320
    PowerLines command, 477
EHANDLER.PS program, 655

Bold page numbers: primary discussion of the topic. Italic page numbers: the topic is illustrated in a figure

Elastic Mode tool, Node Edit roll-up, 172

Ellipse tool, **25**
ellipses, node editing, **173–175**, *173*
ellipsis (…), in menus, 30
embedded .EPS files, printing, 653–654
embedded text objects, 326, *326*
embedding. *See also* Object Linking and Embedding
    editing embedded objects, 749
    embedded objects and paragraph text, 772
    exporting embedded objects, 769–772, *770*, *771*
    linked files versus embedded objects, 747–748, 749–750
EMBOSS.CDR file, 307
embossed text, **306–311**, *307*
emulsion down print option, 644–646, *645*
encapsulated PostScript files. *See* PostScript files (.EPS)
End key, text editing with, 290–291
end objects, in blends, 408, **414–415**, *416*
Enter key, Alt + Enter (Undo undo), 19
The Entrance example, **556–565**. *See also* examples
    the awning, 563–565, *564*
    coloring, 559–560, *560*
    the cutaway view of the corner, 561–563, *562*
    origin of, 556–557, *557*, *558*
    scanning the photo to computer, 558–559, *559*
Envelope roll-up
    Add Preset option, 401
    Create From option, 401–403, *402*
    Keep Lines option, **393–395**, *394*
    mapping options, **395–399**
        example, 397–398, *398*
        Horizontal option, *396*, 397
        Original option, *396*, 397
        overview of, 395–397, *396*
        Putty option, *396*, 397
        Text option, 403
        tips, 399
        Vertical option, *396*, 397
    overview of, 390–393, *391*
    Unconstrained mode, 399–401
envelopes, **390–406**
    applying, 395
    artistic text and, 390
    changing modes, 395
    cloning from objects, 401–403, *402*
    combined objects and, 403
    creating, **390–393**, 401–403
    envelope handles, 391–392
    groups and, 403
    keeping line segments straight option, **393–395**, *394*
    mapping options, **395–399**
        example, 397–398, *398*
        Horizontal option, *396*, 397
        Original option, *396*, 397
        overview of, 395–397, *396*
        Putty option, *396*, 397
        Text option, 403
        tips, 399
        Vertical option, *396*, 397
    mirrored envelopes, 399
    overview of, 390
    for paragraph text, 390, **403–405**, *404*, *406*
    PowerClips and, **507**, *508*
    presets, **401**
    unconstrained envelopes, **399–401**
    wrapping text with, 46–47, 53, 135, 286, **298–306**, 405
ENVTEXT1.CDR file, 299
ENVTEXT2.CDR file, 299–300
.EPS files. *See* PostScript files (.EPS)
EPS (Placeable) file filter, 734–739, *735*, *738*, *739*
EPSF utility, 927–928, 949
Equalize tool, CorelPHOTO-PAINT, 801–802, *802*
erasing, with Shift key, 19

Bold page numbers: primary discussion of the topic. Italic page numbers: the topic is illustrated in a figure

error handler program, for PostScript printers, **655**
examples. *See also* snowboarder
The Diver, **542–553**, *543*
   the background, 544, *545*
   the diver image, 547–552, *548*, *551*
   filling in the landscape, 545–547, *546*, *547*
   on-screen versus printed colors and, 674
   origin of, 544
   overview of, 542, 552–553
dolphin jumping through hoop (PowerClip example), **505–507**, *505*, *506*
Eagle, **568–582**, *569*
   beginning the sketch, 570–571
   blending multiple colors, 576–578, *577*
   the claws, 575–576, *576*
   defining the project, 568–570
   the jet engine, 579–582, *579*, *580*
   sketching the eagle, 573–574
   using XYZ reference lines, 571–573, *572*, 579–581, *580*
   the wings, 574–575
The Entrance, **556–565**
   the awning, 563–565, *564*
   coloring, 559–560, *560*
   the cutaway view of the corner, 561–563, *562*
   origin of, 556–557, *557*, *558*
   scanning the photo to computer, 558–559, *559*
   envelope mapping options, **397–398**, *398*
extruded floor plan, *473*, *473*
fill patterns, **27–29**, *28*
The Huntress, **532–539**, *533*
   the choker, 539
   the face and hair, 535–536, *536*
   the feathers, 534, *535*
   the jeweled headband, 538–539
   the large beads of the headdress, 537
   the medallion, 536, *537*
   on-screen versus printed colors and, 674
   overview of, 532–534
   the scarf, 539
   the small beads of the headdress, 538
Spoon Forest (PowerLines example), **492–494**, *493*, *494*
text styles, **337–347**, *338*
   creating styles, 339–342
   formatting paragraph text, 343–347
   overview of, 337
   setup, 338–339
.EXE files
   location of, 57
   renaming, 897
Export EPS dialog box, 884, 892, *893*
exporting, **752–776**
   artistic text across Clipboard, 772–773, *774*
   AutoCAD .DXF files, 758, *759*
   bitmap images, 763–767, *765*, *766*
   .CGM files, 756–758, *757*
   across Clipboard, 753–754, **769–773**, *770*, *771*, *774*
   CORELFLT.INI file settings for, 88, 775–776
   embedded objects, 769–772, *770*, *771*
   export torture test, **753–756**, *754*, *774–776*
   .GEM files, 761–763, *762*
   HPGL files, 763, *764*
   with Object Linking and Embedding (OLE), 753–754, **769–774**, *770*, *771*, *774*
   overview of, 752–753
   .PCX files, 763–764, *765*, 767
   PostScript files (.EPS), 696, 753–754, **758–761**, *760*, *761*, 774

Bold page numbers: primary discussion of the topic. Italic page numbers: the topic is illustrated in a figure

.TIF files, 763, 765–767, *766*
Ventura Publisher .CAP text, 865–866
Windows Metafiles (.WMF), 753–754, 767–768, *768*, 769
Extract command, Special menu, 912
Extract Contents command, PowerClip submenu, 300, 322
Extrude roll-up, **443–444**, *443*
   Color page, **452–456**
      Drape Fills option, 454, *454*
      Shade option, 455–456
      Solid Fill option, 454–455
      Use Object Fill option, 452–453, 504
   Copy Extrude From option, 464
   Copy VP From option, 463
   Depth page, *443*, 444
   hotkey, 443
   Light Source options, 456-9, *$57*, *458*, *459*
   memory feature, 468
   overview of, 443–444, 468
   Presets page, 469
   Rotation options, 464–468, *464*, *465*, *467*
   Shared Vanishing Point option, 463, 464
   types of extrusions, 444–445, *445*, *446*
   vanishing points in, *443*, 444
   VP Locked to Object option, 462–463, 468
   VP Locked to Page option, 463
extrusions, **442–473**
   Back Parallel and Front Parallel, **444**
   Big Front versus Small Back, **445**, *446*
   child curves and, **460**
   cloning and copying, 463–464
   coloring, **452–456**, 460, 461
      Drape Fills option, 454, *454*
      Shade option, 455–456, 460, 461
      Solid Fill option, 454–455
      Use Object Fill option, 452–453, 504
   cutaway views, *449*, **460**
   drawing speed and, 456
   exercises, 448–452, *449*, *450*, *453*
   extruding text, 136, *137*, *138*

floor plan example, 473, *473*
lighting effects, **456–459**, *457*, *458*, *459*, 460, 461
orthogonal projections, 444
overview of, 53–54, 442–443
parallel extrusions, **447–448**, *448*
as PowerClips, **502–504**, *503*
presets, **469**
rotating, **464–468**, *464*, *465*, *467*
selecting, **451**
separating and ungrouping for manual fills, **461**
shading, **455–456**, 460, 461
in snowboarder exercise, 136, *137*, *138*
types of, **444–445**, *445*, *446*
vanishing points
   common vanishing points, 461–464, 469–472, *470*, *471*
   editing, 452
   in Extrude roll-up, *443*, 444
   overview of, **446–447**
   and rotating extrusions, 468
warping objects, **471–472**, *471*
when to use, **443**

F

F2 key
   Zoom In, 23
   Shift + F2 (Zoom on Selected), 23, 97
F3 key
   Zoom Out, 23
   Ctrl + F3 (Layers roll-up), 108
F4 key
   Fit in Window, 23, 97
   Shift + F4 (Show Page), 23
F5 key
   Pencil tool, 23
   Alt + F5 (Presets roll-up), 256
   Ctrl + F5 (Styles roll-up), 248
F6 key, Rectangle tool, 25
F7 key

Bold page numbers: primary discussion of the topic. Italic page numbers: the topic is illustrated in a figure

Ellipse tool, 25
Ctrl + F7 (Envelope roll-up), 390
F8 key
    artistic text, 25, 294
    Alt + F8 (Rotate), 368
    Ctrl + F8 (PowerLines), 477
    Shift + F8 (paragraph text), 25, 294
F9 key, Ctrl + F9 (Contour), 435
F10 key, Shape tool, 22
F11 key
    Fountain Fill, 27, 197
    Ctrl + F11 (Symbols roll-up), 90
    Shift + F11 (Uniform Fill), 27, 197
F12 key
    Outline Pen, 27, 190
    Shift + F12 (Outline Color), 27
FACES file (07.CDR), 924, 934
Facing Pages option, Page Setup dialog box, 620
fiducial marks, **712**
file filters
    EPS (Placeable) filter, 734–739, *735, 738, 739*
    for importing, 86, 88, 725–726, 734–739, *735*
    PostScript (Interpreted) filter, 734–739, *735, 739*
file formats. *See also* exporting; file name extensions; importing
    importing and, 86, 88
    supported by CorelMOSAIC, 831
file management. *See* CorelMOSAIC
File menu
    Color Manager command, 706
    files listed in, 30
    Import command, 86, 125, 728
    new features in CorelDRAW 4.0, **54–55**
    New From Template command, 252–253
    Open command, 727–728
    overview of, **29–30**, *29*
    Print command, 624
    Update command, 747

file name extensions. *See also* exporting; importing; .INI files; PostScript files (.EPS); Windows Metafiles (.WMF)
.AI, 726, 729–730
.CAP, 864–866, *864*
.CCS, 707
.CDR, 250–251, 730, 775
.CDT, 246, 253
.CGM, 726–727, 730–732, *731, 732,* 756–758, *757*
.CHP, **856–857**, *856, 857, 858,* **859–860**, 862–863, 877
.CMX, 76, 730, **775–776**
.DXF, 730, 758, *759*
.EXE, 57, 897
.GEM, 726–727, 761–763, *762,* 864
.IMG, 864
and importing files, 88
.PAT, 227
.PFB, 889, 891
.PFM, 837
.PUB, 856, *857,* 877
.SHW, 814
.STY, 238, 856, *856,* **860–862**, 866–869, *868*
.TIF, 86–87, 711–712, 744
.TTF, 891
.VGR, 865
.WID, 877
file pointers, in Ventura Publisher, **856**, *857,* 862–863
files. *See also* Companion CD
    listed in File menu, 30
    opening, **96–97**
        versus importing, **727–728**
    printing file information on printouts, **642–643**
    printing to, **626–627**
    saving, **96–97**
    size of bitmap files, 741
    in Ventura Publisher, **854–866**, 869
        caption files (.CAP), 864–866, *864*

Bold page numbers: primary discussion of the topic. Italic page numbers: the topic is illustrated in a figure

chapter files (.CHP), **856–857**, *856, 857, 858*, **859–860**, 862–863, 877
    frames for text and graphics, 857–859
    modularity of, 859
    pointers, 856, *857*, 862–863
    publication files (.PUB), 856, *857*, 877
    versus standard word processor files, 854–855, *855*
    style sheet files (.STY), 238, 856, *856*, 860–862, 866–869, *868*
    text and graphics files, *856*, 862–864, 865–866, 867–869
fill patterns, **194–233**. *See also* Uniform Fill dialog box
    applying, **196–197**
    in CorelDRAW 4.0, 50–51, *52*
    example, 27–29, *28*
    fountain fills, **196**, **206–224**
        conical fountain fills, 50, *51*, 208–211, *208, 209, 220*
        creating, 206–208, *207*, 214, *215*
        defined, **196**
        drawing time for, 210, *210*
        in *Eagle* example, 576–578, *577*
        extrusions and, 456, 460
        linear fountain fills, 208–211, *208, 209, 220*, 469, *470*
        multiple fountain fill effect, 50, *52*, 214, *215*
        presets, 51, 222
        printing, **634–636**
        radial fountain fills, 208–211, *208, 209, 220*, 426–427, *426*
        rainbow fountain fills, 211–213, *213*
        selecting blends, 211–213
        selecting colors, 211, *212*, 216–217, *217*
        in snowboarder example, 120–122, *121*
        square fountain fills, 208–211, *208, 209, 220*
        steps, 51, *52*, 210, *215*, **218–219**, *220*, **634–636**
        types of, 208–211, *208, 209*
        when to use, **223**
    Outline Pen Behind Fill option and, 189, *190*, 313, *314*
    overview of fill tools, **194–196**, *195*
    overview of, **90–91**, *91*
    pattern fills, **194–196**, **224–230**
        defined, **196**
        full-color patterns, 194–196, *195*, **227–228**, *228, 229*
        perspective and, 385
        PostScript patterns, 194–196, *195*, **229–230**, *230*
        two-color patterns, 194–196, *195*, **224–227**, *225, 226*
    printing, **653**
    texture fills, **194–196**, **230–233**, *231*
Fill tool, 27–29, *28*, 91, **195–196**, *195*
film processors, calibrating, **716–721**
filters. *See* file filters
Fit to Page option, Print Options dialog box, 620, 629–630
Fit in Window option, Zoom tool, 23, 97
fitting
    drawings to page and printing, 620, 629–630
    text to paths, 327–330, *329*
Flatness settings, for PostScript printers, 634, *635*, 648–649
floor plan extrusion example, 473, *473*
flowing text. *See* wrapping text
FontBook utility, 928, 950
FontMinder software, 605, **833–836**, *835*
FontNamer utility, 928, 950
FontPower utility, 928, 950
fonts, **273**. *See also* typefaces
FONTS directory (Companion CD), 924, 938–939
    TrueType typefaces in, 925, 935
footnotes, in Ventura Publisher, 871
For Mac option, Print dialog box, 626

Bold page numbers: primary discussion of the topic. Italic page numbers: the topic is illustrated in a figure

format-building desktop publishing
    programs, 849
formatting
    paragraph text, **282–286**, *283*, *288*, *342*
        bulleting, 284
        columns of, 285
        indents, 283–284, *285*
        margins, 282–284, *285*
        spacing, 282
        tabs, 282
        with text styles, 343–347
        wrapping, 46–47, 53, 135, 286, **298–306**, 405
    text, **271–279**. *See also* kerning
        aligning, 274
        character formatting, 271–272, *272*, 278–279, *278*
        sizing, 271, 274
        spacing, 274, *274*, 276–278
        type styles, 274
        in Ventura Publisher, 860–862, **871–872**, 879
Fountain Fill dialog box, 27, 194–196, **206–224**
    Angle option, 218, *220*
    Center Offset option, 218, *220*
    Color Blend options, 211–214, *212*
    Custom option, 578
    Edge Pad option, 221–222, *221*
    hotkey, 27, 197
    overview of, 27, 194–196, *195*, *208*
    PostScript options, 224
    Presets option, 51, 222
    Steps option, 51, *52*, 210, *215*, **218–219**, *220*
    Type drop-down list, 208–211, *208*, *209*
fountain fills, **196**, **206–224**. *See also* fill patterns
    conical fountain fills, 50, *51*, 208–211, *208*, *209*, *220*
    in CorelDRAW 4.0, 50–51, *52*
    creating, 206–208, *207*, 214, *215*
    defined, **196**
    drawing time for, 210, *210*
    in *Eagle* example, 576–578, *577*
    extrusions and, 456, 460
    linear fountain fills, 208–211, *208*, *209*, *220*, 469, *470*
    multiple fountain fill effect, 50, *52*, **214**, *215*
    presets, 51, 222
    printing, **634–636**
    radial fountain fills, 208–211, *208*, *209*, *220*, 426–427, *426*
    rainbow fountain fills, 211–213, *213*
    selecting blends, 211–213
    selecting colors, 211, *212*, 216–217, *217*
    in snowboarder example, 120–122, *121*
    square fountain fills, 208–211, *208*, *209*, *220*
    steps, 51, *52*, 210, *215*, **218–219**, *220*, **634–636**
    types of, 208–211, *208*, *209*
    when to use, **223**
Fountain Steps option, Print Options dialog box, 634–636
four-color color separations, fountain fills and, 216–217, *217*
FPower utility, 928, 950
Frame dialog box, 285
FrameMaker
    versus CorelDRAW, 40
    desktop publishing and, 848
frames
    framing pages with rectangles, 110, 137–142, 620–621
    in Ventura Publisher, **857–859**
frames of text. *See* paragraph text
freehand drawing
    Pencil tool and, 23
    PowerLines and, 478, 482
Front Parallel extrusions, **444**
Full Image option, Open an Image dialog box, 791
full-color patterns, 194–196, *195*, **227–228**, *228*, *229*

full-page rectangles, 110, 137–142, 620–621
fusing blends, 433

G

GALLERY directory (Companion CD), 493–494, 934, 939–941
    BOOK.TXT file, 337
    DIVER.CDR file, 674
    FACES file (07.CDR), 924, 934
    HUNTRESS.CDR file, 539, 674

GDS (Graphic Display System) utility, 928, 950–951
.GEM files
    exporting, 761–763, *762*
    importing, 726–727
    Ventura Publisher and, 761–763, *762*, 864
Ghostscript utility, 928, 951–954
global styles. *See* styles
gradient fills. *See* fountain fills
Graphic Display System (GDS) utility, 928, 950–951
graphic objects
    cataloging. *See* CorelMOSAIC
    overusing, **592–593**
    positioning for printing, 628–629
    printing in tiles, **630**, *631*
    text styles and, 336–337
graphic styles, 41, **237–245**, *237*. *See also* styles
    applying to another object, 241–243, *243*, *244*
    creating and saving, 239–241
    Default Graphic style, 247, 250
    designing the object, 238–239, *239*
    text styles and, 336–337
graphics files, in Ventura Publisher, *856*, **862–864**, 865–866, 867–869
GRAY.PAL file, 202
gray shades, **684–699**. *See also* color
    creating
        PostScript files (.EPS), 696, *697*
        print files, 695
    dots per inch (dpi) and, 684–692, *685*, *686*, *692*, *693*, *694*
    laser printers and, 686–691, *688*, *689*, *690*, *691*
    line screens
        formula for, 698–699
        overview of, 685–691, *686*
        PostScript files (.EPS) and, 696
        for printing slides, 651–652
        Screen Frequency option, 632–633, *637*, 650–651, 695
        setting, 693–699
    lines per inch (lpi) and, 685
    overview of, 684–687
    printer resolution and, 684–687, *685*, *686*
    printing, **632–633**
    in Uniform Fill dialog box, 201
greeking text, **340**
Grid Setup command, Layout menu, 101

grids, 101–102, 909–910
Group command, Arrange menu, 94–95, *94*
grouping
    contours, 438
    objects, **94–95**, *94*
groups
    envelopes and, 403
    selecting inside, 58, *59*
guidelines
    overview of, 101–102, 909–910
    removing, 914–915, *915*

H

halftone options for color separations, 641

handles
    envelope handles, 391–392
    PowerLine pressure handles, 487–489
    rotation and skew handles, **374–375**, *375*
hardware problems, printing and, 646–647
Harvard Graphics, importing from, 731–732, *731*, *732*

headline design, **589–590, 591–592**. *See also* design
    bigger is not better, 589–590
    justification, 598
    the message is senior to formatting, 589, 591–592, *592*, 603
Help
    AutoCAD notes, 730
    overview of, 498
    for Snap tools, 909–910
    for tools, **75–76**
Hewlett-Packard, HPGL files, 763, *764*
hiding. *See also* displaying
    guidelines, 914–915, *915*
    screen elements, **16**, *17*
Home key, text editing with, 290–291
Horizontal envelope mapping option, *396*, 397
hotkeys. *See also* Alt key; Ctrl key; F keys; Shift key
    artistic text, 25, 294
    Character Attributes dialog box, 291
    Combine command, 33
    Convert to Curves command, 33
    Edit Text dialog box, 44–45, 291
    Ellipse tool, 25
    Extrude roll-up, 443
    Fountain Fill dialog box, 27
    Group, 95
    Outline Color dialog box, 27
    Outline Pen dialog box, 27
    overview of, 14–15, **19**
    paragraph text, 25, 294
    Pencil tool, 23
    Pick tool, 22
    PowerLines roll-up, 477
    Preferences dialog box, 19
    Print dialog box, 624
    Rectangle tool, 25
    redrawing screens, 31
    roll-up, 77–78
    Shape tool, 22
    Undo command, 19
    Ungroup, 95
    Uniform Fill dialog box, 27
    Zoom tool, 23, 97
HPGL files, exporting, 763, *764*
HSB color model. *See also* color models
    overview of, **664–665**, *664*, *665*, *666*
    Uniform Fill options, **201–202**
HUNTRESS.CDR file, 539, 674
The Huntress example, **532–539**, *533*. *See also* examples
    the choker, 539
    the face and hair, 535–536, *536*
    the feathers, 534, *535*
    the jeweled headband, 538–539
    the large beads of the headdress, 537
    the medallion, 536, *537*
    on-screen versus printed colors and, 674
    overview of, 532–534
    the scarf, 539
    the small beads of the headdress, 538

I

Illustrator files (.AI), importing, 726, 729–730
Image Alchemy utility, 926, 944
image cataloging. *See* CorelMOSAIC
imagesetters, calibrating, **716–721**
.IMG files, 864
Import dialog box, 86–88, *87*
importing, **86–87, 724–750**
    Adobe Illustrator files (.AI), 726, 729–730
    ASCII files, 88
    AutoCAD .DXF files, 730
    bitmap images, **740–744**, *740*, *742*, *743*
    .CGM files, 726–727, 730–732, *731*, *732*
    clip art, 726–729, *727*, *728*
    across Clipboard, **744–750**
    CorelDRAW .CDR and .CMX files, 730
    CORELFLT.INI file settings for, 88

Bold page numbers: primary discussion of the topic. Italic page numbers: the topic is illustrated in a figure

.GEM files, 726–727
from Harvard Graphics, 731–732, *731, 732*
import file filters, 86, 88, 725–726, 734, *735*
    EPS (Placeable) filter, 734–739, *735, 738, 739*
    PostScript (Interpreted) filter, 734–739, *735, 739*
into Ventura Publisher, **869**
linked data, **744–750**
    creating OLE links, 745–746, *746*
    editing embedded objects, 749
    editing linked files, 748
    linked files versus embedded objects, 747–748, 749–750
    overview of, 744–745
new features in version 4.0, **54–55**, 57, *57*
objects, **86–88**, *87*
versus opening files, **727–728**
overview of, 724–726
PostScript files (.EPS), 75, **733–739**, *735, 738, 739*
rotated bitmaps, 379, 509–510
in snowboarder exercise, 124–126, *126*, 128
text, **323–327**, *324, 325*
.TIF files, 86–87, 744
Windows Metafiles (.WMF), 726, *732, 733*, 749
In Color option, Print Options dialog box, 640
indenting paragraph text, 283–284, *285*
indexes in Ventura Publisher, 870
inflection of curves, 156–157, *157*
.INI files, **900–902**
    CORELAPP.INI, 900
    CORELCHT.INI, 902
    CORELDRW.INI, 900–901
    CORELFLT.INI, 88, 775–776, 901
    CORELFNT.INI, 884, 893–894, 901
    CORELMOS.INI, 902
    CORELMOV.INI, 902
    CORELPNT.INI, 902
    CORELPRN.INI, 891–892, 901–902
    CORELSHW.INI, 902
    CORELTRC.INI, 902
    location of, 57
    WIN.INI, 888–889, 891, 894
installing
    CorelDRAW 5.0, 77
    typefaces, **604–605**, *605*
Interactive Monitor Calibration dialog box, 707–710
interface, **12–21**, *13*. *See also* menus; screens; toolbox
    changes in CorelDRAW 5.0, **71–74**
        drag and drop importing, 73–74, *75*
        Mosaic roll-up, 73
        presets (macros), 72
        Ribbon Bar, 71–72
        square fountain fills, 72, *74*
        Uniform Fill dialog box, 72, *73*
    changes in Ventura Publisher, 874–877, *875, 876*
    color palette, 16
    dialog boxes, **16–20**, *18*
    displaying and hiding elements, **16**, *17*
    overview of, 12–15, *13*
    Ribbon Bar, 14
    roll-ups, 20, *21*
    scroll bars, 16
    status line, 15
    title bars, 14
Interpreted PostScript file filter, 734–739, *735, 739*
Intersection command, Arrange menu, 70, *71*, 903–904
italic type, 274

J

joining nodes and paths, **170–171**
J-Pilot utility, 929, 954
justifying. *See also* aligning
    artistic text, 288–290, *289, 290*

Bold page numbers: primary discussion of the topic. Italic page numbers: the topic is illustrated in a figure

design and, **597–598**

K

Keep Lines option, Envelope roll-up, **393–395**, *394*
kerning
    design and, **606–610**, *609*, *610*
    with CorelKERN utility, **836–837**
    node editing and, 174–175, *174*
    overview of, 274–275, *275*, 278
keyboard shortcut keys. *See* hotkeys
knockouts, color trapping and, 679

L

laser printers. *See also* PostScript printers; printers
    determining printable area in, 623
    gray shades and, 686–691, *688*, *689*, *690*, *691*
layers
    blends and, 415
    overview of, **911**, *911*
    printing problems and, **647**
    in snowboarder exercise, **107–109**, 143
        creating, 108–109, *109*
        defining, 107–108
        hiding, 127
        locking, 117–118
        tips, 143
Layout menu
    Grid Setup command, 101
    Layers roll-up command, 108
    overview of, **32**, *32*
    Page Setup submenu, Display command, 110
    Snap To Grid command, 101–102, 909–910
    Snap To Guidelines command, 909–910
    Snap to Objects command, 909–910
Layout page
    Page Setup dialog box, 620, *621*

Print Options dialog box, *624*, **628–632**, *629*
    Center option, 629
    Fit to Page option, 620, 629–630
    Layout Style options, 630–632, 916–917, *917*
    Position and Size options, 628–630
    Print Tiled Pages option, 630, *631*
leading, 274, 278
Lens roll-up, **513–524**, *513*
    Brighten option, 516, 521
    Color Add option, 516, 520
    Color Limit option, 516, 520
    Heat Map option, 517, 520
    Invert option, 516
    Magnify option, 516, 519, 524
    None option, 517
    overview of, 67, *67*, **513–517**, *513*, *515*
    Tinted Grayscale option, 517, 519–520
    Transparency option, 515
lenses, **513–524**
    applying, 516
    artistic text as lens object, 519
    combining, **517–518**, *518*, **521–524**, *523*
    defined, **513**
    exercises, 514
    tinting, 516
    as windows, 521, *522*
light, color theory and, 659–660, *659*
Light Source options, Extrude roll-up, *458*, *459*
lighting effects, in extrusions, **456–459**, *457*, *458*, *459*, 460, 461
limitations
    in CorelDRAW 4.0, 60–63
    in CorelDRAW 5.0, 77–80
    in CorelMOSAIC, 832
    in CorelSHOW, 813–814
limitcheck errors, PostScript printers, 634, 648–649
limiting use of typefaces, **594–597**, *595*, *596*

Bold page numbers: primary discussion of the topic. Italic page numbers: the topic is illustrated in a figure

Line Caps options, Outline Pen dialog box, 185, 186–187, *188*
line screens. *See also* gray shades
    formula for, 698–699
    overview of, 685–691, *686*
    PostScript files (.EPS) and, 696
    for printing slides, 651–652
    Screen Frequency option, 632–633, *637*, 650–651, 695
    setting, 693–699
line spacing (leading), 274, 278
line styles, **186**
linear fountain fills, 208–211, *208*, *209*, *220*, *469*, *470*
lines, **151–156**. *See also* nodes; Outline Pen dialog box; paths
    creating, 151–154, *154*
    design and, **593–594**
    drawing strategies and, 163–165, *164*
    keeping line segments straight in envelopes, **393–395**, *394*
    ruling lines, **593–594**
    straight line Preferences settings, 154
lines per inch (lpi), gray shades and, 685

linked dimension lines, 907–908
linking, **744–750**. *See also* Object Linking and Embedding
    creating OLE links, 745–746, *746*
    editing linked files, 748
    linked files versus embedded objects, 747–748, 749–750
    overview of, 744–745
Load Template command, Styles roll-up, 248

Lock Contents to PowerClip option, Object menu, 501
long document features, in Ventura Publisher, **870–871**
Look at Me! syndrome, **587–589**. *See also* design
Loop control, Blend roll-up, 418–419, *419*, *420*

M

Mac-ette utility, 929, 955
Macintosh files, printing to, 626
macros. *See also* presets
    in Ventura Publisher, 872
mapping nodes, blends and, **412–413**, *414*, 415
mapping options in Envelope roll-up, **395–399**
    example, 397–398, *398*
    Horizontal option, *396*, 397
    Original option, *396*, 397
    overview of, 395–397, *396*
    Putty option, *396*, 397
    Text option, 403
    tips, 399
    Vertical option, *396*, 397

margins
    for artistic text, 288–290, *289*, *290*
    for paragraph text, 282–284, *285*
marquee boxes, 21, **97**
masks. *See also* PowerClips
    in CorelPHOTO-PAINT, **793–798**
        Color Mask roll-up, 796–798, *797*
        creating masks, 795, *796*
        Mask tools, 793–795, *794*
    masking pages with rectangles, 110, 137–142
    text masks, **314–323**
        creating with Combine command, 68, **315–319**, *319*, 322–323, 512
        creating with PowerClip tool, **319–323**, *322*
        overview of, 68, *68*, *69*, 314–315
Max Width option, PowerLines roll-up, 478
Maximum Number of Points in Curves option, Print Options dialog box, 636, 648
measurement

with dimension lines, 24, *24*, 69–70, **907–909**, *910*
for spacing text, 276–277
units of, 20
MegaEdit utility, 929, 955
menu bar, 14
menus, **29–36**. *See also* interface; toolbox
    Arrange menu, 32–33, *32*
    dimmed commands, 30
    Edit menu, 30–31, *30*
    Effects menu, 33–34, *33*
    ellipsis (…) in, 30
    File menu, 29–30, *29*
    hotkeys, 14–15, **19**
    Layout menu, 32, *32*
    Special menu, 35–36, *35*
    Text menu, 34–35, *34*
    in Ventura Publisher, **874–876**, *876*
    View menu, 31, *31*
Merge Back command, Special menu, 912

merge printing, 909
Microsoft Windows
    Control Panel
        paper size setting, 619
        viewing, 618
    line screen controls, 696
    Windows Metafiles (.WMF)
        exporting, 753–754, 767–768, *768*, 769
        importing, 726, *732*, 733, 749
mirror feature. *See* special effects; stretch and mirror feature
mirrored envelopes, 399
modifying. *See* editing
moiré patterns in color separations, 638–639, *639*
monitors. *See also* screens
    calibrating, **703–710**
        manually, 707–710, *709*
        overview of, 703–706
        with System Color Profile dialog box, 706–707, *706*

fountain fills on, 208
representation of color on, 199, 660, 669, **673–674**
MONOCALIB.BMP file, 705
morphing, with CorelMOVE, 810–812, *811*
mouse
    rotating with, **375–377**, *376*
    secondary mouse button, 291, 370
    stretching and mirroring with, 369–370, *371*
MOVE program, 806, **808–812**
    animating with, 808–810, *809*
    morphing feature, 810–812, *811*
moving. *See also* nudging
    objects, 83–84
    rotation target, 377
    rulers with Shift key, 913, *914*
multiple documents, support for, 77
multiple fountain fill effect, 50, *52*, **214**, *215*
multiple page support, **39–40**, 620

N

naming
    PowerLines, 490–491
    presets, 258–259
navigating in text, **286–291**
    editing controls, 290–291
    on-screen controls, 287, *288*
negative images, printing, **645–646**, *645*
NeoBookPro utility, 929, 955
NeoPaint utility, 929, 955
NeoShow utility, 930, 955–956
nesting PowerClips, *510*, **511–513**, *512*
new features. *See also* CorelDRAW 4.0; CorelDRAW 5.0
    in Ventura Publisher, **873–880**
New From Template command, File menu, 252–253
Nib controls, PowerLines roll-up, **483–484**, *485*

Node Edit roll-up, **167–172**. *See also* Shape tool
    Align tool, 172
    artistic text and, **173–175**, *174*
    Auto-Reduce feature, 168–169, *169*, *170*, 648
    Elastic Mode tool, 172
    joining and breaking paths, 170–171
    rectangles, ellipses and, **173–175**, *173*
    Rotate tool, 171
    Stretch tool, 171
Node Edit tool, CorelPHOTO-PAINT, 795, *796*
node editing
    artistic text, **173–175**, *174*
    in CorelDRAW 4.0, 48
    kerning and, 174–175, *174*
    objects, **173–175**, *173*, *174*
    perspective and, 383
node mapping, blends and, **412–413**, *414*, 415
nodes, **156–162**, 172. *See also* curves; paths
    adding, 913
    aligning, 172
    changing node types, **161–162**
    CorelTRACE and, 825, *826*
    and creating curves and lines, 151–152, *152*, 154
    cusp nodes, 154, **159–160**, *161*
    defined, **150**
    Elastic Mode tool, 172
    and inflection of curves, 156–157, *157*
    joining and breaking, **170–171**
    overview of, 156–157, 172
    PowerLines and, **481–482**, *481*
    rotating, 171
    Shape tool and, 22
    smooth nodes, **158–159**, *160*
    symmetrical nodes, **158**, *159*
NOTES directory (Companion CD)
    overview of, 924, 933, 941
    TYPE.EXE file, 883
nudging. *See also* moving
    kerning and, 175
    objects, 85, *85*
numbering paragraphs, in Ventura Publisher, 870

O

Object Data Manager roll-up, **55–56**, *56*, 912
Object Linking and Embedding (OLE)
    CorelDRAW and, 750
    embedding
        editing embedded objects, 749
        embedded objects and paragraph text, 772
        exporting embedded objects, 769–772, *770*, *771*
        linked files versus embedded objects, 747–748, 749–750
    exporting files with, 753–754, **769–774**, *770*, *771*, *774*
    linking, **744–750**
        creating OLE links, 745–746, *746*
        editing linked files, 748
        linked files versus embedded objects, 747–748, 749–750
        overview of, 744–745
    overview of, 725

Object menu
    Lock Contents to PowerClip command, 501
    Overprint Outline command, 679
    overview of, 55–56
Object Picker tool, CorelPHOTO-PAINT, 793
objects, **82–96**
    aligning, **97–99**, *98*, *99*
    cloning envelopes from, 401–403, *402*
    color trapping and overprinting objects, 679
    combined objects and envelopes, 403
    combining, *94*, *95*

Bold page numbers: primary discussion of the topic. Italic page numbers: the topic is illustrated in a figure

converting to curves, 33, 151, **175–177**, *176, 177*, **330–332**, *331, 332*
copying attributes, 100
creating, **82–83**
creating during preset recording, 258
distributing copies of, 78
embedded text objects, 326, *326*
filling, 90–91, *91*
grouping, **94–95**, *94*
importing, **86–88**, *87*
line screens for selected objects, **696–697**, *697*
moving, 83–84
node editing, **173–175**, *173, 174*
nudging, 85, *85*
outlining, 90–91
overlaying on bitmap images, 741
overview of, 82–83
pasting, **89**, *89*
perspective for multiple objects, 380
printing selected objects, 625
rotating, 84, *84*
selecting, 83, 84
    in groups, 95
    multiple objects, 92, 93
    in Wireframe view, 92, *93*
sizing, 84, 374
skewing, 84, *84*
snapping to, 909–910
templates as starting points for, **251–253**, *252*
text inside, 47
warping, **471–472**, *471*
welding, 58, *59*, **94**, **96**, 96, 128–130
wrapping text around, 46–47, 53, 135, 286, **298–306**, 405
zooming, 22–23, 97
OKFonts utility, 930, 956
one-point perspective, **381–383**, *381, 382*
Open an Image dialog box (CorelPHOTO-PAINT), **790–793**, *790*
    Crop option, 791

Full Image option, 791
Partial Area option, 791–793, *792*
Resample option, 791

Open command, File menu, 727–728
opening
    files, 96–97
    versus importing files, **727–728**
    Outline Color dialog box, 180–182, *181*
    Outline Pen dialog box, 180–182, *181*
Options page, Print Options dialog box, *624*, **632–637**, *633*
    Convert TrueType to Type 1 option, 636–637, 890–891
    Download Type 1 Fonts option, 636–637, 884, 885, 887–889, 890
    Fountain Steps option, 634–636
    Maximum Number of Points in Curves option, 636, 648
    Screen Frequency option, 632–633, *637*, 650–651, 695, 697
    Set Flatness To option, 634, *635*, 648–649
organization charts, **423**, *423*
Original envelope mapping option, *396*, 397
orthogonal projections, **444**
Outline Color dialog box, 27, 181–182, *181*, **190**, 679
Outline Pen dialog box, 27, **180–191**
    Arrows options, 183–185, *184*
    Behind Fill option, 189, *190*, 313, *314*
    Calligraphy options, 188–189, *189*, 477
    Color drop-down list, 186
    Corners options, 186, *187*
    hotkey, 27
    Line Caps options, 185, 186–187, *188*
    opening, 180–182, *181*
    outlining text, **356–359**, *357, 358*
    overview of, 26–27, 91, **180–183**
    perspective and, **385**

Bold page numbers: primary discussion of the topic. Italic page numbers: the topic is illustrated in a figure

Scale With Image option, **189–190**, 372–373, 385
setting defaults, **191**
stretching and, **372–373**
Style drop-down list, 185–186
Widths options, 182–183
outlining
   objects, 90–91
   overview of, 180–182, *181*
   perspective and, 385
   stretching and, 372–373
   text, **356–359**, *357*, *358*
overlaying objects, on bitmap images, 741
overprinting objects, color trapping and, 679

P

page frames, 110, 137–142, 620–621
page layout desktop publishing programs, 849
Page Setup dialog box, *617*, **618–623**, *619*
   Display page, **620–623**, *622*
      Add Page Frame option, 110, 620–621
      Facing Pages option, 620
      Paper Color option, 621–623
      Show Page Border option, 623
   Layout page, 620, *621*
   overview of, *617*, 618–619, *619*
   Size page, *617*, 619–620
PageMaker
   versus CorelDRAW, 39, 46, 238, 359
   .GEM files and, 761–762
   line screen controls, 696
   .PCX files and, 763–764, *765*
   PostScript files (.EPS) and, 758
   Windows Metafiles (.WMF) and, 767
pages. *See also* Page Setup dialog box; printing
   displaying paper size on-screen, 623
   framing with rectangles, 110, 137–142, 620–621
   multiple page support, **39–40**, 620

printing multiple copies of an image on, **630–632**
printing ranges of, **625**
paint programs. *See also* CorelPHOTO-PAINT
   versus drawing programs, **4–8**, *7*, *8*, 817
Paint Shop Pro (PSP) utility, 931, 958
PANTONE colors. *See also* color models
   PANTONE spot color model, 672–673, *672*
   swatch books, 199, 669, **673–674**, 704
   Tinted Grayscale lenses and, 520
Paper Color option, Page Setup dialog box, 621–623
paper size settings, for printers, 619–620
Pappren (Printer's Apprentice) utility, 930, 956
Paragraph dialog box, **282–285**, *283*
   Bullets page, 284–285, *286*
   Indents page, 283–284, *285*
   overview of, 44, *44*
   Spacing page, 274, *274*, 282
   Tabs page, 282
paragraph numbering, in Ventura Publisher, 870
Paragraph Settings dialog box, Ventura Publisher, 861–862, *862*
paragraph text, **281–286**. *See also* artistic text; text
   versus artistic text, 270, **280–282**, 291–294, *293*, **354–355**, *355*
   bulleting, 284
   columns of, 285
   converting artistic text to, **294**
   in CorelDRAW 4.0, 46–47
   in CorelDRAW 5.0, 64
   drawing speed, 282, **354–355**, *355*
   embedded objects and, 772
   envelopes for, 390, **403–405**, *404*, *406*
   formatting, **282–286**, *283*, *288*, **342**
      with text styles, 343–347
   hotkey, 25, 294
   indents, 283–284, *285*

Bold page numbers: primary discussion of the topic. Italic page numbers: the topic is illustrated in a figure

margins, 282–284, *285*
node editing, 298
spacing, 274, *274*, 276–278, 282
tabs, 282
Text tool and, 25
undoing formatting changes, 344
wrapping, 46–47, 53, 135, 286, **298–306**, 405
parallel extrusions, **447–448**, *448*
Partial Area option, Open an Image dialog box, 791–793, *792*
Paste Special dialog box, 746, *746*, 749
pasting. *See also* Clipboard
  objects, **89**, *89*
  traced images across Clipboard, 828
.PAT extension, 227
paths. *See also* curves; nodes
  blending to paths, **420–425**, 431–433
    compound blend to path, **431–433**, *432*
    organization charts, 423, *423*
    reverse step calculation, 421–422
    special effects, 424–425, *424*
  CorelTRACE and, 825, *826*
  defined, **150**
  fitting text to, **327–330**
  joining and breaking, **170–171**
  sizing, 171
  subpaths, **170–171**
pattern fills, **194–196**, **224–230**. *See also* fill patterns
  defined, **196**
  full-color patterns, 194–196, *195*, **227–228**, *228*, *229*
  perspective and, 385
  PostScript patterns, 194–196, *195*, **229–230**, *230*
  two-color patterns, 194–196, *195*, **224–227**, *225*, *226*
PCS (Professional Capture System) utility, 930, 956
.PCX files. *See also* bitmap images
  exporting, 763–764, *765*, 767

Pencil tool
  Bezier curves and, 23, 155–156
  creating lines and curves with, 150, 151–152
  dimension line options, 908
  and erasing with Shift key, 19
  hotkey, 23
  overview of, **23–24**
performance
  contours and, 439
  of CorelDRAW 4.0, 61
  of CorelDRAW 5.0, 64
  drawing speed
    artistic text versus paragraph text, 282, 354–355, *355*
    bitmaps and, 31, 61, *62*, 379
    bold text versus outlined text, 356–359, *357*, *358*
    extrusions and, 456
    for fountain fills, 210, *210*
    paragraph text and, 282
    PostScript versus TrueType typefaces, 352–354, *353*
  importing text and, 327
  PowerClips and, 322
  PowerLines and, 491–492
  print preview and, 628
  text, **350–360**
    adding typefaces, 356, *356*
    artistic text versus paragraph text, 354–355, *355*
    bold text versus outlined text, 356–359, *357*, *358*
    CorelDRAW versus word processors, 359
    PostScript versus TrueType typefaces, 350–354, *353*
  typefaces and, **351–354**, 604–605, *605*
perspective, **380–386**. *See also* special effects
  clearing, 386
  copying, 386
  for multiple objects, 380

Bold page numbers: primary discussion of the topic. Italic page numbers: the topic is illustrated in a figure

one-point perspective, **381–383**, *381, 382*
outlines and, 385
overview of, 380
pattern fills and, 385
Shape tool and, 383
two-point perspective, **383–385**, *384*
vanishing points, 381–382, 384
.PFB files, 889, 891
.PFM files, 837, 888
PHOTO-PAINT. *See* CorelPHOTO-PAINT
PHOTOS.CDR file, 514
Pick tool
    hotkey, 22
    overview of, **21–22**
    toggling with other tools, 913
picture cataloging. *See* CorelMOSAIC
pictures. *See* graphic objects
PICTURES directory (Companion CD), **924, 941–942**
    Chapter 26 examples, 659
    combined special effects example, 524, *525*
    DIVER.CDR file, 674
    HUNTRESS.CDR file, 539, 674
    PHOTOS.CDR file, 514, *515*
    PowerClip example, 511, *512*
    TORTURE.CDR file, 755

Place Duplicates and Clones option, Preferences dialog box, 914
Place Inside Container command, PowerClip submenu, 306, 320
Placeable EPS file filter, 734–739, *735, 738, 739*
planning, design and, **602–603**
PLATE.TIF file, 796, *797*
playing back presets, 257–258, *257*
plotters, HPGL files and, 763, *764*
PlugIn utility, 930–931, 956–958
plus key (+)
    adding nodes with, 913
    for Quick Copy command, 913–914
point sizes, for spacing text, 276–277
pointers, in Ventura Publisher, **856**, *857,* 862–863

Pompousitis, **592–593**. *See also* design
ports, printing problems and serial ports, 647

positioning drawings for printing, 628–629
PostScript files (.EPS)
    versus Adobe Illustrator files (.AI), 729–730
    creating
        for gray shades, 696, 697
        typefaces and, 884, 892, *893*
    exporting, 696, 753–754, **758–761**, *760, 761,* 774
    importing, 75, **733–739**, *735, 738, 739*
    line screens and, 696
    and printing color separations, 638–639
    printing embedded .EPS files, 653–654
PostScript Options dialog box, 224, 696–697, *697*
PostScript patterns, 194–196, *195,* **229–230**, *230*
PostScript printers, **646–656**. *See also* printers
    calibrating, **713–716**
    error handler program, **655**
    Flatness settings, 634, *635,* 648–649
    Fountain Steps setting, 636
    limitcheck errors, 634, 648–649
    line screens and, **695**
    printing copies, 627
    printing curves, 634, *635,* 648–649
    troubleshooting, **646–656**
        bitmaps, 649–651
        complexity and, 647–649
        curves, 648–649
        embedded .EPS files, 653–654
        fill patterns, 653
        hardware problems, 646–647
        layers and, 647
        serial ports and, 647
        slides, 651–652
        slow print or no print, 647
        still won't print, 655–656
PostScript Texture dialog box, 194–196, *195,* **229–230**, *230*

Bold page numbers: primary discussion of the topic. Italic page numbers: the topic is illustrated in a figure

PostScript typefaces. *See also* typefaces
    downloading, 636–637, **888–890**, *889*
    versus TrueType typefaces, **351–354**
        drawing speed, 352–354, *353*
        overview of, 350–351
        print speed, 351–352
POW.CMV file, 810, *811*
PowerClips, **496–513**. *See also* special effects; text masks
    adding bitmap images with, **508–510**, *510*, 743
    containers, **498**
    creating, **497–500**, *499*, *500*
    dolphin jumping through hoop example, 505–507, *505*, *506*
    editing, **500–502**
        Auto-Center Place Inside option and, 501, 507
        grouping and, 501–502
        Lock Contents to PowerClip option and, 501
    envelopes and, **507**, *508*
    Extract Contents command, 300, 322
    extrusions as, **502–504**, *503*
    Help, 498
    nesting, *510*, **511–513**, *512*
    overview of, 68, *68*, *69*, 496–497
    performance and, 322
    Place Inside Container command, 306, 320
    tips, 507
PowerLines, **476–494**. *See also* special effects
    applying, 479, 480, 482
    exercises, 478–480, *479*, *480*
    freehand drawing and, 478, 482
    naming and saving custom PowerLines, **490–491**
    Nib controls, **483–484**, *485*
    nodes and, 481–482, *481*
    overview of, 49–50, *49*, 476–478
    performance and, 491–492
    pressure handles, 487–489
    shaping with Pressure Edit option, **486–490**, *487*, *488*, *490*
    Speed and Spread controls, **482–483**, *483*, *484*
    Spoon Forest example, 492–494, *493*, *494*
    tips, 482, 492
PowerLines roll-up
    Apply When Drawing Lines option, 478
    Max Width option, 478
    Nib controls, **483–484**, *485*
    overview of, **477–478**, *477*
    Pressure Edit option, **486–490**, *487*, *488*, *490*
    Speed and Spread controls, **482–483**, *483*, *484*
PowerType command, Text menu, 34, *35*, 66
PRACTICE directory (Companion CD), 924, 934, **942–943**
    ALBERT.CDR file, 315–322
    BOTTLE.TIF file, 800
    diskette version of, **960**
    DYNO.CCH file, 807, *807*
    DYNO.SHW file, *812*, 813
    DYNOREX.CMV file, 809, *809*
    EMBOSS.CDR file, 307
    ENVTEXT1.CDR file, 299
    ENVTEXT2.CDR file, 299
    PLATE.TIF file, 796, *797*
    POW.CMV file, 810, *811*
    SCUBA.TIF file, 821
    SETTING.CPT file, 798–799, *799*, 800
    SPOON.TIF file, 795, *796*, 799

Preferences dialog box
    Auto-Center Place Inside option, 320, 321–322, 501, 507
    cusp and straight line settings, 154
    Greek Text Below option, 340
    hotkey, 19
    nudge settings, 85
    overview of, 18–19, *18*

Bold page numbers: primary discussion of the topic. Italic page numbers: the topic is illustrated in a figure

Place Duplicates and Clones option, 914
roll-up options, 60
secondary mouse button setting, 291
Undo options, 99–100
Presentation Exchange Data format. *See* .CMX files
presentations, **806–814**
    animation, 808–810, *809*
    charts, 806–808, *807*
    morphing, 810–812, *811*
    overview of, 806
    running, 812–815, *812*
presets, 255–264. *See also* styles
    creating, **256–257**, *256*
        for artistic text, 259–260
        objects during recording, 258
    envelope, **401**
    extrusion, **469**
    fountain fill, 51, 222
    naming, 258–259
    overview of, 255
    playing back, 257–258, *257*
    versus styles, 255, **262–264**
    uses for, 260–262
    when to use, 263–264
Pressure Edit option, PowerLines roll-up, **486–490**, *487*, *488*, *490*
pressure handles, for PowerLines, 487–489
Preview Image option, Print Options dialog box, 628
price, of CorelDRAW 4.0, 62–63
primary colors
    additive primary colors, **661–662**, *661*, *662*
    subtractive primary colors, **663**
Print dialog box, 618, **624–632**, *624*, *625*
    Copies and Collate Copies options, 627
    For Mac option, 626
    new features in CorelDRAW 4.0, **55**, *55*
    overview of, 624–625
    Print Range options, 625
    Print to File option, 626–627
    Printer Color Profile option, 626

Printer and Printer Quality options, 626
selecting printers, 618
Print Options dialog box, *624*, **628–637**
    buttons, 628, *629*, **642–646**, *643*
        Calibration Bars and Densitometer Scale buttons, 644
        Crop Marks and Registration Marks buttons, 643–644
        File Info button, 642–643
        Print Negative and Emulsion Down buttons, 644–645, *645*
    Layout page, *624*, **628–632**, *629*
        Center option, 629
        Fit to Page option, 620, 629–630
        Layout Style options, 630–632, 916–917, *917*
        Position and Size options, 628–630
        Print Tiled Pages option, 630, *631*
    Options page, *624*, **632–637**, *633*
        Convert TrueType to Type 1 option, 636–637, 890–891
        Download Type 1 Fonts option, 636–637, 884, 885, 887–889, 890
        Fountain Steps option, 634–636
        Maximum Number of Points in Curves option, 636, 648
        Screen Frequency option, 632–633, *637*, 650–651, 695, 697
        Set Flatness To option, 634, *635*, 648–649
    Preview Image option, 628
    print preview area, 628, *629*
    Separations page, *624*, **639–642**, *640*
        Advanced Screening dialog box, *624*, 641, *641*
        Auto-Trapping options, 642, 678
        Colors options, 641–642
        Convert Spot Colors to CMYK option, 640–641, 642
        In Color option, 640
        Use Custom Halftone option, 641

Bold page numbers: primary discussion of the topic. Italic page numbers: the topic is illustrated in a figure

print preview area, Print Options dialog
    box, 628, *629*
Print Setup dialog box, **617–618**, *617*, *618*
print speed, PostScript versus TrueType
    typefaces, 351–352
Printer Characterization dialog box, 713

Printer Color Profile option, Print dialog
    box, 626
printer font binary files (.PFB), 889, 891
printer font metric files (.PFM), 837, 888
Printer option, Print dialog box, 626
Printer Quality option, Print dialog box, 626

printers. *See also* PostScript printers
    calibrating, **713–716**, *714*
    color correction feature, 626, 710
    gray shades and resolution of, 684–687,
        685, *686*
    laser printers
        determining printable area in, 623
        gray shades and, 686–691, *688*,
            689, *690*, *691*
        paper size settings, 619–620
        resolution settings, 626
    selecting, **617–618**, *618*, 626
Printer's Apprentice (Pappren) utility, 930,
    956
printing, **616–656**. *See also* Page Setup
        dialog box; pages; Print dialog box;
        Print Options dialog box; Print
        Setup dialog box
    bitmaps, **649–651**
    with blacks and whites reversed,
        645–646, *645*
    business cards, **630–632**, **916–917**, *917*
    calibration bars, 644
    color separations, **637–642**, *639*
        Auto-Trapping feature, 642
        in color, 640
        converting spot colors to CMYK,
            640–641, 642
        custom halftone options, 641
        overview of, 637–639

printing calibration bars and
    densitometer scale, 644
registration and moiré patterns,
    638–639, *639*
selecting separation pages to print,
    641–642
copies, 627
in CorelDRAW 5.0, **74–75**
crop marks, 643–644
curves, 634, *635*, 636, 648–649
densitometer scale, 644
embedded .EPS files, 653–654
with emulsion down, 644–646, *645*
file information on printouts, **642–643**
to files, **626–627**, 695
fill patterns, **653**
fitting drawings to page, 629–630
fountain fills, **634–636**
gray shades, 632–633
to Macintosh files, 626
merge printing, **909**
multiple copies of an image on a page,
    630–632, **916–917**, *917*
negative images, **645–646**, *645*
overview of Print dialog boxes,
    616–617, *617*
positioning drawings for, **628–629**
print preview area, 628, *629*
printing drawings in tiles, **630**, *631*
ranges of pages, 625
registration marks, **643–644**
selected objects, 625
slides, **651–652**
troubleshooting PostScript printers,
    646–656
    bitmaps, 649–651
    complexity and, 647–649
    curves, 648–649
    embedded .EPS files, 653–654
    fill patterns, 653
    hardware problems, 646–647
    layers and, 647

Bold page numbers: primary discussion of the topic. Italic page numbers: the topic is illustrated in a figure

serial ports and, 647
slides, 651–652
slow print or no print, 647
still won't print, 655–656
process color, versus spot color, **671–672**
Professional Capture System (PCS) utility, 930, 956
PROGRAMS directory (CorelDRAW), 902
PSP (Paint Shop Pro) utility, 931, 958
publication files (.PUB), Ventura Publisher, 856, *857*, 877
Publication Manager dialog box, Ventura Publisher, 857, *858*
publication-centered desktop publishing programs, 849
Putty envelope mapping option, *396*, 397

Q

Qpeg486 utility, 931, 958
Quick Copy command, 913–914
Quick Format feature, Ventura Publisher, 879

R

radial fountain fills, 208–211, *208*, *209*, *220*, 426–427, *426*
rainbow fountain fills, 211–213, *213*
Rectangle tool, **25**
rectangles
   framing pages with, 110, 137–142, 620–621
   node editing, **173–175**, *173*
Red/Green/Blue color model. *See* RGB color model
redrawing screens
   artistic text versus paragraph text, 282, 354–355, *355*
   bitmaps and, 31, 61, *62*, 379
   bold text versus outlined text, 356–359, *357*, *358*
   extrusions and, 456

for fountain fills, 210, *210*
paragraph text and, 282
PostScript versus TrueType typefaces, 352–354, *353*
reference guide, CorelDRAW 4.0, 61
registration
   of color separations, 638–639, *639*
   color trapping and, 675
registration marks
   color trapping and, 675
   printing, **643–644**
removing guidelines, 914–915, *915*
RenameTrueType utility, 931–932, 958
renaming .EXE files, 897
Repeat command, Edit menu, 101
Resample option, Open an Image dialog box, 791
reshaping curves, 166
resolution settings
   for printers, 626
   for printing slides, 651–652
retouching tools in CorelPHOTO-PAINT, **801–803**
   Clone tool, 803
   Equalize tool, 801–802, *802*
reusing designs, **602**
Reverse Order command, Arrange menu, 415
RGB color model. *See also* color models
   CMYK color model and, 665–667, *666*, *667*, 668, *668*
   on-screen colors and, 673–674
   overview of, **665–667**, *666*, *667*
   Uniform Fill options, **201–202**
Ribbon Bar, 14
roll-ups
   hotkeys, 77–78
   overview of, 20, *21*
   Preferences settings, 60, *60*, 76, *76*
   in Ventura Publisher, 874, *875*
ROMCAT utility, 932, 958
ROSE.PCX file, 745

Bold page numbers: primary discussion of the topic. Italic page numbers: the topic is illustrated in a figure

rotate and skew feature, **374–380**. *See also* special effects
   constraining rotation, 375–376
   moving rotation target, 377
   overview of, 54, 84, *84*, 368, 369
   rotating with mouse, **375–377**, *376*
   rotating and skewing with Transform roll-up, **377–379**
   rotation and skew handles, **374–375**, *375*
   skewing with mouse, 377, *378*
   stretching and, 379
   tips, 380
rotating
   bitmap images, 61, *62*, 379, 509–510, 651, 741
   blends, 417–418
   extrusions, 464–468, *464*, *465*, *467*
   nodes, 171
rulers, 369, 913, *914*, 915
ruling lines, 593–594
running presentations, 812–813, *812*

S

Save option, limitations, 78
Save Style As dialog box, 334–335, *335*
Save Template command, Styles roll-up, 248, 251
saving
   changed files from Companion CD, 319
   files, 96–97
   graphic styles, 239–241
   PowerLines, 490–491
   styles, 249, 251
   traced images, 827–828
   and Undo command, 100
Scale With Image option, Outline Pen dialog box, **189–190**, 372–373, 385
scaling, bitmap images, 740–741
scanners
   calibrating, **711–713**

   color separations and, 716
scanning
   bitmap images, 650–651
   into CorelTRACE, 819–823, *820*, *823*
   into Ventura Publisher, 879
   text, 828
Screen Frequency option, Print Options dialog box, 632–633, *637*, 650–651, 695, 697
screens. *See also* interface; monitors
   displaying elements of, 16, *17*
   displaying paper size on, 623
   drawing speed
      artistic text versus paragraph text, 282, 354–355, *355*
      bitmaps and, 31, 61, *62*, 379
      bold text versus outlined text, 356–359, *357*, *358*
      extrusions and, 456
      for fountain fills, 210, *210*
      PostScript versus TrueType typefaces, 352–354, *353*
   fountain fills on, 208
   Paper Color setting, 621–623
   representation of color on, 199, 660, 669, **673–674**
scroll bars, 16
SCUBA.TIF file, 821
secondary mouse button
   as hotkey for Edit Text or Character Attributes dialog boxes, 291
   stretch and mirror and, 370
Select All command, Edit menu, 93
selecting
   blends for fountain fills, 211–213
   color models in Uniform Fill dialog box, 197–199, *198*
   color separation pages to print, 641–642
   colors for fountain fills, 211, *212*, 216–217, *217*
   in compound blends, 432
   extrusions, 451
   inside groups, 58, *59*

Bold page numbers: primary discussion of the topic. Italic page numbers: the topic is illustrated in a figure

objects, 83, 84
    in groups, 95
    multiple objects, 92, 93
    in Wireframe view, 92, *93*
    printers, 617–618, *618*, 626
    with Shift key, 92
seminars, **918–919**
separating extrusions, **461**
separations. *See* color separations
Separations page, Print Options dialog box, *624*, **639–642**, *640*
    Advanced Screening dialog box, *624*, 641, *641*
    Auto-Trapping options, 642
    Colors options, 641–642
    Convert Spot Colors to CMYK option, 640–641, 642
    In Color option, 640
    Use Custom Halftone option, 641
Separator program, Ventura Publisher, 879
serial ports, printing problems and, 647

service bureaus
    color calibration and, 721–722
    grayscale printing and, 692, 695–697
    positive/negative and emulsion up/down conversions, 645, *645*
    printing files for, 626
Set Flatness To option, Print Options dialog box, 634, *635*, 648–649
Set Hotkeys dialog box, 342, *342*
setting
    Outline Pen defaults, **191**
    secondary mouse button, 291
SETTING.CPT file, 798–799, *799*, 800
shading
    with blends, **425–429**, *426*, *428*, 434
    extrusions, **455–456**, 460, 461
Shape tool. *See also* Node Edit roll-up
    artistic text and, **173–175**, *174*
    character formatting, 279
    character and line spacing, 278
    cropping bitmap images, 651, 742–744
    hotkey, 22
    overview of, **22**
    perspective and, 383
    rectangles, ellipses and, **173–175**, *173*
    in snowboarder example, 118–119, 129
    shared vanishing points, 461–464, 469–472, *470*, *471*
Shift key. *See also* Alt key; Ctrl key; F keys; hotkeys
    + F2 (Zoom on Selected), 23, 97
    + F4 (Show Page), 23
    + F8 (paragraph text), 25, 294
    + F11 (Uniform Fill), 27, 197
    + F12 (Outline Color), 27, 190
    constraining with
        one-point perspective, 383
        stretches, 370
    envelopes and, 393
    erasing with, 19
    moving rulers with, 913, *914*
    selecting multiple objects with, 92
    text editing with, 290–291
shortcut keys. *See* hotkeys
Show Page Border option, Page Setup dialog box, 623
Show Page option, Zoom tool, 23
SHOW program, **812–814**
    limitations, 813–814
    running presentations, 812–813, *812*
.SHW files, 814
Size option, Print Options dialog box, 628–630
Size page, Page Setup dialog box, *617*, 619–620
sizing
    objects, 84, **374**
    paths, 171
    text, 271, 274
skew feature. *See also* rotate and skew; special effects
    skew handles, **374–375**, *375*
    skewing
        with mouse, 377, *378*

overview of, 84, *84*
with Transform roll-up, **377–379**
stretching and, 379
sky. *See* snowboarder exercise
slide presentations. *See* presentations
slides, printing, **651–652**
Small Back extrusions, **445**, *446*
SMALL.PAL file, 202
smooth nodes, **158–159**, *160*
Snap To Grid command, Layout menu, 101–102, 909–910
Snap To Guidelines command, Layout menu, 909–910
Snap To Objects command, Layout menu, 909–910
snowboarder exercise, **104–144**, *105*, **226–228**. *See also* examples
    cloud, **112–118**
        creating blend, 114–117, *116*
        drawing, 112–114, *113*, *114*
        locking layers, 117–118
    foreground snow, **118–124**
        adding blends, 122–123, *122*, *123*, *124*
        drawing, 118–119, *119*, *120*
        filling slope, 120–122, *121*
    framing, **137–142**
    layers, **107–109**, 143
        creating, 108–109, *109*
        defining, 107–108
        hiding, 127
        locking, 117–118
        tips, 143
    overview of, 104–107, 143–144
    pelican storm pattern fills, **226–228**, *226*, *229*
    sky, **110–111**, *111*
    snowboarder, **124–126**, *126*, *127*
    text, **133–137**
        enveloping, 135, *135*
        extruding, 136, *137*
        stretching, 134, 137, *138*
    tree, **126–132**

adding blends, 131, *132*
adding snow, 128–130, *129*, *131*
importing, 128
overview of, 126–127
Solid Fill option, Extrude roll-up, 454–455
SOUND directory (Companion CD), 924, 934, **943**
Spacebar, Pick tool toggle, 22, 913
spacing
    line spacing (leading), 274, 278
    text, 274, *274*, 276–278, 282
Spacing page, Paragraph dialog box, 282

special effects, **366–387**. *See also* blends; contours; Effects menu; envelopes; extrusions; PowerClips; PowerLines; Transform roll-up; wrapping text
    absolute sizing, **374**
    clearing, 54, **386**, **387**
    combining, **524**, *525*
    in CorelDRAW 4.0, **53–54**
        Blend tool, 53, *53*
        Clear Effects command, 54, 386, 387
        contours, 54
        Copy Effects command, 54
        envelopes, 53
        extrusions, 53–54
        Rotate & Skew tool, 54
        Stretch & Mirror tool, 54
    overview of, 8, *9*
    perspective, **380–386**
        clearing, **386**
        copying, **386**
        for multiple objects, 380
        one-point perspective, **381–383**, *381*, *382*
        outlines and, 385
        overview of, 380
        pattern fills and, 385
        Shape tool and, 383

Bold page numbers: primary discussion of the topic. Italic page numbers: the topic is illustrated in a figure

two-point perspective, **383–385**, *384*
vanishing points, 381–382, 384
rotate and skew, **374–380**
    constraining rotation, 375–376
    moving rotation target, 377
    overview of, 54, 84, *84*, 368, 369
    rotated bitmaps, 61, *62*, 379, 509–510
    rotating extrusions, **464–468**, *464, 465, 467*
    rotating with mouse, **375–377**, *376*
    rotating and skewing with Transform roll-up, 377–379
    rotation and skew handles, 374–375, *375*
    skewing with mouse, **377**, *378*
    stretching and, 379
    tips, 380
stretch and mirror, **369–374**
    constraining stretches, 370
    with mouse, **369–370**, *371*
    outlines and, 372–373
    overview of, 54, 369
    stretching proportionately, **372–373**, *374*
    stretching, rotating, and skewing, 379
    stretching text in snowboarder exercise, 134, 137, *138*
    tips, 372
    with Transform roll-up, **370–372**
tips, **524–526**
Special menu. *See also* Preferences dialog box
    Create Arrow command, 184–185, *185*
    Extract command, 912
    Merge Back command, 912
    overview of, **35–36**, *35*
    Preferences command, 18
    Presets command, 256
    Symbols roll-up, 25–26, *26*, 90, *90*
Speed control, PowerLines roll-up, **482–483**, *483, 484*
Spell Checker, 279, 288, *288*
splitting, blends, 433

Spoon Forest example, **492–494**, *493, 494*
SPOON.TIF file, 795, *796*, 799
spot color, **671–673**, *672*, 674. *See also* color models
    converting to CMYK color model, 640–641, 642
    fountain fills and, 216–217, *217*
    line screens and, 696–697, *697*
    PANTONE spot color model, 672–673, *672*
    versus process color, 671–672
Spread control, PowerLines roll-up, **482–483**, *483, 484*
spreads, color trapping and, **678**
square fountain fills, 208–211, *208, 209, 220*
squeezing text, **311–313**, *312*
start objects, in blends, 408, **414–415**, *416*
status line, 15
steps
    in blends, 117, 410–411, 421–422, 427, 434
    in fountain fills, 51, *52*, 210, *215*, 218–219, *220*, **634–636**
straight lines. *See* lines
stretch and mirror feature, **369–374**. *See also* envelopes; special effects
    constraining stretches, 370
    mirrored envelopes, 399
    with mouse, **369–370**, *371*
    outlines and, 372–373
    overview of, 54, 369
    stretching proportionately, **372–373**, 374
    stretching, rotating, and skewing, 379
    stretching text, 134, 137, *138*
    tips, 372
    with Transform roll-up, **370–372**
Stretch tool, Node Edit roll-up, 171
strings of text. *See* artistic text; text
Style drop-down list, Outline Pen dialog box, 185–186
style sheet files (.STY), Ventura Publisher, 238, 856, *856*, **860–862**, 866–869, *868*

styles, **236–245**, 246–248. *See also* presets; templates
    adding to CORELDRW.CDT, 246, *246*
    changing default style set, **246–248**, 254
    in CorelDRAW 4.0, **40–41**, *41*
    graphic styles, 41, **237–245**, *237*
        applying to another object, 241–243, *243*, *244*
        creating and saving, 239–241
        Default Graphic style, 247, 250
        designing the object, 238–239, *239*
        text styles and, 336–337
    line styles, **186**
    overview of, 236–238
    versus presets, 255, **262–264**
    saving, 249, 251
    text styles, **334–347**
        for artistic text, 335, 337
        creating, **334–335**, 339–342
        example, **337–347**, *338*
        formatting paragraphs, 343–347
        graphic objects and, 336–337
        overview of, 40, *41*
        Save Style As dialog box, 334–335, *335*
    tips, **253–254**
    typefaces for, 253–254
    in Ventura Publisher, 238
    when to use, **243–245**, 262–263
Styles roll-up, 240–241, *241*, 248
subpaths, **170–171**
subtractive primary colors, **663**
swatch books, color, 199, 669, **673–674**, 704
Swimming in the Deep End. *See The Diver* example
Symbols roll-up
    importing from, 128
    overview of, 25–26, *26*, 90, *90*
symmetrical nodes, **158**, *159*
system color profiles. *See* color calibration

T

3-D rendering. *See* extrusions
tables of contents, in Ventura Publisher, 870
tabs, for paragraph text, 282
templates, **245–253**. *See also* styles
    adding styles to, **246–248**, 254
    in CorelDRAW 4.0, 43
    creating, **248–251**
    overview of, 245–246
    as starting points for objects, **251–253**, *252*
text, **270–295**. *See also* text masks; typefaces; Ventura Publisher
    artistic text
        converting to paragraph text, **294**
        in CorelDRAW 5.0, 64, *65*
        creating, **279–280**, *280*
        drawing speed, **354–355**, *355*
        envelopes and, 390
        exporting across Clipboard, 772–773, *774*
        hotkey, 25, 294
        justifying, 288–290, *289*, *290*
        node editing, **173–175**, *174*
        versus paragraph text, **270**, **280–282**, **291–294**, *293*, **354–355**, *355*
        presets for, 259–260
        spacing, 274, *274*, 276–278
        text styles for, 335, 337
        Text tool and, **25**, 270
        when to use, **292**
    color with, **680**
    combining with objects, 95
    converting to curves, **330–332**, *331*, *332*
        typefaces and, 883, **884–887**, *885*, *886*, *887*
    in CorelDRAW 4.0, **40–47**
        defaults, 43–44
        Edit Text dialog box, 44–45
        Paragraph dialog box, 44, *44*

paragraph text, 46–47
text enveloping (wrapping), 46–47, *47*
text flow, 46, *47*
text inside objects, 47
Text roll-up, 45–46, *45*
text styles, 40, *41*
typefaces, 42, *43*
word processing features, 44–45
in CorelDRAW 5.0, **64–66**, **79–80**
artistic text, 64, 65
limitations, 79–80, *79*
paragraph text, 64
text flow, 46, *47*
Text roll-up, 64–65, *65*
typefaces, 42
design and, **590–593**
embedded text objects, 326, *326*
embossed text, **306–311**, *307*
envelopes for wrapping, 46–47, 53, 135, 286, **298–306**, 405
enveloping, 135, *135*
extruding, 136, *137*
fitting to paths, **327–330**
flowing text. *See* wrapping text
formatting, **271–279**. *See also* kerning
aligning, 274
character formatting, 271–272, *272*, 278–279, *278*
sizing, 271, 274
spacing, 274, *274*, 276–278
type styles, 274
greeking, **340**
importing, **323–327**, *324*, *325*
justifying text, **597–598**
kerning
design and, **606–610**, *609*, *610*
node editing and, 174–175, *174*
overview of, **274–275**, *275*, 278
masks, **314–323**. *See also* masks; PowerClips
navigating in, **286–291**

editing controls, 290–291
on-screen controls, 287, *288*
outlining, **356–359**, *357*, *358*
overusing text elements, **592–593**
paragraph text, **281–286**
versus artistic text, 270, **280–282**, **291–294**, *293*, **354–355**, *355*
bulleting, 284
columns of, 285
converting artistic text to, **294**
in CorelDRAW 5.0, 64
creating, **281**, *281*
drawing speed, 282, **354–355**, *355*
embedded objects and, 772
envelopes for, 390, **403–405**, *404*, *406*
formatting, **282–286**, *283*, *288*, 342
formatting with text styles, 343–347
hotkey, 25, 294
indents, 283–284, *285*
margins, 282–284, *285*
node editing, 298
spacing, 274, *274*, 276–278, 282
tabs, 282
Text tool and, **25**
undoing formatting changes, 344
when to use, **292–293**
wrapping, 46–47, 53, 135, 286, **298–306**, 405
performance, **350–360**
adding typefaces, 356, *356*
artistic text versus paragraph text, 354–355, *355*
bold text versus outlined text, 356–359, *357*, *358*
CorelDRAW versus word processors, 359
PostScript versus TrueType typefaces, 350–354, *353*
scanning, 828
in snowboarder exercise, **133–137**
spacing, 274, *274*, 276–278, 282

Spell Checker, 279, 288, *288*
squeezing, **311–313**, *312*
stretching, 134, 137, *138*
Thesaurus, 279
wrapping around objects, 46–47, 53, 135, 286, **298–306**, 405
Text Attributes dialog box, 339, *340*
Text envelope mapping option, 403
text files, in Ventura Publisher, *856, 862–864*, 865–866, 867–869
text frames. *See* frames; paragraph text
text masks, **314–323**. *See also* masks; PowerClips
  creating
    with Combine command, 68, **315–319**, *319*, 322–323, 512
    with PowerClip tool, **319–323**, *322*
  overview of, 68, *68*, *69*, 314–315
Text menu
  Fit Text to Path command, 327–330
  Frame command, 285
  overview of, **34–35**, *34*
  Paragraph command, 274
  PowerType command, 34, *35*
Text roll-up, 45–46, *45*, 64–65, *65*, 271, *271*, 274
text strings. *See* artistic text
text styles, **334–347**
  for artistic text, 335, 337
  creating, **334–335**, 339–342
  example, **337–347**, *338*
    creating styles, 339–342
    formatting paragraph text, 343–347
    overview of, 337
    setup, 338–339
  graphic objects and, 336–337
  overview of, 40, *41*
  Save Style As dialog box, 334–335, *335*
Text tool
  for artistic text, 270, 279
  overview of, **25–26**
  undoing formatting changes, 344

texture fills, **194–196, 230–233**, *231*. *See also* fill patterns
Thesaurus, 279
three-dimensional rendering. *See* extrusions
.TIF files. *See also* bitmap images
  exporting, 763, 765–767, *766*
  importing, 86–87, 744
  scanner calibration and, 711–712
  size of, 741
tiles, printing drawings in, **630**, *631*
title bars, 14
Tool Settings roll-up,
  CorelPHOTO-PAINT, 784–786, *785*
toolbox, **21–29**. *See also* Outline Pen dialog box; Shape tool
  Ellipse tool, 25
  Fill tool, **27–29**, 27–29, *28*, 91, **195–196**, *195*
  overview of, **12–14**, *13*
  Pencil tool, 23–24
    Bezier curves and, 23, 155–156
    creating lines and curves with, 150, 151–152
    dimension line options, 908
    and erasing with Shift key, 19
    hotkey, 23
    overview of, **23–24**
  Pick tool
    hotkey, 22
    overview of, **21–22**
    toggling with other tools, 913
  placing, 60
  pop-up tool help, **75–76**
  Rectangle tool, 25
  Text tool, 25–26
    for artistic text, 270, 279
    overview of, **25–26**
    undoing formatting changes, 344
  Zoom tool, 22–23, 97
TORTURE.CDR file, 755
torture test, export, **753–756**, *754*, 774–776
tracing. *See* CorelTRACE

Bold page numbers: primary discussion of the topic. Italic page numbers: the topic is illustrated in a figure

Transform roll-up, **367–380**, *368*
   Move page, 368, 369
   overview of, 367–369, *368*
   Rotate and Skew pages, **374–380**
      constraining rotation, 375–376
      hotkey, 368
      moving rotation target, 377
      overview of, 54, 84, *84*, 368, 369
      rotated bitmaps, 61, *62*, 379, 509–510
      rotating extrusions, **464–468**, *464, 465, 467*
      rotating with mouse, 375–377, *376*
      rotating and skewing with roll-up, **377–379**
      rotation and skew handles, **374–375**, *375*
      skewing with mouse, 377, *378*
      stretching and, 379
      tips, 380
   Size page, 369, **374**
   Stretch & Mirror page, **369–374**
      constraining stretches, 370
      with mouse, **369–370**, *371*
      outlines and, 372–373
      overview of, 54, 369
      with roll-up, **370–372**
      versus Size page, 374
      stretching proportionately, **372–373**, *374*
      stretching, rotating, and skewing, 379
      stretching text in snowboarder exercise, 134, 137, *138*
      tips, 372
   units of measurement in, **369**
trapping. *See* color trapping
trees. *See* snowboarder exercise
Trim command, Arrange menu, 70, *71*, 405, 497, 513, **905–907**, *907, 908*
TrueType typefaces. *See also* typefaces
   on Companion CD, 925, 935
   Convert TrueType to Type 1 option, 636–637, 890–891
   downloading, 887
   versus PostScript typefaces, **351–354**
      drawing speed, 352–354, *353*
      overview of, 350–351
      print speed, 351–352
TruMatch color swatch books, 199, 669, **673–674**, 704
.TTF files, 891
TWAIN scanner drivers, 819, 820
two-color patterns, 194–196, *195*, **224–227**, *225, 226*
two-point perspective, **383–385**, *384*
Type 1 typefaces. *See* PostScript typefaces
Type Assist dialog box, 34, *35*, 66
Type drop-down list, Fountain Fill dialog box, 208–211, *208, 209*
TYPE.EXE file, 883
type families, **273**
type styles
   boldface type versus outlined text, 356–359, *357, 358*
   creating, 274
typeface management, **882–884**
   adding typefaces, 339, 356, *356*
   CORELFNT.INI file and, 884, 893–894
   CORELPRN.INI file and, 891–892
   downloading typefaces, 636–637, 883, **887–890**
      TrueType typefaces, 887
      Type 1 typefaces, 888–890, *889*
   in Export EPS dialog box, 884, 892, *893*
   FontMinder software, 605, **833–836**, *835*
   installing typefaces, **604–605**, *605*
   overview of, **882–884**
   printer font binary files (.PFB), 889, 891
   printer font metric files (.PFM), 837, 888
   sending text as curves, 883, **884–887**, *885, 886, 887*
   tips, **891–892**
   using resident typefaces, 883, **890–891**
   WIN.INI file and, 888–889, 891, 894
typefaces, **350–360**. *See also* fonts; text
   adding, 339, 356, *356*

Bold page numbers: primary discussion of the topic. Italic page numbers: the topic is illustrated in a figure

boldface type versus outlined text,
   356–359, *357*, *358*
for bullets, 284
defined, **273**
design and, **594–597**, **604–610**
   installing too many, 604–605, *605*
   kerning, 606–610, *609*, *610*
   limiting use of, 594–597, *595*, *596*
   selecting categories of, 606, *607*, *608*
downloading, 636–637, 883, **887–890**
   TrueType typefaces, 887
   Type 1 typefaces, 888–890, *889*
for fitting text to paths, 328–329, *329*
versus fonts, **273**
installing, **604–605**, *605*
overview of, 9–10, 42, *43*
and performance, **351–354**, 604–605, *605*
PostScript versus TrueType, **351–354**
   drawing speed, 352–354, *353*
   overview of, 350–351
   print speed, 351–352
scanned text and, 828
for styles, 253–254
versus type families, **273**
in Ventura Publisher, 877
Zapf Dingbats, 284

U

UltraClip (UC) utility, 932, 958
unconstrained envelopes, **399–401**
underlined type, 274
Undo command
   actions that cannot be undone, **100**
   in CorelDRAW 4.0, 58
   hotkeys, 19
   saving and, 100
   setting levels of, 99–100, 308
   undoing
      Text tool changes, 344
      Weld command, 96

Undo tools, CorelPHOTO-PAINT,
   788–789, *789*
ungrouping
   clip art, 726, 728–729, *728*
   extrusions, 461
Uniform Fill dialog box, 27, **194–206**. *See also* fill patterns
   CMYK color model options, **199–201**, *200*
   color palettes, 201, **202–206**
      creating custom colors, 202–205, *204*, *205*
      custom palettes, 202
      searching for colors, 205–206
   gray shades, 201
   hotkey, 27, 197
   overview of, 27, 194–196, *195*
   PANTONE color library, 672–673, *672*
   PostScript Options dialog box, 696–697, *697*
   RGB and HSB color model options, **201–202**
   selecting color models, 197–199, *198*
   in snowboarder example, 110–111, 114
uniform fills
   defined, **196**
   in snowboarder example, 110–111, 114
units of measurement, 20
Update command, File menu, 747
Use Custom Halftone option, Print Options dialog box, 641
Use Object Fill option, Extrude roll-up, 452–453, 504
user interface. *See* interface
utilities on Companion CD, 924, **925–933**, 943–960
   Alchemy, 926, 944
   CDFont, 927, 944
   Display, 927, 944–948
   DragView, 927, 948–949
   EPSF, 927–928, 949
   FontBook, 928, 950
   FontNamer, 928, 950

Bold page numbers: primary discussion of the topic. Italic page numbers: the topic is illustrated in a figure

FontPower, 928, 950
Ghostscript, 928, 951–954
Graphic Display System (GDS), 928, 950–951
J-Pilot, 929, 954
Mac-ette, 929, 955
MegaEdit, 929, 955
NeoBookPro, 929, 955
NeoPaint, 929, 955
NeoShow, 930, 955–956
OKFonts, 930, 956
overview of, 925–926
Paint Shop Pro (PSP), 931, 958
PlugIn, 930–931, 956–958
Printer's Apprentice (Pappren), 930, 956
Professional Capture System (PCS), 930, 956
Qpeg486, 931, 958
RenameTrueType, 931–932, 958
ROMCAT, 932, 958
UltraClip (UC), 932, 958
VesaView, 933, 958
VuImage, 933, 959–960
utilities in CorelDRAW. *See* CorelMOSAIC; CorelTRACE; FontMinder; CorelKERN
utilities in Ventura Publisher, 879–880

V

vanishing points
   for extrusions
      common vanishing points, 461–464, 469–472, *470*, *471*
      editing, 452
      in Extrude roll-up, *443*, 444
      overview of, **446–447**
      and rotating extrusions, 468
   for perspective, 381–382, 384
VBRUN directory (Companion CD), 923, 924, 926, 960
vector art
   versus bitmap images, **4–8**, *7*, 817
   converting bitmap images to. *See* CorelTRACE
vector drawing programs. *See* drawing programs
Ventura Publisher, **844–849**, **852–880**. *See also* desktop publishing programs
   color separations and, 879
   versus CorelDRAW, 845–848, *846*, *847*
   cross-references, 870–871
   Database Publisher program, 880
   desktop publishing and, **844–849**, 852
   exporting .CAP text, 865–866
   file management, 872–873
   file structure, **854–866**, 869
      caption files (.CAP), 864–866, *864*
      chapter files (.CHP), **856–857**, *856*, *857*, *858*, **859–860**, 862–863, 877
      frames for text and graphics, 857–859
      modularity of, 859
      pointers, **856**, *857*, 862–863
      publication files (.PUB), 856, *857*, 877
      versus standard word processor files, 854–855, *855*
      style sheet files (.STY), 238, 856, *856*, **860–862**, 866–869, *868*
      text and graphics files, *856*, **862–864**, 865–866, 867–869
   footnotes, 871
   formatting tags, 860–862, **871–872**, 879
   .GEM files and, 761–763, *762*, 864
   .IMG files and, 864
   importing files into, 869
   indexes, 870
   long document features, **870–871**
   macros, 872
   menus, 874–876, *876*
   new features, **873–880**
      interface changes, 874–877, *875*, *876*
      listed, 878–879, *878*
      new file formats, 877
      overview of, 873–874

Bold page numbers: primary discussion of the topic. Italic page numbers: the topic is illustrated in a figure

utility programs, 879–880
wish list, 880
numbering paragraphs, 870
overview of, **63**, **853–854**
Paragraph Settings dialog box, 861–862, *862*
.PCX files and, 763–764, *765*
PostScript files (.EPS) and, 758–761, *761*
Publication Manager dialog box, 857, *858*
Quick Format feature, 879
roll-ups, 874, *875*
scanning into, 879
seminars, **919**
Separator program, 879
tables of contents, 870
typefaces, 877
.VGR files, 865
width tables (.WID), 877
Windows Metafiles (.WMF) and, 767
Vertical envelope mapping option, *396*, 397

VesaView utility, 933, 958
.VGR files, 865
video card settings, 706
View menu
    Color Correction command, 626, 710
    Color Palette submenu, Custom Colors command, 205
    Edit Wireframe command, 92
    overview of, **31**, *31*
VP Locked to Object option, Extrude roll-up, 462–463, 468
VP Locked to Page option, Extrude roll-up, 463
VuImage utility, 933, 959–960

W

warping objects, **471–472**, *471*
warranty for Companion CD, vii
Weld command, Arrange menu, 58, *59*, *94*, 96, 128–130
white space, design and, 591, 597
width tables (.WID), Ventura Publisher, 877
Widths options, Outline Pen dialog box, 182–183
WIN.INI file, 888–889, 891, 894
Windows Metafiles (.WMF)
    exporting, 753–754, 767–768, *768*, 769
    importing, 726, *732*, 733, 749
Wireframe view
    selecting objects in, 92, *93*
    in snowboarder example, 115, 125
word processors
    versus CorelDRAW, 359
    versus drawing and desktop publishing programs, 842–843
    features in CorelDRAW 4.0, 44–45
    file structure in, 854–855, *855*
    importing text from, **323–327**, *324*, *325*
workgroup publishing, **848**
wrapping text, 46–47, 53, 135, 286, **298–306**, 405

X

Xpress, versus CorelDRAW, 40
XYZ reference lines, 571–573, *572*, 579–581, *580*

Z

Zapf Dingbat typeface, 284
Zoom tools
    in CorelDRAW, **22–23**, 97
    in CorelPHOTO-PAINT, 786, *787*

Who says typesetting has to be difficult?

Practicality is the key to this expertly crafted and organized insider rundown of the tricks of the typographer's trade. Learn how to estimate the length of a publication, pick up valuable tips on font selection, solve printer problems.

Now available wherever computer books are sold.

384 pages.
ISBN 1246-3

Shortcuts to Understanding.

SYBEX, Inc.
2021 Challenger Drive
Alameda, CA 94501
1-800-227-2346
1-510-523-8233

MAKE A GOOD COMPUTER EVEN BETTER.

350pp. ISBN: 1301-X.

The *PC Upgrade Guide for Everybody* is the no-hassle, do-it-yourself PC upgrade guide for everyone. If you know the difference between a screwdriver and a pair of pliers, this book is for you.

Inside you'll find step-by-step instructions for installing hardware to make your computer even more fun and productive. Add memory chips, CD-ROM drives and more to your PC.

You'll also learn how to diagnose minor PC problems and decide whether to repair or replace faulty components —without schlepping your PC to the shop and paying big bucks.

SYBEX. Help Yourself.

2021 Challenger Drive
Alameda, CA 94501
1-800-227-2346

[1508] Mastering CorelDRAW 5

GET A FREE CATALOG JUST FOR EXPRESSING YOUR OPINION.

Help us improve our books and get a **FREE** full-color catalog in the bargain. Please complete this form, pull out this page and send it in today. The address is on the reverse side.

Name _____ Company _____

Address _____ City _____ State ____ Zip _____

Phone (___) _____

1. **How would you rate the overall quality of this book?**
   - ❏ Excellent
   - ❏ Very Good
   - ❏ Good
   - ❏ Fair
   - ❏ Below Average
   - ❏ Poor

2. **What were the things you liked most about the book? (Check all that apply)**
   - ❏ Pace
   - ❏ Format
   - ❏ Writing Style
   - ❏ Examples
   - ❏ Table of Contents
   - ❏ Index
   - ❏ Price
   - ❏ Illustrations
   - ❏ Type Style
   - ❏ Cover
   - ❏ Depth of Coverage
   - ❏ Fast Track Notes

3. **What were the things you liked *least* about the book? (Check all that apply)**
   - ❏ Pace
   - ❏ Format
   - ❏ Writing Style
   - ❏ Examples
   - ❏ Table of Contents
   - ❏ Index
   - ❏ Price
   - ❏ Illustrations
   - ❏ Type Style
   - ❏ Cover
   - ❏ Depth of Coverage
   - ❏ Fast Track Notes

4. **Where did you buy this book?**
   - ❏ Bookstore chain
   - ❏ Small independent bookstore
   - ❏ Computer store
   - ❏ Wholesale club
   - ❏ College bookstore
   - ❏ Technical bookstore
   - ❏ Other _____

5. **How did you decide to buy this particular book?**
   - ❏ Recommended by friend
   - ❏ Recommended by store personnel
   - ❏ Author's reputation
   - ❏ Sybex's reputation
   - ❏ Read book review in _____
   - ❏ Other _____

6. **How did you pay for this book?**
   - ❏ Used own funds
   - ❏ Reimbursed by company
   - ❏ Received book as a gift

7. **What is your level of experience with the subject covered in this book?**
   - ❏ Beginner
   - ❏ Intermediate
   - ❏ Advanced

8. **How long have you been using a computer?**
   _____ years
   _____ months

9. **Where do you most often use your computer?**
   - ❏ Home
   - ❏ Work
   - ❏ Both
   - ❏ Other _____

10. **What kind of computer equipment do you have? (Check all that apply)**
    - ❏ PC Compatible Desktop Computer
    - ❏ PC Compatible Laptop Computer
    - ❏ Apple/Mac Computer
    - ❏ Apple/Mac Laptop Computer
    - ❏ CD ROM
    - ❏ Fax Modem
    - ❏ Data Modem
    - ❏ Scanner
    - ❏ Sound Card
    - ❏ Other _____

11. **What other kinds of software packages do you ordinarily use?**
    - ❏ Accounting
    - ❏ Databases
    - ❏ Networks
    - ❏ Apple/Mac
    - ❏ Desktop Publishing
    - ❏ Spreadsheets
    - ❏ CAD
    - ❏ Games
    - ❏ Word Processing
    - ❏ Communications
    - ❏ Money Management
    - ❏ Other _____

12. **What operating systems do you ordinarily use?**
    - ❏ DOS
    - ❏ OS/2
    - ❏ Windows
    - ❏ Apple/Mac
    - ❏ Windows NT
    - ❏ Other _____

13. On what computer-related subject(s) would you like to see more books?

_____
_____
_____
_____

14. Do you have any other comments about this book? (Please feel free to use a separate piece of paper if you need more room)

_____
_____
_____
_____

— — — — — — — — — — — PLEASE FOLD, SEAL, AND MAIL TO SYBEX — — — — — — — — — —

SYBEX INC.
Department M
2021 Challenger Drive
Alameda, CA
94501

What You'll Find on the Companion CD

The *Mastering CorelDRAW 5* Companion CD gathers in one place a valuable collection of images, type fonts, utilities, audio tracks, practice files, and Corel product information, making your work with CorelDRAW easier and more fun. Check it out for the following:

- A directory of practice files for following along with the many examples and exercises throughout the book.

- A Gallery directory containing the finished works of prize-winning artists, as well as various professional images that show the possibilities provided by CorelDraw. A good source of ideas and inspiration!

- Audio clips taking you into the mind of a professional CorelDRAW artist as she discusses her approach, her motivation, and her award-winning techniques.

- A directory of Windows and DOS utilities culled from many sources, selected with the goal of making your use of CorelDRAW and related software easier and more productive.

- A multimedia presentation of Corel Corporation's product offerings. Here you can find demonstrations of companion products to CorelDRAW, such as photo CDs and clip art collections.

- A selection of TrueType fonts that you can put to use in all your projects.

You'll also find illustrations detailing the theory and practice of color printing, and technical information and advice concerning potential conflicts with older systems. For more information on using the Companion CD, please refer to **Appendix C**.